Girl Groups

Fabulous Females That Rocked The World

John Clemente

Published by

 **krause
publications**

700 E. State Street • Iola, WI 54990-0001
Telephone: 715/445-2214

Please, call or write us for our free catalog of antiques and collectibles publications. To place an
order or receive our free catalog, call 800-258-0929. For editorial comment and further information,
use our regular business telephone at (715) 445-2214

Library of Congress Catalog Number: 00-104622
ISBN: 0-87341-816-6

Printed in the United States of America

Dedication

This book is dedicated to the memory of Jackie Landry Jackson, one of the original Chantels.

Dear Jackie,
Your positive attitude and shining spirit
will last for all eternity, . . . eternally.

Acknowledgments:

The author would like to thank the following people
who have devoted time and effort into making this book a reality:

My wife, Geralyn and my son, Zachary, all my love and devotion.

My family, John Clemente, Sr. , The Garbushians; Fran, Dennis, Chris & Tommy, The Felius: Joanne, David, & Michael.

The photo wizards: Shauna, Joe and Steve Morello @ Magicolor Photo Lab, Montclair, New Jersey.

The appendix and discography police: Jim Dunn, Karen Efron, John Galindo, Manny Giz, John Grecco, Dave Marston (sergeant), Tony "O" Oetjen, Phantom @ Rutgers, Mitch Rosalsky, Rich Sibello, Joe Sicurella, Ken Thompson, and Elaine Wade.

The deejays who invited me to their shows as a guest and allowed me to play my records and report on these wonderful groups: Frank Gengaro, Tony "O" Oetjen, Dan Romanello, Gordon Skadberg, and Rich Sibello.

My pals at work who were always interested in One Fine Day's progress: Ellin Duggan, Linda Ellenbogen, Rena Green, Cheryl Hoist, Anna Jordan and Carol Porter.

The proprietors of the palaces where I looked over and obtained their wares to do my research and satisfy my craving: Vicki & Steve Blitenthal @ Whirling Disc Records, Nikki Gustafson @ Nikki's Nook, Ronnie and Sandy Italiano @ Clifton Music, George Lavatelli @ Relic Rack, Michael Leighton @ B/W Records, Joe Peel @ Dinosaur Vinyl, Charlie Rigolosi @ Platter World, Robbie & Joel Scherzer @ Robbie Music, Fred Kaplan @ Memory Lane Records, Tanya @ Jerry Ohlingers, Craig Stepneski @ Hackensack Record King, Val Shively and his staff @ R&B Records, Yellowlinda, Inc.

The many people whose contributions brought this publication closer to reality:

John Abbey, Mrs. Herb Abramson, Jimmy Amato, William Baran, Paul Barker, Richard Barrett, Jeff Beckman, Alan Betrock, Philip Black, Gene Bondy, Bob Bosco, Greg Bravo, Eddie Brian, Bob Briskin, Ralph Brown (AFTRA), Pat Brown, Sheila Burgel, Mike Calderullo, Rudy Calvo, Steve Camhi, Brenda & Gary Cape, Sam Carson, Bobby "Blue" Castellano, Elliot Chiprut, Cliftonaires, (Joel Katz, Jack Scandura, Phil Granito, Louis Vinci), David Cole, Arthur Crier, Frankie D., Ann Daniels, Tom DeCillis, Mike DeMirdjian, Tommy Di Bella, Joe & Angie Diomede, Stanley (Mojo) Dixon, Dorn Photo, Earl Edwards, Paul Errante, Frankie Fampa, First Baptist Church Of Coney Island, Donald Gatling, Marv Goldberg, Walt Gollender, Fernando Gonzalez, Randall Grass, Jonathan Greenfield, Phil Groia, Kenneth Higney, Phil Hurtt, Frank W. Johnson, B.J. Jones, Eddie Jones, Artie Kaplan, Kitty Karp, Michael "Doc Rock" Kelly, Paul Kennedy, Mary Jo Kewley, Alan Lee, Gene Leone, Anthony Leong, Beverly Lindsay, Scooter Magruder, Joanne McGuire, Ernie Martinelli, Weldon A. McDougal III, Joe Mirrione, Motown Museum, Laurie Pitcoff, Robert Pruter, Lou Rallo, Michael Redmond, Don K. Reed, Remembrance (Jimie "C" Cicenia, Sandra Gomez, Tony Gomez, Mario Viscardi), Debbie Rensing, Jon Rich, Merlina Rich, Janet Ricci, Angel Rissoff, Chapman Roberts, Ritchie Rome, Jerry Ross, Marty Schein, Tracy Schubert, Phil Schwartz, Derrick Shaw, The Staff of P.S. 21 (The Philip Sheridan School), Yolanda Simmons, Lou Silvani, Amy Stavis, Paul Supia, Mike Sweeney, Luke Tirrell, Kevin Tong, Paul Trefzger, Diva Uscatu, Steve West, Jimmy "the Wiz" Wisner, Steve Yohe, Kenny Young, and Jerry Zwecher.

My thanks and apologies to anyone whom I
inadvertently forgot to extend my appreciation.

Table of Contents

Features:

Foreword

When John Clemente asked me to write this foreword, I really wasn't sure if I'd do it. What would I say . . . You know, female groups were, well, ummm, just female groups, right? And suddenly, I was transported back to my beginnings and I so vividly remembered growing up and listening to and living the male "doo wopp" groups and then, eventually and inevitably, the female groups. The music . . . the sound . . . the records . . . were playing in my head and there I was in the "then" and savoring every minute of it. I remembered what I was wearing and thinking and doing and it's amazing how we never forget any of this. Wow, there were all those "sister" groups (I know I'm going way back, but I must credit these predecessors of what was to come) – The Andrews Sisters, The DeCastro Sisters, The DeJohn Sisters, The Lennon Sisters and The McGuire Sisters! I always felt that their close, tight, and fluid harmonies were a reflection of the closeness and harmony among the sisters themselves (at least that's what I wanted to believe) and that made me happy and I wanted to be one of them. So I picked a part and did just that. And I bet you did that, too, and we immediately became a part of their fun and camaraderie. Ah, yes, sisters, cousins and friends from school and the neighborhood hit the scene and groups like The Chordettes and The Poni Tails filled the airwaves and our hearts and we, naturally, continued to pick a note and sing along. Let's not forget the outfits, dressing the same, dressing a little sexy and all that gook, growing up stuff. We, girls, would live vicariously through these groups and lots of us formed our very own . . . sometimes having as many as a dozen members (after all, we couldn't leave any friends out) . . . and we belonged and we bonded and we had the time of our lives . . . performing at school functions and parties or wherever they'd allow. And, hey, who knows. Maybe we'd be discovered!! Yeah, right!

Realizing the joy and, in my case, the inspiration these groups gave me in my early years, I knew that all I had to do was talk about "feelings" – mine and everybody else's for these wonderful contributors to our musical history. I am so lucky in my career to have been a big part of the "girl group" experience . . . and I must credit Arlene Smith & The Chantels for driving me absolutely crazy and as if that weren't enough, along came Shirley Alston & The Shirelles and I definitely died and went to Heaven. If I had to pick the one female person who had "the big" impact on my musical life, it would be Shirley Alston. When I heard that soulful, innocent, street, sexy sound, I knew I would immerse myself into writing "Pop Music". Yes, I had heard the lead voice I loved and a background group that was straightforward, three part harmony with a slightly uneven unison sound . . . it was so real and unpretentious! I thank you for inspiring me to hone in on my passion for music, vocal harmonies and "a sound".

What were female groups? What was their appeal? Why were they so big?

Why their popularity? I truly feel that the songs were as comfortable and attainable as we felt the groups themselves were. The melodies were easy to sing, the lyrics were easy to relate to, mainly boy/girl love stories, mostly about innocent love and the hopefulness of relationships. Much like the times, nothing was complicated and if the songs were not love-oriented, they were just "fun" songs, like Little Eva's "Locomotion".

It could be that female groups were really a happening. Sometimes I wonder, "what if the male groups continued and did some of the "girl group" records. Would it have worked? I'm not sure of the answer and we'll never know – but if I had to take a guess, I'd say, I think the girls had an edge in their looks, attitude and, naturally, their sound. I don't believe this was an industry plan as much as an evolution . . . and I thank God every day for my part in this evolution, not to mention how proud I am to be linked with the great writers of the day, like Carole King and Gerry Goffin, Barry Mann and Cynthia Weil and Jeff Barry, as well as Bob Crewe (one of my dearest friends), and Bob Gaudio (both of Four Seasons fame), and countless other talented writers and producers, not the least of those being the multi-talented Phil Spector. Almost like the "doo wopp" groups of the 1950s, the female groups just kept coming together. They were mostly friends in school or from the neighborhood and they all had something to say. The race was on in the business for each label to have their signature female group or groups and, in many cases, a producer would manufacture a group, give them a name and very often, enjoy tremendous success with them.

These, many, many groups, so well covered in this book, captured the feelings and tone of a generation. They were powerful and, in many cases, they were raw products . . . mostly, well produced but left with an edge . . . we called it "street". In those days, before MTV, most fans listened to these groups on car radios (mono – but the lucky few had rear speakers), ore on hand-held transistors. You wondered what these groups looked like and anticipated the release of their albums, in large part, for the pictures. When you were lucky enough to see them on Dick Clark's "American Bandstand", or "Shindig" or "Hullabaloo" or Don Kirshner's "Rock Concert" or at The Brooklyn Paramount or Fox Theaters . . . it was orgasmic – always! The boys loved these groups as did the girls . . . there was a lot of "implied" sex on stage, from short skirts to heavy makeup and appropriate body language . . . ALL ATTITUDE!! The boys dreamed that these girls were dateable (and believed that some of them actually might be) and we girls pretended to be one of them and to us, too, the early female groups were accessible (hey, they really were just like us). What a terrific feeling!

In my opinion, looking back to the beginnings of the "the girl group era" gives us the clearest picture of their essence and success, which continues, though somewhat watered-down, today. The innocence and the attainability may be gone, but the sex is more than alive and well, and there are still some signature sounds and, underneath all the electronic arrangements and effects, lies a song that is still simple – basic love stories with the attitude of the changing times AND we can, most of the time, still sing along!

It is also important to remember that many of the artists who performed as female groups were talented singers and, for those who lacked a bit in the ability department, they sure gave us a most memorable sound and, if they were blessed, some groups gave us both! You heard one note and you immediately knew who it was. As a matter of fact, you would never confuse Mary of The Shangri-Las with Ronnie of The Ronettes or Brenda of The Exciters or Judy of The Chiffons or Patti of Patti LaBelle and the Blue Belles . . . and long reign their differences! Their individuality and uniqueness were enhanced by their collaborations with arrangers like Artie Butler and engineers like Brooks Arthur and Larry Levine, who got the most out of the recording sessions. And let us take our hats of to the insight and talents of the producers, who knew how to get the best out of all the components.

The females of Motown . . . The Supremes, Martha Reeves and The Vandellas, The Marvelettes . . . Hello, Philly, hello, Orlons . . . Spector's "harem" with The Crystals, The Ronettes, Bob B. Soxx & The Blue Jeans . . . Red Bird's The Dixie Cups, The Shangri-Las and . . . let's not forget the group that could do it all, the one and only Pointer Sisters . . . I must remember this is a foreword, and I cannot list all the wonderful groups that deserve mentioning and I apologize to all of you that live in my heart and not in this paragraph. In some cases, the groups became so popular, that just one of them could instantly legitimize and bring respect and profitability to a record label. I believe that if you had to pick one word to sum up the greatness and popularity of the female groups, it would be that more than anything, they were FUN!

John Clemente has done a thorough and exhaustive job in researching the history of these groups. From their formation and through their careers, he has uncovered facts and anecdotes that are interesting and revealing to both the industry insiders and the fans of the groups. A really enjoyable read for everyone that takes you back to a simpler time and place – and thank you very much, John, for taking me back in time and reminding me of my age (only kidding).

In my show, "Leader of the Pack", the opening starts with the infectious drum beat to "Be My Baby" – and the audience roars with memories and recognition – while the narrator says: 'It's a hot August night in 1963 and wherever you were and whatever you were doing, the radio was playing this song.' Everyone sings along, everyone is transported back to that moment in time, everyone is happy and in a "fun" mode . . . everyone is young and innocent again. And, thank you, female groups for this and, how lucky am I to have been able to contribute to making people sing and be happy!

Ellie Greenwich
February, 2000

Introduction

When I first got the idea to put together a book about female vocal groups, I had to think long and hard about what I was going to present. Was it going to be a few perfunctory paragraphs on each group? Would it cover a general history of the groups and their hits? The path most interesting to a music lover or a record collector would be an accurate history of how a group came together, where it intended to go in its career and what the circumstances were surrounding its demise, and, in many cases, its resurrection. I knew that when I came across any information for any of these groups, it never seemed like enough data to satisfy my curiosity. I realized that what I had to offer had to go a step further than what had come before, if it was going to have sufficient validity.

Originally, the book started out as a list of female groups and their related record labels. The idea for the list came from my appearance on a series of radio shows, where I featured items from my record collection. In October of 1992, I was asked to be a guest on The Rhythm and Blues Group Harmony Review, hosted by Dan Romanello, who was then working on the show with Neil Hirsch. Earlier in the year, I had called the station to talk to Dan about some female group cuts he had played. Dan and I had discovered that we had a mutual affinity for the sounds of female group harmony. Although I had listened to other collectors talk about different records from their collections, I had never before envisioned being a guest on a show like this. Truthfully, I didn't think I had it in me, but after the first show, I was comfortable presenting my records. Dan was encouraging and the response from listeners was positive, despite criticism from "purists" who felt that too much female vocal group music would detract from what they surmised was the sole focus of the show. These same critics felt that there was not enough material to sustain the venue as a subgenre of vocal group music. We did not agree.

Despite the negativity from some pockets of group harmony collectors, to our surprise, more and more people came forward, less reluctantly testifying to their personal interest in the genre. Dan suggested that since I seemed to have absorbed a multitude of facts and other tidbits about the groups I presented, maybe I should consider writing a book about these groups. With the exception of female groups who have had monster hits, none have had extensive coverage in any other documentation, outside of isolated articles in collectors' magazines. At first I thought, 'what a great idea', but writing a book would be time consuming, and I didn't think I could commit to that amount of time. As a consolation to myself and to thwart the notion that there weren't enough female groups to go around, I decided to keep a running list of female groups and their related labels. Soon the list expanded from 1950s and 1960s groups to 1970s groups and beyond, including vocal harmony duets. This is now the appendix of the book.

In 1995, The United In Group Harmony Association (UGHA), an organization dedicated to preserving the history of 1950s and 1960s vocal group harmony music, was holding its sixth annual hall of fame induction and The Chantels were among the honorees. This marked the first time that a female vocal group was being inducted. Knowing that I was dabbling with information about female vocal groups, Ronnie "I" Italiano, the organization's founder and president, asked me to obtain information for a feature to be presented in "Harmony Tymes," a UGHA-associated magazine that was active during the 1980s, but had remained dormant for several years. Ronnie had intended to reactivate the publication, so he wanted a special feature for the second initiation. After meeting and interviewing group members, I worked on the article, having had ample time before the October 1st deadline. Unfortunately, the plan for the magazine was shelved due to numerous production problems. When it became clear that these problems were insurmountable, I decided that my article on The Chantels was to be the foundation for a collection of biographies of female vocal groups, a collection that I would gather on my own.

It was difficult getting started for several reasons. First, I had to decide which groups were going to be included. Was it going to be just groups from the 1950s or 1960s, or would it extend beyond? Was I going to include pop groups or just R&B and R&R groups? Was I going to include groups who had mostly big hits or who remained locally popular? Would there be the inclusion of solo artists who consistently sang with female backing? The logical choice was to make a list of all the groups that I enjoyed the most, regardless of the era. The inclusion of the few solo artists were those whose body of work I felt fit the group harmony criteria; beginning and ending a recording career making group records with female backing. Second, I needed a strategy that was going to make this project different from the endeavors that had preceded it, yet be completely marketable from a publishing standpoint. I decided that I wanted to obtain information only from the group members, using their words amidst narrative passages. Of course, this meant I had to find group members. Some groups on which I had decided were still performing, but many were not. Since I was trying to find women, I had to take into account the fact that most women change their names when they marry, so tracking through information services was made that much more difficult. Using the network I had available to me through UGHA, I started asking people who were in the business, both then and now. One member had a sister who sang in a group, which he managed. Another person was still friendly with a member from another group. When that person was contacted, she knew someone else. One producer whose record label was still active after almost thirty-five years knew the whereabouts of the groups on his label. Gradually, the task became less arduous, and, with each successful contact, I became more confident that I could "pull rabbits out of the hat."

By the time I was ready to search for a publisher, I had amassed information on about twenty-five groups, most with significant input from group members, contributing many facts never before published. Every effort was made to contact as many group members as possible for their contributions to this project. Unfortunately, there were instances where members, for various reasons, did not wish to participate, where the whereabouts of members were unknown, or where few original members were still living. In some cases, those close to the scene, a writer, producer or accompanist gave pertinent data. If these resources were not available for an entry, extensive research and examination of recorded material summed up the group's contribution to the music world. Obtaining photos for some groups was tedious, because original photographic material had been misplaced, destroyed or simply never existed. Due to these circumstances, there are a few entries in the book without pictorial representation. On the positive side, however, many of the photos provided for this book are either rare or never before seen pictures of the artists. These representations alone merit the existence of a book of this nature. Almost all the group members are identified in the photos and vocal positions for many group members are listed. Discographies feature most, if not all the works by the group and many works by individual members. After the completion of the chapter, each contributing group member was given a draft for perusal and critique, something not usually afforded to performers. In return, many artists got back to me with corrections and additions. Therefore, most historical portrayals are reported to the artists' satisfaction. I am honored to have written historical accounts bearing the artists' approval.

Five years of blissful dedication have gone into the production of this book. I was afforded the opportunity to meet and speak with dozens of entertainers whose works I admire as a fan and emulate as an artist. Whether one enjoys the stark sounds of the 1950s, the production-oriented sounds and sweet soul of the 1960s, or the melodic and rhythmic sounds of the 1970s and 1980s, in this book, there is a group for every taste. I hope you enjoy reading it as much as I have enjoyed putting it together. I owe a debt of gratitude to the artists, and to you, my fellow fans. Your enthusiasm for female vocal groups has prompted me to make this publication my dream come true.

John Clemente
March, 2000

The Andantes

Members:

(1961-72) Marlene Barrow, 2nd Soprano
Louvain Demps, 1st Soprano
Jackie Hicks, Alto

A well-rounded backing vocal should be smooth, cool, searing, and rich in its tones and range. Motown Records had such a group singing backing vocals—The Andantes. They accompanied such greats as Marvin Gaye, Kim Weston, The Four Tops, Vandellas, Supremes, Marvelettes, Temptations and Holland-Dozier. They were Motown's female group, used almost exclusively for backing vocals (frequently with no label credit). They were a most prominent sound on vinyl, yet their identity was anonymous.

Berry Gordy had started Motown Records with a few hundred dollars borrowed from family members. Through his talents as a songwriter and the intuitive ability to spot talent, he built his company from a small independent label to one of the most influential and fastest growing businesses in the entertainment industry. When the company first began, however, everything was run on a shoestring. Motown cut corners by having the staff do anything and everything they were capable of doing, write songs and make the coffee; handle distribution and answer phones; operate the recording equipment and be a chauffeur. Gordy learned early on to utilize everything (and everyone) to the fullest potential.

Louvain Demps came to Motown Records in 1959, just as the company was getting started. She had been out of Pershing High School a couple of years. Her parents knew of her vocal abilities and wanted her to study opera. Much to their vexation, Louvain elected to sing Rhythm & Blues, the music that all the teenagers were listening to. At the insistence of her friend, Little Willie John, Louvain started going to auditions. Motown put out the word that they would record anyone who had the money to pay for the session. Louvain and a friend took the offer. Louvain recollects, "When Marv Johnson's record came out, they were offering recording contracts, or anybody that wanted to cut a record to pay $100. My girlfriend, Rhoda Collins (Howard) had written a song but she couldn't sing. She wanted me to do it. I cut my record, which really didn't do anything."

Although the song that Louvain recorded was not released, Motown offered her a job as one of the backing vocalists for the few artists they had on the roster at the time, Barrett Strong, Amos Milburn, Marv Johnson, The Satintones and Mabel John. One of her first assignments at Motown was singing on "Money", a big hit for the company. From then on, it seemed like the sessions were endless.

As The Rayber Voices, Raynoma Gordy, Brian Holland, Robert Bateman and William "Sonny" Sanders, both of The Satintones, sang the backing vocals on many early singles at Motown. After their writing and administrative duties took precedence, those voices included anyone available on staff who could sing. In her case, Louvain replaced Ray. This way, costs were kept to a minimum by having artists doing double duty. Louvain remembers, "We would go to Motown in the morning and stay the whole day. The Rayber Voices did most of the work."

In 1960, Richard "Popcorn" Wylie first came to Motown to record some demos in the hopes of signing with the company. "Popcorn" brought three friends with him to help out with the vocals. Judith (Marlene) Barrow, Jackie Hicks and Emily Philips came along to help out their friend. Popcorn did record a handful of singles for Motown as Popcorn and The Mohawks, but didn't care for the long term deal he was offered, so he left the company, taking his friends with him. Jackie remembers that they were just there to lend their friend a helping hand, but wound up with an offer that they were not expecting, "He (Popcorn) was trying to get a contract.

The Andantes, backstage with Kim Weston after a concert, 1965, (L-R) Jackie Hicks, Weston, Louvain Demps, Marlene Barrow. (Photo courtesy of Louvain Demps)

Things didn't work out for him, so he went elsewhere. When he left, we left too, but they started contacting us for vocals and handclaps. We weren't interested, but they wore us down."

The young ladies had provided backing vocals for local artist Billy Kent. When this trio (Philips, Hicks, and Barrow) who called themselves The Andantes had come to Motown, Berry Gordy was struck by the fact that the group learned their parts quickly. He finally recruited the capable trio for his company. Emily Philips and Marlene were married and Marlene was expecting her first child. Emily's husband was in the service and when she decided to join him where he was stationed, it was suggested that Louvain join with Marlene and Jackie. At first, Emily's sister Edith filled in for her, but Edith was not interested in a long-term commitment, so Louvain became the third member, permanently. Marlene was satisfied with the union, stating, "We were quick studies. We had good memories and we could sing. Louvain had a high voice, so she slipped right into the top spot—it was a perfect blend."

Together, the trio had a beautiful, irresistible blend, with overtones that were almost operatic. The Andantes were lending their voices to recordings for other artists, but they never ruled out having their own name on a recording.

One of The Andantes' first assignments was providing backing vocals for Eddie Holland's "Jamie." Later, on Mary Wells' "Laughing Boy", The Andantes received billing on the record label, but more often than not, The Andantes did not receive a label credit. This treatment differed from other groups who did vocal backing like The Love Tones or The Vandellas. Attempts at single releases were novelty items like "What Goes Up, Must Come Down", released under the name Holland-Dozier. Motown also used The Andantes to experiment with sounds made popular by other companies. Motown tried to achieve the Phil Spector sound by pairing The Andantes with The Marvelettes on "Too Hurt To Cry, Too Much In Love To Say Goodbye" and billing the single as The Darnells. The Andantes sang the harmonies while The Marvelettes sang the unison behind a duet lead by Gladys Horton and Wanda Rogers.

Over the next few years, numerous, outstanding examples of The Andantes' presence on recordings were the opening chords to The Four Tops' "Ask The Lonely" and the cresting line in the superb B-side by The Supremes', "Standing At The Crossroads Of Love." As far as having a career of their own, the trio would have welcomed it, but the chance never came. In fact, only one singles appeared under The Andantes' name during their tenure at Motown. In 1964, "Like A Nightmare" was released on Motown's VIP records. Anne Bogan, who had come to the label with Harvey Fuqua, was brought in to sing the lead on the dynamic song, which possessed a driving beat and forceful vocals. Louvain thinks that Motown made too many assumptions concerning The Andantes capabilities as lead singers, "They didn't even ask any of us if we could sing the lead."

The single had much potential, but was allowed to languish in favor of groups who made live appearances.

Motown did not consider The Andantes a performing group. Motown valued them in the studio. As a result of Motown's apathy toward the single, few copies exist today. "Like A Nightmare" is considered one of the rarest Motown singles on the collectors' market.

The existence of The Andantes on recordings by other artists was part of Berry Gordy's plan to have a sound that no other company could duplicate. Andantes' vocals were utilized the same way that Motown used their session musicians, for specific enhancements particular to the Motown sound. All Motown musicians and vocalists were forbidden to record for any other record company. However, this did not stop Jackie and Marlene from recording backgrounds for Jackie Wilson on some of his big hits, including "Higher and Higher." Marlene expresses the sentiment that The Andantes felt at the time, "Berry did not want anyone else to have his sound, but if you want anything exclusively, you have to pay exclusively."

In addition to backing Jackie Wilson, The Andantes did much work in Chicago with The Dells, John Lee Hooker, Bobby "Blue" Bland and Jerry Butler. Louvain recalls even taking Supreme Mary Wilson to sing on a John Lee Hooker session. Louvain did not join Jackie and Marlene on the sessions for Jackie Wilson. The third person was singer Pat Lewis, a former member of The Adorables, who recorded for the rival Detroit label, Ric-Tic/Golden World. When that company was taken over by Motown, Lewis became a substitute Andante, along with future Dawn member Telma Hopkins. Louvain recalls preparing the ladies for sub work, "Pat Lewis and Telma Hopkins started with us; they were groomed under us."

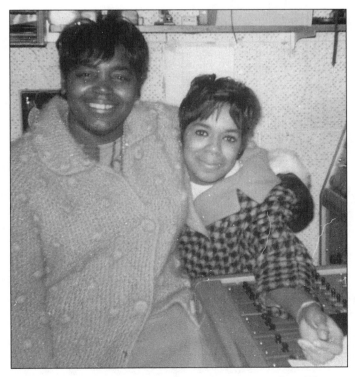

Jackie and Marlene enjoy a break at the Motown studios. (Photo courtesy of Louvain Demps)

The Andantes often shone on recordings behind Motown's solo artists. Marvin Gaye's "Ain't That Peculiar" and Brenda Holloway's "When I'm Gone" are just a handful of examples of The Andantes' exemplary work. Mary Wells' recording of "My Guy" was the first smash single with Andantes backing. The only chance that the group had to sing at a live performance was with Kim Weston, whom they backed regularly, in addition to her recordings. The Andantes' abilities would serve the Motown machine in other ways, as well.

As Motown Records moved forward and the company and its acts became bigger, the importance of having in-house musicians and vocalists to keep the wheels turning became more and more important. In the mid-60s, Motown was an extremely busy place. In the studio, The Andantes filled in for groups who were on the road. Therefore, the release of recordings adhered to a timely schedule. The Andantes were working so much, filling in on recordings by other Motown artists, they had their own office in the building. By 1966, The Motown sound was becoming more homogenized. The Andantes' strong voices were blended with backgrounds to fill out the sound on everyone's recordings. On some occasions, vocal accents were provided through overdubbing. On other occasions, The Andantes stood at one mike while the other group stood at another and the vocals were blended together. Many times, The Andantes' backing would be favored. Some groups were finding it hard to approximate this sound in live performance. Taking this

into consideration, The Temptations asked that the existence of Andantes' vocals on their recordings be stopped. As far as artist billing was concerned, the performing groups provided the image for the public and the framework for premium recordings. The Andantes were session people, like the guitarist or the piano player. They received salaries and were paid session fees.

During 1966, there was much trouble brewing within the ranks of Motown's premier female group, The Supremes. Motown was preparing Diana Ross for her solo career. This did not sit well with Florence Ballard, who began missing performances. Many times, Marlene Barrow was often tapped to be a last minute stand-in for the ailing Ballard before her departure from The Supremes. Starting in 1967, The Andantes were used on all singles by The Supremes, replacing Mary Wilson and Cindy Birdsong, until Diana's departure. This employment was a way of stylistically separating Diana Ross from her group mates, preparing the record-buying public for Diana Ross as a separate entity. Marlene did not consider her temporary position in The Supremes as an offer to replace Florence Ballard; "I stood in during the time that she (Ballard) formally left the group. I think that they had Cindy in mind from the start, but they had to straighten out everything with the contracts. I knew the songs, so they didn't have to teach me the songs. I also fit her gowns."

Jackie saw things a little differently. She feels Marlene could have had the spot if she so chose, "I think they were considering Marlene, but if Marlene was to join The Supremes, she'd have to leave The Andantes and tour, which is something she didn't want to do."

Marlene came pretty close to a favored position, filling in on important dates like the dress rehearsal for The Supremes' show at The Copacabana, staged at The Basin Street East in Boston, as well as shows scheduled in other prominent venues.

As a unit, The Andantes continued to impress, particularly with their background work for Marvin Gaye and The Four Tops. They performed seemingly effortless call and response vocals on "I Heard It Through The Grapevine", a supportive chorus on "Bernadette" and the chorus of tears on Stevie Wonder's "Purple Raindrops."

However, by the end of the 1960s, the work began to slow down. One of their last efforts was to supply backing vocals for Wanda Rogers, her work originally slated as a solo LP for her, then assigned the title of "The Return of The Marvelettes." New, more self-contained artists were joining the Motown roster. Still, Louvain remembers the sessions as fairly abundant, "Even in the final hours there, we did so much stuff we didn't know what was coming out. We did some recordings with Rare Earth…and did work with Ashford & Simpson. Motown simply never offered to take us to California."

Berry Gordy performed less as a hands-on company head and delegated more authority to others. The company was starting to diversify and the employee roster was growing. Gordy was planning more involvement in the movies. When it was evident that Motown was moving to Los Angeles for good, many of the artists were not asked to join the move. When Motown finally relocated in 1972, many of

Louvain on the cover of her recent LP. (Photo courtesy of Louvain Demps)

the musicians and vocalists were left in Detroit, including The Andantes. Jackie recounts how unceremonious the move was, "It wasn't so much that they moved, because we didn't want to go, nor were we asked to."

By 1973, The Andantes were finding work less and less frequently in Detroit. This was certainly not because they were not wanted, but when Motown left Detroit, they took the Detroit music scene with them. The Andantes were still in demand at United Studios, but it was no match for the level of work that they received while at Motown. After Motown departed, Louvain received an offer for a contract with ABC-Dunhill Records, the label that The Four Tops signed with after Motown went west. Unfortunately, the deal fell through. Eventually, Louvain accepted work that was being offered in Atlanta, Georgia. Her departure finally split The Andantes, who had stayed a cohesive team for such a long time.

During the 1970s, Louvain recorded for GRC Records in Atlanta with Mike Thevis on a project called "Gatsby", in which her voice was overdubbed five times. She then joined The Richard Law Singers, making live appearances in Nashville and Atlanta and recording the soundtrack for the movie "Black Starlet" in 1974. They also sang behind the famous Harlem Globetrotter Meadowlark Lemon. Louvain's memorable soprano also graced recordings by Jonathan Edwards and Loleatta Holloway. Louvain has recorded jingles for the local news and the acclaimed show "Look Up Atlanta." In addition, she worked with Telma Hopkins and Joyce Vincent backing Joe Hinton. Louvain ultimately moved south to take advantage of the plethora of work she had found. In addition to her singing, Louvain is employed as a governess and has also found fulfillment as an evangelist.

Marlene and Jackie worked for awhile in Detroit, but eventually gave up singing as a full-time job. Marlene then settled down to raise her family in Detroit. Jackie also lives in Detroit. Jackie and Louvain are two of the former Motown artists who come out for the annual fundraisers that Esther Gordy Edwards sponsors for the Motown museum, housed at the original location of Motown Records on W. Grand Boulevard. In 1987, The Andantes got together with other former Motown artists, The Velvelettes, Carolyn Crawford, and Mary Wilson, to record for Ian Levine's Nightmare Records, interestingly, named for The Andantes' single. They recorded a version of "Reach Out and Touch", with Pat Lewis joining them for this session and, in 1994, Louvain went to London to record as a soloist for Levine, recording the LP, "Better Times."

As for the part the group played in Rock & Roll history, The Andantes would like more recognition for their roles as an essential part of what made the sound of Motown. Recordings from Motown's golden age are continually repackaged and sold, with previously unreleased product being available to the public. The Motown Corporation has been sold numerous times, and is now part of a large conglomerate, Polygram. The Andantes see their involvement as part of the driving force that entices new generations of listeners to possess Motown products. The Andantes provided enhancing vocals for many Motown singles, having as much of an important place in the Motown studios as Earl Van Dyke and The Funk Brothers Band, forming the sounds that would define a generation of recordings known as "The Sound of Young America."

The Andantes Discography

45s	Label	Number	Year
Like A Nightmare/If You Were Mine	VIP	25004	1964
Reach Out and Touch	Nightmare	--	1987
(as The Darnells w/The Marvelettes)			
Too Hurt To Cry, Too Much In Love To Say Goodbye/Come On Home	Gordy	7024	1963
(as Holland-Dozier w/The Four Tops)			
What Goes Up, Must Come Down/Come On Home (inst.)	Motown	1045	1963
(w/Billy Kent)			
Take All Of Me/Your Love	Mahs	0002	1961
(w/Amos Milburn)			
I'll Make It Up To You Somehow/My Baby Gave Me Another Chance	Motown	1038	1963
(w/Mary Wells)			
Laughing Boy/Two Wrongs Don't Make A Right	Motown	1039	1963
The Rayber Voices w/Barrett Strong			
I'm Gonna Cry/Whirlwind	Tamla	54033	1960

LPs			
Louvain Demps			
Better Times	Nightmare	--	1994

(There are thousands of recordings for Motown Records where The Andantes remain unaccredited.)

The Angels

Members:

The universally understood story of a teenage girl telling a fresh boy to stop hitting on her and threatening to send her huge, hulking boyfriend after him to inflict retribution came across quite effectively when three girls from New Jersey told the tale in their signature song, "My Boyfriend's Back." The renown of this song is just the tip of the iceberg for the group who made it notable, The Angels.

The group began singing as The Starlets in Orange, NJ in 1960. They were a quartet instituted by sisters Barbara

Astro Records   THE STARLETS   Personal Management
TOM DeCILLIS
Elizabeth 3-0468   N. J.

Before they were Angels, they were Starlets, 1960, (clockwise from top left) Phyllis (Jiggs) Allbut, Barbara Allbut, Linda Malzone, Bernadette Carroll. (Photo courtesy of Tom DeCillis)

and Phyllis (Jiggs) Allbut. Prior to forming a group, Barbara and Jiggs grew up singing for fun. As time progressed, the sisters honed their talents by singing songs which Barbara had written. Barbara and Jiggs were born on the same day, two years apart. On one occasion for their birthday, Barbara and Jiggs received some money, so they went to a local recording studio to record some of Barbara's songs. While they were there, they happened upon a portly, cigar-chomping man named Bob Minute who wanted to know if they would record his songs. The two girls agreed, so he took them to another, more elaborate studio to record his compositions.

The girls displayed their natural abilities in the studio, and soon other people who Barbara and Jiggs met while on these musical excursions would ask them to record demos. It was through this ever-growing network that the two sisters met one of their soon-to-be groupmates for The Starlets, Bernadette Carroll. Bernadette came to the group through songwriter and producer Tom DeCillis, whom the girls met while recording in Linden, New Jersey. Linda Malzone came into the group after becoming friends with Barbara at WABC (where they both worked) and Tom became the group's manager.

Barbara played the piano and knew how to arrange, so she put the group's songs together and also taught Jiggs, Bernadette, and Linda how to sing harmony. She wrote a song called "Where Is My Love Tonight," and with Tom DeCillis producing, The Starlets recorded it and the standard, "P.S. I Love You," with Linda singing the plaintive leads. The single was placed with Astro Records, a tiny Newark label, co-owned by Vince Burke, Don Smith and Marty Ostroff. According to DeCillis, Astro's owners were jazz enthusiasts and not interested in Rock & Roll. They didn't know what to do with the label.

Tom offered his help to promote The Starlets single. Through his efforts, "P.S. I Love You" gained local airplay and soon Canadian-American Records offered to distribute the single. Meanwhile, Astro released another single, "Romeo Loves Juliet/Lonely Tambourine." At this time, the girls were busy doing demos and backing vocals for other artists. Bernadette had dropped out as a full-time Starlet to pursue a solo career. She recorded one single for Tom DeCillis' Julia Records, "My Heart Stood Still," and one for Tommy Falcone's Cleopatra label before recording her big hit on Laurie Records in 1964, the bouncy "Party Girl," with Tom DeCillis co-producing. Linda Malzone also left The Starlets and was replaced by Linda Jankowski, who was introduced to Barbara and Jiggs by Tom's wife. When the time came to renew contracts, DeCillis, busy with other efforts, released them.

In 1961, through the Canadian-American connection, the trio signed with Caprice Records, co-owned by Neal Galligan, arranger Hutch Davie and singer/songwriter Gerry Granahan. The Starlets decided on a name change at this time. After sifting through magazines and taking friendly suggestions, they decided on The Blue Angels, but quickly shortened it to The Angels.

The Angels' first effort at the label was the recording of another standard, the very beautiful "Til," flipped with another of Barbara's compositions, the dreamy "A Moment Ago," published through Tom DeCillis' Tee Dee Music. Linda lent her crisp, clear lead to both sides, using it effectively for these wistful ballads. Although it took time, "Til" made it to the top of the charts.

Since another hit was now needed for the group, their producers sent them to Philadelphia to hear some songs. The group sat with songwriter Morris Bailey, and after listening to many songs, decided on the intense "Cry Baby Cry." It was released in early 1962. Its flip, the charming "That's All I Ask of You," was another endearing tune co-written by Gerry Granahan and Wes Farrell. "Cry Baby

Cry" broke into the top 40 and was a huge hit in the New York area. As a result of these premium productions, The Angels began getting work recording demos and singing backup on records for other artists. They also recorded jingles and radio spots, which certainly kept their voices at the forefront of New York radio.

Before Peggy Santiglia joined The Angels, she came into the music business while still in high school. Always a prolific writer, Peggy wrote songs about her friends, their boyfriends and the cars they drove. "Black And White Thunderbird," "Ronnie Is My Lover," and "Too Young To Date" were some of Peggy's songs. She and two of her friends, Denise Ferri and Arlene Lanzotti, formed a group called The Delicates while still at School #8 in Belleville, NJ in 1959. The group had gotten their name because one of the girls' parents ran a delicatessen on Union Ave. The trio's first recording was for Tender Records in 1959. One day, Peggy and Denise skipped school to pitch one of Peggy's tunes to their favorite deejay, Murray the K. They walked into the station's office and told Murray's secretary that they had an appointment. Peggy remembers the story, "I played hooky from school and got on a bus in the middle of winter with Denise. I'm sure they knew we did not have an appointment. They brought us up to him, he recorded us, and we listened to ourselves on the radio that night."

From that moment on, The Delicates were Murray's sweethearts. Through him they met Billy Mure and

The Angels on American Bandstand, 1962, (from left) manager Tom DeCillis, Linda Jankowski, Barbara Allbut, Dick Clark, Jiggs Allbut, songwriter Morris Bailey. (Photo courtesy of Tom DeCillis)

Don Costa, who produced them for United Artists Records. The Delicates spent most of their time at Murray's studio coming up with songs tailored for him. One result was a song based on the language Murray used with the teenagers. It was called "Meusurray," released in 1959 on the United Artists subsidiary, Unart Records. Peggy also wrote Murray's "Submarine Race Watchers' Theme."

The Delicates performed at many engagements around the New York/New Jersey area, once doing a summer tour with teen heartthrob Paul Anka. The Delicates frequently shared the bill with The Starlets. The Delicates admired The Starlets' intricate arrangements and their deft handling of standards like "Pennies From Heaven;" meanwhile The Delicates were performing covers of novelty tunes like "Western Movies." Under the direction of

producer Don Costa, The Delicates' recorded lightweight pop tunes like "Your Happiest Years," and "Flip, Flip" with pleasant, temperate harmonies, nothing to compare with the songs and arrangements Peggy would be fronting in just two years. The Delicates kept themselves in the public eye locally, appearing at various functions in their hometown of Belleville, along with another hometown act, Connie Francis.

By 1961, The Delicates had gone over to Roulette Records to record three singles. Arlene had dropped out of the group in 1960, so the act was now a duo. The initial single for Roulette was a Country and Western flavored tune entitled "Little Ship." This song was provided by the talents of Doc Pomus and Mort Shuman, already responsible for The Drifters' "This Magic Moment" and Elvis Presley's "His Latest Flame." The second single for

The belles from Belleville, The Delicates, 1959, (L-R) Arlene Lanzotti, Peggy Santiglia, Denise Ferri. (Photo courtesy of Peggy Santiglia Davison)

Roulette was a version of The Cleftones' "Little Girl Of Mine," appropriately retitled "Little Boy Of Mine," flipped with "Dickie Went And Did It." One more single, "I Don't Know Why," was released during 1961. Although all of The Delicates' singles enjoyed local airplay, they fell short of making the national charts.

In addition to being a Delicate while still in high school, Peggy was also commissioned as a staff writer at April-Blackwood Music in New York. Now, instead of leisurely writing ditties for herself and her friends, she was being paid to write songs on demand. She was paired with a host of different writers, many of whom were older, veteran songwriters. They had written what had come to be known as "standards." Some notable songwriters with which Peggy wrote were Ben Raleigh and Jean Thomas. Peggy found it amazing that what she wrote was turned into large orchestrations complete with string and horn sections. Peggy also found herself being utilized as a session singer for demos and jingles. On these occasions she worked with Barbara and Jiggs who were also hired for background. The girls thought that they blended very well, both vocally and socially. A unique bond was forming between these three young girls, a bond which would have more significance than the girls realized at the time.

During 1962, The Angels were quickly becoming one of the top female groups in the country. Ironically, after two successful ballad hits in a row, the group's production team decided on another direction, recording a novelty version of "Everybody Loves A Lover" flipped with the uptempo "Blow Joe." Fortunately, the group recovered from that move. They recorded another ballad, "I'd Be Good For You" flipped with the timely, "You Should Have Told Me." Unfortunately, these singles did not restore the group to the charts.

The Angels were having better luck with the more lucrative and sure-footed session singing. It was on one of these sessions that Barbara and Jiggs became friendly with the hatchling writing and production company of Richard Gottehrer, Robert Feldman and Jerry Goldstein. "FGG" had been signed to various publishing houses before going out on their own. "FGG" worked with Gerry Granahan, producing the last Caprice single for The Angels. When the songwriters cornered a deal with Smash Records, The Angels followed their new production team. FGG bought out the group's contract from Gerry Granahan. Granahan released an album of their singles on Caprice and two more singles, one on Caprice, the recycled "A Moment Ago" flipped with a version of the standard "Cotton Fields," and one on Ascot Records, "Cotton Fields" flipped with "Irresistible."

Before the move to Smash Records, disagreements within the group resulted in Linda's resignation. Linda continued recording as a soloist under the name Carol Lynn Brent. Barbara and Jiggs now needed a lead singer to replace Linda. The sisters had become friendly with Peggy after working with her at recording sessions for backgrounds, and remembered how well the trio meshed, both on a personal and creative level. When Peggy's contract was up with Don Costa and The Delicates, she immediately filled the spot vacated by Linda.

The Angels, now exclusively with FGG, scored with a song that had been written after one of the team heard some girl in the street yelling at a boy. She was threatening this guy with a visit from her strapping beau. The result was the inimitable "My Boyfriend's Back." The song was a stone smash right from the start. The song begins with a spoken intro by Peggy, accompanied by rhythmic handclapping to get one's attention. The tone in Peggy's voice sounds like she's jabbing her index finger right into this guy's shoulder. The backing vocals soon join to tell this boor what is in store for him now that he's crossed the line. All at once these girls are ganging up on him, heralding the fate which is about to beset this teenage masher.

The feelings delivered by "My Boyfriend's Back" were the first of their kind in the genre. This trendsetting song became one of the most played records of its time and is even still being used today, both in its original form and as a parody, most notably in the rock opera, "Godspell," a testimony to its entrenchment in American musical society. Twenty years later Richard Gottehrer was still taking cues from his original production, using obvious elements on The Go-Go's "We Got The Beat" in 1981. It was a hit of such magnitude that it was almost inescapable. Jiggs tells how the song became ubiquitous, "The biggest thrill was hearing the song air on the three biggest stations in the New York area. Once we were about to ride through the Lincoln Tunnel and the song came on, so we pulled over until it was finished . . . we had to hear it."

Gracing the B-side was the more traditional sounding, "(Love Me) Now." The song featured a rare lead by Barbara, and is noted among collectors because of the clearly audible sounds of objects being thrown onto the floor during the mix-down. This was FGG's attempt to deter the disc jockeys from flipping the record over. Jiggs reported that they just ran around the studio throwing every object not nailed down, even one of those heavy, standing ashtrays. The sounds do not appear on the LP version.

With the success of "My Boyfriend's Back," the group was scheduled to sing on all the popular music shows, including American Bandstand, as well as popular talk and variety shows. The Angels graced the screen on shows such as "The Tonight Show" and "Kraft Music Hall."

The Angels were also scheduled to sing their song on "The Ed Sullivan Show" and Peggy's grandmother made the girls' dresses. Peggy recalled receiving a phone call from the staff at the theater, leaving a message that the date had been moved up. The dresses that the group was to wear weren't ready, so the girls sang on "The Ed Sullivan Show" with their dresses pinned at the hems and in the back. But this wasn't the only time the girls faced "exposure." On Buddy Deane's show in Baltimore, as the group was starting the intro to "My Boyfriend's Back," they started shaking their bodies, and several adults called in to say they thought it was crude.

The girls were now treading the fast-paced world of the business of Rock & Roll, cutting demos, meeting new people and attending parties with music industry bigwigs. Of course there were the Rock & Roll shows,

The Delicates, 1961, (L-R) Denise, Peggy. (Photo courtesy of Peggy Santiglia Davison)

Peggy's first photo session as an Angel, 1963, (L-R) Barbara, Peggy, Jiggs. (Photo courtesy of Peggy Santiglia Davison)

namely those sponsored by Murray The K, who, of course, welcomed The Angels with open arms. Peggy and Jiggs always enthusiastically anticipated their experiences at these various shows and affairs. It was Barbara who was always the cautious one and the member of the group who would keep everyone else in check.

After the initial success of "My Boyfriend's Back," the girls thought that their follow-up should continue the story of the boy bothering the girl and getting his just desserts. The Angels recorded a song Peggy had co-written called "The Guy With The Black Eye," which would have been an appropriate song to come on the heels of "My Boyfriend's Back." Their opinion fell on deaf ears and the follow-up was the Spectoresce "I Adore Him," which shared chart action with its flip, "Thank You And Goodnight," a gorgeous, dreamy ballad, which perfectly fit the group's sound and lent itself to the end of many a disc jockey show. "The Boy With The Black Eye" ended up on the group's first Smash LP, "My Boyfriend's Back." The third single from Smash was the frenetic "Wow Wow Wee" and its seasonal flip, "Snowflakes And Teardrops." This pairing was the last single to chart. "Wow Wow Wee" tells the story of how a girl sets out to hook the boy of her dreams (while making him think it was his idea).

The Angels' singles had clever, teenage lyrics, which always had a succinct story line. These songs were carefully crafted Rock & Roll tunes, with Peggy's fanciful leads for the ballads and gutsy sounds for the jump tunes. The altitudinous backing vocals soared to the highest places on the musical scale. Bernadette Carroll was often brought in to round out the chords in the backgrounds. Although meticulously produced, the singles were not making the impact of earlier efforts by the group, however.

In 1964, The Angels released three singles. The first single, released in April, was The Beatles salute, "Little Beatle Boy," flipped with the amusing vocal version of Al Hirt's "Java." Just in time for those hot summer nights, FGG induced an innocent, yet seductive quality from Peggy's voice with the next single, the incredibly heavenly "Dream Boy," released in July. For the flip, FGG jumped on the blue beat bandwagon with the Caribbean-flavored "Jamaica Joe." The final single for 1964 received an updated arrangement by Leroy Glover, while borrowing guitar elements from Duane Eddy, giving "The Boy From Cross-town" a Motown-inspired groove made famous on songs like "Dancing In The Street." "World Without Love," taken from an earlier session, again taps into the sweet, sensual quality in Peggy's voice.

The songs were basic Angels' formulas and well worth the effort for a voice like Peggy's. Peggy was also corralled to record a solo single produced by Bob Crewe and neighborhood friend Frankie Valli. Originally slated as an Angels single, "Snowman" and "Give Your Love," which Peggy co-wrote (as Peggy Farina), was released as Peggy Sans on the Vee Jay subsidiary, Tollie Records,

The Angels in their famous balloon dresses, 1963, (L-R) Peggy, Barbara, Jiggs (Photo courtesy of Peggy Santiglia Davison)

Bernadette Carroll, 1964. (Photo courtesy of Sheila Burgel)

after Peggy added some extra vocals to the original backgrounds. Despite these marvelous singles and an album, "A Halo To You," The Angels did not return to the charts for 1964. After watching their superior efforts go nowhere, The Angels did not record under their own name for almost three years.

As 1964 and 1965 drew on, The Angels were thinking of themselves less and less as pop chart toppers. They were finishing various musical projects under pseudonyms, while concentrating on their emerging nightclub act. The results of one of these sessions were singles released as The Beachnuts, who were actually The Angels with FGG and Jean Thomas. FGG had their own studio recordings on the charts as The Strangeloves, who recorded "I Want Candy" and "Cara-Lin" on Bang Records. This was one more angle to try. The Beachnuts' theme revolved around, of course, the beach. One significant single by the studio group on Bang was "Out In The Sun," featuring call-and-response lines by the two groups with a tropical beat underlining the vocals. Actually, upon listening to follow-up efforts by the studio-concocted group, it is dubious that The Angels are on any follow-up recordings.

With no significant events occurring for The Angels, Peggy took a leave of absence from the group in 1965. She was replaced by Toni Mason. Toni's voice possessed a spirited quality, certainly changing the more lucid tones of the group's tight harmonies. This trio recorded three singles for Congress Records, not as The Angels, but as The Halos, the most celebrated single being their lithesome version of "Since I Fell For You." These productions employed all the current trends; a Motown-influenced version of Jimmy Reed's "Baby What You Want Me To Do" and the British Invasion-flavored "Hey, Hey Love Me." Unfortunately, the singles lacked cohesiveness and didn't make an impact. As the group's chart success waned, they concentrated their efforts on their live act, not even bothering to sing the hits which put them at the forefront of pop music just two years before. Jiggs reflects on that time: "We changed our name to The Halos and sang in supper clubs. There was a time when we didn't do our own songs. There was no nostalgia back then. It wasn't until the revival that we started singing our hits again."

Although the camaraderie was there for the three women, Toni's lack of experience within a group made it difficult for The Halos to achieve the right blend. She stayed for about two years.

At this same point in time, Peggy found herself completing more and more studio work. United Artists was recording Patty Duke, then a teenage television star. It was common practice to cast any teenage TV or film star

The Angels, 1976, (from top) Barbara, Peggy, Jiggs. (Photo courtesy of Peggy Santiglia Davison)

Jiggs and Peggy in the 1980s. (Photo courtesy of Peggy Santiglia Davison)

as a singer, whether they could sing or not. Peggy remembers Patty standing at the microphone wrapped in a fur coat. At the end of the session, after Patty had left, Peggy sang to all the tracks. The producer, Jack Gold and arranger Arnold Goland blended just enough of Peggy's leads with Patty's to make them sound more "beautiful." The result was "Don't Just Stand There." Also during this period, Peggy was part of one of the most famous backgrounds in Rock and Roll history, composing the arrangement and backing Lou Christie on his huge hit, "Lightning Strikes," along with Bernadette Carroll and fellow Delicate, Denise Ferri. Jiggs also helped Lou Christie on "Rhapsody In The Rain" and later, in 1969, with "I'm Gonna Make You Mine." Sometimes someone would call for one person to fill in backgrounds, so group members took turns.

Barbara and Jiggs kept the group going in Peggy's absence, commissioning Mason, former Pixies Three member Debra Swisher and Bernadette Carroll to front the group in varying rotations for their club shows. Coincidentally, FGG had produced a version of "Thank You And Goodnight" with Debra Swisher on the Bang subsidiary, Boom Records, in 1965. Peggy completed another project as a singer/songwriter, a series of recordings that were released on Dyno Voice Records as Jessica James and The Outlaws. "We'll Be Makin' Out/Lucky Day," "Give Her Up, Baby/Come Closer" and a version of "Blue Skies" were the cuts by this fictitious group, but the cut which stands out for Peggy is a version of "Dixie," which was banned because promoters in some

radio markets feared it would cause a problem, in light of the civil rights movement. Peggy emphasizes that this was certainly not their intention, "This recording was among the best of what I did with Bob Crewe and Bob Gaudio. The original orchestrations were unique. Some stations would not accept it, yet Jose Feliciano's version came out a short time later."

Also, during her leave of absence from The Angels, Peggy put together a nightclub act that she took to various clubs around New York. One night at The Bitter End, Peggy was introduced to the powers behind The Serendipity Singers by Fred Weintraub, owner of the club. They were looking for a rock vocalist to round out their troupe. Peggy spent some time as part of their ensemble. Peggy recorded one album with The Serendipity Singers entitled, "Love Is A State Of Mind. This album yielded one single on United Artists, Neil Diamond's "The Boat That I Row." She also continued her efforts as a songwriter. Co-writing (as Peggy Farina) with Bob Gaudio, Peggy penned "Beggin" for The Four Seasons and "September Rain" for one of Frankie Valli's solo efforts. Peggy considers her efforts as an extension of her capabilities as a singer, "When I wasn't with the group, it wasn't because I didn't like The Angels. My mission for myself was to expand my horizons as a singer. I was combining rock and jazz."

With Debra and Bernadette fronting The Angels during 1967-68, the sound of the group was altered. They were starting to lean more toward a pop sound. This was evident in the assemblage of singles the group recorded

THE ANGELS

Peggy and Jiggs in the 1990s. (Photo courtesy of Peggy Santiglia Davison)

Appearing as a trio, 1998, (L-R) Jiggs, Barbara, Peggy. (Photo courtesy of Peggy Santiglia Davison)

for RCA Records. Chart success with these singles was elusive. Songs like "I Had A Dream I Lost You" and "The Boy With The Green Eyes" were seriously mild in comparison to the singles of just a few years before. Jiggs doesn't look unfavorably upon the RCA years, however, "Every recording time was really great. We loved going into the studio, but the records at RCA didn't do much. We were just having a really good time." Since The Angels were still concentrating on their nightclub act, the trio was not especially concerned about not having a hit record.

In 1969, Peggy returned to the group. The Angels were still recording as a back-up vocalists during 1970, when Peggy was asked to be the lead singer for a studio group called Dusk which was being produced by Hank Medress of The Tokens and former Cameo-Parkway writer/arranger, Dave Appell. The singles were recorded during 1970-71 with Peggy and a studio group. Two of the four, "Angel Baby" and "I Hear Those Church Bells Ringing," made the national charts, becoming staples in the top 10 in some local markets. The other singles were "Treat Me Like A Good Piece Of Candy" and "Point Of No Return."

Peggy and Barbara were asked if they wanted to be a part of another project that the producers were undertaking. The producers had a companion project to Dusk, appropriately called Dawn, a studio group with Tony Orlando singing lead. The first Dawn recording, "Candida," had become a hit, so the studio group needed to become a real group. After singing backup on Dawn's next hit single, "Knock Three Times," Peggy and Barbara were asked if they wanted to be part of Dawn, but that would have meant putting The Angels on hold. They passed, so Telma Hopkins and Joyce Vincent got the jobs.

The Angels' lineup of Peggy, Barbara and Jiggs continued their club work throughout the 1970s. They recorded one more single in 1974 on Polydor Records. They had been contacted by former Toys producer Denny Randell, who had an idea for a single which he wanted The Angels to record. One tune was a version of Marvin Gaye and Tammi Terrell's hit, "You're All I Need To Get By," flipped with the light Country and Western song, "Papa's Side Of The Bed," produced by Ray Dahrouge. The group continued with their appearances in nightclubs and what was now becoming "The Nostalgia Cir-

cuit." In 1978, Peggy recorded a Brazilian album under the name Fantasia, featuring Peggy Santiglia, entitled, "Fantasia Carnivale," which was sold in foreign markets. It yielded the dance single, "Go On And Dance/Sweet, Sweet City Rhythm," a big hit in South America. It was released on TK Records, then a red-hot company featuring many prominent singles of the disco era. Jiggs was also busy with acting, modeling and doing voice-overs for well-known products such as Thom McAnn Shoes and The Money Store.

As the 1970s drew on, Barbara decided she had enough of the grind of keeping a performing group running, and decided to retire from The Angels. Lana Shaw, a singer who Peggy had met while she was in The Serendipity Singers, was commissioned for the group. Lana was an experienced group singer and had also done studio work and jingles, as both Peggy and Jiggs had done. Lana performed with The Angels for about a year.

After Lana left the group, Peggy and Jiggs decided not to replace her. Barbara does come back for an occasional show, however. The focus of the group's act has changed over the years. Both Jiggs and Peggy know how to update vocal and musical arrangements in order to keep them current and relevant to all audiences. During recent years, Peggy and Jiggs have continued to build a superior night club act, concentrating on their own personal strengths as singers and not just as part of a group. Peggy has guest starred on The High School Sweethearts' CD, "Passing Notes." The artist is Peggy's niece, Cynthia. Barbara has taken to writing new songs for The Angels, one of which they've been singing in their act, and which they hope to record. Jiggs is optimistic about another venture, "We'd like to start our own publishing company. If the songs don't do anything for us, they're great demos to send around."

The Angels' undertakings have taken them all around the world. The popularity of the group and their material has kept them in the public eye, years after many of their contemporaries faded from the music scene. Actually, The Angels never left. They bravely rode all the crests in the popular music industry, evolving as necessary, yet they still evoke the same feelings now as in 1963 when they first warned us that he went away and you hung around. Watch out!

The Angels Discography

45s	Label	Number	Year
(The Delicates)			
The Johnny Bunny/My First Date	Tender	818	1959
Black And White Thunderbird/Ronnie Is My Lover	Unart	2017	
Meusurry/Ringa Ding		2024	
Flip Flip/Your Happiest Years	United Artists	210	1960
Too Young To Date/The Kiss		228	
Little Ship/Not Tomorrow	Roulette	4321	1961
Little Boy Of Mine/Dickie Went And Did It		4360	
I Don't Know Why/Strange Love		4387	
(as The Starlets)			
P.S. I Love You/Where Is My Love Tonight	Astro	202/203	1960
Romeo Loves Juliet/Lonely Tambourine		204/205	

45s	**Label**	**Number**	**Year**
(The Angels)			
'Til/A Moment Ago	Caprice	107	1961
Cry Baby Cry/That's All I Ask Of You		112	1962
Everybody Loves A Lover/Blow Joe		116	
You Should Have Told Me/I'd Be Good For You		118	
Cotton Fields/A Moment Ago		121	1963
Cotton Fields/Irresistible	Ascot	2139	
My Boyfriend's Back/Love Me Now	Smash	1834	
Thank You And Goodnight/I Adore Him		1854	
Wow Wow Wee/Snowflakes And Teardrops		1870	
Little Beatle Boy/Java		1885	1964
Dream Boy/Jamaica Joe		1915	
Boy From Cross-town/World Without Love		1931	
I Had A Dream I Lost You/What To Do	RCA	9129	1967
Go Out And Play/You'll Never Get To Heaven		9246	
You're The Cause Of It/With Love		9404	
The Modley/If I Didn't Love You		9541	1968
The Boy With The Green Eyes/But For Love		9612	
Merry-Go-Round/So Nice		9681	
Papa's Side Of The Bed/You're All I Need To Get By	Polydor	14222	1974
(The Halos)			
Do I/Just Keep On Loving Me	Congress	244	1965
Since I Fell For You/You're Never Gonna Find		249	
Baby What You Want Me To Do/Hey, Hey Love Me		253	
(as Dusk)			
Angel Baby/If We Just Leave Today	Bell	961	1971
I Hear Those Church Bells Ringing/I Cannot See To See You		990	
Treat Me Like A Good Piece Of Candy/Suburbia U.S.A. (inst.)		148	
Point Of No Return/--	--		
(as Angie & The Chicklettes w/Jean Thomas)			
Treat Him Tender, Maureen/Tommy	Apt	25080	1964
(as The Beach Nuts w/Jean Thomas and FGG)			
Out In The Sun (Hey-O)/Someday Soon	Bang	504	1965
Peggy Santiglia (as Peggy Sans)			
Snow Man/Give Your Love	Tollie	9018	1964
(as Jessica James and The Outlaws)			
Give Her Up, Baby/Come Closer	Dyno Voice	213	1965
We'll Be Makin' Out/Lucky Day		220	1966
We'll Be Makin' Out/Lucky Day	Bronco	220	
Blue Skies/--	--		
Peggy Santiglia w/The Serendipity Singers			
The Boat That I Row/--	United Artists	50168	1967
(as Fantasia feat. Peggy Santiglia)			
Go On And Dance/Sweet, Sweet City Rhythms	TK Disco	102	1978
Bernadette Carroll			
My Heart Stood Still/Sweet Sugar Sweet	Julia	1106	1962
Heavenly/Laughing On The Outside	Cleopatra	5	
All The Way Home I Cried/Nicky	Laurie	3217	1963
Party Girl/I Don't Wanna Know		3238	1964
Happy Birthday/Homecoming Party		3268	
One Little Lie/The Hero		3278	
Circus Girl/Don't Hurt Me		3311	1965
He's Just A Playboy/Try Your Luck		3320	
Linda Jankowski (as Carol Lynn Brent)			
Rose Of Washington Square/My Man	Congress	213	1963
Toni Mason			
One More Tear/Love Theme From "The Sandpipers"	Jubilee	5571	1965
LPs			
And The Angels Sing	Caprice	1001	1962
The Angels Sing Twelve Of Their Greatest Hits	Ascot	13009	1963
My Boyfriend's Back	Smash	7039	
A Halo To You	Smash	7048	1964
(as Fantasia feat. Peggy Santiglia)			
Fantasia Carnivale	TK	--	1978
(Peggy Santiglia with The Serendipity Singers)			
Love Is A State Of Mind	United Artists	6619	1967

Honey And The Bees

Members:

(1965-72) Nadine Felder, Lead
Jean Davis
Gwendolyn Oliver
Cassandra (Ann) Wooten

The sounds of group harmony experienced a meta-morphosis during the 1960s. Basic songs with simple chords were performed on the streets of American cities during the 1950s. Many were takes on street songs made up by aspiring singers, some of which became national favorites when recorded.

As new ideas for group harmony singing changed with public tastes, producers and arrangers orchestrated more composite treatments for R&B, most notably with strings and horns. Philadelphia held the strongest link between stark harmonies of the 1950s and sweet, inter-twining harmonies and steady, seamless unison of the 1960s, amidst imposing orchestration. Fine examples of this style are evident in records by Eddie Holman, The Larks, Delfonics and Ambassadors, among others. Female groups also engaged in this brand of soul harmony. A prime example of the genre is the serene sounds of the soul quartet, Honey and The Bees.

This Philadelphia group originated in 1965, recording a single for Academy Records, "Two Can Play The Same Game/Inside O' Me." According to songwriter Phil Hurtt, who co-wrote "Two Can Play The Same Game," the group that recorded the Academy single disappeared shortly after its release.

The concept of recording a group with this sound was not forgotten, however, as the name was revived a year later with a different lineup of singers, lead by Nadine Felder, sister of singer/songwriter Allan Felder. The other members were Jean Davis, Cassandra Ann Wooten, and Gwendolyn Oliver. This configuration began record-ing for Arctic Records in 1966. The first single for Arctic was the Kenny Gamble tune, "One Time Is Forever." A year later, the quartet proved they were no flash in the pan with their interpretation of Allan Felder's moving ballad, "(You Better) Go Now." The production is ripe with clever production cues like the violin intro and gui-tar kicks before the refrain. Honey and The Bees singles are noteworthy for both resonant harmonies and conge-nial unison supporting Nadine's crystalline soprano lead. Bobby Martin provides viable musical arrange-ments for both the ballad side and it's uptempo B-side, "Why Do You Want To Hurt The One Who Loves You."

More singles followed on the eclectic record label. "Love Addict," "Together Forever" and a splendid ver-sion of "Sunday Kind Of Love" were released in 1969. All these creative renditions did not benefit from the rewards of chart action.

After Arctic Records folded, Honey and The Bees made a brief stop at North Bay Records for a Christmas tune, the jovial "Jing Jing A Ling" co-written by Philadelphia song-sters Norman Harris and Jimmy Bishop. This single con-tains audible cues for Vince Montana's production of "Christmas Time" recorded with The Salsoul Orchestra in 1976. It was paired with a timely arrangement for Auld Lang Syne, the beginning chime reminiscent of early 1960s Philadelphia sound made popular by The Dreamlovers' "When We Get Married." The celebratory tunes were sub-sequently leased to Chess Records for release. After this, the group would once again change labels.

The next stop for Honey and The Bees productions were with Josie Records in New York, starting with the reassuring love anthem, "Help Me (Get Over My Used To Be Lover)," an engaging dance tune with a thumping tempo. The group banked on tearful ballads, with the contrary "Love Can Turn To Hate" and the somber "What About Me." A clever medley of Teddy Randazzo productions compacted into a smooth version of The Royalettes hit "It's Gonna Take A Miracle" netted the group some local chart action in Philly and New York. Honey and The Bees then recorded two singles for Bell Records, including the revealing "Has Somebody Taken My Place." With nothing happening for these two sin-gles, the group dispersed in 1972.

After the demise of Honey and The Bees, two members of the group continued with studio session work during the early 1970s. Songwriter and arranger Ritchie Rome was the conductor of an orchestra in Philadelphia that was recording dance tracks for the new brand of uptempo soul emerging from Philadelphia and other major cities in the 1970s, disco. Rome headed an ensemble that had joined forces with French producer Jacques Morali to record a disco version of the Latin standard, "Brazil."

When the record was released, the orchestra was dubbed The Ritchie Family, after its conductor. Session singer and future Sweetheart of Sigma, Barbara Ingram recorded the vocals for the single, which became an enor-mous hit early in 1975. An album followed, filled with the fusion of lush orchestral arrangements and the steady, hi-hat disco beat. Since Barbara had no desire to go out on the road to promote the single, former Honey and The Bees members Cassandra and Gwendolyn were selected to be the vocalists to front the orchestra. These two ladies and Cheryl Mason Jacks would become the faces identified as The Ritchie Family.

In 1976, The Ritchie Family recorded their next single, a reprise of earlier dance floor hits called "The Best Disco In Town," co-written by Rome, Morali, Henri Belolo and songwriter Phil Hurtt. This medley was the second smash for the orchestra. An LP based on an Arabic theme was released to capitalize on the single's success. A photo of Cheryl, Cassandra and Gwen, all decked out in Middle Eastern regalia, graced the cover. Successful tours and two more albums followed, the mildly successful "Life Is Music" followed a more traditional approach, depicting the ladies in gowns and furs, even labeling their names over their pictures on the back cover.

Their best selling LP, however, was "African Queens," a frantic, non-stop succession of sizzling summer disco tracks compacted into one wild mix. This LP was based on African Themes, describing in details the virtues of Nefertiti, Cleopatra and the Queen of Sheba. A bubbling version of Martin Denny's "Quiet Village" and the dizzying effects of "A Summer Dance" anchored itself in the top 10 disco LPs in the summer of 1977 and stayed on deejays' platters for over a year.

However, as a blind testimonial of image over substance in the world of disco, professional dancers who could also sing replaced Cheryl, Cassandra, and Gwen in The Ritchie Family in 1978. This oriented the orchestra for live shows with more choreographed movement and theatrics. Morali's statement at the time was that The Ritchie Family was a concept, therefore subject to changes of this nature, claiming the vocalists were not the central focus of the act. Jacks and Wooten returned to studio work, featured as backing vocalists for John Lennon and Yoko Ono on Double Fantasy and Yoko's subsequent solo ventures.

Although their benefaction was sporadic, Honey and The Bees proved to be among Philadelphia's best representations of supreme sweet soul, their talent enhanced, but never tempered by the songwriters and producers who directed them, even amidst changing musical styles. The sounds of Honey and The Bees are a true illustration of classic Philadelphia female soul harmony.

Honey And The Bees Discography

45s

	Label	Number	Year
Inside O' Me/Two Can Play The Same Game	Academy	114	1965
I'm Confessin'/One Time Is Forever	Arctic	118	1966
(You Better) Go Now/Why Do You Hurt The One Who Loves You		141	1968
Love Addict/I'll Be There		149	1969
Together Forever/Dynamite Exploded		152	
Sunday Kind Of Love/Baby Do That Thing		158	
Jing Jing A Ling/Auld Lang Syne	North Bay	303	
Jing Jing A Ling/Auld Lang Syne	Chess	2088	
Make Love To Me/Please Have Mercy Baby	Josie	1017	1970
Help Me (Get Over My Used To Be Lover)/Please Have Mercy Baby		1020	
Make Love To Me/People Need Each Other		1023	
Come Get It/Love Can Turn To Hate		1025	
We Got To Stay Together/Help Me (Get Over My Used To Be Lover)		1028	1971
It's Gonna Take A Miracle/What About Me		1030	
That's What Boys Are Made For/Has Somebody Taken My Place	Bell	217	1972
Leave Me Alone/Song For Jim		299	

(as The Ritchie Family)

	Label	Number	Year
The Best Disco In Town/Part 2	Marlin	3306	1976
Life Is Music/Lady Luck		--	1977
A Summer Dance/Quiet Village		--	1977

LPs

	Label	Number	Year
Love	Josie	4013	1970

(as The Ritchie Family)

	Label	Number	Year
Arabian Nights	Marlin	2201	1976
Life Is Music		--	1977
African Queens		--	1977

The Blossoms

Members:

(1955-58) Fanita Barrett (James)
Gloria Jones
Annette Williams
Nanette Williams

(1958-60) Fanita James
Gloria Jones
Annette Williams
Darlene Wright

(1961-63) Fanita James
Gloria Jones
Darlene Wright (Love)

(1963-64) Fanita James
Darlene Love
Gracia Nitzsche

(1964-75) Fanita James
Jean King
Darlene Love

(1975-80) Alex Brown
Fanita James
Jean King

Every phenomenal Rock & Roll record has the same ingredients: a catchy melody, driving beat, simple yet effective lyrics, and a memorable lead vocal. Last, but certainly not least, are the backing vocals that turn more than a few listeners on to songs without them even realizing it. One group of singers whose job it was to catch the listeners, not only caught them, but held them there wanting more. This is the story of The Blossoms, a group that became famous by staying out of the limelight.

The Blossoms were formed in 1954 in Los Angeles, California. Gloria Jones, Fanita Barrett (James), fraternal twin sisters Annette and Nanette Williams, Pat Howard and Jewel Cobbs all attended Fremont High School in Los Angeles. Fanita and Jewel had been in the glee club together at Edison Junior High School.

When the girls attended Fremont, Fanita and Jewel met the twins in the chorus. Pat and Gloria soon joined the group. This sextet was originally named The Dreamers. The girls palled around with fellow student Dexter Tisby, himself a member of the locally popular group, The Penguins, who had a hit with the memorable, "Earth Angel." Gloria Jones recounts how the group fell in with the other musically inclined students at Fremont, "We were always around school singing. We would occasionally sing with another girl, Beverly Thompson who sang with The Flairs. We got to know Dexter. He's the one who brought us to Richard."

Richard Berry was having emergent success as a songwriter and as a jazz and R&B soloist. The young singer liked the sextet of young girls. Barely out of high school himself, Richard was quickly making a name for himself as a smooth baritone crooner and The Dreamers complemented him perfectly. He began using them as backing vocalists on his recordings for Flair and RPM Records. Johnny Otis, the famed disc jockey and orchestra leader, spotted the girls at a high school talent show. One of their first appearances was for his radio show on KFOX in 1955. Not long after this appearance, Pat and Jewel turned their attentions to other activities in their lives. The group quickly became an efficient quartet.

The Dreamers developed an harmonic tone that was crystal clear and

THE ECHOES

Mable Weathers' Agency
7622 1/2 So. Vermont
Los Angeles 44, Calif.

Darlene's first group, The Echoes, 1957, (not in order, from top) Darlene Wright, Ed DeVold, Elmo Jones, Marzetta Freeman, Mosely Carter)

mesmerizing in its clarity. Every note was sung in perfectly aimed "oohs," and when their words were sung, it was like a recitation. Everything they sang was done in three or four-part harmonies with either Fanita or Nanette taking the occasional lead. The Dreamers weren't interested in making a name for themselves as a primary group. Happy being backing vocalists, they played both an integral and primary part of Richard Berry's recordings. Beginning with a version of Harry Warren and Mack Gordon's standard gem "At Last," The Dreamers backed Richard Berry on three singles for Flair, one single for RPM and one single for Flip. Gloria says the group liked the creative freedom they were allowed in the background, "…we would make everything three or four-part harmony. We made Richard the sweet part of our group."

Also, The Dreamers lent their signature sound to other solo artists like Eloise Brooks and Etta James. Perhaps the most memorable recording by the group under their original moniker was the enchanting "Do Not Forget" and its compatible flip, "Since You've Been Gone," both penned by Richard Berry. In a true California style, the girls blow their way through each phrase, putting their unique intonations on every chord. Nanette could not sing lead on this session, so Jennell Hawkins took her place. Jennell is an accomplished organist as well as an engaging singer and had recorded duets with Richard Berry on RPM before rising to fame with her 1962 hit, "Moments." The Dreamers' ability to sing in any configuration allowed them to garner work singing for different labels under assumed names. Gloria occasionally sang as a member of Richard Berry's Pharaohs. Gloria, Annette and Fanita recorded two singles for Class Records under the pseudonym The Rollettes. "Sad Fool" and "More Than You Realize/Kiss Me Benny" were two efforts which, unfortunately, went by unnoticed, but the efforts of the singing group did not. Recording under assumed names was to become the group's way of life.

Another reason for The Dreamers' success came from their ability to deftly sing any style of music. This ability made them much in demand as session singers for a variety of artists. Vocal coach Eddie Beal mentored this latent sense of style. Dexter Tisby had introduced him to the group in 1955. Under the aegis of Beal, the group learned about more structured chords and close harmony. They also became adept at singing pop, jazz and country. Fanita tells how the group's abilities expanded under his direction: "Eddie taught us four and five part harmony. Eddie is the one that got us the deal with Capitol Records."

Through Eddie's management, the group was signed to Capitol Records for one year. One condition of the new deal was that they change their name. The company may have thought the group needed a more feminine-sounding name. The A&R man at Capitol named the group The Blossoms after noticing their different skin tones. He said they looked like a bouquet in bloom.

During the group's stay at Capitol in 1957, Nanette Williams had married and was expecting her first child. Fortunately, Fanita found her replacement singing at a wedding. The voice that Fanita heard not only would complement the group's versatile harmonies, but would provide them with a very distinct lead. Fanita knew that Darlene Wright was destined to be a Blossom from the moment she heard her sing the first note, "I found Darlene at St. Paul's Baptist Church. My friend, Delores Perkins told me about this girl who sang. I said to the girls, 'let's go and hear this girl. When we heard her, we knew.'"

At 16 years old, Darlene would soon become the new sound of The Blossoms. No stranger to group harmony singing, Darlene had been honing her skills as a session singer on records by Sam Cooke and Clydie King, then known as Little Clydie. Darlene also recorded two singles with The Echoes for Combo and Specialty Records.

The Blossoms' tenure at Capitol was ephemeral, with only three singles to their credit. The first single "Move On," lead by Nanette, was close enough to a true R&B California rocker, but its flip, "He Promised Me," lead by Fanita, leans over almost to pure pop. Next came "Have Faith In Me/Little Louie." "Have Faith…" is a beautiful ballad casting the group back into their standard California blow harmonies. This song is closest in feel to "Do Not Forget." Fanita's polite, breathy vocal adds charm to the lilting ballad. One more single, "No Other Love/Baby Daddy-O" followed in 1958, with Darlene taking her first lead as a Blossom. As it happened, their most successful Capitol recording was not as artists, but as backing vocalists for the casual vocal delivered by Ed Townsend on "For Your Love." For many years, fans assumed that a pop chorale provided the backing vocals.

THE BLOSSOMS — EXCLUSIVE CAPITOL RECORDING ARTISTS

The Blossoms, 1957, (clockwise from top left) Fanita James, Gloria Jones, Annette Williams, Nanette Williams.

The Blossoms' recordings for Capitol were quite a departure from the California R&B they were singing behind Richard Berry and Etta James. Their reputation to mutate their sound into other genres of music was being utilized to its fullest potential. Capitol Records, however, did not know how to promote them as primary artists. This special ability to be versatile also made them misunderstood by the major labels.

A short stay at RCA under the name The Playgirls during 1959 and 1960 yielded two very unusual singles, "Hey Sport/Young Love Swings The World" and "Sugarbeat/Gee But I'm Lonesome." "Hey Sport" is straight out of a pop song book with an incongruous response by Darlene at the chorus, belting out a decidedly R&B "So what!" "Sugarbeat" was a minor chart item, featuring a pop chorus and skating rink organ. Again, Darlene saves the song from pop obscurity with her trademark "oh yeahs" in the verse. The beautiful "Gee, But I'm Lonesome" was penned by future Beach Boy Bruce Johnston, who nagged Gloria until she presented the song to the group; "Bruce would come by my house often and say how he wished we would record his song (he never wore shoes). He used to date Annette, and when he came to her house, her father said, 'Can I see your driver's license?' That always made us roar with laughter."

During 1959 and 1960, members of the group were married and began saving their places in The Blossoms in a round-robin fashion. Although a hit record would have been nice, the ladies found their present situation more to their liking, so they could be at home with their families. They did not have to travel or do tours, something a steady hit-making group must do to support its efforts. They certainly met their share of celebrities, a source of bland pop fodder in the recording industry. Many young stars and teen idols would be corralled to record whether they could sing or not. Gloria recalls the girls drooling over Jimmy Darren when he came in to record "Angel Face" and the group, credited on this single as The Four Blossoms, thought he was delightful, "When Jimmy came in to record, we all thought he was so cute. He was very nervous because he had never recorded before." We also met Chuck Connors who had just gotten his show, "The Rifleman."

The Blossoms were also the favored angelic voices on another television star's only hit, Shelley Fabares' "Johnny Angel." At this time, Darlene says, work began picking up, "After the Darren sessions, we became more in demand. We rehearsed in this big building, where other singers were also rehearsing. They needed background singers and would ask Eddie. He'd say 'let The Blossoms do it.'"

In 1961, the girls signed with Challenge Records. The group was a trio by this time—Darlene, Gloria and Fanita. Unfortunately, the ladies were already running into problems at the new label. Gloria remembers how this chain of events sent everyone scrambling: "We were all set for our first session for Challenge. Darlene had fought with her husband that morning and he wouldn't let her go to the session, so we had to get someone to take her place. For the life of me, I can't remember the girl's name who sang lead on the song, but it became a hit."

The unknown singer is rumored to be Jenelle Hawkins, but the lead does not sound like her. The Blossoms, with the "unknown" singer on lead had a mild hit with their first Challenge single, an answer record to Ernie-K-Doe's "Mother In-Law" aptly entitled "Son In-Law." Ironically, the single wasn't even supposed to be a Blossoms single, as original pressings have the group billed as The Coeds. Two more singles followed in 1961 and early 1962, "The Search Is Over/Big Talkin' Jim" and the willowy styled "Write Me A Letter."

None of the follow-ups made any chart impact. The group was indifferent. Darlene had two children by this time, and both Fanita and Gloria

BOB B. SOXX & THE BLUE JEANS

Bob B. Soxx & The Blue Jeans, 1963, (L-R) Bobby Sheen, Darlene, Fanita.

were married. Their plethora of session work was keeping them working and leaving them with flexible hours, although work was becoming more abundant. They backed literally hundreds of artists like Sam Cooke, Jimmy Darren, Roberta Shore, Shirley Gunter, Carolyn Daye, veteran cowboy Gene Autry and Duane Eddy. Part-time Blossoms soon joined the fold. Singers Carolyn Willis, Edna Wright, Darlene's younger sister, and Gracia Nitzsche, wife of young arranger Jack Nitzsche joined the coterie of session singers who would be the regulars at Gold Star Studios, the place where most Rock & Roll sessions were cut. Nanette and Annette also returned for occasional sessions. The situation of constant studio work together with the ability to adapt their voices to any vocal style were quickly catapulting The Blossoms to the status of the most in-demand session singers of their time. Their reputation afforded them another chance to record a single, this time with Columbia's Okeh subsidiary. "I'm In Love/What Makes Love" haplessly sank without a trace. Another chance was on the horizon, given to the group for the same reasons, but this chance would make The Blossoms famous in voice only.

On a summer morning in 1962, The Blossoms got a call that they had a session at Gold Star to record a song for a producer who had been on the East Coast recording The Crystals. His name was Phil Spector. He had a song he thought was a sure fire hit, and he might release it under the Blossoms' name. Spector had stated that The Crystals were not available to fly out to Los Angeles for the session, so the studio group was used. However, when the record came out, the song was billed as The Crystals, an established New York group with two hits to their credit and a controversial new song bubbling under the Hot 100. The Blossoms were paid a session fee, but they had asked for triple scale. The song, "He's A Rebel," written by Gene Pitney as an intended follow-up to The Crystals' "Uptown," was a smash hit, featuring Darlene's raging lead. Although the group could not reap the benefits of having a hit single, they established an ongoing relationship with Spector that would last for three years.

Later in 1962, The Blossoms were again recruited by Spector to sing another two songs, one with singer Bobby Sheen. The first was a twangy, soul-inspired version of the Disney classic, "Zip A Dee Doo Dah," with Bobby doing an early Drifters' inspired lead. This single was credited to a makeshift group called Bob B. Soxx & The Blue Jeans. The second was another teen tale of undying love for a less than perfect guy. "He's Sure The Boy I Love" was intended to be a Blossoms single, as a reward for their work on "He's A Rebel." The single came out, again credited as a Crystals single. Darlene, Bobby and Fanita had signed contracts with Spector after "He's A Rebel," but this snub of The Blossoms would always be in the back of their minds.

At the beginning of 1963, Phil made good on a promise to record Darlene as a soloist, releasing "(Today I Met) The Boy I'm Gonna Marry." The label credit did not read "Darlene Wright," but the new moniker assigned by Spector himself, "Darlene Love." Darlene also lent her lead vocals to another song credited to Bob B. Soxx & The Blue Jeans, "Why Do Lovers Break Each Other's

Hearts?" Darlene was still wary of Spector's motives, so she hesitated on signing as a soloist, "We always talked about him signing me. I told him I wasn't going to do any more work as The Crystals."

The Blossoms were on every single and potential single Spector put out for almost the entire run of his label. They didn't ignore the multitude of concurrent session work available to them with other producers. Gloria, Nanette and Carolyn recorded as The Girlfriends with David Gates, producing a top 60 hit for Colpix Records called "My One and Only Jimmy Boy." They also backed Dorothy Berry on her singles for Challenge Records. Darlene was participating in recordings as part of her contracted studio work with Liberty Records. The Victorians' recording of "What Makes Little Girls Cry," produced by David Gates and Perry Botkin Jr., was one of many Spector sound-alikes. As far as The Blossoms were concerned, there was so much work, Darlene says that it had to be regulated; "We were doing up to four or five sessions a day and that almost killed us; so we decided to only do just three sessions a day. Some of our sessions were five hours a day, 10:00 to 3:00 in the morning."

After a few public appearances, Darlene and Fanita did not want to be on the road as Bob B. Soxx & The Blue Jeans, so Gloria and Carolyn appeared as the group on the road. Later, Lillian Washington took Gloria's place. The outside interests involving The Blossoms disgruntled Spector, who wanted "his" voices for his productions only.

DARLENE LOVE

Darlene Love as a soloist, 1963.

Spector continued his work with the group during 1963, mostly with Darlene on lead and various Blossoms and Bobby Sheen on backup. An LP entitled "Zip A Dee Doo Dah" by Bob B. Soxx & The Blue Jeans has cuts showing the studio work by these configurations. He even recorded Edna Wright as the second harmony voice on "Wait 'Til My Bobby Gets Home." The Blossoms recorded songs that came out as the backgrounds for Crystals and Ronettes records with those groups' lead singers out front. Spector was not making good on his allusion to giving The Blossoms a chance to have a hit with their name on it. By the end of 1963, Gloria Jones grew more frustrated with Spector's ways in the studio. At the time Spector was recording his now famous Christmas LP, "A Christmas Gift For You," Gloria left the session without recording anything because she got tired of waiting around. Gloria would eventually become pregnant and leave The Blossoms as a performing member. Gracia Nitzsche took her place permanently.

Fortunately for the Rock & Roll world in 1964, television was becoming a more viable medium of communication with the ever-growing populace and was looking to present music for young audiences, a multiplying and viable source for advertisement potential. Producer Jack Good, responsible for England's "Ready, Steady, Go" music show, was commissioned to produce a nationally syndicated show for ABC-TV. He tapped into the enclave of session musicians and singers available to him on the West Coast. Many of these musicians were to be a part of this new show called "Shindig" and The Blossoms were to be included. The group was designated to sing backup for many of the acts appearing on the show. They would also have an occasional solo spot. The archaic and ridiculous notion that blacks were not to be shown on television was becoming a thing of the past, albeit slowly. There was a stipulation, however, that the backing trio must be an all black group. Gracia Nitzsche was white. One of the other session singers on the scene, Jean King, was chosen to be the third Blossom.

The Blossoms backing Marvin Gaye on The TAMI Show, 1965, (L-R) Jean King, Darlene Love, Fanita James.

The Blossoms appeared weekly on "Shindig," garnering their own spots as well as being the resident backing vocal group. This trio continued working with Spector before their abrupt split in 1965. Ongoing disagreements over Darlene's outside work interests eventually ended The Blossoms' association with Spector. The Blossoms had passed up some golden opportunities to work with other labels and producers, most notably at Atlantic Records, in order to work for Spector, a move that Fanita regrets, "Not going with Atlantic was one of the biggest mistakes that The Blossoms ever made."

After "Shindig" folded in 1966, the group signed to Reprise Records, where they recorded a handful of carefully crafted productions under the auspices of veteran rocker Jimmy Bowen. Songs like "That's When The Tears Start" and "Good, Good Lovin'" established the group in the soul/Motown groove of the day. The Blossoms did not stay long at Reprise, but did stay long enough to back Frank Sinatra on "That's Life." Darlene says that, at this point, the ladies wanted to see success as primary artists; "We were trying to have a hit record. At that time, they didn't know where to put us. We could sing anything. Who would think of recording 'If'? We always had a full orchestra at Reprise."

The year of 1967 brought many changing trends in popular music, and vocal group music was no exception. Rhythm and Blues artists were experimenting with hybrid versions of songs, mixtures of Rhythm & Blues and folk rock, containing more reflective lyrical content. Producer Lou Adler, who founded Dunhill Records, was starting a new label on the West Coast called Ode Records and had recruited many songwriters from Don Kirshner's now defunct Dimension Records complex, who had moved west to work for Screen Gems. Carole King had traveled to California to continue her songwriting and eventually recorded for Ode. Laura Nyro was supplying songs for the Ode complex, and The Blossoms had joined the Ode roster just in time to record a version of Nyro's "Stoney End," flipped with a version of Aretha Franklin's "Cry Like A Baby." The song was released twice, once in 1967 and again in 1969.

Unfortunately, by that time, Barbra Streisand had her hit with "Stoney End" and The Blossoms' version was forgotten. The group then recorded one single for MGM, a version of Sam & Dave's "You Got Me Hummin'." Once again, their mark at the label was as backing vocalists, behind Righteous Brother Bill Medley on his hit, "Brown Eyed Woman."

The Blossoms continued to carve a niche as session vocalists throughout 1969 and 1970. They released some adequate cover versions of tried and true songs like "You've Lost That Loving Feeling" and "Soul and Inspiration." In 1972, The Blossoms' most triumphant accomplishment under their own guise was the release of the critically acclaimed album entitled, "Shockwave." "Shockwave" contained something for everyone's taste, a version of James Taylor's "Fire and Rain," some neo-Motown, like "Cherish What Is Dear To You" and sturdy R&B ballads like Bill Withers' "Grandma's Hands." The trio was pictured on the cover amidst a very earthy setting. Many of the songs on the LP became singles. Despite the creative success, no singles charted. Although they needed to go where business was most lucrative, Fanita feels that they never stayed long enough at any one label to make a significant impact, "We started touring with Tom Jones in 1969. When you move, you lose. When we went on the road, we lost the studio work. We went around the world three times with Tom Jones."

The last vestige of many attempts to secure an image for themselves as primary artists came with a continued association with MGM during 1973-74. None of this material ever saw the light of day. By this time, the group yielded to its main impetus, providing superior backing vocals for other artists. They worked extensively in Las Vegas for Elvis Presley, Paul Anka, Tom Jones and Dionne Warwick. Unfortunately, internal conflicts came to a head during an extensive tour with Dionne Warwick. These events caused a rift within the group. Darlene saw it coming. "We weren't getting along. We couldn't get our lives together as a group anymore."

This turn of events marked Darlene's departure from the group in 1975. The Blossoms continued with former Raelett, Alex Brown, in Darlene's place. They had a brief association with Epic Records in 1977, recording the pleasant, "Walking On Air."

After departing The Blossoms, Darlene pursued a contract with Gamble and Huff on their red-hot Philadelphia International Records. That road wound up leading her back to none other than Phil Spector. During this period she recorded "Lord If You're A Woman" for Warner/Spector Records.

Darlene dropped out of the entertainment industry for a few years to concentrate on family life. After a series of jobs which she found were not her true calling, Darlene decided to resume her life as a singer. When she returned, however, she found that the recording business had changed significantly. Many of her former associates had disappeared, leaving her to reestablish herself as a solo artist.

Darlene's first major move was to headline at New York City's Bottom Line Café in 1982, appearing with her old chum Gloria Jones and Ula Hedwig on backing vocals. Several more appearances across the country netted her a chance to appear in Ellie Greenwich's life story, "Leader Of The Pack," both off and on Broadway. This triumph led to a role in a less successful stage version of "Carrie," based on the novel by Stephen King. Columbia released her LP, "Paint Another Picture" in 1987. Sporadically, Darlene appeared on several independent CDs, including one with Lani Groves.

Other appearances, notably a revue in 1994 based on her life and movie roles in the Lethal Weapon series have put Darlene on top and kept her there, where she belonged many years before. In 1998, Darlene published, "My Name Is Love," a successful book, recounting her days as a singer. Darlene also released "Unconditional Love," a Gospel CD, produced by Gospel great, Edwin Hawkins. She is currently auditioning for roles in the movies and is negotiating a deal for a movie based on her life.

Darlene Love, 2000. (Photo courtesy of Darlene Love)

Fanita James has kept The Blossoms going over the years, with various personnel changes, making her living providing reliable backing vocals for big name artists on tour. The last incarnation of the group, with Cynthia Woodard, recorded two songs for Dave Antrell's Classic Artists Records in 1989. Fanita retired The Blossoms in 1990. Gloria and Fanita most recently provided backing vocals for Doris Jackson's Shirelles. Gloria kept working, attending to family life, holding what she deems just about every job in every profession, never getting too far from being a singer.

"When there wasn't any singing work available, I just went ahead and did something else. I always held a job in another area."

Gloria and Carolyn Willis lent their backing vocals for Charles Thomas and The Watts 103rd St. Band in 1998.

Gloria wants to let everyone know that she is not the Gloria Jones who recorded "Tainted Love" and "Heartbeat." Gloria, Annette and Nanette made a special appearance with Richard Berry shortly before his death in 1996, at the Southern California Doo Wop Society's monthly meeting. Fans were treated to versions of "Good Love" and "Together." Gloria is now a caseworker with the city of Los Angeles. Sadly, Jean King passed away from a heart attack in 1983.

The Blossoms are permanently woven into the fabric of Rock & Roll through their diversified efforts, their voices gracing thousands of popular records for over thirty years. The Blossoms have conclusively proven that it wasn't necessary to be out front in order to be out front.

The Blossoms Discography

45s	Label	Number	Year
Move On/He Promised Me	Capitol	3822	1957
Have Faith In Me/Little Louie		3878	1958
No Other Love/Baby Daddy-O		4072	
Son In-Law/I'll Wait	Challenge	9109	1961
Write Me A Letter/Hard To Get		9122	
The Search Is Over/Big Talking Jim		9138	1962
I'm In Love/What Makes Love	Okeh	7162	
Things Are Changing/same	EEOC	T4LM 8172	1965
Things Are Changing/Please Be My Boyfriend (Crystals)		T4LM 8172-1	
That's When The Tears Start/Good, Good Lovin'	Reprise	0436	1966
My Love Come Home/Lover Boy		0475	
Deep Into My Heart/Let Your Love Shine On Me		0522	
Good, Good Lovin'/Deep Into My Heart		0639	1967
Stoney End/Wonderful	Ode	101	
Wonderful/Cry Like A Baby		106	
Tweedlee Dee/You Got Me Hummin'	MGM	13964	1968
Stoney End/Wonderful	Ode	125	1969
You've Lost That Lovin' Feeling/Something So Wrong	Bell	780	
Soul And Inspiration/Stand By		797	
I Ain't Got To Love Nobody Else/Don't Take Your Love		857	1970
One Step Away/Break Your Promise		937	
Touchdown/It's All Up To You	Lion	108	1972
Cherish What Is Dear To You/Grandma's Hands		125	
Cherish What Is Dear To You/Shockwave		125	
Walking On Air/There's No Greater Love	Epic	50434	1977
Lonely Friday Night/The Last Letter	Classic Artists	110	1989
(as Bob B. Soxx & The Blue Jeans)			
Zip A Dee Doo Dah/Flip and Nitty	Philles	107	1962
Why Do Lovers Break Each Other's Hearts/Dr. Kaplan's Office		110	1963
Not Too Young To Get Married/Annette		113	
Not Too Young To Get Married/--	Collectables	3204	1983
Why Do Lovers Break Each Other's Hearts/Zip A Dee Doo Dah		3209	
(as The Coeds)			
Son In-Law/I'll Wait	Challenge	9109	1961
(as The Crystals)			
He's A Rebel/I Love You Eddie (NY group)	Philles	106	1962
He's Sure The Boy I Love/Walkin' Along (La La)		109	
He's A Rebel/--	Collectables	3200	1983
He's Sure The Boy I Love/--		3202	
(as The Dreamers w/Richard Berry)			
At Last/Bye Bye	Flair	1052	1955
Daddy Daddy/Baby Darling		1058	
Together/Jelly Roll (no group)		1075	
Wait For Me/Good Love	RPM	477	1956
Do I Do/Besame Mucho	Flip	339	1958
(as The Dreamers)			
Do Not Forget/Since You've Been Gone	Flip	319	1956
Do Not Forget/Since You've Been Gone	Flip	354	1961

45s

	Label	Number	Year
(as The 4 Blossoms w/Jimmy Darren)			
Angel Face/I Don't Wanna Lose Ya	Colpix	119	1959
(as The Girlfriends)			
My One and Only Jimmy Boy/For My Sake	Colpix	712	1963
(as The Playgirls)			
Hey Sport/Young Love Swings The World	RCA	7546	1959
Gee, But I'm Lonesome/Sugar Beat		7719	1960
(as The Wildcats)			
What Are We Gonna Do In '64/3625 Groovy St.	Reprise	02531	1964
(as The Rollettes)			
Sad Fool/Wham Bam (Googie Rene Orch.)	Class	201	1956
More Than You Realize/Kiss Me Benny		203	
Darlene Love			
My Heart Beat A Little Bit Faster/(Today I Met) The Boy I'm Gonna Marry	Philles	111	1963
(Today I Met) The Boy I'm Gonna Marry/Playing For Keeps		111	
Wait 'Til My Bobby Gets Home/Take It From Me		114	
A Fine, Fine Boy/Nino and Sonny (Big Trouble)		117	
Christmas (Baby Please Come Home)/Harry and Milt Meet Hal B.		119x	
Stumble And Fall/(He's A) Quiet Guy		123	1964
Christmas (Baby Please Come Home)/Winter Wonderland		125	
Christmas (Baby Please Come Home)/Winter Blues		125	
Too Late To Say You're Sorry/If	Reprise	0534	1966
Christmas (Baby Please Come Home)/Winter Wonderland	Warner-Spector	0401	1976
Lord, If You're A Woman/Stumble and Fall		0410	1977
Today I Met The Boy I'm Gonna Marry/Strange Kind Of Love	Collectables	3210	1983
Wait 'Til My Bobby Gets Home/Stumble And Fall		3211	
River Deep, Mountain High/Leader of The Pack (Annie Golden)	Elektra	7-69647	1985
He's Sure The Man I Love/Everybody Needs	Columbia	38-07984	1987
All Alone On Christmas/--	Fox	10003	1993
Darlene Love (w/The Echoes)			
Aye Senorita/My Little Honey	Combo	128	1957
Over The Rainbow/Someone	Specialty	601	
Darlene Love (w/The Victorians)			
What Makes Little Girls Cry/Climb Every Mountain	Liberty	55574	1963
You're Invited To A Party/Monkey Stroll		55656	1964
Happy Birthday Blue/Oh What A Night For Love		55693	
Monkey Stroll/If I Loved You		55728	

EPs

	Label	Number	Year
(w/Bob B. Soxx & The Blue Jeans/Darlene Love)			
Christmas EP	Philles	X-EP	1963

LPs

	Label	Number	Year
(as The Dreamers w/Richard Berry)			
Richard Berry & The Dreamers	Crown	371	1962
Shockwave	Lion	1007	1972
(as Bob B. Soxx & The Blue Jeans)			
Zip A Dee Doo Dah	Philles	4002	1963
Jean King			
Jean King Sings For The In Crowd	Hanna-Barbera	8505	1966
Darlene Love			
He's A Rebel (as The Crystals – 2 cuts)	Philles	4001	1962
A Christmas Gift For You		4005	1963
Today's Hits By Today's Artists		4007	1964
Phil Spector's Greatest Hits	Warner/Spector	9104	1977
Rare Masters	Phil Spector Int'l. (UK)	2335 236	1977
Live at Hop Singh's	Rhino		1982
Wholehearted	Love	01	1983
Paint Another Picture	Columbia	40605	1987

CDs

	Label	Number	Year
A Rhythm & Blues Christmas Vol. 4	Collectables	5525	1994
Darlene Love			
Unconditional Love	Harmony	--	1998

Patti Labelle & The Blue Belles

Members:

(1962-67) Patricia Holte (Labelle) Sarah Dash Nona Hendryx Cindy Birdsong	*(1967-70)* Patti Labelle Sarah Dash Nona Hendryx	*(as Labelle)* *(1971-76)* Patti Labelle Sarah Dash Nona Hendryx

They convey sounds as touching as songbirds on the sill in the early morning, or as jolting as that same morning's first cup of coffee. These are the sounds of Patti Labelle and The Blue Belles, a group whose body of work has taken them through many creative changes in their career. Initially, they were chosen to cover another group's clandestine work, but would prove their own exceptional abilities above and beyond the heights of the expectations of anyone who has ever hoped to make it in the music business.

The story of The Blue Belles starts in Philadelphia in the early 1960s when a shy, unassuming little girl named Patsy Holte found her own voice by listening to her brother's records and began singing with the hopes of making it big.

From the moment she gained attention with her commanding voice and uninhibited style, "Patti" knew early on that this is what she wanted to do with her life. Patti spent time hanging out with her junior high school pals at the roller rink to hear deejay Georgie Woods play records. Patti also joined the junior choir at her church, where one day she conjured the courage to sing a solo. The real push to become a professional singer was when Patti won first place in her high school talent show. The audience applause fueled Patti's desire to be on stage.

Encouraged by the rise of female groups in the early 1960s, Patti joined with a group of girls to form a quartet called The Ordettes. In 1960, Patty, Jean Brown, Yvonne Hogen, and Johnnie Dawson rehearsed in their living rooms and performed at many local functions in their neighborhood. Patti's church singing had netted her a positive reputation among young people and adults alike. Through a friend of Jean's mother, the girls auditioned for Bernard Montague, a promoter who was placing acts on the local club circuit. Since female groups were hot at the time, he wanted one in his repertoire. After intense rehearsals under his direction, The Ordettes appeared at the Orchid Ballroom and brought down the house. This led to a string of local one-nighters

Patti LaBelle & The Blue Belles, 1963, (clockwise from top) Sarah Dash, Patti LaBelle, Nona Hendryx, Cindy Birdsong.

that would often leave the high-schoolers exhausted for classes the next day.

As time went by, other aspects of life took away The Ordettes one by one. One replacement for Johnnie was Sundray (Sandra) Tucker. Sandra was the daughter of Ira Tucker of the famed Gospel group, The Dixie Humming-birds. Sandra was plucked from The Tonettes, another group that Bernard Montague was managing. After Jean and Yvonne left to get married, Patti and Sandra stayed on as soloists with Mr. Montague's revue until replacements could be found for the departed group members. After weeks of auditions, Montague found two girls from Trenton, New Jersey who were singing in a group called The Del Capris. He convinced Nona Hendryx and Sarah Dash to join him and placed them in The Tonettes. When it became apparent that The Tonettes were not cohesive, Nona and Sarah became Ordettes.

The Ordettes were handling quite a load of bookings, churning out supreme performances wherever they appeared. The Ordettes worked with The Bill Massey Band, a capable local outfit. As the needs of the group changed, Mr. Montague assigned the duties of refinement and choreography to Morris Bailey, a musician/songwriter who scored his first writing success with "Cry Baby Cry" for The Angels in 1962. Bailey rehearsed The Ordettes incessantly. The hard work paid a high dividend, because the group was revered on the local scene. As the bookings increased, the need to be on top of their game also increased. Nona, Sarah and Patti dropped out of high school, getting their diplomas at a later date. Sandra's parents, however, wouldn't hear of it, so she was forced to resign her position in The Ordettes. Through a contact with another one of Mr. Montague's acts, Cindy Birdsong, a singer from Camden, New Jersey, came to Philadelphia to audition for the group. All concerned knew she was in before she finished her audition. The hopes of the group continued to rise.

Under Bernard Montague's direction, The Ordettes traveled all over the eastern United States, working wherever they could, every day of the week. The group's big break came when Morris Bailey told the group he arranged for a local record producer to hear them sing.

Arranger and songwriter Bobby Martin, who would one day become famous as one of the forces behind The Sound of Philadelphia in the 1970s, was associated with car salesman Harold B. Robinson, who was also a self-proclaimed music man. Robinson had a recording studio in the basement of his showroom. He had approached another female group a few months before, to ask if they would record with his outfit. The Starlets, from Chicago, were in Philadelphia to promote their minor hit, "Better Tell Him No." At first, they turned Robinson down, saying they were already signed to Bill Sheppard and Carl Davis on Pam Records. Robinson assured them he could work out the details and they naively believed him. Normally, the group was a quintet, but only four had been on tour at the time of recording. The Starlets recorded some sides for Robinson before departing for Chicago.

Robinson released one single, a version of "I Sold My Heart To The Junkman" on his brand new Newtown Records. Knowing he couldn't release the single with The Starlets' name on the label, he called the artist The Blue Belles. When the record started to take off, Robinson needed a group to promote the single. This is where The Ordettes came in. At the audition, they were asked to sing the song, which was familiar both as a standard, and because the new version was already being played on the radio.

At first, Robinson refused to hear the group because he thought that visually, Patti was too plain looking to front the group. He left the room before they sang, but returned when he heard their sound, particularly Patti's lead. The Ordettes were signed on the spot as The Blue Belles. The Ordettes' plans to record were about to come true. Other, harsher realities were about to come true, too.

As the popularity of "I Sold My Heart To The Junkman" grew, The Blue Belles were asked to appear on "American Bandstand" to promote the single. Jane Hall, one of The Starlets, heard from her mother that a group was on "Bandstand" promoting the single that The Starlets recorded. Maxine Edwards, who sang the lead, also heard from her mother, who told her that the record was taking off down south.

As the Chicago contingency went into action, so did Robinson. He had Patti, Cindy, Nona and Sarah record a version of "Junkman" note for note with the first version. By the time this matter reached the courtroom, accusations were flying all over the place between Robinson, Phil Terry, Bobby Martin, The Starlets, Carl Davis and

PATTI LaBELLE
and the BLUEBELLES

Patti LaBelle & The Blue Belles, 1966, (clockwise from top) Patti, Nona, Sarah, Cindy. (Photo courtesy of Yellowlinda, Inc.)

Bill Sheppard. The Blue Belles were caught in the middle, for they had not done anything illegal, but were part of the proceedings anyway. When the smoke cleared, everyone was compensated. This matter facilitated, in part, the name change to Patti Labelle and The Blue Belles. Patsy Holte received her stage name and the group now concentrated on building their own reputation on the circuit.

The Blue Belles continued recording for Newtown for another year, proving they could handle any style of music. First came the "Junkman" sound-alike, "I Found A New Love," then the mashed potato-oriented "Tear After Tear," and "Academy Award" which gave only a hint of both the harmonic capabilities of the group and Patti's compelling and powerful lead.

Dramatic ballads like "Go On (This Is Goodbye)" and standards like "Where Are You" and "You'll Never Walk Alone," the song Patti had sung when she won her first high school talent show, would become the group's signature style during their early years. One notable chart topper that showcased the group's talents is the endearing and ironically sorrowful "Down The Aisle," appropriately nicknamed "the wedding song." On a day that should be the happiest for a bride, the mixture of vocals and instrumentation evoke the saddest of emotions, perhaps the bittersweet feelings of life passing from one stage to another.

The group's second chart single was originally placed with King Records, then released locally on Newtown, which is why the release number is out of sequence. The Blue Belles released two LPs, unusual for a small label in the early 60s. Their first album contains a collection of some of their singles as well as stellar album cuts, particularly the intense "Have I Sinned." The second LP was a Christmas tribute in The Blue Belles style, "Sleigh Bells, Jingle Bells and Blue Belles." Despite these attempts to further the group's recording career, Harold B. Robinson was only interested in making money and had no real grasp on the music business. When The Blue Belles efforts did not prove as lucrative as he had hoped, he sold his record company after two LPs and about twenty single releases.

The Blue Belles contract was picked up by Cameo-Parkway, who re-released "You'll Never Walk Alone/Decatur Street" in late 1963. The single had been the last release for Robinson's company, the name augmented to Nicetown Records. At the more established Parkway Records, however, the single charted. The balance of Patti Labelle and The BlueBelles' tenure at Cameo-Parkway fostered an LP and two more singles. The Blue Belles recorded the lamenting, "One Phone Call," backed with the wistful, "You Will Fill My Eyes No More," and profound versions of "I Believe" and "Danny Boy," the latter tune giving this impressive group another chart single. Another master arranger, Ritchie Rome, had been brought in for these singles. The Blue Belles did not stay long at Cameo-Parkway, for opportunity was knocking on the stage door, this time from Atlantic Records.

Since The Blue Belles' bread-and-butter was coming from live shows, the group crammed in their live performances as a packer would can sardines. Fortunately, the group was always well received, so the group's tours on the Chitlin Circuit continued. After so many performances in Harlem, The Blue Belles were nicknamed "The Sweethearts of The Apollo." Although The Blue Belles worked constantly, it seemed that the money was not always commensurate with their talents. Between booking agents, management and living expenses on the road, what was left over at the end was almost not worth the effort. The group needed a big hit to sustain them.

During 1965, The Blue Belles were scheduled to participate in an American tour as one of the opening acts for The Rolling Stones, who were riding high on the success of The British Invasion. Since the band was already known for their behavior, Mr. Montague and his wife, who was now the girls' chaperone, warned the quartet to be mindful of their own behavior. After the successful, twelve-month tour, Patti Labelle and The Blue Belles were back on the circuit. Not long after their return, representatives from Atlantic Records approached The Blue Belles to sign a contract. Since their act was both polished and vintage R&B, this is what Atlantic was looking for to join the stellar 1960s roster of other artists like Barbara Lewis, Solomon Burke, The Drifters, The Young Rascals and Wilson Pickett. By the end of 1965, The Blue Belles had themselves another recording contract.

The years with Atlantic Records didn't prove as fruitful as the group had hoped. For almost five years, The Blue Belles worked with capable producers like Bert Berns, Ritchie Rome, Bob Finiz and Don Davis. The first single, written by Lori Burton and Pam Sawyer, was "All Or Nothing" which netted the group a mild chart placing. The song possessed the typical formula for the group, a ballad that dramatically builds to a stratospheric climax. The group also backed Wilson Pickett on his hit, "634-5789." What followed for 1966 and 1967 were soul standards of pop rock hits like "Groovy Kind of Love" and tried and true standard formulas of "Over The Rainbow," "Unchained Melody" and "Ebb Tide."

Interesting treatments were evident in "Patti's Prayer," "I'm Still Waiting" and the departure from the usual in the 1967 single, "Oh My Love" penned by Sam Bell and Lorraine Ellison. This song is much more ethereal than most Blue Belles productions, allowing the backing vocals to rightfully shine through, especially Sarah's pinpointed, laser-like first soprano. Likewise for its flip, "I Need Your Love," one of Nona Hendryx' earliest writing efforts.

Despite these valiant attempts, the only other chart single that Patti Labelle and The Blue Belles achieved while at Atlantic was a cover of Trade Martin's "Take Me For A Little While." Lack of consistent chart toppers didn't stop the group from continuing as a premium in-person attraction. The group made a trip to London, playing all the clubs and appearing on television on the British answer to "American Bandstand," "Ready, Steady, Go." The Blue Belles were well received and kept in touch with Vicki Wickham, one of the producers.

During 1967, Atlantic Records fussed over a new acquisition, Aretha Franklin, who turned the industry upside down with a cover version of Otis Redding's "Respect." Aretha had spent five years with Columbia Records, but they didn't know how to market her unique voice and style. Now that she was making musical history at Atlantic, she gained a preferred position at the company. Also, another, more profound change came to The Blue Belles in 1967.

Cindy Birdsong accepted an offer from Motown Records to replace Florence Ballard in The Supremes (at the time the top female group in the world). Cindy had to make a decision right away and chose the option that would immediately further her singing career. Even though the group was disheartened by her sudden departure, they carried on. Sandra Tucker briefly took Cindy's place for live performances, but eventually, after working closely for years as a quartet, Patti Labelle and The Blue Belles were now a trio.

By 1969, the priorities at Atlantic were artists like Aretha Franklin, as well as Percy Sledge, Led Zeppelin and Dusty Springfield. The Blue Belles' contracts with Atlantic and with Mr. Montague were coming to an end. The business affairs of the group were in complete disarray. In desperation, their business decisions were made in haste and for a brief time, they wound up with dubious management. Fortunately, the old connection with Vicki Wickham paid off, for when she heard that The Blue Belles were available, Wickham jumped at the chance to manage them. After untying some knots, Vicki became the group's new manager. Envisioning bold steps for the group in terms of direction, Wickham would take The Blue Belles onto another plateau.

Under Vicki Wickham's direction, not only would the group change their name, but their image and musical direction as well. The group was renamed Labelle and their music would be a mixture of R&B and rock, with deeper, more socially conscious lyrical messages about life and love. At first, Labelle's visual image was that of the white rock bands—casual, down home dress.

At the behest of designer Larry LaGaspi, however, the trio cashed in on the glamour rock images of the early 1970s. LaGaspi designed outlandish stage outfits to go with the sound and message of Labelle's music. Space suits, feathers and studs, a conglomeration of flash was the new basis for Labelle. The transformation worked beyond anyone's expectations, especially Patti's, who at first rejected the changes. Labelle became known for their elaborate stage outfits as well as their music.

The launching pad for Labelle came as the opening act for The Who in New York. Their two albums for Warner Bros. and one for RCA met with critical acclaim, but no commercial success. Singles like "Morning Much Better" and "Pressure Cookin'" were a far cry from the lush sounds of standard love ballads that The Blue Belles used to sing. A positive glimmer for Labelle's career was in 1971, when the group backed singer/songwriter Laura Nyro on a collection of R&B hits entitled, "Gonna Take A Miracle." The LP was a refreshing take on early Rock & Roll standards. Labelle performed with Nyro at Carnegie Hall. There were more refreshing surprises to come.

By 1974, Labelle had quite a following, with thousands of new admirers as well as loyal fans from their days as Blue Belles. Nona Hendryx was now coming into her own as a songwriter and was drawing much praise for her introspective lyrical slants. Even though Nona was writing material for the group, the next single, written by Kenny Nolan and veteran producer Bob Crewe, would catapult the group to the apex of the industry. "Lady Marmalade (Voulez Vous Coucher Avec Moi, Ce Soir?)" was the story of a New Orleans lady of the evening. Produced by acclaimed songwriter Allen Toussaint, the song took the popular music world by storm. It connected with the R&B crowd, bearing the gritty feel of down home blues and the instrumentation that astounded the hard rock enthusiasts. "Lady Marmalade" soared to the top spot on the charts, winning the award for best R&B recording of 1974. The accompanying LP, "Nightbirds" established Labelle as a force to be reckoned with.

Looking to hold on to their long awaited success, Labelle became more cautious with the business end of their affairs. They started their own publishing company, Gospel Birds, as well as a production and management company. Success continued for the group, playing to a sold-out crowd for their "wear something silver" show at New York's Metropolitan Opera House, a first for a rock group. On the strength of the success they worked hard for, the group embarked on a world tour. Another forceful single followed, "What Can I Do For You." Two more LPs were released in 1975 and 1976. Unfortunately, "Phoenix" and "Chameleon" could not repeat the commercial success of "Nightbirds."

The state of radio programming in the 1970s made it impossible for Labelle's material to gain the proper airplay. Radio stations couldn't typecast Labelle, therefore, programmers ignored them. What a shame, because, in

LABELLE

The transformation to Labelle, 1975, (L-R) Sarah, Patti, Nona. (Photo courtesy of Vicki Wickham/Take Out Productions)

addition to their seasoned vocals, Nona Hendryx' writing ability still continued to impress with songs like the visionary "Phoenix" and the thought-provoking "Who's Watching The Watcher." Even with plans being made for another album and more touring, life in the fast lane was taking its toll. Caving into internal conflict, creative differences and growing personal problems, Labelle disbanded in 1976, ending a fourteen-year professional association between Patti Labelle, Nona Hendryx and Sarah Dash. The trio had stuck with each other through many ups and downs. This was the end of the line.

Since 1976, the ladies that made up Patti Labelle and The Blue Belles/Labelle have gone on to achieve high levels of success both in and out of the music industry. Sarah Dash recorded for Don Kirshner's label, having a disco hit with the driving "Sinner Man," in 1978. Sarah has made numerous guest appearances on vinyl with Alice Cooper, The Rolling Stones, and her old pal, Patti Labelle.

Nona Hendryx continues to sing and write songs. She has recorded for Epic and RCA, releasing the underground club hit "Busting Out" with Material, a local New York band, which led to the production of her second LP, "Nona." In 1983, she scored a minor hit with Ellie Greenwich's "Keep It Confidential," as well as collaborating on numerous independent projects with Talking Heads and the former David Johanssen, now known as Buster Poindexter. Nona has also lent her voice to political causes, as part of The Artists United Against Apartheid. Nona has a recurring role on Showtime's series, "Linc's." She has composed a classical score for the play, "Oak and Ivy," which opened at the Arena Stage in Washington DC. She is in the running for both a Grammy

for "Rock This House" and an Emmy for her work on "Children of The World," a song featured in the Disney animated children's special, "People." Nona's film and theatrical scores have been part of numerous productions. Nona is currently the head of her own production/logo company, Free Records.

Cindy Birdsong enjoyed immense success with The Supremes from 1967-71 and again in 1975-76. Cindy left show business and entered into the ministry. She currently resides in the western United States.

Patti Labelle has enjoyed the most recording success as a solo artist and is an international star. Patti has had numerous chart hits since 1977, including 1984's monster success, "New Attitude" and "On My Own," a duet with Michael McDonald. Patti has appeared in numerous movies, notably "The Color Purple" and on television. She has opened her own cabaret as well as having written a book about her life, entitled "Don't Block The Blessing." Patti Labelle and The Blue Belles were inducted into The Rhythm and Blues Hall of Fame in 1999.

The Blue Belles worked their way up from Chitllin Circuit staples to the "Sweethearts of The Apollo" to the next wave of the future as Labelle. Only a handful of vocal groups like The Dells and Little Anthony and The Imperials made the change from one musical genre to the next and were successful with the change. The Blue Belles' professional experience had allowed them to transform themselves from one phase of their career to the next, not necessarily with ease, but with strength and with vision, becoming Labelle and blending into the substance of popular music, true "chameleons" of Rock & Roll.

Patti Labelle & The Blue Belles Discography

45s	Label	Number	Year
I Sold My Heart To The Junkman/Itty Bitty Twist (Starlets)	Newtown	5000	1962
Pitter Patter/I Found A New Love		5006	
Go On (This Is Goodbye)/I Found A New Love		5006	
Tear After Tear/Go On (This Is Goodbye)		5007	
Cool Water/When Johnny Comes Marching Home		5009	1963
Love Me Just A Little/Pitter Patter		5010	
Academy Award/Decatur Street		5019	
Down The Aisle/C'est La Vie	King	5777	
Down The Aisle/C'est La Vie	Newtown	5777	
You'll Never Walk Alone/Where Are You	Nicetown	5020	
You'll Never Walk Alone/Decatur Street		5020	
You'll Never Walk Alone/Decatur Street	Parkway	896	
One Phone Call/You Will Fill My Eyes No More		913	1964
Danny Boy/I Believe		935	
All Or Nothing/You Forgot How To Love	Atlantic	2311	1965
Over The Rainbow/Groovy Kind Of Love		2318	1966
Ebb Tide/Patti's Prayer		2333	
Family Man/I'm Still Waiting		2347	
Take Me For A Little While/I Don't Want To Go On Without You		2373	1967
Always Something There To Remind Me/Tender Words		2390	
Unchained Melody/Dreamer		2408	
Oh My Love/I Need Your Love		2446	
Wonderful/He's My Man		2548	1968
Dance To The Rhythm Of Love/He's Gone		2610	1969
Pride's No Match For Love/Loving Rules		2629	1970
Trustin' In You/Suffer		2712	
(as Labelle)			
Morning Much Better/Shades Of Difference	Warner Bros.	7512	1971
Moonshadow/If I Can't Have You		7579	1972

45s

	Label	Number	Year
Ain't It Sad It's All Over/Touch Me All Over		7624	
Mr. Music Man/Sunshine	RCA	0157	1973
Going On A Holiday/Open Up Your Heart		0965	
Lady Marmalade/Space Children	Epic	50048	1974
What Can I Do For You/Nightbirds		50097	
Messin' With My Mind/Take The Night Off		50140	1975
Far As We Felt Like Goin'/Slow Burn		50168	
Get You Somebody New/Who's Watchin' The Watcher		50262	1976
Isn't It A Shame/Gypsy Moths		50315	
Lady Marmalade/Messin' With My Mind		69180	1989
Turn It Out/Inst.	MCA	55113	1995

Sarah Dash

	Label	Number	Year
Sinner Man/Look But Don't Touch	Kirshner	4278	1978
(Come and Take This) Candy From Your Baby/Do It For Love		4281	
Ooh La La, Too Soon/If You Don't Play, I Can't Sing		4286	1980
When You Talk To Me/--	RCA	--	1990
Low Down, Dirty Rhythm/--	Unidisc	--	1994

Nona Hendryx

	Label	Number	Year
Everybody Wants To Be Somebody/--	Epic	50479	1977
Busting Out/Inst.	ZE	--	1981
Keep It Confidential/Dummy Up	RCA	13437	1983
I Sweat (Goin' Through The Motions)/--	--	--	--
B-Boys/- Moving Violations		--	1985
Baby, Go Go/Drive Me Wild	EMI-America	43028	1987
Why Should I Cry/Funkyland	EMI-America	8382	1987

Patti Labelle**

	Label	Number	Year
Love Me Just A Little/The Joke's On You	Newtime	515	1964
Joy To Have Your Love/Do I Stand A Chance	Epic	50445	1977
You Are My Friend/I Think About You		50487	
Little Girls/You Make It So Hard To Say No		50583	1978
Teach Me Tonight/Quiet Time		50550	
Save The Last Dance For Me/Eyes In The Back Of My Head		50573	
It's Alright With Me/My Best Was Good Enough		50659	1979
Music Is My Way Of Life/It's Alright With Me		50659	
Love And Learn/Love Is Just A Touch Away		50763	
Release/Come And Dance With Me		50852	1980
I Don't Go Shopping/Come And Dance With Me		50872	
Don't Make Your Angel Cry/Ain't That Enough		50910	

LPs

	Label	Number	Year
The Apollo Presents The Blue Belles	Newtown	631	1963
Sleigh Bells, Jingle Bells and Blue Belles		632	
On Stage	Parkway	7043	1964
Over The Rainbow	Atlantic	8119	1966
Dreamer		8147	1967
At The Apollo	Upfront	129	1970

(as Labelle)

	Label	Number	Year
Labelle	Warner Bros.	1943	1971
Moonshadow		2618	1972
Pressure Cookin'	RCA	10205	1973
Nightbirds	Epic	33075	1974
Phoenix		33579	1975
Chameleon		34189	1976

Sarah Dash

	Label	Number	Year
Sarah Dash	Kirshner	35477	1978
Ooh La La, Sarah Dash		36207	1980
Close Enough	--	--	1981
You're All I Need	EMI	--	1988

Nona Hendryx

	Label	Number	Year
Nona Hendryx	Epic	34863	1977
Nona	RCA	4565	1983
The Art of Defense	--	--	1984
The Heat	--	--	1985
Female Trouble	EMI-America	17248	1987
Skindiver	Private Music	--	1989
You Have To Cry Sometime (w/Billy Vera) (CD)	Shanachie	9001	1992
Transformation: The Best Of Nona Hendryx (CD)	Razor & Tie	--	1999

Patti Labelle**

	Label	Number	Year
Patti Labelle	Epic	34847	1977
Tasty		35335	1978
It's Alright With Me		35772	1979
Released		36381	1980
Best Of Patti Labelle		36997	1982

**Since ample documentation exists on Patti Labelle's discography, this listing ends with her departure from Epic Records.

The Bobbettes

Members:

(1957-61)	Reather Dixon, 2nd Alto/2nd Lead	*(1961-80)*	Reather Dixon
	Helen Gathers, Baritone		Emma Pought
	Emma Pought, 1st Alto/1st Lead		Jannie Pought
	Linda "Jannie" Pought, 2nd Soprano		Laura Webb
	Laura Webb, 2nd Soprano	*(1981)*	Reather Dixon
			Emma Pought
			Laura Webb

Catchy ditties and Rock & Roll scats make up the tunes that gave this group their start in the music business. As time went by, they graduated to singing smooth, driven soul sounds. This musical ability combined with a keenly-honed stage presence keeps them in demand as a fervent attraction in any venue. This is the description of the talents of the versatile Bobbettes.

The Bobbettes story began at I.S. 155 on 99th St. in Harlem, where the girls had fun singing in the halls, after school in the glee club, and in their church. The name of their group was the Harlem Queens. They had even made up a song for a teacher (his name was Mr. Lee) whom they had in school.

Originally, the seven member group used to get together just to sing the popular songs of the day, but it was getting too confusing to have so many members. Founders, Reather Dixon and Emma Pought, decided they should trim the group to five. Who should they

THE BOBBETTES

JACQUES BENBASSAT

JAMES A. DAILEY
PERSONAL MGR.

The Bobbettes enjoying their first hit in 1957, (L-R) Jannie Pought, Reather Dixon, Emma Pought, Laura Webb, Helen Gathers.

choose? The girls decided only the five best would go on singing in the Harlem Queens. The group was finally pared down to Reather, Emma, her sister Jannie, Helen Gathers and Laura Webb, who won her place as the fifth member.

The group dispels the theory that they didn't like Mr. Lee; that they made up this song to put him down. Reather says the original song was actually a true description of what he looked like.

"He had these thick horn-rimmed glasses, so we said he was four-eyed. He knew the song was about him and he didn't care."

James Dailey, who managed another group, The Ospreys, heard the girls and thought they had a great deal of potential. He brought the group to Atlantic Records. Ahmet Ertegun and Jerry Wexler liked the group's sound, thinking that no one would believe that the voices coming from these young girls, ages 11-15, were not those of adult women. Ertegun and Wexler asked the girls to sing the original song they had, and after careful listening, asked the group to turn the lyrics into love lyrics. The group quickly rewrote "Mr. Lee" to make him the object of their desire. The punchy tune was recorded in early 1957, using Emma and Reather simultaneously as lead singers. Group members Helen and Emma penned three more tunes for the session. Reggie Obrecht shared writing credit for his orchestration.

Within a few weeks of its release, "Mr. Lee" started to gain steady airplay. Once it arrived, the song scored high on both the pop and R&B charts. "Mr. Lee had an infectious guitar hook right from the start, with startling, interspersed "twangs," like a rock-a-billy tune. The voices pick up the beat like a well-rehearsed street rhyme. The record was now a radio favorite. None of the group members were ready for instant stardom. Emma recounts walking down the street, having just graduated from junior high school, when she stopped in disbelief as she heard her own voice on the street.

"I'll never forget it. I graduated that day. I had on these black patent leather shoes, my first high heel shoes, and I was walking down that street. At the time, I think it was fifteen cents for the bus. I was just trying to figure out how I was going to get back home. Along 125th Street, they played records outside. You could hear the music. I heard this song and I kept saying 'that sounds like me, . . . nah, that's not me'. I went up to the store and they played it louder and louder. I said, 'that's us!' I took off those shoes and I started running. I got that bus and by the time I got to the building where we lived, my mother and everybody in that building knew about it. People were sitting in my mother's living room and they were talking about 'Mr. Lee'."

From the day Mr. Lee became a hit, the girls were now part of the fast-paced Rock & Roll world. Reather says even Mr. Lee didn't believe the song on the radio was actually by the same girls.

"I remember when Mr. Lee heard the finished song of "Mr. Lee" for the first time. He was ecstatic. He called Jannie and me out of our class to make sure it was the same song we had sung for him a couple of months

before, when it was derogatory about him. He said he just wanted to make sure it was the same song, because he thought someone had stolen our song."

The Bobbettes experienced a lot of firsts. They were indeed the youngest female group (collectively) to have a hit single, for which they received gold records. They were readily recognized for their outstanding abilities, earning them the Billboard awards for most promising group of 1957. "Mr. Lee" was not just a one-shot happenstance. The girls were asked to come up with other songs for them to sing. Laura credits Atlantic heads Ahmet Ertegun and Jerry Wexler with recognizing the group's numerous talents: writing, comedy, and dancing. It was often stated that they were far ahead of their time.

"It was Ahmet and Jerry who believed in us. He's the one who really pushed us to write our own material. Because we had no musical training, we wrote what was in our hearts. Sometimes in the studio, we had to hum to the musicians so they would understand how we thought a certain part of the arrangement should be."

Of course, this meant being under pressure to come up with another hit like Mr. Lee. Now they were writing for the company, where money was being made. It was not just for fun anymore. Also, there were now longer rehearsals.

Sometimes the girls would get together to write. One person would come with a piece of paper with three lines written and they would build on that. The songs like "Speedy" and "Zoomy" were based on various boyfriends. The group would write out the lyrics and relate the melody to Reggie Obrecht, who wrote the lead sheets. He'd then give the sheets to Ray Ellis, who composed the orchestration. It was not as much fun writing when one was on a time limit. Their day-to-day lives also changed as they went from junior high school into The Professional Children's School. Touring kept them away for months at a time. Reather laughs as she envisions the departing scene of the tours, "We would go on the Chitlin Circuit for months at a time. All the girls would be crying, their parents would be crying and I'd be like 'bye Mom!'"

The Bobbettes toured constantly in the United States and The West Indies. Often they would be the youngest act on the bill. The group performed alongside many other popular performers like LaVern Baker, Sam Cooke, Dion and The Belmonts, The Drifters, Frankie Lymon and The Teenagers and Annie Laurie. On one Apollo show, they backed all the solo performers on the bill. The Bobbettes stage shows were thrilling, involving singing and naturally choreographed dancing, comedy routines and sight gags. One routine involved four of the girls leaving the stage while Reather remained, still singing. Eventually, the group would come back out to take their bows and drag Reather off the stage.

The Bobbettes singles that followed Mr. Lee were pleasant imitations either in lyric or in arrangement. "Come-A Come-A," "Speedy," "Zoomy," and "Rock and Re Ah Zoll" had the "Mr. Lee" feel, much to the group's dismay. They wanted to break out of the mold since this formula was no longer working as a viable hit maker. Bluesy ballads like "The Dream" and "Don't Say Goodnight" were more to the group's liking. An especially endearing tune that the group recorded while at Atlantic was a ballad, written by Emma and her childhood sweetheart, David, who eventually became her husband. The song's vocal arrangement was different than most of the songs they recorded for Atlantic, using one member to provide a vocal bass line, an arrangement usually reserved for male groups. The sauntering ballad was aptly entitled, "You Are My Sweetheart," recorded at The Bobbettes last session for Atlantic. With no more hits forthcoming, the group decided to leave James Dailey and pursue other opportunities for the group. Laura's brother, Joe Webb, began managing the group. The Bobbettes reached the end of their contract with Atlantic and signed with George Goldner's End complex in 1960.

Before the group's departure from Atlantic, the girls recorded one more Mr. Lee song entitled "I Shot Mr. Lee." When the group signed with Goldner, they were assigned to the short-lived Triple-X subsidiary. There they recorded an updated version of "I Shot Mr. Lee." The two versions competed on the charts, the Triple-X version winning the duel. The group had its second chart entry. During this time, Helen Gathers decided to stop performing with the group, although she recorded with them for a short time afterward. By 1961, she had left permanently. It was also during their tenure at Triple-X that The Bobbettes began their association with songwriter/producer Teddy Vann.

Between 1960 and 1962, the group recorded for a variety of labels, including Galliant, King, End and Gone. Emma states that everyone wanted The Bobbettes, "Many labels wanted to record us. We never wanted for a record deal."

It was Teddy Vann's finesse with the group that would sustain them from 1960 through 1965, making creative recordings for Jubilee and Diamond Records. These recordings included a version of "Close Your Eyes" and a tribute to the producer called "Teddy." The group continued to write songs for themselves, such as "Looking For A Lover," and Emma's "I'm Stepping Out Tonight." The sound of the group was constantly being updated to keep them relevant to changing musical tastes and fickle record buyers. The group hadn't had a strong hit since 1961, when they recorded an answer record to Chris Kenner's hit, entitled "I Don't Like It Like That." In 1966, with RCA Records, the group recorded a driving version of Bobby Womack's "It's All Over Now," flipped with the Motown-inspired "Happy Go Lucky Me," penned by Emma. Joe Webb was now producing. Although this was a promising start, the group recorded only one more single for RCA, and stayed out of the recording studio for a few years.

Always in good voice, the ladies concentrated on their stage shows, playing places like the Apollo and several clubs in the New York area. They were featured many times on Dick Clark's "American Bandstand." It was the development of the skills of performing live and keeping an audience entertained that would see the group through the 1960s. The Bobbettes played the club circuit, utilizing skills they learned performing as little girls on the Chitlin Circuit. The group performed in places such as Grossing-

ers, the Sands and Laurel's. The ladies admit that the pace was grueling and the pay often fell short of what they felt they should have been earning. They worked nightly at a club in Brooklyn called The Monte Carlo, and spent a few years working at other local nightspots in New York City. For a time, family matters temporarily splintered the group. Emma and Reather worked with another lady, Mattie La Vette, as The Soul Angels, but eventually found their way back to The Bobbettes.

In 1971, the group decided it was time to go into the recording studio again. Working with the production team of Joe Webb, Donald Height, Dennis Williams and Eddie Jones, they recorded a handful of timely soul tunes for Mayhew Records. In 1977, the group recorded and released another Bobby Womack tune, "Check It Out," on Bareback Records, as The Sophisticated Ladies. The ladies felt that The Bobbettes needed an updated sound and image. The single enjoyed some success in England.

In 1980, a tragedy nearly halted the group for good. Jannie was killed in an accident while visiting a friend in Jersey City, New Jersey. The loss of their sister and friend was brutal, but the group moved forward. After trying several new singers as a fourth member, the ladies thought it best to remain a trio. One more single was released in 1981, after a much-publicized reunion show at Radio City. Since that time, the group has refrained from recording.

During the 1980s and 1990s, The Bobbettes have performed sporadically, appearing at the Nassau Coliseum, The Stage at Julia Richmond School, and The United In Group Harmony Association meetings. Their love of singing and performing has provided the group with an open link to world of pop music. They each received a platinum record from Atlantic Records for the featuring of "Mr. Lee" on the soundtrack of the hit movie "Stand By Me." "Mr. Lee" was also featured with other early Atlantic R&B artists in the movie "The Big Town" with Matt Dillon. They receive regular royalty checks rightfully due them for their songwriting efforts when they were with Atlantic Records. This was the result of intense negotiations with the company and their fortitude paid off. The group would consider recording again, but it would have to be with a producer whom they feel will make the efforts worthwhile. Emma puts it frankly: "If someone like Babyface wanted to work with us, we wouldn't turn him down."

Reather Dixon Turner now lives in Astoria, NY and works for a mail-order house. Emma Pought Patron is an office manager with The Human Resource Association of New York City. Now retired, she currently lives in Manhattan. Laura Webb Childress also resides in Manhattan and is a customer-relations liaison with Virgin-Atlantic Airways. Although Helen Gathers gave up performing, she is still in touch with the group. The Bobbettes feel blessed to have had such a fruitful life and career. Laura happily reflects on the first days of the group, "Those were my best years. One thing I did like about the shows was that we were children having fun. I did everything, out of control, doing everything I wanted to do, that I never had the chance to do before. I had fun doing it; I was a big kid. We didn't realize what we were getting into. All we knew is that we'd get on stage and have fun. If something happened backstage and it was funny, we'd bring it on stage and we'd still be laughing about it, but we're still singing."

Even now, The Bobbettes never tire of performing and entertaining, making throngs of fans happy by singing all their tunes. Of course, the requests for "Mr. Lee" are forthcoming for every performance. The ladies sing it with as much gusto as when they were little girls poking both fun and honor at a teacher whose quirky demeanor and horn-rimmed glasses were the inspiration for a Rock & Roll classic.

The Bobbettes Discography

45s	Label	Number	Year
Mr. Lee/Look at the Stars	Atlantic	1144	1957
Speedy/Come-A Come-A		1159	
Zoomy/Rock And Ree-Ah-Zole		1181	1958
The Dream/Um Bow Bow		1194	
Don't Say Goodnight/You Are My Sweetheart		2027	1959
I Shot Mr. Lee/Untrue Love		2069	1960
I Shot Mr. Lee/Billy	Triple-X	104	
Have Mercy Baby/Dance With Me Georgie		106	
Oh My Papa/I Cried	Galliant	1006	
Teach Me Tonight/Mr. Johnny Q	End	1093	1961
I Don't Like It Like That/Part 2		1095	
I Don't Like It Like That/Mr. Johnny Q	Gone	5112	
Oh My Papa/Dance With Me Georgie	King	5490	
Looking For A Lover/Are You Satisfied		5551	
My Dearest/I'm Stepping Out Tonight		5623	1962
Over There/Loneliness	Jubilee	5427	
The Broken Heart/Mama Papa		5442	
Teddy/Row, Row, Row	Diamond	133	
Close Your Eyes/Somebody Bad Stole De Wedding Bell		142	1963
My Mama Said/Sandman		156	1964
In Paradise/I'm Climbing A Mountain		166	
You Ain't Seen Nothin' Yet/I'm Climbing A Mountain		181	1965
Teddy/Love Is Blind		189	
Having Fun/I've Gotta Face The World	RCA	47-8832	1966
It's All Over/Happy Go Lucky, Me		47-8983	
All In Your Mind/That's A Bad Thing To Know	Mayhew	712297/98	1971
Tighten Up Your Own/Looking For A New Love		37	1972
It Won't Work Out/Good Man		861/62	1974
--(disco 12" only)		--	--1981
(as The Sophisticated Ladies)			
Check It Out (Part 1)/Good Man	Mayhew	532	1977
Check It Out (Part 1)/Part 2 (12 inch single)			
Check It Out (Part 1)/Good Man	Bareback	353	
(as The Soul Angels)			
It's All In Your Mind/The Ladies Choice (inst.)	Josie	1002	1969

The Chantels

Members:

(1957-59) Arlene Smith, Lead
Lois Harris, 1st Soprano
Sonia Goring, 2nd Soprano
Jackie Landry, 1st Alto
Renee Minus, 2nd Alto/Bass

(1961-62) Annette Smith, Lead
Sonia Goring
Jackie Landry
Renee Minus

(1963-64) Sandra Dawn, Lead
Sonia Goring
Jackie Landry
Renee Minus

(1965-66) Renee Minus, Lead
Sonia Goring
Jackie Landry
Helen Liebowitz (Powell)

(1970) Arlene Smith, Lead
Renee Minus
Sonia Goring
Jackie Landry

April 8, 1995, Symphony Space, New York City. It is time for the Fifth Annual United In Group Harmony Hall Of Fame Awards Ceremony, the event that honors the much overlooked R&B vocal groups for their achievements and contributions to American music.

The audience goes silent. The music begins. Four silhouettes move out onto the stage. The lights go on and a familiar musical intro starts. The audience hears the angelic harmonies of "Look In My Eyes." The crowd goes wild. A brief intermission, then another musical prelude. A familiar figure takes the stage. The crowd starts screaming and fans holding cameras stampede to the front of the theatre. Five people have just taken the stage who have not stood on stage together in over twenty-five years. It is the reunion of the five original Chantels, and they're singing "Maybe." Thousands of

Before they recorded, The Chantels backstage at The Apollo for Amateur Night, 1956, (L-R) Sonia Goring, Lois Harris, Jackie Landry, Renee Minus, Arlene Smith. (Photo courtesy of Jackie Landry)

fans have dreamed about the opportunity to once again hear these icons of female vocal group harmony. On this night the dream had come true.

The Chantels originated in the junior choir at St. Anthony of Padua on 166th Street and Prospect Ave. in The Bronx. The group took their name from a rival school, St. Francis de Chantal. The girls had known each other since the second grade, with the exception of Renee, who was a bit younger. The group of girls who had sung together was pared down from twelve members, coming and going, to the five girls, ages 12-16, who rehearsed at Arlene's house after choir rehearsals on Sunday. Unfortunately, singing Rock and Roll songs during choir time had gotten Jackie and Sonia kicked out of the choir for singing, as Sister Richard Marie put it, "that skip 'n jump stuff!" The nuns who ran the choir played an important part in The Chantels' understanding of music. The girls were taught to play piano and other instruments, as well as being taught to sight-read music. Musically, though, the girls were influenced by the popular Rhythm & Blues vocal group sounds of the day. They listened to groups like Frankie Lymon & The Teenagers, The Valentines and The Cookies, especially The Cookies' "In Paradise."

One evening, the girls were on their way to a Rock and Roll show in Manhattan. Jackie recalls the scene, "We were all dressed alike, white blouses with aqua skirts and bucks." We had taken the train to get downtown. In those days you could do that."

While passing a rehearsal studio, they were spotted by a young man on the corner who wanted to know if they sang. They replied "yes" and he immediately brought them up to the studio to prove it. While singing, they spotted on the street, Richard Barrett, Ronnie Bright, and David Clowney, songwriters and members of one of their favorite groups, The Valentines. The five girls immediately ran downstairs, leaving the young gentleman in the dust.

At first Richard didn't believe they actually were a singing group. They were so young, but they were dressed alike. He said, "sing something." They broke into the street version of what was to become "The Plea." Barrett told the group they sounded great, that he would contact them, and they would put something together. Weeks went by, and after not hearing a word from him, Jackie got hold of his home address and wrote him. Jackie wanted to know what had happened to the plans they made. They were serious about what he said. Was he?

After meeting the group a second time, Richard spoke to George Goldner, head of Gee-Rama Records for whom The Valentines recorded. It was decided that the group would record for Goldner's complex, but it would be on his newly formed label, End Records.

Richard had thoroughly rehearsed the group before going into the studio. These were the days before sel-sync, so a perfect take was what he wanted. The result of that session was "He's Gone" and "The Plea." Released in mid-1957, "He's Gone" made #71 on the national charts. The tune immediately captures your ear with the chime off, then the soft blend of The Chantels' young voices, and finally, the lead grabs you and holds you until the end of the song, when the group signs off the

way they came in. Nothing like it had come before. Its flip side is just as enchanting; one of the best stroll records ever. The Chantels were excited to have a record of their own on the radio. Life didn't change much. Little did they dream their next recording would be a song which many vocalists would forever hold paramount.

"Maybe" is one of those songs that was a trend-setting first. No other record had sounded like this before. From its thunderous piano intro, through Arlene's emphatic lead, to its call and response ending, the performance is truly captivating. "Maybe" reached #15 nationally. The flip side, "Come My Little Baby," is a lighthearted rocker with Jackie and Sonia sharing a duel lead.

If life didn't change after the first single, it certainly would now with two chart records to The Chantels' credit. Preparations were now being made for the group to appear locally, and to go on tour as well. This meant that they would have to leave school and receive private tutoring. Lois' mother would have none of this. Lois always recorded with her group while on End, but she did not tour if it meant being far away overnight. Lois reflects on the decision concerning her fate, "I was in my senior year of high school. The nuns in the school and my mother thought it (touring) would jeopardize my graduation."

This is why there are two sets of photos, some with five members and some with four. Jackie did make it a point to write to Lois while on tour and tell her everything the group was going through, "Lois' mother stuck to her guns, and I remember she cried, but I wrote her letters to let her know what we were doing. I remember being upset because I was homesick." However, once Lois graduated in 1958, she was able to participate in the tours.

According to Jackie, the tours were grueling. Drive into a city by bus, do a show or two, then onto the next city, mostly within one day. In addition to Barrett, Arlene's father, Ray, would accompany the group on some tours. Also, Renee's mom, Thelma Minus, would chaperone and offer her words of encouragement and support. The girls certainly did need looking after. They were so young and they were always the only female group on the tours. Much to the girls' dismay, they would get locked in their rooms.

The fun part of the tours was that The Chantels were billed with some of their favorite performers such as The Tuneweavers, LaVern Baker, Lee Andrews and The Hearts, Little Anthony and The Imperials, and Little Willie John. It was at one of their first performances at the famed Apollo Theatre that The Chantels shared the bill with young Bobby Darin when he first introduced "Splish Splash." He was introduced to the crowd by another first-timer at The Apollo, Murray The K.

Meanwhile, Chantels material continued to impress. 1958 continued with the release of "Every Night/Whoever You Are," and "I Love You So/How Could You Call It Off." Both songs reached #39 and #42 respectively. "Every Night" was a pleasant reinterpretation of "Maybe" and "I Love You So" delivers a much more dramatic version of the tune originally done by The Crows, with the background vocals soaring high in the sky. "Whoever You Are," written by Royal Roost recording artist Fran Manfred, implores young lovers to stay together, and "How Could You Call It Off" breaks your heart with the tale of a bride almost left at the altar. The rest of the year was rounded out with the singles, "Sure Of Love/Prayee," "Congratulations/If You Try," and "I Can't Take It/Never Let Go."

"Sure Of Love" and "I Can't Take It" had what would fondly be regarded as The Chantels' formula. These songs contain Arlene's beseeching lead with a message of teen angst, while her girlfriends supportively back her up, painting surety for "Sure Of Love," with its steady unison in both the beginning and end, and, in "I Can't Take It," sorrow and despair. "Never Let Go," written by Carmen Taylor, put the group in an up-tempo groove. "Congratulations" was in keeping with "The Plea" as another great stroll tune, but the killers among these tunes were "If You Try," written by Flamingo Nate Nelson, and "Prayee." These productions feature much more of the group, probably because the group is reciting a pattern instead of "oohs and aahs." During "Prayee," Renee is performing a rarity among female group recordings; she's singing bass.

It was in 1958 that End records also released The Chantels' first LP, "We Are The Chantels." This release is a compilation of the group's first six singles. The first of two covers for the LP featured the group on the cover sporting full peach colored dresses with sashes, tammy hats worn way back on their heads, white gloves and charm bracelets. The girls are dressed for Church, in keeping with their church choir sound. The second cover, the more common "Jukebox Cover," looks like something out of a Sandra Dee movie.

The sound of The Chantels is what group harmony fans regard as part of the New York vocal group sound. Unfortunately, none of the great tunes after "I Love You So" charted. This was when Barrett and Goldner decided on a change in musical direction. The Chantels had flirted with pop tunes on one of the two EPs also issued during 1958, recording "I'll Walk Alone" and "C'est Si Bon." During their live shows, the group performed songs such as Frank Loesser's "My Darling," and Johnny Mathis' "It's Not For Me To Say." The Chantels were taught a special arrangement of "It's Not For Me To Say" backstage at a show by none other than the mighty Dells, who were impressed that a group so young could tackle the intricate arrangement. However, they made the mistake of performing The Dells' arrangement for a show. Needless to say The Dells were no longer impressed. They were also no longer on speaking terms with The Chantels.

The year 1959 saw many changes within The Chantels, as well as changes at Goldner's complex. The group only released one single on their own, "I'm Confessin'/Goodbye To Love," and a cover of The Fleetwoods' tune, "Come Softly To Me," with Richard Barrett on lead. "I'm

The Chantels, 1958 (L-R) Arlene Smith, Renee Minus, Sonia Goring, Jackie Landry, Lois Harris.

Confessin" is a pop tune with The Chantels stamp, and "Goodbye To Love" represents a new direction in melody for the group. This tune was co-written by Cameo-Parkway's Kal Mann. The song was successfully covered two years later by The Marcels, appearing as the flip side of "Blue Moon." It was at this time that the group discovered that the Gee-Rama complex was bankrupt. George Goldner had sold controlling interest in the corporation to Roulette Records. The Chantels and their parents were told that End Records would be no more and that they were released from their contracts. At this time, the girls returned to their lives and went back to school. Arlene stayed in The Professional Children's School. Lois had started college. Sonia and Renee attended Morris High School, the school that many other members of Morrisania vocal groups attended, and Jackie attended St. Helena's in The Bronx. In fact, after returning to school, Jackie was worried, "The school told me I couldn't leave now that I was back in. They said because I missed schoolwork, being out on the road. If I didn't stay in school this time, they wouldn't let me graduate on time."

During 1960, the complex that Goldner had pioneered was indeed going strong, but under the new ownership of Roulette Records. The End and Gone labels were now divisions of Roulette. The company continued to release Chantels recordings on End and Gone. (Actually, Rama Records was laid to rest in 1957, Gee Records in 1958, only to reappear in 1961. Gee and End were also used as reissue labels. By 1963 all would be gone, with the exception of End releasing sporadic singles between 1963-66.) The Chantels recording of "Whoever You Are/How Could You Call It Off" was released in 1960, along with another Chantels-backed Richard Barrett recording, "All Is Forgiven/Summer Love," both previously recorded in 1958 and '59. "All Is Forgiven" accentuates the group's high and lilting blend.

Richard Barrett was busy producing another female group in 1960, The Veneers. The Veneers were also a New York group, a quartet from the East Village, consisting of lead singer Annette Swinson Smith, her sister Valerie Swinson, and their cousins, Lorraine and Barbara Joyner. Barrett once again captured a specific sound, this time with harmonies lower and more spread out. The two wonderful sides by The Veneers, "Believe Me/I" were released on Barrett's short-lived Princeton label. The Veneers, without Annette, went on to become Jackie Wilson's Wilsonettes, backing him live. Lead singer Annette's destiny would be different.

After The Chantels' run with End, they thought, "that was that!" Upon graduation from high school, Jackie had landed a job in a bank. Lois had finished her education and was planning to marry. Sonia and Renee were still in high school. After the recordings for End, Arlene decided to go solo, cutting three single releases between 1961 and 1963. Arlene's first solo effort was for Big Top records, with a new young producer from L.A. named Phil Spector. The two songs, "Love, Love, Love" and "He Knows I Love Him Too Much," were cover tunes. The former was a hit for The Clovers in 1956, and the latter was a version of the concurrently released song by the Phil Spector-produced Paris Sisters. Her next two singles, "Everything/Good

Girls," on the Roulette-Spector related Spectorious records, and "Mon Cherie Au Revoir/To Live My Life Again," reunited her with her old label, End, and with Richard Barrett, who produced the sessions.

In 1961, about a year after Jackie started her job in the bank, she was contacted by Sonia. Richard Barrett had called and said he had a hot new tune that would be perfect for The Chantels sound. Jackie immediately said "yes." Arlene, also just out of high school, could not rejoin the group because she was already contractually bound to her deal with Big Top. Apparently, the girls were not ready to call it quits. It seems Richard Barrett wasn't ready either. Annette Smith of The Veneers was auditioned and immediately commissioned to be the new lead for The Chantels. The Chantels were going to sing again.

Richard Barrett struck a deal with Carlton Records to release the material he was producing with the groups that he was also managing, The Chantels and Little Anthony and The Imperials. The Chantels had missed national attention on the charts for almost three years. The first of the girls' three releases for Carlton was the song that had excited them so much upon hearing it, the very beautiful "Look In My Eyes." This angelic tune captures your attention from the opening, with the guitar playing that bass-line riff so familiar in group harmony records, and the sweet, dynamic strings that instantly carry you away. The song momentarily stops. Enter the vocals. Something familiar, yet different is heard from the song. Those heavenly church-choir vocals that we heard behind Arlene's powerful lead were now up front, and were everything they were in 1958, with a new sophistication. Annette's lead appears only at the bridge. Many have said Annette sounds like Arlene. Annette does have a similar range, but is slightly deeper and more nasal,

The Chantels on tour as a quartet, 1958, (top) Arlene (bottom, L-R) Sonia, Jackie, Renee.

giving her voice a sound all its own. The Chantels debut single on Carlton reached #19 on the pop charts. Its flip was the Drifterish-sounding "Glad To Be Back," certainly an appropriate title at this time. The Chantels were again on their way.

The Chantels' chart success led to Carlton releasing two more singles and an album during the group's stay at the label. End also released an album to capitalize on the group's newly found success. The End LP, entitled "There's Our Song Again," featured the balance of The Chantels' End material plus the two Veneers songs. The Veneers' cuts were also released on End as a single, but under The Chantels' name. The second Carlton single was "Well I Told You/Still." "Well I Told You" is an answer record to Ray Charles' "Hit The Road, Jack," a departure from typical Chantels recordings because it was not a ballad. Fans have commented that this tune can be best appreciated when heard in live performance. It brings the crowd to its feet. This single charted at #29. "Still" was true to the group's wistful ballad style. The last single for Carlton was "Here It Comes Again/Summertime," issued in early 1962. "Here It Comes Again" took styling cues from "Look In My Eyes," but with more of a lead vocal. On The Chantels' version of the Gershwin tune "Summertime," Annette delivers a beautiful, soft-sung jazz lead as the background conjures up the image of hanging out on a hot summer night. "Here It Comes Again" bubbled under the Hot 100 at #118.

The Chantels co-starring at The Apollo, 1958. (Photo courtesy of Jackie Landry/Marty Schein)

On the strength of the singles, the group was again in demand. The Chantels started touring again. Carlton released an album entitled "The Chantels On Tour" which featured their singles, an album cut and also some material by The Imperials and former Del Viking, Gus Backus. It was at this time that Jackie left to have her son. An old neighborhood friend, Yvonne Fair, prior to her early 1970s Motown fame, took Jackie's place on the road, but Jackie always appeared on record. It was also at this time that Annette left the group, also to have a baby. Enter future Platters vocalist Sandra Dawn. With "Dawn" singing lead, The Chantels left Carlton and travelled over to Luther Dixon's newly formed Ludix label. Luther had just left Scepter records where he had tremendous success writing and producing for The Shirelles. He produced this session for The Chantels. Their association with Luther Dixon yielded two singles for the Ludix label. The first, "Eternally/Swamp Water," put the group back on the charts in 1963, topping out at #77. "Eternally" revisits the days of "Maybe" and "The Plea" with a strong lead and superb choral background, but with an updated arrangement. "Eternally" garnered airplay on the East coast, with heavy attention from the Philadelphia area. It would be The Chantels' last chart record. The follow-up was "That's Why You're Happy," a sweet-sounding copy of The Shirelles' "Soldier Boy." The up-tempo "Some Tears Fall Dry" has arranger Teddy Randazzo working on the sound he would perfect a year later with The Royalettes and Little Anthony and The Imperials. The single went by barely noticed.

From 1962-66, The Chantels toured extensively on the East coast and in Canada, playing an endless amount of clubs and college fraternity houses. The roster of live Chantels was ever changing with Jackie and Annette attending to family business. Helen Leibowitz was used on the live dates, and also Yvonne Fair. Leibowitz, also known as Helen Powell, was a former member of The Impacts. She had also sung with Barbara English and The Fashions. The deal was, though, that when Jackie returned, someone had to leave. With this arrangement, the group was able to continue performing, keeping their basic sound intact. The Chantels were also a self-contained group at this point, travelling with their own band, The Dayton Selby Trio, a combo out of Brooklyn, made up of a man and two women: Dayton Selby, keyboards, Wylena Barton, sax, and Paola Roberts, drums. The advantage of having their own band saved The Chantels the trouble, and often the embarrassment, of having to work with a series of house bands who weren't familiar with their material or sound. It was unusual to watch almost all women on stage, especially behind the instruments. By this time, The Chantels were definitely a polished group, not only singing their hits, but intricate arrangements on standard material, giving the group a more well-rounded appeal. This certainly became apparent while the group was appearing at a week long engagement at the Royal Theater in Chicago. Duke Ellington was also appearing. He did not care for being on the bill with a "Rock & Roll" act. Jackie reflects, "We sang an arrangement of "Autumn Leaves," that our orchestra leader, Sammy Lowe, taught to us." Duke Ellington also had the song in his act, so he asked us not to perform it, but we had learned it and we were going to use it."

For the first few days of the show, Ellington wouldn't even listen to their performance. He couldn't, however, turn off his ears. When he heard the group sing their arrangement, he relented, and nodded his approval.

The Chantels' "frat days" were days of excitement, with the group performing at one frat house while The Imperials were at another house, and yet another act at a third house on fraternity row. In addition to performing their hits, The Chantels performed big party songs such as Little Willie John's "Fever," "When The Saints Go Marchin' In," and "Splish Splash." The Chantels' continuing autonomy would eventually separate them from their one-time mentor, Richard Barrett.

Differences between Richard Barrett and The Chantels were becoming more apparent. They disagreed on choice of material and arrangements. They disagreed on management and production decisions. By 1964, The Chantels were no longer little girls, but adults, quite capable of making their own decisions. Barrett had moved his operations back down to Philadelphia in 1963. This parting of the ways began with the Ludix singles, with Luther Dixon, not Richard Barrett, producing the sessions. Barrett's priorities were already shifting. By 1964, Barrett was busy producing records for Harold Melvin and The Blue Notes, Sheila Ferguson, and the group who would eventually achieve the greatest fame in the 1970s under

his direction, The Three Degrees (of which Ferguson became a member). Barrett did, however, offer to shop the group around and get them a deal. He had arranged for The Chantels to record some sides for Capitol Records. Capitol had released "Eternally" in Canada. The potential to record for a major label certainly must have seemed inviting. Cast in a seriously pop role, the group recorded standards associated with Disney, such as "Someday My Prince Will Come." The Chantels were not happy with this direction. This treatment made them sound much too removed from their R&B roots. These sides were not released. It would have been interesting to see what direction the group's career would have taken had these sides been issued.

By 1965, The Chantels were now totally self-managed. Richard Barrett had fulfilled his offer to find a good deal for them. The group was to work with Philadelphia carmogul turned producer Harold B. Robinson, who had worked with Patti LaBelle and The Bluebelles on Newtown Records. Sandra Dawn had left to replace Barbara Randolph in The Platters. Randolph had replaced Zola Taylor in The Platters in 1962. Sandra Dawn enjoyed success from the three chart entries for The Platters during 1966-67. Robinson would record The Chantels on the Twentieth Century Fox subsidiary, TCF/Arrawak, with Renee now singing lead, and Helen Leibowitz in a permanent position in The Chantels' lineup. The single was a reworking of the Eddie Jones-penned tune "Take Me

The Chantels after topping the charts with "Look In My Eyes", 1961, (standing, L-R) Sonia, Annette Smith, Renee. (seated) Jackie. (Photo courtesy of Yellowlinda, Inc.)

The Chantels, 1996, (clockwise from top left) Sonia, Jackie, Ami Ortiz, Lois, Renee. (Photo courtesy of Marty Schein)

As I Am." Its flip, "There's No Forgetting You," deftly showed the fusion of soul with a light amount of jazz. Unfortunately, the record did nothing to change the group's chart impact. In 1966, The Chantels hooked up with Robert Moseley and one-time Motown and then-current Red Bird producer Robert Bateman. Bert Keyes handled the arrangements. "You're Welcome To My Heart/Soul Of A Soldier" and "Indian Giver/It's Just Me" were both released on the MGM subsidary, Verve Records. A Motown-sounding version of "You're Welcome. . ." had been recorded a year earlier with Bateman's arrangement on the Blue Cat label by another female group, The Bouquets. The Chantels' Verve sessions were soul-inspired treatments. Although Renee delivers an honest and effective lead, little use is made of the group's wonderful harmonies. The dirge-like tempo for "Your Welcome. . . " is uninspiring. Predictably, these records did not achieve success.

In 1967, after being on the road for almost ten years, The Chantels finally decided to call it quits and turn their attention to other aspects of their lives. They had certainly had better luck than most groups who have one or two hits, make a few personal appearances, and then fade into obscurity. The original Chantels were briefly reunited for a single on RCA in 1970, under the supervision of Los Angeles-based promoter Clarence Avant, Horace Ott, Lockie Edwards and former Solitaire-turned record executive Buzzy Willis. "I'm Gonna Win Him Back/Love Makes All The Difference In The World," features Arlene's lead with prominent background vocals over contemporary arrangements. "Love Makes. . ." features the writing efforts of Sandy Linzer and Denny Randell, the duo responsible for hits by The Toys and The Four Seasons. Despite photo sessions taken at the Uni-

sphere in Flushing Meadow Park and a promotional push, the record sank.

Even if the RCA single didn't put The Chantels back on the radio, it did put them back on the club circuit for two years. Arlene elected not to join them, so Christine Iron took her place. They appeared at Dante's, a club in Queens. The affair was sponsored by the Policemen's Club. Sonia's husband, Ray Wilson, was a member. They also made appearances at cabaret clubs like The Fantasy East in The Bronx, which catered to other R&B acts such as The Harptones. One can also hear Jackie, Sonia and Lois singing back-up on "Party People," by The Jimmy Castor Bunch during the late 1970s. They also appeared for a radio interview with Bobby Jay on WWRL in New York City.

In 1972, Jackie Landry Jackson became a court reporter and a teacher of court reporting in White Plains, NY. Jackie made her home in Yonkers, NY, until her death on December 23, 1997, from breast cancer. Lois Harris Powell is a mental health nurse practitioner in private practice. Lois heads a program in which she counsels students. Lois also sings with a classical chorus, The Hudson-Putnam Valley Singers, who perform throughout the Westchester County area. She resides in Hartsdale, NY. Arlene Smith still lives in The Bronx, where she also teaches elementary school. Arlene picked up the ball for the group in the late 1970s and regularly performs around New York, reprising her Chantels songs with the help of back-up singers. Her fans have christened her the "Queen Of Doo Wop." Sonia Goring Wilson is a special education teacher and lives in Florida. Renee Minus White lives in Tarrytown, NY, and is the fashion and beauty editor for Harlem's acclaimed Amsterdam News. Annette Smith lives in Manhattan, where she designs her

The Chantels at The Tarrytown Music Hall, Tarrytown, NY, 1996. (Photo courtesy of Marty Schein)

own clothing and jewelry. In 1996, Annette finished a new CD with producer Jerry Zwecher. The Chantels achieved another high honor by being among the 1996 inductees into The Rhythm And Blues Foundation Hall Of Fame. The original group received their awards in Los Angeles in February of that year. It was a thrill for them, not only to be formally recognized in the world of pop music, but to be reunited with people they haven't seen since their days of touring, such as The Isley Bros., The Flamingos, and Betty Everett, who were also inductees.

After their 1995 induction into the UGHA Hall Of Fame, The Chantels decided to come back onto the music circuit. The group has been making personal appearances in New York, New Jersey, Philadelphia and Pittsburgh. They have played to sold-out houses at the Tarrytown Hall Of Music in Tarrytown, NY. They have done radio interviews on The Rhythm & Blues Group Harmony Review on WFUV-FM with Dan Romanello and on Ronnie I's R&B Party on WNYC-FM. Arlene is having success with her solo career and her emerging involvement in the theater. Joining the rest of the group is a fabulous new singer, Amy Ortiz. She definitely fits The Chantels' image with her clear, powerful voice, her charming wit and her stately good looks. The

Chantels, including both Arlene and Amy, were part of a successful showcase of group harmony singing, with other veteran artists like The Marcels, The Skyliners and Gene Chandler, recorded for PBS in March of 1999 and presented during the fall fundraiser. The Chantels were part of the Great Day In Harlem photo shoot with other pioneer R&B personalities, including their one time mentor, Richard Barrett. The group was also in Washington, DC for the photo's dedication at The Smithsonian Institution in February, 2000.

The Chantels' music has had a tremendous impact on the female group harmony sound, as well as on American music in general. Even today the group is modest about their impact on American music and what their songs mean to their fans. Lois remembers her reaction to a fan's comments at a recent show.

"I was so in awe of the people who knew all of our records. One man told me at a show that it was "I Love You So" that got him back from Vietnam. When he was in a fox hole and scared, he would think of that song."

With so many pivotal R&B songs to their credit, songs that have influenced a host of singers both past and present, The Chantels have deservedly taken their rightful place in the annals of Rock & Roll, past, present, and future.

The Chantels Discography

45s

	Label	Number	Year
He's Gone/The Plea	End	1001	1957
Maybe/Come My Little Baby		1005	
Every Night/Whoever You Are		1015	1958
I Love You So/How Could You Call It Off		1020	
Sure Of Love/Prayee		1026	
Congratulations/If You Try		1030	
I Can't Take It/Never Let Go		1037	
Goodbye To Love/I'm Confessin'		1048	1959
Whoever You Are/How Could You Call It Off		1069	1960
Believe Me/I(Veneers)		1103	1961
There's Our Song Again/I'm The Girl		1105	
Look In My Eyes/Glad To Be Back	Carlton	555	
Well I Told You/Still		564	
Summertime/Here It Comes Again		569	1962
Eternally/Swamp Water	Ludix	101	1963
That's Why You're Happy/Some Tears Fall Dry		105	
Take Me As I Am/There's No Forgetting You	TCF/Arrawak	123	1965
You're Welcome To My Heart/Soul Of A Soldier	Verve	10387	1966
It's Just Me/Indian Giver		10435	
Love Makes All The Difference In The World/I'm Gonna Win Him Back	RCA	74-0347	1970

(Richard Barrett and The Chantels)
	Label	Number	Year
Come Softly To Me*/Walking Through Dreamland (No Group)	Orchid	5004	1959
Come Softly To Me*/Walking Through Dreamland (No Group)	Gone	5056	1959
Summer Love/All Is Forgiven		5060	1960
Summer Love/All Is Forgiven*	Crackerjack	4012	1963

* Some pressings do not mention the group

LPs

	Label	Number	Year
We Are The Chantels	End	301	1958
The Chantels		301	1958
There's Our Song Again		312	1961
The Chantels On Tour	Carlton	144	1962
The Chantels Sing Their Favorites	Forum	9104	1964
Arlene Smith And The Chantels	Murray Hill	000385	1987

EPs

	Label	Number	Year
I Love You So/Prayee/Sure Of Love/How Could You Call It Off	End	EP201	1958
C'est Si Bon/Memories/ I'll Walk Alone/Congratulations		EP202	

The Charmettes

Members:

(1963-65)   Clara Byrd
Minnie Ponder
Betty Simmons

Hey! Hey! Hey! How do you get the attention of the radio audience? Record three nightingales amidst a blend of guitars, saxophones, drums and chimes. This is not an unusual arrangement for 1963, but special to a singing threesome and their producers, whose relentless efforts led to success.

Kenny Young was new to the writing and music production world. In 1963, he teamed with producer Ron Oehl and the duo sought to make their mark in the bustling music scene in New York City. Young had written a song called "Please Don't Kiss Me Again" and the pair needed an act that would properly present the material.

THE CHARMETTES

PERSONAL MANAGEMENT
YOUNG & OEHL

Those singing nurses, The Charmettes, 1963, (L-R) Minnie Ponder, Clara Byrd, Betty Simmons. (Photo courtesy of Kenny Young)

Ron's girlfriend knew of a trio of young nurses who all worked at the same hospital and sang for fun. She suggested to the songwriters that they audition the girls. (This was Kenny Young's first production, so, of course, he hoped that his first effort would have positive results.)

Young and Oehl brought the group into the studio and recorded two songs with Clara Byrd singing the lead. She possessed that New York nasal twang so prevalent in other New York area productions. Record buyers could identify with the "next-door-neighbor" quality of her voice, combined with sweet sounding "ahs" and signature "heys" in the background.

"Please Don't Kiss Me Again" was a genuine bow to both teenage naiveté and adolescent awakening. This sentiment was still being expressed years later in songs like Bruce Springsteen's "Fire," successfully conveyed by The Pointer Sisters in 1979. In the Charmettes case, the virtuous tune, with its bashful message, made it all the way into the top ten in New York in October of 1963, and just snagging the national charts. This was certainly regal satisfaction for Kenny Young, who tells of how difficult it was to initially get the record placed: "Ron and I went to fourteen record companies before Al Stanton at Kapp Records asked us to remix "Please Don't Kiss Me Again." So I just overdubbed Clara Byrd's voice over the stereo mix and 'voila', a master was approved for release and accepted by the radio audience as a favorite tune."

The success of The Charmettes' maiden single prompted another production from the team of Young and Oehl. In 1964, the second Charmettes effort was released. Rock & Roll instrumentation was bolder in the face of the British Invasion, so "Ouzi Ouzi Ooh" donned a heavier production. The same innocent lyrics proclaimed an exuberant tale of adolescent courtship. The flip side dabbled in the "good girl loves the bad boy" territory. In "He's A Wise Guy," the young girl goes against her parents' wishes and dates a roughneck because she can see through his tough exterior. "He's A Wise Guy" has a Latin sounding arrangement with its Cha Cha beat and salsa flutes. This was a departure from the group's initial single.

In 1964, Kenny Young's stature in the music business changed dramatically when he and his new songwriting partner, Artie Resnick, wrote a number one tune for The Drifters, the beach lovers' anthem, "Under The Boardwalk." Resnick joined in for the third and last Charmettes single in 1965. "Stop The Wedding/Sugar Boy" was a double-sided surprise. The single was an adroit move toward the soul category. This time, the innocents showed they had grown up, their voices possessing a haughty attitude, the message more forcefully delivered. The production was placed with World Artists Records, home to Chad and Jeremy and Reparata and The Delrons. Again, the record did well locally. Unfortunately, the ladies had other plans, returning to their lives as medical caregivers soon after the single's release.

Kenny Young continued his writing and producing efforts, writing hundreds of songs, some recorded by legendary artists like The Drifters, The Sapphires and Herman's Hermits. Young and Resnick produced an up-and-coming Bernadette Peters for ABC-Paramount Records, as well as The Goodnight Kisses for Atco and Reparata and The Delrons for Mala. Kenny Young moved to England in 1969, where he has since lived, still pursuing his craft. The Charmettes stepped briefly into the limelight, contributing three fresh voices to the music industry and helping express teenage declarations to the world.

The Charmettes Discography

45s	Label	Number	Year
Please Don't Kiss Me Again/What Is A Tear	Kapp	547	1963
Ouzi Ouzi Ooh/He's A Wise Guy		570	1964
Stop The Wedding/Sugar Boy	World Artists	1053	1965

The Chiffons

Members:

(1962-69) Pat Bennett
Judy Craig, Lead
Barbara Lee
Sylvia Peterson, Lead

(1975) Pat Bennett
Barbara Lee
Sylvia Peterson

There isn't a music fan alive that doesn't remember the nonsense syllables uttered by four young girls singing a 1963 song called "He's So Fine." "Doo Lang" became a part of Rock & Roll jargon when The Chiffons made the song their own and took pop radio by storm.

The Chiffons were formed at James Monroe High School in The Bronx around 1960. Their story started when Ronnie Mack, a young songwriter, heard the group sing. Mack wrote songs for all the groups in his Soundview neighborhood. None of the girls had sung in a group before, with the exception of Sylvia, who had been a member of Little Jimmy and The Tops. The Tops had recorded "Puppy Love" on Len Records in 1961, which Mack had written.

The Chiffons were originally a trio, Judy, Pat and Barbara. They would just get together to sing for fun. Ironically, none of the girls were very interested in singing as a career. Judy wanted to become a dancer. Also, their influences were not popular Rock & Roll groups of the day, but jazz artists like Nancy Wilson and Nina Simone. Taken by their unique sound, Ronnie asked the group to record a song he had written called "He's So Fine." At first the girls balked, but after some persuasion, Ronnie won them over. He also suggested they take in Sylvia as a fourth member. The song featured Judy's warm, urbane lead. After recording the song, Ronnie shopped it around to several companies. He found a home for the song at Bright Tunes Productions, a company owned by The Tokens.

The Tokens were artists in their own right, recording the smash, "Lion Sleeps Tonight," as well as other chart items. The Tokens had founded Bright Tunes for their own creative output as producers, and The Chiffons were their first act. Bright Tunes, in turn, struck a deal with Laurie Records, which released "He's So Fine." This was the group's first in a series of singles and LPs for Laurie and the Bright Tunes. There was another group, possibly out of LA, named The Chiffons, who had brief chart action in 1960 with a version (same tracks) of The Shirelles' "Tonight's The Night," on Big Deal Records. Reissue LPs, some as early as 1964, feature the other group's songs, but the pictures are of the New York Chiffons. They are not the same group.

The success of "He's So Fine/Oh My Love" was well deserved. "He's So Fine" is full of catch phrases, including the introductory "doo langs." It's impossible to forget the lyrics. That lead-in became so identifiable with The Chiffons; it was used as a background pattern for other songs sung by the group. Additionally, it inspired The Tokens to write a song called "The Doo Lang" for Andrea Carroll.

Unfortunately, Ronnie Mack did not see The Chiffons achieve this creative success. After penning one more tune for the group, he died of complications from Hodgkin's Disease. The Tokens were now producing The Chiffons recording sessions. The group's second single was the Ronnie Mack-penned "Lucky Me." Its flip was The Tokens' writing and production number, "Why Am I So Shy," with Sylvia on lead. Sylvia's voice was much different from Judy's. Judy's lead is smooth and aloof, while Sylvia's lead is quintessential and well phrased, with a clear, winsome tone. Having two leads varied the recordings, yet kept the overall Chiffons sound intact.

The Tokens were only in their twenties, but already had a clever discernment for the music business. If a group they were producing had a hit with an A-side written by someone else, their B-side would go right along with it. Unfortunately for "Lucky Me," it was closely patterned after "He's So Fine," yet had no outstanding hooks so it did not chart. The Tokens quickly rushed out another single, mining a song from the Aldon Publishing Company, home of the tremendously successful Dimension Records and the successful songwriting team of Gerry Goffin and Carole King. They already had a fortuitous track record with dozens of artists, among them, Little Eva, The Cookies, Bobby Vee, The Shirelles, Big Dee Irwin and Steve Lawrence. The Tokens obtained a demo of a song called "One Fine Day," with Little Eva singing lead and The Cookies singing backup. The Tokens used the same tracks, erased Little Eva's lead, intermingled The Chiffons vocals with The Cookies vocals on the beginning backgrounds, and recorded over the rest, leaving Carole King's pounding piano intro. They recycled "Why Am I So Shy" for the B-side. The musical tracks of "Why Am I So Shy," including The Chiffons backing vocals, found yet another home on Big Top Records, with Andrea Carroll's voice on lead.

The next single to chart in 1963 was a song co-written by George Kerr, Sidney Barnes and The Tokens. George Kerr was a member of The Serenaders, and was now chief writer and A&R man of Motown's New York Office. "A Love So Fine" was a reworking of a song called "Boyfriend" which Kerr had written for The Serenadettes, a distaff counterpart to his own group, released on Enrica Records in 1961. The song provided yet another novel pattern for The Chiffons' backing vocals, "bomp bom, sic a lic." It's flip was The Tokens' penned ballad, "Only My Friend."

THE CHIFFONS

The Chiffons, 1963, (L-R) Sylvia Peterson, Barbara Lee, Patricia Bennett, Judy Craig.

Many of The Chiffons' B-sides and album cuts were songs that The Tokens had recorded as artists. Interspersed with these successful singles during 1963 were two albums, "He's So Fine" and "One Fine Day." Both albums contained mild cover versions of popular songs of the day, 50s favorites, and more Chiffons versions of Tokens singles. Included in the albums are versions of "See You In September," "Teenager In Love" "ABC-123," "When I Go To Sleep At Night" and "Will You Still Love Me Tomorrow." Even Barbara got a rare lead on "Why Do Fools Fall In Love."

The Chiffons were riding so high at this time that The Tokens actually had the group cover their own sound by recording two singles, released as The Four Pennies on the Laurie subsidiary, Rust Records. These singles, "My Block" and "When The Boy's Happy," The Tokens' tribute to the Spector sound (complete with instrumental flips), featured Sylvia on lead. "When The Boy's Happy" was written by Ellie Greenwich and Jeff Barry. The formula worked so well that the next official Chiffons single was the Barry-Greenwich-Tokens effort entitled, "I Have A Boyfriend," which gave the group their fourth Top 40 single. It was considered one of the best "Wobble" records in New York. The Wobble was a New York line dance similar to The Stroll. The flip was the formulaic "I'm Gonna Dry My Eyes." One more single, "Easy To Love/Tonight I Met An Angel," was released before the end of the year.

The Chiffons now had eight singles and two LPs to their credit. Four of the eight singles released climbed into the Top 40, two of them going Top 10, with "He's So Fine" hitting Number 1. The group was working with a team of proven young writers and producers. They had access to some of the best material in the Rock & Roll world. Their manager was (and still is) the assertive Ernie Martinelli.

Unfortunately, the group was in dispute with The Tokens over choice of material and over distribution of production monies. The Chiffons entered into a lawsuit to free themselves from their contract with The Tokens. The court ruled in their favor. The girls were now ready to work for someone whom they felt understood in what direction the group wanted to go. Regrettably, it seemed that The Chiffons were now bad news for production companies. The group is certain that they were blackballed. No production company wanted to take a chance on a group that had sued to get out of a contract and won. This unhappy state of affairs left The Chiffons in limbo. They no longer had creative backing behind them or a label to record for. Without a forthcoming follow-up to their hits, the momentum would be lost. In 1964, during the time that the group was in litigation, two singles were issued. The first single, "Sailor Boy/When Summer's Through," sustained a mid-chart placing on the pop charts. The second song, "What Am I Gonna Do With You/Strange, Strange Feeling," did not make the charts. Both A-sides were the collaborative writing efforts of Gerry Goffin and Russ Titelman. The Cookies and Skeeter Davis also recorded the latter single.

The immense talent of The Chiffons was not lost on the executives at Laurie. In 1965, The Chiffons signed directly to the label, where they worked under the guises of Doug Morris and Elliot Greenberg. The recordings continued at Allegro Sound with Brooks Arthur at the controls. Hank Medress said that he still supervised The Chiffons recordings during this period. Chiffons singles continued to sport the "Bright Tunes Productions" label as well as Tokens-written B-sides. From a creative standpoint, this certainly wouldn't hurt the group's chance at another hit. Also, here was a chance for a change in direction. The Chiffons first session for Morris and Greenberg yielded the Ashford and Simpson-composition, "The Real Thing," flipped with a piece that was decidedly laden with instruments and echo, called "Nobody Knows What's Goin' On." The former was pulled so not to create a battle on the charts with the Tina Britt version, both out in the Spring of 1965. "Nobody..." took off, but stalled at the outer reaches of the national charts, although it did well in New York, reaching the top 20. The next single, "Tonight I'm Gonna Dream," with its neo-Spector sound, did not chart at all. The Chiffons were busy making personal appearances, including a cameo in the movie "Disk-O-Tek Holiday," where they performed "Nobody...". Their next single would put them back on top.

Many hear "Sweet Talking Guy" as a Motown variant. Actually, it is New York sounding, an ongoing attempt during the mid-60s to keep the Brill Building sound alive, relying on violins and big band intros. "Sweet Talking Guy" supplanted itself firmly in the top ten. Its success spawned two sound-alike tunes, "Out of This World" and "Stop, Look and Listen," which also received airplay and chart action. Also, Morris and Greenberg used the group on backing vocals for "The Next In Line" by Hoagy Lands.

Outside of the Motown groups and The Four Seasons, not many vocal groups, especially female, were able to sustain success throughout the ever-changing sound of mid-60s pop rock. The Chiffons' renewed success was proof that the right match of singers, producers and songs could still work, even in the face of many more self-contained groups. But then Laurie got careless, releasing singles meant for the albums, like a version of "My Boyfriend's Back" and "March," a B-side staple from the Tokens' library. Gems like "Just For Tonight" and Ernie Maresca's "Dream, Dream, Dream" were overlooked either for release or proper promotion. "Just For Tonight" did chart in Canada. This aloof approach created a downward spiral on the charts, from which The Chiffons would not recover.

As the 1960s drew to a close, The Chiffons were recipients of the writing efforts of Irwin Levine and Toni Wine, who wrote a beautiful ballad entitled, "Love Me Like You're Gonna Lose Me," featuring countering leads by Judy and Sylvia. The song was timely, and foreshadowed future success for the songwriting duo, who in a year's time would have a big hit with "Candida" by Tony Orlando and Dawn.

Meanwhile, in 1969, The Tokens had decided to release all the old sessions of The Chiffons that they had in the vault. The B.T. Puppy LP, "Secret Love" produced a single, "Secret Love" with Sylvia leading, backed by the ubiquitous "Strange, Strange Feeling." The album sports more of The Tokens premium production work, containing songs like Ronnie Mack's "Love Of A Lifetime" and Goffin/Wine/Kornfeld's "Now That You're My Baby." No alternate versions of any Chiffons recordings exist. Hank Medress said that Judy would always get her lead vocal in one take. These sessions were recorded during 1963 and 1964. When The Tokens began a production deal with Buddah Records, they released one more Chiffons single in 1970, a version of "So In Love." The Chiffons' current recordings were more and more sporadic. Tired of the business hustle, Judy Craig left the group in 1971.

Although The Chiffons were slipping from earshot, their sound was still exercising its influence. At one point, on an extended tour, the group crossed paths with George Harrison, even sharing a bill for a time on a show. According to their manager, Ernie Martinelli, the tour lasted several weeks, and Harrison's musical mind must have sopped up what he heard, because his "My Sweet Lord" was a carbon copy of "He's So Fine." Eventually, Ronnie Mack's estate had to face off with Harrison in court over American rights to the song. Although Mack's estate won in the U.S., George Harrison still holds international rights. For a lark, The Chiffons recorded "My Sweet Lord" and Laurie released it as a single in 1975. "One Fine Day" had jumped back on to the British charts in 1972.

One more Laurie single, the belated "Dream, Dream, Dream," was released in 1976, a marvelous tune, perfect for 1967, when it was recorded, but obviously anachronistic during the disco era. The Chiffons continued to forge ahead, making club and television appearances on some of the first revival circuit shows with other veteran groups like The Penguins and The Dell Vikings.

Throughout the 1970s and 1980s, The Chiffons continued making personal appearances, both in the US and Europe, although their publicity remained decidedly reserved. Judy stayed out of the group until the untimely death of Barbara Lee in 1992 at age 48. After a nasty stage accident, Sylvia decided to retire from the music business. Sylvia was replaced by Connie Harvey, a noted session singer, whose credits include the popular 1979 disco album, "Poussez." Connie also recorded backing vocals for Billy Idol and other artists both in America and abroad. This trio continues to entertain the masses with their body of catchy, hook-laden ditties. Judy's lead voice continues to be outstanding. Although the ladies have chosen other careers for their life's work, performing as The Chiffons has never gone away. Their records were continually repackaged by Laurie Records in various forms for the last two decades, until Laurie was finally sold to Capitol Records. The group's timeless recordings and perennial appearances are proof that audiences possess the constant craving for what The Chiffons deliver, a feeling and sound that is "so fine."

The Chiffons Discography

45s

	Label	Number	Year
He's So Fine/Oh My Lover	Laurie	3152	1962
Lucky Me/Why Am I So Shy		3166	1963
One Fine Day/Why Am I So Shy		3179	
A Love So Fine/Only My Friend		3195	
I Have A Boyfriend/I'm Gonna Dry My Eyes		3212	
Easy To Love/Tonight I Met An Angel		3224	
Sailor Boy/When Summer's Through		3262	1964
What Am I Gonna Do With You/Strange, Strange Feeling		3275	
Nobody Knows What's Going On/The Real Thing		3301	1965
Nobody Knows What's Going On/Did You Ever Go Steady		3301	
Tonight I'm Gonna Dream/The Heavenly Place		3318	
Sweet Talking Guy/Did You Ever Go Steady		3340	1966
Out Of This World/Just A Boy		3350	
Stop, Look and Listen/March		3357	
My Boyfriend's Back/I Got Plenty O' Nuttin'		3364	
Keep The Boy Happy/If I Knew Then		3377	1967
The Next In Line/Please Don't Talk About Me (w/Hoagy Lands)		3381	
Just For Tonight/Teach Me How		3423	
Up On The Bridge/March		3460	1968
Love Me Like You're Gonna Lose Me/Three Dips of Ice Cream		3497	1969
Secret Love/Strange, Strange Feeling	B.T. Puppy	558	
So Much In Love/ Strange, Strange Feeling	Buddah	171	1970
My Sweet Lord/Main Nerve	Laurie	3630	1975
Dream, Dream, Dream/Oh My Lover		3648	1976

(as The Four Pennies)

	Label	Number	Year
When The Boy's Happy/Hockaday Part 1	Rust	5070	1963
My Block/Dry Your Eyes		5071	

LPs

	Label	Number	Year
He's So Fine	Laurie	2018	1963
One Fine Day		2020	1963
Sweet Talking Guy		2036	1966
Secret Love	B.T. Puppy	1011	1969
Everything You Always Wanted To Hear by The Chiffons But Couldn't Get	Laurie	4001	1974
The Chiffons Sing The Hits of the 50s & 60s		4016	1979

The Clickettes

Members:

(1958-59)	Barbara English, Lead Charlotte McCartney, 1st Soprano Trudy McCartney, 2nd Soprano Sylvia Hammond, Alto	*(1960)*	Barbara English, Lead Jeanne Bolden, 1st Soprano Barbara Saunders, 2nd Soprano Sylvia Hammond	*(Fashions)* *(1961-62)*	Barbara English, Lead Jeanne Bolden Helen Powell (Liebowitz) Barbara Saunders

According to vocal group folklore, this is how the tale is told. Male groups gathered on street corners or in after-school centers and sang harmonies, hoping to attract the attention of females and, eventually, the record companies. Female groups did not hang out. They were formed as companion groups to the males. How about a female group that came up with their own songs and arrangements and did so with a unique style and phrasing all their own? Such is the case of the fabulous Clickettes, young ladies with voices of savvy style and grace.

THE CLICKETTES

The Clickettes, 1959, (clockwise from top left) Trudy McCartney, Charlotte McCartney, Shirley (?), Barbara Jean English, Sylvia Hammond. (Photo courtesy of The Clickettes/Marv Gold-

The story of The Clickettes (or Clicketts/Click-etts, as some record labels have the name spelled) began when 16 year-old Barbara Jean English moved from Philadelphia to New York City with her mother and step-father, settling on the east side of Manhattan in 1957. The family had previously moved to Philadelphia from South Carolina.

Barbara Jean was tired of moving around. The prospect of having to make new friends in another city was making her feel quite morose. She began putting her thoughts to melodies she had rolling around in her head. Barbara's family knew she liked to sing, and because Barbara was normally shy, her mother encouraged it. Once the family had settled into their new home, Barbara was enrolled at Yorkville Vocational High School at 88th St. and York Ave. To pass the time on the bus ride from home to school, Barbara and her friend, Roberta Alloway, would make up lyrics to Barbara's melodies. By the time the bus pulled up to the school, the shy, yet emotional teenager had written her first song. It was entitled "Lover's Prayer."

Sylvia Hammond was born and raised in New York City, where she lived with her mother, brother and sister. Sylvia never missed an opportunity to listen to the radio. She would sing along to anything with backgrounds and found that she not only had an ear for harmony, but could also sing any part with ease. In junior high school she joined the glee club, but had not thought seriously about starting a group until she entered high school.

Charlotte and Trudy McCartney were born and raised in The Bronx. They grew up singing in church. Trudy credits her love of singing to her early experiences, "We sang with a church group called the Gospelettes. Our parents, Charles and Mabel McCartney were so supportive of our goals, and so proud."

One day at school, Barbara heard a group of girls rehearsing some songs in one of the stairways. She thought they sounded so good, but was too shy to ask if she could join them. After weeks of trying to figure out a way to approach them, Barbara finally decided the best way to do it was to ask them if they could come up with a background to a song she wrote. Barbara figured that they would take her more seriously if she were less direct about trying to "crash" the group.

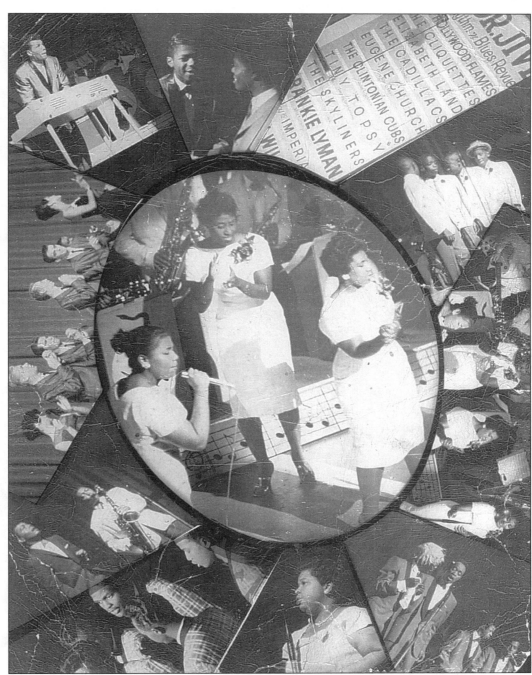

The Clickettes, co-starring in a star-studded spectacular at The Apollo, August, 1959, (clockwise from top right) The Clintonian Cubs, The Clickettes, The Cadillacs, Liz Lands, Little Anthony & The Imperials, Tiny Topsy, The Skyliners, Eugene Church, Frankie Lymon. (Photo courtesy of Trudy McCartney Cunningham)

The girls told her that they would have to hear the full melody line if they were to come up with the right background. Barbara knew this was it. She opened her mouth and started to sing "...Lo-ord, show me if he... really loves me...." Sylvia was so impressed with Barbara's lead she soon thereafter left her group to form one with Barbara. Sylvia recounts how the quartet actually came together. "I was singing with one of my classmates, Nellie Brazeal. We didn't have a real group together at that time, but were trying to start one. While we palled around together, we would sing as a duo. When anyone came along as we sang in the hallways, stairways or in front of the cafeteria and started singing with us, we'd welcome it. Trudy joined in one day outside the cafeteria, and from then on we continued to meet. One day we were all singing in the hallway, and began listening to Barbara sing. We liked what we heard."

In a short time, a trio containing Barbara, Sylvia and Trudy was formed. Charlotte attended Walton High School in The Bronx, where the McCartneys lived. Charlotte was brought in to round out the group.

The Clickettes with Trudy leading on "Mr. Lucifer", a song written for the stage by Johnnielouise Richardson. (Photo courtesy of Trudy McCartney Cunningham)

The yet unnamed group began regular rehearsals after school. After awhile the girls decided on using the name The Bouquets. They had acquired a manager at this point, a man named Gordon King. King had produced a demo of the girls singing one of Barbara's tunes, "But Not For Me." King then took the group over to Broadway's Brill Building, located on the corner of 49th St., where groups abounded in the hallways hoping for a record deal. King kept the group waiting for hours while he shopped their demo. Some stations already had a copy of this song and were playing it on the air. The group was even corralled to sing background on a song recorded by a new singer from The Bronx named Bobby Darin. The song, "Now We're One," was released on Atco as The Rinky Dinks.

One cold day, the group was waiting outside the Brill Building for Gordon. Zell Sanders, owner of J & S Records spotted them, huddled in the doorway, trying to stay warm. Zell was enjoying her success with Johnnie & Joe's "Over The Mountain," recorded by Joe Rivers and Johnnielouise Richardson, Zell's daughter. Zell asked the girls if they were a group. When they replied "yes," she asked them to sing for her. They sang two of Barbara's compositions, "But Not For Me," and "Lover's Prayer." Zell directed the group to meet at her house, then on Tiffany St. in The Bronx.

Zell was starting a companion label to J & S that her daughter Johnnielouise would manage. The label was called Dice, possibly because she knew it would be a gamble. At first, Zell was planning to have the girls become the next configuration of Hearts. Zell was already famous for firing entire groups and she was already on her third generation of Hearts. The group would have none of that, however. They would have their own identity. In keeping with the theme of the new label, the group was rechristened The Clickettes, for the click of the dice, and because, as Trudy puts it, "our harmony just 'clicked'." One variant of the label pictures a hand rolling a pair of dice. Right from the start, Barbara remembers how grueling rehearsals were; "We rehearsed from five to seven days a week, certainly no less than six days. Zell wanted to make sure we sounded perfect, that our diction was perfect."

Charlotte remembers singing endlessly, not just for rehearsal's sake, but for fun, "We would harmonize anywhere and everywhere—on trains, buses, in school and studio hallways. We remember day after day doing our homework on the train after school on our way to practice. School was always our priority."

In September of 1958, after some rehearsing, The Clickettes were ready to record. Most of the group's recordings were done at Bell Sound. It was decided that although "Lover's Prayer" was a strong song for the group, Zell wanted to go with "But Not For Me" flipped with "I Love You I Swear." Zell had purchased the master of "But Not For Me" from Gordon King and used it for one side of the group's first single. The musical accompaniment at the session was usually no more than four pieces, allowing the true sound of the group to come through. The group often had the song in two or three takes. Unfortunately, Zell could not move the record. The group's follow-up,

another teenage ballad, "A Teenager's First Love," and its amusing flip, the rocking "Jive Time Turkey," again failed to break the way Zell had intended. Zell also used the group to back a young boy (identity unknown) and released the single, "Louella," as The Avalons.

The Clickettes would net creative and commercial recognition with their next few releases. In 1959, "Because Of My Best Friend" told an engaging story of a young girl who trusted her best friend with her guy. The song was sung in a call and response style. It's flip, "To Be A Part Of You" was another dreamy ballad containing a message from a girl to her guy. One can hear the unique blend of the very street background vocals with the stylized approach and specific diction of Barbara's lead. This single would be The Clickettes' biggest commercial success, becoming a two-sided hit in Philadelphia. Barbara feels that the group's sales were strongest in Philly because of the laid back feel of the songs, a style favored in Philadelphia.

The next single also enjoyed airplay in the Northeast. "Warm, Soft And Lovely," a cover of a Johnnie & Joe tune that J & S had released a year earlier, was written by song man and Hearts' piano player, Rex Garvin. The Clickettes version was fuller, with more voices singing in group harmony, showing their now established style. A moving, uptempo number, "Why Oh Why," with Trudy on lead harmony was the flip. "Why Oh Why" was also previously recorded by Johnnie & Joe. The Clickettes' recordings were very unique because the group had originated their sound. They had no direct influences. Their sound was culled from various kinds of singing styles. It was this style which Zell herself would instruct her other female groups to adhere to.

One more single was issued in 1959 when "Lover's Prayer" was finally released. From its simple piano intro to its plucked guitar lead-in, the song promptly invokes visions of a warm summer night and a young girl's wistful dreams. Barbara's sincere lead, combined with the group's high, almost kitten-like calls and warbling runs, put the song over the top. Her plea was every teenage girl's message. It's flip was the similar, but more soft-sung "Grateful." Barbara was honing her skills as a songwriter, a craft that would later serve her well. Songwriting credits usually went to Barbara and Johnnielouise.

Despite the originality and creativeness of The Clickettes recordings and their local success, they failed to make a significant chart impact. Amazingly, "Lover's Prayer" didn't do well nationally for the group, but it is most definitely a collector's favorite. In 1995, Felix Hernandez, host of National Public Radio's successful and critically acclaimed "Rhythm Review," voted "Lover's Prayer" onto The 25 Best Vocal Group Records survey. Zell had even attempted (but not succeeded) to cash in on the victories of The Clickettes sound with a group from The Bronx, The Teen Clefs. "Sputnik/Hiding My Tears With A Smile" was released on Dice, right on the heels of "Lover's Prayer." A CD released by Gotham Records has this single listed as two unreleased Clickettes sides. The closest The Teen Clefs ever came to being The Clickettes was that one of their members posed in The Clickettes' only publicity photo.

This string of successful local hits put the group on a run of personal appearances along the eastern seaboard. The Clickettes only public appearance prior to their success was at a contest in New Jersey, in 1958, where the group beat out The Shirelles for first place. As the airplay for their records increased, the group became more in demand. The Clickettes played to standing-room-only crowds at The Uptown Theater in Philadelphia, where "To Be A Part Of You" was #1 on regional playlists. The famed Apollo Theater, The Royal Theater in Baltimore, and The Howard in Washington D.C. were also successful venues for the group, appearing with other notables like The Skyliners and Jackie Wilson.

Surprisingly, the girls were unaware of the magnitude of their popularity. At one show at New York's Apollo Theatre, during the summer of 1959, The Clickettes were on a star-studded bill with The Skyliners, The Cadillacs, Liz Lands, The Clintonian Cubs, Little Anthony and The Imperials, and Eugene Church. Trudy recalls her astonishment, "What's amazing is that we were stars and we didn't even know it. We even appeared with Frankie Lymon, among others. Our mother recalls the first time she came to see us perform. The women were falling out, fainting and screaming for Frankie Lymon. She couldn't believe that when we came out the men were doing the same thing for us, hanging over the balcony, yelling and screaming at the top of their lungs."

Barbara Jean English

Barbara Jean English, 2000. (Photo courtesy of Barbara Jean English)

As all performers before them, The Clickettes soon learned about the hard life of the road. Pulling one-nighters in several places for short periods of time made everyone tired and homesick. The girls would all be cramped into one room in a guest house in order to save money. Living on a steady diet of chicken wings combined with little rest can definitely weaken one's immune system. One evening before a performance Barbara discovered she was coming down with a cold and was beginning to get hoarse. One of the road managers for The Skyliners gave Barbara an elixir that was sure to make her "feel better." The next thing Barbara knew she was on stage pouring out her heart and soul to the audience feeling no pain in the process, as Barbara vividly describes:

"I had a sore throat and singing at these shows meant doing three or four shows a day, six or seven days a week. Jimmy Beaumont of The Skyliners was also sick. I don't remember if it was his sister or the girl in the group who gave me cough syrup with codeine. Well, I'll tell you, it had me sailing. There were bars in the dressing rooms and I was swinging from them. I was on my knees on stage, like the male singers. It was probably not even a phrase where one should be begging. I came off stage, and Zell looked at me and said, 'What were you doing? You were terrible!' I was probably cracking. She said it would freeze my throat and I wouldn't feel anything. Well she was right. I didn't feel anything!"

Upon leaving the stage, she received quizzical looks from her contemporaries. Apparently Barbara no longer felt hoarse, but the audience heard it just the same. Excellent stage presence and bravado made up for more than a few swallowed notes.

Another lesson learned by The Clickettes is one that has stayed with Barbara throughout her professional career. Early on, Zell Sanders instilled in her acts the importance of maintaining the highest possible standards in order to make it. For this group of young girls this always meant a top-notch appearance; "As far as the attire was concerned, she instilled in us to be ladies. If a pin was found in your bra, Zell would fine you. The crinoline had to be cleaned and starched. Zell was a general. She cracked the whip."

This sentiment of complete professionalism was never more apparent as on the night The Clickettes were on stage at The Apollo performing a frenetic dance routine to "Why Oh Why" when one of the girls' pants suits split wide open in the back. They had to finish the performance. Every time their backs went to the audience, these wild hand motions covering their rear ends would ensue. At the end of the performance they wiggled off stage. Zell took one look at the ripped pants and freaked. The next day all four outfits were in the trash. Sure it could be fixed, but that would be below the standards which Zell wanted. Another time, Trudy cracked the heel off her shoe when coming down the stage steps at the Apollo, but, regardless, the show went on.

After the local success of The Clickettes' material on Dice, they decided to leave Zell Sander's label. Growing disagreement over Zell's handling of the group prompted the girls to seek management elsewhere. The group went over to Guyden Records in 1960, recording "Where Is He?," a song written by Chantels' Svengali, Richard Barrett. The flip side, "The Lone Lover," was a novelty tune written by the group on the bus en route to a job in Philadelphia, with some help from veteran songwriter Otis Blackwell.

An interesting attribute of The Clickettes was that there actually were seven girls, though they only performed as a quartet. During their recordings on Dice, the McCartney sisters were not allowed to do the overnight tours. Jeanne Bolden and Barbara Saunders did the live dates. Another girl named Shirley (her last name escapes everyone) also occasionally did live dates. She was fortunate enough to appear in the group's only known publicity photo. Shirley was a member of fellow Dice stablemates, The Teen Clefs. She did no recording with the group. Right before The Clickettes moved to Guyden, Charlotte and Trudy left for good to continue their education. Jeanne and Barbara then conveniently dropped into their spots, with almost no change in sound.

Following the group's Guyden single, The Clickettes switched labels again in 1961, moving to Morty Craft's Warwick label. It was at this time that The Clickettes found out that they could no longer call themselves The Clickettes. Zell Sanders exercised her right to retain the group's name, the name she had originally given them.

When the Warwick recording was released, the label read "The Fashions." The group members now, besides Barbara, were Jeanne, Barbara Saunders and a new member, Helen Powell Liebowitz, a former member of The Impacts who would eventually perform and record as one of The Chantels. Helen replaced Sylvia.

"Dearest One," written by Richard Barrett, was a beautiful, Latin-tinged number with Barbara's unique lead with sweet vocals from the backup. It was flipped with the bluesy "All I Want." After one release on Warwick, the group's next release, "Fairy Tales/Please Let It Be Me," was released on Elmor Records. Other renditions of "Fairy Tales" were eventually recorded by The Capri Sisters and The Spaniels.

In 1962, another move to Morris Levy's Roulette complex and yet another name change occurred. The record label now read "Barbara English and The Fashions." This billing set the stage for Barbara English's solo career. Roulette released "We Need Them," a great dance tune with a mashed potato beat and a 'can't live with men/can't live without them' message. The flip was "Ta Ta Tee Ta Ta," written by Arthur Crier, a member of The Halos, famous for "You're A Nag." Arthur sings bass on this single. Arthur was also managing Barbara at the time. One more Roulette single followed, but neither song met with overwhelming success. Barbara forged ahead, determined to make a living in the music business.

The Clickettes getting together for a holiday reunion, 1996, (clockwise from left) Sylvia, Charlotte, Barbara, and Trudy. (Photo courtesy of Trudy McCartney Cunningham)

The name of The Clickettes was resurrected for a single released on Checker Records in 1963. The song, "I Just Can't Help It," borrows some cues from The Essex "Easier Said Than Done." The singers on the session were Lezli Valentine, Marlina Mars and Iggy Williams, all members of Zell's Hearts/Jaynetts group. The master numbers for the Checker release are Tuff master numbers consecutive with the master numbers of The Hearts' "I Understand Him." Zell owned the name of The Clickettes and would apply it if she felt it would be financially sound. However, no one noticed the single.

With her Clickettes days behind her, Barbara took a job as a receptionist for Aaron Schroeder Publishing, to be close to the action. She lent her unique vocals to cutting demo records for various labels and songwriters. This kept Barbara's voice in shape, netted her financial security and also placed her at the forefront for new songs. She certainly was in good company in these circles, recording dozens of demos along with Arthur Crier's Halos, The Cookies, Tony Middleton and Lenny Welch. This position also gave Barbara the chance to continue with her songwriting. With Al Cleveland, she wrote "Mr. Heartbreak" for Cathy Saint, who recorded for Leiber and Stoller's Daisy label (the forerunner to the Red Bird complex).

There was one song in particular for which Barbara cut the demo in 1963, not only lending her voice, but her style as well. She was sure this would be a break as a solo artist. Barbara was then working with producers Jimmy Radcliffe and Aaron Schroeder. She asked them to release her version of this song, but the producers said that it was already promised to a young 16-year old girl from New Jersey who was signed with an influential, major label. When the single was released on Mercury Records, it indeed did contain Barbara's stamp. The artist? Lesley Gore. The song? "It's My Party." This song was also recorded by, but never released by The Crystals.

Sylvia had left The Clickettes in 1961, but had a yearning to sing a couple of years later. In 1963, she contacted Johnnielouise, who put her together with Gloria Gilbert. One of Zell's artists, Ada Ray (Kelly) introduced Sylvia and Gloria to Jehoshabeth (Jay) Dunston. They formed a trio that Johnnielouise was going to manage. When Johnnielouise was slow in securing the group a deal, they struck out on their own. The group met with Samson Horton one day outside the Brill Building and decided to sign contracts with him and his songwriting partner, Bobby Adams. The duo had a company called Samada Productions. Christened "The Loreleis" by the production company, the trio of young ladies recorded, "Why Do I Put Up With You/Strange Way" for Brunswick Records. The group rehearsed feverishly and garnered some studio work, but never followed up their initial single. Sylvia attributes this to the saturation that many performers encountered from struggling production companies, "Mr. Horton had a lot of other writing commitments that he had to work on, due to advance payments, and it seemed to us that he had become disinterested. Mr. Adams decided to take over. Through him, we came in contact with another music arranger, Horace Ott, who wrote the music to two songs written by Mr. Adams for

The Loreleis. They were "Years From Now" and "Sad Song." I don't know why, but we never got a chance to record them." Eventually, Jay left the group and was replaced by Dora Brooks. Shortly thereafter, the group disbanded.

Barbara continued to make her living as a singer and a songwriter during the 1960s. She recorded two singles for Reprise Records, and one for Warner Bros., before recording her Northern Soul stomper, "Sittin' In The Corner" for Aurora Records, an uptempo dance classic. Things began to slow down for Barbara during the late 60s. Then, in 1971, she signed on as the premier artist of John Krowlovich's new label, Alithia Records, under the supervision of Lou Toby.

Barbara had recorded a song entitled, "So Many Ways To Die," from the film, "The Arrangement." In fact, the tune had actually been in the can for a couple of years before being heard, which led to the offer to record again. Barbara released numerous singles and two LPs for the label between 1971 and 1974.

Her second album, entitled "Barbara Jean English," was produced by the veteran singer-songwriter-producer George Kerr. Kerr had written songs and produced for The Escorts, The Chiffons, and his own group, The Serenaders. No stranger to producing female voices, George worked with the great talent, Linda Jones. The singles produced with Barbara made a significant impact on R&B stations and charts. Barbara's more noteworthy singles during this period were a cover of Dionne Warwick's "Don't Make Me Over," "Guess Who," and "Breaking Up A Happy Home." In 1979, on Zakia Records, Barbara released a tune which made a considerable showing on the then red-hot disco circuit. "I'm Dancing To Keep From Crying" featured Barbara's great vocals amidst basic, yet absorbing, dance tracks. The session was produced by Herschell Dwellingham. The song garnered major airplay on New York stations WLIB and WWRL, as well as being a staple on the club disc jockeys' Disconet. This web was where jocks made sure the hottest sounds were being played in all the happening clubs by passing along their finds to other club jockeys. A few years later, Barbara followed with more dance recordings released in England. Produced by Kevin Robert on Blue Chip Records, "It's Better If You Don't Get To Know Me," was released in England in 1990.

In June of 1996, Barbara and Trudy appeared as guests on "The R&B Review" with Dan Romanello on WFUV-FM, at Fordham University. There they discussed their glory days as Clickettes, and were thrilled to hear their songs on the radio once again (some of which they hadn't heard in over thirty years). Trudy, Charlotte and Sylvia appeared with Frank Gengaro and Gordon Skadberg on The R&B Serenade out of Hofstra University on Long Island. There they told interesting stories and signed autographs. Unfortunately, the group is not in possession of all of their material. With the exception of their strongest singles, most Clickettes songs have not been reissued.

For many years, Barbara has been a successful cabaret singer. She makes her home in Fort Lee, New Jersey. Her wonderful phrasing certainly makes her voice suited for the sounds of pop, jazz and R&B. She plays to packed houses in The Catskills, Atlantic City, Puerto Rico, Monte Carlo, on cruise ships and in countless cabarets in and around New York City. Barbara has always made her living as a singer, singing sophisticated sounds now with as much gusto as she did when she was singing songs about teen angst. Charlotte graduated from high school and went straight to nursing school. She and her family live in Florida and she is a registered nurse. Jeanne Bolden also lives down south.

Trudy once had an offer to sub in Patti LaBelle and The Blue Belles, but turned it down. Instead, Trudy went to business school and made a career in banking. She is now settled in Jamaica, Queens. Sylvia is a homemaker, living in Manhattan. Helen Powell passed away in December of 1997.

On June 6, 1999, in Harlem, New York, The Clickettes were part of the Great Day In Harlem photo shoot with numerous pioneer R&B groups. The group was also present at the photo's dedication at The Smithsonian Institution in February, 2000. On the strength of this renewed visibility on the part of The Clickettes, Barbara, Trudy and Sylvia officially regrouped in 1999, with Lorraine Joyner of The Veneers joining as the fourth member. The Clickettes played to an enthusiastic Washington D.C. crowd at MJ's Meeting Place just outside the capital in Capitol Heights, Maryland, sharing the bill with the Spaniels for a New Year's eve gala, thrilling the audience with fresh renditions of their group harmony classics. The Clickettes have also appeared at Luci's Place, in Harlem and on the Heroines of R&B concert series presented by Ronnie "I," at New York's Symphony Space. Viewed as the unsung champions of Rhythm and Blues female group harmony, The Clickettes are justifiably receiving their due as part of the history of Rock & Roll. The Clickettes are figured among the singers who personified the voices of 1950s New York City female group harmony. The Clickettes have certainly left their distinct mark on Rock & Roll vocal group music, and for this we are truly "grateful."

The Clickettes Discography

45s

	Label	Number	Year
But Not For Me/I Love You I Swear	Dice	100	1958
Jive Time Turkey/A Teenager's First Love		83/84	
To Be A Part Of You/Because Of My Best Friend		92/93	1959
Warm, Soft And Lovely/Why Oh Why		94/95	
Lover's Prayer/Grateful		96/97	
Where Is He/The Lone Lover	Guyden	2043	1960

(as The Avalons)

	Label	Number	Year
Louella/You Broke Our Hearts	Dice	90/91	1958

(as The Fashions)

	Label	Number	Year
Dearest One/All I Want	Warwick	646	1961
Fairy Tales/Please Let It Be Me	Elmor	301	1961

(as Barbara English and The Fashions)

	Label	Number	Year
We Need Them/Ta Ta Tee Ta Ta	Roulette	4428	1962
Bad News/Fever		4450	

Barbara Jean English

	Label	Number	Year
I've Got A Date/Shoo Fly	Reprise	0290	1964
Small Town Girl/Tell Me Like It Is		0349	1965
Because I Love Somebody/Good Times Gone	Warner Bros.	5685	
(You Got Me) Sittin' In The Corner/Standing On Tip Toe	Aurora	55	1966
Love's Arrangement/--	Alithia	6035	1971
So Many Ways To Die/Danger Signs		6041	1972
I'm Sorry/Li'l Baby		6042	
Don't Make Me Over/Baby I'm A Want You		6046	
You're Going To Need Somebody To Love/All This		6053	1973
Coming Or Going/Love's Arrangement		6059	1974
Guess Who/Breaking Up A Happy Home		6064	
I'm Dancing To Keep From Crying/Inst.	Zakia	--	1979
It's Better If You Don't Get To Know Me/--	Blue Chip	--	1990

(as The Rinky Dinks w/Bobby Darin)

	Label	Number	Year
Now We're One/Early In The Morning	Atco	6121	1958

(The Loreleis w/Sylvia Hammond)

	Label	Number	Year
Why Do I Put Up With You/Strange Way	Brunswick	55271	1964

LPs

Barbara Jean English

	Label	Number	Year
So Many Ways	Alithia	9102	1972
Barbara Jean English		9105	1973

The Cookies

Members:

(1954-56)   Dorothy Jones, 1st Soprano
Beulah Robertson, 2nd Soprano/Lead
Ethel (Darlene) McCrea, Alto/Baritone/Bass

(1956-59)   Dorothy Jones, 1st Soprano
Margie Hendrix, 2nd Soprano/Lead
Darlene McCrea, Alto/Baritone/Bass

(1960-65)   Margaret Ross, Lead/Soprano
Dorothy Jones, Lead/Soprano
Earl-Jean McCrea, Lead/Alto

(1966-67)   Margaret Ross
Dorothy Jones
Darlene McCrea

During the early 1960s, there came the dawn of the producer era. A handful of successful songwriters and producers were churning out pop hits faster than one could blink. Within this creative enclave, there existed a trio of females who lent their unique vocal capabilities to a singular body of recordings. What is not well known is that this same ensemble appeared on dozens of other recording sessions in New York City during the 1950s and 1960s, both in their own right as artists, and as prominent background vocalists for other artists who received more acclaim for their efforts. What The Blossoms were to background vocals on the West Coast, The Cookies were to musical settings on the East Coast.

The Cookies were formed around 1954 in Coney Island, New York. The founding members of the group, Dorothy Jones, her cousin Beulah Robertson and Ethel (Darlene) McCrea all sang in the choir at The First Baptist Church of Coney Island on Mermaid Ave. Dorothy started singing as a little girl growing up in Montclair, South Carolina. She would attend Children's Day at her church. Dorothy's mom was lead soloist, so it was expected that Dorothy would sing at church functions. Dorothy was an only child, so she would often pass the time entertaining herself. Singing and going to the movies were Dorothy's passions. She often dreamed that one-day she would indeed be gracing the stage as a performer.

Eventually, Dorothy's family moved north and settled in Brooklyn. Dorothy was now surrounded by the profusion of Rhythm and Blues abounding in New York City. Dorothy became fast friends with The McCreas who lived a block away. Dorothy and Ethel, known as Darlene, knew each other from Mark Twain Junior High, which they attended.

Dorothy and Darlene's influences were from singing gospel and listening to the popular Rhythm and Blues groups of the day. Darlene's brother played guitar and Darlene sang. When the girls were in high school they joined the church choir. They would spend evenings sitting in the house just singing. The girls didn't take much notice, but the adults would tell them how good they sounded. It was this kind of encouragement that led to the group's official formation. Dorothy relates the story: "Darlene, myself and some neighborhood friends used to sing on the street

COOKIES

Direction
SHAW ARTISTS CORPORATION
565 Fifth Avenue
New York 17, New York

The Cookies, 1954, (L-R) Beulah Robertson, Darlene McCrea, Dorothy Jones. (Photo courtesy of Yellowlinda, Inc.)

and in the park. Later we joined the First Baptist Church choir. People would hear us sing and tell us we had beautiful voices. One day Beulah started singing with us and she really had a voice. People recommended that we go to the Apollo amateur night."

After a few "official" rehearsals, the group entered the famed Talent Night at the legendary Apollo Theatre in Harlem. To the girls' shock, they won 3rd place in the contest. A young Joe Tex had come in first, and a Detroit group called The Flairs had come in 2nd. Jesse Stone, then a talent scout, heard the group's performance and asked them if they would like to sign with a record label. The girls promptly said yes. Through Jesse's connections, he planned to record the group for Lamp Records, a subsidiary of Aladdin Records out of California. Other East Coast artists had singles placed with Lamp: The Cues, The Mello-Fellows and a female soloist named Margie Hendrix.

The group's first recording session was done at Aladdin's studios in New York around August of 1954. The group recorded two songs for Lamp entitled "All Night Mambo," a song to fit the then current trend of Latin dances, and "Don't Let Go" a gentle ballad with glowing harmonies. Jesse Stone and Howard Biggs wrote the material the group would record. It was Stone who also christened the group "The Cookies."

A few months later, The Cookies signed with Atlantic Records. Their first session for Atlantic in early 1955 yielded "Later, Later/Precious Love" (two mild jump tunes written by Jesse Stone and Winfield Scott, then staff writers for Atlantic). It was the group's second release in 1956 that would make them the sweethearts of the studio. "In Paradise," co-written by fellow Atlantic artist and songwriter Carmen Taylor, invokes the feeling of stepping into an enchanted garden and all you want to do is dream. With the aid of The Cues in the backdrop, The Cookies conjured the images of a tropical island. The song found its way to the charts. Also, the melodic tune was covered by Otis Williams and The Charms. Its flip, the equally charming "Passing Time," features the male vocal helpers as a bass line, and also features bass pickups by Darlene, something unusual for a female voice to do in 1956.

"Passing Time" is a noteworthy song because it was the first effort published by two young Brooklyn songwriters, ages 16 and 20. Neil Sedaka and Howard Greenfield had their first song placed on the flip of a single, which charted. "Passing Time" also received much local airplay. This sparked the beginning of a professional relationship between Sedaka and The Cookies. Later on, as his stature in the music business grew, Neil employed The Cookies as background singers on his own records. The Cookies' professional prestige was accelerating and they were asked to appear on The Arthur Godfrey Show. However, the offer was rescinded. Darlene remembers the reason: "A neighbor of ours had gotten us an audition with Arthur Godfrey's show. However, we were required to read music, but we didn't. Right before we were scheduled to appear, the performance was called off."

The Cookies continued to record for Atlantic, releasing one more single in 1956, the "In Paradise" sound alike, but still pleasant, "Down By The River." This song features the emergent voice of Darlene on the tag line in the bridge. Its flip, Jesse Stone's "My Lover," contains the usually warm group harmony The Cookies displayed. On "Down By The River," their third recording for Atlantic, the group sings in their usual tight, neo-Andrews Sisters group harmony, but a tag line at the end of the bridge reveals Darlene's distinctive baritone voice. Little sister Earl-Jean used the same style on the bridges of later hits like "Chains" and "Don't Say Nothin' Bad."

The history of The Cookies has often been shrouded in mystery. Many believed the group who recorded for Atlantic in the 1950s and the Dimension group during the 1960s, have no lineage to each other. This misnomer is due to the fact that from 1958 to 1962 The Cookies did not release any singles under their own name, and that two thirds of the group branched off to form another group.

The sound of the group, however, is unmistakable. The common threads in both groups are founding member Dorothy and sisters Darlene and Earl-Jean. In fact, the sisters looked and sounded so much alike, many Rock & Roll historians reported that they were one and the same person.

There was one change which slightly altered the sound of the group during their tenure at Atlantic. Right before the last Atlantic single under their own name, Beulah had a falling out with Jesse Stone and was fired. She was greatly disappointed, because she never got to perform with the group on stage since recording the Lamp single. This incident involving Beulah would open an irreparable rift between Stone and the girls. Margie Hendrix, whom Jesse had recorded for Lamp, was

The Cookies at the Atlantic Studios, 1955, (L-R) Darlene, Beulah, Dorothy. (Photo courtesy of Yellowlinda, Inc.)

recruited for the group. Margie replaced Beulah for the last Atlantic single. The balance of The Cookies tenure at Atlantic was filled with background sessions for every other major artist on Atlantic at the time. Their first recording as session vocalists was for Big Joe Turner's "Honey Hush." The group also lent their superb vocal abilities to records by La Verne Baker, Ruth Brown, Chuck Willis and Ray Charles.

Within the time frame of 1957, the group issued a lone single on Josie Records entitled "King Of Hearts," another tune contoured for The Cookies by Neil Sedaka and Howard Greenfield. The deal with Josie Records was through the auspices of Earl Carroll of The Cadillacs. The Cookies had been touring with The Cadillacs and they became friends. The Cadillacs, of course, were enjoying much success at the label. Margie sang the lead. Its flip, the catchy "Hippy Dippy Daddy" was written by Darlene and Margie. This single showcased an updated style of the Lamp single, while retaining the feature of the male voices, this time, The Cadillacs, for the bass lines. The Cookies were also backing Varetta Dillard on RCA, earning a label credit on the pop-swing tune, "Star Of Fortune," and its fanciful flip, "Rules Of Love."

Like The Blossoms on the West Coast, The Cookies didn't merely sing back-up, they were often an integral part of the song. Producers didn't ask for The Cookies because they wanted background singers, it was because they wanted The Cookies.

Performing as The Raeletts, 1960, (L-R) Pat Lyles, Margie Hendrix, Gwen Berry, Darlene McCrea.

In fact, The Cookies were so in demand as session singers that their own careers were on hold. Also, the group couldn't get a solid deal as artists themselves, because the problems with Jesse Stone had escalated. He eventually washed his hands of the group. His wife tried managing them for a time, but her lack of experience would not sustain The Cookies a fortuitous place in the music world.

It is at this time that two-thirds of the group accepted an offer to become Ray Charles' back-up group after they backed him on "Yes Indeed." In 1958, Margie and Darlene, along with Pat Moseley, became Raeletts, sealing the fate of the first incarnation of The Cookies. It is Margie's powerful voice that is heard answering Ray on the second chorus of the grinding hit, "Night Time Is The Right Time." Dorothy was pregnant at the time and did not join them. She was also not sure that she wanted to disband The Cookies.

Ray Charles had big tour plans for his new backing group. He had renamed the new configuration and had added Gwen Berry to the lineup. Pat's mother, Pat Lyles, managed the group from thereon (and even replaced her daughter in the group for awhile). Darlene and Margie were now part of the incessant gallop of life on the road. Darlene found the life of a musician on the road much too fast-paced for her taste. She recalls the shock of having to deal with shady musicians, strange towns and lost luggage.

Charles would find musicians under the influence of drugs and fire them on the spot. Charles himself had been detained after a gig in Boston, so the tour was delayed. He fired and rehired the ladies at will. He did eventually ask Darlene to return. She toured on and off as a Raelett until 1969. Her 1959 Roulette single, "You Made A Fool Of Me," made some noise, earning Darlene some local appearances, including a spot on Clay Cole's show. The segment was cut at the last minute because the scene showed Darlene lying on a lounge chair in what was deemed a "seductive" pose. Darlene continued between session work and singing intermittently with Charles, even appearing with him in the British movie, "Ballad In Blue," (also called "Blues For Lovers") before officially rejoining The Cookies in 1965.

Dorothy was deeply disappointed that The Cookies were breaking up after developing such a strong reputation in the business. True, she was pregnant at the time of the offer from Charles, but she also felt the trio had a reputation of their own and she did not want to give that up.

The Cookies, however, had already left a lasting legacy. Not only was there still talk around town that The Cookies sang prime back-up, but Darlene's little sister, Earl-Jean and Dorothy's cousin Margaret had sat in on the rehearsal sessions and had picked up all the harmonies. Earl-Jean and Margaret had amused their friends singing in school for fun, even though Earl-Jean in particular had found performing a little nerve racking. Margaret had to hold her hand while they sang. Still they found this opportunity enticing.

Without realizing it, Dorothy inadvertently had her next group of Cookies all ready and waiting. They could not yet tour because Earl-Jean and Margaret were still in high school. Dorothy's mother was Margaret's guardian so it took some convincing by Dorothy, but upon their graduation in 1960, Margaret and Earl-Jean officially became Cookies. Dorothy recalls the events leading to the group's revitalization; "There was a two-year period when I didn't work. I had changed my mind about joining The Raeletts after Darlene came back. By then Ray had already hired someone else. I was not working at all. About 1960, Neil called me. He'd kept my number. He asked if we were still together. He had a girl who needed vocalists for a new artist she discovered. I said I'd see what I could do. I asked my mother if Margaret could sing with us and Margaret suggested Earl-Jean."

Margaret thought it was perfectly natural for Earl-Jean and her to step into the empty spots. They attended many of the group's practice sessions. Margaret saw this as the perfect choice; "We knew that Darlene and Margie had gone on as Raeletts. We would stand in during rehearsals. We knew the parts so well."

Neil Sedaka called Dorothy and asked her to lend her vocals for a Tony Orlando session, but he needed a group. As a young working mother, Dorothy aptly treated The Cookies as a business. Not one to ignore opportunity knocking for the second time, Dorothy had swiftly and cleverly organized the second incarnation of The Cookies. Margaret and Earl-Jean joined Dorothy to garner the benefits of a steady stream of quality background chores, attaining the same sound by using voices that were so closely related to the first set of Cookies.

This set of Cookies deftly took care of background duties on what would become ""Halfway To Paradise" and "Bless You" in 1961. Meanwhile, Atlantic had once again released "In Paradise/Passing Time" in 1960. Through Neil, the group was introduced to King, Don Kirshner and Al Nevins at the newly emerging Aldon publishing house. Nevins, a trumpet player popular during the 1940s and Kirshner, a fledgling songwriter had been collaborating on songs since 1956.

The Cookies' introduction to the Aldon family was the beginning of the group's prosperous relationship with the then husband/wife songwriting team of Carole King and Gerry Goffin, who were Aldon staff writers. Carole immediately fell in love with Earl-Jean's alto, Gerry with Dorothy's robust 2nd soprano. Along with Margaret's youthful 1st soprano, this group of Cookies once again proved that there were three capable and distinctive leads packaged into one forceful trio.

One day at a rehearsal at Carole's house, Dorothy started singing a version of "Will You Still Love Me Tomorrow." Carole and Gerry were so taken that they tailor-made a song called "Taking That Long Walk Home" for Dorothy and released it as her solo effort with Cookies' back-up on Columbia Records in July of 1961.

The Cookies, 1962, (L-R) Dorothy Jones, Earl Jean McCrea, Margaret Ross. (Photo courtesy of Gordon Skadberg)

The arrangement sported a similar treatment to that of "…Tomorrow."

Its flip, the dramatic and powerful "It's Unbearable" was equally impressive. This single showed that Dorothy had promise as a singer who could cater to an adult contemporary audience as well as teenage record buyers. By 1962, The Cookies had reestablished themselves as a premier backing group for the vocal talents of La Verne Baker, The Drifters, Mel Torme, Edie Gorme, Neil Sedaka, Tony Orlando, and Ben E. King, among others. More importantly, The Cookies were once again at the receiving end of superior songs from one of the most prolific songwriting teams of the 1960s.

After a few years of placing their songs with artists at different labels, the Nevins/Kirshner team decided to form their own record label, Dimension Records. The Cookies' first single on Aldon's new label during 1962 was "Chains," a lyrically solid song with a soft but moving groove. The Cookies' no nonsense delivery countered the swinging tempo of the song, pushing it straight into the Top 20 nationally.

Its flip was another successful attempt to feature Dorothy as a lead vocalist. With a melody very much like "It's Unbearable," but containing stark musical arrangements and fuller backing vocals, the very emotional "Stranger In My Arms" brings Dorothy to the height of her vocal abilities. Dorothy delivers the revelation to her

The Cookies backstage at The Baby Grand, Harlem, NY, 1963, (L-R) Earl Jean, Margaret, Dorothy's mom, Elease Jones, Dorothy. (Photo courtesy of The Cookies)

lover that she is aware of the fact that he is distancing himself from her, and without actually telling him, inferring that he had better do something about it. If it wasn't clear with her Columbia single, it certainly was with this effort that Dorothy's voice was not just for kids.

At the beginning of 1963, The Cookies again reached the top of the charts with "Don't Say Nothin' Bad," a song with call-and-response verses and tough-talking lyrics deftly delivered by Earl-Jean. It was their second hit within six months, and the group was riding high. The Cookies were now an integral part of the machinery at Aldon, lending just as much significant input to the songs as Goffin/King and the musicians who accompanied them on the sessions. Its flip, "Softly In The Night," was a Philadelphia area favorite. Dorothy is also very fond of this song and thinks it should have been a hit on its own. Aldon quickly released the next Cookies single to capitalize on success. Although "Will Power" was a pleasant enough song with its Country and Western feel, it lacked the drive or spirit of their first two releases.

The flip side, "I Want A Boy For My Birthday," written by veteran songwriter Sylvester Bradford who brought us "Tears On My Pillow," was a more timely piece with its light cha-cha beat and teenage lyrics. This single did not chart high. The label of this single would be the first to show a new association for Dimension Records, Screen Gems Publishing. By the end of 1963, Dimension had released one more Cookies single, the conventional "Girls Grow Up Faster Than Boys," which featured mock Four Seasons styled bass lines convincingly delivered by Earl-Jean, while Dorothy and Margaret shared a lead vocal. The more interesting side was "Only To Other People," featuring a sincere vocal delivery by Margaret, with an atmospheric musical arrangement for the backdrop, easily one of the group's best efforts. It was co-written by Toni Wine, Art Kornfeld and Gerry Goffin.

The secret of Dimension's creative success was due in part to its utilization of the same session men as well as its loyal writing staff. Like Motown and Philles, Dimension had its core band like sax man Art Kaplan, drummer Gary Chester and Harry Licowski on violin, akin to a family. Like the rest of the family, the girls were also hard at work in the studio singing backup or cutting demos for other artists to ponder as their next hit. Every day, the group would be in the studio from early in the morning until the afternoon. During one session, Dorothy, pregnant with her daughter, remembers almost having the baby at the studio; "We were working so hard. We stayed in the studio seven days a week for twelve hours. I was pregnant with my daughter, Rochelle. I think it was a King Curtis session. After coming from the studio, about fifteen minutes after lying down, I was in labor."

These sessions were grueling, but actually they were labors of love. Margaret says it was exciting being in the thick of the action, "Doing backgrounds and doing our own thing was hectic. At least three to four times a week, we were never home. We would be in the studio 18-24 hours, but we enjoyed what we were doing."

The group was always cut with the trio in the background in addition to the lead vocal. Sometimes Little Eva was recruited as the fourth voice, even on the group's own singles. The group had talked about adding Little Eva as the fourth Cookie, but it never happened, for Little Eva became popular on her own. Dimension released some of The Cookies' demos, along with other demos by Little Eva and Carole King on the Dimension LP entitled "Dimension Dolls." Fans are treated to The Cookies' versions of "On Broadway" and "Foolish Little Girl." Other demos were released under a pseudonym, The Palisades, for Chairman Records. "Make The Night A Little Longer," featuring Margaret's virtuous lead, eventually got passed to Dionne Warwick and The Shirelles.

The Cookies also spent much time on the road doing all those one-nighters Rock and Rollers were famous for during the 1950s and 1960s. According to Margaret, it seemed like an endless loop of either recording in the studio or performing short stints in many cities. It was quite an exhausting schedule and sometimes took its toll on the group members. During one "Show Of Stars" tour, Dorothy was confined to a hotel bed under doctor's orders. A girl named Isabelle took her place for the concert dates and photo shoots. The Cookies were always in good form back in New York. They definitely rose to the occasion of their continuing success by becoming the live poster girls for Aldon's operations. The group would often dress alike, sporting leopard coats with matching hats and gloves, and parade down Broadway near The Brill Building, much to the delight of Al Nevins. Not only did his record label churn out great records, he had a built-in publicity team besides.

Beginning in mid-1963, a change took place at Aldon which would eventually spell the end for Dimension Records. A few months earlier, Don Kirshner had struck a deal with Columbia-Screen Gems to acquire the label, with Don becoming the executive vice president in charge of publishing of the new company and Al Nevins was hired as a consultant. Certainly, Kirshner thought of this as furthering his career in the music business (and it did). This would mean broader exposure for the many staff writers at Aldon in terms of movie and television work. But what would this mean for the artists signed to Dimension Records?

From a financial standpoint, by late-1963, Dimension was emitting fewer and fewer records which were placing in the Top 40. Outside acts were now being recruited for the label, with much of the product coming in from the West Coast. At the end of 1963, Dimension released singles by those associated with their new labelmate, Colpix Records.

The product from Dimension was still quality material. The Cookies continued their contributions to songs by Little Eva and Big Dee Irwin, rounding out 1963 with "The Christmas Song/We Wish You A Merry Christmas." Also, The Cookies were completing background sessions for Freddie Scott, backing him on his successful "Hey Girl" and "Where Have All The Flowers Gone" during late 1963 and early 1964 for Colpix. Meanwhile, balancing a career and family was not easy for The Cookies, who were all married by now. This created internal problems. Despite the conflicts, they forged ahead, continuing to record dozens of demos and masters, to this day not sure if some ever actually came out, and with so much overdubbing, it is sometimes unclear whose voice actually ended up on the final product.

The next single, issued in 1964, pulled out all the stops when it comes to music of this genre. Darlene had joined in sharing background chores with The Cookies. "Baby, Baby I Still Love You" was not issued under The Cookies' name, but as The Cinderellas. The song displays an effective, updated style of the Dimension sound. The inspiring quick-strumming guitar intro drives straight to a heartfelt lead vocal by Margaret with thunderously climaxing vocals in the background. Margaret's vocal versatility is certainly shining on this single, and "Baby, Baby . . ." is a highly sought after collectors' item today.

Its equally brilliant flip, "Please Don't Wake Me" was a demo for The Ronettes to consider as their next single, but Phil Spector rejected it. It is easy to imagine The Ronettes singing this song. Some Spector touches were included on this version by The Cookies, including his signature intro.

A conspicuous change in the Aldon cast was used for this session, including newcomer Russ Titelman, who wrote and produced the single with Barry Mann and Cynthia Weil. This powerful performance with Margaret made some noise on New York radio and was also released in England on Colpix Records. However, the group didn't even know the song had been released. Margaret relates her surprise, "When Carole and Gerry wrote the songs, we did the demos. We had no idea that the (group) name would be changed, but it was us."

The Cookies' final single for Dimension under their own name paired them with Goffin-King-Titelman. "I Never Dreamed" employs the updated arrangements featured on The Cinderellas single, but with much milder lyrics. The flip side was a demo of "The Old Crowd" which had been lying around since Lesley Gore took it for her own. This single also went by unnoticed. Less and less time and effort were being spent on promotion for Dimension releases. One can only speculate that business was winding down and the company no longer was interested in promoting their acts, knowing that Dimension would eventually be absorbed into Colpix which was part of Screen Gems. Colpix would eventually turn into Colgems, the home of America's answer to The Beatles, The Monkees.

Meanwhile, Gerry Goffin was concentrating efforts on two singles for Earl-Jean, released on Colpix Records during 1964. Always a fan of Earl-Jean's voice, Goffin longed to try her out as a solo artist and scored the first time out, reaching the Top 40 with Earl-Jean's original version of "I'm Into Something Good." For this effort, Earl-Jean was able to sing breathy, yet effective highs, in contrast to singing the novelty bass line on "Girls Grow Up Faster Than Boys." The record made the Top 40, and was heard and appreciated by British producer Mickie Most who insisted that Herman's Hermits, one of the new British Invasion bands, cover this song. Their version surpassed Earl-Jean's on the American charts and made number 1 in England. "We Love And Learn" was a pleasant, jazzy-sounding flipside.

Her second single, "Randy/They're Jealous Of Me" was an equally affable set of tunes, the stronger side being "They're Jealous…." These tunes did not feature the rest of The Cookies on back-up. Darlene and Carole took care of backgrounds for these singles. She felt that, "A solo career was never my intent. It was just done as another project. I never imagined my lead voice as being particularly likable or special." Ironically, this modesty comes from someone who has one of the most discernible and enviable voices in female Rock & Roll history.

With the ultimate demise of Dimension Records on the horizon in 1965, Goffin and King began placing their efforts with other labels. Three more sides waxed by The Cookies were released, but again, not under the name of The Cookies. Once more, Darlene was called in for overdubs. A pair of warm, melodic songs was released in the fall of 1964, on the Fontana record label, a Mercury subsidiary.

Originally, the single was slated to be released on Smash Records, another subsidiary, hence, the presence of a Smash release number, out of sequence with the regular Fontana numbering system. "One Wonderful Night" was very much in keeping with The Cookies' Dimension catalog, with its clap-along beat. This side received airplay in New York. The real sleeper is the danceable "She Don't Deserve You," a hot item on the Northern Soul scene in England. Both sides were led by Margaret who uses her regular vocals for "One Wonderful Night," and a higher, breathier style for "She Don't...." In fact, the two voices sound so different many collectors thought that the leads were done by two different singers. Their second single as The Honey Bees was "Some Of Your Lovin'/You Turn Me On Boy," another Goffin-King production, again placed with Fontana Records. None of the group members recognize the lead singer, but The Cookies are on backing vocals. Dusty Springfield heard it and recorded it as a single a year later.

After Dimension folded, Dorothy found it difficult to negotiate new deals with other record companies. They did, of course, find background work, most notably on Len Barry's monster hit "1-2-3." Earl-Jean decided she had enough of the grind of road trips and endless studio time, so she left The Cookies in 1965 to concentrate on family life. Darlene, on hiatus from The Raeletts, took her place. In 1967, after almost two years of being without a label to call home, The Cookies negotiated a deal with Bright Tunes Productions, who were in reality The Tokens. The Tokens had just cut a deal with Warner Bros. Records to release their own productions. They hit the first time out with "Portrait Of My Love."

For Bright Tunes, The Cookies recorded a version of the traditional folk song "All My Trials," with Margaret on lead amidst a folksy-sounding arrangement, with mandolins and flutes. The flip, "Wounded," was a Tokens-penned tune which featured beautiful counterleads. These were two very timely productions; an unusual pairing of voices and style. The second single was a novelty tune called "Mr. Cupid." Neither single met with commercial success, so The Cookies' association with Bright Tunes was brief. With the obligations of their personal lives looming larger, The Cookies decided to lay their singing and recording pursuits to rest, ending one of the most fruitful careers in Rock & Roll. The Cookies had added their vocal accents to countless records for 13 years. An era had ended.

Margaret and her husband, Ronnie Williams, settled back in Coney Island, where they raised their two sons. Margaret worked for the New York City Department of Health and Hospital Services until her retirement in 1998. She is very active in her church choir and sings at occasional events.

Dorothy and her family moved to Columbus, Ohio in 1970, where she and her husband, Bill Johnson, reared their twelve children. Dorothy also became active at her church. Today, Dorothy is retired from her job with the Ohio Bureau of Permits.

Earl-Jean and her husband, Grandison Reavis, moved south to Raleigh, North Carolina. Darlene McCrea Jackson lives in Newark, New Jersey where her husband is pastor of The Community Chapel Of Christ. Margie Hendrix stayed with Ray Charles as part of his band. Sadly, she died of a drug overdose in New York in 1966. Mercury Records continued releasing her material after her death. Beulah Robertson did not perform after her stay with The Cookies was cut short. She died from cancer in 1987.

In 1997, The Cookies appeared as guests on WFUV's "Group Harmony Review" with Dan

The Cookies reunited in the WFUV studios at Fordham University, Bronx, 1997, (L-R) Darlene, Dorothy, Margaret, and Earl-Jean.

Romanello out of Fordham University in New York to talk about their career. They have taken steps to retain royalty rights to their songs, and now that both Dorothy and Margaret are retired, they have taken their act on the road once again, performing at selected shows. Margaret, Dorothy, and Dorothy's daughter Rochelle, have appeared on several benefit shows for other artists. Earl-Jean and Darlene have devoted their lives to the Church and have no plans to perform secular music at this time.

The Cookies' body of work for Dimension and Warner Bros. has been reissued, as well as the work they recorded under pseudonyms. Audiences would surely look forward to being treated to The Cookies' distinct vocal abilities once again, a sound that helped weave the fabric of pop music, especially during the early 1960s. With such a sound body of recordings behind them, one must admit, there's nothin' bad you can say about The Cookies.

The Cookies Discography

45s

	Label	Number	Year
Don't Let Go/All Night Mambo	Lamp	8008	1954
Later, Later/Precious Love	Atlantic	1061	1955
In Paradise/Passing Time		1084	1956
Down By The River/My Lover		1110	
King Of Hearts/Hippy Dippy Daddy	Josie	822	1957
In Paradise/Passing Time	Atlantic	2079	1960
Chains/Stranger In My Arms	Dimension	1002	1962
Don't Say Nothin' Bad/Softly In The Night		1008	1963
Will Power/I Want A Boy For My Birthday		1012	
Girls Grow Up Faster Than Boys/Only To Other People		1020	
I Never Dreamed/The Old Crowd		1032	1964
Wounded/All My Trials	Warner Bros.	7025	1967
Mr. Cupid/Hang My Head And Cry (Big Guys)		7047	

(as The Cinderellas)

	Label	Number	Year
Baby, Baby I Still Love You/Please Don't Wake Me	Dimension	1026	1964

(as The Honey Bees)

	Label	Number	Year
One Wonderful Night/She Don't Deserve You	Fontana	1939	1964
Some Of Your Lovin'/You Turn Me On Boy		1505	1965

(as The Palisades)

	Label	Number	Year
Make The Night A Little Longer/ Heaven Is Being With You	Chairman	4401	1963

(as The Stepping Stones)

	Label	Number	Year
I Got My Job Through The New York Times/The Nearness Of You	Philips	40108	1963

Margie Hendrix

	Label	Number	Year
Every Time/Good Treatment	Lamp	8002	1954
Let No One Hold You/A Lover's Blues	Tangerine	940	1964
Baby/Packin' Up	Mercury	72420	1965
The Question/I Call You Lover But You Ain't Nothin' But A Tramp		72673	1967
Restless/On The Right Track		72701	
Don't Destroy Me/Jim Dandy	Sound Stage-7	2624	1968
Somebody's Gonna Plow Your Field/Your Mama's Recipe		2631	1969

Dorothy Jones

	Label	Number	Year
It's Unbearable/Taking That Long Walk Home	Columbia	42062	1961

Ethel (Darlene) McCrea (as Darlene McCrea)

	Label	Number	Year
You Made A Fool Of Me/You	Roulette	4173	1959
My Heart's Not In It/Don't You Worry Baby	Tower	104	1964
I Feel A Little Bit Better/Soulful Feeling	Jubilee	5524	1965

Earl-Jean McCrea (as Earl-Jean)

	Label	Number	Year
I'm Into Something Good/We Love and Learn	Colpix	729	1964
Randy/They're Jealous Of Me		748	

(with La Verne Baker)

	Label	Number	Year
Substitute/Learning To Love	Atlantic	1176	1958

(with Ray Charles)

	Label	Number	Year
Yes Indeed/I Had A Dream	Atlantic	1180	1958

(with Varetta Dillard)

	Label	Number	Year
Star Of Fortune/Rules Of Love	RCA	47-7144	1958

LPs

	Label	Number	Year
Dimension Dolls	Dimension	1001	1963

*There are numerous recording where The Cookies remain unaccredited.

The Crystals

Members:

(1961)	Dolores (Dee Dee) Kenniebrew, 1st Soprano Patricia (Patsy) Wright, 2nd Soprano/Lead Barbara Alston, 1st Alto/Lead Myrna Gerard, 1st Alto Mary Thomas, 2nd Alto		Patsy Wright, 2nd Soprano Delores (La La) Brooks, 1st Alto/Lead Barbara Alston, 1st Alto/Lead Mary Thomas, 2nd Alto	*(1964)*	Barbara Alston La La Brooks Frances Collins Dee Dee Kenniebrew
(1961-63)	Dee Dee Kenniebrew, 1st Soprano	*(1963)*	Barbara Alston La La Brooks Dee Dee Kenniebrew Patsy Wright	*(1965-66)*	La La Brooks Frances Collins Dee Dee Kenniebrew
				(1967)	Barbara Alston Dee Dee Kenniebrew Mary Thomas

Great moments in Rock & Roll history that have anything to do with vocal groups, female groups in particular, seldom include the period of 1960-64. Why is the moment when Phil Spector produced his first record by The Crystals never seen as the porthole it actually was? Musical notables such as Brian Wilson, Sonny Bono, The New York Dolls, Patti Smith and Blondie refer to this time period as the time that they found their own musical voices. This crucial time in Rock & Roll history is the beginning of the marriages of specific songwriters collaborating with specific producers to formulate specific sounds.

Most documentation seems to go straight from Elvis to The Beatles, with a well-deserved mention of the beginnings of Motown. Those who weren't there would think vocal groups in general didn't even exist in earnest, and you can't blame it on the lack of chart action. The role of the producer certainly loomed large. Especially large was Phil Spector, the producer who saw himself more as the artist, than the artists themselves. So begins the story of The Crystals, the group that was the pivot in Spector's plan for Rock & Roll styling.

The Crystals were formed in Brooklyn, NY in 1960. Barbara Alston grew up on Lexington Ave. in Bedford-Stuyvesant. She attended Central Commercial High School, but didn't like it, so she transferred to Maxwell High School where she met and became friends with Mary Thomas and Myrna Gerard. Originally the yet unnamed group was a trio, just singing for fun with no

The Crystals, 1961, (L-R) Barbara Alston, Mary Thomas, Patsy Wright, Dee Dee Kenniebrew, La La Brooks. (Photo courtesy of John Grecco)

real plans to do any recording. The trio did win a school talent show singing The Five Satins' "In The Still Of The Night."

Barbara's uncle, Benny Wells, knew the girls sang for fun, and was trying to put a singing group together for recording. He knew of two girls who were interested in being in a group, Patsy Wright and Dolores (Dee Dee) Kenniebrew.

Dee Dee had come to Benny Wells' attention through her mother, Mrs. Henry. Dee Dee's mom had her time in the spotlight when she and her sister used to sing on the radio when they were children. Dee Dee recalls how her mother played an important part in her joining the group: "I came to the group because my mother worked at the school, a junior high school called P.S. 73. There was a guy in the neighborhood by the name of Benny Wells who used to use the music room in that school after school hours to rehearse some of the singers he was interested in getting recorded and he decided he wanted to

start a girl's group. He asked my mother if she knew any teenage girls that sang. She said, 'Well, I have a daughter at home and she sings around the house. Maybe you'd like to give her a listen, and if you like her, we could talk about it'. So that's how I came to be in the group."

After some convincing, he got the quintet to rehearse after school. The girls rehearsed at the after-school center, where many teens spent their afternoons. Benny's taste leaned more toward Modernaires' type harmonies. He would give the group these songs to sing so that they might develop their musical ears. His aim was to start the group off singing at weddings, bar mitzvahs and clubs in The Catskills. The girls were soon approached by Patsy's brother-in-law, a fledgling songwriter named Leroy Bates who had a song entitled "There's No Other (Like My Baby)" he thought would be perfect for them to record. The girls agreed, and they began rehearsing the song, an uptempo number sporting a group vocal. When the song was thoroughly rehearsed, Wells took the group

THE CRYSTALS   PERSONAL MANAGEMENT
SCANDORE & SHAYNE

EXCLUSIVE XXXX MANAGEMENT
WILLIAM MORRIS AGENCY, INC.
SINCE 1898 THE AGENCY OF THE SHOW WORLD
NEW YORK   BEVERLY HILLS   CHICAGO
LONDON   PARIS   ROME   MADRID

The Crystals, 1963, (L-R) Patsy, Dee Dee, La La, Barbara.

into Manhattan to sing the song with the hope of having someone record them. The girls decided on their name by choosing the name of Patsy's niece, Crystal.

The group came to the attention of Phil Spector in New York where they were auditioning "There's No Other" at the offices of Hill and Range Music. Phil Spector was passing by while the group was singing, and heard something he knew would be the ingredient for a hit. After introductions, Spector began working with the group that he saw as his chance to create his own productions.

Phil heard a different treatment for Bates' uptempo tune, telling the girls to slow it down, that it would sound better as a dreamy ballad. He also felt the song needed a single lead for the verses. He wanted to know who would take the lead.

Ironically, none of the eager singers were eager to be the lead. It was decided that he could get the best lead for this song from Barbara. Spector coached her; obtaining exactly the mood he felt would fit the song and her voice. The girls were very happy with the results. He then hustled the group into the studio in June of 1961 to record. Barbara, Mary and Myrna came straight from their prom to the session, still in their prom dresses. Barbara recalls that night. "Myrna, Mary and I came straight from the school to the studio. Phil knew exactly what he wanted to do. He got us in the studio and gave us specific directions. I didn't want to do lead on the song. It was fast and Phil made us slow it down."

Phil was very particular about his arrangements. He had the group sing the song over and over again, until they were more than rehearsed—they were hoarse. Then, he turned down the lights in the studio and prompted the girls to sing in their softest voices. From the moment Barbara delivers her first line in the most gentle, somber voice, she breaks your heart, reinventing the tale of adolescent love. Its flip, "Oh Yeah, Maybe Baby," was written by Spector, with Hank Hunter, and was the intended A-side, with its adventurous, Latin sound, so popular in the early 60s. Patsy was given the lead on this one, mainly to keep her out of the background because she had a bit of a pitch problem, which is evident on her shaky, yet effective lead.

Spector produced three groups as per his agreement with Hill and Range; The Ducanes, The Creations and The Crystals. The master of The Creations went to Jamie Records and The Ducanes to George Goldner's Goldisc label. Spector decided, unbeknownst to the heads of Hill and Range, that he was going to keep The Crystals master to start his own record label, Philles Records, a combination of Phil's name, and his business partner, Lester Sill. There was an unwritten understanding that The Crystals were to become artists on Big Top Records, but Spector signed them directly, much to the dismay of the Bienstocks (heads of Hill and Range), when they found out that Phil had taken The Crystals for himself.

The monies used to record The Crystals were part of a deal that Phil had struck with Liberty Records. Although "Oh Yeah, Maybe Baby" was Spector's intended hit, the public liked the more familiar tones of the ballad side. "There's No Other" climbed into the Top 20 in the fall of 1961. The Crystals now had one hit to their credit. Benny Wells continued to manage the group, but his role as manager was becoming increasingly tenuous because, compared to Spector and the people he met who were already in the business for several years, he was a novice, with no idea on how to get the group the best deal. Certainly the girls were happy to have a hit, but beyond that, they didn't have much foresight. None of the concerns that both Wells and the group would later have were apparent at this time.

Since Spector now had a group he felt he could mold into his creations, his next step was to secure another hit with them to further wrest controlling interest of his new venture from his partner. Lester Sill was making recordings that Phil felt were a waste of the company's time and money.

Spector wanted total control. "There's No Other" had hit the Top 20. He knew another hit would further ensure his stature in the business. Spector secured a song from Don Kirshner and Al Nevins' successful Aldon publishing house. "Uptown" was written by Barry Mann and Cynthia Weil. In the interim between the recording of "There's No Other" and the group's subsequent personal appearances, Myrna Gerard had married right out of high school. Although she had recorded some songs that were eventually included on an album, she left the group in November of 1961.

Delores "La La" Brooks grew up on Marion St. in Brooklyn. La La was in possession of a forceful voice at a very young age, singing lead in a Gospel quartet called The Little Gospel Tears at the age of seven with her sister Lorraine, her brother James, and niece Theresa. The young singers made the rounds to different churches, being well received by parishioners.

La La also spent her time listening to the radio, singing along with some of her idols like Brenda Lee, Baby Washington and Maxine Brown. She would convince her mother to take her to Rock & Roll shows to see her favorite performers. La La attended P.S. 73, and used to hang around at the after-school center. Many neighborhood people used the after school center to enjoy recreation and use the school's music room. One afternoon, La La was singing to herself in the hallway when she heard a piano playing. She walked into the room where a man was playing the piano. La La admits she didn't stand on ceremony. "I said to the man, 'Can I sing along?' and he said, 'Can you?' I said yes and sang 'Gee Whiz'."

Little did La La know that song was inadvertently the audition for her entry into the world of popular music. She was heard by Dee Dee Kenniebrew's mom, the school secretary. La La recounts the event. "Dee Dee's mom heard me singing and said, 'Was that you with the big voice? How would you like to join a singing group, The Crystals?' I knew who they were, so I asked Mrs. Henry to ask my mom. One day she came by our house and my mom said yes."

Since the group knew that they needed a replacement for Myrna, they decided that it should be someone with the ability and the desire to be out front. They were fortunate that Mrs. Henry had discovered La La. Her first assignment was at a Murray The "K" Christmas show.

The group had decided she would lead from now on, but for some reason, Phil Spector did not want La La as The Crystals' lead voice. Perhaps he thought her voice too gospel-oriented for the direction in which he wanted to take his productions.

For a time, Spector would continue to use the reluctant Barbara as his lead singer, against her wishes. Barbara recalls, "I was not interested in singing lead or being out front. La La was a natural out front. We brought her into the group specifically to sing leads, but for some reason Phil was against using her on lead."

The augmented group was ready to record their second Philles single. "Uptown" did not disappoint on chart action, going all the way to number 13. It's flip was the blasé, "What A Nice Way To Turn Seventeen," part of a deal to secure "Uptown" from the successful Aldon publishing company. Barbara's soft-spoken intro and relaxed delivery, coupled with the Latin beat and Mann and Weil's hard-hitting lyrics, sold the song. Efforts were under way to complete both Philles' and The Crystals' first long player, "The Crystals Twist Uptown." Myrna was on hand for the completion of the album and so was La La, so the album was actually the work of six Crystals, although Myrna is not pictured on the cover, and has never taken publicity photos with the group. The first LP for the label was released in 1962. It featured their hits, some B-side fillers, and the original version of "On Broadway," brought to national attention a year later by The Drifters.

The Crystals were now at the top of their game and were making many personal appearances to perform their two monster hits. La La's mother immediately enrolled La La in the Mace Professional Children's school. She and Dee Dee were the only members not out of high school at this time. Actually, at 14, La La had just entered high school. She'd have to do her homework on the road and send it in. La La found the road trips a bit rough because she was younger than the rest of the girls.

Barbara, Mary and Patsy were of legal age, so they went to parties and were not the least bit interested in babysitting or helping with homework. Amusingly, La La recalls that the older girls would boss her around or tease her, "They would say to me, 'It's time for you to go to bed now', and I would cry and say that I didn't want to, or when I had something to say, I would be told 'oh, be quiet' and of course I wouldn't be quiet. Dee Dee would help me with my homework, though."

Either Mrs. Henry or Mrs. Wright was often the girls' chaperones on the tours. They played the circuit of theatres in Philadelphia, Baltimore, Washington, D.C. and Chicago, as well as The Apollo. Once they were out in the audience listening to their favorite singing stars, now they were performing alongside Sam Cooke, James Brown, The Coasters, Dee Clark, The Orlons and The Drifters.

Phil Spector's plan of having a hit with The Crystals' second single had been successful. He was gaining more and more momentum toward his aim to have Philles for himself. Although nobody really knows why Spector chose "He Hit Me" for the girls' next single, speculation by many say it was a way to scare off his conservative business partners.

When the group heard the song, they were not happy with its blatant lyrics, but they complied because they were now signed to Philles for five years. Dirge-like in their executions, "He Hit Me," and its equally melancholy flip, "No One Ever Tells You," were interesting productions, if not hit material. Barbara's impervious leads delivered what Spector wanted; a matter-of-fact

The Crystals on their tour of England, February 1964, (L-R) La La, Barbara, Frances Collins, Dee Dee. (Photo courtesy of John Grecco)

approach to a controversial subject. Perhaps this is what put off programmers. Parents were not happy with it, especially after it gained airplay. La La was well aware of everyone's attitude toward the song. "After we recorded 'He Hit Me', many people hated it. My mother wouldn't let me play it in the house. I remember Cousin Brucie playing it and making comments about it over the air."

Dee Dee thinks that regardless of the lyrical content, no one in the group appreciated the stylistic direction in which Phil went with these recordings. "They were kind of down, laid back type of droning things that we really didn't care for, but we didn't have much say so. We were happy we didn't have to sing that, because had they become hits we would have had to sing them."

After being issued, the record actually started climbing the charts, bubbling under the Top 100. It proved to be too strong and did not survive the barrage of complaints received by radio stations to ban it. Spector pulled the record. His next move would have to be grandiose.

The veneer on the relationship between Phil and The Crystals was starting to crack. Needless to say they were not happy over "He Hit Me," and their original manager, Benny Wells, had little control at this point over the group's direction. The group was already looking to free themselves from Phil's clutches. Having officially signed contracts with him only after "There's No Other" was a hit, they were to be bound to him for a long time. The group started to question Spector's methods and motives. Spector was incensed at this show of will from individuals he felt were his proteges. It was just one more reason for him to start moving his operations to the West Coast, away from rivals, union rules concerning overdubbing and stubborn session musicians. He was busy contemplating his next hit. He had heard a demo of a Gene Pitney song called "He's A Rebel" and grew very excited. This would be The Crystals' next hit.

Phil had made the decision to record this single out on the West Coast. He felt comfortable at Gold Star where he had recorded his early hits with The Teddy Bears. At this point, The Crystals were feeling frustration toward Spector at his not wanting to use La La for leads. Another frustration was that the group now had two hits, but weren't seeing any money from these hits. Spector told the girls that groups don't make any money from records, but from personal appearances. Barbara says Phil's actions forced the girls to depart from their quiet roles in the shadows. "Our show of strength was to not fly out for the session. We certainly weren't afraid to fly because we were already touring and would eventually fly to England. We were trying to make a stand against him."

They never dreamed that Phil would go so far as to release a single with The Crystals name on it that wasn't really them singing. Phil was in a hurry to get the jump on this song he felt would wait for no one. Phil recorded the single with The Blossoms, then Darlene Wright, Fanita James and Gloria Jones. Also, the production style was moving toward Phil Spector's ever-mounting wall of sound. The Crystals were on tour when they heard the song on the radio. Needless to say they were shocked. They had to learn the song for the tour, but Barbara's voice was not the same type and style as Darlene's lead. With her Gospel background, La La was the only member who could carry it off. She took the lead to "He's A Rebel" on stage. When Spector duplicated his handy work with "He's Sure The Boy I Love," again recording The Blossoms and releasing the single billed as The Crystals, La La's vocal prowess certainly was an asset when it came time to sing this new hit live. Although the group was incensed over the apparent charade on record, La La was confident about her ability to pass it off on stage. "I didn't worry about sounding like Darlene on stage. The only thing I did was practice the spoken intro to "He's Sure The Boy I Love" in the mirror so I could sound like her, because I had a Brooklyn accent and she was from California."

Both "He's A Rebel' and "He's Sure The Boy I Love" further solidified The Crystals career. Phil had also repackaged their first LP as a new one, calling it "He's A Rebel." Some tracks were replaced with the title track and "He's Sure The Boy I Love." The album jacket had a quote that read "guest vocalists." If the group was questioning Spector about his incitements before these singles and subsequent LP, they were to now launch an all out war in their list of complaints against him on their behalf. One key component of what the girls wanted did come out of Spector's use of The Blossoms for alleged Crystals' records. Spector eventually acquiesced to using La La as the lead singer. Spector even had them sing a throwaway song called "(Let's Dance) the Screw," to fulfill a contractual obligation. The group saw this recording as a complete waste of their time. Their dissatisfaction with product and monies earned on royalties were looming larger. La La felt left out of this sentiment because, at 15, she was solely interested in making records.

With Spector's productions increasing in magnitude, he needed a voice that would mesh with his productions, yet retain a quality of its own. Barbara Alston's tender, and at times, almost insouciant voice, well suited to Spector's earlier productions, would be lost in the upbeat, frenetic productions to come. The answer, of course, was to finally utilize the girl who was duplicating versions of "He's A Rebel" on stage. Spector had found a way to evoke what he wanted from La La's fiery delivery, yet keep her voice tempered within his pop production. Spector had cut another single with his West Coast singers, but wasn't satisfied with the results, so he used La La by default.

The result was tremendous. "Da Doo Ron Ron" hits like a blast of cold, compressed air, leaving the listener breathless. Spector's production brings all the elements of a good dance record to the forefront, and its simple, easy to remember lyric sticks in mind of anyone who comes in contact with the record. This was the wall of sound taken to its height, a stellar production, catchy song and superior vocals.

As for the backing vocals during this period, stories conflict over who actually wound up on the finished single. La La says that starting with "Da Doo Ron Ron," she never again recorded with the rest of the group. Whether or not this means that The Crystals weren't actually on any future sides beyond "He Hit Me" is open to speculation, although "I Love You Eddie," the flip side of "He's A Rebel," was The Crystals. Barbara says the group most certainly did record on all the singles. Phil cut all of La La's leads separately. Gloria Jones of The Blossoms says she as well as the other Blossoms and studio singers recorded back-ups for songs that came out as Crystals records. Experts on recording and production techniques state that given the equipment Spector had to work with in 1963, he couldn't possibly have mixed East and West Coast backing vocals onto one master. He must have had two versions of the same song and would later decide which one he would release.

There was always augmentation, such as overdubbing, but there are glaring examples of extra or specific voices on some productions. One can clearly hear Cher's distinctive voice as the bottom note on the backing vocals of "Da Doo Ron Ron," as well as La La's overdubs in the background of "Little Boy" and "I Wonder." With more and more echo shoveled onto the productions, it is often anyone's guess as to who is actually on the finished product. The third Crystals LP, "The Crystals Sing The Greatest Hits, Volume 1," was another reworking of their first LP, restoring old cuts, replacing others with their current hit and featuring "guest vocalists" on cuts like "The Twist" and "Mashed Potato Time." Albums meant nothing to Spector. It was merely another way to capitalize on success.

The Crystals were now feeling their way through their career in the dark. From day to day, they didn't know what to expect. The feud with Spector over his roulette-wheel approach to their releases and growing disagreements over money was too much for the morale of the group. He even resorted to divisiveness by trying to play off La La against the rest of the group, by treating her to special gifts. Once he bought her a dog. La La feels that because of her age, she was less concerned with money matters than with just having fun singing, with less reason to question Phil or his motives.

This was not so with Mary Thomas, who was the first one to leave the group, at the behest of her boyfriend, who knew of another group that needed a singer. Mary left in mid-1963 and soon joined a quartet of girls called The Butterflys, who recorded two bright singles for Red Bird Records, "Goodnight, Baby/The Swim," and "I Wonder/Gee Baby Gee," in 1964. Ironically, this group's sound was very close to the sound of the earlier Crystals efforts, recording songs written by Ellie Greenwich and Jeff Barry and being produced by Greenwich/Barry and Steve Venet.

By the fall of 1963, Phil was readying his most famous compilation featuring all the artists on his roster. Production was to begin on "A Christmas Gift For You," a collection of Christmas standards featuring the Spectoresce touch. The Ronettes were given cutesy tunes like "Sleigh Ride" and "I Saw Mommy Kissing Santa Claus." Bobby Sheen showed off his Clyde McPhatter-like voice on "The Bells of St. Mary's." Darlene Love put her signature voice to "Winter Wonderland" and the only original Christmas tune on the LP, "Christmas (Baby Please Come Home)."

The Crystals received the storybook songs like "Rudolph The Red-Nosed Reindeer," and "Parade Of The Wooden Soldiers." Neither of those approached the depth and power that was evoked on the fire and brim-stone version of "Santa Claus Is Coming To Town." La La's intro is that of an older sister putting her little brother to bed with tales of a kindly old man bearing goodies who's coming to visit him. That image of night-time tranquility was immediately obscured by big sister's ardent message to be good or else. The Crystals' version was obviously the blueprint for versions by Michael Jackson and Bruce Springsteen. Ironically, the group was not happy with the songs thrust upon them for the Christmas LP. (Dee Dee refers to them as "the kiddy songs.")

As far as the single recordings were concerned, it seems the balance of The Crystals' output at Philles was already laid out. Since the arrival of The Ronettes at Philles, The Crystals were not getting the attention they used to get. "Then He Kissed Me" was released in September of 1963 and had done well for the group. A marvelous single, it strutted a more galloping pace than "Da Doo Ron Ron," just as much, if not more echo, and once again featured La La's commanding lead vocal. Two more releases followed. "Little Boy" was released in December of 1963, barely scraping the charts at #92. Not as melodic as most Greenwich/Barry/Spector compositions, the song seems to have a mismatched backbeat. It's obvious that no care was taken on the decision to release this as the follow-up to a top ten hit. In England, Spector dispensed with the cautionary instrumental B-side and issued "Little Boy" flipped with a version of "I Wonder," which suffered from most of the same shortcomings as "Little Boy." These were not terrible records, but not hit caliber when compared to The Crystals' earlier efforts.

The next Crystal to leave the fold was Patsy Wright. As well as being dissatisfied with the group's position at Philles, Patsy was also under pressure to improve her pitch. A few weeks before Christmas, Patsy left the group. This was especially upsetting for The Crystals because they were about to embark on their first overseas tour. The Crystals were ready to go on a three-month European tour when Patsy left, so a replacement was quickly needed. By this time, Mel and Joe Scandore were managing the group. One evening, Mel happened upon a friend of his whom was producing a jazz dance show called "Twistarama USA." The large troupe was booked in Paris for two months with such stars as Lola Falana and a featured singer named Freda Payne.

Frances Collins, a dancer on the show, happened to be in the right place at the right time. Born in Harlem, New York and raised in South Jamaica, Queens, Frances had never sung before. When her producer impulsively offered her services, she was stunned. Frances tells the story. "The producer of Twistarama took a small group of us to dinner one night after the rehearsal. While sitting there, his friend, Mel came in and when he saw us he came over to greet his friend. When the producer of our show said 'How's everything', Mel stated, 'I'm upset because The Crystals have a contract to leave for England in a couple of weeks and I can't find a replacement. They either look the type but have no passport, or have a passport but look too old for the group.' The producer thought for a moment then said, 'I have a large group of dancers going to Europe. They all have passports.' He looked over at me and said, 'Take Frances, she looks young enough.' I was absolutely shocked. I said, 'but I'm not a singer, I'm a dancer!'"

The manager urged the teenage Frances to at least audition for the group. She did so, hesitantly, but wound up getting the job. It would be this quartet of girls who would sustain the group's popularity in England while Spector allowed their recording career to flounder in the United States.

In England and Scotland, The Crystals toured endlessly. Also on the bill were Manfred Mann, Johnny and The Pirates and Heinz. The group had shows booked almost every night for three months. They attended press conferences and television shows. The Beatles had just arrived in The United States and commented that they were very disappointed they could not meet one of their favorite groups, because The Crystals were on The Beatles' home turf for three months. According to group members, they played shows in almost every town in England. Manfred Mann acted as the backup band for the group on several occasions. Everywhere they went, The Crystals were mobbed by adoring fans. They were

THE CRYSTALS

The Crystals, 1966, (L-R) Dee Dee, Frances, La La, guitarist Ronnie (?). (Photo courtesy of Yellowlinda, Inc.)

the toasts of the town. Fans would greet them at shows with gifts, tokens of their appreciation. This adoration was a true telling of the impact that the group had on British musical tastes.

After returning from a successful tour of England, the group had to return to battle with Phil. In the spring of 1964, Spector released The Crystals' last single for Philles, "All Grown Up." This song, a raucous production with a surf-like theme, was a loose answer to Chuck Berry's "Almost Grown." It had been in the can for awhile. Spector had released it in response to Ellie Greenwich and Jeff Barry's plans to release their version of the song with The Exciters. When The Crystals version was released in late March, Greenwich and Barry decided not to go with their version. Although there was no competition from The Exciters' version on the charts, this single fared even worse than "Little Boy" did, scoring only #98 on the national charts. One more recording session took place in the summertime. Spector recorded some songs with his newfound songwriting team, Vinnie Poncia and Pete Andreoli, responsible for wondrous songs like "(The Best Part Of) Breakin' Up" and "Do I Love You," recorded by The Ronettes.

Spector spent an unusual amount of time on a song called "Please Be My Boyfriend," taking great care with the arrangement. In a surprise move, he used Barbara for the lead once again. The song surfaced only as the B-side of a test pressing by The Blossoms, recorded for the EEOC, entitled "Things Are Changin'. After that session, the relationship between the two factions was through.

The Crystals finally exacted their release from Spector at the end of 1964, obtaining a severance fee of $5,000, with the stipulation that they not ask him for any future monies. Their manager took them over to United Artists Records to work with producer Paul Tannen and arranger Charlie Calello. Before the group had their first session for UA in July of 1965, Barbara Alston had married and left the group to have a baby, so the Crystals were now carrying on as a trio.

The first session yielded four songs, "My Place," "You Can't Tie A Good Girl Down," "You'll Know When The Right Man Comes Along," and "I Got A Man." However, UA delayed release of any material until September. With so many new artists and sounds jumping onto the music scene in 1965, The Crystals were becoming frustrated by their lack of chart action. The trio continued to make live appearances at colleges and in clubs at almost all points in the United States, but were always asked to sing their Philles hits.

The Crystals were absent from the top of the charts for almost two years by the time UA decided on "My Place/You Can't Tie A Good Girl Down" as the first single. La La received a featured mention on the record label. Outside of some New York airplay, the record didn't budge, so the company delayed releasing another single on the group. Another session yielded four more sides, including some input from the up-and-coming songwriting team of Nick Ashford and Valerie Simpson. La La had met Valerie at a party one night and asked her to write a song for The Crystals. The result was "Are You Trying To Get Rid Of Me Baby," a mild soul song with the

rhythmic progression of the more popular Motown tunes with a Trade Martin arrangement. The more interesting side was its flip, held over from the first session. "I Got A Man," written by Toys songsters Sandy Linzer and Denny Randell, was made for La La's voice, and she tears it up, singing it like a vamp coming on to a group of sailors in a smoky juke joint. Solid backing vocals complete this bluesy number. This second and final UA release for the group was issued in February of 1966. Three sides from their second session remained in the can until their release during the 1980s on an LP of unreleased UA material (which also features The Exciters' version of "All Grown Up"). With no action happening with their singles, The Crystals left UA in 1966.

During 1966, many factors brought about the end of The Crystals lineup as it was. Dee Dee and La La were the youngest of the original group, and now they were out of high school. Everyone was going in different directions. La La was planning to marry and Frances had to be sent home from a tour in Chicago because she was having a nasty withdrawal from diet pills she had been taking. Tired of the road, Frances decided to settle down to raise her son, Gregory. With everyone's priorities changing, it was time to put the group to rest, albeit temporarily. Dee Dee went on to try singing as a soloist. In 1967, Dee Dee's chauffeur had to run an errand to his brother's recording studio. It turned out that Barbara

THE CRYSTALS

315 WEST 57th STREET
NEW YORK, N.Y. 10019

SUITE 20D (212) 246-7134

Apostol Enterprises Ltd.

The Crystals, 1972, (clockwise from top left) Barbara, Dee Dee, Mary. (Photo courtesy of Yellowlinda, Inc.)

was already in the studio cutting demos, so Dee Dee went up to the studio to say hello.

The label owner of Michelle Records, Bill Pemberton and the producer, Don French, suggested that Dee Dee and Barbara record something together. They called Mary and decided to record for Pemberton's small label. Their sole single, "Ring A Ting A Ling/Should I Keep On Waiting," was far away from what was being produced at that time. Dee Dee puts it bluntly. "From the moment I heard them I knew they were not going to be hits. The producer tried to keep us in that bubble gum thing. They did not have their fingers on the pulse of what was going on in music at the time." This superfluous single marked an end to the career of The Crystals as a recording unit. Dee Dee married Bill Pemberton and stayed out of singing for a few years.

During the late 1960s, Barbara Alston and Mary Thomas continued to garner studio work as independent singers. In 1968, Mary and Barbara lent their background vocals for a recording by an eighteen-year old singer named Teri Nelson. Originally from Harlem, NY, Nelson was seeking a contract as a soloist, but wound up having her only release for Kama Sutra Records promoted as a group. According to Nelson's former manager, Steve Camhi, she was offered a deal by Super K Productions for a year. Barbara remembers recording the single "Sweet Talkin' Willie," but said she wasn't aware that an album called "Sweet Talkin' Teri" by The Teri Nelson Group had been released. She recorded the back-ups

La La Brooks, 2000. (Photo courtesy of La La Brooks)

along with Mary, Betty Cooper and Ona Lee. Barbara's distinct vocal is easily heard in the background. They are pictured along with Nelson on the album's front cover sporting psychedelic maxi dresses. Not happy with her lot at Kama Sutra, Teri Nelson was gone after one year.

With only a three-year break, Dee Dee kept The Crystals going, working extensively with a series of different configurations of original members and replacements. Dee Dee, La La, Barbara and Mary did regroup for a Madison Square Garden show in 1971. Dee Dee had been working with two girls as The Crystals in the islands, but let them go in order to work with the original group. La La dropped out after her token appearance at Madison Square Garden. Dee Dee, Barbara and Mary continued, touring in Europe, Australia and New Zealand until 1974, when Barbara, after an especially exhausting tour, returned home to be with her family and Mary, pregnant with her first child, retired from the music business.

Since it seemed that the lust for the sound of The Crystals hadn't waned in the late 1970s, Dee Dee recorded two cuts for a Nashville reissue label, Gusto Records, with convincing Spector-like backing tracks. A version of "He's A Rebel" with La La on lead, albeit a more mature La La, surfaced on an LP, "American Dream The 1960s," out of Minneapolis from 1980. Spector himself had reissued the real thing many times in England during the 1970s and 1980s with his "Wall Of Sound" series.

A tempting attraction for collectors was the nifty two-box set of color plastic 45s, issued in conjunction with Collectibles Records in 1983. In 1986, Dee Dee and La La got together at the behest of a fan, Kirk Beasley, who wanted them to rerecord some of their old hits. He produced the session at Masters Touch Studios in Nashville. The other two vocalists on the project were Darlene Davis and Gretchen Gale Prendatt. They basically did a reprise of cuts from their "He's A Rebel" LP, plus other hits like "Da Doo Ron Ron" and a version of "The Boy I'm Gonna Marry." The vocals were commendable, but the instrumentation was the antithesis of what Spector had achieved.

Dee Dee continued with the group, working with Peggie Blue and Louise Bethune, their only publicity shot featured on the cover of the Phil Spector Wall of Sound series issued in England in the mid-70s. Dee Dee continued with rotating configurations of Crystals, doing live dates and appearing on Sha Na Na's weekly television show, singing "Da Doo Ron Ron." She forged ahead, winning the name of The Crystals from Spector and working under it to this day, featured as the only original member. Dee Dee's Crystals are a mainstay on the nostalgia circuit. Dee Dee has one daughter.

Barbara Alston raised her four children and runs her own business from her home in North Carolina. Mary Thomas Anderson still resides in Brooklyn, where she and her husband raised their two children. Patsy Wright married and moved to the West Coast.

Frances Collins settled back in Queens, NY after her tenure as a Crystal. She joined The National Black Theatre, where she danced, acted, wrote poetry, recited and taught dance and Black history to schoolchildren. She also became a Muslim, taking the name Fatima. Graduating from New York University in 1976 with a degree in

Dance Therapy, she now owns a dance studio in Miami Beach, Florida. Fatima Johnson Gueye is married with two sons. Her son, Chaka, is Prodigy, part of the popular rap duo, Mobb Deep.

La La went into modeling and acting, garnering parts in the Broadway plays "Hair" and "Two Gentlemen of Verona" with Clifton Davis. She married noted jazz drummer Idris Muhammed, and herself became Sakinah Muhammed. They lived in Teaneck, New Jersey, then moved to Vienna, Austria, where they raised their four children. La La was host of her own radio show in Austria called "C'mon Everybody." She appeared at the Fat Boy Saloon to a sellout crowd in New York City in October of 1997, singing her Crystals hits as well as her own contemporary songs, backed by a powerhouse gospel quartet of singers and seasoned musicians including her husband. La La was joined by a host of notables including Ben E. King, Isaac Hayes and Maxine Brown. With her children now grown, she has reemerged as a soloist, traveling all over the world to sing once again.

The Crystals body of work established them as crucial components in the conglomeration that makes up popular music. Although, admittedly, they were not always willing proponents of the Wall of Sound, one cannot imagine the wall standing without them. Forever encased in the wall are these young voices, the voices of 1960s teen radio at its height.

The Crystals Discography

45s

	Label	Number	Year
Oh Yeah, Maybe Baby/There's No Other	Philles	100	1961
Uptown/What A Nice Way To Turn Seventeen		102	1962
He Hit Me/No One Ever Tells You		105	
He's A Rebel/I Love You Eddie		106	
He's Sure The Boy I Love/Walkin' Along (La La La)		109	
The Screw Pt. 1/The Screw Pt. 2		111	1963
Da Doo Ron Ron/Git It (Inst.)		112	
Then He Kissed Me/Brother Julius (Inst.)		115	
Little Boy/Harry (From W. Va.) and Milt (Inst.)		119x	
All Grown Up/Irving (Jaggered Sixteenths) (Inst.)		122	1964
I Wonder/Little Boy (UK only)	London	9852	
Please Be My Boyfriend/Things Are Changing (Blossoms)	EEOCT4LM	8172-1	1965
My Place/You Can't Tie A Good Girl Down	United Artists	927	
I Got A Man/Are You Trying To Get Rid Of Me Baby		994	1966
Ring A Ting A Ling/Should I Keep On Waiting	Michelle	4113	1967
Da Doo Ron Ron/Then He Kissed Me	Gusto	2090	1979
Rudolph The Red-Nosed Reindeer/I Saw Mommy Kissing Santa Claus (Ronettes)	Pavillion	8-03333	1981
He's A Rebel/He Hit Me	Collectibles	3200	1983
Then He Kissed Me/--		3201	
Uptown/He's Sure The Boy I Love		3202	
All Grown Up (Alt.)/Da Doo Ron Ron		3203	
There's No Other		3204	

The Butterflys w/Mary Thomas

	Label	Number	Year
Goodnight Baby/The Swim	Red Bird	10-009	1964
Wonder/Gee Baby Gee		10-016	

Teri Nelson Group

	Label	Number	Year
Sweet Talkin' Willie/The Backside	Kama Sutra	245	1968

LPs

	Label	Number	Year
The Crystals Twist Uptown	Philles	4000	1962
He's A Rebel		4001	
The Crystals Sing Today's Hits		4003	1963
A Christmas Gift For You		4005	
Today's Hits By Today's Artists		4007	1964
Phil Spector's Greatest Hits	Warner/Spector	9104	1977
Rare Masters	Phil Spector Int'l. (UK)	2335	1977
American Dream The 60s (version of "He's A Rebel")	Excelsior	6017	1980
He's A Rebel	Jango	777	1986
Teri Nelson Group w/Barbara Alston & Mary Thomas			
Sweet Talkin' Teri	Kama Sutra	--	1968

EPs

	Label	Number	Year
Christmas EP	Philles	X-EP	1963

CDs

	Label	Number	Year
La La Brooks			
La La Brooks and Friends	BMG Ariola	--	1996

The Darlettes

Members:

(1961-63) Dianne Christian, Lead
Gale Noble, Soprano
Shirley Crier, Alto

Making a big long line and dancing back and forth, "walking like an Egyptian," "hitchhiking" and "sweeping the floor." Every party held in every basement or living room in The Bronx, in 1962, exhibited happy revelers doing the fashionable new dance called "The Wobble," brought to the mainland New York borough by three of its hometown daughters, The Darlettes.

The Darlettes were from the Morrisania section of The Bronx, which was the stomping ground for many a top-notch vocal group. The Darlettes grew up listening to The Chords, Wrens, The Chantels, and Lillian Leach and The Mellows. Shirley Crier's older brother, Arthur, was a member of The Chimes and The Mellows. Arthur later achieved the most success as the bass in The Halos (Craftys), who recorded "Pretty Little Angel Eyes," with Curtis Lee. The girls were not able to "hang out," so Shirley had to be content to listening to Arthur's group rehearse at their house.

The Darlettes all lived within a block from each other on Tinton and Union Aves. between 166th and 167th Streets. Shirley attended Morris High School in The Bronx. Dianne Christian and Gale Noble attended Central Commercial in Manhattan, which is now the site of Norman Thomas High School. They frequently attended the talent competitions at P.S. 99 on Stebbins Ave. With an older brother who was a successful singer and songwriter, it seemed natural that Shirley would eventually sing in a group. With her mom's blessing, Gale at 17, was already hanging around The Brill Building getting session work, providing hand claps to records made by Ben E. King, among others. Dianne was considering a career in modeling.

It was at this time Arthur became active in managing several groups, so, of course he would manage and write for The Darlettes. At first, the group was using the name The Rosettes. Arthur had co-written their first single, "You Broke My Heart." It was released on Al Silver's Herald record label. This tune had a shuffling "mashed potato" sound. Arthur used his experience in the business to train the girls. Gale remembers rehearsals as grueling, "Arthur would have us working in the community center after school. We would ask

The Darlettes, 1962, (clockwise from top) Dianne Christian, Shirley Crier, Gale Noble. (Photo courtesy of Dianne Christian Toppin)

him to give us a break and he would say, 'No, you have to get it perfect'."

The group anxiously waited to hear their song on the radio. Shirley attributes the girls' acute anxiety to their youth: "At the age we were, we thought of stardom. It was great. Rocky G. played with WLIB and he plugged the record. We were on the street by the candy store when we heard it and we just started screaming."

Their second single saw the name change, temporarily, to Diane and The Darlettes, since Dianne was primarily singing lead. Arthur's group, The Halos, was recording for Dunes Records, so he got the group a chance to record with the company, then associated with Big Top Records.

The group's first single for the label was patterned after a fashionable Bronx dance entitled "The Wobble," that the teenagers strutted at parties. The Wobble was a dance done in two lines with each line facing each other. This was similar to The Stroll, but no one walked down the middle of the rows. Instead, dancers would make gestures as the lines moved back and forth. One was a Popeye gesture, like a hitchhiker. Another was an imitation of Egyptian hieroglyphics, with one hand held up and the other down with fingers pointing. The third step was to "sweep the floor," bending as you moved and letting your fingers touch the ground. The girls figured a song named after such a popular dance would at least take off locally. The song and it's flip, "Just You," did merit some airplay, but unfortunately did nothing. "The Wobble" featured Arthur on bass. Arthur often guest-starred on songs he wrote for other artists, notably female artists. He also sang bass on Barbara English and The Fashions' "Ta Ta Te Ta Ta."

"Just You" featured a dual lead by Dianne and Shirley. "Just You" was also the flip of The Darlettes' next single. "Here She Comes" was written by the highly successful

Dianne as a soloist, 1964. (Photo courtesy of Dianne Christian Toppin)

Dianne with The Liberty Belles, 1967, (L-R) Terry Whittier (?), Dianne, Marva Sasso. (Photo courtesy of Dianne Christian Toppin)

THE LIBERTY BELLES
SHOUT RECORDING ARTISTS

MANAGEMENT
HORIZON PROMOTIONS, INC.
225 W 57TH ST N Y N Y

songwriting team of Ellie Greenwich and Jeff Barry. This song features some tough-talking lyrics warning a girl to stay away from Dianne's boyfriend. Gale sings the high octave above Dianne's lead. Stan Shulman produced the session and Alan Lorber arranged the music. Shirley says that the group did not like "Just You" because at the time of its recording all three of the girls had colds and couldn't get the sound they wanted with their voices cracking. Shirley relates the events, "I didn't like 'Just You', but I liked it when Gale sang it. She got hoarse and couldn't do it that day. I think it sounds better now than it did then."

The Darlettes were also lucky enough to be called in to cut demo records when the coveted spot held by The Cookies was available. If The Cookies were on tour, The Darlettes would be asked to fill in. The Darlettes did very little touring. They promoted themselves at local clubs and on radio stations. They did do a television spot in Connecticut, and their record was rated on Dick Clark's famed "American Bandstand." However, the girls did not see The Darlettes as a true career for them; it was just fun. After the local success of "Here She Comes," Shirley got married and moved to Texas. Dianne was busy cutting demos and releasing solo recordings, thus marking the end of The Darlettes.

At this time, Dianne began working with Feldman, Goldstein and Gottehrer, the writing and producing team who were having chart success with The Angels' "My Boyfriend's Back." Dianne cut demos and recorded singles for Smash and Bell Records. Dianne had the ability to adjust her voice to any singing style, which made her in demand as a demo and session singer. The production team could vary their styles on her singles as a result of her talent. She made quality records with the FGG team, including the jumpy "Has Anybody Seen My Boyfriend," for Smash Records in 1963: "I went for an audition for about 500 people and I was one of the singers they selected. This led to the Liberty Belles. I also did jin-

Dianne and her Delights appearing in The Carribean with singer Vince (?), late 1960s, (L-R) Dianne, Rosalind Gooding, Vince (?), Helena Johnson, Oreal Brown. (Photo courtesy of Dianne Christian Toppin)

gles with Bert DeCoteaux for Kool Cigarettes, and Canada Dry. I had met Bert through FGG."

Other marvelous records followed, starting with "Wonderful Guy," for Bell Records in 1964, the Northern Soul classic "Little Boy/Why Don't The Boy Leave Me Alone," also for Bell, in 1965. She also recorded a song released under a pseudonym, with Patti Lace & The Petticoats, backing her. The song, "I Want You To Be My Boyfriend" was leased to Josie Records as The Chic-Lets. Dianne recorded with two other groups, Diane and The Delights and The Liberty Belles who recorded one single for Shout Records in 1967. Dianne worked with The Delights extensively, in and around New York, and in the Caribbean. As a soloist, she also appeared at The Apollo Theatre, The Hunt's Point Palace and at Peg Leg Bates and Swan Lake in upstate New York. After a few more years of singing in bands, doing local gigs, Dianne gave up singing to raise her family.

Gale continued to make her mark in the recording industry, going out as a solo act under the supervision of a production company. During the late 60s, she appeared at Harlem's Apollo Theatre, singing a version of "You'll Never Walk Alone," and made the cover of Cash Box magazine as a promising new artist. As Gale sang on stage, her mother in the audience, she discovered something from her mom's cheers, "My mother was more excited than I was. For me it was fascinating. I knew I could sing. When I got to sing, I felt great."

Gale recorded some material to be released with the help of a production company she was working with. One afternoon at rehearsal, the producer made some suggestions to Gale that were not going to be part of the deal. Disgusted by this turn of events after she had worked so hard, Gale decided to quit show business for good.

Today, Shirley Fields is a mother of three and is a health technician with the Veterans Hospital in The Bronx. Dianne also resides in The Bronx. Gale Noble lives in Manhattan and works for The Department of Veteran Affairs. In 1996, Gale's brother surprised her on the day of his wedding by reuniting her with Shirley at the reception. They had not seen each other for over thirty years. In 1999, Dianne, Gale and Shirley decided to reunite and began rehearsals with the hopes of performing once again. Arthur is once again at the helm. The Darlettes were fortunate enough to be in with the best writers and producers during their brief career in Rock & Roll, making their mark by recording a small, yet eclectic group of memorable records.

The Darlettes Discography

45s	Label	Number	Year
(as The Rosettes)			
You Broke My Heart/It Must Be Love	Herald	562	1961
(as Diane and The Darlettes)			
Just You/Wobble	Dunes	2016	1962
The Darlettes			
Here She Comes/Just You	Dunes	2026	1963
Diane Christian			
Has Anybody Seen My Boyfriend/There's So Much About My Baby That I Love	Smash	1862	1963
Wonderful Guy/It Happened One Night	Bell	610	1964
Little Boy/Why Don't The Boy Leave Me Alone		617	1965
The Chic-Lets			
I Want You To Be My Boyfriend/Don't Goof On Me	Josie	919	1964
The Liberty Belles			
Shing-A-Ling Time/Just Try Me	Shout	209	1967

The Delltones

Members:

The Enchanters
(1952-53)
Pearl Brice
Rachel Gist
Frances Kelly
Della Simpson, Lead

The Delltones
(1954-55)
Gloria Alleyne (Lynne)
Sherry Gary
Frances Kelly
Della Simpson

(1955-56)
Shirley (Bunny) Foy
Della Simpson
Renee Stewart
Algie Willie

Hail to one of the forerunners of many female R&B vocal groups, The Delltones. As The Enchanters, this prototypical foursome ushered the way for other female vocal groups like the (early) Blue Belles and The Hearts.

The Enchanters, 1952, (clockwise from top left) Frances Kelly, Pearl Brice, Della Simpson, Rachel Gist, (Photo courtesy of Della Simpson Griffin)

Their mixture of jazz and blues gained them the attention of a prestigious record executive. Their equal handling of jazz ballads and bluesy swing tunes astounded and entertained audiences all over America.

Della Simpson was born in the South and raised in Jamaica, New York. At an early age, Della had a hankering to be on stage. She grew up listening to the radio, taking in all the sounds she heard from the big band singers, especially her idol, Billie Holliday. She and one of her friends, with whom she worked, decided to put a group together. Della recalls how she just made up her mind one day, "I always liked show business. I liked Billie Holliday. I was working with another girl and we decided to put a group together and sing. Any place they would let us sing, we would sing."

The duo recruited two more ladies and named themselves The Enchanters. The quartet started working with piano player Chris Towns, who wrote and arranged songs for the group. The group attracted much attention because, at the time, in 1952, most vocal groups were male groups. The Enchanters were among the first female groups in the early 1950s who were singing R&B. The group and their piano player booked themselves into every venue available to them. One particular club allowed the group to hold rehearsals there, during off-hours. Della made the bold move of calling Jerry Blaine, owner of Jubilee Records, inviting him to attend a show. Jubilee Records was home to another group of Della's singing heroes, The Orioles. She told Blaine to come down and check out the act, never thinking he would actually come. When he walked in the room, the ladies recognized him and they almost fell off the stage.

The DELL-TONES

The Delltones, 1954, (top) Della (bottom, L-R) Gloria Alleyne (Lynne), Sherry Gary, Frances Kelly. (Photo courtesy of Della Simpson Griffin)

Blaine was impressed with their singing and Towns' arrangements. He signed them to Jubilee Records.

The first single for The Enchanters was the sentimental ode to a lover, "Today Is Your Birthday," released in 1952. "...Birthday" showcases Della as a warm, supple singer, caressing each line with reverent tenderness. This ballad was flipped with the blues rocker, "How Could You" which shows that The Enchanters could also jump with the best of them. Della's purposeful lead voice and a fervent group convincingly sell this side. The Enchanters started touring off of the critical acclaim and local success that the single generated. The group began making the rounds of the theatres on The Chitlin Circuit, The Apollo in New York, The Howard in Washington, DC and The Royal in Baltimore, winning kudos from the audiences. Jubilee issued the second single, following the same formula as the first single. Chris Towns' "I've Lost" and the woeful "Housewife Blues" met with a comparable reception.

The Enchanters became associated with revered groups like The Four Buddies and The Wanderers. The Enchanters' arrangements were based on these groups that they favored. In fact, Four Buddies members Ollie Jones and Luther Dixon had written "How Could You" for the ladies. Also, Della became good friends with the legendary Sonny Til.

The versatile quartet also tackled Four Freshman tunes and sang songs in French. The group was looking to be taken seriously and was proud of a sound they felt was diversified. At Jubilee, The Enchanters realized that they were big fish in a bigger pond. They were not receiving the attention afforded male groups like The Orioles or The Marylanders. After two singles with Jubi-

The Delltones with their accompanists, 1956, (L-R) Della, Bunny Foy, bassist Gloria Bell, Renee Stewart, Algie Willie, pianist Chris Towns. (Photo courtesy of Della Simpson Griffin)

THE DELL-TONES

lee, the group left the label. During this time, Rachel Gist left the group and was replaced by Gloria Alleyne. Other personnel changes would soon follow, with new member Sherry Gary replacing Pearl Brice. These substitutions also facilitated their name change to The Delltones.

In 1953, the first effort recorded under the new group name was for Brunswick Records, the glorious "My Heart's On Fire" and the demure "Yours Alone" featuring Gloria on the bridge. Another single, "I'm Not In Love With You," followed on Rainbow Records in 1954. At this time, The Delltones hooked up with Jimmy Forrest and his Night Train Revue, sharing the bill with many Rhythm & Blues luminaries like Spo-Dee-O-Dee and Jimmy Smith. Oddly, the songs were now being released with the group billed as The Delltones, but some stage cards still billed the group as The Enchanters. (This must have caused confusion for those fans seeking to buy their records. Some placards even show the group designated The Enchanteers.) There were abundant venues where the group was playing on the bill with musicians like renowned jazz saxophonists Illinois Jacquet and Arnett Cobb. The Delltones performed countless shows, traveling all over The United States and Canada.

The next stop for The Delltones was Sol Rabinowitz's Baton Records where they recorded two singles. Gloria Alleyne and Sherry Gary had left the group. This final incarnation of Della's group included Bunny Foy, Algie Willie and Renee Stewart. Stewart is the author of the celebrated R&B street anthem, "I Call To You" and a member of a short-lived female group, The Solirettes. Gloria Bell, a former bassist with Duke Ellington's band, also joined as an accompanist. The group continued to tour for a time and even got a chance to sing on The Arthur Godfrey Show, where they delighted the producers at the audition. Optimism turned to disappointment, however, when The Delltones were told they couldn't sing any songs from their cache of material because they sounded too white. The group was relegated to sing a song they didn't care for just to net an appearance on the show. Since their hearts weren't into the tune, the group didn't give their all. Della remarks on the song that the group dutifully sang, "That's not what we were about, so of course we didn't win."

Eventually, The Delltones dissolved due to marriages and families taking priority over the stage. Gloria Alleyne became Gloria Lynne, working for years as a soloist, recording her hit version of "I Wish You Love" in 1964. Lynne is a continuing force in the jazz world. Della

went out on her own for many years with her own organ and sax combo, sharing the bill with singer Etta Jones. When Jones had her hit version of "Don't Go To Strangers" in 1961, her touring pace changed, so Della became the sole feature on many scheduled dates. Della had married The Orioles' piano player and session musician, Paul Griffin. When Paul wanted Della to put the breaks on her career, she took time off to raise her family: "When I married Paul, he wanted me to take time off. After we broke up, I started making the rounds again. I was scheduled to sing at The Blue Book on 146th Street and St. Nicholas Ave. for two weeks and wound up staying for years."

After being rediscovered by group harmony enthusiast Louie Silvani in 1994, Della, Frances and Bunny made an appearance on Dan Romanello's Rhythm & Blues Group Harmony Review at Fordham University's WFUV-FM in New York. There they answered questions and conveyed facts about The Enchanters and The Delltones for the listening audience. Della put a new group of Delltones together that year, including original Enchanter Frances Kelly and new members Annette St. John and Gwen Michael. This quartet has made numerous appearances at Ronnie I's United In Group Harmony Association (UGHA) concerts and were included on The Heroines of R&B concert at Symphony Space in October of 1995, with The Chantels, The Jewels and Vikki Burgess, among others. Della intends to continue to quench her thirst for entertaining. She hasn't lost her sense of wit and spontaneity. Despite a hasty rehearsal with the house band before the show, she needed some quick guidance from her accompanists during the performance, so she excused herself from the microphone while Frances, Annette and Gwen repeated their pickup lines, "We had started to sing and I had to ask the band what song we were singing. I didn't recognize the song. Everybody thought it was part of the act."

In addition to The Delltones, Della continues to appear in jazz clubs in and around New York City, both as a soloist and as an accomplished drummer. She has graduated from playing the tom toms to playing the whole drum kit. Della is also mentioned in the Encyclopedia of Jazz. The Enchanters/Delltones took a daring step forward when they decided to compete on a circuit usually reserved for men. Others soon followed in the footsteps of one of the pioneering female ensembles of vocal group music.

The Delltones Discography

45s	Label	Number	Year
(as The Enchanters)			
Today Is Your Birthday/How Could You	Jubilee	5072	1952
I've Lost/Housewife Blues		5080	
(as The Delltones)			
My Heart's On Fire/Yours Alone	Brunswick	85015	1953
I'm Not In Love With You/Little Short Daddy	Rainbow	244	1954
Baby Say You Love Me/Don't Be Too Long	Baton	212	1955
My Special Love/Believe It		223	1956

Reparata & The Delrons

Members:

(1964-65)	Mary "Reparata" Aiese, Lead Carol Drobnicki Sheila Reilly	(1965-70)	Mary "Reparata" Aiese Nanette Licari Lorraine Mazzola	(1970-93)	Mary "Reparata" Aiese Nanette Licari Cookie Sirico

A heady concoction of young voices and girlish innocence professing unremitting love was the sound of Reparata & The Delrons. A group whose fresh delivery and simplistic harmonies netted them a special niche in female group history.

The story of Reparata & The Delrons started in 1963 at St. Brendan's High School in the Midwood section of Brooklyn, New York. Sheila Reilly, Carol Drobnicki, Margie McGuire, Cathy Romeo and lead singer, Mary Aiese started singing at Knights of Columbus dances for fun, just getting up out of the audience and singing acappella. Through an acquaintance, they came to the attention of Steve and Bill Jerome who owned a record store and recording studio in Bay Ridge, Brooklyn. The brothers had a production company called Realgood Productions. The Jerome brothers auditioned the quintet of girls. They decided to record them independently, then shop the master around to prospective labels. Margie McGuire dropped out almost immediately after plans were made to record, to go steady with her boyfriend.

Cathy Romeo was dropped because she could not sustain her note in the group. Also, the producers thought she did not fit the group's image because she was a bit overweight. Mary Aiese confesses that because the young group was so anxious to have a recording deal that they rationalized any decision the producers made for them, "We convinced ourselves that Cathy was not a good singer, but at that time we would have sold our own mothers down the river. I told her that if we became famous, I would buy her a Corvette."

Their first single, "Your Big Mistake/Leave Us Alone" was placed with Laurie Records in 1964. Unfortunately, the record did nothing. For this single, the group was billed simply as The Delrons. The producers thought the name needed more femininity. They asked the girls if they could come up with a name to add to The Delrons. After tossing around some suggestions, Mary suggested "Reparata," her confirmation name. The producers thought it fit nicely in front of The Delrons. It was appropriate for Mary because she was the lead singer. Thus, her stage name was born.

For the group's next single, the Jerome brothers placed them with World Artists Records. The girls recorded their first big hit, "Whenever A Teenager Cries," written by Ernie Maresca, the man who brought Dion's big hit to the Rock & Roll world, "The Wanderer." "Whenever A Teenager Cries" was such a big hit in the New York area, that the producers followed the single with an album of the same name. The group successfully covered the popular tunes of the day, most notably their version of the Four Seasons' "Bye Bye Baby." Their second single, released in early 1965, was the tale of unconditional love, "Tommy." The single was the second hit for Reparata & The Delrons. This new-found popularity netted the group a spot on a tour for Dick Clark. The tour was particularly long and grueling. When they returned, "Tommy" was scurrying up the charts. Not wanting to lose the momentum that was building on the group, the Jeromes immediately planned a two-month tour, to begin just days after returning from the first excursion. The grueling pace was excessive for Sheila and Carol. The thought of being sent out on the road so soon after returning from their first tour was too much, so they simply refused to do the second tour. Reparata had to do the forty-seven day tour by herself, making excuses on stage for the absence of the other two girls. Originally, they were to meet her at a certain point in the tour, but further disagreements with the Jerome brothers put an end to Sheila and Carol's days as Delrons. Reparata said that after their return from the first tour she never saw them again. It was surely a task carrying this part of the show by herself, but Reparata pulled it off. Some of her mates on this tour were The Rolling Stones, Little Anthony & The Imperials, The Ikettes and Lou Christie. From this tour, Reparata and Lou would remain friends.

World Artists continued to release singles throughout 1965, "A Summer Thought/He's The Greatest" and "The Boy I Love/I Found My Place." In fact, in anticipation of her possible continuance as a solo artist, "A Summer Thought" was billed simply as Reparata. However, upon her arrival from the second tour, a search would begin for a new set of Delrons. Reparata had known several girls who sang well enough to ask them if they wanted to be the next incarnation of Delrons. She decided to ask Nanette Licari, with whom she had sung informally on previous occasions, while the two were still in high school. Nanette accepted, recalling just missing out on the chance to form the first group with Reparata: "I went to high school with Mary and we used to sing, just fooling around. Then they changed classes and we weren't together anymore. She started singing with other girls. The other girls didn't want to do the tours anymore, so Steve Jerome wanted to put another group together. Mary and I were friends, so she called me and asked if I wanted to do it."

Lorraine Mazzola was Reparata's neighbor from down the street. They also attended Brooklyn College together. Lorraine possessed a good voice and appearance. She also said yes to the offer to become a Delron.

EXCLUSIVE
RCA VICTOR RECORDING ARTISTS

REPARATA
and
THE DELRONS

World United Productions
1595 Broadway N.Y.C.
CI 5-4735

*Reparata & The Delrons, 1966, (L-R) Lorraine Mazzola, Nanette Licari, Mary "Reparata" Aiese.
(Photo courtesy of Paul Errante)*

Unfortunately, none of the singles World Artists had released during the scramble for new Delrons were hits, so they and the other popular act on the roster, Chad & Jeremy, were released. The label shut down by the close of 1965. The Jeromes shopped the group to other labels, striking a deal with RCA in November of 1965.

At first, Reparata & The Delrons were elated at the thought of being placed with RCA, a major label. This meant bigger budgets, access to better material and superior recording facilities. But as so many artists learned in the past, the group simply got lost among the myriad of artists on the RCA roster. They recorded some marvelous singles while at RCA, including the Ellie Greenwich/Jeff Barry penned, "I'm Nobody's Baby Now," and the atmospheric "I Can Hear The Rain." None of the half-dozen singles released by the label charted. The group stayed with RCA about 14 months. Also, with no more hits coming, the group was no longer asked to be a part of the big Rock & Roll tours.

Reparata & The Delrons now had the unenviable task of relying solely on personal appearances for exposure. The group did not have their own backing band, so they had to depend on the house bands to provide instrumentation. Often, the bands were inexperienced and unfamiliar with many tunes at all, let alone Delrons songs. The group had to sing whatever the band knew. Reparata recalls one torturous experience: "One place had a band where the only song they knew was 'Land Of 1000 Dances,' so we wound up doing a 30-minute version of that song."

The ladies' fortunes seemed to change somewhat when they signed to the Amy/Mala/Bell complex in September of 1967, where five singles were released. The group was still under the direction of the Jerome brothers and arranger John Abbott. These singles include an ardent version of "I Believe" and a catchy song, co-written by Kenny Young, the man who penned "Under The Boardwalk." "Captain Of Your Ship," released in 1968, depicts late 60s pop at its best. The arrangement utilizes acoustic guitars and an organ, giving the song a folksy feel, over a mostly group vocal.

Its flip, "Toom Toom," was equally enchanting. "Captain . . ." climbed the charts in England, creating demand for the group overseas. The ladies immediately embarked on a three-country tour of England, Germany, and Poland. The group was mobbed during this tour, making appearances nightly, signing autographs, and granting interviews. This attention gave the group renewed hope that their career was not waning to oblivion.

Nanette says that the group was elated to have this chance to travel abroad, not once, but twice: "When we went overseas, the first tour was for three weeks. When we had Easter break, we went back for three months. I took some time off from school. Terry Ellis and Chris Wright, who became Chrysalis Records, planned the tour. They had Ten Years After over here and we were in Europe. We helped them get established in America."

Despite the fuss they created in Europe, when Reparata & The Delrons returned to the United States, it was back to making personal appearances at small clubs in Connecticut, New Jersey, and Long Island, working for a pittance of what they deserved. Their production team could not come up with another chart record, so at the close of 1968, Reparata & The Delrons again switched record companies to Kapp Records. Out of the three singles released during 1969, only a cover of The Ronettes' "Walking In The Rain" showed promise. Waiting in the wings, however, was another vocal group. Jay and The Americans, who were enjoying success with 1950s and early 1960s cover versions, beat Reparata & The Delrons to the charts with their rendition of "Walking In The Rain" (reaching the Top 20).

Etched in the deadwax of subsequent pressings of Jay and The Americans' singles was the apologetic message, "Sorry, Reparata." This was the final straw for a group that had consistently maintained high standards while struggling to survive in the increasingly competitive world of pop music. With nothing to satisfy the group in their present situation, Reparata & The Delrons decided to take a break from the music business.

During 1970, the Jerome brothers still believed in Mary Aiese's talents, so Reparata was now a solo performer. She recorded "There's So Little Time/Just You" for Big Tree Records in 1971, and a version of "Octopus's Garden" for Laurie Records in 1972. By 1974, Lorraine, Nanette and new Delron, Cookie Sirico were busy cutting demos. Through her place of employment, Lorraine had an offer from a singer/songwriter who was just coming into his own, named Barry Manilow. He had heard one of the group's demos and liked it. He told Lorraine that he needed backing vocalists for his act. Lorraine wanted the group to audition, but Nanette and Cookie were not interested, "Lorraine was working for 'The Morning Show.' She had a lot of contacts. She wanted us to go with Barry Manilow, but Cookie and I passed it up. I didn't want to leave home and go on tour. Lorraine was all excited. She really wanted to do it."

Nothing was happening with The Delrons, so Lorraine went with the blessings of the other ladies. Reparata was in the midst of releasing another single on Polydor Records entitled "Shoes." It was an engaging song with a European disco beat, and it gained popularity both here and abroad. Just as the single was climbing the charts, Mary got a call from a lawyer, telling her to stop using the name Reparata because someone associated with Barry Manilow says she is the "real" Reparata. Polydor, not wanting to be in the middle of a lawsuit, pulled the single.

What ensued next for Mary was a nightmare. She telephoned Lorraine to ask about what was going on. Lorraine assured Mary that it would be taken care of. Not only was it not resolved, Mary received notice that Lorraine was taking her to court over the rights to use the name "Reparata." Lorraine had been singing lead in The Delrons in Mary's absence, so she perpetuated the idea that she was Reparata.

Over the next few years, Mary and her husband spent thousands of dollars trying to prove that she held the right to be called Reparata. Meanwhile, Lorraine was still using it where she could to her advantage. One night, Mary received a call from her old pal, Lou Christie, who told her to turn on the television. Lorraine was on a late night talk show, masquerading as Reparata. In the end, Lorraine never showed up in court for the battle. Mary regained her rightful title, but not before it cost her the right to use the name "Reparata" when she needed it to promote herself.

Many people in the industry who were aware of the charade simply shook their heads and said nothing. Sadly, this level of apathy keeps many bogus artists out there, continuing to fool an unsuspecting public. Fortunately, the distasteful experience did not sour Reparata's love of performing.

During the 1970s, despite the legal woes, Reparata reformed the group with Cookie and Nanette, playing to appreciative audiences in and around New York City. Reparata & The Delrons are featured performers at many shows in their native Brooklyn where many remember them from the early days. Nanette Licari stayed until 1993, when Judy Jay replaced her. Nanette Licari, a schoolteacher, now sings with The Tercels. Singer Lauren Stitch also sang as a Delron for a short time. Sheila Reilly moved to the West Coast where she teaches school. Carol Drobnicki passed away during the 1970s. Reparata has

also made her living as a New York City schoolteacher and resides in Brooklyn with her family.

In recent years, Reparata & The Delrons have done some recording, including a jingle for Mr. G, the weatherman on WCBS-FM, New York. "Tommy" was used to honor baseball great Tommy LaSorda. Promoters hire Reparata & The Delrons because they know that people are going to see a top-notch group. The group has honed its performing skills so well. Every arrangement from their backup band, every dance step and every song is chosen with care. The group performs their hits as well as favorite female group songs like "Leader Of The Pack" and "Boogie Woogie Bugle Boy," showing the crowd that they can handle any vocal arrangement. Reparata sometimes thinks of retiring the group, but she credits the camaraderie of her fellow Delrons and her band with keeping her in the business. Her only regret is not taking charge when the group was new, but everything is a learning experience, and surely the present group is enjoying the benefits of Reparata's sometimes hard-learned lessons. The quality of Reparata & The Delrons proves that it takes pressure to make a diamond.

The Delrons Discography

45s

	Label	Number	Year
(as The Delrons)			
Your Big Mistake/Leave Us Alone	Laurie	3252	1964
Reparata & The Delrons			
Whenever A Teenager Cries/He's My Guy	World Artists	1036	
Tommy/Mama Don't Allow		1051	1965
A Summer Thought/He's The Greatest		1057	
The Boy I Love/I Found My Place		1062	
I Can Tell/Take A Look Around You	RCA	47-8721	
I'm Nobody's Baby Now/Loneliest Girl In Town		47-8820	1966
He Don't Want You/Mama's Little Girl		47-8921	
The Kind Of Trouble That I Love/Boys And Girls		47-9123	1967
I Can Hear The Rain/Always Waitin'		47-9185	
I Believe/It's Waiting There For You	Mala	573	
Captain Of Your Ship/Toom Toom		589	1968
Saturday Night Didn't Happen/Panic		12000	
You Can't Change A Young Boy's Mind/Weather Forecast		12016	
Heaven Only Knows/Summer Laughter		12026	
That's What Sends Men To The Bowery/I've Got An Awful Lot Of Losin' You To Do	Kapp	989	1969
We're Gonna Hold The Night/San Juan		2010	
Walking In The Rain/I've Got An Awful Lot Of Losin' You To Do		2050	
Reparata			
There's So Little Time/Just You	Big Tree	114	1971
Octopus's Garden/Your Life Is Gone	Laurie	3589	1972
Whenever A Teenager Cries/--	North American	2024	1974
Shoes/Song For All	Polydor	14271	1975

LPs

	Label	Number	Year
Whenever A Teenager Cries	World Artists	3006	1965

The Deltairs

Members:

(1957-58)   Barbara Thompson, Lead
Thelma Stansbury, 1st Soprano
Carol Stansbury, 2nd Soprano
Shirley Taylor, Alto
Barbara Lee, Bass

In 1957, female Rock & Roll groups were considered unusual. An even rarer occurrence was for a female group to sing an arrangement normally reserved for male groups. One such group sang a mellifluous melody featuring a five-part arrangement, with one of the ladies singing the bass riffs, another preeminent touch by a female group in the field of Rock & Roll.

The Deltairs, a quintet from Jamaica, Queens, got their start singing for fun like many young singers who had come before, utilizing their ability to sing brilliant harmonies to duplicate sounds they heard sung by their favorite artists that were being played on the radio. Orig-

inally a quartet, sisters Thelma and Carol Stansbury were from Queens. Shirley Taylor was originally from Brooklyn, then moved to Queens. Barbara Lee was from Brooklyn. Barbara Thompson, also from Brooklyn, came to the group a little later. The Deltairs sang with their friends in front of their apartment building in The South Jamaica Houses in South Jamaica. Carol was the leader of the group, as well as their resident songwriter, who wrote original material for The Deltairs. Carol remembers getting together for a singing jam session with other groups living in the neighborhood: "We used to sit out on the benches and sing. We used to sing with the boy groups. Our brother group was The Five Sharps."

While attending Samuel Huntington Junior High School, The Deltairs did a lot of work producing their own shows, both at the school and at the youth center in their neighborhood. All their friends from the neighborhood would attend. As the young ladies entered high school, they honed their singing skills on standards like "Danny Boy" and "You'll Never Walk Alone," the latter winning them the honors of second place at a talent show for The Boys and Girls Club in Brooklyn.

Prior to The Deltairs recording, they formed an association with bandleader and producer Al Browne. Browne had started in the music business in the 1940s with a small combo. By the mid-50s, Browne conducted an orchestra and was working with many groups popular in the New York City area. Carol met him at her place of employment. She recalls that he encouraged the group to perform and offered them the opportunity to sing with his band, "Al used to work for the Workman's Compensation Board and I worked there, too. I told him about my group and he asked us to sing at a club. He took my word that I had a good group. He had a band and we used to sing with his band at different places, like The Baby Grand on Eastern Parkway in Brooklyn."

Through an arrangement made by Browne, The Deltairs first recording was with Ed Portnoy's Ivy Records. The group had Carol's originals that they had rehearsed, but had never performed in public. For recording, Carol selected a song at random from a roster of tunes that the quintet was rehearsing.

"Lullaby of The Bells" begins with the sedate resonance of a guitar and chimes. The

THE DELTAIRS

WELLS-BAUM
HY 1-6281

The Deltairs, 1957, (L-R) Carol Stansbury, Shirley Taylor, Barbara Thompson, Thelma Stansbury, Barbara Lee.

listener is tranquilized almost before the song begins. Barbara Lee's resounding bass imparts the vocal introduction and the group's warbling harmonies smoothly carry the song, as does Barbara Thompson's soprano lead. A haunting saxophone weaves in and out of the whispering blend of voices. A summer breeze couldn't make the listener feel any more composed.

An uptempo rocker, "It's Only You Dear," co-written Al Browne and Oliver Hall, graces the B-side. It features an exchange of responses between the group and the bass. The experience of Al Browne's orchestra shows in the production of the two sides. Browne was no novice when it came to showcasing group singers without compromising the presence of his band. Many vocal groups records by The Crests, The Miller Sisters and The Heartbeats benefited by the inclusion of Al Browne's orchestra. The Deltairs were no exception. Carol's divine composition of "Lullaby Of The Bells" became a staple on New York radio in the summertime of 1957. Naturally, the group was elated when they heard "Lullaby of The Bells" on the radio: "We were excited about hearing it. I think we were in one of our houses when we heard it. We were screaming and carrying on."

On the strength of "Lullaby of The Bells," The Deltairs made the rounds on the Chitlin Circuit, performing at the Apollo Theater in New York, the Uptown in Philadelphia, and the Howard in Washington, D.C. They performed alongside other luminaries like Jackie Wilson, The Moonglows, Bo Diddley and Big Maybelle. Carol's mother made many of their stunning outfits. According to observers at concerts that featured The Deltairs, these five majestic young ladies appeared in green velvet gowns, highlighted only by stage lighting. It was as if their presence was a reverie, like shadows seen by a child already half asleep.

The Deltairs' next single for Ivy was "Standing At The Altar." Some vocal arrangements from "Lullaby . . ." were prescribed for this strolling number, also written by Carol. A mambo flavored number, "I Might Like It" was the intended A-side, written by George Weiss, who would later write for The Jaynetts. Neither song met with the success of the first single. Also absent from this single was the creative input of Al Browne's band, although Carol doesn't recall any other band's backing besides Browne's.

Ed Portnoy had been managing the group, but The Deltairs were not happy with his business practices.

After a year, they left Ivy Records and went over to the London subsidiary, Felsted Records. At Felsted, they recorded the amiable "Who Would Have Thought It" in 1958.

With no success from this recording effort, the group moved on. Their next collaboration was with singer/songwriter Lincoln Chase for his small Hamilton label. One single, "You're Such A Much," was released, but to the group's surprise, the label credited the quintet as The Tranquils. The name change was probably an attempt by the record label to avoid confrontation over the name "Deltairs." After only four singles, The Deltairs did not make any subsequent recordings.

Despite their absence in the studio, The Deltairs continued to perform, appearing at local nightspots and in talent contests. Not satisfied with the business acumen of others, Carol began managing the group, getting them premium bookings at Jerry's Tip Top Supper Club in Queens, opening for the immortal Sammy Davis Jr. For these venues, the ladies called on their ability to handle standards and exercised their vocal versatility by switching parts in order to vary the overall sound and potential of the group. Over time, other commitments like marriages and families took over their lives, marking an end to the career of The Deltairs.

In 1973, Carol opened Karizma Studio, a cultural arts center that held classes in modeling, dance, karate, sewing, drama and exercise. The studio, located in Jamaica, Queens, was open for nine years. In 1988, Carol Stansbury Johnson moved from New York to Virginia, giving modeling classes and producing fashion shows. Consequently, she opened her own beauty salon, as well as starting her own line of face and body products called Emage-1, which she runs with her son and her niece. Carol also models and trains other models to work in fashion shows. Thelma Stansbury Lemon also moved south, settling in Maryland. The other members of The Deltairs still live in the New York area. Carol reflects positively on her tenure as a Deltair, "We had fun. We were all very musically talented and had fun. Our voices blended as one and the harmonies were tight."

Lovers can still close their eyes and lean together, listening to the vanguard of carillons giving way to five virtuous voices chiming an emphatic "ding dong." Sweet dreams.

The Deltairs Discography

45s	Label	Number	Year
Lullaby of The Bells/It's Only You Dear	Ivy	101	1957
Standing At The Altar/I Might Like It		105	1958
Who Would Have Thought It/You Won't Be Satisfied	Felsted	8525	
(as The Tranquils)			
You're Such A Much/One Billion, Seven Million And Thirty Three	Hamilton	50005	1958

The Dixie Cups

Members:

(1964-67) Barbara Ann Hawkins
Rosa Lee Hawkins
Joan Marie Johnson

There wasn't a time in the spring of 1964 that one could escape the soft sounds of young female voices emanating from every radio. The Dixie Cups, a trio of young Louisiana ladies who came to New York in search of music industry success, were singing about getting married. Not only did they triumph; they recorded one of the most enduring female group anthems of all time.

Barbara Ann Hawkins, Rosa Lee Hawkins and Joan Marie Johnson started singing at a young age, just for fun. Their hometown of New Orleans, Louisiana was an enviable place to be for musical influences, with jazz and blues abounding from every nook and cranny.

As The Mel-Tones, the young ladies started singing at various events around town, and sang backup for their close friend, Art Neville of The Neville Brothers. Drummer Joe Jones noticed them at a talent show. Jones thought highly of the sound of the young group and decided to try striking a deal for them in New York. Jones had a hit single in 1960 called "You Talk Too Much." The song was originally released on the local Ric label, then was picked up for national distribution by Roulette Records. It was then that Jones became associated with George Goldner. In 1964, Goldner became associated with producers Jerry Leiber and Mike Stoller, who were thinking of starting a new label to promote their productions.

Jones didn't contact Leiber and Stoller immediately. He called around to other producers that he had met while in New York, like Sylvia Robinson. Eventually, Jones negotiated the deal with Goldner and The Mel-Tones were on their way. The only remaining loose end was to get the girls' parents to agree to let the trio come to New York. With their parents' blessings, the group arrived in New York in early 1964.

Songwriters Ellie Greenwich and Jeff Barry had worked with Leiber and Stoller while producing for United Artists Records. The husband and wife team was signed to Leiber and Stoller's Trio Music company. Their next assignment for Leiber and Stoller was to come up with a hit for the new group from New Orleans. Ellie and Jeff had worked on a song with Phil Spector called "Chapel of Love." Spector had recorded the song with The Ronettes, The Crystals and Darlene Love, but was not satisfied with any of the versions he recorded with his artists. Since Ellie and Jeff held two-thirds of the writing credit, they decided to try out the song on The Mel-Tones. Barbara tells that, initially, when the songwriting duo played the song for them, they weren't impressed,

"They said, 'we have some songs for you to hear.' They played it for us on the piano and we said, 'Do you want us to sing that?' When they said yes, we said, 'Is that the way you want us to sing it?' Ellie said, 'No, sing it like you want to.' We decided to sing 'Chapel of Love' the way it was recorded."

It was also suggested that the group change its name from The Mel-Tones to Little Miss and The Muffets, but by the time their first single hit the stores, the group from Dixie was aptly billed as The Dixie Cups. Only after the single was finished, was the decision made to place it with Red Bird Records, the name of Leiber and Stoller's new label. The new company had released only one other single so far, an instrumental. "Chapel of Love" would establish Red Bird in the industry. The song's production was straightforward, with demure bells and accenting horns. The group alternated between relenting unison and gentle harmonies. Fellow label mate Alvin Robinson was the guitar player. The Dixie Cups had returned to New Orleans when the single started to pick up airplay, "We just happened to be listening to the radio and we heard it. That's when we got the call from Leiber and Stoller to come back; we had a hit on our hands."

Ellie says that Phil Spector balked when he was told that "Chapel of Love" would be recorded and released. He did not, however, try to release a competing version, as he had done with The Crystals' version of "All Grown Up," when a version by The Exciters was scheduled for release. No other version of "Chapel of Love" existed on vinyl until the LP, "Presenting The Fabulous Ronettes," was released at the end of 1964. As Barbara recalls, "The Dixie Cups' version shot to number one all over the country by the summertime of 1964, right in the middle of The British Invasion, "Chapel of Love" broke through The Beatles' chart items and reclaimed the charts for American groups."

Although Joe Jones received production credits for "Chapel of Love," Ellie and Jeff actually produced and The Dixie Cups came up with the arrangement, with help from Wardell Quezerque. Earl King Johnson's "Ain't That Nice" appeared as the B-side. The next single, an equally warm, melodious tune, also sported the Leiber and Stoller production label. Like "Chapel of Love," "People Say" also featured sparse arrangements and decorous vocals. The group almost recites the adolescent lyrics deftly provided by Greenwich and Barry. This song also reached the top 20. The next two singles

The Dixie Cups, 1964, (L-R) Barbara Ann Hawkins, Joan Marie Johnson, Rosa Lee Hawkins.

"You Should Have Seen The Way He Looked At Me" and "Little Bell" did not climb as high on the national charts, but enjoyed a positive reception, both landing on the local charts in New York and in nearby regions.

The Dixie Cups were soon appearing on all the popular tours, including Dick Clark's Caravan of Stars. They made guest appearances on teen dance shows like Lloyd Thaxton and on Clay Cole, where they not only sang, but also participated in the many skits Cole would perform for the television audience. The girls wore many outfits, appearing in alluring stretch pants and high heels or Native American costumes.

Their live stage shows usually contained a little bit more of the down home qualities they portrayed in their native New Orleans, in addition to the images captured by their hits. One song that clearly identified them with their Louisiana roots was their final hit for Red Bird. "Iko Iko," a traditional New Orleans folk song, was recorded almost by accident at the tail end of a recording session. The song is done acappella, with the exception of a calypso box and a few other impromptu percussive instruments. At first, "Iko Iko" was a hit in Europe before hitting in America, but soon made its mark on American shores.

Initially, Earl King Johnson's "I'm Gonna Get You Yet" appeared as the B-side. On subsequent pressings, the Barry-Greenwich composition of "Gee Baby Gee" appears as the B-side. The group had only one album entitled "Chapel of Love," repackaged as "Iko Iko" in 1965.

The Dixie Cups were enjoying their success as a result of the efforts at Red Bird, but Joe Jones was not satisfied with his lot at the company. He had secured a production deal at ABC-Paramount Records that would give writing, arranging and production credit to him. Wardell Quezerque came on board sharing co-arranging credits with Jones. Jones continually made deals like this without the knowledge or consent of the group. When The Dixie Cups found out what had happened and that they were no longer signed to Red Bird, they were anxious about their future. They knew the track record of Leiber, Stoller, Greenwich and Barry. They had no idea what would be in store for them now. Their worst suspicions would be confirmed within the next few months of 1965.

By mid-1965, Joe Jones had taken The Dixie Cups from Red Bird and brought them to ABC-Paramount, as per his agreement with the label. Red Bird was moving full speed ahead with the group whose success would eclipse every other act on the roster, The Shangri-Las. As a signal to the departure of The Dixie Cups, Red Bird reflexively responded by issuing one belated single, a reworking of The Ronettes', "Why Don't They Let Us Fall In Love,"

retitled for the hook line, "Gee The Moon Is Shining Bright." This was coupled with the recycled, "I'm Gonna Get You Yet." The two sides had appeared on The Dixie Cups' LPs. The single went nowhere.

Jones quickly discovered his ill-fated move after a few weeks at ABC-Paramount. The first Dixie Cups release was an unsuccessful attempt at capitalizing on the allure of "Iko Iko." "Two Way Poc A Way" did not possess the spontaneity of "Iko Iko." A series of less successful singles followed, including the incredulous "ABC Song." None of these singles were featured in The Dixie Cups' live act. The Red Bird hits were what the audiences wanted to hear. In fact, the group performed songs deliberately aimed to refrain from the image of the ABC-Paramount singles. Despite an LP entitled, "Flying High," the balloon was steadily losing air. The group was also fed up with what they saw as Joe Jones' increasingly dubious business practices.

Barbara feels that Red Bird also exercised some of its industry muscle; "I don't know what went on with ABC-Paramount. We didn't have a chance at ABC because of Joe. The reason the records didn't do as well was because they were pulled. Once Red Bird talked to ABC, the records didn't get a chance to do anything."

The Dixie Cups continued on the cabaret circuit in New York until 1968, when the group decided to pack up and return home to New Orleans. Although The Dixie Cups did not record after 1967, they continued to perform in concert. The Dixie Cups have performed on stage with other renowned New Orleans artists like The Neville Brothers and Irma Thomas. Throughout the 1970s and 1980s, they lent their musical skills to countless concerts and benefits.

They had parted ways with Joe Jones, who persistently tried to stop the group from using their name. Jones had laid claim to the name, although he had no legal hold. For years, his claim prevented The Dixie Cups from performing at prestigious venues like the New Orleans World's Fair.

Finally, someone called his bluff. After briefly going by the augmented spelling of "Dixi Kups," they finally won out. Joan Marie Johnson retired from the music business in the late 1960s. Barbara Ann and Rosa Lee are still going strong, having sung to audiences in just about every state in the union. Barbara now runs the business of The Dixie Cups, keeping a watchful eye on the fruits of their labors. "Chapel of Love" has been an enduring recording for many years, marked as the song for all whom have decided to take the big step. "Chapel Of Love" evokes ardent thoughts among those who recall when they walked down that wedding aisle—ain't that nice?

The Dixie Cups Discography

45s

	Label	Number	Year
Chapel of Love/Ain't That Nice	Red Bird	10-001	1964
People Say/Girls Can Tell		10-006	
You Should Have Seen The Way He Looked At Me/No True Love		10-012	
Little Bell/Another Boy Like Mine		10-017	
Iko Iko/I'm Gonna Get You Yet		10-024	1965
Iko Iko/Gee Baby Gee		10-024	
Gee The Moon Is Shining Bright/I'm Gonna Get You Yet		10-032	
Two Way Poc-A-Way/That's Where It's At	ABC-Paramount	10692	
What Goes Up, Must Come Down/I'm Not The Kind of Girl		10715	
ABC Song/That's What The Kids Said		10755	
Love Ain't So Bad/Daddy Said No	ABC	10855	1966

LPs

	Label	Number	Year
Chapel of Love	Red Bird	20-100	1964
Iko Iko		20-103	1965
Flying High	ABC-Paramount		1966

Nella Dodds

Is it possible for a fourteen-year old girl to influence the decision of a major record company? It is when she's decided to effectively cover one of its songs. High school freshman Nella Dodds had that distinction during her brief, but creative career in the mid-1960s. Her record company aptly provided her with female groups to augment her sweet, quintessential sound.

Nella Dodds was born Donzella Pettijohn in Havre de Grace, Maryland, the town on the Susquehanna River that also brought the music world soul singer Arthur Conley. According to disc jockey Sam Carson, Donzella was only fourteen in 1964 when she accompanied her uncle and his group to New York to pitch and record some songs he had written. It was their intention to sing the songs for prospective record executives. Upon arriving in New York, Donzella's uncle made the rounds to the various record companies on Broadway. One stop that proved fruitful was at Scepter/Wand Records, home of The Shirelles, Maxine Brown, Dionne Warwick, Chuck Jackson and a host of other successful artists. While the

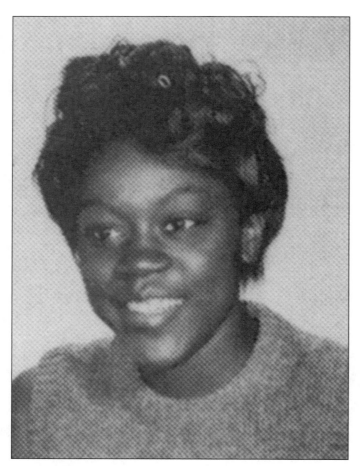

Teenage Nella Dodds in high school, 1965. (Photo courtesy of Sam Carson)

group was trying to sell songs, Donzella was hanging around the office, singing to herself.

Record mogul Florence Greenberg, the owner of the Scepter/Wand complex, overheard Donzella leisurely vocalizing as she waited for her uncle's group to finish taking care of business. Florence Greenberg discerned a distinguishing quality in Donzella's voice. Greenberg told Donzella's uncle that she couldn't use the songs or the group, but she would like to record Donzella. This was certainly an unexpected turn of events. It seems the impetus of the trip had changed. Donzella was nonplussed, but excited at the thought of recording. Florence Greenberg's offer was accepted. Donzella was given a few songs for rehearsal and asked to return.

Not long after her maiden voyage to New York, the day came for Donzella's first recording session. She brought with her much enthusiasm, but more importantly, she was armed with potential material to record. In Donzella's possession was an LP by a group that had kicked Motown Records into high gear just a few months before. Donzella had in her hands a copy of the album, "Where Did Our Love Go," by The Supremes.

The Detroit trio was riding a crest, having had a number one hit with the title track and with "Baby Love," now on the charts, and soon to be number one. Donzella was interested in recording a cut from the album entitled, "Come See About Me." Donzella's voice contained some of the tonality of a voice like Diana Ross, right down to the slightly nasal attribute that identified Ross. Donzella felt the song was right for her and the producers concurred. "Come See About Me" was recorded with the instrumentation almost perfectly matching the original Motown track. The session was complete with a female backing group, a feature that would grace most of Donzella's future recordings. It was flipped with a Kenny Gamble composition, the sentimental "You Don't Love Me Anymore."

Within a few weeks, "Come See About Me" entered the Hot 100 and was gaining airplay around Baltimore and Philadelphia, and showed promise for attention in other major cities as well. It was Greenberg who changed her name to the shortened "Nella Dodds" before the single's release.

Nella's first recording procured everyone's attention. Sam Carson remembers the administration at Havre de Grace High School taking pride in Nella's work by broadcasting "Come See About Me" over the public address system. As fate would have it, the version also caught the attention of Berry Gordy, who was not going to be beaten on the charts with his own material, especially with something he had not considered for single release. Motown rush-released The Supremes' version of "Come See About Me," their momentum still speeding with "Baby Love" having reached the top spot.

Since any record bearing the Motown label was like a gold doubloon, the deejays promptly forgot about

Nella's version and played the original. It breezed past Nella's rendition, which had halted in the Top 80. The impromptu Supremes single became the third of five number one singles in a row for the rallying group. Despite this defeat for Nella, there was still confidence in her style and ability, so productions for the young teen continued.

Although her initial single had been sidetracked, Nella's producers thought it best to stay inside the parameters of the Motown sound-alike arena. Nella's second single was a swinging, light-sounding number called "Finders Keepers, Losers Weepers," similar to the sounds of Mary Wells and Chicago singer Jackie Ross. Its flip, "A Girl's Life," was also cast in true pseudo-Motown style, borrowing cues from The Miracles' hit, "That's What Love Is Made Of." Nella had local success in New York with this one, albeit briefly. Since her recordings were regionally popular and, because of her age, personal appearances by the young artist were restricted to weekends. The session that produced "Come See About Me" was recorded in New York. Afterwards, Nella recorded in Philadelphia. Her recordings were joint ventures of Wand Records and the producing and writing efforts of Kenny Gamble, Jimmy Bishop and Luther Randolph under their Dynodynamic Productions, with the association of Johnny Stiles and Weldon MacDougal III. This group of associates was on the verge of forming its own record labels, Arctic and Harthon, as well as leasing productions out to more established labels like Scepter/Wand and Cameo/Parkway. Bishop also became Nella's manager. For the third single, the production team came up with another play on idioms called "Ps and Qs." Stylistic approaches more akin to Philadelphia productions were on the horizon.

Nella's next single was destined to send everyone to the dance floor. "Come Back Baby," written by Kenny Gamble and Jimmy Bishop, is more in keeping with elements present in many East Coast productions. The song opens with a heralding saxophone, and is further augmented by flutes, violins and prominent percussion, keeping Dynodynamic Productions at the productive forefront with groundbreaking singles, which would continue with future recordings by The Victors and Eddie Holman. The forceful dance tune was flipped with the mild "Dream Boy," and released in 1965. Two more recordings followed in 1966 and early 1967, including an endearing version of Carla Thomas' "Gee Whiz." Upon her graduation from high school, Nella decided to turn her attentions to other aspirations and retired from the music business.

Today, Donzella is a minister in the Baltimore area. She holds a special fondness for her brief recording career and the fact that her good taste in songs prompted a major resolve from a record industry giant.

Nella Dodds Discography

45s	Label	Number	Year
Come See About Me/You Don't Love Me Anymore	Wand	167	1964
Finders Keepers, Losers Weepers/A Girl's Life		171	
Ps and Qs/Your Love's Back		178	1965
Come Back Baby/Dream Boy		187	
Gee Whiz/Maybe Baby		1111	1966
Honey Boy/I Just Gotta Have You		1136	1967

The Emotions

Members:

(1965-70) Jeanette Hutchinson
Sheila Hutchinson
Wanda Hutchinson

(1970-74) Theresa Davis
Sheila Hutchinson
Wanda Hutchinson

(1974-77) Jeanette (Hutchinson) Hawes
Sheila Hutchinson
Wanda Hutchinson

(1977-85) Pamela Hutchinson
Sheila Hutchinson
Wanda Hutchinson

(1985-87) Adrianne Harris
Sheila Hutchinson
Wanda (Hutchinson) Vaughn

The EMOTIONS

The Emotions, 1970, (L-R) Sheila Hutchinson, Wanda Hutchinson, Theresa Davis. (Photo courtesy of Yellowlinda, Inc.)

Ever wonder what the magic garden would sound like with mother earth singing three-part harmony? Look no closer than the cherubic sounds of The Emotions. This sister act cut their teeth on Gospel tunes and grew into three young ladies who transformed their style from its Gospel roots to smooth sensible songs with advice about love, life, and womanhood.

The Emotions were sisters from Chicago who began their singing careers as little girls, part of a gospel trio with their father, who played guitar. Wanda, Sheila and Jeanette were called The Hutchinson Sunbeams. The girls and their dad traveled to various churches, singing popular Gospel tunes for the congregations. They developed quite a reputation in the Gospel community, appearing on local Gospel television programs. Joe Hutchinson recognized the talent in his daughters and knew one day they would be appreciated on a much larger scale.

When the girls became young ladies, the family unit moved easily from Gospel into soul in the mid-1960s. As teenagers, the sisters already had their own brand of crisp, high harmonies, which they exercised at their first recording of secular music. They had much practice, because their father rehearsed them on the classics as well as Gospel.

As an accomplished, self-taught musician, Joe Hutchinson also wrote songs for his daughters. It was at this time that dad decided to stay out of the performing end of things and take on the role of manager, as well as songwriter. The Emotions began their recording career in secular music with one single for the Vee Jay subsidiary, Tollie, the pleasant "Good Old Days," billed as The Sunbeams. Their dad suggested that they call themselves The Emotions, since that is precisely from where they drew their vocal power. The Tollie single didn't attract much attention, but the talents of The Emotions didn't go unnoticed. In 1967, the independent Brainstorm Records picked up the trio. Here, they released the frenetic "I Can't Stand No More Heartaches," backed by the Chicago styled, "You'd Better Get Pushed To It," written by the elder Hutchinson. Brainstorm Records eventually was absorbed into Twin Stacks Records in 1968. The Emotions recorded five sides for the label, including the emphatic "Brushfire," and the heartfelt "Never Let Me Go." With distribution by the Bell Records organization, the three singles were widely available to appreciative audiences.

The Emotions' recordings were different from other group efforts because they were formulated mainly from the impetus of group harmony, with intermittent leads, so everyone had a chance to be heard as a soloist, thereby varying the sound. The Emotions' intricate weaving in and out of the high harmonies amidst the diversified lyrical content identifies the different sentiments of love, joy, reflection, regret, passion and guilt, all the feelings their name suggests. The emotive qualities of their alpine voices did not come from street smarts, but from strong, down-home sensibilities. It was through these insights that The Emotions were picking up a rapidly increasing audience that followed their live act, even if their records weren't selling in high volume. It was through one of their personal appearances that an offer was made to take The Emotions' recording career to another level.

Earthier sounds in soul were gaining more and more popularity in the mainstream. Stax Records in Memphis had developed quite a reputation in this vein by the late 1960s. The label sported such soul luminaries as The Mad Lads, Otis Redding, Carla and Rufus Thomas, William Bell, Sam & Dave, Booker T. & The MGs, Jeanne & The Darlings and Isaac Hayes. Heartfelt soul was the main ingredient in the recordings laid down at Muscle Shoals Studios, served as a down-home dish like fried chicken with collard greens. The Emotions were asked to join the roster of acts flocking to Stax Records to match their talents with the capabilities of the core of musicians recording this raw brand of R&B. The Emotions signed and were placed on Volt Records in 1969.

The first single released by the trio was "So I Can Love You," produced by Isaac Hayes and David Porter. The

The Emotions, topping the charts in 1976, (L-R) Jeanette, Sheila and Wanda.

inviting tune, penned by Sheila, made both the pop and R&B charts. Other successful singles followed, like the catchy "The Best Part Of A Love Affair," the guilt-ridden "Stealing Love" and the light "Heart Association." Each recording covered so many different angles on a love theme, that The Emotions seemed more like actresses than singers, playing a different part in every new musical anecdote.

The spiritual effect of Emotions singles was that of a boat ride, with the waves carrying the listener up and down, with sudden swells between relaxing swings. Among all the ups and downs felt in their music, one can't help hearing the strength and fortitude in the voices of The Emotions, no matter how much of a picture of devotion or despair they paint. A changing of the ranks had occurred in 1970 when Jeanette (now Hawes) left to have a baby. Theresa Davis, a former member of Our Ladies of Soul, replaced her and the group didn't miss a step.

During 1971 and 1972, more singles scanned the range of passions, from the innocence of "Show Me How" and "From Toys To Boys" to the despair of "Blind Alley" and "Running Back and Forth." The group also recorded interesting seasonal tunes like "Black Christmas" in 1970 and "What Do The Lonely Do At Christmas?" in 1973. The Emotions consistently hit the R&B charts and there seemed no end to their tenure at the Stax/Volt complex. The sweet sounding "Put A Little Love Away," opened 1974, followed by "Baby I'm Through." Altogether, The Emotions released seventeen singles and numerous LPs for the Stax/Volt empire. The group was shocked when they were told that the company was faltering and would cease production. Theresa Davis recorded one single as a soloist for Stax before the label shut its doors in 1975.

The Emotions continued with their live act during the mid-70s, especially since they were now without a record label. Jeanette had rejoined the group in 1975. It wasn't long after the touring started again that the ladies were introduced to Maurice White of Earth, Wind and Fire, who expressed an interest in working with the group. The first joint effort of The Emotions and EWF produced the LP, "Flowers," which yielded the double-sided hit "I Don't Want To Lose Your Love/Flowers." The updated showcase of the fabulously skyward harmonies of The Emotions, combined with the driving dance beats of EWF, reckoned the group with the next generation of R&B enthusiasts. The Emotions had significant input on this production as writers and vocal arrangers.

Contemporary dance tunes and lofty ballads were interspersed with quick takes on their Gospel roots with "We Go Through Changes" and the perennial standard, "God Will Take Care Of You." "Flowers" was the appetizer to the enormously successful second LP, entitled "Rejoice," another nod to their Gospel beginnings. "Rejoice" contained the number one song of 1977. "The Best Of My Love" has all the ingredients of a supreme pop tune, a great lyrical hook, excellent production and instrumentation, and celestial vocals to carry the song. The popularity of The Emotions was so great that Fantasy Records, who had taken over all the Stax material, reissued the Volt LPs during 1978 and 1979.

The Emotions continued their association with EWF and joined with them at the end of the decade to produce one of the hottest dance singles of 1979. The infectious "Boogie Wonderland" kept all disco dancers on the floor for endless hours. The Emotions now toured with Earth, Wind and Fire, as well as with The Commodores. Jeanette bowed out of the tour when she became pregnant with her second child. Another Hutchinson sister, Pamela, replaced her for the tours and some recordings. The Emotions' association with EWF lasted until 1982. The trio recorded for the small, independent Red Label Records, producing the critically acclaimed singles, "You're The One" and "Are You Through With My Heart." In 1985, Adrianne Harris replaced Pamela. The Emotions then signed a contract at Motown Records. Unfortunately, their stay at Motown was not successful, so their tenure was brief. By this time, though, Wanda and Sheila were looking to change pace and settle down. Despite a vast following still on their heels, The Emotions elected to concentrate on family life in 1987.

Jeanette now spends her days writing songs and recording commercial jingles. Wanda and Sheila are also exercising their vocal prowess once again. The Emotions produced their own show in Los Angeles, chronicling their excursion from Gospel roots to their pop stardom. Joe Hutchinson passed away in the late 1980s. The Emotions' sincerity has shone proudly in all their recordings. Their sweet harmonies are the pulse of their versatile vocal abilities. The success of The Emotions' career is due to the fact that they were always a cohesive family unit, bound by endless energy, talent and grace, qualities that gave them the reserves to enable listeners everywhere to "rejoice."

The Emotions Discography

45s	Label	Number	Year
(as The Sunbeams)			
Good Old Days/Sing A Song	Tollie	9022	1965
The Emotions			
I Can't Stand No More Heartaches/You Better Get Pushed To It	Brainstorm	125	1967
Brushfire/Somebody New	Twin Stacks	126	1968
Never Let Me Go/I Can't Control These Emotions		129	
Brushfire/I Love You But I'll Leave You		130	
So I Can Love You/Got To Be The Man	Volt	4010	1969

45s

	Label	Number	Year
The Best Part Of A Love Affair/I Like It		4021	
Stealing Love/When Tomorrow Comes		4031	
Heart Association/The Touch Of Your Lips		4045	1970
Black Christmas/Inst.		4053	
You Make Me Want To Love You/What You See Is What You Get		4054	1971
If You Think It/Love Ain't Easy One Sided		4062	
Show Me How/Boss Love Maker		4066	
My Honey and Me/Blind Alley		4077	1972
I Never Could Be Happy/I've Fallen In Love		4083	
From Toys To Boys/I Call This Loving You		4088	
Runnin' Back (And Forth)/I Wanna Come Back		4095	1973
Runnin' Back (And Forth)/Peace Be Still		4100	
What Do The Lonely Do At Christmas/Inst.		4104	
Put A Little Love Away/I Call This Loving You		4106	1974
I Wanna Come Back/Baby, I'm Through		4110	
There Are More Questions Than Answers/Any Way You Look At It		4113	
Flowers/You've Got The Right To Know	Columbia	10347	1976
I Don't Wanna Lose Your Love/Flowers		10514	
The Best Of My Love/A Feeling Is		10544	1977
Don't Ask My Neighbors/Love's What's Happenin'		10622	
Shouting Out Love/Baby, I'm Through	Stax	3200	
Smile/Changes	Columbia	10791	1978
Walking The Line/Whole Lotta Shakin'		10828	
Time Is Passing By/Whole Lotta Shakin'		10828	
Any Way You Look At It/ Baby, I'm Through	Stax	3205	
What Do The Lonely Do At Christmas/Inst.		3215	
Ain't No Doubt About It/Walking The Line	Columbia	10874	1979
Laid Back/What Is The Name Of Your Love		11134	
Where Is Your Love/Laid Back		11205	
When You Gonna Wake Up/Turn It Out	Arc/Columbia	02239	1981
Here You Come Again/Now That I Know		02535	
You're The One/I Can Do Anything	Red Label	001	1984
You Know I'm The One/You're The Best		001-2	
You Know I'm The One/Are You Through With My Heart		101-3	
Miss Your Love/I Can't Wait To Make You Mine	Motown	1784	1985
Eternally/If I Only Knew Then		1792	

(w/Earth, Wind and Fire)

	Label	Number	Year
Boogie Wonderland/Inst.	Arc/Columbia	10956	1979

Theresa Davis

	Label	Number	Year
No Way/If I Were You	Stax	0247	1975

EPs

(w/Ramsey Lewis and Deniece Williams)

	Label	Number	Year
Three With Spirit–I Don't Wanna Lose Your Love	Columbia	BTS 36	1976

LPs

	Label	Number	Year
So I Can Love You	Volt	6008	1970
Untouched		6015	1971
Flowers	Columbia	34163	1976
Rejoice		34762	1977
Sunbeam		35385	1978
Sunshine	Stax	4100	
So I Can Love You		4110	
Untouched		4112	
Chronicle		4121	1979
New Affair	Columbia	37456	1981
Sincerely	Red Label	001-1	1984
If I Only Knew	Motown	6316	1985

The Exciters

Members:

(1961-74)   Carolyn (Carol) Johnson, Alto
Brenda Reid, Lead
Herbert Rooney, Tenor
Lillian Walker, Soprano

Sheer exuberance is always the central focus of every ounce of material The Exciters ever recorded. Their urgent lead and steady, gospel-like harmonies of the backgrounds weaved a special vocal web, capturing hoards of listeners with every note. They auditioned for Leiber and Stoller and had a monstrous hit with their first single. "Tell Him" was an immediate smash, written by another newcomer to the music scene, Bert Berns. Together, this team would reach a series of creative climaxes.

The Exciters formed in Jamaica, Queens in 1961. All of the young ladies, Brenda Reid, Sylvia Wilbur, Carolyn (Carol) Johnson and Lillian Walker, were still in high school. Brenda conveys that it was Lillian who had the desire to be in the music business: "We were all fifteen years old. Lillian is the one who started the group. It was her dream to be on the stage, Lillian and her friend, Sylvia Wilbur. They asked me because I had a piano, but I couldn't play. Carol got into the group after I got in."

Lillian was happy to finally meet someone who was as serious about singing as she and Sylvia were. The group began rehearsing at Brenda's house. Lillian and Sylvia knew that Brenda was interested, but didn't realize Carol wanted in until they heard her singing, "Sylvia and I were trying to start a group, but every time we would get somebody, they would only last a month or two. We were the only two that were serious. Brenda's mother got us together. She invited us to her house. Carol used to just sit there and listen to us sing. One day, Brenda went to the store and we stayed in the basement. Carol was singing quietly to herself. I said 'You sing?' She said yes, so I said, 'you want to be in the group?'

Carol was sure her time would come eventually; "I kind of figured that everybody knew. I assumed they knew I wanted to sing." Now that the quartet was solidified, rehearsals were at Brenda's house on a regular basis. A friend of theirs, Clayton "Dickie" Williams, who was also a singer, often came by to listen to the group rehearse. One day, another young man came by looking for Dickie, his friend, Herbert Rooney.

Herb was a songwriter, as well as a singer. He and Dickie had been a part of a local group, The Beltones. The group's recording

The Exciters, 1964, (L-R) Lillian Walker, Brenda Reid, Carol Johnson, Herbert Rooney. (Photo courtesy of Gordon Skadberg)

of "I Talk To My Echo" emanated from radios all over the New York area in 1957. Dickie and Herb were now members of The Masters. They had recently recorded "A Man Is Not Supposed To Cry" for George Goldner's End Records.

Herb heard them rehearsing in Brenda's mother's real estate office. Brenda remembers how, initially, Herb made light of their talents, "My mother's office was by the front door, where we rehearsed. Herb came by looking for Clayton. He pulled up in his 1957 Buick. He asked what we were doing. We said we were singing. He said, 'you call that singing?'

Of course, all the girls wanted to beat him. Herb explained that while he thought they had good voices, they were not singing like a group. Herb, Clayton and fellow Master Andrew Pope began coming by on a regular basis to help the girls with harmonies and arrangements and write original material for them. Herb was a few years older than the young ladies were, so they took full advantage of his experience and his talents. Soon, the quartet became known as The Masterettes, companion group to Herb's ensemble. The Masterettes accompanied The Masters to many local gigs. They even had a manager, Mr. Banks, the father of David Banks, another one of The Masters. After preparing the group with two songs, "Never Ever" with Sylvia leading, and "Follow The Leader," led by Brenda, Herb thought it was time the girls showcased their talents on the stage. Lillian remembers the long preparation for the day that The Masterettes would finally go public; "The Masters were popular in the community and they would take us to their shows. We wanted a show of our own. A couple of months went by. They rehearsed us every day. They finally told us we were ready."

The first gig for The Masterettes was at The Hillside Theatre in Queens, opening for The Masters, Baby Washington, Sam & Dave and fellow Jamaica residents, Shep & The Limelites. Brenda recalls the support that The Masterettes received from all their neighborhood friends: "A lot of our friends heard through the grapevine and came down to see the show. We had never sung in front of anybody before. We opened the show. We brought the house down."

Carol decided at that moment, she was exactly where she belonged, "Our first time on stage was very exciting and I knew it was what I wanted to do. I never desired to lead. I was satisfied with doing background."

Indeed, the response that The Masterettes garnered after their first appearance was the remuneration they were waiting for. When The Masters recorded their next single, they took The Masterettes with them. Both groups recorded for Cecil Bowen's Le Sage label, out of Brooklyn. The Masterettes recorded "Never Ever" and "Follow The Leader," the two songs they had performed at the show.

Now that The Masterettes were established with a single of their own, other opportunities came their way. Rennie Roker, the brother of Wally Roker of The Heartbeats, had approached the group backstage after the show at The Hillside and expressed an interest in the group joining the management team he formed with

Wally and orchestra leader Al Sears. Roker also wanted to introduce the group to the songwriting and production team of Jerry Leiber and Mike Stoller, forever fans of raw Rhythm and Blues, who were having immense success (ironically) with Jay and The Americans. The Masterettes were already signed with Mr. Banks. When they approached him about this new offer from Roker, he released them, having nothing to counteroffer.

The Masterettes were all set to take Roker's bid when Sylvia announced that she was leaving the group. Sylvia was to be married soon and this next step did not figure into her marriage plans. She was replaced with another singing friend, Penny Carter. This quartet, accompanied by Herb, who was now the group's spokesman and piano player, made their way to the door of producers Leiber and Stoller. For the audition, The Masterettes sang two of Herb's compositions, "I Feel" and "Nothing Beats A Try." The sincere and identifiable quality of the lead, coupled with the tight, blow harmonies struck a chord with the renowned producers. Carol is convinced that singing the originals helped cinch the audition, "When we went to the audition, we sang songs that Herb had written. I think that helped, because then they could hear our sound. You can't really hear a person's sound until you sing your own songs. Your own sound really develops when you have your own material."

Despite the marvelous material, Leiber and Stoller did not select any of Herb's songs for recording. The Masterettes were given three items as they left the audition that day. One was a contract for them to sign. The second item was a song called "Tell Him," a song recorded by Johnny Thunder (as Gil Hamilton). The tune had a catchy message, but had not gotten a positive reaction from the record buying public. The Masterettes did not think much of it, either. Lillian recollects that the girls tried to convince Herb that they didn't want to do it, "We couldn't wait to get out of the office and say we hated it. We said we'd stick together, but it never worked on Herbie. We'd go back to the office and tell them we don't like the song and they'd say, 'yeah, yeah, learn the song.' We almost missed it because we didn't even want to do the song."

The third item on Leiber and Stoller's agenda was to change the name of the group because they didn't want to run into problems over the name Masterettes, since the girls had recorded under it. The group was hereby christened The Exciters. The girls took their contracts home for their parents to sign. Right before the group was to record, though, Penny dropped out. She blamed it on her father not wanting to sign, but the group thinks she just got cold feet. Herb said he would fill in at the recording date. Since Herb sensed more opportunity knocking here than at The Masters' door, his presence as the fourth member quickly became permanent.

The assertive "Tell Him" was written by Bert Berns. Berns had been writing for about a year and singing as Russell Byrd, for Wand Records. He wrote "Tell Him" and credited the song to another one of his pseudonyms, Bert Russell. Bert found prosperity with his first writing effort, "A Little Bit Of Soap," recorded by The Jarmels in 1961. Teacho Wiltshire arranged The Exciters' records.

The Exciters, 1969, (L-R) Brenda, Carol, Lillian, Herb. (Photo courtesy of Gordon Skadberg)

The veteran orchestra leader's extensive use of strings sweetened the production, offsetting the church-like harmonies of the group. In a sea of "Should I?" or "Shouldn't I?" records for females, "Tell Him" had a message to forego the indecisiveness so apparent in songs tailored for girls. The lady conveys her feelings first hand. Brenda's confident voice sells the song. This exhilarative tune made it into the top five in early 1963.

Although the group was a quartet, there is no evidence of an outstanding male part on any Exciters records. Having a male in the group provided a unique visual image, since The Orlons were the only other group at the time with one male as a member. Herb Rooney was a tenor, and his voice fit right under Carol's alto and Lillian's soprano, providing a unified triad. Brenda's identifiable lead is the voice that inspired Dusty Springfield to leave her group, The Springfields, and become a soloist. Dusty had indicated in interviews that when she heard Brenda singing "Tell Him," she decided that was the kind of singing she wanted for herself. The Exciters were definitely a prized package.

After taking the pop charts by storm with "Tell Him," the group continued showcasing their blended voices with Brenda's inspirational lead on their next single. Leiber and Stoller went to another, relatively new and talented songwriter for the second recording, "He's Got The Power." Ellie Greenwich had been working with Leiber and Stoller for a few months. She penned the song with her partner, Tony Powers. Ellie has nothing but praise for Brenda's voice, categorizing her as a flawless performer.

Unfortunately, "He's Got The Power" did not chart high nationally, although it was a New York favorite. An LP was now in order for The Exciters. The production team showcased songs from both proven and promising songwriters of the day, among them, Ellie Greenwich, Burt Bacharach, Hal David and Van McCoy. Brenda and Herb also contributed as songwriters, showing that they could keep pace. The LP features their propelling song, "Remember Me" and the tender ballad, "Goodnight, So Long."

For the third Exciters single, the production team tried to return to the formula of "Tell Him" with the similar sounding "Get Him." When this formula yielded only a mild hit, Ellie and her new partner and husband, Jeff Barry, provided another single.

"Do Wah Diddy" was a driving rocker and a sure-fire hit for the group. Unfortunately the timing was bad, as the country was mourning the death of President Kennedy. The country was at a standstill and, as Brenda conveyed in a radio interview in 1989, no new, upbeat tunes were featured during this time. The song was covered a year later by Manfred Mann and became a number one hit for them.

While at United Artists, The Exciters recorded five singles and one LP, featuring wonderful versions of "It's Love That Really Counts" and "A Handful Of Memories," songs already attempted by Dionne Warwick, The Shirelles and Baby Washington, but given The Exciters' touch. Their last single for UA, "We Were Lovers," provided another cover for British Invasion artist Sandra Barry in 1965.

Another Greenwich/Barry composition that showed promise was "All Grown Up," but was left unreleased. Brenda and Herb were also shopping songs around to different record labels, hoping to get something placed. They often felt compelled to give up the publishing rights just to get the songs out there in the hope that someone would have a hit with one of them. Brenda and Herb's business relationship was now officially personal as well.

The Exciters signed with Morris Levy's Roulette Records in 1964, having parted ways with Leiber and Stoller due to management conflicts. This also precipitated a management change to Carmine Di Noia. While at Roulette, The Exciters worked with the production team that made hits for Elvis Presley, Hugo Peretti & Luigi Creatore.

The group scored a minor hit with their first Roulette single, a version of The Frankie Lymon and The Teenagers song, "I Want You To Be My Girl (Boy)." Three more singles, including two "Tell Him" sound-alikes, "Just Not Ready" and "There They Go" did not enter the national charts. Both Sammy Lowe and Teacho Wiltshire arranged the sessions at Roulette. Bert Berns was called in to produce their last single for Roulette. The Exciters would eventually follow Bert Berns to Bang Records in late 1965. Roulette released a belated compilation LP in 1966. Lillian relays that The Exciters were confident about their ability to land record deals, even though they had only one monster hit.

Producers knew of the group's talent and wanted the chance to produce their next big hit, "It seemed like it became a challenge that people were going to get a hit for us. We never had to go begging for a record deal. We'd say 'Exciters' and they'd say 'sign 'em up'."

Another perk for being a talented, versatile group was that The Exciters had the admiration of their contemporaries. Besides the American groups, this adoration came from the British Invasion groups as well. When one of the booking agents for The Beatles tour was hunting down records in Queens. He inquired about The Exciters after seeing their record album in a store. The owner hooked him up with Herb, who made arrangements for the group to meet the tour in San Francisco.

The Exciters were now part of The Beatles American tour in 1964, joining a brilliant lineup that included The Righteous Bros., Fats Domino, Clarence "Frogman" Henry and Jackie DeShannon. The Exciters found The Beatles to be like every other act on the tour, talented young people who enjoyed making music. Lillian reminisces about one leg of the tour where The Exciters, The Beatles and some of the other artists sat for hours talking about their musical influences: "We had a layover in Key West. The Beatles rented out the whole motor inn. About midnight, some people went up to the pool. We got into a big conversation about music and they told us about how they liked music by black singers. There was a room over to the side of the swimming pool. We would sing and they would play their instruments. They played jazz, classical, R&B, pop. They were blowing our minds with this talent. When we got back to New York, we knew no one could say they were only a little Rock & Roll band."

Another down home touch to this tour was the inclusion of Brenda's mom as a chaperone. She took film footage of everyone rehearsing on the airplane and whipped up batches of home cooked meals for everyone. Even though it seemed everyone sustained a high comfort level, a more nerve-racking element of the tour was dealing with the adoring, overzealous Beatles fans. One evening, according to Carol, The Exciters were awakened out of their sleep when some fans broke into their motel room looking for The Beatles, saying they heard the band was eating a late night snack in The Exciters' motel room: "We were sleeping and these girls were breaking into our apartment. One girl was Miss Teenage America, and she was with her mother. We just ushered them out. You'd be surprised how many parents were pushing their daughters to be with The Beatles. I was outraged."

After the tour, when The Beatles were in New York, The Exciters visited the band at The Plaza, armed with one of Mrs. Reid's meals for the fabulous four. The Exciters walked past the throngs of screaming fans and into the hotel. Malcolm, one of the tour managers, would meet the group at the front desk and escort them up to the room.

The Exciters were also part of another phenomenon, although a bit less celebrated than a Beatles tour in 1964. They were the first group to have videos made to accompany "Tell Him" and "He's Got The Power." This early form of the music video, called the scopotone, would roll inside of jukeboxes while the record played. Brenda relates how the group shot the video at a zoo in Paris, while on a tour. While filming at the lion's pit, which was not enclosed, the photographer had the bright idea to make the lion move by throwing pebbles at him, "A man named Mr. Miller had the idea for scopotone. We were at The Olympian Theatre in Paris. We were the first American group to do a video. We're pointing at the lions and they're looking at us and walking back and forth. Lillian and Mr. Miller jumped in this car and it was going around in a circle."

The pebbles hitting the lion caused it to run toward the singers. Mr. Miller and Lillian jumped into a nearby auto, causing the driver to panic and yell at them in rapid-fire French to get out. The group preferred to settle back in to the recording studio after this workout.

The first effort by The Exciters while at Bang Records was a version of Bert's first big success, "A Little Bit Of Soap." It had been a hit for The Jarmels in 1961 and a hit for Garnett Mimms in 1964. The Exciters' version reached the middle of the charts in early 1966, but climbed no higher. Berns was now at the helm, producing and Artie Butler was the arranger. Carol feels that Berns and The Exciters were a natural pairing, "We kind of seeked each other out. We had a good match. We had success with his first song and we thought we could recapture that."

Berns tried another tune for the second single. "You Better Come Home," previously recorded by The Isley Brothers, features trumpets and great guitar licks. The group rises to the occasion, singing over a production tailored more for a garage band than a vocal quartet. In fact, in the same year, a garage band called The Head Lyters recorded a version of "You Better Come Home" for Wand

Records. The Exciters' hybrid version was tightly executed. The Exciters' next two singles were released on the Shout subsidiary during 1966 and 1967. Writing credits go to Herb, Brenda and former fellow Beltone Andrew Pope, as well as Berns and Jerry Ragovoy. Brenda's dramatic delivery on "You Got Love" is a foreshadowing of Ragovoy's work by Janis Joplin.

Although there were no huge hits since "Tell Him," record companies still recognized the enormous talents of The Exciters and the potential for hit singles. Continuing their long association with Teacho Wiltshire, The Exciters signed to RCA in 1968. Songwriter and former Four Fellows member Larry Banks co-produced with Wiltshire. RCA recorded many vocal groups like The Chantels, Moonglows, Main Ingredient and Friends of Distinction during the time period of 1968-72. The label released two Exciters singles, including the frenetic, "Blowing Up My Mind," followed by their only LP for RCA, "Chitlins and Caviar." Anyone who ever suspected that Herb didn't really sing, can hear his soulful tenor on two cuts, "You Got Me" and "A Year Ago." With Brenda in the backgrounds, the group's power is increased. The LP won critical praise. With no hits, unfortunately, the group left RCA in 1970. Carol thinks more attention to their recordings would have put them over the top, "The RCA album never took off; we never got the airplay we should have gotten. I don't think they promoted it the way they said they would."

While concentrating their efforts on personal appearances, both in America and abroad, despite no hits in seven years, The Exciters moved on to Today Records, this time with Herb producing, releasing a single, "Life, Love and Peace," and another album, "Black Beauty."

This production featured timely musical innovations, like organs and wah-wah guitars. The group then moved to the reactivated Fargo Records, recording a soulful version of Gilbert O'Sullivan's tearful tune, "Alone Again, Naturally." The Exciters could not find chart success despite the relentless efforts of the group and their producers. The members were also going through personal life changes. In the early 1970s, Brenda took maternity leave and was replaced with her sister, Janice or with Penny Carter.

When Carol left, Herb and Lillian handled backgrounds as a duo. Eventually, The Exciters needed to be put aside in favor of other aspects of life. The act broke up in 1974. At the pace The Exciters were moving, Lillian states that everyone eventually needed a rest, "I became burned out. After awhile, I started to feel like a robot. The whole time I was in the group, I was never absent and never late."

Brenda and Herb Rooney, together since the earlier days of the group, continued recording as Brenda and Herb, working with British producer Ian Levine to record a song called "Reaching For The Best" in 1975, a fantastic song which was very popular in England. The singing duo reunited with Hugo & Luigi on their H&L record label in 1977. They recorded a few singles, including a superb disco version of "I Who Have Nothing," a song that The Exciters used to perform in their live act. A beautiful mid-tempo number, complete with recitations,

"Tonight I'm Gonna Make You a Star," was a song well suited to Brenda's voice.

This incarnation of the talents that were The Exciters showcased Herb as a vocalist as well. These ventures were undertaken in between raising their children, so Brenda & Herb remained a local act in the New York area. In the late 1980s, Brenda and Herb tried to revive The Exciters. They reformed the group using their children as vocalists and backup musicians. The revamped Exciters played an exuberant show at New York's Bottom Line and conducted numerous radio interviews.

In the early 1990s, Brenda again worked with Ian Levine and re-recorded "Reaching For The Best," as well as other tunes released only overseas. After this brief resurgence, Brenda retired to devote her life to her church. Herb Rooney passed away in the early 1990s. Brenda and Herb's son, Corey, is better known as the distinguished Mark C. Rooney, Senior Record Executive of Sony Music, overseeing such acts as Mary J. Blige, Mariah Carey and Mark Anthony.

Brenda continues with her work for the needy where she worships. Lillian is a guidance counselor for the New York public school system. Carol is an account clerk for G&G Retail in New York. The Exciters have appeared on WRHU's R&B Serenade with Gordon Skadberg and Frank Gengaro to share their recollections with the listening audience. The ladies have not ruled out the possibility of The Exciters' return to the stage.

The Exciters shaped a series of the most refreshing productions ever recorded on vinyl. Two important facts are a testament to the group's musical integrity; that they lasted longer than many vocal groups, especially when chart success was not always forthcoming, and that they were able to weather stylistic changes in popular music, never once sounding awkward or stale in the mix. The work of The Exciters holds up, play after play. Phenomenal talent will always stand the test of time.

The Exciters Discography

45s

	Label	Number	Year
as The Masterettes			
Never Ever/Follow The Leader	Le Sage	716	1961
The Exciters			
Tell Him/Hard Way To Go	United Artists	544	1962
He's Got The Power/Drama Of Love		572	1963
Get Him/It's So Exciting		604	
Do Wah Diddy/If Love Came Your Way		662	
We Were Lovers/Having My Fun		721	1964
I Want You To Be My Boy/Tonight, Tonight	Roulette	4591	
Just Not Ready/Are You Satisfied		4594	1965
Run Mascara/My Father		4614	
There They Go/I Knew You Would		4632	

45s

	Label	Number	Year
A Little Bit Of Soap/I'm Gonna Get Him Someday	Bang	515	
You Better Come Home/Weddings Make Me Cry		518	1966
You Got Love/Number One	Shout	205	
Soul Motion/You Know It Ain't Right		214	1967
If You Want My Love/Take One Step (I'll Take Two)	RCA	47-9633	1968
Blowing Up My Mind/Don't Know What You're Missing		47-9723	1969
Life, Love And Peace/--	Elephant V Ltd.	5	1970
Life, Love And Peace/Learning How To Fly	Today	1002	
Do What You Think Is Right/Don't It Just Make You Feel Good			1971
Alone Again, Naturally/--	Fargo	1400	1972
Brenda & Herb			
I Who Have Nothing	H&L	--	1977
Tonight I'm Gonna Make You A Star		4699	1978
The Beltones w/Herb Rooney			
I Talk To My Echo/Oof Oof	Hull	721	1957
The Masters w/Herb Rooney			
A Man Is Not Supposed To Cry/Look Out	End	1100	1961
Crying My Heart Out/I'm Searching	Le Sage	714	

LPs

	Label	Number	Year
Tell Him	United Artists	3264	1963
The Exciters	Roulette	25326	1966
Chitlins and Caviar	RCA	4211	1969
Black Beauty	Today	--	1971

CDs

	Label	Number	Year
Reaching For The Best	Hot Records	-- (import only)	1995

First Choice

Members:

(1972)   Rochelle Fleming, Lead
     Annette Guest
     Wardell Piper
     Mulaney Star

(1973)   Rochelle Fleming
     Annette Guest
     Wardell Piper

(1973-75)   Rochelle Fleming
     Annette Guest
     Joyce Jones

(1975-78)   Rochelle Fleming
     Annette Guest
     Ursula Herring

(1978-80)   Rochelle Fleming
     Annette Guest
     Debbie Martin

Biting commentaries with no-nonsense lyrics and a tough-as nails delivery. This is the attitude with which First Choice sold their social messages, compiling a powerful and cohesive string of hits. Their hit, "Armed and Extremely Dangerous," tells the listener that they'd better heed the warning or else.

First Choice formed at Overbrook High School in Philadelphia in 1970. Lead singer Rochelle Fleming, with good friends Annette Guest, Wardell Piper and Mulaney Star sang for fun at the somewhat famous Philadelphia high school. The gospel roots in their energetic voices are clearly heard. Rochelle grew up in a family where singing in their church choir was important . An audition for Georgie Woods at WDAS brought them to the attention of songwriters/producers Norman Harris and Allan Felder. The producers cut one single with the group, "This Is The House" which was released on Scepter Records in 1972. The single did not chart, so this marked the end of Mulaney's involvement in the group. However, the performance of this powerful unit proved that First Choice was a force to reckon with. Harris and Felder placed the next production with Thom Bell's Philly Groove Records. Philly Groove had scored with numerous records by The Delfonics.

The following session for First Choice, co-produced by manager Stan Watson and Norman Harris, yielded a wicked single, complete with sirens, bullhorns and full orchestration. "Armed and Extremely Dangerous" exploded onto urban radio. As the vocals enter, Rochelle's soaring, larger than life voice delivers the story with a street sensibility, while Annette and Wardell chant their agreement in the background.

Before the single had a chance to break out, Wardell exited the group. Wardell had success in the 1970s with the disco hit, "Captain Boogie." She was replaced by Joyce Jones. Meanwhile, the single generated enough enthusiasm to net the group an album. First Choice's first LP did very well, yielding two more singles, "Newsy Neighbors," and "Smarty Pants."

First Choice, 1973, (L-R) Annette Guest, Rochelle Fleming, Joyce Jones.

These popular singles exhibited the same qualities as "Armed . . ." and were still receiving airplay well into 1974.

The producers extended the instrumental breaks, giving the musicians, and vocalists, a chance to showcase their talents. These mixes were tailor-made for the underground dance club scene, not yet called "disco." The Philadelphia session men on the LP, "Armed and Extremely Dangerous," included, Norman Harris, Ron Baker, Earl Young, Roland Chambers and Bobby Eli, all just beginning to make their mark as the musicians who make up "the Sound of Philadelphia."

First Choice was now making the rounds of all the popular dance shows including "American Bandstand" and "Soul Train." The idea of the good girl loving the wrong man was such a strong image for the group, the producers kept it going with their next single and album. "The Player" fared well on the pop charts, although the LP did not yield as many hit singles. Again, the group apprises the listening audience of the escapades of fictitious friends and neighborhood characters, positioning themselves as urban narrators for accounts like "The Player" and "Guess What Mary Jones Did."

In 1975, Philly Groove's association with Bell ended. Warner Bros. Records picked up a distribution option. In the interim, Joyce Jones exited the group. She was replaced by Ursula Herring. For their only album for Warner Bros., "So Let Us Entertain You," a change in image had the ladies sporting gowns and feather boas. Stan Watson is credited as the producer of this project. One single, "Yes, Maybe No" received major airplay in the now burgeoning disco scene. The single did not have sufficient power to keep the group at the forefront of the 1970s music scene. The next album would take care of that.

During the mid-70s, discos rise in popularity prompted the recording industry to concentrate heavily on dance tracks. Producers of R&B artists were concerned because the uptempo soul singles had achieved a niche of their own, the dance charts (or the hot deejay action). Not only were good vocals expected to sell a song, dance mixes were becoming more extensive to keep crowds out on the dance floor. Since radio was still geared to the three minute single, extended dance tracks on albums meant more people would opt to buy the LP for the elongated mixes. Salsoul Records formed in late 1975 and early on, the label had a hit with a disco version of Helen O'Connell's standard, "Tangerine," by The Salsoul Orchestra.

Salsoul Records was owned by the Kayre Bros., Joe, Stan, and Ken. The label name was taken from a 1970s Joe Bataan single, recorded for their Mericana label. Salsoul was the musical blending of Salsa and Soul. Through orchestra leader Vince Montana, the New York based label had a direct link to Philadelphia talent, where Montana worked. Producers and songwriters like Norman Harris, Ron Kersey, Earl Young, Ron Baker, Ron Tyson and Allan Felder were writing and producing material for acts now signed to The Salsoul complex. Norman Harris' new label, Gold Mind, became a Salsoul affiliate.

Salsoul and Gold Mind were not only releasing LPs and 45s, but 12" 45rpm extended singles, previously dj onlys , now sold to the general public. The new labels boasted veteran soul singer Loleatta Holloway, her husband, Floyd Smith, The Salsoul Orchestra, and First Choice, whose new album, "Delusions" was released on Gold Mind. This LP contains cut after cut of musical extravaganzas. From this excitable LP came two monster dance singles, "Doctor Love" and "Let No Man Put Asunder." Metaphoric lyrical phrases abound and inescapable pulsations keep dancers on the dance floor. Invigorating backing vocals chant and Rochelle's lead ascends above it all.

Producers hitting upon the right formula were able to net club play for many of their artists at once. Disc jockeys at local clubs were becoming just as important as producers, stringing together beats for nonstop disco dancing. The radio was no longer the only medium to surmount. First Choice records conquered it all. "Delusions" and its singles stayed popular in the discos for almost a year and a half.

In the spring of 1978 "Delusions" momentum waned and Ursula left the group. Rochelle and Annette went back to their old Overbrook High School directory, remembering a fellow classmate, Deborah Martin, who became a member of Brenda and The Tabulations when Brenda Payton changed her backing group from all male to all female. Brenda again reconfigured her Tabulations in 1976. The opportunity to have someone experienced at group singing was a favorable one. In the fall of 1978, the single, "Hold Your Horses," was released without an LP.

For the next First Choice single, there was a notable change in the production lineup. German producers Thor Baldursson, Mat Bjoerklund and Pete Bellotte were brought in to put together the next First Choice product, along with dj turned master mixer, Tom Moulton. They were part of the European disco scene that seized the opportunity to corner the American dance music market after Donna Summer's huge hit, "Love To Love You," that Bellotte co-produced with Giorgio Moroder.

Hereafter, the sound achieved by these producers using heavily synthesized sounds was called Eurodisco. This sound, combined with the vocal talents of First Choice, produced a rival LP to "Delusions."

In early 1979, "Hold Your Horses" was released. Almost every track on the LP was released either as a 45 or 12" dance single. Also, numerous remix packages were available to club jockeys. "Double Cross" and "Love Thang" were the most popular songs from the LP.

Through all the mixes and re-mixes of the records, Rochelle, Annette, and Debbie's voices wore it well. They were sometimes crying out, sometimes humming, all with deliberate tones conveying messages of love, both gained and lost, in a decidedly fiery fashion, complementing what disco was about, physical and emotional love, passionate movement and body language. Six years after their debut, First Choice's limitless prowess was stronger than ever.

As the 1970s became the 1980s, new sounds were infiltrating disco music. Faster tempos and Rock-influenced instrumentation were recognizable in dance music. Artists in music areas other than R&B wanted part of the lucrative action.

First Choice's final album for Gold Mind was decidedly mellower than the tracks on "Hold Your Horses." One track, "Pressure Point," received advanced airplay in late 1979. When the album came out, only "Breakaway" and "I Can Show You" approached the vitality of the group's previous efforts. Sadly, the album did not create the amount of excitement that was First Choice. This was their last recording.

Rochelle Fleming went on to have a well-deserved solo career, cutting intermittent singles between 1985 and 1994. She has a large following in the gay community. Rochelle performs at clubs and colleges on the eastern seaboard. First Choice staged a rare appearance in 1986 at the Gay Pride Parade In Harlem, NY. Annette Guest and Joyce Jones are now involved with their churches. Jones has recorded some gospel material. Bits of First Choice recordings, especially "Let No Man Put Asunder," are sampled in songs by contemporary artists. Because of this, there is a renewed interest in First Choice material. First Choice is lauded as one of the most influential and trend-setting female vocal groups of the 1970s. Their influence is extensive and well deserved. Their fans have chosen wisely.

First Choice Discography

45s

	Label	Number	Year
This Is The House/One Step Away	Scepter	12347	1972
Armed and Extremely Dangerous/Gonna Keep On Lovin' Him	Philly Groove	175	1973
Smarty Pants/One Step Away		179	
Newsy Neighbors/This Little Woman		183	1974
The Player/Part 2		200	
Guilty/Wake Up To Me		202	
Love Freeze/A Boy Named Junior		204	
The Player/Part 2		250	
Yes, Maybe No/Gotta Get Away	Warner Bros.	8214	1976
Let Him Go/First Choice Theme		8251	
Doctor Love/I Love You More Than Before	Gold Mind	4004	1977*
Indian Giver/Love Having You Around		4009	
Hold Your Horses/Now I've Thrown It All Away		4017	1978
Double Crossed/Gamble On Love		4019	1979
Love Thang/Great Expectations		4022	
Breakaway/House For Sale		4023	1980
Let No Man Put Asunder/remix (12" only)		397	1983

*Some singles were available as 12" extended mixes.

Rochelle Fleming

	Label	Number	Year
Love Itch/--	Prelude	700	1985
Danger/--	Cutting	300	1994

Wardell Piper

	Label	Number	Year
Captain Boogie/Long Version	Midsong Int'l.	1001	1978
Super Sweet/Don't Turn Away From Me Baby		1005	1979

LPs

	Label	Number	Year
Armed and Extremely Dangerous	Philly Groove	1400	1973
The Player		--	1974
So Let Us Entertain You	Warner Bros.	2934	1976
Delusions	Gold Mind	9500	1977
Hold Your Horses		9502	1979
First Choice		--	1980

Wardell Piper

	Label	Number	Year
Wardell Piper	Midsong Int'l.	1009	1979

Members:

(as The Gypsies)

(1964)   Lesley Johnson
           Betty Pearce

(1965-66)   Viola Billups
           Betty Pearce
           Ernestine Pearce
           Shirley Pearce

The Flirtations

(1966-67)   Viola Billups
           Betty Pearce
           Ernestine Pearce
           Shirley Pearce

(1967-74)   Viola Billups
           Shirley Pearce
           Ernestine Pearce

(1974-86)   Loretta Noble
           Ernestine Pearce
           Shirley Pearce

They were cute pixies, making lightweight soul records. An offer from an eager producer turned them into American sensations in both England and Europe. To say they were quintessential is to say that they were the marked representation of pop soul, making an imprint through two producers hoping to bring a brand of American soul to the European shores. The Flirtations figure into the plans of European musician/producer Wayne Bickerton and his songwriting partner, Tony Waddington.

The Flirtations formed in New York City in 1964. The group consisted of sisters Betty, Ernestine and Shirley Pearce, along with good friend Lesley Johnson. The group was barely in their teens when they began singing after school and at parties. After many compliments from well wishers, the suggestion was made for the group to record. The quartet billed themselves as The Gypsies and began recording at Hy Weiss' Old

The Flirtations starting out as The Gypsies, 1965, (not in order) Ernestine Pearce, Shirley Pearce, Betty Pierce, Viola Billups.

Town Records for songwriters and producers, Randy Stewart and Ray Evans. Stewart was once a member of The Fiestas, who recorded "So Fine." Now, he was a staff writer at Old Town.

The group's first effort, "Hey There, Hey There," did nothing, but their sophomore single, "Jerk It," made some noise on the national charts and was a favored dance record in New York, with its Motown-inspired thumping rhythm, akin to The Supremes' "Where Did Our Love Go."

The true testament of what a girl wants was related in "Diamonds, Rubies, Gold and Fame," which graced the flip side. For the second single, Lesley Johnson exited the group and was replaced by Viola Billups. It is inconsistent that their next single would be entitled "It's A Woman's World," since the group posed for their first publicity shot wearing shell blouses and flared pants, looking like junior high school innocents. One more single was released on Old Town in 1965 before the group left, concentrating primarily on their live act, figuring to parlay it into clubs.

The Gypsies performed often, mainly on the strength of "Jerk It." As the girls grew into young ladies, they decided the name of The Gypsies was too stolid. Seeking a bolder image for themselves, the group made the name change to The Flirtations in 1966. Also in 1966, Caprice Records released one more single on the group, billed as The Gypsies. The group forged ahead under their new moniker.

The group's first assignment as The Flirtations was working under the wing of the legendary Herb Abramson, co-founder and former owner of Jubilee and Atlantic Records. Abramson was now a free-lance producer and worked with The Flirtations on a heavy-duty soul number called "Change My Darkness Into Light." The sound was so different from their normally reticent voices that upon hearing it, many questioned that it was actually the same group. It seems that the leads were rotated to vary the sound. J.J. Jackson and Sidney Barnes wrote the songs and arranged the session. They had been writing for several years, producing songs for The Chiffons and The Shangri-Las, as well as providing songs for Motown's New York offices. It was about a year before Jackson would become a star on his own with "But, It's Alright." His gem for The Flirtations was their most soulful single to date. It's flip, "Natural Born Lover," takes a page from the Mary Wells scrapbook. The group worked with Abramson, Jackson and Barnes through the team's previous association with Hy Weiss, Randy Stewart and Ray Evans. After two auspicious singles under Abramson's direction, the group went on its own.

Arthur (Wayne) Bickerton grew up in Liverpool, England. As a teenager, Wayne was swept up in the same mania as all the other teenage guys, singing and playing Rock & Roll on the bass guitar. Music lovers in Liverpool were interested in American R&B as well as guitar-oriented music. The Beatles took their brand of hybrid garage music to American audiences, creating the most pivotal musical influences of our time. Wayne hooked up with former Beatle Pete Best, recording a version of "Boys" which was released in The United States on

Cameo Records. Wayne sang the lead vocal. Wayne traveled to America and became a session musician in New York, working with Luther Dixon. Wayne was influenced especially by American soul. Wayne longed to have creative input with American soul artists, female groups in particular. As Wayne moved further and further into the music business, he became associated with Deram Records, a subsidiary of the Decca corporation, which also distributed London Records and its related labels. Wayne's realization of recording a black American female group was not far away.

The Flirtations were touring, despite not having had a major hit in The United States. Their stage shows had become polished and their repertoire extensive as they performed their modest hits, and Rock & Roll classics. When Wayne was introduced to the group after a show in England, he knew that his plans could come true, "I met The Flirtations through an agent I knew in London. We wanted to record a black female group. They were not connected to anyone at the time. We met and talked about doing some things with Tony Waddington."

Wayne and his songwriting partner, Tony Waddington, began collaborating with the group in 1968. Betty Pearce had exited the group in 1967, so The Flirtations were now a trio. Ernestine sang the lead with her firm, assured voice.

The Flirtations' first single with Wayne as producer was "How Can You Tell Me?" This maiden recording used late 60s Motown-inspired instrumentation. The crowded, but danceable arrangement was released in America on the Parrot subsidiary. The record did not gain any attention. The second single would give The Flirtations their first bona fide hit. "Nothing But A Heartache" begins with a dramatic guitar and piano, and steady drum beat. The more evenly spread instrumentation allows the vocals to command more attention. This single was a hit both in America and abroad and gave The Flirtations' career a firmer foundation. In the scheme of pop musical history, the team of Bickerton and Waddington, with arranger Johnny Harris, lead the way for English producers, "Everything was recorded in England. We were the first white producers to have an African American act on the charts."

The production team followed the hit with more fabulous tunes like the driving "Need Your Loving" and the longing "South Carolina." The sound of The Flirtations singles was just rough enough to attract those looking for a harder-edged

sound, while still beguiling enough for the pop fan. Wayne recalls that the sound of The Flirtations was wielding so much influence that even the inimitable Tom Jones covered one of their singles: "Tom Jones had the record "Can't Stop Loving You" and cut it on an album after The Flirtations had their single. Tom was very big at the time. I think the two versions crossed paths on the charts."

The Flirtations were enjoying prosperity on the European circuit, especially in England, appearing at such legendary places as Talk of The Town and The Palladium. The more steady gigs consisted of smaller clubs where the ladies performed their perfectly honed cabaret act. The LP, "Nothing But A Heartache," had been released and a few more singles continued to impress. The production team changed the formula for the last Deram single, "Give Me Love, Love, Love," which once again proved that slowing the beat created a more driving groove. Actually, this side was written and produced by John Hunter. Wayne and Tony took credit for the sweet soul side left over from another session. "This Must Be The End of The Line" was complete with a soft-sung lead and wispy backing vocals.

In 1970, after a series of prevailing singles, Wayne Bickerton left The Flirtations and Decca and went to Polygram Records. While at Polygram, Wayne enjoyed success with The Rubettes and Mack and Katie Kissoon. The Flirtations recorded one of Wayne's songs for Polygram in 1972, but recorded only sporadically after their run on Deram Records. In 1977, the trio jumped on the Disco bandwagon and recorded the pulsating "Earthquake," which met with medium success both in England and America. In 1999, the Pearce sisters were still performing and readying an updated recording of "Nothing But A Heartache." Dr. Wayne Bickerton found success in other facets of the music business, becoming chairman of The Performing Rights Society as well as chairman of the publishing house, SESAC International.

The Flirtations' overseas success inspired homegrown versions of American female groups like Sylvia and The Sapphires. Employing basic soul chords and hooks, plus a healthy dose of guitar, flutes and strings, the records were strong in their appeal on both sides of the Atlantic. Through The Flirtations' works, Bickerton and Waddington characterized the best of pop soul, a mixture that proved to be both an enduring and enticing formula.

The Flirtations Discography

45s	Label	Number	Year
(as The Gypsies)			
Hey There, Hey There/Blue Bird	Old Town	1168	1964
Jerk It/Diamonds, Rubies, Gold and Fame		1180	1965
They're Having A Party/It's A Woman's World		1184	
Oh I Wonder Why/Diamonds, Rubies, Gold and Fame		1193	1966
Look For The One Who Loves You/Oh Girl	Caprice	8442	
The Flirtations			
Change My Darkness Into Light/Natural Born Lover	Josie	956	
Stronger Than Her Love/Settle Down	Festival	705	1967
How Can You Tell Me?/Someone Out There	Parrot	40028	1968
Nothing But A Heartache/Christmas Time Is Here Again	Deram	85036	
Nothing But A Heartache/How Can You Tell Me?		85038	
South Carolina/Need Your Loving		85048	1969
Keep On Searching/I Wanna Be There		85057	
Can't Stop Lovin' You/Everybody Needs Somebody		85062	
Give Me Love, Love, Love/This Must Be The End of The Line		7531	1970
Hold On To Me Baby/Love A Little Longer	Polydor	15047	1972
Earthquake/(long version)	D and D	5501	1977
Read All About It/Remix	Passion	1267	1986
LPs			
Nothing But A Heartache	Deram	18028	1968

The Go Go's

Members:

(1980-85) Charlotte Caffey, Keyboard/Lead Guitar/Vocals

(1990-91) Belinda Carlisle, Vocals

(1994-95) Gina Schock, Drums/Percussion

(1997-99) Jane Wiedlen, Rhythm Guitar/Vocals
Kathy Valentine, Bass Guitar/Lead Guitar

The master complaint about music of the 1970s is that most of it was hands down dull. Most rockers had enough of the mindless thumping of disco music on FM radio and the bland droning of saccharin icons on AM radio. Many musicians decided to look to their roots and reinvent what originally enticed them to create music.

By the end of the decade, the bands that dominated the rock underground began to surface and reclaim pop radio. Many artists were qualified to fill the void. Danceable, feel-good Rock & Roll was needed here. Out came new artists like X, The Ramones, Talking Heads, Television, Blondie and The B52s—musicians who weren't afraid to reference The Ventures, Link Wray, The Ronettes and other artists who inspired them.

Elvis Costello, Madness, The Selector, XTC and The English Beat were bands out of the UK, who were never afraid to embrace the music of past decades. They were equally successful riding the crest of the new wave. As the 1980s began, these artists moved more into the mainstream, even adapting certain rhythms from the previously reviled disco era, making their music more all encompassing. One female band from Los Angeles possessed these qualities, plus the earnest dispositions of 1980s women who were doing things for themselves. Although more liberated, these feelings were similar to the passions of the early 60s females, posed with the questions facing impending adolescence. Different from the extreme sounds of The B52s or the existential attitudes of Blondie, The Go Go's put a spring back in everyone's step with tried and true messages, riffs and chord changes.

The formation of The Go Go's began during the late 1970s. All members had previously been playing around LA with various bands, some that recorded for independent labels. The music of choice for the instrumentalists was usually ensconced in heavy metal and punk, with a shot of the blues thrown in for good measure. It was from this circuit that The Go Go's conglomerated.

Rhythm guitarist Jane Wiedlin had been a soloist under the name Jane Drano. Lead guitarist Charlotte Caffey recorded with The Eyes and Belinda Carlisle was the vocalist for The Germs. This trio got together to form The Misfits, along with two more members, Elisa Bello and Margot Olivierra. After the band changed its name to The Go Go's, Bello and Olivierra departed. Enter bass guitarist Kathy Valentine, from a band called The Textones and

The Go Go's, (L-R) Belinda Carlisle, Jane Wiedlin, Gina Schock, Kathy Valentine, Charlotte Caffey.

freelance drummer Gina Schock. The Go Go's cohesive lineup was complete by the end of 1980.

During the early 1980s, American acts like The Go Go's and The Stray Cats were breaking new singles in England first. Once established in the English market, the material was subsequently released in America. The Go Go's first effort, "We Got The Beat/How Much More" was produced by Paul L. Wexler and written by Jane and Charlotte, who would often write their own material for the burgeoning group. This initial single was originally marketed in England and released on Stiff Records in 1980. The single met with favorable success in the UK, so IRS Records picked up the band in America.

Veteran producer Richard Gottehrer, whose track record for hits was a mile long and still growing, stepped in for "Beauty and The Beat," the band's first LP and subsequent single "Our Lips Are Sealed." Richard started his career working as a New York songwriter and producer, making Rock & Roll history by co-writing and producing one of the most enduring female group singles ever, the timeless, "My Boyfriend's Back" with The Angels in 1963.

In 1981, Gottehrer and his partner Ron Freeman duplicated the work Richard had done twenty years earlier with The Angels, picking up on the vocal tones of Belinda, Charlotte and Jane, and their similarities to the female blends of an earlier era. With its splendid guitar playing, positive drumming and sincere vocal, "Our Lips Are Sealed" established The Go Go's in The United States. The single's success prompted a cover version in 1982 by Fun Boy Three. Member Terry Hall had co-written the song with Jane. A remixed version of "We Got The Beat" was released as the second single for IRS in the states. The singles and LP rocketed The Go Go's to the top of both the pop and the newly impacting college charts. The band was now in the fast track.

The Go Go's second LP, "Vacation," provided more of the same power pop that had originally launched the band, sporting the impetuous title track as its primary single. Extensive touring and other personal appearances now prevailed. The fun-loving sounds of the group were anthems for every free-spirited female in America, so it's no wonder that The Go Go's became the heroines of progressive pop. The unstoppable unit traveled in America and abroad for almost two years before recording their third album, "Talk Show," in 1984, which yielded their last immensely popular single, "Head Over Heels."

Not only do The Go Go's pay tribute to their immediate influences, but exercise abandon on songs like the Ventures inspired "Surfing and Spying," well done cov-

The Go Go's, (L-R) Kathy, Jane, Charlotte, Gina, Belinda.

ers of The Shangri-Las classic, "(Remember) Walking In The Sand" and The Capitols' "Cool Jerk." As far as their audience was concerned, the party train was nonstop.

Unfortunately, the pressures of touring and creative differences lead to Jane Wiedlin's exit from the band shortly after the release of "Talk Show." Paula Brown replaced her for the live dates. Medical problems also plagued the band members at this time. Gina Schock was having heart problems and Kathy Valentine needed surgery on her hand. After considering the turn of events, Charlotte and Belinda decided to disband The Go Go's in 1985.

Jane Wiedlin introduced herself to the music world as a soloist in 1985 with the album "Jane Wiedlin." From the debut LP came the brilliant rocker, "Blue Kiss," as her first single. Two more albums, "Fur" and "Tangled" followed. In 1996, Jane formed a band called froSTed, with which she currently performs. In recent years, Jane has provided songs to other artists, as well as lending her voice to various cartoon shows, most notably "King Of The Hill."

Charlotte Caffey continued honing her stellar songwriting and producing abilities, providing input for contemporary artists like Jewel and Courtney Love. Charlotte and Belinda Carlisle worked together on Belinda's solo efforts. After the breakup of The Go Go's, Belinda gained an extremely successful solo career, releasing numerous singles and LPs. Her most lucrative singles have been "Mad About You," "I Get Weak" and

"Heaven Is A Place On Earth." Presently, Belinda retains a strong following overseas and she resides in England.

Charlotte writes with Jane and performs with her as Twisted and Jaded. Gina Schock has formed her own bands, House of Schock and K-Five. Gina also writes television commercials and film scores. Gina has played as a drummer with Kathy Valentine's band, The Delphines, which was formed in 1992. Within The Delphines, Kathy has played with such notables as Brian Setzer, Seal and Charlie Sexton, artists who were in turn, admirers of hers.

Since the initial breakup of the band, The Go Gos have reformed for tours and sporadic recordings in 1990, 1994 and 1997. The band released two CDs, "Greatest Hits" and "Return To The Valley of The Go Go's," which contains previously unreleased demos. It seems that the members of The Go Go's value the moments that they had when they first formed and are able to recapture that for specific periods of time. The situation works well since all are involved in their own projects. The sound of The Go Go's seems like the culmination of all good time music that has come to pass. Go Go music is sheer, danceable amusement, a fine representation of the reawakening of pure Rock & Roll in the 1980s. The fact that The Go Go's can intermittently reform and play for loyal, waiting fans shows that their sound has resilience and has maintained its place in mainstream pop music.

The Go Go's Discography

45s	**Label**	**Number**	**Year**
Our Lips Are Sealed/Surfing and Spying	IRS	9901	1981
We Got The Beat/Can't Stop The World		9903	
We Got The Beat/Our Lips Are Sealed (Picture Record)		8001	
Vacation/Beatnik Beat		9907	1982
Get Up and Go/Speeding		9910	
This Old Feeling/It's Everything But Party Time		9911	
Head Over Heels/Good For Gone		9926	
Turn To You/I'm With You		9928	1984
Mercenary/Yes Or No		9933	
We Got The Beat/Our Lips Are Sealed		8690	1990
Vacation/Cool Jerk		8691	
Belinda Carlisle			
Mad About You/I Never Wanted A Rich Man	IRS	52815	1986
Band Of Gold/----			
I Feel The Magic/From The Heart		52889	1987
Since You've Gone/same		17262	
Heaven Is A Place On Earth/We Can Change	MCA	53181	
I Get Weak/Should I Let You In		53242	
Circles In The Sand/We Can Change		53308	1988
I Feel Free/Should I Let You In		53377	
Leave A Light On/Shades Of Michelangelo		53706	1989
Summer Rain/Shades Of Michelangelo		53783	
Window Of The World/It's Too Real	Virgin	17598	1993
California/In Too Deep		19941	1998
House of Schock/w Gina Schock			
World Goes 'Round/Middle Of Nowhere	Capitol	44135	1988
Love In Return/Middle Of Nowhere		44202	
Jane Wiedlin			
Blue Kiss/My Traveling Heart	IRS	52674	1985
Rush Hour/The End Of Love	EMI-Manhattan	50118	1988
Inside A Dream/Song Of The Factory		50145	

LPs

Beauty and The Beat	IRS	70021	1981
Vacation		70031	1982
Talk Show		70041	1984
Go Go's Greatest Hits		--	1990

Belinda Carlisle

Belinda	IRS	5741	1986
Heaven On Earth	MCA	42080	1987
Runaway Horses		6339	1989
Live Your Life, Be Free		--	--
Greatest Hits		--	--
Real		--	--
A Woman And A Man		--	--

House of Schock (w/Gina Schock)

House of Schock	Capitol	--	1988

Jane Wiedlin

Jane Wiedlin	IRS	5638	1985
Fur		--	1986
Tangled	EMI-Manhattan	--	1987
From Cool Places To Worlds On Fire		--	1989

CDs

Return To The Valley of The Go Go's	MCA	--	1994
Good Girl/The Whole World's Lost It's Head		--	1995

Delphines (w/Kathy Valentine)

Woo Woo Woo	--	--	--

froSTed (w/Jane Wiedlin)

Cold	Geffen	--	1996

Graces (w/Charlotte Caffey)

Perfect View	--	--	--

Maureen Gray

During the early 1960s, Philadelphia was a hot spot for new directions in popular music. Cameo-Parkway Records was enjoying success with its dance-oriented sounds, and both Chancellor and Swan Records had reigning teen idols like Frankie Avalon, Fabian and Freddie Cannon. Philadelphia's record business had its fingers on the pulse of favored trends and fads of the now rapidly changing sounds of Rock & Roll. One artist from this region came to encompass almost every trend in pop music, catering to as many people as possible by combining teen pop with fabulous female group backing. Although much younger than her contemporaries, through her talents and the talents of her producers, her records would set the stage for other Philadelphia classics.

Maureen Gray was born in New York City in 1949. Maureen was singing almost from the time she was born. Singing was a way for young Maureen to communicate. Her first public performance took place while heading across town on a city bus. Her mother, Louise, was very encouraging. Maureen recounts; "My mother was very supportive of what I was doing. She was interested in music; she liked singing."

Madara and White's 12-year old singing sensation, 1961. (Photo courtesy of Maureen Gray)

Being a fan of music herself, Louise taught Maureen classics, like songs from "Showboat." Relatives also introduced Maureen to West Indian rhythms. By the time Maureen was five, her mother was putting her in shows for children. Louise entered Maureen in a show at Carnegie Hall. She sang "Steam Heat" and "I Get Ideas."

When Maureen was seven, she and her mom stayed in New Jersey, near relatives. Maureen would sing with her cousins, listening to the popular music of the day, namely Ray Charles, Little Anthony & The Imperials, Mary Wells and The Chantels. Maureen's uncle knew Jocko, the famous deejay, so Maureen was often treated to hearing popular acts at a local roller rink where she and her cousins would go skating. After about a year, her mother's job relocated, so they moved to Philadelphia.

There was a record store on 60th Street that Maureen frequented. She spent endless amounts of time there, listening to all the new releases. One day, songwriters/producers John Madara and David White walked in. They heard Maureen singing and liked what they heard. They asked her if she wanted to make a record. Maureen agreed, and, after the formalities were taken care of with Maureen's mom, she was on her way to the recording studio.

John Madara and David White were fairly seasoned producers and writers by the early 1960s. David White was a former member of Danny and The Juniors. He had cowritten their big hit, "At The Hop" with Madara and Artie Singer. Now they were independent producers striking deals with various labels by producing finished masters for release. Maureen was only 12, and her voice had a distinctive quality not found in their older acts. Her songs would have to be carefully crafted.

Madara and White leased Maureen's first recording to Bob Marcucci's Chancellor Records. Maureen remembers little about her first recording session, except that there were a lot of grown-ups around. Of course, to a 12-year old, a high school senior can seem much older. This is what she remembers most about her unknown female backing group, a group that would back her on most of her recordings. Maureen's other guests in the studio included Fabian and Frankie Avalon. To her, they weren't the stars that everyone else knew, but to a 12-year old, just regular guys hanging around.

Madara and White decided that Maureen's first single should hit the junior high crowd straight between the eyes, and released a two-sided gem. "Today's The Day" features a catchy shuffling drum beat, complete with "shop shop shoo wopps" in the background, borrowed from the Shirelles manic B-side, "Boys." The production utilized strings and rhythmic drums. It's flip, the grinding, pounding ballad, "Crazy Over You," completes this two-sided teen angst package. Maureen's strong voice sells both sides convincingly. The lyrics were simplistic and the melodies catchy. "Today's The Day" received local airplay.

Madara and White were so confident about "Today's The Day," that they recorded a sound-alike song with Maureen entitled, "Remember Me." Although the lyrics and some chords were different, it was an attempt to capitalize on the mild success of the first single, however, Chancellor delayed releasing "Remember Me."

For Maureen's second single at Chancellor, Madara and White decided to have members of Danny and The Juniors back Maureen on a novelty tune entitled, "Come On and Dance," with its twist-inspired beat and its inviting lyrical delivery. Maureen recalls: "I remember John and David coaxing me to sing a gruffy, 'Come on, come on, come on'."

The flip side features Maureen on another ballad, "I Don't Want To Cry," complete with both soft-spoken lines and a crying break, reminiscent of Jackie and The Starlites', "Valerie." Danny and The Juniors repeated their involvement on Maureen's last single for Chancellor, a comparable cover of The Students classic, "I'm So Young." Unfortunately, neither of these singles met with commercial success.

With no lasting success for Maureen at Chancellor, Madara and White's next stop was Landa Records, home to The Stompers and Billy and The Essentials. Maureen's first single was a song about a popular dance called "Dancin' The Strand." The song borrows obvious cues from The Chantels' "Maybe." Maureen casts a heartfelt lead while retaining that junior-high quality in her voice. She certainly convinced the record buying public, as " . . . Strand" made it to the pop charts, receiving much airplay in many local markets like Philadelphia and Pittsburgh. Its follow-up, "People Are Talking," tried to capture the same intensity, but it was not as melodic as " . . . Strand" and did not chart. "Oh My" flipped both singles on Landa.

Maureen was, of course, making personal appearances at shows and record hops, becoming the envy of all her junior high school chums. Little did they know that the envy was reciprocal, as a schedule for a 13-year old performer left little time to do what other young teens did, like going around with friends to parties and shows, "I would go to the record hops, and all my peers were out dancing, and I'd have to get on the stage and perform."

On the weekends, Madara and White kept her busy. Maureen's love of singing and entertaining kept her going and she knew she had the support and understanding of her mother. Maureen's arrangement with Madara and White would be considered conflict of interests these days, because they were not only her producers and managers, but they took care of bookings and provided legal consultation. Maureen's mother had considered leaving them several times, but was often convinced to stay on.

The next label that released Maureen Gray recordings was Mercury Records. Madara and White had several of their productions leased to Mercury, like Anthony and The Sophomores' nostalgic anthem, "Play Those Oldies Mr. Dee Jay," and The Pixies Three lively song, "Birthday Party." The duo was even contracted to provide a song for a young girl just a couple of years older than Maureen, but with a track record of three hits under her belt.

Lesley Gore recorded "You Don't Own Me" after hearing Maureen sing it for her, Maureen having learned it as a possible venue for release. Maureen released "The Story Of My Love/Summertime Is Near," another two-sided jewel, featuring Maureen's utilization of two completely different styles of voice. " . . . Story" is reminiscent of the capacity of "Dancin' The Strand," and "Summertime . . ." contains the light, swinging elements found in early Motown productions of Marvelettes singles.

One more single, the Spectoresce "Goodbye Baby," was released in early 1964. Maureen then announced to her mother that she no longer wanted to be in show business; she wanted to go back to being a regular young girl. At the tender age of 15, Maureen decided to exit the record business.

After deciding not to continue with a recording career, Maureen finished school, took some time to travel and settled down in California for awhile. She tried to reunite with Madara and White for a project, but was unsuccessful. In 1969, Maureen moved to England where she resumed her recording career, backing such notables as John Lennon and Bob Marley. She sang with and recorded with several rock bands in England and The Netherlands during the 1970s and 1980s. Maureen is now part of a band called Girl and The Boys, whom are currently recording and performing in New York City. Maureen looks back fondly on her days as a young artist, and sees it as a conduit to what she is doing now. Maureen believes that the work of all artists is to make themselves fully known. Rock & Roll enthusiasts know very well what indelible contributions Maureen had made to the world of pop music.

Maureen Gray Discography

45s	Label	Number	Year
Crazy Over You/Today's The Day	Chancellor	1082	1961
I Don't Want To Cry/Come On And Dance		1091	
I'm So Young/There Is A Boy		1100	1962
Dancing The Strand/Oh My	Landa	689	
People Are Talking/Oh My		692	
Remember Me/Slop Time (acetate)	Guyden	2072	
The Story Of My Love/Summertime Is Near	Mercury	72131	1963
Goodbye Baby/I'm A Happy Girl		72227	1964
Dancing The Strand, (no lead vocal)	Jamie	919	1972

The Hearts

Members:

(1955-56)	Hazel Crutchfield (Anderson)
	Forestine Barnes
	Louise Harris
	Joyce West
(1956)	Hazel Anderson
	Louise Harris
	Thaddus McLean
	Joyce West
(1956-57)	Anna Barnhill
	Justine "Baby" Washington
	Theresa Chatman
	Joyce Peterson

(1957-58)	Tiffany St. Ann (King?)
	Betty Harris
	Mandy Hopper
	Theresa Chatman
	Lezli (Green) Valentine
	Mary Green Wilson
(1959-60)	Ruth Artis
	Louise Harris (Murray)
	Marie Hood
	Mandy Hopper
	Lezli Valentine

(1961-63)	Theresa Chatman
	Cynthia Cox (Felder)
	Louise Murray
	Marie Hood
	Lezli Valentine
(1970)	Cynthia Felder
	Yvonne Bushnell
	Johnnielouise Richardson
(1970)	Cynthia Felder
	Mary Jefferson
	Lavergne Ray

During the early days of post-war Rhythm & Blues, many established record companies would not sign Rhythm & Blues or "race" acts to their labels. If they did, a new label was created to release these records and, in most cases, was treated as the specialty market it was at the time, with very little attention paid to the artists. These attitudes prompted the rise of many, local R&B labels that would produce and promote their own artists. Since these labels did not enjoy the same distribution as the majors, proprietors were forced to hustle their own product. Also, like most aspects of American life in the 1950s, the music business was still a man's domain.

Zelma "Zell" Sanders, a security officer by day and self-determined record mogul by night was to become the pebble in the shoe of the male-dominated record business, getting to the deejays with her "in your face" attitude. This was a must, for she had to work twice as hard to be taken seriously. Zell established J&S Records with a group that reflected her "women can do what the men do" attitude. This is the story of The Hearts.

This account begins in Harlem, NY, autumn of 1954, when a trio of young girls stood on the corner of 122nd St and Lenox Ave., harmonizing some of the songs that male groups were crooning throughout their neighborhood. Joyce West, Forestine Barnes and Hazel Crutchfield felt that they could match the guys note for note. This group of girls came to Zell's attention after an appearance at the Apollo Theatre, arranged by Frank Schiffman.

Zell was looking to try her luck producing a group for the burgeoning Rhythm & Blues market. After some rehearsals, the trio decided they needed a fourth member. Through a mutual friend, Roxanne Winfield, Louise Harris was asked to join the group. Louise had been singing for a few years, and had won a contest at the Apollo

The Hearts, 1956, (L-R) Theresa Chatman, Anna Barnhill, Justine "Baby" Washington, Joyce Peterson, Rex Garvin.

Theatre when she was eight. Louise had to get permission from her mother, since she was still in junior high school. Zell even recruited a young neighbor to be the girls' accompanist on piano, Rex Garvin. The entire act was between twelve and fifteen years old.

It was unusual to hear young girls singing in a style usually reserved for male groups. Some female groups did exist in the field of Rhythm and Blues, most notably, Shirley Gunter and The Queens, a quartet from Los Angeles who zoomed to the top of the R&B charts with "Oop Shoop" in 1954. There were other female groups signed to labels at this time. The Enchanters were signed to Jubilee Records in 1952, and The Cookies were recording for Lamp Records in 1954. A quintet of ladies called The Blue Belles had a single entitled, "Story Of A Fool/Cancel The Call," released by Atlantic in 1953. (This group had no relation to Patti LaBelle's Bluebelles a decade later.) The Hearts were the next female group after The Queens to have a song on the R&B charts.

Zell placed the group with Sol Rabinowitz's Baton label in early 1955. "Lonely Nights," a grinding testament of lost love, soon climbed the R&B charts and the young group was suddenly in demand. The girls rehearsed at Zell's house after school and during vacations. Rex Garvin, lovingly referred to as "maestro," arranged all the songs for the group.

Joyce West possessed a sassy lead that exuded sauciness on the torchy, pop ballad and the swinging jump blues tune, "Oo Wee," with a touch of a gutsy grind in her voice. Louise contributed the unforgettable hook in the bridge, "you great big lump of sugar." The lyrics tell of the yearnings of uncertain love, exuding penned-up energies caused by roller coaster relationships, sung with the insights of middle-aged dance hall molls, ironically delivered by 15-year olds.

In fact, this formula would see the group through their tenure with Zell. The vocals were matched with the full sound of the Big Al Sears Orchestra, featuring such session notables as Sam "The Man" Taylor and Mickey "Guitar" Baker. Since the group was so young, they did not perform in clubs, but did theater dates like The Apollo, and never traveled too far. The Hearts performed "Money Honey" and "Blue Moon" in addition to their hit. Zell was putting her "perfection in appearance and performance" notions into effect, imposing fines if standards were not met. She wanted her girls to be the icons of female R&B.

The group's next recording session yielded the compelling single "All My Love Belongs To You/Talk About Him Girlie." The latter sported a call and response title hook. Louise took the lead for the blues inspired "Gone, Gone, Gone" and the group adapted the Ink Spots standard "Until The Real Thing Comes Along" which was recorded at their first session.

Neither of these singles met with the success of "Lonely Nights." The group stayed with Zell for about a year. The youngsters were having a good time and not really serious about being in "the business." Louise remembers how her actions led to the demise of the first incarnation of The Hearts. "I was young and I didn't want to do all the rehearsals that Zell wanted us to do, so I wouldn't show up. Zell wanted to replace me, but the rest of the girls said they wouldn't sing without me, so that was the end of that group."

Zell certainly wasn't going to waste the reputation The Hearts had started building. The only logical thing to do was to get another group of girls to be The Hearts. She held auditions and assembled Joyce Peterson, Theresa Chatman, Anna Barnhill and Justine Washington, known as "Baby."

This second group of Hearts recorded the classic "Disappointed Bride," the pinnacle of The Hearts' style. The song begins with a staggered horn section and drum beat not unlike a slow march. Justine's half-sung, half-spoken recitation keeps the listener waiting for this female preacher to deliver her sermon.

"Going Home To Stay," also delivers a considerable amount of grandiosity and independence in its message. It was the last recording the group would do for Baton. This single did very well in local markets. Hardly anyone noticed that the group was a completely different lineup.

Where Joyce West's voice was coy and semi-sweet, Baby Washington's voice is candid and imposing. Distinct in style and broad in execution, Baby Washington's voice often breaks out of the ensemble. Actually, it was not her first choice to be in a group, but the opportunity to sing and record drew Justine to the audition. She admired Zell's way of handling things: "I heard that auditions were being held for this group, so I went to 125th Street, next to Carr's Studios, to try out. Zell was a shrewd businesswoman. Right from the start, she was strict about rehearsal times and dress codes."

Confident in her ability to mold a group to her liking, Zell no longer worried about individual group members. This came in handy when she found herself in disagreements with anyone over business matters. She wouldn't waste time haggling, she'd just replace anyone who couldn't make rehearsals, keep up with the fast pace or complained about money.

The second group of Hearts accomplished just what Zell had hoped. They continued the momentum created

The Hearts, stepping out with unidentified friends, 1959, (L-R) Marie Hood, Lezli Valentine, Mandy Hopper. (Photo courtesy of Lezli Valentine)

by the first group, performing at countless shows. This group recorded the jingles for disc jockey Georgie Hudson. One more Baton single, "He Drives Me Crazy/I Had A Guy," recorded by the first group, was released.

After her deal with Baton Records ended, Zell decided it was time to start her own record company, J&S Records. She lost the big band sound of the Al Sears Orchestra, and acquired the full, bottom-heavy, piano laden arrangements that would come to signify the J&S sound. Many of the musicians working for Zell on the J&S singles were non-union. Zell was now managing two groups, The Pre-Teens and The Gospel Wonders, who started up the label in late 1956, followed by another acquisition, The Plants. The Hearts first single on J&S was "Dancing In A Dream World," a song not very neatly executed, but Baby Washington's lead makes it interesting. A handful of Baby Washington-led singles was released, like "You Needn't Tell Me, I Know."

Eventually, Washington embarked on her solo career while still under the Zell's direction. Baby's solo efforts, such as "I Hate To See You Go," put her in a LaVern Baker-type mold, with backing by The Plants. With no success for her solo efforts, Baby Washington accepted an offer from Ben Fowler's Neptune label. She had made his acquaintance through a member of her band. She had a monster R&B hit in 1959 with "The Time," which established her as a solo performer, her genuine desire.

After Baby Washington's departure, another young woman who answered the call would replace her. Lezli Valentine was out of school and working as a stenographer for the State Liquor Board when she joined Zell's company. Theresa introduced her to Zell and Lezli was soon part of The Hearts.

Lezli Valentine, 1960. (Photo courtesy of Lezli Valentine)

Other new members were Betty Harris, Mandy Hopper, and Tiffany St. Ann (this is what she was called). This was almost a total reworking of the second group, essentially making a third group. Mary Green Wilson joined as a part-time Heart.

So determined was Zell to succeed, the image and sound of this group began exceeding the identity of the individual members. (Zell had tried to recruit The Clickettes to be the new Hearts, but they declined.) Lezli's tender lead fronted eclectic songs like "If I Had Known" and "There's No Love At All." Lezli's voice was sweet, like Joyce West's, but higher.

It was thought that Rex sang the low notes on these singles, but Ann provided the bottom end. This formation stayed for about a year, until Louise Harris returned in place of Ann and Marie Hood replaced Betty Harris. Ruth Artis joined the fold here, too.

They recorded one song not placed with J&S, but on Argyle Records, a label this group owned with Zell. The artist was billed as Ena Louise and The Hearts, Louise taking her mother's name for this single. "From A Cap and A Gown/A Prisoner To You" is an enchanting single, featuring Louise's rich lead.

Confusion exists about recording personnel for three reasons. First, there were several different groups of Hearts. Leads within each formation, though, remained fairly constant. Joyce West led the first group of Hearts with Louise Harris taking an occasional lead. Baby Washington led the second group, with occasional leads by Anna Barnhill. Lezli led the third group, with an occasional lead by Mandy Hopper. Louise was Ena Louise for the fourth group.

Another reason for the mix up is because Zell would intermittently release songs left in the can by a previous lineup. Third, J&S had a random numbering system, making it difficult to tell which singles actually came first. Depending upon Zell's base of operations, labels sport several addresses including 125th St. in Manhattan, Tiffany St., Washington Ave., Anthony Ave. and Nelson Ave. in The Bronx. Zell would often employ subs for photos if members weren't available. On one occasion, Mandy was late coming to a photo shoot, so Zell got her upstairs neighbor to stand in for Mandy.

As the 1950s drew to a close, members of The Hearts were turning their attentions to family matters, getting married and having children. One single in the can, "A Thousand Years From Today," led by Ruth Artis, was released in 1960. This single was resurrected in 1970 on Zells Records. Another single, "Suffering With My Heart" was released on J&S in 1960, but gave label credit to The Endeavors.

Substitutes were necessary to employ for live dates and, as it turned out, recording sessions. A most capable stand-in was Cynthia Cox, also known as Cindy Felder. Cindy was commissioned to perform with Lezli and Marie at a show in Connecticut with The Isley Bros. This netted her a lead on the last Hearts single for the parent J&S label, "I Couldn't Let Him See Me Crying," released in 1961. This made the fifth group of Hearts. Cindy also recorded "As The Years Go By/Hi Ho The Merry-O" as Hartsy Maye, a name previously bestowed upon Zell's old station wagon.

The Hearts disappeared as a recording group for almost two years, although they continued making personal appearances. The name resurfaced on two singles in 1963, one a mild chart item called "Dear Abby." Lezli provided the Ann Landers-like voice for the bridge. Because money wasn't always forthcoming, day jobs and other obligations kept members away. Zell turned her attentions to some soloists she was working with, and managing her daughter, Johnnielouise Richardson, in the successful duo of Johnnie and Joe, with Joe Rivers.

The truth is that Zell was running out of funding for her projects. Too much wheeling and dealing put her in financial trouble. She had to give away pieces of her pie in order to keep recording. Lezli recalls how J&S Records began faltering, "Zell had good ideas, but she sold herself, her labels and songs down the drain. Even if she buried money, too many people knew where to dig."

The authorities at Chess Records would put her back on track within two years, when she enjoyed chart action with her most commercially successful single since "Over The Mountain." A variation on a nursery rhyme called "Sally Go 'Round The Roses," was recorded with another female group, The Jaynetts. Zell didn't have to look too far for this group. Remaining members of The Hearts were only too happy to oblige.

Justine "Baby" Washington was the most successful former Heart, going on to have many pop and R&B hits throughout the 1960s and 1970s. She recorded for a variety of record labels, usually under the direction of either Juggy Murray or Clarence Lawton. She is sometimes credited as Jeanette, although she has no idea why. Justine is currently working on a new CD with Juggy.

Lezli, Marie and Louise stayed on as members of The Jaynetts. Joyce West Watson and Anna Barnhill Gore settled in upstate New York to raise families. Theresa Chat-

The Hearts, 1962, (top) Theresa Chatman. (bottom, L-R) Marie Hood, Cindy "Hartsy Maye" Felder, Louise Murray. (Photo courtesy of Louise Murray)

man became a minister. Forestine Barnes worked with Harptones accompanist Raoul Cita in the late 1950s. She has since passed on.

Betty Harris went on to have solo success with her single "Cry To Me" and I'm Evil Tonight" among others. Rex Garvin weathered all the changes in the group, remaining their accompanist, as Rex put it, "mainly to meet girls." Rex was the original harmony voice on "Over The Mountain, Across The Sea." He moved south, working through the years with various bands. Rex now resides in Georgia.

Zell did revive the name of The Hearts once more in 1970. She re-released "A Thousand Years From Today/I Feel So Good" and, in addition, came up with a new release, "Do You Remember," with Cynthia, Johnnielouise and Yvonne Bushnell.

Zell went so far as to release an LP entitled "I Feel So Good," mostly filled with older Hearts material. The members shown on the cover and credited with the recording are Cynthia Felder, Mary Jefferson and Lavergne Ray, but it is probable that only Cynthia actually recorded anything connected with the release.

This final attempt fell on deaf ears, despite Zell's on-vinyl challenge to the deejays that "we're going to sock it to you." The Hearts enjoyed their time in the spotlight, overreaching outstanding individual input to pioneer a distinctive style and sound in female vocal group harmony.

The Hearts Lead Personnel

Song	Vocal	Year
Lonely Nights	Joyce West (bridge – Louise)	1955
Oo-Wee	Joyce West	
All My Love Belongs To You	Joyce West	
Talk About Him Girlie	Joyce West	
Gone, Gone, Gone	Louise Harris	
Until The Real Thing Comes Along	Joyce West	
Going Home To Stay	Baby Washington	1956
Disappointed Bride	Baby Washington	
I Had A Guy	Joyce West	
He Drives Me Crazy	Joyce West	
Dancing In A Dreamworld	Baby Washington	1957
You Needn't Tell Me, I Know	Baby Washington	
So Long Baby	Anna Barnhill (lead/spoken bridge)(bridge - Johnnielouise)	
You Say You Love Me	Baby Washington	
I Want Your Love Tonight	Group Vocal	
Like Later Baby	Betty Harris w/Kenny Curry	
There's No Love At All	Lezli Valentine	1958
Goodbye, Baby	Mandy Hopper	
If I Had Known	Lezli Valentine	

Song	Vocal	Year
There Are So Many Ways	Lezli Valentine	
You or Me Has Got To Go	Lezli Valentine	1959
My Love Has Gone	Lezli Valentine	
From A Cap and A Gown	Louise Harris	
A Prisoner To You	Louise Harris	
Suffering With My Heart	Lezli Valentine	1960
I Got The Feeling	Lezli Valentine	
A Thousand Years From Today	Ruth Artis	
I Feel So Good	Ruth Artis	
You Weren't Home	?	
I Couldn't Let Him See Me Crying	Cynthia Cox (Felder)	1961
As The Years Go By	Cynthia Cox (Hartsy Maye)	1962
Dear Abby	Lezli Valentine (spoken bridge)	1963
I Understand Him	Lezli Valentine	
Don't Let Me Down	?	1970
Do You Remember	?	

The Hearts Discography

45s	Label	Number	Year
Lonely Nights/Oo-Wee	Baton	208	1955
All My Love Belongs To You/Talk About Him Girlie		211	
Gone, Gone, Gone/Until The Real Thing Comes Along		215	
Going Home To Stay/Disappointed Bride		222	1956
I Had A Guy/He Drives Me Crazy		228	
Dancing In A Dream World/You Needn't Tell Me, I Know	J&S	1657	1957
So Long Baby/You Say You Love Me		1660	

45s

	Label	Number	Year
I Want Your Love Tonight/Like Later Baby		1626/1627	1958
If I Had Known/There Are So Many Ways		10002/10003	
My Love Has Gone/You Or Me Has Got To Go		425/426	1959
There's No Love At All/Goodbye Baby		4571	
A Thousand Years From Today/I Feel So Good		995	1960
I Couldn't Let Him See Me Crying/You Weren't Home		1181	1961
Dear Abby/Inst.	Tuff	370	1963
I Understand Him/Inst.		373	
A Thousand Years From Today/I Feel So Good	Zells	3377	1970
Don't Let Me Down/Do You Remember		3378	

(as Ena Louise and The Hearts)

	Label	Number	Year
From A Cap And A Gown/A Prisoner To You	Argyle	1635	1959

(as The Endeavors)

	Label	Number	Year
Suffering With My Heart/I Got The Feeling	J&S	254	1960

(as Hartsy Maye & Group)

	Label	Number	Year
As The Years Go By/Heigh Ho The Merry O	Zell	4397	1962

Betty Harris

	Label	Number	Year
Cry To Me/I'll Be A Liar	Jubilee	5456	1963
His Kiss/It's Dark Outside		5465	
Twelve Red Roses/What'd I Do Wrong	Sansu	455	1967
I'm Evil Tonight/Nearer To You		466	
Can't Last Much Longer/I'm Gonna Git Ya		471	1968
Trouble With My Lover/Ride Your Pony		480	

Baby Washington*

	Label	Number	Year
Congratulations Baby/There Must Be A Reason	J&S	1604	1957
Aha/Been A Long Time Baby		1607	
Every Day/Smitty's Rock		1656	
I Hate To See You Go/Knock Yourself Out		1613	1958
I Hate To See You Go/Knock Yourself Out		1632	
I Hate To See You Go/Knock Yourself Out	Checker	918	1959
The Time/You Never Could Be Mine	Neptune	101	
The Bells/Why Did My Baby Put Me Down		104	
Work Out/Let's Love In The Moonlight		107	
Medicine Man/Tears Fall		120	1960
Too Late/Move On		121	1961
Nobody Cares/Money's Funny		122	
My Time To Cry/Let Love Go By	ABC-Paramount	10223	
There You Go Again/Don't Cry Foolish Heart		10245	
Go On/No Tears	Sue	764	1962
A Handful Of Memories/Careless Hands		767	
Hush Heart/I've Got A Feeling		769	
That's How Heartaches Are Made/There He Is		783	1963
Leave Me Alone/You And The Night And The Music		790	
Hey Lonely One/--		794	
I Can't Wait Until I See My Baby/Who's Going To Take Care Of Me		797	1964
The Clock/Standing On The Pier		104	
Move On, Drifter/It'll Never Be Over		114	
You Fool/Run, My Heart		119	
I Can't Wait Until I See My Baby/Who's Going To Take Care Of Me		124	1965
Only Those In Love/The Ballad Of Bobby Dawn		129	
No Time For Pity/There He Is		137	
White Christmas/Silent Night		149	1966
You Are What You Are/Either You're With Me		150	
Silent Night/White Christmas	Veep	1274	1967
I Know/It'll Change	Sue	4	1968
Hurt So Bad/Get A Hold Of Yourself	Veep	--	1969
Hold Back The Dawn/Think About The Good Times		1297	
Is It Worth It/Happy Birthday	Chess	2099	1970
I Don't Know/I Can't Afford To Lose Him	Cotillion	44047	1969
Breakfast In Bed/--		44055	
Let Them Talk/I Love You Brother		44065	1971
Don't Let Me Lose This Dream/I'm Good Enough For You		44086	
Forever (w/Don Gardner)/--	Master Five	9103	1972
Can't Get You Out Of My Mind/--		9104	
I've Got To Break Away/You (Just A Dream)		9107	1973
Lay A Little Lovin' On Me (w/Don Gardner)/--		9110	
Can't Get Over Losing You/ Care Free		3500	1974
Can't Get Over Losing You/I Wanna Dance	AVI	253	1978
I Know I'm Losing You/Bring It On Home To Me	Law-ton	500	1986

*Some recordings are billed as Jeanette "Baby" Washington or Justine Washington.

LPs

Hearts

	Label	Number	Year
I Feel So Good	Zells	337	1970

Baby Washington

	Label	Number	Year
That's How Heartaches Are Made	Sue	1014	1960

The Honey Cone

Members:

(1969-73) Shelly Clark
Carolyn Willis
Edna Wright, Lead

Many social changes had taken hold in America during the 1960s and early 1970s. Crises facing American society had fostered many revisions. War was still raging in Southeast Asia and man had landed on the moon. Television had become more candid in style and approach and popular music reflected evidence of political concerns and the sexual revolution, the thoughts of the younger generation pondering its arrival. The role of women in American society was quite a departure from the stereotype that had been ten years before. Women were making their own way in the world. They had the same wants and needs as their male counterparts. Women were eager to please their partners but only if the feelings were reciprocated. The modern 1970s woman wouldn't hesitate to move on if her needs weren't being met.

A particular trio from Los Angeles came across with the universal message of modern women everywhere. They were sassy, sexy and enticing, confident, head strong, and, best of all, independent. These women conveyed the message that wanted their men, but didn't need them loud and clear. Don't mess with the likes of The Honey Cone; the most assured vocal group of the twentieth century.

The Honey Cone was born out of an offer from a very famous songwriting team from Detroit to a group of well-known session singers from Los Angeles. The songwriting team of Brian Holland, Eddie Holland and Lamont Dozier were cutting their ties with Motown Records and in the process of starting their own labels in 1968. Although Holland-Dozier-Holland were still in dispute with Motown over monies owed them, they were determined not to be derailed by this turn of events. HDH wanted to run a company that was to their greatest financial advantage. At Motown, they felt that they deserved a bigger share of the pie, but weren't getting it. The songwriters, who wrote some of Motown's

Carolyn's first group, the one and only Girlfriends, 1963, (L-R) Carolyn Willis, Gloria Jones, Nanette Williams. (Photo courtesy of Ken Thompson)

biggest hits, had been put on hold during court proceedings for over a year, but in 1969, it was time to break out once again. They had heard about a trio of young ladies singing on recording sessions in Los Angeles and set out to make the trio an offer to sing as a bona fide vocal group.

As a young girl, Edna Wright started singing in her father's church. As she grew into young adulthood, Edna followed in the footsteps of her older sister, Darlene, who had made a name for herself on the LA session circuit as a versatile background singer. By the time Edna's sister became popular as Darlene Love, Edna was helping out on sessions that Phil Spector was recording at Gold Star Studios in Los Angeles. On one particular session for Darlene, Edna sang the harmony line to her sister's lead on "Wait 'Til My Bobby Gets Home."

Edna continued getting work, using her voice on records with fictitious groups made out of session singers, besides popular and up-and-coming artists like Jan and Dean, The Beach Boys, Terry Melcher and Sonny and Cher. One of these recordings, a version of "Yes Sir, That's My Baby," released as Hale and The Hushabyes, features Edna's outstanding vocal responses on the refrain. Edna was also part of a Gospel group called The Cogic Singers, who recorded and released a handful of sides. Edna's major role as a soloist came when she signed to Ed Cobb's Champion Records in 1965. Edna recorded two singles, including the musical tale "The Touch of Venus" under the pseudonym Sandy Wynns. Not comfortable as a solo artist, Edna reverted to the more stable environment of session work after releasing two more singles during 1966 and 1967.

As a child, Carolyn Willis moved with her family to Los Angeles from the East Coast. Carolyn's brother, Fred, helped draw his little sister to the musical world. Fred was a member of the versatile group, The Calvanes. He knew many of the other young performers from high school, most notably, an adaptable group of young ladies backing singer Richard Berry, calling themselves The Dreamers. They eventually became The Blossoms. Through Fred's contacts, Carolyn entered the world of recording. Carolyn also knew Edna Wright from school and worked with her on occasion. Carolyn found that she liked the diversity of recording dates as opposed to the restraints of being a member of a regular singing group, "I started singing and recording out of high school. The first singing job I had was with the Spector sessions. I was really never part of a group."

This was trial by fire. Carolyn's first major assignment was to go out on the road as part of Bob B. Soxx and The Blue Jeans. Bobby Sheen, Darlene Love and Fanita James had been involved in the successful recordings, but didn't want to be on the road, so Carolyn and Blossom Gloria Jones made the personal appearances. When Gloria decided she had her fill, Philadelphia session singer Lillian Washington took her place. Carolyn and Lillian are pictured with Bobby on the cover of Phil Spector's celebratory holiday LP, "A Christmas Gift For You." Carolyn was not fond of being a live Blue Jean, "I didn't like the experience of being on the road. I wanted to be in the background."

Carolyn did feel complacent enough to collaborate with Blossoms' Gloria Jones and Nanette Williams on a single for a young producer named David Gates. Not surprisingly, the single with all the talent behind it was released on Colpix Records in late 1963 and began climbing the charts. "My One and Only Jimmy Boy," with the trio billed as The Girlfriends, bounced its way up to the top 50 nationally and to the top 25 in New York: "We had done studio work for David Gates. The record became a hit. We had intended to go forward with The Girlfriends, then President Kennedy was assassinated."

Unfortunately, November of 1963 was not a premium time for new singles to hit the charts. America was immobilized by the killing of President John F. Kennedy. Many promising new singles fell into a void. The Girlfriends recorded two more sides, "Baby Don't Cry" and "I Don't Believe In You," that were slated for release on Colpix in early 1964, but never came out. Gloria became pregnant and left The Blossoms as a full time member. Carolyn went back to her first love, session singing, which would see her through the 1960s.

Before working solely as a vocalist, Shelly Clark became involved in stage performance at a very young age: "My first professional appearance was at the age of four, in New York, so I guess you could say I was a stage child. I sang and danced with my brother, Ilya, until high school. We were called The Clark Kids."

As well as appearing on stage in the hit musical "House of Flowers," Shelly recorded at the age of eight, singing on an album released by Columbia Records called "Calypso Songs for Children." Upon graduation from high school, Shelly entered the University of Southern California on a scholarship program for talented singers. While Shelly attended USC, she worked as a session vocalist to make some money. While in this circle, she met Carolyn and Edna.

Through her work as a session vocalist, Shelly was afforded the opportunity to try out for the famous Ike and Tina Turner Review. In her own living room, Shelly auditioned for Ike Turner's assistant, Ann Kane. Kane had heard about Shelly's session work and wanted to try her out. Shelly was hired on the spot. Shelly never recorded as an Ikette, but was a part of the road tour with Sherell Brooks (?) and Ann Thomas.

She traveled with the Ike Turner Review for about a year, until a bus crash in Wichita, Kansas ended Shelly's days as an Ikette. She and two musicians were hospitalized for awhile, so the tour recruited other people to take their place and went on.

By 1968, Carolyn was still busy singing on sessions and providing backing for a variety of other artists. When Holland-Dozier-Holland decided it was time they formed their own company, they needed premium acts to continue in the tradition to which they were accustomed, having hits. Carolyn, Edna and another session singer, Julia Tillman, were spotted singing behind Lena Horne on her television special.

Normally, Carolyn was happy staying in the backgrounds, collecting steady session fees and not worrying about being on the road. Since Los Angeles session musicians were a small clique, the versatile singer never wanted for work. Carolyn relates how she and the other ladies decided to step into the limelight: "I had to be talked into The Honey Cone. We had Julia Tillman, another girl before Shelly. We were doing background work for Lena Horne. It was her first television show. We were singing all the way back with the orchestra, but Lena wouldn't have it. She brought us up front. From that show is where someone got the idea for The Honey Cone."

Edna and Carolyn were continuing with session work and live appearances singing background. Julia Tillman had gone on to other projects, so Shelly auditioned and joined as the third member. She had been working as a dancer, part of Little Richard's stage show. After an appearance subbing for The Blossoms on The Andy Williams Show, Eddie Holland called them and asked them to come to Detroit. Originally, Eddie Holland had asked Edna to be an artist on his emerging Hot Wax Records, but Edna preferred being with a group. Although Carolyn and Shelly were wary because of HDH's negative reputation with their artists concerning both creative and

financial matters, they decided to go along anyway. The contemporary sounding name of The Honey Cone was bestowed upon them.

The first efforts in the studio by The Honey Cone yielded the pumping single, "While You're Out Looking For Sugar," written and produced by Ronald Dunbar and Edith Wayne. Its sure-footed beat and forewarning lyrical content was the formula for all future successful Honey Cone singles. The record made an incredible impact in many local markets across America, but failed to really break out, nationally. The second single, "Girls It Ain't Easy," with its superb harmonies, met a similar fate. Shelly had acting experience, and since nothing of note was happening with The Honey Cone, she auditioned and was hired as one of The Nabors Kids on "The Jim Nabors Hour" in 1969. Another single, "Take Me With You," went by unnoticed. The fourth attempt at a hit by the fierce trio soon forced Shelly to reconfigure her schedule.

After hearing the next single by The Honey Cone, the classified section never sounded so alluring. "Want Ads"

HONEY CONE
HOTWAX RECORDING ARTIST

Direction Of:
CREATIVE ATTRACTIONS
3125 Cadillac Towers
Detroit, Michigan 48226

The Honey Cone, early seventies flower power, 1970, (from top) Carolyn Willis, Edna Wright, Shelly Clark. (Photo courtesy of Shelly Clark White)

THE HoneyCone

The Honey Cone posing for the 90s reunion, (L-R) Carolyn, Shelly, Edna. (Photo courtesy of Shelly Clark White)

begins with Edna's announcement of her special ad placement, "wanted, young man, single and free." Carolyn and Shelly soon join in on her periodical lament. "Want Ads" exploded onto the charts in 1971. The Honey Cone were now a hot property, having joined the ranks of other hit makers at Hot Wax/Invictus Records like Freda Payne, The Chairman of The Board, Glass House and The Flaming Ember. Suddenly, the talented trio took a sudden thrust forward into rehearsing, recording and performing. Shelly found the experience grueling, but exciting, "I remember lots of traveling, rehearsing and being tired all the time. It's okay when you are young. As a matter of fact, it's lots of fun, but as time goes on, you start to question whether it's worth it or not."

The Honey Cone was just starting to venture to new musical heights. They made countless personal appearances on teen dance shows like "American Bandstand" and "Soul Train," but also on shows with a wider audience range like "Sonny & Cher" and "The Tonight Show." The tours included the famed Apollo Theatre and The Twenty Grand in Detroit.

The group did so well and was so much in demand that Shelly had to leave "The Jim Nabors Show" after appearing for three seasons. She had to come up with her own replacement, so Alex Brown took her place. "Want Ads" was the onset of a run of very successful singles. Greg Perry was now producing the group, with songs tailor made for them by Perry and Chairman of The Board leader and former Showman, Norman "General" Johnson.

The premise of "Want Ads" was patterned after a formula most effectively used by Motown songwriter Smokey Robinson. Robinson's most adhering lyrics were titles that were based on variations of popular sayings or phrases. The staff writers at Hot Wax/Invictus followed the same formula and were also very successful with it. The sound-alike song "Stick Up" was The Honey Cone's next release. It also rode favorably up the charts, on the coattails of "Want Ads" "Stick Up" employed a similar musical structure, plus the incongruous nonsense tag line, "boom, boom, shaka lacka, boom, boom, boom, boom, which caught the ears of the bubble gum set everywhere.

The group then reached the apex of their success with the all out grooving stomper, "One Monkey Don't Stop No Show." Again, a well planned title, with no-nonsense lyrical content, in keeping with the new 70s woman, drove the single straight into the top 20, the third chart topper for The Honey Cone in a year and a half. Obligatory LPs, featuring their hits and popular songs of the day, accompanied most of the singles. Edna and Shelly shared leads on some of the LP cuts.

After the success of "One Monkey Don't Stop No Show," three more singles with the message of modern woman were released. "The Day I Found Myself" tells the tale of a woman coming into her own after emerging from the shadow of her overbearing male companion. "Sitting On A Time Bomb" and "Innocent 'Til Proven Guilty" were also fine efforts, but the tried and true formula for Honey Cone singles was wearing thin.

An esoteric version of Smokey Robinson's "Ooh, Baby Baby" was selected as one side of a single, enjoyable for its unpredictable movements, but too complicated for mass consumption. "Ace In The Hole" was probably the intended A-side. The group's next and last single, "Woman Can't Live by Bread Alone," tried to get back to the vitality of The Honey Cone's first few singles, but it was too late. Changing designs for Rhythm and Blues had already begun, with the tendency toward strings and steadier beats, culminating in what eventually would be regarded as disco. The road to hitsville became harder.

Besides the floundering of the singles for the group, other factors were bringing about the eventual disintegration of The Honey Cone as well. At first, the undertaking was fun for everyone, but then the grind of rehearsing, touring and recording became too much for Carolyn. Never quite happy with the material that the group was recording, increasing tensions within the group and with Holland-Dozier-Holland helped Carolyn make her decision to exit The Honey Cone in 1973. As Carolyn so succinctly puts it, "I got tired of the material and left." Carolyn was the unofficial vocal arranger for the group.

An inherent musician from an early age, Carolyn writes music, plays piano and has perfect pitch. The simplistic sounds of the material recorded by the group no longer interested her. Edna and Shelly tried replacements, but the energy shared by the original group was gone. When Edna grew discontent with HDH, she didn't show up for recording sessions. The company reserved the right to replace vocalists on recordings, so that's just what they did, sealing the fate of The Honey Cone.

Things weren't going much better for HDH. They were having business difficulties by the mid-70s, and despite hits by many outstanding recording artists between 1969 and 1973, the Hot Wax/Invictus complex folded in 1974. They tried to cash in on the burgeoning disco craze by briefly reviving Hot Wax in 1976, with a Honey Cone single involving none of the original members. "Someone Is Always Messing Up A Good Thing," featured singer Sharon Cash, and went away unnoticed. Popular music had taken another turn, away from those that previously reveled in its glory.

Fortunately, the trio that was The Honey Cone, had much experience as singers and as much clout in the music industry to fall back on after their successful run as a pop group ended. Edna recorded her own album entitled, "Oops, Here I Go Again," for RCA Records in 1977. She also went back to session work, appearing on record and in live performance with Annie Lennox, Whitney Houston, Steely Dan, Ray Charles and with her sister, Darlene Love, appearing on Darlene's 1987 LP, "Paint Another Picture." Edna is married to songwriter and producer Greg Perry, the man who produced many of The Honey Cone's singles.

Carolyn continued to work in the studios, recording jingles for Toyota, American Airlines and Max Factor. She has appeared on vinyl with Melissa Manchester, Boz Scaggs, Steely Dan and with Stanley Turrentine, for which she often received vocal arranging credit. Carolyn has appeared on the soundtracks of "Butterfly" and "A Star Is Born" with Barbra Streisand. Carolyn was also the featured guest vocalist on Seals and Croft's big hit for Warner Bros., "Get Closer" in 1976. Her photo graces the picture sleeve of the 45-rpm single, "I had gone in to do the background work. They needed someone to sing the lead. I had never done leads. I said, 'me'? They (Seals and Croft) were very nice people to work with. I received my session fee, but after the record hit, I also received royalties. They were always honest."

After a few years on hiatus, living in the Midwest, Carolyn returned to Los Angeles in 1997 and picked up her session singing career by joining Blossom/Girlfriend Gloria Jones on a recording session with Charles Wright and The Watts 103rd St. Band. Shelly has also continued with her singing, recording and performing with Tom Jones, Harry Belafonte, Richard Harris and Cab Calloway.

Shelly worked for Eddie Murphy Television as a production coordinator and casting director. Shelly formed W&W Management Company that represents entertainers and sports figures. Shelly is married to Verdine White of Earth, Wind & Fire. She also manages some of the business affairs of EWF. In the 1990s, Carolyn, Shelly and Edna attempted a reunion of The Honey Cone, went all out for rehearsals and had publicity photos taken. Unfortunately, too many old feelings resurfaced, causing Carolyn to once again withdraw from the project. Mary Russell (Leon's wife) was considered as a replacement, but the project fell apart. Still, Shelly doesn't regret a thing about The Honey Cone: "I can honestly say it was one of the highlights of my life and I wouldn't have traded it for all the rice in China. I learned so much and was able to use what I learned in later years. Life is a culmination of great and not so great experiences."

What better couriers could have delivered the messages of independence than Carolyn, Edna and Shelly, three strong and self-reliant women? The Honey Cone were the spitfires of the music world in the early 1970s, proving that women can be packaged as effectual forces as well as enticing sex symbols. The Honey Cone made powerful pop statements inside of two and a half minutes, helping to illuminate the path all women were taking from now on, the satisfaction of their own wants and needs.

The Honey Cone Discography

45s	Label	Number	Year
While You're Out Lookin' For Sugar/The Feeling's Gone	Hot Wax	6901	1969
Girls, It Ain't Easy/The Feeling's Gone		6903	
Take Me With You/Take My Love		7001	1970
Take Me With You/When Will It End		7005	
Want Ads/We Belong Together		7011	1971
Stick Up/V.I.P.		7106	
One Monkey Don't Stop No Show/Part 2		7110	
The Day I Found Myself/When Will It End		7113	1972
Sitting On A Time Bomb/It's Better To Have Loved and Lost		7205	
Innocent 'Til Proven Guilty/Don't Send Me An Invitation		7208	
Ooh, Baby Baby/Ace In The Hole		7212	
Women Can't Live By Bread Alone/If I Can't Fly		7301	1973
Somebody Is Always Messing Up A Good Thing/The Truth Will Come Out		9255	1976
Carolyn Willis (w/The Girlfriends)			
My One and Only Jimmy Boy/For My Sake	Colpix	712	1963
(w/Seals and Croft)			
Get Closer/Don't Fail	Warner Bros.	8190	1976
Edna Wright (w/ The Cogic Singers)			
It's A Blessing/Since I Found Him	Simpson	273	1964
(as Hale and The Hushabyes)			
Yes Sir, That's My Baby/Quetzals (Inst.)	Apogee	104	1964
Yes Sir, That's My Baby/Jack's Theme (Inst.)	Reprise	0299	1964
Yes Sir, That's My Baby/Bee Side Soul (Inst.)	York	408	1967
(as Sandy Wynns)			
The Touch Of Venus/A Lover's Quarrel	Champion	14001	1965
Yes, I Really Love You/Love Belongs To Everyone		14003	
I'll Give That To You/You Turned Your Back To Me	Simco	30001	1966
Love's Like Quicksand/How Can Something Be So Wrong	Canterbury	520	1967

LPs			
Take Me With You	Hot Wax	701	1969
Sweet Reply		706	1970
Soulful Tapestry		707	1971
Love, Peace and Soul		713	1972
Edna Wright			
Oops, Here I Go Again	RCA	--	1977

The Ikettes

Members:

(1961-62) Delores Johnson (Flora
Williams)
Eloise Hester
Josephine Armstead

(1962-66) Venetta Fields
Robbie Montgomery
Jessie Smith

(The Mirettes)

(1966-70) Venetta Fields
Robbie Montgomery
Jessie Smith

When Ike Turner asked Annie Mae Bullock to join his traveling show in 1958, musical history was in the making. Ike changed her name to Tina Turner, creating the alliance of one of the most intense on and off stage relationships in Rock & Roll history. Although the initial influences of Ike & Tina Turner weren't realized until Tina's 1980s rise to stardom. They were a viable underground force in Rhythm & Blues, especially to arriving bands both during and after the British Invasion.

Tina's presence in the limelight was captivating, accumulating electrifying energy with every movement. In order to intensify this presence, dancing singers were employed to further enhance what Tina had created for her frenzied shows. The Ikettes were part of The Ike & Tina Turner Revue and were every inch a show-stopping feature on the review.

The idea surrounding the creation of The Ikettes was to provide both a full sound and maximum interaction on the stage during one of Tina's frantic singing testimonials. Tina's persona as a kind of musical Pentecostal minister had already been established with her early hit, "A Fool In Love." One of the voices asked to be on that single was a young lady named Robbie Montgomery, a former member of The Rhythmettes. She was introduced to Ike Turner when she was a part of Art Lassiter's band, The Ardettes. Robbie was not yet a permanent member of Tina's backing group. The original voices that became The Ikettes on vinyl were hired mainly to sing backgrounds for Tina on her singles.

The strength of the presence that evolved into The Ikettes garnered the group some singles of their own for Atco Records in 1962. Recorded in late 1961, their maiden single, "I'm Blue," kept all the soulsters on the dance floor, while singing the signature background hook, "gong, gong, gong," charting in the process. This trio was mainly a studio group consisting of Delores Johnson (who also went by the name of Flora Williams), Eloise Hester, and singer/songwriter Josephine Armstead, who went on to collaborate with Nik Ashford and Valerie Simpson. This trio was not interested in touring, and since the review traveled many miles all over the United States, and Ikettes were probably hired from major cities. For a time, though, The Ikettes were an entity unto themselves.

Initially, Ike Turner based the review in New York, where he and Tina had their recording contract with Juggy Murray's Sue Records. Ike and Tina Turner Records were enjoying local airplay and chart action in New York which led to national recognition with such hits as "A Fool In Love," "Poor Fool" and "Tra La La La La," songs prominently featuring a female background group. They did not receive a credit on the record label. When the Murray association ended, Turner moved the band's home base to Los Angeles. Robbie Montgomery became a permanent member and moved with the act, receiving top billing as the lead vocalist in The Ikettes, including mention on one single, "Crazy In Love." Since Ike Turner was enterprising, he continued to bill and record The Ikettes as a separate unit. The group's solidification wouldn't happen until 1964.

When The Ike Turner Review's settled in Los Angeles, The Ikettes received special attention. Touring with the review, they had become fixed members of the organization. Turner recorded the ladies with the revived California label, Modern Records, which released six singles by the trio. Brill Building residents Steve Venet and Toni Wine provided some of The Ikettes' Modern material. Venet and Turner would co-produce.

The first single, "Camel Walk," did nothing, but the second effort, a lively track called "Peaches and Cream," made both the pop and R&B charts. By this time, The Ikettes were the threesome of Robbie Montgomery, Jessie Smith and Venetta Fields. In addition to being Ikettes, Montgomery and Fields enjoyed work as session singers in Los Angeles. More recognition followed with "Fine Fine Fine" and "How Come." The Ikettes singles were basic mixtures of Rock and Blues, bump-and-grind dance singles, not overly indulgent on the productions, much more roots-oriented music, with a live sound.

What a surprise when the third Ikettes single, "I'm So Thankful," swept onto the charts in late 1965. It was smooth and polished, with a swaying beat with backing vocals as light as angel cake. The song was written by Marc Gordon and Frank Wilson, two writers heading the Motown Records production chores out in Los Angeles and having success producing Motown artist Brenda Holloway. "I'm So Thankful" stood alone as an example of lustrous glamour for The Ikettes, succeeded by rousing versions of "Sally Go 'Round The Roses" and "Da Doo Ron Ron."

In late 1965, Ike Turner made a deal with Phil Spector to record Tina for Philles Records, where she recorded the glorious "River Deep, Mountain High." The Ikettes were also placed on Spector's Phi-Dan label, which issued "What'cha Gonna Do," yet another simplistic Blues-flavored tune. Surprisingly, The Ikettes that were having the hits were not featured in the movie, "The Big TNT Show," a concert on film produced by Spector. It is open to speculation whether this was the beginning of the end for The Ikettes.

Tina and The Ikettes, strutting on The Big TNT Show, 1965.

6592-13

The trio was planning to break away from Ike Turner's outfit and bill themselves as The New Ikettes. Ike prevented them through legal entanglements, and they changed their name to The Mirettes. The trio recorded a roster of medium soul records, including covers of "The Real Thing" and "Stand By Your Man," before breaking up in 1970. Robbie Montgomery and Venetta Fields continued with their ultimately successful careers as much-in-demand session vocalists.

Turner now needed replacements for The Ikettes. He commissioned his assistant, Ann Cane to mine the Los Angeles circuit of session singers. Among these vocalists, Cane heard about a young lady singing backgrounds while going to school on a scholarship at USC. Talented Shelly Clark was asked to audition for a place in The Ikettes.

After an audition in her living room, Shelly joined the tour as a singer and dancer in 1966. She was joined by Sherell Brooks (?) and Ann Thomas, nicknamed Tomez. As was Ike Turner's tradition, the shows were always high-powered with alternating constant movement and vocal play. Shelly remembers the pace as galvanizing: "The atmosphere in the 1960s was small clubs, lots of smoking and men, but a high energy show. Being a dancer, I could keep up with her (Tina) very well, but she would dance most men and women right off the stage. Also, you couldn't move your hips front and back in the clubs back then, so most routines had side-to-side hip gyrations. If you missed a step or your hair or outfit was not together, it was an automatic $5.00 fine. Talk about a tight ship!"

Shelly's tenure with The Ike & Tina Turner review came to an abrupt halt during one tour when the bus in which the band was travelling hit a pole and turned over in Wichita, Kansas. Shelly recounts how she almost lost her life, "The bus crash in Wichita, Kansas was due to the bus driver falling asleep at the wheel because he was also the lighting director for the show, so he never got to rest. We hit a telephone pole and rolled over twice. I fell out of the bus. Al McKay, the guitarist, ran down the embankment to find me. I was hospitalized in Kansas with two other musicians. The tour recruited new artists and went on without us."

Shelly ended her days as a touring Ikette in Kansas. After her recuperation, she eventually went on to become part of the immensely successful female singing group, The Honey Cone. For The Ike & Tina Turner review, indeed, the show must go on. There was never a cohesive Ikettes group after 1968.

Other recording or live Ikettes have included Jackie Stanton, P.P. Johnson and Pat Powdrill. Most singles released under the name Ikettes have been recycled recordings from their earlier days. Venetta Fields went on to record backing vocals for "A Star Is Born" with Barbra Streisand. She joined Martha Wash, Izora Armstead, Maxine Waters and Julia Tillman as one of The Weather Girls, recording the 1983 disco hit, "It's Raining Men".

Robbie Montgomery also recorded with Barbra Streisand, The Rolling Stones and Stevie Wonder. Also, Robbie joined Dr. John on his successful single, "Right Place, Wrong Time" in 1972. In the mid-1980s, Montgomery returned to her place of birth, St. Louis, MO, where she enjoys a prominent following in the local clubs, as well as appearances on numerous European tours. Shelly Clark married Verdine White of Earth, Wind & Fire. In addition to session singing, Shelly works as part of the empire that keeps Earth, Wind and Fire in business.

All members of The Ikettes were consummate professionals in their own right, something Ike obviously looked for, if his review were to continue as a prime attraction. Even today, the aura of energy and excitement exuded by The Ikettes is reflected in the talents of modern female groups like TLC, En Vogue and SWV. The Ikettes represented an integral and most exuberant component of The Ike & Tina Turner Review.

The Ikettes Discography

45s

	Label	Number	Year
I'm Blue (The Gong Gong Song)/Find My Baby	Atco	6212	1961
Troubles On My Mind/Come On and Truck		6223	1962
Heavenly Love/Zizzy Zee Zum Zum		6232	
I Had A Dream The Other Night/I Do Love You		6243	
Crazy In Love/Pee Wee	Teena	1701	1963
Prisoner In Love/Those Words		1702	
Here's Your Heart/Inst.	Innis	3000	1964
Camel Walk/Nobody Loves Me	Modern	1003	
Peaches 'n' Cream/The Biggest Players		1005	1965
Fine Fine Fine/How Come		1008	
I'm So Thankful/Don't Feel Sorry For Me		1011	
Sally Go 'Round The Roses/Lonely For You		1015	1966
Da Doo Ron Ron/Not That I Recall		1023	
Down Down/What'cha Gonna Do	Phi-Dan	5009	
Beauty Is Just Skin Deep/Make Them Wait	Pompeii	66683	1968
I Want To Take You Higher/--	Liberty	56177	1970
Camel Walk/Nobody Loves Me	United Artists	50866	1971
Two Timin' Double Dealin'/I'm Just Not Ready For Love		51103	1972

(as The Mirettes)

	Label	Number	Year
He's All Right With Me/Your Kind Ain't No Good	Mirwood	5514	1966
Now That I Found You Baby/He's Alright With Me		5531	1967
In The Midnight Hour/To Have Somebody	Revue	11004	
The Real Thing/Take Me For A Little While		11017	1968
First Love/I'm A Whole New Thing		11029	
Help Wanted/John's Big Chance	Minit	32045	
Stand By Your Man/If Everybody'd Help Somebody	Uni	55110	1969
Ain't You Tryin' To Cross Over/Heart Full Of Gladness		55126	
Ain't You Tryin' To Cross Over/Whirlpool		55147	
Ain't My Stuff Good Enough/Season To Be Free	Zea	50002	1970

(as Ike & Tina Turner & The Ikettes)

	Label	Number	Year
So Blue Over You/So Fine	Innis	6667	1968

(as The Mirettes w/Nate Turner)

	Label	Number	Year
Sweet Soul Sister/Rap, Run It Down	Uni	55161	1969

LP

	Label	Number	Year
The Mirettes			
Whirlpool	Uni	73062	1970

The Jaynetts

Members:

(1963-64)	Ethel Davis	(1964-66)	Evangeline Jenkins
	Louise (Harris) Murray		Linda Jenkins
	Selena Healey		Georgette Malone
	Marie Hood		Johnnielouise Richardson
	Ada Ray Kelly		
	Marlina Mars (Mack)		
	Lezli Valentine		
	Mary Green Wilson		
	Iggy Williams		

Lezli and Marie in the studio recording "Sally Go Round The Roses", 1963. (Photo courtesy of Lezli Valentine)

By the 1960s, production values in the music business were changing. The record business was on its way to becoming less hit or miss in its approach. There was now a union of producers, performers and songwriters working to make records commercially viable. Zell Sanders, president of J&S Records, created The Hearts by mixing, matching and even recreating entire groups. Using a round-robin approach, she used all the female singers available to her. A second group was necessary to keep everyone working. This is how The Jaynetts became the daughter group of the initiatory Hearts.

By 1963, Zell Sanders had her good ideas and not much else. She was living in The Bronx, with a heavy hand in the music business, producing soloists Rita Zell and Clarence Ashe. She was also managing Johnnie and Joe. Besides J&S, Zell had a few short-lived labels, Scatt, Dice, and Argyle; Dice being the most successful. A new subsidiary called Zell's Records also showed promise. However, Zell was borrowing money to keep the projects afloat. She had The Hearts, but by this time the group had splintered. Zell wanted to retain all the girls she recorded as Hearts. Zell's forte had always been female vocal groups. Naturally, she thought of having other female groups to pick up the extra members, so everyone could work. Lezli Valentine had come up with a name: "Zell wanted another girl group in addition to The Hearts because the 'on leave' ladies were returning and she didn't want anyone stranded. She said to me, 'Lezli, give me a name.' I said "J" for J&S, and Aynetts for my middle name, Anetta. I had no idea she would use it. I had given Zell the name "Jaynetts" several years prior to her releasing Sally'. "

Zell first used the name "Jaynetts" to put out two songs by the Baby Washington-led Hearts that had been in the can since 1957. The record, "I Want To Be Free/Where Are You Tonight" was released on J&S as The Jaynetts right after acquiring a new set of Hearts in 1958. Zell wouldn't use the name again for five years.

Now that Zell had enough members for two groups, she needed product. Songs based on fairy tales and nursery rhymes, like "Zip A Dee Doo

Dah" and "How Much Is That Doggie In The Window," were all the rage in 1963. Zell just manufactured her own brand. As a favor to the Chess brothers, Zell welcomed a producer sent by them from Chicago. Abner Spector and his wife, Lona Stevens, came to New York to work with Zell on her productions.

Chess had some financial input on these productions which were not released on J&S, but on Spector's Tuff Records. The first single was based on a reworked nursery rhyme. "Sally Go 'Round The Roses" took its bizarre message all the way to #6 on New York playlists in the fall of 1963, as well as becoming a national hit. "Sally. . ." was unlike any single on the radio. It featured Lezli, Marie and Louise, with overdubs by Lezli. This would begin a two-year collaboration with Abner Spector. Lezli contributed a few lines to the song. Artie Butler polished off the arrangement. Writing credits went to Zell, Lona and George David Weiss.

All the female group singles on Tuff were recorded by a nucleus of ladies taking turns in the studio, with three girls cast as the road group. The core of The Jaynetts was Lezli, Louise and Marie, with occasional fill-ins by Cindy Felder, Marlina Mars, Iggy Williams and Selena Healey, among others. Zell had even pieced together the photo

for the group's album using a photo of Lezli and Ethel and matching it with a picture of an unknown young lady. Zell recorded a soloist named Ada Ray (Kelly) on the dramatic "I No Longer Believe In Miracles," where she breaks down crying on the song's bridge, only to be coaxed back by Zell herself. Ada was part of the road group of Jaynetts with Ethel Davis and Johnnielouise. Ethel became a soloist also, recording under the name Vernell Hill. Her only single, "Long Haired Daddy," was released on Tuff in 1964.

Lezli recorded one single with Marlina and Iggy as a revived version of The Clickettes for an "Easier Said Than Done" sound-alike called, "I Just Can't Help It." Another member, Mary Green Wilson, also recorded "Spoiled" as Mary Sue Wellington. Various configurations of singers recorded as The Poppies, Patty Cakes, and Z-Debs, either on Tuff or Roulette. The group also backed Clarence Ashe on his take of "Dancing In A Dream World." Despite several attempts to repeat the

The Jaynetts getting ready for the road, 1963, (L-R) Lezli Valentine, Marie Hood, pianist Charles Landers, Ethel "Vernell Hill" Davis. (Photo courtesy of George Lavatelli/Lezli Valentine)

Johnnielouise Richardson, with Joe Rivers, as Johnnie & Joe.

success of The Jaynetts' hit, none met with overwhelming success, so all the singers eventually went their separate ways.

Disgusted with the sundering of her acts and the lack of attention her singles were receiving, Zell made another change when she moved to upstate New York in 1965. She recorded Johnnielouise as The Jaynetts with another group of singers from Tarrytown on the revived J&S label. The singers were related to Fred Nixon, a friend of Zell's. This group, Johnnie, Linda Jenkins Evangeline Jenkins and Georgette Malone had six interesting singles, including an updated sound on "Sally . . ." called "Cry Behind The Daisies" and the Fred Kaplan-produced "Who Stole The Cookie." The J&S numbering system

TWO HEARTS

CONTACT:
LOUISE MURRA
212-234-3123

Two Hearts, Louise Murray and Donald Gatling, 2000. (Photo courtesy of Louise Murray)

remained haphazard, vaguely related to the different addresses where Zell lived.

In 1966, Lezli Valentine joined Sylvia Robinson's All Platinum Records where she had significant input as a recording artist, songwriter and gal Friday for the complex. Lezli recorded "The Coward's Way Out" and "I Won't Do Anything Except For My Baby" in 1968. Lezli's feistiness always paid off: "I enjoyed recording 'I Won't Do Anything'. Larry Roberts was writing and playing chords on his guitar, but he kept stopping at the same word. I was Joseph Robinson's secretary at the time. Finally, I went into Larry's office and announced, 'I am going to show you how this is supposed to sound!' I did, and since the tune was incomplete, I added La, la la, la la la la la—ooh, how I love him. He liked it and so did Sylvia."

Lezli Valentine eventually retired from the music business and went into the ministry. She currently resides in Ohio. Marie Hood moved to the Midwest and now works for the postal service.

Louise married and settled down in Manhattan to raise her family. She and her husband, Donald Gatling, currently perform as Two Hearts, appearing at various shows in and around New York City. The husband and wife team also sing in a gospel choir. Marlina Mars became Marlina Mack, enjoying brief success by replacing Francine Barker in Peaches & Herb.

Zell made yet another attempt to start a new label in early 1972, called Junior Achievement Records. Lezli helped her out by recording a tune to kick off the label. Health problems prevented Zell from putting her all into this project, so it fell by the wayside. Zell moved to Albany, where failing health kept her out of the recording business permanently. She passed away in St. Barnabus Hospital in New York in 1976.

Johnnielouise suffered a stroke and met an untimely death in 1988, at the age of 43. Since then, the master tapes of J&S have been ensnared in legal red tape, leaving master recordings languishing and many singles never reissued. The determination of one woman to make it in the music business lasted two decades. Zell's accomplishments are a tribute to her fortitude, an eye for talent, and a feel for what she loved best, the music.

The Jeynetts Discography

45s

	Label	Number	Year
I Wanted To Be Free/Where Are You Tonight	J&S	1765/66	1958
Sally Go Round The Roses/Inst.	Tuff	369	1963
Keep An Eye On Her/Inst.		371	
Snowman, Snowman Sweet Potato Nose/Inst.		374	
There's No Love At All/Tonight You Belong To Me		377	1964
Cry Behind The Daisies/Is It My Imagination	J&S	1177	
Chicken, Chicken, Cranny Crow/Winky Dinky		1468/69	
Peepin' In And Out The Window/Extra Extra, Read All About It		1473	1965
Who Stole The Cookie/That's My Baby		1477	
Looking For Wonderland, My Lover/Make It An Extra		1686	
Vangie Don't You Cry/My Guy Is As Sweet As Can Be		4418/4419	

(as The Clickettes)

	Label	Number	Year
I Just Can't Help It/Inst.	Checker	1060	1963

(as The Patty Cakes)

	Label	Number	Year
I Understand Them/Inst.	Tuff	378	1964

(as The Poppies)

	Label	Number	Year
Johnny Don't Cry/Inst.	Tuff	372	1963
There's No Love At All/Johnny Don't Cry	(promo only)	377	1964

(as The Z-Debs)

	Label	Number	Year
Changing My Life For You/I Would If I Could	Roulette	4544	1964

Vernell Hill

	Label	Number	Year
Long Haired Daddy/Sometimes Love	Tuff	381	1964

Marlina Mars

	Label	Number	Year
Johnny's Heart/The Correct Form	Capitol	4922	1963
Just For The Book/I Thought I Knew Me		4997	
It's Love That Really Counts/Just Another Dance	Okeh	7213	1964
Inside I've Died/I'm Gonna Hold On (To Your Love)	MGM	13404	1965
Put My Love On Strike/Give Your Love To Me		13482	1966

Louise Murray

	Label	Number	Year
For Some/The Love I Give	Verve	10376	1966

Ada "Cry Baby" Ray

	Label	Number	Year
I No Longer Believe In Miracles/Give Our Love A Chance	Zell's	252	1963
I Cried To Be Free/Oh Come Back Baby		260	1964

Mary Sue Wellington

	Label	Number	Year
Spoiled/Save A Little Monkey	Tuff	400	1964

Lezli Valentine

	Label	Number	Year
I Won't Do Anything/Coward's Way Out	All Platinum	2308	1968
Who Said To Make It Legal/--	Junior Achievement	--	1972

LPs

	Label	Number	Year
Sally Go 'Round The Roses	Tuff	13	1963

The Jelly Beans

Members:

(1964)	Elyse Herbert		*(1965)*	Elyse Herbert
	Maxine Herbert			Maxine Herbert
	Alma Brewer			Alma Brewer
	Diane Taylor			
	Charles Thomas			

The echo of every teenage girl's heart was the resounding vow to get the guy of her dreams. She knows everything about him, who his friends are and where she can go to get a glimpse of him. No song depicted this sentiment better than "I Wanna Love Him So Bad" sung in the classic New Jersey teen style of The Jelly Beans.

The Jelly Beans were formed while attending various schools in Jersey City, NJ. Charles Thomas, the only male and the oldest member, directed the group and sang bass, countering the girls' high harmonies. Diane Taylor, Alma Brewer and Maxine Herbert attended high school together. Maxine's sister, Elyse, was still in junior high school when she was recruited to be the group's lead singer.

The quintet performed at dances and other local spots in Jersey City when they caught the attention of Bill Downs. Downs thought enough of the group's talent to become their manager. Through Downs' connection to songwriter Steve Venet, The Jelly Beans netted an audition at a new label formed by Jerry Leiber and Mike Stoller called Red Bird Records. The group was given a song written by Steve, Ellie Greenwich and Jeff Barry, entitled "I Wanna Love Him So Bad." The single contributed to an auspicious beginning for the fledgling label.

"I Wanna Love Him So Bad" hit the top ten in the summer of 1964. The group was quickly added to many Rock & Roll tours happening that summer. At the end of one tour, the group was hustled into the studio for a follow-up single. The sophisticated "Baby Be Mine" was a mid-chart placing in the fall of 1964.

With two chart singles to The Jelly Beans' credit, Red Bird started selecting songs for a planned LP. Many tracks were recorded for the album tentatively entitled "Baby Be Mine," named after the second single. Ellie Greenwich, Jeff Barry and Steve Venet co-wrote original songs for the long player, as well as covers of Barry/Greenwich tunes already recorded by other artists, like "Do Wah Ditty," "Here She Comes," "Chapel Of Love" and the already released version of "The Kind Of Boy You Can't Forget."

However, Charles Thomas had a hankering to get into the music business as a producer, and his musical tastes did not coincide with the material that the group was being given. Also, Diane Taylor was not interested enough to stay with the group, so she dropped out. The group did not remain with Red Bird and left in the middle of this project.

As a result, The Jelly Beans album was shelved. By this time, The Dixie Cups had scored four chart items for Red Bird and The Shangri-Las were just taking off. Another female group, The Butterflys, garnered chart action with "Goodnight Baby," so The Jelly Beans were hardly missed at Red Bird. A few months later, in the fall of 1965, they resurfaced as a trio, Alma, Maxine and Elyse. Their driving dance cut, "You Don't Mean Me No Good," and it's wistful flip, "I'm Hip To You," kicked off the miniscule Eskee Records. Charles Thomas wrote the songs and produced the session, but did not sing on the sides. Frank Owens and Eskee's A&R man, Sid Shaw, did the arrangements. An interesting note is that this label used the same numbering configuration as Red Bird. Today, this single enjoys more popularity on the British Northern Soul circuit than it did in its initial release.

The Jelly Beans' flirt with fame was short-lived, as they disappeared from the music world after the Eskee single. Their shelved album was finally released as part of a compilation of Red Bird material in the 1980s, "The Red Bird Story, Parts 1 & 2." The only group member to stay in the music business was Charles Thomas, who, throughout the 1960s, worked as an independent producer, working with The Manhattans and other local groups. Success for The Jelly Beans was fleeting, but the impact of their singles was long-lasting.

The Jelly Beans Discography

45s

	Label	Number	Year
I Wanna Love Him So Bad/So Long	Red Bird	10-003	1964
Baby Be Mine/The Kind Of Boy You Can't Forget		10-011	
You Don't Mean Me No Good/I'm Hip To You	Eskee	10001	1965

LPs

	Label	Number	Year
The Red Bird Story Volume 2	Charly	CDX 19 (UK only)	1987

THE JELLY BEANS   RED BIRD RECORDS

Exclusive Management
Bill Downs
410 W. 115 St., N.Y.C.
UN 5-9795

The Jelly Beans, 1964, (L-R) Maxine Herbert, Elyse Herbert, Charles Thomas, Alma Brewer.

The Jewels

Members:

(1961-63) Sandra Peoples (Bears)
Margie Clarke
Carrie Mingo
Grace Ruffin

(1964-68) Sandra Bears
Margie Clarke
Martha Harvin
Grace Ruffin

(1968-Pres.) Sandra Bears
Margie Clarke
Grace Ruffin

A jewel is, by definition, an ornament or precious stone or metal, given a high value. It also means a person who is greatly revered and appreciated. The Jewels have graced the nation's capital with their fantastic harmonies and impeccable sense of timing and style, both in recordings and on stage. How appropriate that this talented group hails from a place so loaded with monuments saluting great American treasures.

The Jewels were formed at Roosevelt High School in Washington D.C. in 1958. Sandra Peoples and Grace Ruffin lived on the same street. Sandra and Grace met Carrie Mingo at their church where they sang together in the choir. Margie hooked up with the other girls in school. They all blended, both in voice and in personality. It was almost fateful that these four schoolgirls would make singing their pastime of choice.

They all came from musical backgrounds. Margie's sisters sang in local groups and both Sandra and Grace had brothers who were members of vocal groups. Grace's cousin was the inimitable Billy Stewart. It was

through Billy and recording star, Bo Diddley, that the group started its career in entertainment. At first they called themselves The Impalas. Margie remembers the trend toward the name: "Car groups were popular at the time. At first we were going to call ourselves The Renaults, but we decided on The Impalas."

The Impalas started singing around town, doing talent shows and getting jobs at nursing homes and military shows under the guise of Captain Rumsey, a military officer who ran these shows for the benefit of the military bases nearby. He hired a bus and took The Impalas and other artists around to perform. Often, these shows were for free, but the group gained the chance to hone its stage skills in the process.

Bo Diddley was already an established recording artist by the early 1960s. He made his home in Washington, D.C. and kept a small recording studio in his basement. This is where all the young talent in D.C. gravitated, and The Impalas were no exception. According to Grace, these gatherings attracted many talents: "Everybody

The Four Jewels, 1962, (L-R) Sandra Peoples, Grace Ruffin, Margie Clarke, Carrie Mingo. (Photo courtesy of The Jewels)

knew that Bo Diddley had a studio in his basement where he would record, so people would go to his place. We recorded "For The Love Of Mike" and "I Need You So Much" in his basement. We also backed him on "Hey, Bo Diddley" and "Bo Diddley The Lover.""

Two other people who frequented Bo Diddley's basement were Bob E. Lee and James Hopp. The group was introduced to them through these meetings. Lee wanted to produce The Impalas. Hopp became their manager.

The potential product for this group was amazing, since all members were capable of taking the lead spots without any change in dynamics in the backgrounds. Two songs were recorded in the fall of 1961. "For The Love Of Mike" was lead by Grace and "I Need You So Much" featured Margie taking the lead. Fellow singer Chester Simmons, who was a member of The Rainbows and The Marquees, penned "For The Love Of Mike." Through an arrangement with Bo Diddley, the single was released on Checker Records, a subsidiary of the Chess complex in Chicago. Chess also liked another tune, "Dear Miss Lovelorn," which was kept for future release. The prospect of The Impalas having their first single issued on a prestigious label with a proven track record seemed promising, but the record failed to score any points on the charts.

Not phased by the lack of success with the group's first effort, Bob E. Lee continued to record The Impalas, this time with plans to release the records on his fledgling Start record label. The first recordings produced "Loaded With Goodies," lead by Carrie and "Fire," lead by Sandra. By the time the release of the first Start single was ready, a name change was pending. Not wanting to be confused with another group of the same name, The Impalas became The Four Jewels, a more feminine designation.

"Loaded With Goodies" picked up local airplay. With a favorable, local hit to their credit, The Jewels received offers to join the tours on what became known as the "Chitlin Circuit," The Apollo Theater in New York, The Uptown in Philadelphia, The Howard in Washington

D.C., and The Royal in Baltimore. They did all the one-nighters, sharing the bill with their favorite artists, like Mary Wells, The Temptations and Barbara Lewis. On one tour, they were corralled to sing backup for Barbara Lewis.

By this time, Chess Records renewed its interest in The Four Jewels. The group went to Chicago to record some sides at the Chess studios. Bo Diddley and some of the girls' mothers accompanied them. This session generated "Dapper Dan" and "Time For Love." "Loaded With Goodies," a lilting ballad, was paired with "Dapper Dan" and released on Checker. Sandra recalls the song's battle for the number one position on many regional playlists: 'Loaded With Goodies' was locally popular. It traded off the top spot with 'Our Day Will Come' by Ruby & The Romantics. One week it would be 'Loaded With Goodies' at number one, then the next week, 'Our Day Will Come' was number one. They would switch off."

The group also backed Billy Stewart on "Reap What You Sow." The Jewels were developing quite a reputation for their superb stage shows as well as their masterful vocals, with precise, well-blended blow harmonies. James Hopp saw to every detail concerning his charges, including what they would be wearing on stage. Bob E. Lee released two additional singles on Start, the heartfelt "Johnny Jealousy," backed by "Someone Special" and the reminiscent "All That's Good," backed by the bouncy, "I Love Me Some You." Also, the group was utilized to sing backup for Jimmy D. on "Dream World" and was duly billed as The

The Four Jewels on stage, 1963, (L-R) Martha Harvin, Sandra, Grace, Margie. (Photo courtesy of The Jewels)

Manager
SMOKEY McALLISTER

THE JEWELS
Dimension Records

Direction
SHAW ARTISTS CORPORATIO
565 Fifth Avenue
New York 17, New York

Opportunity knocks for The Jewels, 1964, (L-R) Sandra, Grace and Martha.

"D"-Lites. Despite being marvelous singles, they did not approach the success of "Loaded With Goodies."

During 1963, the group's schedule grew busier. Carrie had married and was growing tired of the frenzied pace of touring. She no longer wanted to be on the road. She left the group in 1963 and was immediately replaced by another school chum, Martha Harvin. This quartet made the last trip to Chess to record the uptempo tune, "That's What They Put Erasers On Pencils For," given at the same time to another female group, The Gems. Margie led this number, which was paired with "Time For Love" and released in early 1964.

The group continued with a crowded itinerary of personal appearances at colleges, cabarets and military bases, reminiscent of the days with Captain Rumsey. Their association with Bob E. Lee had ended, so they recorded one single for Tec Records in 1964, a soulful version of The Spaniels tune, "Baby It's You," containing an acrobatic scat by Margie.

One night after a gig in 1964, a gentleman named Smokey McAllister approached the group. He professed to be a manager with connections in New York. He told the group that if they came to see him, he could do something for them. Since they were without a manager at this point, they accepted McAllister's offer. Grace recollects the turn of events, "Smokey McAllister saw us at a show and told us that if we came to New York, he would help us. He lived in New Jersey, so we met him in New Jersey and went into New York. He became our manager."

The group's operations were now temporarily based in the New York area. Margie did not tour with the group at this time, although she was featured on the recordings. This precipitated a name change to The Jewels, since their new publicity pictures featured only Sandra, Grace and Martha. Smokey McAllister struck a deal with Don Kirshner's Dimension Records, home of the hit makers, Little Eva and The Cookies.

By this time, Dimension Records was using independent producers for its product because the in-house teams of songwriters and producers at the former Aldon complex were in the process of moving West. Gene Redd, former member of The Fi-Tones Quintet, produced The Jewels first session, which yielded "Opportunity" and "Gotta Find A Way," the latter written by McAllister. Upon its release, "Opportunity" took off, climbing into the middle reaches of the national charts. The song was the biggest selling single that The Jewels had and provided a venue for a broader spectrum of touring possibilities for the group.

One evening, at a performance at The Apollo Theatre, a familiar figure watched as The Jewels performed on stage. The group was about to be given a special opportunity to be part of a most extraordinary entertainment package. James Brown kept a watchful and critical eye on the young ladies as they exploited their knowledge of

The Jewels in the 1980s, (L-R) Margie, Sandra, Grace. (Photo courtesy of The Jewels)

THE FABULOUS
JEWELS
The Finest in Entertainment
(202) 232-6470   (301) 336-7989   (202) 291-7532

Almost 40 years in the business, 2000, (L-R) Sandra, Grace, Margie. (Photo courtesy of The Jewels)

showmanship and unique stage presence. It was a moment Sandra will never forget: "Big performers came to see upstarts, smaller acts, at The Apollo Theatre. We received a standing ovation. He (Brown) sent his bodyguard to see us backstage, then he asked us to join his act. We were under contract to Smokey, so we said no. Later on, when our contract ended, he came to see us in D.C. We asked him if he was still interested."

James Brown was still very much interested. The Jewels were free of their obligations to Smokey McAllister, so they joined The James Brown Revue. In late 1964, Brown produced one single for them on Federal Records, a version of the Gene and Eunice hit, "This Is My Story." Another, belated single was released by Dimension in 1965, a version of Clarence Henry's "But I Do," flipped with "Smokey Joe's," a song written by newcomers Nikolas Ashford and Valerie Simpson, still a few years away from their fame at Motown.

Meanwhile, The Jewels were learning the finer points of hard work from travelling with the revue. When they weren't on stage entertaining, they were rehearsing. This is what made James Brown's shows incomparable. The group was often featured on stage, beside other featured artists such as Bobby Byrd and horn player Fred Wesley. After a tour filled with interesting times and relentless efforts, The Jewels retired from the revue in 1967. They continued their association with Brown, and were featured on some recordings, including the anthem, "Say It Loud, I'm Black and I'm Proud," "Don't Be A Dropout" and a rare answer record called "Papa's Left Mama Holdin' The Bag."

After leaving James Brown, The Jewels continued to perform in between raising their families. They remained a source of superior entertainment in cabarets and clubs around their native Washington D.C., performing their exquisite material, as well as superb covers of songs made popular by Mary Wells, Creedence Clearwater and Tina Turner. Martha Harvin elected to stay with James Brown's show and is still with him to this day as a featured vocalist. Carrie Mingo stayed out of singing for awhile, then joined The Velons from the late 60s until the late 80s.

In 1985, Sandra, Grace, Margie and Carrie recorded an album of all their tunes, recreating each song exactly as it was done in the early 1960s. This made all their material available on one album, including "Dear Miss Lovelorn." The original sits in the Chess Records vault, unreleased to this day. The LP was released on B.J. Jones' BJM label. In 1996, The Jewels celebrated their 35th anniversary in show business. It was a gala affair attended by mostly friends and family. All five members of The Jewels were in attendance. Notes of recognition were sent from the mayor, Bo Diddley and James Brown, who sent a congratulatory video.

After celebrating almost forty years in the business, The Jewels have no intentions of slowing the pace. The ladies have made numerous appearances on Ronnie I's Heroine's Of R&B concert series, as well as performing at the annual Ladies Night hosted by Ronnie's United In Group Harmony Association.

In June, 1999, The Jewels were part of the Great Day In Harlem photo shoot among other pioneer R&B groups. The Jewels also performed at the dedication at The Smithsonian Institution in February, 2000. Their recordings are often featured on collectors' shows like Dan Romanello's Rhythm and Blues Group Harmony Review and The Rhythm and Blues Serenade, hosted by Gordon Skadberg and Frank Gengaro. Their years as performers afford them the ability to give advice to other groups just starting out. Margie's thoughts on the subject are direct: "This message is for female groups. Your stage presence is important. Sex sells, but you should show just enough and leave the rest to the imagination."

The achievements of The Jewels are far-reaching, their talents unsurpassed. Just one look and one listen will be proof enough that the value of these Jewels is priceless.

The Jewels Discography

45s	Label	Number	Year
(as The Impalas)			
For The Love Of Mike/I Need You So Much	Checker	999	1961
(as The Four Jewels)	Start	638	1962
Loaded With Goodies/Fire		638	1963
Johnny Jealousy/Someone Special		641	
All That's Good/I Love Me Some You	Checker	1039	
Loaded With Goodies/Dapper Dan		1069	1964
Time For Love/That's What They Put Erasers On Pencils For	Tec	3007	
Baby It's You/She's Wrong For You Baby			
(as The "D"-Lites w/Jimmy "D")	Start	643	1963
Dream World/Jeanie			
The Jewels	Dimension	1034	1964
Opportunity/Gotta Find A Way	Federal	12541	
This Is My Story/My Song	Dimension	1048	1965
Smokey Joe/But I Do	Dynamite	2000	1966
Papas Left Mama Holdin' The Bag/This Is My Story			

LPs	Label	Number	Year
Loaded With Goodies	BJM	001	1985

The Joytones

Members:

(1956) Vikki Burgess	*(1956)* Vikki Burgess	*(1956-65)* Vikki Burgess
Margaret Moore	Margaret Moore	Margaret Moore
Estelle Harper	Barbara Brown	Lynn Middleton

Perhaps among the most revered of all vocal groups are the groups that came out of Harlem, New York. Many careers were made and broken on the historical, regal, and often mean streets of mid and upper Manhattan. Out of the myriad of street corner singers were certain groups which had definitive characteristics all their own.

It seems that there was a certain network of groups as The Harptones and The Lyrics under the supervision of musical impresario Raoul Cita. It certainly stood to reason that Cita would have a stable of beautiful, talented female voices to complement his stable of male crooners. This is the story of The Joytones, a deliberate blending of quality, experience and sound.

Lucille (Vikki) Burgess grew up near 119th and Eighth Ave, honing her vocal skills from the recordings of her favorite singer, Dinah Washington, as well as groups like The Orioles and The Five Keys. She was familiar with the popular sounds of her neighborhood and was good friends with the sister of Clyde McPhatter, The Drifters' lead. Clyde had written a song called "Lucille" to honor her as a family friend.

Her first venture into the world of entertainment came when she went to audition for a part in a vocal quartet, known as The Charmers. Vikki attended the audition with her mother. The group knew when they saw her that the svelte 17 year-old with the full-bodied alto voice would be a great front for their group.

The Charmers were then signed to the Central record label. Their efforts at a session yielded two singles, "The Beating Of My Heart/Why Does It Have To Be Me" and

Vikki's first group, The Charmers, 1953, (L-R) George Daniels, Alfred Todman, Vikki, James Cooke, Eugene "Sonny" Cooke. (Photo courtesy of Vikki Burgess)

"Tony, My Darling/In The Rain," with Vikki leading the A-sides. Unfortunately, these superb recordings did nothing to further the group's career. This marked Vikki's exit from The Charmers. She had only been a recording member of the group. They never performed live. Without Vikki, the group went on to record two singles for Timely Records with Eugene "Sonny" Cooke singing lead.

Following her short stay with The Charmers, Vikki was a part of a short-lived group called The Solirettes. The members of this group at the time were Vikki, Renee Stewart, Lillian Maebelle and Myrna Hamilton. They had been a companion group to The Gaynotes and Solitaires. The quartet recorded one song for Hy Weiss' Old Town label. The recording was a version of "I Call To You," written by Stewart. The song had been previously recorded by The Fi-tones and The Mellows. Recorded in 1955, the song remained in the can until its release on a compilation CD.

Vikki and Renee also worked with Della Simpson (Griffin) as part of Griffin's Delltones, with Renee staying on as a recording member. Vikki's association with The Joytones was precipitated by an introduction one night to Raoul Cita, backstage at The Apollo. He had heard her sing "The Nearness of You," and wanted to meet her. Vikki seized the opportunity to sing with the reputable Cita. Vikki sang "The Glory of Love" for her audition with Cita. This auspicious audition made Vikki a member of The Royale Cita Chorus. Vikki remembers her audition: "They were looking for another singer to join The Joytones. I had to go and audition for Cita after meeting him at the Apollo. We all used to gather there at 55 W. 119th Street."

She then turned her attentions to working in various configurations of groups in the Cita arena. One subgroup that was good for three singles on George Goldner's Rama label was The Joytones. There were actually three different groupings of Joytones for the 1956 recordings, with Vikki and Margaret Moore as the common threads.

The first configuration with Estelle Harper recorded the bluesy testament, "All My Love Belongs To You," flipped with the jumpy, "You Just Won't Treat Me Right." The group had a change in the lineup with Barbara Brown replacing Estelle for the next single, the bouncy "Gee What A Boy," flipped with the weepy "Is This the End." The final incarnation of the trio was for their third single when Lynn Middleton (Daniels) replaced a pregnant Barbara Brown.

The Joytones are perhaps best known for their poignant version of "My Foolish Heart." Its flip is the frantic, "Jimbo Jango." This record is the rarest of the Rama singles. The last trio of Joytones did three shows at The Apollo to standing room only crowds. One noteworthy show featured an all-star roster from the Gee/Rama Records complex, with The Joytones, The Teenagers, Cleftones, Valentines, and Harptones.

The Joytones, 1958, (from top) Lynn Middleton, Vikki Burgess, Margaret Moore. (Photo courtesy of Vikki Burgess)

VIKKI and EDDIE BARNES

Vikki and her husband Eddie Barnes, late 1960s. (Photo courtesy of Vikki Burgess)

After the group's run of singles, they concentrated on personal appearances and studio work. Later, in 1958, The Joytones (Vikki, Lynn and Margaret) recorded another song for Raoul Cita on a short-lived label, Reno Records. The song was a mellow tune entitled "Please Believe Me, I Love You." The single, however, was released as The Hi-Lites. Cita decided to change the group's name at the last minute. Lynn also recorded with The Lyrics, The Vibraharps and The Harptones.

Not too soon after recording the Reno single, Vikki gave birth to her daughter. The rest of the group did not record or perform without her, so The Joytones were put on indefinite hold until Vikki returned. Upon her return, the group once again performed studio work.

One of their more interesting assignments came when they were called to perform on a Ray Charles recording. Charles did not have his regular stable of Raeletts available, so The Joytones were called in to perform. Charles was adamant about the sound he wanted. He needed the normally stylized Joytones to be more strident. The final result was "Alexander's Ragtime Band."

Although The Joytones were making the right connections, that single needed to put them on top was elusive. Vikki says their last attempt at a hit single was in 1965 on Coed Records through their involvement with Billy Dawn Smith, "Billy Dawn was handling us at this time. We did studio work for about three years until Billy Dawn got us recorded with Coed Records."

"This Love," was co-written by Tony Middleton, former lead singer of The Willows who recorded the 1956 hit, "Church Bells May Ring." This new Joytones single utilized lilting violins, mesmerizing backgrounds, and the breathy, cooing lead voice of Lynn Middleton. Unfortunately, Coed was on its last leg, and the single was not promoted. Margaret Moore remembered the reaction of radio programmers, "At the time we were trying to get airplay for the record, The Supremes' sound was popular, so the radio stations wanted something with a sound similar to that."

This last effort for the group did not move programmers. Soon after, The Joytones went their separate ways. Although "This Love" was released again, twice, with the group billed as Love Potion, the time for its sound's viability on pop radio had passed.

After the group folded, Vikki did backup work for producer Juggy Murray and sang a few commercial jingles, most notably for Lark cigarettes and the sales pitch, "I Got My Job Through The New York Times." Vikki and her husband, Eddie Barnes, put together an act promoting Vikki as a soloist, singing the bluesy torch songs she admired so much as a teen. Vikki performed at The Palisadium and was the first act to appear at The Binghamton Boat in Edgewater, New Jersey, when it first opened.

For many years she and her husband were staples on the cabaret scene at Resorts, The Catskills and at various lounges of many premium hotels in New York City. Her most notable club appearance was at the famed Jimmy Weston's, where Vikki entertained in front of many Hollywood stars like Frank Sinatra. Vikki received rave reviews for her performances from Rex Reed.

After Eddie's untimely death, Vikki continued on her own, putting together her own band, Greg Hunter, piano; Carol Coleman, bass; and Yogi Horton, drums. With the advent of disco for the masses and changing tastes for nightlife, the abundance of lounges waned in the late 1970s. Vikki gave up singing on a regular basis and took a job outside the music business.

In 1991, Vikki was brought back into the limelight to recollect her days as a

Ms. Victoria Barnes

Vikki as a soloist, 1975. (Photo courtesy of Vikki Burgess)

The Joytones reunion at UGHA, 1992, (L-R) Vikki, Margaret, Lynn. (Photo courtesy of Ralph Corwin)

member of The Charmers and The Joytones. She accompanied Jimmy Merchant of The Teenagers to a radio segment of The Rhythm & Blues Group Harmony Review at Fordham University's WFUV in New York. This led to The Joytones' regrouping for one last time when they appeared at one of The United In Group Harmony Association's all-star concerts in 1992. Vikki also reprised her songs with a group of Charmers (aka The Sheps) at subsequent UGHA concerts.

Lynn Middleton Daniels performed globally with Ramon Loper's Platters during the late 1960s and 1970s. She then became known as Sugar Grier, performing in many Harlem nightspots during the 1980s. She rejoined The Harptones during the early 1990s, helping to once

again present the group's reputable talents. Unfortunately, she passed away in 1994.

Margaret Moore moved out of New York City for a time, before returning to New York and joining Cita in a series of musical projects as the group Feelings during the 1970s. Margaret passed away in 1996.

Vikki recalls her days as a Joytone with genuine fondness for the music, the company, and for the chance to do what came naturally, which was singing. The Joytones will be remembered as one of the featured threads of an intricately woven fabric of songs and raw talent that blanketed the streets of New York during the 1950s. Theirs are the talents and efforts of a certain time in musical history, part of the continuum of American music.

The Joytones Discography

45s	Label	Number	Year
The Joytones			
You Just Won't Treat Me Right/All My Love Belongs To You	Rama	191	1956
Gee What A Boy/Is This Really The End		202	
My Foolish Heart/Jimbo Jango		215	
This Love/I Wanna Party Some More	Coed	600	1965
(as The Hi-Lites)			
Please Believe Me, I Love You/Sweet And Lovely	Reno	1030	1958
(as Love Potion)			
This Love/Mr. Farouk (inst.)	TCB	1601	1968
This Love/Moby Binks	Kapp	979	1969

Candy & The Kisses

Members:

(1964-69)   Jeanette Johnson
            Beryl Nelson
            Suzanne Nelson

They're doing the Twist, the Fish, the Fly, the Popeye, and the Monkey. You name it, and it was a dance. By 1964, teenagers performed so many new dances, 1959 seemed like a million years ago when dancers were only demonstrating variations on the Lindy. Producers were so in touch with songs the record buying public wanted, they could create more and more product overnight, including dances that didn't even exist yet. Out of a masterful realm of creative forces came The 81, a localized dance that no one is still quite sure how it goes, but the song soared onto the charts in 1964, presented by a trio of cooing teens named Candy and The Kisses.

Candy and The Kisses started as many vocal groups did, singing after school and at parties in their native New Jersey. Lead singer Beryl Nelson, her sister Suzanne and her cousin Jeanette Johnson, were influenced by the multitude of musical talent emanating out of the radio. In late 1963, the yet unnamed group got a chance to sing backing vocals for singer/songwriter Ernestine Eady on her hip single for Junior Records, "The Change." Eventually, the group found its way to the offices of Cameo-Parkway Records, home of The Orlons and The Dovells. Producer Jerry Ross thought much of the quintessential threesome fronted by Beryl's astute voice. According to Ross, he christened the group Candy and The Kisses for their maiden single. The name had been used a year earlier on an isolated single by a California female group, but the two have no relation.

Ross, with Joe Renzetti and arranger Jimmy Wisner, listened carefully to what was working among female group sounds at the time and developed a Kenny Gamble/Jerry Ross song into a pseudo-Motown groove. "The 81," based on an obscure dance step, made it into the top 50 in the fall of 1964, with higher charting positions on regional play lists. Many people thought it was the next Martha and The Vandellas single. It's flip "Two Happy People" sounds like homage to Red Bird Records productions, like "Chapel of Love." Both songs contained a sprightly feeling about them.

Despite an auspicious start for Candy and The Kisses, they did not record a follow-up single until a few months later. In 1965, Renzetti and Ross reworked two songs written by songwriters Vinnie Poncia and Pete Andreoli, songs that Phil Spector had used when he was associated with the songwriting duo. "Soldier Baby of Mine," a previously recorded, unreleased track by The Ronettes, was selected for Candy and The Kisses. The group provided beguiling vocals amidst a catchy production, with a mandolin intro and a processional hi-hat drum, to match the "soldier boy" lyrics.

Ross then paired the group with singer Harriet Laverne to form Honey Love and The Love Notes, recording the pleasant "We Belong Together" and another song, "Mary Ann," previously recorded by The Crystals, but left in the can. "Soldier Baby of Mine" was backed by a moving production called "Shakin' Time," a fine example of go-go music at its best. The song opens with wild bongos and a (fake) live crowd. Intermittent trumpets herald each chorus.

This was a production worthy of carrying Cameo-Parkway safely into soul music. However, this was not to be. It is open to speculation whether or not the company pushed the record, but by this time, it was obvious in the trades that Cameo-Parkway was in trouble. Other, less creative product was crowding the roster and key producers were leaving the fold.

Ross, Renzetti and Wisner went over to ABC-Paramount, where they had success with The Sapphires. Candy and The Kisses were now forced to either stay at the company and be paired with new producers or jump ship. At this time, "The Change," by Ernestine Eady, was picked up for release by Scepter Records. By the middle of 1965, Candy and The Kisses were also signed to Scepter Records and then another Love Notes single was released by Cameo in 1966.

The group's tenure at the New York label was spent under the direction of Jovalnick Productions, the name given the co-producing and writing talents of Jo Armstead, Valerie Simpson, and Nik Ashford. The first effort for the group by the up and coming songwriters was "Keep On Searchin'," a raucous dance number. The pleasant flip, "Together," was written by another future Motown team, Pam Sawyer and Lori Burton. "Together" was much more pacific than the A-side, with appeasing shifts between unison and harmony.

The production team decided to center on the group's softer side for the second single, "Sweet and Lovely." The song contained ingredients later found in Ashford and Simpson's efforts at Motown, such as establishing the tune with cautious, relenting rhythms, then intensifying it with tempo and orchestration changes. The result was a rhythmic sway.

For the B-side, Ashford-Simpson-Armstead gave a nod to a Shangri-Las' tune by having the group record their rendition of tough love called "Out In The Streets Again." One more single was produced for Scepter; a version of The Shirelles classic, "Tonight's The Night" released in 1966. The song features a progressive beat, with lounge band horn modulations after each chorus. Although the production team tried to establish a style for the group, the singles did not yield any lasting success. A few months later, Ashford and Simpson were the stars of Motown, flushed with success over their hit song recorded by Marvin Gaye and Tammi Terrell, "Ain't No Mountain High Enough" and Candy and The Kisses were looking for a new record label. The trio made another stop at Decca in 1968, recording "Chains of Love." The group continued as Sweet Soul, recording one single for Mercury before exiting the music business for good, in 1969.

Candy and The Kisses recordings showed a precise mixture of sound and technique, with the help of their producers, the group showed capabilities for quite a few musical styles. Even though no one remembers exactly how to do The 81, audiences are glad to groove to a song that keeps them moving every time it's dropped onto a record player.

Candy And The Kisses Discography

45s	Label	Number	Year
The 81/Two Happy People	Cameo	336	1964
Soldier Baby (Of Mine)/Shakin' Time		355	1965
Keep On Searchin'/Together	Scepter	12106	
Sweet and Lovely/Out In The Streets Again		12125	
Tonight's The Night/The Last Time		12136	1966
Chains of Love/Someone Out There	Decca	32415	1968
(as Honey Love and The Love Notes)			
We Belong Together/Mary Ann	Cameo	380	1965
(as The Love Notes)			
Baby Baby You/Beg Me	Cameo	409	1966
(as Sweet Soul)			
If You Love Him/Oh No, Oh No	Mercury	72415	1969

Little Eva

During the early 1960s, starting with the Twist, new dances were popping up like wildflowers. Sometimes a song about a dance would precede the dance itself. One dance in particular had teenagers moving across the dance floors like runaway trains. This inspirational stomp was aptly entitled "The Locomotion", brought to you by a singer who had come to New York City armed with ambition and a voice, looking for employment. With the aid of extraordinary backing by one of the era's most popular female groups, she was thrust to the forefront of the world of Rock & Roll. With no time for introductions, Little Eva burst onto the music scene, singing what would become one of the most enduring songs of our time.

Eva Narcissus Boyd was born in Bellhaven, North Carolina in 1943. As a teenager, her first trip to New York was in 1961, but she didn't stay. Eva traveled North again in 1962, to find a job, any job. Her brother's wife had a friend, Earl Jean McCrea, who joined a trio of young ladies getting work singing background vocals at recording sessions in New York. The group was The Cookies. Little Eva tells of her first encounter: "My brother's wife knew Earl Jean. Earl Jean had informed her producers, Carol King and Gerry Goffin, that I was coming north for a job and that I could sing."

And sing she did. At first, Eva landed a spot in The Cookies, singing demos with the group. She also accepted a job babysitting for Goffin and King's two children. Carole King and Gerry Goffin would often rehearse their songs at home. Eva picked up on what they were doing and sang along. This song, intended for Dee Dee Sharp's follow up to "Mashed Potato Time," sounded so good with Eva singing it, the songwriting duo decided to let her record the song. She was tapped to record what

would become a major release for Dimension Records, and for Little Eva as a "new artist." This launched Little Eva's solo career. The song was "The Locomotion."

The song begins with a blaring intro of horns and drums. The production possessed an infectious rhythm, besides a hook line from the onset. Eva's youthful vocal sold the dance, while The Cookies provided the call and response backing vocals, which is a hook unto itself. This also became a ready-made dance for the teenagers.

With the advent of teen dance shows, new dances like the Locomotion, Watusi and Mashed Potato were joining the Twist on the list of crazes sweeping the country. "The Locomotion" went straight into the top ten in early 1962. Little Eva's "job" was now being Little Eva. Her overnight success was secretly a dream come true: "'Locomotion' overwhelmed me as a singer. I mean, I had dreamed about it and talked about it. I had even written an essay about it. You hope that it would happen. I got to travel all over America, England and Paris."

The Cookies would soon enjoy their own success as artists, but were always guests on Little Eva's records. Occasionally, Little Eva would still be the fourth voice in the background. Little Eva recorded a string of creative, if not always commercially successful songs for Dimension, while managing an extensive touring schedule in America and in England. "Keep Your Hands Off My Baby" was the next successful single in 1962 after "The Locomotion."

An album entitled, "Locomotion" was released, as was "Dimension Dolls," a compilation of demos sung by Little Eva, The Cookies, and Carole King. "Keep Your Hands Off My Baby" did well in the big cities. "Let's Turkey Trot" and "Old Smokey Locomotion" did not fare as well. Perhaps the second most successful single of Little Eva's career was her impromptu duet with Big Dee Irwin on his version of "Swinging On A Star." The duo also recorded a Christmas single together.

More adventurous productions were staged with Little Eva's more interesting singles, like "The Trouble With Boys," "What I Gotta Do" "Just A Little Girl" and "Please Hurt Me." During this period, Eva was immersed in her personal appearances. She did not bother herself with the business side of entertaining because she was young, making a living at something she loved to do. Even Eva's sister headed for New York to sing. Idalia Boyd recorded a single, "Hula Hoppin'," featuring Little Eva and The Cookies on backups. Idalia's career was not as lasting as Eva's was.

In early 1964, plans had been made to phase Dimension Records out of existence. Screen Gems absorbed Aldon Publishing in mid 1963. Now the big push was on Colpix Records, Screen Gems' main label. Al Nevins, now in failing health, relinquished his control of the company to Don Kirshner, but stayed on as a consultant. Many of the songwriters at Dimension were getting ready to travel West to write for television, in which Screen Gems had heavy involvement. The writers were going to receive exposure to a wider array of opportunities. The artists were basically left to fend for themselves.

Little Eva did manage to record a song which gained television exposure, "Makin' With The Magilla," was fea-

LITTLE EVA

Little Eva doing The Locomotion, 1962.

tured in an episode of the Hanna-Barbera cartoon show, "Magilla Gorilla." Anyone of elementary school age at this time fondly remembers hearing the song on this prime time cartoon show.

When the operations for Dimension were rapidly being shut down, outside producers with finished masters were used as output for the label. Little Eva recorded "Taking Back What I Said," her final single for Dimension in early 1965. Goffin and King did not produce this single. Jack Lewis produced and Charlie Calello arranged. Chip Taylor, then a fledgling songwriter, still a year away from "Wild Thing," took writing credits on both sides. When Eva came back from a tour, she heard the news that Al Nevins had passed away. Nevins was her supporter at Dimension and always made sure Little Eva got her due. She also found that her contract was sold to Bell Records, the company that pressed and distributed Dimension Records. There she worked with Robert Feldman, Jerry Goldstein and Richard Gottehrer, releasing a version of Ben E. King's "Stand By Me" in 1965, on Amy Records, a Bell subsidiary.

During 1965, Eva was still touring on the strength of "Locomotion," appearing on ABC's "Shindig" and "Hullabaloo." Her stage shows were lively and full of emotionally charged versions of many of her recordings.

Eva's next chance at making a record was with producer Creed Taylor at MGM. The output here is a departure from the material for which Eva was known. "Just One Word Ain't Enough" was a guitar licking, soul-inspired piece that surprisingly downplays the tougher aspect of Little Eva's voice. "Bend It" was actually an attempt at another dance record. The second single, "Everything Is Beautiful About You, Boy" exhibited all the ingredients of premium uptempo soul. By contrast, Eva's voice conveyed its more gentle qualities.

By 1968, Eva was working with writer/producer John Lombardo and producer/arranger Jerry Gross and was managed by Roy and Julius Rifkin. She recorded three singles for Spring Records. One was an adequate cover of The Shirelles' "Mama Said," flipped with another temperate, rhythmic tune, "Something About You, Boy."

Eva's later records were firmly rooted in contemporary R&B and her vocal exuded more maturity. These emergent qualities came together with her next single, "Night After Night." Renewed boldness plus new polish exuding from Eva's lead, together with an audacious track, melded Little Eva's vocal into her best production since her days with Goffin/King. It would be her last record.

By the beginning of the 1970s, Little Eva was disillusioned with the entertainment industry. When the hits were no longer forthcoming, she garnered more club work, but was constantly dogged by what she considered unscrupulous business practices, out and out cupidity and pilferage of what was due her monetarily by many in the business.

Little Eva married and gave up recording to raise her family, returning to North Carolina and settling in Kinston. Always religious, she spent her time with her church. For many years, she ran a restaurant, Hanzie's Grill, where she was discovered by "People Magazine" in 1991. Gary Cape, head of Gary Cape Management saw the article in "People" and contacted Eva. He wanted her to perform again and offered to manage her. At first Eva was resistant. It took some convincing on Gary's part: "Gary had taken a survey and people wanted me to come back. I finally consented to talk to Gary, but nothing convinced me to do it. Gary sent me these contracts and I let them sit for eight months. I didn't want to compromise my beliefs. I was devoted to the church."

With Gary's solid management behind her, Little Eva finally agreed to go back to the stage. She has made personal appearances at The Meadowlands in New Jersey, The Wisconsin State Fair, and has toured overseas as a package with Bobby Vee, making stops in England, Scotland, Wales, The Netherlands and Germany. At first, Little Eva admits she was nervous about going back on stage, but her love of singing and entertaining once again took over her system, and she is as relaxed on stage as the day she embarked on her first tour. The wide-eyed little girl who came to New York in the early 1960s to look for work is still on the job.

Little Eva Discography

45s

	Label	Number	Year
The Locomotion/He Is The Boy	Dimension	1000	1962
Keep Your Hands Off My Baby/Where Do I Go?		1003	
Let's Turkey Trot/Down Home		1006	1963
Old Smokey Locomotion/Just A Little Girl		1011	
The Trouble With Boys/What I Gotta Do		1013	
Please Hurt Me/Let's Start The Party Again		1019	
Makin' With The Magilla/Run To Him		1035	1964
Takin' Back What I Said/Wake Up John		1042	1965
Stand By Me/That's My Man	Amy	943	
Just One Word Ain't Enough/Bend It	Verve	10459	1966
Everything Is Beautiful About You Boy/Take A Step In My Direction		10529	1967
Mama Said/Something About You Boy	Spring	101	1969
Night After Night/Something About You		107	1970

(as Little Eva Harris)

	Label	Number	Year
Get Ready – Uptight/Mr. Everything	Spring	704	1968

(w/Big Dee Irwin)

	Label	Number	Year
Swinging On A Star/Another Night With The Boys	Dimension	1010	1963
The Christmas Song/I Wish You A Merry Christmas		1021	

LPs

	Label	Number	Year
The Locomotion	Dimension	4001	1962
Dimension Dolls		4002	1963

Love Unlimited

Members:

(1972-79)   Glodean James
               Linda James
               Diane Taylor

During the early 1970s, soul sounds were becoming more earthy and gritty. In a small corner of the R&B world, there remained a need for sweet, lush and polished soul. Melodies that could rock lovers to sleep, wrapped in each other's arms. If a rift between two sweethearts forced them apart, just the opening movement in one of these songs could rebond the two feuding paramours. Although all this sentiment seems a little syrupy, there really was a market for songs that invoked such feelings. Love Unlimited, a glamorous and lustrous group of females, along with their director and mentor, Barry White produced such euphonious confections.

In mid-1960s Los Angeles, singer/songwriter Barry White was trying his hand at producing. After the breakup of his group, The Atlantics, in 1966, Barry got into producing, recording a soft, bird-like vocalist named Felice Taylor. Felice was a former member of The Sweets, who recorded "The Richest Girl" for Valiant Records. White and fellow songwriter Paul Politi produced two singles for Mustang Records, home of the celebrated Bobby Fuller Four. Taylor's take on "I'm Under The Influence of Love" and "It May Be Winter Outside" sounds like a caricature of Diana Ross' voice amidst pseudo-Motown productions. In fact, the melody to "It May Be Winter Outside" bears a striking resemblance to The Supremes' "Everything Is Good About You," but, in 1966, Motown was the sound to emulate.

White's production takes the popular sound a step further by frosting the dancing beat with swirling violins. The producers took their cue from Phil Spector, and paired each single with an instrumental B-side, giving the public another taste of the instrumentation available on the A-side, but without the vocalist. This was a prophecy of things to come, since in the 1970s, tracks were extended for more dancing time. After the releases for Felice Taylor, Barry White turned his attentions elsewhere.

Twin sisters Linda and Glodean James started singing for fun in their San Pedro, California neighborhood located just south of busy Los Angeles. The sisters had joined the school glee club and followed in their mother's footsteps, by singing at their local church. The girls formed a group with some school friends, and appeared at the usual venues, parties, and dances, but never seriously considered doing anything beyond that scope of events. Upon graduation from high school, the group broke up. It wasn't until a few years later that Glodean's friend, Andrea Sprewell, asked her to sing backup on a project she was working on with a producer named Barry White. Glodean recruited her sister Linda and another girl, Diane Taylor.

This trio was part of the group that sang in high school. The ladies decided it was time to go beyond the living room stage of singing and agreed to meet Andrea at her house for a rehearsal. When they arrived, Barry White was already there. When he heard them, he thought highly of their sound.

After the project with Andrea was finished, the group was impressed with White's ability to write and arrange. Since mutual admiration now existed, the factions decided it was in everyone's best professional interest to work together.

The first order of business was finding a new name. Some ideas were passed around, and it was decided that the name should be in keeping with the songs the group would sing and their style. What better name was there for the group than Love Unlimited? After all, White would soon be presenting himself as the deep-throated master of love, so his counterparts would do the same, showcasing themselves as warbling cherubs filled with unremitting adulation for their mates.

The first production released as a single was "Walking In The Rain With The One I Love." The track starts with office friends saying goodbye, and as we follow the young lady's trip home, it begins to rain and her thoughts turn to her significant other. This romantic interlude unfolding on vinyl worked well for the group, placing them on the R&B charts in 1972. The single was also a smash in the UK.

Under the influence, Love Unlimited, 1972. (Photo courtesy of Sandra Gomez)

The follow-up single, "Is It Really True Boy, Is It Really Me," continues the surreal dream of existing in a world where everyone's dreams of happiness come true. The rich mixture of the high voices and Barry White's production soon earned him the title of "The Black Mantovani." Love Unlimited's debut LP was a series of love stories on vinyl. White was so successful with Love Unlimited's singles and their album, aptly named "Love Unlimited," he named his Love Unlimited Orchestra after them. The only negative hitch was that their record label, Uni Records, was being absorbed into a new company, MCA Records. Unlike label mates, Elton John and Neil Diamond, Love Unlimited did not join the new label. They moved over to 20th Century Fox Records, where Barry White had signed on as a solo artist.

Further success followed with the second album, "Under The Influence of Love Unlimited," which had two singles to its credit. Updated versions of "It May Be Winter Outside" and "Under The Influence of Love" were released during 1973 and 1974, keeping the trio visible on the music charts and television shows like Don Cornelius' Los Angeles based "Soul Train."

Through the emerging disco scene breaking in major cities, Love Unlimited singles were staples on djs' turntables, rousting lovers from their seats to end the night of revelry with a slow grind to a sweet love song. Most singles had an instrumental B-side, to showcase the orchestra. The singles did well, but did not climb as high on the charts as the next record, a production that would borrow elements from tried and true love songs from the past.

Passions were firing up as Love Unlimited recorded their third album, "In Heat," released in 1974. The first single, "I Belong To You," is clearly inspired by old love songs like Ed Townsend's "For Your Love" and The Chantels' "The Plea," while invoking a feeling of sultry seduction and passionate angst. The single made it to the national top 30. A second single bearing the same sentiment, "Share A Little Love In Your Heart," followed.

By 1974, passions had also heated up for Glodean and Barry, as they became husband and wife. His successful career as a lamenting crooner amidst the ambient sounds of the ever-growing Love Unlimited Orchestra was going full speed ahead. The momentum gained by Love Unlimited would not always be as forceful.

Barry White and The Love Unlimited Orchestra were appearing at concerts all over the globe. This provided less time for the vocal trio than before. Running off the success of "I Belong To You," another album wasn't released until 1976. Barry struck a deal with Columbia to distribute his new Unlimited Gold Label. The next two Love Unlimited LPs were released on this label. "He's All I Got" yielded one single, "I Did It For Love," which failed to attract sufficient radio action.

The group was absent for almost two years until the vibrant disco single, "High Steppin', Hip Dressin' Fella," from the LP, "Love's Back," an album seeking to reintroduce the group in 1979. The single is reminiscent of the early 1970s, with its "I love the neighborhood hunk" message. The production featured an updated tempo, driven by the piano and high hat drums, perfect for dancing the Hustle. Once again, Barry White's old writing partner, Paul Politi, and former Motown producer Frank Wilson collaborated on this effort. Dance clubs featured the 12-inch extended tracks and the shorter version received extensive radio play. Unfortunately, Love Unlimited did not benefit from this next hit and disbanded within a year.

Linda James married in 1978 and soon after the group's breakup, moved to Europe. Sadly, Diane Taylor died in 1985 after a battle with cancer. Glodean and Barry recorded some duets together, and she continued to tour with him. In recent years, Barry White and his music have enjoyed a huge resurgence, mainly because of the renewed interest in 1970s disco.

The music of Love Unlimited embodied what their name implied. With song after song filled with luxuriant musical scoring and lyrics professing undying and unselfish love, these three soaring voices, dressed elegantly, like exquisite hostesses, became the poster girls for what we now call "mood music." And with Love Unlimited, the mood was always right.

Love Unlimited Discography

45s

	Label	Number	Year
Walking In The Rain With The One I Love/I Should Have Known	Uni	55319	1972
Is It Really True Boy, Is It Really Me/Another Chance		55342	
It May Be Winter Outside (But In My Heart It's Spring)/It's Winter Again (Inst.)	20th Century	2062	1973
Under The Influence Of Love/Inst.		2082	1974
I Belong To You/And Only You		2141	
Share A Little Love In Your Heart/Love You So, Never Gonna Let You Go		2183	
I Did It For Love/Inst.	Unlimited Gold	7001	1976
High Steppin' Hip Dressin' Fella/Inst.		1409	1979

Barry and Glodean White

	Label	Number	Year
I Want You/Our Theme	Unlimited Gold	02087	1981
You're The Only One For Me/This Love		02419	
Didn't We Make It Happen, Baby/Our Theme		70064	

LPs

	Label	Number	Year
Love Unlimited	Uni	73131	1972
Under The Influence of Love Unlimited	20th Century	414	1973
In Heat		443	1974
He's All I've Got	Unlimited Gold		1976
Love's Back		36130	1979

The Marvelettes

Members:

(1961-63) Katherine Anderson
Juanita Cowart
Gladys Horton, Lead
Georgeanna Tillman
Wanda Young (Rogers), Lead

(1963-65) Katherine Anderson
(Schaffner)
Gladys Horton
Wanda Rogers
Georgeanna Tillman

(1965-67) Katherine Schaffner
Gladys Horton
Wanda Rogers

(1967-70) Katherine Schaffner
Anne Bogan
Wanda Rogers

THE MARVELETTES

The marvelous Marvelettes, 1961, (L-R) Juanita Cowart, Georgeanna Tillman, Gladys Horton, Wanda Young, Katherine Anderson.

Is it possible to be both provincial and outstanding? A group of talented, homespun girls from Inkster, Michigan, a bucolic town outside of Detroit proved this to be true. A chance appearance at a school competition netted five girls a chance to make a move that would keep them forever in the minds of all who listened to Rock & Roll radio throughout the 1960s. The marvelous Marvelettes left their indelible stamp on a string of recordings forever etched in pop music history.

The roots of The Marvelettes began in Inkster, Michigan, a small town outside of Detroit. Gladys Horton grew up listening to popular music on the radio. Gladys enjoyed singing and did some writing as well. As Gladys grew into a young lady, she gravitated to friends who also had a love of music and a flair for singing. At fourteen, Gladys joined with some friends; Jeanette McClaflin, Juanita McClaflin and Rosemary Wells, to sing in a group called The Del-Rhythmetts.

The informal group recorded "Chic-A-Boomer," a light, Latin-tinged rocker for the tiny JVB Records in 1959. Outside of local airplay, nothing came of the single. Gladys' yearning to perform did not dissipate as quickly.

Gladys' ongoing predilection to sing and perform drew her to the talent shows given at Inkster High School where she enjoyed seeing the abundant talent exhibited by all the young people. However, the talent of a particular contestant,

Georgia Dobbins, especially caught her attention: "I started going to the talent shows before I was in high school. I would always see Georgia. Every year she was on and every year she won. One year she had an all-girl band, with a horn and a piano, doing Bill Doggett's 'Hold It'." Gladys was impressed by Georgia's ability to be versatile and to pick out winning material and arrangements and vowed that she would soon put together a winning team of her own.

In 1960, when Gladys entered high school, she joined the glee club and, of course, planned to enter the annual talent contests. One year, when the notices for the next show were posted, Gladys went to work, selecting members for a group to perform in the competition. By this time, Georgia had graduated, but Gladys asked her to join her group. Gladys also asked Katherine Anderson, with whom she sang in the glee club.

The group quickly grew to a quintet, with Georgeanna Tillman and Juanita Cowart, other members from the school chorus, also joining the fold. With the exception of Georgia, all the girls were sophomores and juniors. Gladys says the group jokingly dubbed themselves The Casingyettes, (can't sing yet) because they felt they needed more polish. This particular talent show was special, because the winners would win an audition for Motown Records, the Detroit label that had a smash hit with a song called "Shop Around" by The Miracles. The girls were apprehensive, but they weren't going to miss this chance. Juanita recalls the group's decision to compete, "We had heard that there was going to be a talent show at Inkster High School and that a talent scout would be there from Motown, searching for new talent. We decided to enter."

By the time they reached the stage, they were still calling themselves The Casingyettes. As it turned out, The Casingyettes came in fourth. Even though this position didn't qualify them for the audition, the student advisor, Shirley Sharpley, insisted that the young ladies be included in the trip to Detroit. Berry Gordy, Motown's president, liked the group, but told them they needed original material to record. The young ladies would have an original song upon their return to Motown.

The group planned their next rehearsal, but Katherine says they weren't sure what their next step would be in preparing for their return to Motown. Georgia arrived at rehearsal with William Garrett, an acquaintance who wrote songs. Georgia wanted to augment a song in his cache called "Please Mr. Postman." She recalls: "We were doing material by girl groups of that time. Georgia went out and found this gentleman that did a little writing. His specialty was mostly blues. She went through his briefcase and found this song. She changed the wording to make it more conducive to R&B. We had a nice mailman that we had known for a long time named Mr. Johnson, so it was fitting that we do this song."

The way Georgia had reworked the song caused the rest of the group to take notice. They became more positive about their impending date with Motown. The group rehearsed "Please Mr. Postman" with Georgia on lead. The group auditioned the song for Motown, contracts were drawn up and a recording date was set. To Gladys' surprise, shortly before the recording session, Georgia came to her house to announce that she was opting out of the group, "Georgia's mother was sick with a bad back, and Georgia made it clear that she was not going to leave her mother if we had to tour. Georgia wanted me to sing the lead, so she taught me the song."

The prospect of singing lead at the session made Gladys somewhat nervous. The group also had to find a replacement for Georgia. Gladys asked Wanda Young to take Georgia's place. Wanda, like Georgia, was a couple of years older than the others, had graduated, and was

The Marvelettes, 1964, (L-R) Wanda, Gladys, Georgeanna, Katherine.

not quite sure of her professional direction, so she accepted the position in the group. This quintet made the trip to Motown for the session in the spring of 1961.

The production of "Please Mr. Postman" featured many background musicians who were also on the verge of successful careers. Brian Holland and Robert Bateman were just beginning to exercise their skills as songwriters. They made some adjustments to the song and, in turn, took part of the writing credit. Likewise for the flip side, "So Long Baby," written by Wanda's brother, James. Wanda sang the lead for the B-side. The drummer on the session was a young man who had come from a Washington D.C. group called The Marquees. For two years, this group had been the new Moonglows, singing behind Harvey Fuqua. Marvin Gaye was now a soloist and drummer for the budding Motown Records. Gladys, still apprehensive about the last minute changes for the session, found relief from

Florence Ballard, a member of another new group at Motown, The Supremes: "Florence came in with Mary [Wilson] while we were recording. When we took a break, Florence asked the producer if she could have a couple of minutes coaching me, because of the adlibs she heard, she felt they would add to the song."

With Florence's suggestions, Gladys felt more at ease. After a few outtakes, the record was finished. Gladys' strong delivery, with pert background responses, sold the song. Everyone thought the group sounded "marvelous," so the final, finishing touch was Berry Gordy's change of the name "Casingyettes" to the more commercial sounding "Marvelettes."

"Please Mr. Postman" did not sound like anything else on the pop charts. The entire production absolutely moves the listener. In 1961, musical styles were changing. Influences from blues and Gospel were becoming more of a driving force in popular music, no longer confined to Rhythm & Blues. Strangely, it took some pushing to get the tune to climb the charts.

Once the public heard it, though, they couldn't get enough. The record shot to number one and soon, sound-alike songs were popping up on other labels. The Marvelettes' sound was showcased on a following LP, also entitled, "Please Mr. Postman." This album included their hit, the ballad written by Wanda's brother, a cover of The Supremes song, "I Want A Guy" and several other covers of songs recorded by other Motown artists, like The Satintones' "Angel" and Barrett Strong's "I Apologize." Motown was one of the few Rock & Roll labels to feature albums. Motown used the postman theme with the group's next single, "Twistin' Postman" in 1962, which made the Top 40.

By mid-1962, The Marvelettes were Motown's most consistent hit makers. Gladys wrote the group's third Top 40 hit, "Playboy," cashing in on the theme of "girls warning girls." This delightful single placed the group in the Top 20. The fourth single didn't disappoint, clearly shouting the fictitious number, "Beechwood 4-5789" (which many teenagers called just for a lark). A tender ballad, "Someday, Someway," graced the B-side. Flip side ballads were common practice for Marvelettes singles. For the next single, "Strange, I Know," the ballad won the airplay, although the uptempo "Too Strong To Be Strung Along" was the intended A-side, and did receive some attention.

Although her voice was facilitating the popularity of the group's records, Gladys' credits Motown's intuitive

THE MARVELETTES
Tamla Recording Artists

The Marvelettes, still making hits as a trio, 1966, (clockwise from top) Katherine, Gladys, Wanda.

skill with helping them acquire star status, "We had the hits, but they had the experience. There was an intelligence down there that you wouldn't believe. Everything ran smoothly."

Motown felt that to properly present its artists, they must capture attention on stage as well as in recording, so choreography became an important part of the group's stage preparation. The group was able to use these dance routines effectively, with Gladys singing her lead, then spinning off into the background while Wanda advanced to the forefront to present her lead tune.

As The Marvelettes acquired more hits, Motown became more conscientious concerning stage presence and costumes for its act. In the beginning, The Marvelettes took care of their own choreography. Motown's ritual of personal refinement and precisely-timed dance routines for its early artists would come awhile later. Motown used the early trialing as a springboard for packaging and promoting future acts. Ironically, these considerations would both help and hinder the career of The Marvelettes.

The Marvelettes were now headlining Motown's Motortown Revues that were appearing in every major city in America. This was a chance to give exposure to all the Motown acts, while keeping the cost of touring to a minimum. An interesting note to one of The Marvelettes' early tours was that Florence Ballard of The Supremes took the place of Wanda Rogers, who was expecting a child. This fulfilled contractual requirements and was helpful in maintaining the group's image, for which Gordy was a stickler.

The entertainers made many stops in numerous cities in a relatively short period of time. The regularity of these one-nighters was arduous, often amid conditions that were far less than perfect. This proved to be too much for Juanita Cowart. Juanita relates how she became sidetracked by infirmity, "I became ill and had to be hospitalized. After I was given a clean bill of health in every way by my doctor, I wanted to continue singing with the group, but was not allowed to. Even though I wasn't traveling with the group, whenever they were in town, I would go to the studio with them to record. Some of the songs that I last recorded was 'Locking Up My Heart', 'Forever', etc."

Juanita ended her career as a performing member of The Marvelettes in 1962, although she continued recording as a member until the beginning of 1963. Katherine explains the group's decision to forge ahead without searching for a replacement for Juanita, "The pace we had to endure and the conditions that we had to live under were not like the comforts of home and community. Too much was happening too fast. We decided not to replace Juanita. We wanted to keep the group as original as possible."

The Marvelettes were also feeling the strain of competition from other female groups at the company. Their main rivals were The Supremes, whose style and grace caught the company's eye, even though, in 1963, The Supremes still had no hits. The Supremes would eventually take the company to other levels of success in the entertainment industry. Motown did not seek to develop the raw vocal talents of The Marvelettes. For them, the company would simply focus on the group's two lead singers, the reputation the group built, and the records they generated.

Marvelettes singles for 1963 continued to impress, although they did not climb as high on the pop charts as previous singles. Marvelettes LPs were released at an unusually quick pace. The Marvelettes album sales were better than average for the time. The Marvelettes had five LPs released between 1961-63, including "Playboy," "Sing The Hits of 1962," "Marvelous Marvelettes" and a live album that includes stage recitation by Gladys. One single, "Locking Up My Heart/Forever" received dual airplay, thus canceling each other out in sales. "My Daddy Knows Best" and "As Long As I Know He's Mine" reached only the middle of the pop charts. One can speculate that it was the luck of the draw on which the group's fate teetered.

In the fall of 1963, Motown decided to experiment with The Marvelettes' sound, recording and releasing a single by the group on Gordy Records. The song features Gladys and Wanda singing lead harmonies, while the group sings in unison response. The background harmonies are provided by Motown's in-house backing group, The Andantes, whose powerful, gospel-like blow tones sound nothing like the untrained, sometimes unblended harmonies of The Marvelettes. The single, "Too Hurt Too Cry, Too Much In Love To Say Goodbye," was released as The Darnells, with "Come On Home," on the B-side, featuring The Andantes on vocals. For whatever the reasons Motown had for applying this augmentation, the practice continued on subsequent singles by The Marvelettes. Producers embellished recordings with either echo, or use of The Andantes as an enhancement. This practice was not exclusive to Marvelettes singles. Motown eventually employed vocal embellishments by The Andantes on many records by other Motown artists to create a specific sound and to make sure record releases were generated in a timely manner, if a group happened to be on tour.

Quality recordings continued into 1964, with two Smokey Robinson productions, "He's A Good Guy" and "You're My Remedy." The latter was the first A-side to feature Wanda exclusively on lead. The single features heavy echo on the background harmonies. The Marvelettes had an interesting blend of voices, leaning toward the high end, each with a distinctive tone, sometimes causing an uneven mixture, as in "A Need For Love." The treatment worked on songs like "Postman" and "Beechwood 4-5789," but would not do for the smoother, more standardized sounds to come. The big hit for 1964, "Too Many Fish In The Sea," features each of the quartet on their own, in the sound-off before the refrain, Gladys, Georgeanna, Katherine and Wanda, in that order. There is also the presence of male voices on the record.

This was their first top 30 song in over a year. The Marvelettes recall turning down material which was eventually given to The Supremes, material that became hits. At Motown, it was not an uncommon event for artists to sing on or to record each other's songs, the same tune with the same backing tracks. Many tracks were done in order to save time and money, as well as for publishing purposes. Motown covering Motown could net a hit by two different artists on the same song, thereby doubling the return. According to Gladys, Motown always offered the artists a variety of material, "When the writers came to you, they would first ask, 'do you like the song?' Then we would choose what we wanted."

Motown thought it a gainful practice to link artists to specific producers in the hopes of spawning a successful creative relationship. Most groups at Motown found a match with a particular writer/producer whose productions were tailored for the group.

As far as The Marvelettes were concerned, everyone had a hand in producing them. When they first came to the company, Brian Holland and Robert Bateman were their main producers. After Bateman left the company, Mickey Stevenson took his turn producing Marvelettes records. In 1963, Brian Holland and Lamont Dozier handled Marvelettes sessions. Smokey Robinson produced them in early 1964, then Norman Whitfield, Clarence Paul and Ivy Joe Hunter in 1965. None of these associations provided consistent hit making, until Smokey worked with the group using Wanda as the primary lead.

In fact, after "Too Many Fish In The Sea," Gladys would no longer be used for A-sides. The sounds of the group were changing. Not only had they lost Juanita as a result of touring demands, but also, Georgeanna, suffering from sickle cell anemia, often could not meet touring or scheduling demands. For The Marvelettes' first tour of England, Belgium and The Netherlands, the group went out as a trio. Too ill to continue, Georgeanna eventually left the group in 1965. Whatever the configuration, Smokey Robinson would contribute to The Marvelettes' longest run of successful singles since Brian Holland and Robert Bateman produced them during 1961-62.

Smokey Robinson took great care in writing and producing all acts under his direction, and The Marvelettes were no exception. Using Wanda's breathy, sultry voice on "Don't Mess With Bill," Smokey achieved a most supple delivery. Smokey used the formula for another single, "You're The One," but it didn't work a second time. The next single features Smokey's most clever use of metaphor. "The Hunter Gets Captured By The Game" is memorable for its lyrical implications. Cover versions by Candi Staton, Blondie, and Grace Jones have honored the song's timeless message.

For single releases, Motown rarely covered the work of a songwriter who was not a part of the corporation. In an unusual move, Motown used an entry from the Van McCoy songbook for the next single, a version of "When You're Young And In Love," produced by James Dean and William Weatherspoon. Evidence of blending Marvelettes backgrounds with Andantes voices on this string of recordings is apparent.

In 1967, Gladys Horton was planning to marry and settle down. Since Gladys had been orphaned as a child, this move in her life was an important one to her. She decided to leave The Marvelettes.

Wanda had been handling the leads, so the change went unnoticed on vinyl. Anne Bogan replaced Gladys in the group. She is pictured on the group's next LP, "Sophisticated Soul." No stranger to group singing, her

group, The Challengers III, recorded for Harvey Fuqua's Tri-Phi label in 1961-62. Anne also recorded singles with Harvey billed as Harvey and Anne.

When Motown absorbed Fuqua's labels in 1963, Anne became a Motown artist. She was the lead voice on The Andantes' "Like A Nightmare," the only Motown single bearing their name as the primary artist. In the two years with The Marvelettes, her formidable lead was featured on only one single, "I'm Gonna Hold On As Long As I Can." Five singles and two albums were released after Gladys left. The first post-Gladys single, "My Baby Must Be A Magician," charted high, and again featured Smokey Robinson's magical twist on lyrics. After that, The Marvelettes never again entered the Top 40, despite superb singles like "Here I Am Baby" and "Destination: Anywhere," a favored single in England, written and produced by Nik Ashford and Valerie Simpson. Seemingly, the group was promoted on the road, but allowed to languish in the studio. By 1969, problems within the structure of The Marvelettes took its toll and, in 1969, the group disbanded. Katherine felt that there were no options left for The Marvelettes, "There were internal problems in the group. Because of The Supremes, we were put on the back burner. I didn't feel that I had the full and total support of the company. It seems they all had one focal point. Everybody got pushed back so that one person could go forward."

In addition, Smokey Robinson produced an album intended for Wanda Rogers to showcase herself as a soloist in 1970. When the LP was released, it was entitled "The Return of The Marvelettes." The two subsequent singles released in 1970 and 1971 were also released as Marvelettes' singles. This came at a time when fanfare was bestowed on Diana Ross' departure from The Supremes and her continuing with a solo career. Smokey's project with Wanda was not given preferred status. Katherine was asked to participate in a photo shoot for "Return of The Marvelettes," but was not asked to record the album, and wanted no part of the charade, "They had called to ask me if I would come in and do a photo session, but they wouldn't help me with internal problems."

Wanda Young had married Bobby Rogers of The Miracles early in her career. She continued as a Marvelette in between raising her family. After leaving Motown, she attempted a revival of her career, teaming for a time with Gladys, but it never materialized.

Having female singers juggling family life with life in the entertainment business was probably another reason for Motown to forego the career of The Marvelettes. Juanita Cowart retired from The Marvelettes in 1963 and married in 1964. Juanita and her husband Larry Motley are active in their church and in community affairs in Inkster. Juanita says that it was a splendid surprise for her church choir when they found out her musical history, "When they found out that I was an original Marvelette, I led a song."

Georgeanna Tillman married Billy Gordon of The Contours. She died from complications of sickle-cell anemia and Lupus Disease in 1980. Anne Bogan continued her association with Harvey Fuqua, singing in a trio called Love, Peace and Happiness, which Harvey produced for RCA in the early 1970s. They were part of a larger band, New Birth, that had successful R&B singles such as "I Can Understand It" and "Never Can Say Goodbye."

Katherine Anderson Shaffner co-wrote "I Don't Want To Do Wrong" for Gladys Knight and The Pips. Katherine states that the song came from her life story. She received a gold record. Katherine revels in her days as an entertainer. She is happy to grant interviews and participate in radio programs to discuss The Marvelettes, but has no desire to return to the stage.

Gladys Horton moved around the country for awhile, eventually settling back in Los Angeles. She raised her three sons and now runs a beauty salon in California. Gladys has appeared as herself and as G Lady and Good Friends. After being out of the music scene for a time, Gladys has resumed her touring schedule, the sound of her robust voice still very much in demand.

Today, groups of Marvelettes tour the country, but have no connection to the original members, a practice that Katherine and Gladys, as well as other fellow entertainers, find appalling. For many years, legalities prevented the original Marvelettes from using the name they helped make famous. Veteran group singers marched on Washington D.C. in 1998, lobbying to get the trademark laws changed so original members have some rights concerning the use of a group name.

In 1999, a court ruled that original recording members of groups should be able to benefit from the use of a name they helped build to prominence. The original Marvelettes were inducted into The Rhythm & Blues Foundation's Hall of Fame in 1995, an accolade they so rightly deserved. According to Katherine, the success of Motown is owed in part to The Marvelettes having that first hit, "Motown became even more known once we hit with 'Please Mr. Postman'. In my opinion, where Motown wanted to go, The Marvelettes came in and kicked the door open. Had we not hit with 'Postman', there would have been more preparation for a million seller and they would not have been prepared when it did come."

Blazing a trail so others may find their way is not always an enviable position. The Marvelettes helped many others in the Motown Corporation go forward, but they're best remembered for telling the world to "wait"!

The Marvelettes Discography

45s

	Label	Number	Year
Please Mr. Postman/So Long Baby	Tamla	54046	1961
Twistin' Postman/I Want A Guy		54054	1962
Playboy/All The Love I've Got		54060	
Beechwood 4-5789/Someday, Someway		54065	
Strange, I Know/Too Strong To Be Strung Along		54072	
Locking Up My Heart/Forever		54077	1963
My Daddy Knows Best/Tie A String Around Your Finger		54082	
As Long As I Know He's Mine/Little Girl Blue		54088	
He's A Good Guy/Goddess Of Love		54091	1964
You're My Remedy/A Little Bit Of Sympathy, A Little Bit Of Love		54097	
Too Many Fish In The Sea/A Need For Love		54105	
I'll Keep Holding On/No Time For Tears		54116	1965
Danger, Heartbreak Dead Ahead/Your Cheating Ways		54120	
Don't Mess With Bill/Anything You Wanna Do		54126	
You're The One/Paper Boy		54131	1966
The Hunter Gets Captured By The Game/I Think I Can Change You		54143	
When You're Young And In Love/The Day You Take One, You Have To Take The Other		54150	1967
My Baby Must Be A Magician/I Need Someone		54158	
Here I Am Baby/Keep Off, No Trespassing		54166	1968
Destination: Anywhere/What's Easy For Two Is So Hard For One		54171	
I'm Gonna Hold On As Long As I Can/Don't Make Hurting Me A Habit	54177		
That's How Heartaches Are Made/Rainy Mourning		54186	1969
Marionette/After All		54198	1970
A Breath Taking Guy/You're The One For Me, Bobby		54213	1971

(as The Darnells w/The Andantes)
Too Hurt To Cry, Too Much In Love To Say Goodbye/Come On Home Gordy		7024	1963

The Del-Rhythmetts w/Gladys Horton
Chic-A-Boomer/I Need Your Love	JVB	5000	1959

LPs

	Label	Number	Year
Please Mr. Postman	Tamla	228	1961
Marvelettes Smash Hits Of 1962		229	1962
Marvelettes Sing		229	
Playboy		231	
Marvelous Marvelettes		237	1963
Marvelettes Live On Stage		243	
Marvelettes Greatest Hits		253	1966
Marvelettes		274	1967
Sophisticated Soul		286	1968
In Full Bloom		288	1969
Return Of The Marvelettes		305	1970
The Marvelettes Greatest Hits		--	1975

The Orlons

Members:

(1961-63) Marlena Davis, lst Soprano/Lead
Rosetta Hightower, 2nd Soprano/Lead
Shirley Brickley, Alto/Lead
Stephen Caldwell, Baritone/Bass/Lead

(1964) Rosetta Hightower, Lead
Sandy Person
Shirley Brickley
Stephen Caldwell

(1964-65) Rosetta Hightower
Sandy Person
Shirley Brickley

(1965) Rosetta Hightower
Yvonne Young
Shirley Brickley

(1966-67) Rosetta Hightower
Audrey Brickley
Shirley Brickley

During the 1960s, the city of Philadelphia generated many a trend-setting musical note, but none echoed more distinctively and with such diversity as the sounds of The Orlons. For six years The Orlons transcended many R&B genres, delivering all with sincere gusto. With Rosetta's no-nonsense lead on the group's get-down dance tunes, The Orlons were the icons for every dance craze along the eastern seaboard. But this group was much more than just singers of a bunch of dance fad songs. They were one of the most prolific group of singers of their time and, unfortunately, very underrated.

The Orlons started life as a quintet of girls singing for fun in junior high school. This quintet originally included Rosetta Hightower, Marlena Davis, Shirley Brickley and Shirley's sisters, Audrey and Jean. This proficient singing group called themselves Little Audrey and The Teenettes. Since Mr. and Mrs. Brickley were musically inclined, with Mrs. Brickley an accomplished pianist and Mr. Brickley proficient on the guitar, it was only natural for their daughters to gravitate in a musical direction. At first, they were a living room group, but soon began appearing at local teen night spots in and around Phila-

THE ORLONS

The Orlons first photo, 1961, (L-R) Stephen Caldwell, Marlena Davis, Rosetta Hightower, Shirley Brickley.

delphia during 1958 and 1959. But, when eager promoters tried to drive the young girls into bars and adult clubs, Mr. and Mrs. Brickley applied the brakes.

Audrey could not appear in clubs at age 13. Jean decided she could take it or leave it, but the three remaining girls did get together on occasion, just to flex their vocal chords. One evening, while Shirley, Rosetta and Marlena were rehearsing at Shirley's house, they were overheard by Shirley's neighbor, Stephen Caldwell. Steve was an equally talented singer; singing in a six-man group called The Romeos, who were well known in the neighborhood, although they never recorded. Steve came over just to "jam" and before the night was over, the singers knew they had a sound worth pursuing. Thus, The Orlons were born.

The Orlons were originally named in keeping with another group, The Cashmeres, who then changed their name to The Dovells. Len Barry was a pal from Overbrook High School, who sang lead for the popular singing group who had signed with Cameo-Parkway Records and scored with their first recording, "The Bristol Stomp." It was on Len's recommendation that The Orlons secured an audition at the company. Initially, Steve was the lead singer of the group with the three girls backing him. After hearing the group sing, Cameo thanked them and sent them home.

The Orlons were asked back two more times before Cameo agreed to give them a shot. At first, they only wanted the three girls, but the trio would not sign without Steve. Apparently this was a sign that the powers at Cameo were going to reconfigure the singing order of the group. Steve recalls the final audition: "What Cameo-Parkway had decided was that they were looking for a female lead singer. The next audition we did the same tunes. They asked each girl to lead. The girls were not used to doing lead, so they were overcome. They were looking at me like, 'What do we do?'."

When The Orlons first arrived at Cameo, the label didn't quite know what to do with them. Kal Mann, who would be working with the group knew that he wanted only hits. Since all members were capable of singing effective leads, all were potential candidates for leading their maiden effort. For the group's first single, Kal Mann tried a soft, sultry lead for the A-side. A tune penned by Kal Mann, "I'll Be True," was waxed with Marlena's gentle lead. A "soldier boy"-type song, it did well locally, but Cameo failed to break the record nationally. Its flip is the engaging "Heart, Darling Angel"; replete with a warm baritone/bass intro by Steve, following with Rosetta's marked lead, surrounded by harmony. The song was co-written by Steve and Shirley. Initially, the company did not want to record "Heart, Darling Angel," but acquiesced to the group since the tune was to be a B-side. Steve had other songs he had written for the group, but unfortunately, the company dismissed them as not commercial enough.

Cameo was only interested in the recordings. They did not want to concern themselves with the group's image or live performances. Even though a man named Nat Siegel managed the group for a time, almost from the onset, Steve was responsible for getting the group to their gigs on time and making sure that the girls had everything they needed for their shows, basically acting as a road manager. This left little time to take care of Steve the singer, even though he was also an integral part of the group. Steve fulfilled his duties with great responsibility, even down to carrying the girls' luggage and, on occasion, acting as a bodyguard against overzealous male fans.

Since "I'll Be True" had made only local static, Cameo next tried Shirley on lead for the group's second single, "Happy Birthday, Mr. 21." This tune was written by Billy Myles. Myles found success as a writer with "Tonight Tonight," recorded by The Mello Kings in 1957. "Mr. 21" is another of the handful of ballads deftly handled by the group, and is highly sought after by collectors. Shirley does an equally convincing job on the flip, "Please Let It Be Me."

Again, Cameo failed to score a hit with the two-sided ballad single. Still, the songs were great selections to sing at the group's live shows when they appeared in and around Philadelphia. With no big hits to their credit, The Orlons were performing local gigs as well as being asked to lend their voices to backgrounds on records for other Cameo artists. One significant single was for a young lady who herself started as a guest vocalist on "Slow Twistin'" by Chubby Checker. Dee Dee Sharp was ready to record "Mashed Potato Time" and vocalists were needed in the background. Cameo asked The Orlons to do it, but Steve and Marlena, thinking that the company was already focusing too much on Dee Dee, refused. Rosetta and Shirley did not agree. They sang the backups with Shirley's sister Audrey. The trio was paid a session fee. The record was a smash hit.

Little did The Orlons realize at the time that they, too, would not have much longer to wait. Audrey's excitement ran in a different direction, as she tells it: "Even though Shirley was only a year and a half older than me, she was allowed to stay in the group and sing in clubs. I was excited about singing on a record. It was on a Sunday morning. Shirley woke me up and said, 'Do you want to make a record?' Dee Dee Sharp's voice wasn't even on it yet. We sang to an instrumental background. I got paid $35. After that, I was asked to sing background on other records as part of a party background."

Kal Mann and Bernie Lowe were convinced that another change in musical direction was in order for The Orlons. Ballads didn't seem to put the group on the national charts and this was the production team's only concern. Since dance crazes were the thing during the early 1960s, Cameo-Parkway had naturally jumped on the bandwagon. They had scored big time with Chubby Checker's version of "The Twist" (twice) and The Dovells' "Bristol Stomp." Now the production team had one more dance tune to their credit, "Mashed Potato Time."

It was time for The Orlons to step in that direction. Their third single was based on another early 1960s dance, the Watusi. The Vibrations had netted a hit with a song about the dance. The title of The Orlons' song would be "The Wah-Watusi," a play on the vocal arrangement of the song. Again, the production team switched lead vocalists, putting Rosetta on the lead breaks. Marlena led the flip, a dreamy, Fleetwoods-like ballad called "Holiday Hill." Rosetta's biting soprano on "The Wah-Watusi" sounds quite different from the treatment she gives ballads. Her voice has the toughness needed for the dance-tune style. Apparently the formula worked, driving "The Wah-Watusi" straight into the Top 20.

With a hit record to their credit, The Orlons were now considered one of Cameo-Parkway's premier vocal groups, along with The Dovells. Since Kal Mann, Bernie Lowe and arranger Dave Appell were purely business-minded, they knew that the formula that worked for The Orlons with their first hit was not to be tampered with.

The Orlons riding the crest of their hits, 1963, (from left) Marlena, Stephen, Rosetta, Shirley (seated). (Photo courtesy of Stephen Caldwell)

The Orlons, 1964, (clockwise from top left) Sandy Person, Shirley, Stephen, Rosetta.

Again, conjuring up a horn-blowing, hand-clapping arrangement, Mann, Lowe and Appell hit paydirt once more with "Don't Hang Up," a song, which gives Steve one of the best tag lines in Rock & Roll. His frog-like "Oh no's" countering the girls' recitation of the title line is the perfect hook. Actually, Steve's frog voice was done as a lark during a recording session. The producers liked it so much, they asked him to keep doing it, and it was a key factor in The Orlons' recordings ever since.

There is a level of consolation in the fact that Steve's altervoice is so significant. Steve was not asked to lead any singles, despite the fact that he possesses a smooth baritone lead, which is evident on aptly chosen cover tunes on the albums, such as Ed Townsend's "For Your Love," and the superior cover of The Lovenotes' "Tonight." His ability to turn the notes, yet achieve total continuity in a song, is one evident factor that Cameo-Parkway was not tapping into the abundant talent available in The Orlons.

Since the powers at Cameo were not going to tamper with success, Rosetta was again chosen to sing the solo lines. She also sang the stroll-oriented tune on the flip, "The Conservative." "The Conservative" was designated as the A-side on the single, but was pushed aside by the uptempo number. Mann and Lowe were sure of Rosetta's piquantly powerful leads for the dance tunes. She was a good shouter. After Rosetta's success on the solo lines for the first two hits, none of her group mates would get the chance to sing lead on any other Orlons singles.

After "The Wah-Watusi" and "Don't Hang Up" hit the top of the charts, The Orlons were destined to record what had come to be known as discotheque records; pure foot-stomping fun, capable of keeping club crowds on the dance floors for hours. The Orlons certainly didn't mind this assignment. They were ecstatic to sing it all, the dance songs, the novelty records, the covers and the ballads. They were entertainers, which is what the group was happiest doing. Early on in their quest for finding recognition in the world of music, Mr. Brickley had insisted that they grab the opportunity to sing professionally while they were young. Shirley's father also didn't hesitate to point out that there were very few options for them at that point in time, and that this chance might never come again. Steve admits to having been a wild teenager, and he credits both Mr. Brickley and The Orlons for giving him music as his focal point.

At the beginning of 1963, The Orlons again saw themselves at the top of the charts with "South Street," a song written about a happening hangout in South Philly. Like its predecessors, the song featured alternating group vocals and Rosetta's solo accents, amidst handclaps, horns and drums. Many songs, including "South Street," were written on the spot and the group improvised around the tune which Kal Mann sang. "Them Terrible Boots" is another product of this improvisation. Originally called "Bad Shirt," the lyrics of the song are about some guy who thinks he's so cool, but gets ripped to shreds about his wardrobe. The tag line features Steve's infamous frog voice. From the sound of the atmosphere in the studio, it seems that having fun with the songs was one of the primary ingredients in many successful sessions for The Orlons.

Usually, Cameo followed up a hit single by an artist with an LP. When "The Wah-Watusi" scored high on the charts, an album of the same name was issued. The package contained their hit, the first two ballad singles and some tasty covers, easily the group's best LP. "Don't Hang Up" was accompanied by Cameo's famous "All The Hits" compilations by The Orlons. "South Street" had its own LP, filled with "location" songs.

The group had free reign for the songs selected for B-sides and LPs, since the recipe for the singles was pretty much set. At the onset of the 1960s, Rock & Roll was still very much a singles-oriented business. Cameo, like Motown, saw a market for LPs, releasing endless strings of their own "Greatest Hits" packages, with artists singing other labelmates' hits, as well as covers of popular songs of the day.

Cameo-Parkway even ventured into theme albums, releasing a surf album, with all the major acts singing beach songs. The Orlons' contributions to the LP, "Everybody's Gone Surfin'," were a cover of The Beach Boys' "Surfin'" and a scream of a song with Steve singing lead in his frog voice called, "Mister Surfer." Although they were not as marketable as the singles, these records were a lot of fun. The company was more lenient with these collections since there were no plans to market them as singles.

Cuts that appeared on The Orlons albums were usually the tunes that the group showcased during their live shows. The Orlons were a performing group before they were a recording group, so they had polished cover tunes all ready to go when called upon for album filler. One can bet that since this was the other group members' chance to shine on record, they took their performances quite seriously.

Another tune that did well for The Orlons in 1963, was a premium cover of the Gary U.S. Bonds tune, "Not Me." This song was part of a repertoire that the group performed during live shows. They were singing it in between takes at a session. Mann and Lowe liked what they heard and recorded it. It was their next single. When it hit, Cameo issued an album of the same name. The LP "Not Me" is in keeping with the other Orlons LPs, most notably "The Wah-Watusi" LP, containing a hit and selected covers done with paramount style.

As the group came to know exactly what the company wanted for album cuts, Mann and Lowe usually sent The Orlons to the studio by themselves; they trusted the judgment of the group that much. Steve recalls when the group was recording "For Your Love," they used a new studio, and the engineers were having trouble in the control room getting the right sound, so the group had to sing the song again and again. Steve remembers losing patience: "The new studio was on 17th

The Orlons, 2000, (L-R) Lillian Washington Taylor, Jean Brickley Maddox, Stephen Caldwell, Audrey Brickley. (Photo courtesy of Stephen Caldwell)

and Jackson in South Philly. Two old guys were working the controls. With all the other big studios around, why we wound up at this apartment, we don't know. They were unprepared. The mikes had no screens. I really said 'or' instead of 'for'. Everybody said it came off well, but I didn't think so. I started expressing myself."

Steve said that this was a breakout tune for the group at live shows, so they wanted the recorded version to match the zest of their live rendition. Needless to say, after several takes, the song was losing its magic. The engineers became annoyed with the group. After telling the new engineers where to go, the group chose the next decent take, and that is the performance heard on the "Not Me" LP. The group was not satisfied with this take. As consolation to themselves, at The Apollo Theatre on New Year's Eve, 1963, with their parents in the audience, the group belted out what Steve hails as the best performance of "For Your Love" they ever did. They received a standing ovation.

Not only did Cameo-Parkway almost single-handedly corner the market on Rock & Roll LPs, but also, the singles of the hitmakers were almost always attractively packaged in picture sleeves. Due to the singles' popularity, many of the Cameo-Parkway sleeves still abound. Lavishly-colored publicity photos were used to adorn these sleeves.

The Orlons were ready for their photo shoots with a hint of every style. Their costumes ranged from the semi-formal pink dresses for the girls and white jacket for Steve used on the sleeve for "Don't Hang Up" and their "All The Hits" LP, to the gold lame dresses and British-looking suit for Steve, displayed on one of their foreign EPs.

The Orlons had costumes for any look. Steve remembers seeing a particular suit in the window of a clothing store outside The Royal Theatre in Baltimore. He and his guitarist, Roland Chambers, liked the suits and needed some new stage wear. They went into the store and the proprietor offered them a great deal if they would take the suit in different colors, so they now had this suit in red, blue, and green, and turned the collars in for the desired effect. The suits were a huge hit on stage and likewise for publicity photos—image was everything.

Speaking of image, there was also another, newly found form of exposure for Rock & Roll groups during the early 60s, the television dance program. Since they were from Philadelphia, The Orlons had a close relationship with Dick Clark, who hosted the by-then nationally syndicated dance show to end all dance shows, "American Bandstand." Not that the Philadelphia groups received so much special attention, but Clark always had a spot in his heart for talent which came from the town where Bandstand originated.

The Orlons, as well as other acts appearing on the program, would lip-sync their songs during their personal appearance, and reap the benefits of their own hometown status. Clark was always glad to have the group as guests and helped their career along whenever he could be of service. The Orlons were certainly worthy of this ministration.

As 1963 carried through, the Cameo-Parkway machine was moving full speed ahead with The Orlons in the driver's seat, as they scored with two more singles, the infectious, Motown-inspired "Crossfire" and the frenetic "Bon Doo Wah." They also tried their hands at singing a staunch arrangement of a song Billy Jackson and Jimmy Wisner wrote called "Don't Throw Your Love Away," a song containing hints of the style that Burt Bacharach made popular with Dionne Warwick.

A few months later, the tune would be picked up and changed to accommodate one of the new British Invasion bands, The Searchers, who had a huge hit with the song. Despite forages in other musical directions, The Orlons' dance-oriented singles still served them well. These productions had come to have the distinction of being the ultimate "party" records. Since The Orlons put much effort into their live shows, these songs certainly helped kick things into high gear, with

the group moving and shaking all over the stage. In keeping with the company's ability to churn out hits faster than one could blink, The Orlons had just recorded "Crossfire," the company released it and it quickly climbed the charts. There was one hitch. There was no dance called the "Crossfire." The Orlons were required to make it up as they presented it on stage one night at The Apollo Theatre. The sheet music was rushed to the back-up musicians.

The band played the already speedy song so fast that the group found it impossible to spontaneously choreograph. They could barely catch their breath to sing the song, let alone make up a dance, so The Orlons usual routines on stage became the dance known as "Crossfire." Cameo followed up this single with the obligatory LP, "Biggest Hits, The Orlons." Also, to cash in on the group's current appeal, a single was released under the name Zip & The Zippers. The A-side, entitled, "Where You Goin' Little Boy," features a typical Orlons formula. In an unusual move, "Gig" features Steve as a soloist telling the story of a bored jazz musician having to play Rock & Roll at a recording session. The amusing song is a mixture of typical Cameo-Parkway riffs and jazz interludes. It was issued on the Cameo-affiliated Pageant label.

Since The Orlons had experience on stage, they knew how to improvise. They encouraged everyone to have a good time. Many times this would be done under the worst of circumstances. They would all pile into the station wagon at the start of their road trips, and always end up in places with the most extreme weather conditions imaginable. Their manager would book them in Vermont in the dead of winter, and Florida during a heat wave.

One tour in particular gave the group a good laugh and the audience more than they paid for. The Orlons were booked to do a show in Burke, Florida. When the group arrived, they found that the room in which they were to perform had no air conditioning. The show must go on, so the group started the show on time. It seems that Shirley was entertaining the room so intently, she hadn't noticed that her hairdo had fallen all around her head and her mascara had started to run. As Shirley was singing her heart out, she looked over at Steve. He had stopped singing and was in a fit of hysterical laughter. The group took it in stride and finished the performance, but the girls wore wigs after that show.

Another time that the group displayed their infinite professionalism was when the girls had overslept, and were due at a show for Murray The K at The Brooklyn Fox Theatre. The show was to start at 8:30 and the acts had to be there at least an hour before time. Steve tried several times to wake the girls and finally had to go to the theatre by himself. Murray asked where the rest of the group was and Steve said they would be along shortly. A little before curtain time, Rosetta, Shirley and Marlena came rushing into the stage area, slightly disheveled, but ready to perform. The Orlons never disappointed their fans.

Despite the group's success on the charts, the wear and tear of the tours and endless performing were beginning to exact their price. Growing differences between the girls caused Marlena to resign from the group in October of 1963. Sandy Person, the wife of one of the musicians who performed with the group's back-up band, replaced her. Sandy's first assignment with The Orlons was to record an album of cover songs appropriately entitled, "Down Memory Lane." Steve recalls that this was one of the times that the group was coming in off of a tour, so the tracks were laid out before time.

When the group recorded the vocals, some of the keys were too low, but the group recorded these tunes anyway. The brilliance of their voices was lost in this process. Considering the quality of previous Orlons LPs, it is a surprise that Cameo-Parkway would package the group in this manner. This effort would be the last Orlons long player.

The year of 1964 brought significant changes for The Orlons, as well as the industry of Rock & Roll as a whole. The first single release for the group was "Shimmy Shimmy," another link in the chain of dance-craze themes, flipped with a mild, Latin-tinged "Everything Nice." The next single for The Orlons was a tune inspired by Ray Charles' "What'd I Say," called "Rules Of Love" complete with the live crowd screaming in the background. This was the last Mann-Appell tune for The Orlons. The more interesting side of this single was the no-holds-barred, boppin' version of the Elvis Presley classic, "Heartbreak Hotel."

This killer "B" should have been the A-side. The treatment of the song is completely transposed into The Orlons' style, without losing one ounce of the song's original intent. The arrangement moves in waves, cresting in hooting harmonies on the refrain, then letting down gently to melodic unison for the verses and bridge, with Rosetta's effective lead in the forefront, her grinding accents working to potential.

This creative turn was one of the many signs that The Orlons, as well as other artists at Cameo-Parkway, could easily move into the soul idiom. Happening concurrently with the mining of this new creative vein was the purchase of the Cameo-Parkway complex by record distributor Alfred Rosenthal. The push for the new product at Cameo-Parkway didn't seem strong enough to sustain the favored acts. Rosenthal also hired fledgling record mogul Neil Bogart, then a singer known as Neil Scott, to manage the label. Neil would eventually find success running Casablanca Records.

The Orlons, as well as Chubby Checker, The Dovells, Dee Dee Sharp and The Tymes, continued to record for Cameo-Parkway, but were no longer receiving the considerations which would keep them at the top of the charts. This turn of events was certainly not due to a lack of available production and writing talents. Various prominent New York and Philadelphia producers came in to work with the groups. Bob Crewe and Charles Calello worked with The Orlons on their next single, "Knock Knock," a novel update on a party theme containing Steve's infamous frog voice on alternating lead with the trio, flipped with "Goin' Places," an energetic song with obvious Crewe/Calello touches.

With Crewe's solid production talents behind it, this issue was the group's last chart single and, coincidentally, Steve's last single with the group. He had worked so hard to maintain their stature in the business, he had forgotten about his own abilities as a singer and songwriter. He certainly wasn't content to be just the "frog-voice" forever. Steve left The Orlons in November of 1964.

Despite the misguided direction in which the management was steering Cameo-Parkway, premium product was in store for The Orlons, although they would never again enjoy chart success. The group closed out 1964 with a two-sided soul stir-rer. One of the initial writing and producing efforts of Kenny Gamble and Leon Huff, "I Ain't Comin' Back" delivers a cha-cha groove with superb vocal efforts by the group.

It's flip, the pulsating "Envy," was written by Ugene Dozier, marking one of the many Conlo Productions on Cameo. "Envy" is currently popular at the Northern Soul dance parties in England. "I Ain't Comin' Back" was recycled as the B-side for the next single in early 1965, the more conventional "Come On Down, Baby Baby," co-written by Wes Farrell and orchestrated by Hutch Davie. "Don't You Want My Lovin'," another Gamble-Huff composition, was an adventurous track for the group, employing a heavy blues beat and twanging rock guitars.

The second side, "I Can't Take It" was co-written and arranged by Thom Bell, the man who would eventually bring us The Stylistics. Each of the girls takes turns singing lead on this dramatic chant. This was the first ballad on vinyl for the group in almost three years.

For this single, Yvonne Young replaced Sandy Person. The girls were still making live appearances, despite their absence on the charts. They even appeared in an episode of "Burke's Law" playing (what else) singers where one of them gets "bumped off" in a nightclub.

The last single issued by Cameo was another Conlo Production written by veteran Motowner Barrett Strong. "No Love But Your Love" was a pleasant mid-tempo tune, flipped with the recycled "Envy." Without the solid backing of their record label, none of these singles released in 1965 made a dent in the ever-changing music charts. It certainly wasn't for lack of trying on the part of the group. Cameo-Parkway was a sinking ship, despite scoring a major hit with "96 Tears" by ? and The Mysterians in 1966. With the departure of The Tymes and The Dovells having occurred a year earlier, The Orlons, along with Chubby Checker and Dee Dee Sharp, left the label in 1965.

Through his main business as a distributor, Rosenthal distributed a few local labels through the Cameo-Parkway complex, such as Windy C, Moon Shot and Calla Records. For one single, The Orlons' next home was Calla Records, under the auspices of Ritchie Rome, Billy Jackson and Jimmy Wisner. In fact, Jackson and Wisner were producing and arranging for many of the former Cameo-Parkway acts like The Tymes for MGM, and Len Barry for Decca, respectively.

The Orlons' single for Calla, "Spinning Top," was fervent and swirling from start to finish. It did very well in Philadelphia, New York, and Baltimore during 1966, but failed to break nationally. The flip was a version of Dionne Warwick's "Anyone Who Had A Heart." The group had previously sung this tune as an accappella number in their live act. At this time, Audrey became a permanent member, replacing Yvonne. The group maintained their association with Jackson and Wisner, who moved the group to ABC Records for their last two singles in 1967.

The first was a temperate ballad with the signature of the Philadelphia sound written all over it. "Keep Your Hands Off My Baby," used modern instrumentation while planting the overall feel of the song in a firm bed of sophisticated soul. The B-side, "Everything," exhibited a more conventional formula for mid-60s soul. The second single for the label was the bouncy "Once Upon A Time," also a staple on the Northern Soul circuit in England.

For the backside, Jackson-Wisner reached back into the Cameo-Parkway catalog for an updated version of Bobby Rydell's "Kissin' Time," using Joe Renzetti to conduct the musicians. These singles for ABC were well produced and orchestrated by two of the most consistent producers in the business at that time, but they went nowhere. The group had signed an agreement to make three appearances in England. Audrey remembers these trips as the deciding factor in Rosetta's eventual departure, "People over there were telling us that we should stay. We were told we could make a lot more money than we were already making, but Shirley and I were homebodies. We wanted to stay close to home. After the second trip, Rosetta told us that when we returned for the third time, she would be staying."

Seeking opportunities for herself as a singer elsewhere, Rosetta left The Orlons in 1967, thus marking the end of the group's recording career, ending a six-year run of very cogent and versatile vocal group records. Rosetta began picking up work as a background and session singer. She was fortunate enough to back up Joe Cocker on his huge hit of The Beatles' cover, "With A Little Help From My Friends" in 1967. Sunni Wheetman and Madeline Bell completed the trio.

Rosetta became part of a group of female soul singers who found steady success singing backgrounds on recordings abroad, along with Madeline Bell and Doris Troy. Rosetta eventually moved to England where she became popular in her own right. She wrote and recorded two songs for Epic Records in 1970. "Go Pray For Tomorrow/Why," were two message songs written in the vein of the rock-opera songs many singers were recording during this period. She also married her producer, Ian Green. Today, she resides in England.

After Rosetta's departure, Shirley and Audrey continued with The Orlons in several configurations during the late 1960s and 1970s through their association with the Norman Joyce Agency. Some of the local singers who sang with The Orlons during this period were Jimmie Lewis, Ella Mae Hilton and ex-Velvelette Sandra Tilley. Another, most notable member was first cousin to the Brickleys, Lillian Washington. Lillian was a talented session singer who went out on the road with Bobby Sheen and Carolyn Willis as Bob B. Soxx and The Blue Jeans in 1963. It is she who is pictured standing alongside Bobby and Carolyn on the cover of "A Christmas Gift For You," the famous Phil Spector Christmas LP. Lillian also sang on the session. The Orlons remained visible as a performing group around the Philadelphia area until, tragically, Shirley was killed by an intruder in her Philadelphia home in 1977.

After leaving The Orlons as a performer in 1964, Steve continued to manage them for a time. Steve forged ahead in the music business, writing songs and managing various acts. Steve briefly handled another trio of ladies. He tried to market them to Billy Jackson, who was by this time an independent producer, but disagreements with Jackson over the handling of the group forced Steve to abandon the project. Steve sat on the school board in Philadelphia for 27 years, drives a school bus, is shop steward for the drivers union, and operates his own auto body shop (by appointment only). He, his wife, Louise, and their children live in Philadelphia. One evening, Steve was made aware that a group calling themselves The Orlons was performing at The Penn's Landing Club in Philadelphia. He and Marlena decided to check it out. After reviewing this "group," Steve and Marlena looked at each other and decided that the real Orlons should stand up. They officially reactivated the group in 1988, once again turning out stellar performances and reclaiming the group whose name and reputation they built. Marlena stayed with The Orlons until her death from cancer in 1993.

Steve currently heads a most interesting group of Orlons. Audrey Brickley joins Steve in the present lineup, as well as her sister Jean, reminiscent of their days as Little Audrey and The Teenettes. Once again, rounding out this powerful group is their cousin Lillian Washington (Taylor). They consistently bring down the house at the Rock & Roll shows with command performances that capture and enrapture, just like in the old days. Steve enthusiastically reports with pride, "At this point The Orlons have fared very well for their comeback and have been appreciated at each venue they've played. We deserve to be recognized for the material we did and our live performances. We did accomplish something a lot of acts did not do. We had four top ten records in one year."

Steve is still battling to keep the bogus group of Orlons from using the name. Apparently, the ignorance of some promoters and club owners keeps this group out there. Cameo-Parkway was sold for a second time in the mid-60s to Allen Klein, who changed the company's name to Abkco in the 1970s. Steve is negotiating a deal with Abkco that will hopefully lead to the legitimate rerelease of all The Orlons' material. Steve stands firm in what he believes The Orlons, both past and present, deserve for their role in popular American music, which will ensure that The Orlons continue to maintain their premium stature in the chronicles of Rock & Roll.

The Orlons Discography

45s

	Label	Number	Year
I'll Be True/Heart, Darling Angel	Cameo	198	1961
Happy Birthday, Mr. 21/Please Let It Be Me (w/organ)		211	1962
(B2 in deadwax, possibly dj only)			
Happy Birthday, Mr. 21/Please Let It Be Me (w/strings)		211	
The Wah-Watusi/Holiday Hill		218	
Don't Hang Up/The Conservative		231	
South Street/Them Terrible Boots		243	1963
Not Me/My Best Friend		257	
Crossfire/It's No Big Thing		273	
Bon-Doo-Wah/Don't Throw Your Love Away		287	
Shimmy, Shimmy/Everything Nice		295	1964
Rules Of Love/Heartbreak Hotel		319	
Knock, Knock/Goin' Places		332	
I Ain't Comin' Back/Envy		346	
Come On Down, Baby Baby/I Ain't Comin' Back		352	1965
Don't You Want My Lovin'/I Can't Take It		372	
No Love But Your Love/Envy		384	
Spinnin' Top/Anyone Who Had A Heart	Calla	113	1966
Keep Your Hands Off My Baby/Everything	ABC	10894	1967
Once Upon A Time/Kissin' Time		10948	

(as Zip & The Zippers)
	Label	Number	Year
Where You Goin', Little Boy/Gig	Pageant	607	1963

Rosetta Hightower
	Label	Number	Year
Go Pray For Tomorrow/Why	Epic	10727	1970

LPs*

	Label	Number	Year
The Wah-Watusi	Cameo	1020	1962
All The Hits		1033	
South Street		1041	1963
Not Me		1054	
Biggest Hits		1061	
Down Memory Lane		1073	
Everybody's Gone Surfin'	Parkway	7035	
The Girl Groups Are The Best	Pricewise	4004	1965
(Please Let It Be Me)			

* (Orlons cuts also appear on various "All The Hits" compilations issued by Cameo-Parkway on Cameo and Wyncotte Records)

The Pixies Three

Members:

(1963)   Midge Bollinger   (1963-64)   Bonnie Long
           Kaye McCool   Kaye McCool
           Debra Swisher   Debra Swisher

Their voices are sweet and their records filled with mirth. This describes the stimulating, teenage voices of The Pixies Three, a group formed not in accordance with the usual high school acquaintance, but as youngsters living side by side, so by the time they were teenagers, they were masterful entertainers on stage. With their producers, they became adept at delivering their refreshing harmonies on vinyl.

The Pixies Three formed in Hanover, Pa. in 1957. Two neighbors, Debra (Deb) Swisher and Kaye McCool would play together, then corral their friends into putting on shows in Debra's driveway. The elementary school youngsters soon formed a club called The "All Around The World" club. The ensemble would act, sing, dance or do whatever it could to entertain parents, friends and neighbors. As time went on, Kaye and Deb solidified their act by practicing the popular tunes of the day, winning a talent show in 1957 singing The Everly Brothers' "Bye Bye Love."

The girls called themselves The K-D-Dids. They accompanied themselves on ukuleles. The girls recruited a third friend and neighbor, Midge Bollinger, in 1958, so they could round out the act by singing three-part harmony. They even went so far as to modify their name to

The Pixies Three enjoying success with "Birthday Party", 1963, (L-R) Kaye McCool, Debra Swisher, Midge Bollinger. (Photo courtesy of John Grecco)

The K-D Mids. Their parents were very supportive and chauffeured them around to local Kiwanis, American Legion shows and fairs. The girls liked what they were doing and it was a job they had on weekends. Deb's mom was the group's acting manager. All the girls went for singing lessons and Kaye took piano lessons. Deb had been taking singing lessons as a toddler, "I started taking singing lessons when I was five years old. My mother said I was singing around the house all the time. The teacher would put me in another room and make me project, so I learned volume control."

A key turning point for the young group came when Deb's mother got them a spot on the acclaimed Ted Mack's Amateur Hour in 1960. This was now a step up in stature for the trio, and they didn't disappoint, turning in an endearing version of Annette Funicello's "Tall Paul," winning top prize two times. Of course, they made sure that the mail-in votes made it to the station because they helped fill out all the postcards. Kaye remembers the hard work and sacrifice that it took, "I was in the ninth grade. I had the lead in the school play. We won the contest, so the school had to postpone the play. It was the first time we ever sang with an orchestra."

From here on in, the group was going to perform in every room and at every event that they could get a booking. Every weekend the girls would pile into the car and go to work. They did this year-round, even during the summer, where Deb's mother rented a bungalow in Atlantic City. The girls performed at The Steel Pier, Tony Grant's Stars of Tomorrow and at various functions that

The Pixies Three, 1964, (L-R) Debra, Kaye, Bonnie Long. (Photo courtesy of The Pixies Three)

would allow the prepubescent trio. The group did not participate in activities that their contemporaries did because they always worked on the weekends, but they always had each other.

The group performed nonstop for about four years before recording. All three were now in high school at Eichelberger High School which became Hanover High. One evening in 1963, Mrs. Swisher arranged to have the group sing at a venue that was noted for attracting producers and A&R men who were looking for new talent. After the performance, they were approached by successful songwriters/producers John Madara and David White, who had success placing their two most favorable acts to date with the Chicago based Mercury Records. Anthony and The Sophomores and Maureen Gray enjoyed local success in Philadelphia and were making outstanding records with Madara and White. After business formalities were taken care of, it was agreed that the girls would record for them. It was decided that the group should change its name to The Pixies, after a popular haircut. Unfortunately, another female group from New York laid claim to the name. Instead of giving it up, they augmented it, christening themselves The Pixies Three.

The first single fielded for the Madara and White team was an upbeat ditty entitled, "Birthday Party." It featured a bubbly tempo with crisp, clean vocals delivering the birthday wish, with lead vocals by Midge. The song jumped onto the pop charts. The flip, "Our Love," written by Kaye, concerns the trials and tribulations of her relationship with her childhood sweetheart. Now things were really taking off for the fortuitous trio, and, of course, they had their parents' support behind them. Their performances were still limited to the weekends, because they were still in school. Deb recalls that they had to write papers on their experiences. What experiences they were, performing with all their favorite artists. The girls downplayed all this hobnobbing to their school friends, because they just wanted to be like everyone else.

The next Pixies Three single to grace the charts was "442 Glenwood Avenue," again a bouncy, party number. Its flip, the Spector-sounding "Cold, Cold Winter," also made the national charts. Now the group had two hit singles to its credit, one a double-sided smash. Both singles were issued with picture sleeves. Surprisingly, the group was not thinking in terms of a long musical career. This was still a weekend job. The girls were so used to each other, they were like family. Little did they dream that their spin of success would endure a temporary lurch.

With two hit singles to their credit, plans were being made to have the group record a full-length LP. They were still busy touring, making the rounds to promote their latest hit. In November of 1963, the group was driving to Baltimore to appear on Buddy Deane's dance show when they saw cars screeching to a halt on the highway. Deb's mother stopped the car to see what was going on. Everyone got the sad news that President Kennedy had been killed. She called the show and it had been cancelled. The trio had grown up together and lived with each other during world shattering events.

The young ladies were slated to record their album in February of 1964, when Midge announced that she was withdrawing from The Pixies Three. Everyone was rather shocked at Midge's news. Midge enjoyed entertaining, but as she got older, it seemed less important to her than other events on the horizon. All the girls had boyfriends and as Midge's relationship with her beau blossomed, her desire to perform regularly became less serious. Deb remembers how she cried when Midge decided to go.

Despite their feelings over the departure of their adopted sister, Deb and Kaye had to find a replacement. They were under contract to record this album. They held auditions, listening to just about everyone in town. Best suited for the position to replace Midge was Bonnie Long. Bonnie had rehearsed with the group in the past for the purpose of subbing if the need ever arose. The work paid off. Bonnie had the unenviable job of learning all the songs the group was set to record for the LP in just two weeks. No stranger to singing, Bonnie recounts the start of her foray into The Pixies Three, "Singing ran in the family. I grew up listening to my mother and her sister sing. I sang at talent shows and at church. Deb and I were friends from church. The first big show I did was in New York City with Dionne Warwick and Santo & Johnny. Dionne said being a little nervous is good, because if you're not, then you're too sure of yourself. It keeps you on your toes being a little nervous."

THE PIXIES THREE
The Original Mercury Recording Artists

Pixies Three, 2000, (L-R) Debra, Kaye, Bonnie. (Photo courtesy of The Pixies Three)

At the end of their performance, they held hands to bow, then very quickly, exited the stage. The only problem was that they were still holding hands. Deb ran one way, Bonnie, the other and practically tore poor Kaye in half. There were many memorable shows and tours with notable artists like Roy Orbison, The Angels and The Four Seasons.

"Party With The Pixies Three" was recorded over two days at Mira Sound Studios with Brooks Arthur at the engineering board and Leroy Lovett contributing the arrangements. The group graces the cover, with party decorations set in the background. Mercury wanted the group to pay for male models to come in to pose for the picture, but the group would have none of that. Deb and Kaye's boyfriends and Bonnie's brother made the trip to have their images shown on the cover. In the end, the photo of the guys in the background was blurred. Party hoots and handclaps were provided by anyone available at the studio that day. Most songs recorded had the party theme, including wonderful covers of "Sixteen Candles," "Party Lights" and "Happy, Happy Birthday Baby." Their next single was taken from the LP, a cover of The Crows' "Gee." This single gave the group their final chart single, reaching the bottom of the top 100.

The group's next effort was a song based on an English dance called "The Hootch." The company didn't realize though, that "hootch" meant drinking. The promotion department changed direction and "Summertime U.S.A." was then actively promoted. The beach music flip was an effective dance tune, calling all teenagers to the beach upon its release in June. Next came the standard, "Love Walked In," followed by the sweet soul-oriented "Love Me, Love Me." Although the records had an unwavering style and premium production values, these singles did not pick up airplay and failed to make a dent in the charts. Mercury Records did not pick up the group's option and released The Pixies Three at the end of 1964.

Despite the production team's attempt to update the sound of The Pixies Three, Kaye felt that too many new sounds were jumping onto the playlists. The sound of The Pixies Three was quickly becoming dated. The British Invasion monopolized the pop side of Rock & Roll. In response, Kaye said for months afterwards, she listened to nothing but soul music. There were a few promising prospects, like a preliminary deal with Cameo-Parkway Records and a solid song written for them by Len Barry called "1-2-3." Barry had written it with The Pixies Three in mind. With no airplay for their last two singles, the group did not want to go through shopping around for a new deal and decided to part ways. Perhaps, if they had recorded "1-2-3," the fate of The Pixies Three might have taken a different turn.

After the breakup of The Pixies Three, Kaye stopped performing, although she did study music theory in college and wrote a symphony. She married her high school sweetheart, who was in the navy, and they traveled around, living in different parts of the country. Bonnie returned to Hanover and sang with The Chimes, a local group that performed in clubs and at private parties, singing popular R&B covers by Lulu, Aretha Franklin and Dionne Warwick, and Bonnie also did solo work at weddings. Deb also returned to Hanover, her mother continuing to push her career as a solo artist. Deb recorded a single for Robert Feldman, Jerry Goldstein and Richard Gottehrer on Boom Records, a resounding cover version of The Beach Boys tune, "You're So Good To Me," flipped with an FGG standard, "Thank You and Goodnight." It was Deb's association with FGG that landed her a job in The Angels in 1966, "One afternoon, I came home from school after a final and received a call from Jiggs Allbut of The Angels. She asked me to try out for The Angels. I thought she was kidding. My mother told me to call her back and tell her we would come to New York. My mother left me in New York and I never returned to Hanover."

Deb stayed with The Angels for three years. They had been The Halos for a year and Peggy was still on a leave of absence, working with The Serendipity Singers. Deb shared lead chores with Bernadette Carroll, including some singles for RCA, including "Boy With The Green Eyes" and "The Modley." Although most of Deb's work with the group involved live shows, they did make television appearances as guest hosts on The Mike Douglas Show and Dean Martin's variety show. Deb remained with The Angels until a stopover show in Oklahoma in 1969, where she met her first husband, a musician. Deb stayed in Oklahoma, making a living for years singing in various bands, notably Bare Facts and Granddaddy, playing whatever the current musical trend. She also did some recording, singing two gospel tunes she sang as a child, and a country tune entitled, "You Bought The Shoes That Just Walked Out The Door," for a local label. Deb has never stopped performing.

In 1991, a graduating class of Hanover High School was celebrating its 25th reunion. Deb and Bonnie were attending and Bonnie was on the reunion committee. They got the notion to sing at their reunion, and while everyone was in town for the event, a special perfor-

mance of the hometown girls was being planned. Deb and Bonnie rented the Elks hall and were going to surprise Kaye. They planned an impromptu rehearsal of which Kaye was apprehensive, "I had not sung out of the shower in 27 years. I drove around the block, debating whether or not to go in."

The ladies agree that all doubt melted away when they opened their mouths to sing and heard that "sister harmony." The Pixies Three sound was still there after all these years. The Pixies Three resumed performing that weekend and have not stopped, making personal appearances up and down the northeastern corridor, greeted by loyal fans wherever they appear. They recorded a CD, "Then and Now," which is available at their shows. It contains a mixture of some vintage hits and songs they perform in their live act. Although their appearance on the charts was short-lived, the group contributed their influence in the continuum of popular music. Kaye recalls a startling introduction to a present-day vocal group, "There are some current groups who have the sound that we had. When I first heard Wilson-Phillips, I nearly wrecked the car!"

Debra Swisher Horne and her husband continue to make their home in Edmond, Oklahoma. Deb has continually made her living as a performer. In addition to the reformed Pixies Three, Deb occasionally sings with a band. Kaye McCool Krebs lives in Virginia Beach with her husband and two daughters. Bonnie Long Walker still resides in Hanover, Pa. with her husband and sings in her church choir. Midge Bollinger Neel lives in Florida. Deb, Kaye and Bonnie practice for their performances by tape. Knowing each other's voices so well, there is no problem envisioning what the finished product will sound like on stage. The talents of The Pixies Three evoke a unique enthusiasm for singing and performing. The ladies plan to deliver their vibrant sound for as long as time will allow.

The Pixies Three Discography

45s	Label	Number	Year
Birthday Party/Our Love	Mercury	72130	1963
442 Glenwood Avenue/Cold, Cold Winter		72008	
Gee/After The Party		72250	1964
The Hootch/It's Summertime USA		72288	
Love Walked In/Orphan Boy		72331	
Love Me, Love Me/Your Way		72357	
Debra Swisher			
You're So Good To Me/Thank You and Goodnight	Boom	60001	1965
God Is So Good/I Found The Answer	CTE	00002	1980?
You Bought The Shoes That Just Walked Out The Door/Strong Willed Woman Proud Eagle		17759	1985?

LPs			
Party With The Pixies Three	Mercury	20912	1964

CDs			
Now and Then	No Label	--	1995

The Pointer Sisters

Members:

(1972-77)	Ruth Pointer	(1978-Present)	Ruth Pointer
	Bonnie Pointer		Anita Pointer
	Anita Pointer		June Pointer
	June Pointer		

The Pointer Sisters are as gutsy as a Gospel chorus, raunchy as barroom maids and smooth as warbling songbirds. This diversity is the main contribution for their longevity in the music business. The ladies' ability to appeal to all audiences is evident by their confidence onstage and their choice of material in the studio. Throw in a bit of theatrics and you have a multitalented group of singers, who captivate fans and are ready for any challenge.

This talented, musical family started out in Oakland, California singing in their father's church. The sisters sang under the guise of their parents who were none too happy about the prospect of the young ladies singing secular music.

As the 1960s drew to a close and the 1970s took shape, an underground movement in music was borrowing from the styles and sounds of the 1940s. Bette Midler had made it the focus of her act prior to her recording in 1972, singer/songwriter Joni Mitchell showed evidence of the style in her work, and an upstart band called The Manhattan Transfer recorded an offbeat, 40s-styled LP for Capitol Records in 1970.

Anita, Bonnie and little sister June harnessed their vocal prowess to sing secular songs, providing backgrounds for local artists. Prior to recording in late 1971, Ruth decided to add to the harmonies, making the group a quartet. The sisters attracted the attention of Atlantic Records, where they

The Pointer Sisters, 1940s glamour and camp, 1973, (L-R) Ruth, Anita, Bonnie, June.

recorded two singles, including a country soul song entitled, "Tulsa County," early evidence of the group's broad musical influences.

With no action from the Atlantic singles, they signed with Blue Thumb Records in 1973. They had an interesting, nostalgic look, beckoning back to the 1940s, wearing tailored, broad shouldered suits and floral dresses, and holding long cigarette holders. The cover of their first LP, "The Pointer Sisters," shows their portrait painted in the tints of old photographs. The music was reflective of that era, swinging, retro songs like "Little Pony," "Steam Heat" and "Salt Peanuts." The group also wrote original songs featuring a 1940s touch, like "Jada." All songs featuring Andrews Sisters type harmonies.

Although much of their appeal came from this style, it was the group's contemporary, stripped down soul offerings that put them on the pop charts. "Yes We Can Can," written by New Orleans great Allen Toussaint hit the top twenty in 1973. Their association with Blue Thumb lasted three years, yielding "How Long (Bet'cha Got A Chick On The Side)" and a killer version of "Wang Dang Doodle." The singles held spots on the pop, R&B and country charts. One single, "Fairy Tale" won a Grammy Award in the country category. The sisters' knack for flamboyant theatrics landed them a part in the movie "Car Wash" in 1976.

In 1977, the group would experience a metamorphosis. Bonnie decided to leave the group to go solo. Her husband, Jeffrey Bowen, was a producer at Motown Records. He had worked with The Temptations. Bonnie released two LPs, yielding one disco hit, "Free Me From My Freedom (Tie Me To A Tree)." The bigger hit came from material reflective of the Motown artists of the 1960s.

Bonnie recorded The Elgins' "Heaven Must Have Sent You," both in a cover version, featuring a great scat, and a disco version. The straight version went Top 20, while the disco version was a smash hit in the clubs. On the strength of the previous singles, Bowen recorded another album of mostly Motown covers, featuring a disco cover of "I Can't Help Myself (Sugar Pie Honey Bunch). The rest of the album was filled with versions of "Come See About Me," "When The Lovelight Starts Shining Through His Eyes," with special lyrics added by Bonnie, and "Nowhere To Run." It was released in late 1979. Even though both LPs charted, the formula had worked once, but not twice. Soon thereafter, Bonnie and Jeffrey left Motown Records.

The remaining sisters worked with pop vocal producer Richard Perry in 1978, who had produced acclaimed recordings by Martha Reeves and scored big with Manhattan Transfer. The sisters were assigned to Richard's Planet Records, a subsidiary of RCA. Since the group was anxious

The Pointer Sisters, going strong in the 1990s, (L-R) Ruth, Anita, June.

GALLIN · MOREY · ASSOCIATES
8730 SUNSET BOULEVARD   PENTHOUSE WEST   LOS ANGELES, CALIFORNIA 90069

The Pointer Sisters

MOTOWN®

to branch out from their previous musical associations, Richard leaned the sessions more toward Rock than R&B. Almost immediately, the hits started coming, starting with a heartfelt version of Bruce Springsteen's, "Fire," which reached the Top 10 in the Summer of 1978.

Success continued with the Gospel-flavored "Happiness," another Allen Toussaint effort, in 1979, and the girl-group sounding ditty, "He's So Shy" in 1980, co-written by

veteran Brill Building employee, Cynthia Weil. The Pointer Sisters were now the hottest female pop group in the United States, continuing their success with "Slow Hand," and "Holding Out For Love" in 1981-82.

Their next release, "So Excited" was placed on the parent RCA label. The single, "I'm So Excited" did not immediately take off. In 1983, their LP "Breakout" garnered a million in sales. Another string of hits followed, "Automatic," "Jump" and "Neutron Dance."

"I'm So Excited" was again featured on "Breakout" and a subsequent second pressing single was issued on Planet, now with an RCA numbering sequence. This time it was a hit. The string of solid, dance-inspired hits kept people hopping in clubs and at parties for almost two years. "Neutron Dance" was featured in the opening sequences of the film "Beverly Hills Cop." The sisters returned to the charts in 1985 with "Dare Me."

The Pointer Sisters were often guests on high profile television programs like "The Carol Burnett Show," "Gimme A Break" with Nell Carter, and "Johnny Carson." The group has been featured on numerous variety programs televised from around the country.

June Pointer got her solo cue for one LP, as did her sister Anita. One of June's songs, "Little Boy Of Mine" was featured in the hilarious comedy, "National Lampoon's Vacation." The Pointer Sisters continue to play to capacity crowds in Atlantic City, Las Vegas, and at other major venues across the country. Although their chart action has waned in recent years, they have a solid foundation of diverse recordings and the reputation of being able to charm any audience, which makes them constantly in demand.

Their diverse vocal talents and flair for theatrics certainly paid off. In 1996, the sisters were part of a revival of "Ain't Misbehavin'," the musical based on the songs of Fats Waller. They received rave reviews for the competent handling of the Waller tunes. There is always an aura of energy around The Pointer Sisters. They have achieved superstar status. Their cumulative power is well expended. Theirs is the intensity to fuel the stars.

The Pointer Sisters on the road in "Ain't Misbehavin'", 1996.

The Pointer Sisters Discography

45s	Label	Number	Year
Don't Try To Take The Fifth On Me/Tulsa County	Atlantic	2845	1972
Destination, No More Heartaches/Send Him Back		2893	
Yes We Can Can/Jada	Blue Thumb	229	1973
Wang Dang Doodle/Cloudburst		243	
Steam Heat/Shakey Flat Blues		248	1974
Fairy Tale/Love In Them There Hills		254	
Live Your Life Before You Die/Shakey Flat Blues		262	1975
How Long (Bet'cha Got A Chick On The Side)/Easy Days		265	
Going Down Slowly/Sleeping Alone		268	
You Gotta Believe/Shakey Flat Blues		271	1976
Having A Party/Lonely Gal		275	1977
I Need A Man/I'll Get By Without You		277	1978
Fire/Love Is Like A Rolling Stone	Planet	45901	
Happiness/Lay It On The Line		45902	
Blind Faith/The Shape I'm In		45906	1979
Who Do You Love/Turned Up Too Late		45908	
He's So Shy/Movin' On		47916	1980

45s

	Label	Number	Year
Es Tan Timido/Cosas Especiales		47918	
Could I Be Dreaming/Evil		47920	
Where Did The Time Go/Special Things		47925	1981
Slow Hand/Holding Out For Love		47929	
What A Surprise/Fall In Love Again		47937	
Got To Find Love/Sweet Lover Man		47945	
Should I Do It/We're Gonna Make It		47960	
American Music/I Want To Do It With You		13254	1982
I'm So Excited/Nothing But A Heartache		13327	
All Of You/If You Wanna Get Back Your Lady		13430	
American Music/I'm So Excited	RCA	13485	
I Need You/Operator	Planet	13639	1983
Automatic/Nightline		13730	
Jump/Heart Beat		13780	
I'm So Excited/Dance Electric		13857	
Neutron Dance/Telegraph Your Love		13951	
Baby Come and Get It/Operator		14041	
Dare Me/I'll Be There	RCA	14126	1985
Twist My Arm/Easy Persuasion		14197	1986
Freedom/Telegraph Your Love		14224	
Gold Mine/Sexual Power		5062-7	
All I Know Is The Way I Feel/Translation		5112-7	1987
Mercury Rising/Say The Word		5230-7	
Be There/Inst.	MCA	53120	
He Turned Me Out/Translation	RCA	6865-7	1988
I'm In Love/Uh-Oh		8378-7	
Power Of Persuasion/Inst.	Columbia	38-08015	
Friends' Advice (Don't Take It)/Radio Edit	Motown	7-902	1990
Tell It To My Heart/Don't Walk Away	ERG	17637	1993

Anita Pointer

	Label	Number	Year
Overnight Success/Love Me Like You Do	RCA	5291-7	1987
More Than A Memory/Have A Little Faith In Love		6847-7	

Bonnie Pointer

	Label	Number	Year
Free Me From My Freedom/Inst.	Motown	1451	1978
Heaven Must Have Sent You/LP Version		1459	1979
I Can't Help Myself/I Wanna Make It In Your World		1478	
Deep Inside My Soul/I Love To Sing You		1484	1980
There's Nobody Quite Like You/Your Touch	Private I	04449	1984
Premonition/Tight Blue Jeans		04658	
There's Nobody Quite Like You/The Beast In Me		04819	1985

June Pointer

	Label	Number	Year
Always/Ready For Some Action	Planet	13522	1983
Don't Mess With Bill/I Understand		13592	
Tight On Time/Fool For Love	Columbia	68748	1989

Ruth Pointer

	Label	Number	Year
I Need You/Enemies Like You And Me (w/Billy Vera)	Epic	08115	1988

LPs

	Label	Number	Year
The Pointer Sisters	Blue Thumb	48	1973
That's A Plenty		--	1974
Having A Party	Blue Thumb	6023	1977
Energy	Planet	--	1978
Priority		--	1979
Special Things		--	1980
Black & White		--	1981
So Excited	RCA	4355	1982
Break Out		4705	1983
Back To Back		--	1984
Contact		5487	1985
Serious Slammin'		6562-1	1987
Right Rhythm	Motown	6287	1990

Bonnie Pointer

	Label	Number	Year
Bonnie Pointer	Motown	911	1978
Bonnie Pointer		929	1979
Heavenly Bodies	Private I	3993	1984

June Pointer

	Label	Number	Year
Little Sister	Planet	4508	1983

Anita Pointer

	Label	Number	Year
Love For What It Is	RCA	6419-1	1987

Shirley Gunter & The Queens

Members:

(1954-55) Shirley Gunter
                Lula B. Kenney (Piper Alvez)
                Lula Mae Suggs
                Blondean Taylor

The term "queen" means a royal or reigning female head of state. This term is an apt title for a quartet that belongs at the top of the realm of female Rock & Roll vocal groups. Shirley Gunter & The Queens' brand of California styled R&B possessed an endearing flavor, while packing quite a punch. Their jumpy "Oop Shoop," light in its delivery, but heavy in the infectious way it grabs the listener, is a standard by which many female group recordings would be measured.

The Los Angeles-based group began their career as many groups did, informally meeting with their friends in and after school. All the girls lived in the same neighborhood. Blondean Taylor and Shirley Gunter also knew each other from high school. Lula Mae Suggs was a couple of years older, having graduated already and Lula B. Kenney (now known as Piper Alvez), the youngest member of the group, was still in junior high school. (For years, rumors

The Queens, 1955, (clockwise from top left) Blondean Taylor, Lula Mae Suggs, Lula B. Kenney (Piper Alvez), Shirley Gunter. (Photo courtesy of Yellowlinda Inc.)

persisted that Zola Taylor of The Platters was once a member of Shirley Gunter & The Queens. This is not true.) Beginning in the fall of 1953, rehearsals convened at Shirley's house, where the girls polished their sound.

Since there were no female groups to counter the abundance of male groups in the Los Angeles area, the presence of Shirley Gunter & The Queens was conspicuous, their style parallel to patterns used by male groups who had their roots in the blues. Shirley Gunter & The Queens certainly had supreme influences surrounding them. Other singers who eventually formed groups like The Hollywood Flames, The Chimes, The Robins, The Penguins, Jesse Belvin and Richard Berry and The Dreamers were some of Shirley Gunter & The Queens contemporaries.

Although none of the young ladies had previously been in a group, Shirley had been sufficiently exposed to the emerging scene of California Rhythm and Blues by her brother, Cornel Gunter, who was having local success with his group, The Flairs. The Flairs were signed to Flair Records. Flair and its sister label, Modern Records, owned by Joe and Saul Bihari, were enjoying ongoing popularity, specializing in popular Blues and R&B. These sounds would shape West Coast R&B and Rock & Roll for years to come. When Shirley Gunter & The Queens signed to Flair Records in 1954, little did they dream that they would officially be crowned the distaff heralds of West Coast R&B. Shirley possessed a nimble, stimulating lead, featuring perfect enunciation. This delivery, surrounded by warm vocal harmonies, provided the style that netted the group a chart single with their first recording.

Released in late 1954, "Oop Shoop" catches the listener with its effervescent beat and its free and easy opening vocal riff. Shirley furnishes the message with a girlishly zealous expression. "Oop Shoop" began getting airplay in and around Los Angeles, then broke out across the country, featured on other radio stations that played R&B music. The group went from singing in Shirley's living room to becoming radio and recording stars almost overnight. Shirley Gunter & The Queens were now in demand for personal appearances. Piper recalls all the excitement surrounding the fledgling group's sudden success, "We were excited about hearing ourselves on the radio. Wow! We worked all over L.A. and the surrounding area and went on tour with Roy Milton, The Penguins, The Flairs, Mickey Champion and Camille Howard."

The single rapidly climbed the R&B charts, landing the group on the cover of Cash Box. Another, more impressive feat was the accomplishment of being the first female group with a chart hit. Shirley Gunter & The Queens were officially crowned the first female group in R&B. The group's next single featured another first, members of a female group who were writing their own material. Their big R&B hit was followed by another frenetic tune, "You're Mine," and its flip, the doleful ballad, "Why," both co-written by Shirley and Blondean. With a second, similarly executed single to their credit, the gifted quartet continued making personal appearances on television as well as in live performance.

Shows like The Al Jarvis Show and the burgeoning "American Bandstand" brought Shirley Gunter & The Queens to thousands of admiring fans. Their pleasant, second single failed to match the impact of "Oop Shoop," however. Two more singles were released in 1955, but neither one met with any success. The talented young ladies found that their second big single was elusive. After a recording life of about eighteen months, other

Shirley Gunter & The Queens

Together for a Queens reunion, 1990, (L-R) Piper Alvez, Shirley Gunter, Patty Gunter. (Photo courtesy of Piper Alvez)

facets of life warranted the members' considerations. Shirley Gunter & The Queens disbanded in 1956.

Shirley went on to record three singles with The Flairs in 1956, including the jazzy "Ipsy Opsy Ooh" and the splendid "Fortune In Love." Shirley continued to record in the late 1950s and sporadically, in the 1960s. Shirley worked with her old label mates, The Dreamers, who, by 1958, were rising to fame as the premier backing group, The Blossoms. The Blossoms join Shirley on her atmospheric song, "Believe Me," which was released on Tender Records in 1958. Shirley currently resides in Las Vegas, Nevada. Both Blondean Taylor and Lula Mae Suggs have passed away. Piper Alvez continued in show business for years, becoming one of the first black dancers and showgirls working in Las Vegas. Piper worked as a dancer for Motown for a time, appearing in a show at The Copacabana in New York with Marvin Gaye. During March of 1980, Piper was asked to step into the role of singer again, for a tour with one of the most celebrated vocal groups of all time, the fabulous Platters, "I was on tour with Paul Robi's group for six months and we had a wonderful tour. I got a call from Paul that his singer had a heart attack on the plane en route to Sidney, Australia and he asked me to replace her."

Piper's talents as a singer and dancer have taken her around the world. Piper is currently performing as a singer, covering Jazz, R&B and show tunes. Piper also exercises her talents as a songwriter, penning "Loving You" for Johnny Nash and publishing it through her own publishing company, Sag Scorpio Music. She is also completing a book for publication. Piper currently lives in Los Angeles with her daughter, Koi, and her son, Ricardo. In July of 1990, Shirley Gunter & The Queens made their first public appearance in thirty years at the One Summer Night concert hosted by California's Doo Wop Society. Piper, Shirley and Shirley's sister, Patty, reprised the classic songs of Shirley Gunter & The Queens for devoted and appreciative fans.

Although the existence of Shirley Gunter & The Queens was brief, their influence on popular music is far reaching. Without the efforts of this pioneering group, other female groups would have found the road to success narrow and a little bit bumpier. Scores of groups that followed in their footsteps owe these trailblazers a nod of gratitude. Hail to Shirley Gunter & The Queens, the paragons of female Rhythm and Blues and Rock & Roll.

Shirley Gunter & The Queens Discography

45s	Label	Number	Year
Oop Shoop/It's You	Flair	1050	1954
You're Mine/Why		1060	1955
Baby, I Love You So/What Difference Does It Make		1065	
That's The Way I Like It/Gimme, Gimme, Gimme		1070	
Shirley Gunter w/The Flairs			
Ipsy, Opsy Ooh/How Can I Tell You	Flair	1076	1955
I Want You/Headin' Home	Modern	989	1956
Fortune In Love/I Just Got Rid Of A Heartache		1001	
Shirley Gunter			
Believe Me/Crazy Little Baby	Tender	511	1958
Stuck Up/You Let My Love Grow Cold	Tangerine	949	1969

The Quintones

Members:

(1958-61)   Roberta Haymon, Lead
Phyllis Carr, 1st Soprano
Jeanne Crist, 2nd Soprano
Carolyn (Cissy) Holmes, Alto
Kenny Sexton, Bass

For young people growing up in America during the 1950s, life still consisted of many simple choices. One grew up, finished high school, got married and settled down to raise a family. As time progresses, we can reflect on how those choices became greatly expanded, but in 1958, marriage and family were the choices for most young people. For decades, popular music has acted as the window of young hearts. If you want to know what a sixteen-year old was thinking in 1958, just consult the music charts. One particular group of Pennsylvanian youngsters not only sang about the thoughts of a youthful heart, but also created their own teen homage to those feelings, recording a smash single in the process. "Down The Aisle of Love" is a bona fide Rock & Roll processional hymn, sung by the tender teen voices of The Quintones.

The Quintones all hailed from York, Pennsylvania. In 1957, while juniors at William Penn High School, friends Phyllis Carr and Jeanne Crist decided to gather singers to start a vocal group, like those they listened to on the radio. The pair had sung for fun both at home and at school since they were little girls, but now they wanted something a bit more serious and concrete. As their interest in popular music had grown, so had their ambition to find a set of singers to create the right blend that they'd been trying to perfect since they were about eight years old. The duo asked their friends in school and recruited a sophomore to sing with them. Carolyn Holmes, known to her family and friends as Cissy, was secured to sing alto to complement Jeanne and Phyllis' high harmonies.

Now that the girls had a working triad to create their puerile blend, they needed a contrasting element in the group. Kenny Sexton joined the group of young girls, finding a place to exercise his baritone/bass voice. At the same time, the group acquired a young accompanist, Ronnie Scott. Ronnie was the group's resident piano player and arranger. Only a handful of vocal groups had an arranger who was a contemporary. The group was completed when they found the perfect voice to front their exuberant consonance. Young Roberta Haymon was schooled on singing while attending her church. Roberta possessed a controlled, expressive voice emitting enough emotion to cautiously entice her listening audience.

Now, with a cohesive lineup in place, the group practiced often at the Crispus Attucks Center, tightening their harmonies and working out songs they had written while Ronnie made adjustments to their elementary arrangements. The group was originally called The Quinteros, then altered the name to The Quintones. The skillful quintet displayed their emerging talents at parties and dances in York. At one such dance for The Odd Fellows Hall, a gentleman named Sonny Pendleton heard the group and felt they had potential. Pendleton arranged for The Quintones to audition for a popular deejay named Paul Landersman who played R&B in Harrisburg for stations WCMB and WHGB. Landersman sponsored dances at a few nightclubs and it was at a club named Dance Land's event that the group showed up and sang for the popular deejay. Landersman decided on the spot that he wanted to manage them.

Paul began gathering his forces and arranged to have The Quintones record their first session. Early in 1958, the group met at the Reco-Art Studio in Philadelphia to record some of their originals. The Quintones recorded four songs, "Bells," "I Try So Hard," "Please Dear" and "Stars." For the group's first single, Landersman paired "Bells" and "I Try So Hard" and scheduled them for release on his PL Records. The shrewd deejay reconsidered, however, arranging a deal with David Rosen who was the regional distributor for Chess Records. Through Rosen, The Quintones' maiden single was released on Chess with two obvious changes in the label credits. The first was the innocuous change of the title of the A-side from "Bells" to "Ding Dong." The second change was the more calculated augmentation in the assigning of the writing credits to J. Stein, an anonymous writer who, if the record became a hit, would stand to earn a royalty from both sides. On the pro-

THE QUINTONES

The Quintones, 1958, (clockwise from top left) Jeanne Crist, pianist Ronnie Scott, Roberta Haymon, Kenny Sexton, Phyllis Carr, Carolyn (Cissy) Holmes. (Photo courtesy of Phil Schwartz)

duction of "Ding Dong," the sound of the group is pleasant enough, but the band behind them seems clumsy and not in time with the singers. Despite its haphazard arrangement, the unrefined single made a mild impact on regional playlists and afforded The Quintones the opportunity to tour.

Amidst the endless stream of one-nighters while on tour, The Quintones worked on a song that would become their second and most popular single. The song was based around the wedding march, complete with an organ intro of "Here Comes The Bride." Upon the group's return to their native region, The Quintones again entered the studio, intending to record the song they had written on tour, now entitled, "Down The Aisle of Love," which included all the ingredients Ronnie had whipped up for the arrangement.

Since "Ding Dong" had done marginally well and the group gained valuable experience performing with house bands, the productions of "Down The Aisle of Love" and a reworked version of "Please Dear" were more polished and assured. Seasoned musicians like Doc Bagby were available for the Quintones sophomore studio excursion. From the moment the first movements of the organ are heard, the listener is gliding.

If this angelic A-side was the ceremony, the flip side was the reception, the festive mambo, "Please Dear," led by Cissy; a perfect song for letting loose. The two sides were leased to Red Schwartz and Irving Nathan's Red Top Records. The small label was already enjoying success with the rocking testament of love, "Oo Wee Baby" by The Ivy Tones. Red Top now had its second big hit. "Down The Aisle of Love" began gaining popularity, but would eventually flounder without the proper exposure. When the fabulous ballad exhausted its local possibilities, Paul took the record to Dick Clark, who agreed to place the song on one of the labels in which he had a financial stake, Hunt Records. Hunt was distributed nationally by ABC-Paramount Records, who had already made a national smash out of another single, "At The Hop," by Danny and The Juniors, taken from Singular Records, another local Philadelphia label. In return for the placement, Dick Clark was assigned almost all of the publishing rights. Clark was the host of the immensely successful American Bandstand, and at this time, having a vested interest in record labels was not legally considered a conflict of interest.

Dick Clark began pushing "Down The Aisle of Love," playing it every day on his local broadcast of "American Bandstand" and on its national version on the weekends. The Quintones appeared on "Bandstand" to promote the single. The combination of a winning single and an extensive presentation schedule sent "Down The Aisle of Love" up the national charts in the summer of 1958. The sales of the single on Hunt Records were reported just under a million copies. The level of popularity of the single meant that The Quintones would once again tour. They began the rounds of The Chitlin Circuit as well as fancier clubs and dates in the US and Canada. The group appeared with other notable artists of the day, like The Danleers, Bobby

Hendricks, The Olympics, The Chantels and The Spaniels. While on tour, the group's next single, "What Am I To Do/There'll Be No Sorrow" was released on Hunt Records. The same configuration remained with Roberta leading "What Am I To Do" and Cissy leading "There'll Be No Sorrow." Both sides were similar in sound to their predecessor, but did not possess as familiar a message as "Down The Aisle of Love." The single was not well received.

As time went on, Paul Landersman and The Quintones were no longer seeing eye to eye on money matters. As a result of the increasing friction, Landersman turned the management of the group over to promoter Irv Hahan. Hahan continued the association with Red Top Records during 1959. The final single for The Quintones was a supple rendition of Edna McGriff's "Heavenly Father," lead by Roberta, and a re-recorded version of Jeanne Crist's original composition of "Stars," now called "I Watch The Stars," lead alternately by Roberta and Jeanne. This single equaled the creative success of "Down The Aisle of Love," but was affected by the lack of national attention for the single. Under Hahan's direction, the group toured for about two more years. In 1961, the Quintones recorded some material that was to be handled by the Cameo-Parkway complex, but the deal did not come to fruition. Kenny and Ronnie got drafted and Roberta got married, thus marking the end of their career as York, Pennsylvania's leading stars.

Today, Jeanne Crist lives in the Harrisburg area. Kenny Sexton and Ronnie Scott moved west and settled in California. Paul Landersman owns Myra Music Co. in Harrisburg. As of this writing, the BMI archive lists Paul Landersman as the sole writer of both "Ding Dong" and "I Try So Hard." After intermittent attempts to regroup, The Quintones finally succeeded in the late 1980s.

Original members Cissy, Phyllis and Roberta joined forces with Phyllis' brother Vince to put together the group that enchanted so many with their blend of cherubic voices. The reformed Quintones made appearances in their hometown of York, as well as playing to appreciative crowds at several meetings of New Jersey's United In Group Harmony Association.

The Quintones were also among the headliners at the fabulous Lead East weekend, an extensive tribute to the 1950s, given yearly over the Labor Day weekend in Parsippany, New Jersey. As the 1990s opened, The Quintones newly gained momentum allowed them to work as a featured house attraction at many venues in Pennsylvania, performing as a total entertainment package, singing popular songs of the day as well as their proven hits.

Sadly, the group disbanded once again after the death of Roberta Haymon in 1997. The Quintones made a handful of lasting recordings. Their timeless classic, "Down The Aisle of Love," will never go out of style. The Quintones realized their teenage dream to be singing sensations, and in the process, bestowed upon the music world the ultimate Rock and Roll wedding march.

The Quintones Discography

45s	Label	Number	Year
Ding Dong/I Try So Hard	Chess	1685	1958
Down The Aisle of Love/Please Dear	Red Top	108	
Down The Aisle of Love/Please Dear	Hunt	321	
What Am I To Do/There'll Be No Sorrow	Hunt	322	
Heavenly Father/I Watch The Stars	Red Top	116	1959

The Raindrops

Members:

(1963-65) Ellie Greenwich
Jeff Barry

In 1963, there were many quality female groups having chart success with vibrant, creative songs written by some of the more clever composers in the business. What happens when you're an inventive writer, proficient singer, master producer and maker of demos capable of being released "as is" on their own? It's one thing to be a group out on the road with two hits to your credit, but what if your job is to write for an apt and active publishing house? Your responsibility is to develop hit songs for other artists, but you find yourself a singer in a group with one problem—there is no group! This is the tale of a very successful "group" that possessed all of these features. This is the portrait of Ellie Greenwich and her studio creation, The Raindrops.

The Raindrops was the brainchild of songwriters Ellie Greenwich and Jeff Barry. They didn't even know they had a group until label heads and producers clamored for the finished demo.

Ellie Greenwich grew up in Brooklyn, NY, then moved to Levittown, NY when she was just entering junior high school. Ellie loved music and played the accordion and, later, the piano. She also enjoyed listening to her favorite tunes on the radio. Ellie was a prolific writer at an early age and began writing songs while in her early teens. Through a deal made by a friend in the music business, she recorded a single at RCA in 1958 entitled "Cha Cha Charming/Silly Isn't It." Ellie had written "Silly Isn't It" when she was 14.

By 1960, Ellie was cutting demos and some records with her new boyfriend, Jeff Barry. By late 1962, Ellie and Jeff were married, and Ellie was working for songwriters Jerry Leiber and Mike Stoller's Trio Music. Ellie had hooked up with the temperamental Phil Spector with her first writing partner, Tony Powers. They were supplying songs for The Exciters, Darlene Love, Bob B. Soxx and The Blue Jeans and Beverly Warren. When Ellie and Jeff began collaborating, they also wrote songs for those artists as well as The Crystals and The Shirelles.

Ellie and Jeff were coming into work one day, trying to come up with a song for the Philadelphia group, The Sensations. The Sensations were coming off two monster hits, "Let Me In" and "Music, Music, Music," and needed a strong follow-up to keep them on the charts. Ellie and Jeff had written a song called "What A Guy" on the train coming in to work and had cut the demo that morning. The song had the same tempo as "Let Me In" and was sure to capture the feel of that song. Unfortunately for The Sensations, fate stepped in and they were not to be part of a certain chain of events.

When Ellie and Jeff played the demo of "What A Guy" for Leiber and Stoller, they flipped out, saying that the record has to come out. Phil Spector was there at the time and demanded the song. Ellie was perplexed, to say the least. There was no record; it was just a demo with Ellie's voice overdubbed a few times and Jeff providing a bass line. Leiber and Stoller arranged for the demo to be released on Jubilee Records.

They had to come up with a name for the ad hoc group. Ellie suggested Raindrops, derived from the Dee Clark record. The single with "It's

The Raindrops, 1963, (L-R) Ellie Greenwich, Jeff Barry, Laura Greenwich. (Photo courtesy of Ellie Greenwich)

So Wonderful," another demo on the B-side, took off, making the Top 40 nationally and breaking the Top 10 in local markets, particularly in New York, Philadelphia and Detroit.

Having a hit single on the charts was pleasing, except for one thing. There were now invitations to make personal appearances but there was no group. The simple solution was to get one. Ellie asked her sister, Laura, who, as Ellie puts it, "had no choice, I begged her to do it."

Ellie also asked a young teen singer that was under Ellie's wing, Beverly Warren. Ellie had already written a song for Beverly entitled "It Was Me Yesterday." Beverly was rehearsing with Jeff and Ellie, so Ellie asked Beverly to join. A young man named Bobby Bosco rounded out the quartet that was to be the Raindrops road group.

There wasn't much touring, just on weekends, mostly, but the group had to promote the singles. This made Ellie a very busy person, what with the responsibilities of a new marriage, songwriting with Jeff and Phil Spector as well as collaborations for other artists under Trio, but this was Ellie's life; it was her job.

Unlike some of the projects Ellie had done with Jeff in the past, these Raindrops singles had more of a Rock & Roll edge than the pure pop Ellie had done as Ellie Gee and The Jets and Kellie Douglas. When they showed up to do shows, some promoters didn't believe that they were The Raindrops, expecting to see a black group. Since two singles had already hit just on the strength of being well done demos, Ellie and Jeff decided to actively produce the next single, "That Boy John." Ellie had strong feelings for this single, since it had an auspicious beginning; "It was moving very quickly. It would have been a very good record for us. That was the one record I really thought (and the company thought) would go over the top. Then, John Kennedy was assassinated and the record was pulled."

Although it charted, the association of the record's title sealed its fate in November of 1963. The flip side, "Hanky Panky," had life as a single for a female group called The Summits and would later be the debut single for Tommy James and The Shondells. The continued success of The Raindrops prompted Ellie and Jeff to put together an impromptu LP of singles, demos and quickly recorded filler for mass consumption. Wonderful demos of "Da Doo Ron Ron," "Not Too Young To Get Married" and "That Boy Is Messing Up My Mind" received exposure to the public. The next single, in 1964, was a cover of The Monotones' "Book Of Love" flipped with "I Won't Cry," written by Ellie and recorded a year earlier by Mary Ann Lewis on Coral Records. This single was a mild chart item.

During 1964, Ellie and Jeff were the premier writers and producers at the newly formed Red Bird Records. The attention paid to that endeavor was more far reaching than the handful of Raindrops singles being produced, and since it was not the duo's main intention to be recording artists and performers, they did not entertain the idea of The Raindrops becoming a Red Bird act. This was this deal and that was that deal.

Two more singles emerged during 1964. "Let's Go Together" did not chart, but the fictitious group bounced back with "One More Tear" flipped with a demo of "Another Boy Like Mine" covered by Red Bird stars, The Dixie Cups. The idea had run its course. One more single came out in early 1965, a cover of Jesse Stone's "Don't Let Go" almost as an afterthought. Ellie and Jeff's bets rested on Red Bird, so Raindrops records were not a priority venture.

Ellie did release one single under her own name on Red Bird, the dramatic "You Don't Know," a wonderful soap opera on vinyl. Again, since her primary job at Red Bird was as a writer/producer, the single was not actively promoted. It did, however, establish Ellie as a viable recording artist, an annotation that would be a marked feather in her cap when Red Bird began having business problems. When Ellie and Jeff left Red Bird, they joined friend Bert Berns at Bang Records, producing songs for budding artist Neil Diamond.

At this time, Ellie ended her three-year marriage to Jeff Barry, although they continued their professional association. Ellie and Jeff resumed writing songs for Phil Spector in 1966, notably "I Can Hear Music" and "River Deep, Mountain High." In 1967, Ellie recorded a single for United Artists, which led to an LP entitled "Ellie Greenwich Composes, Produces and Sings," containing a variety of songs, some written and produced by Ellie and Bob Crewe. Ellie's backing vocalists for the project included Mickie Harris, Melba Moore, Valerie Simpson, and The Sweet Inspirations.

Ellie recorded as The Meantime for Atco and as The Fuzzy Bunnies on Decca. She also had singles under her own name on Bell, producing with Mike Rashkow, and

Ellie and Jeff in the offices of The Brill Building, 1964. (Photo courtesy of Ellie Greenwich)

on Verve, the latter accompanied by a critically acclaimed LP in 1973, "Let It Be Written, Let It Be Sung," produced by Steve Feldman and Steve Tudanger and arranged by Artie Butler. With the advent of Carole King's "Tapestry," and the rising popularity of Laura Nyro, every singer/songwriter was then encouraged to record their own material. Ellie readily admits that this was an album she was kind of coaxed into recording, that it was just not the right venue for her. Ellie would use her talents for other purposes.

In 1976, Ellie's superior prowess as a backing vocalist was featured on Blondie's first LP, singing the backing tracks to "In The Flesh" and "Man Overboard," and on their fourth LP, "Eat To The Beat," singing on two top 40 singles, "Dreaming" and "Atomic." The Greenwich-Barry catalogue was also being foraged in 1977, with Shaun Cassidy's version of "Da Doo Ron Ron" and Mink De-Ville's cover of "Little (Boy) Girl" being released as singles. Ellie has continued her songwriting efforts writing for pop artists like Cyndi Lauper and former Blue

Belle/Labelle member Nona Hendryx, as well as commercial jingle writing. More recently, on Blondie's CD, "No Exit," homage is paid to Ellie by the inclusion of a version of "Out In The Streets," a reprised version of a 1975 Blondie single. In 1983, "Leader Of The Pack," a musical review based on Ellie's life, played to sold-out crowds at New York's Bottom Line, before being picked up to open on Broadway, revitalizing the career of Spector star Darlene Love. Throughout all the planning, changes and deals made, Ellie always managed to make herself available to fans. Both in person and through articles and television interviews she exuded candor and warmth. She is currently working on a book about her life.

The fresh sound of The Raindrops was just a stripe in the rainbow of the work of Ellie Greenwich, containing the same honest, emotional and true elements applied to all of her work. This is why Raindrops recordings are able to stand up by themselves with little augmentation, unadulterated pop rock at its best.

The Raindrops Discography

45s

	Label	Number	Year
What A Guy/It's So Wonderful	Jubilee	5444	1963
The Kind Of Boy You Can't Forget/Even Though You Can't Dance		5455	
That Boy John/Hanky Panky		5466	
Book Of Love/I Won't Cry		5469	1964
Let's Go Together/You Got What I Like		5475	
One More Tear/Another Boy Like Mine		5487	
Don't Let Go/My Mama Don't Like Him (Inst.)		5497	1965

Ellie Greenwich

	Label	Number	Year
You Don't Know/Baby	Red Bird	10-034	1965
I Want You To Be My Baby/Goodnight, Goodnight	United Artists	50151	1967
A Long Time Coming/Neki-Hokey		50278	1968
I Don't Want To Be Left Outside/Ain't That Peculiar	Bell	855	1970
Sad, Old Kind Of Movie/That Certain Someone		933	
Maybe I Know/Goodnight Baby/Be My Baby	Verve	10719	1973
Chapel Of Love/River Deep, Mountain High		10724	

(as Ellie Gaye)

	Label	Number	Year
Cha-Cha Charming/Silly Isn't It	RCA	7231	1958

(as Ellie Gee and The Jets)

	Label	Number	Year
Red Corvette/I Go You Go	Madison	160	*1961*

(as Kellie Douglas)

	Label	Number	Year
My Mama Don't Like Him/Big Honky Baby	RCA	8005	1962

(as The Definitive Rock Chorale)

	Label	Number	Year
Mirrors Of Your Mind/Get On With It	Philips	40486	1967
Variations On A Theme Called Hanky Panky/Picture Postcard Wild		40529	1968
I Love You/5:17	Bell	844	1969
I Hear The Grass Singing/Let Me Be Forever		889	1970

(as The Fuzzy Bunnies)

	Label	Number	Year
The Sun Ain't Gonna Shine Anymore/Lemons & Lime	Decca	32364	1968
Strength To Carry On/Make Us One		32420	1969
No Good To Cry/Heaven Is In Your Mind		32537	

(as The Meantime)

	Label	Number	Year
Friday Kind Of Monday/Right Back Where I Started From	Atco	6524	1967

LPs

	Label	Number	Year
The Raindrops	Jubilee	5023	1963

Ellie Greenwich

	Label	Number	Year
Ellie Greenwich Composes, Produces and Sings	United Artists	6648	1968
Let It Be Written, Let It Be Sung	Verve	5091	1973

THE RAINDROPS

Raindrops abound, (clockwise from left) Laura, Jeff, Ellie; Laura, Ellie, Jeff; Raindrops on the road, Ellie, Bobby Bosco, Beverly Warren. (Photo courtesy of Ellie Greenwich)

The Ronettes

Members:

(1961-66)	Veronica (Ronnie) Bennett Estelle Bennett Nedra Talley	*(1973)*	Ronnie Spector Chip Fields Denise Edwards

They were urban hot and they were urban cool. This is the only way to describe a female group that became the epitome of Rock & Roll style. They sounded superb, worked with the best producer in Rock & Roll history, made timeless records and became part of Rock & Roll royalty. Ladies and gentlemen, as their premiere album cover exclaimed, "presenting the fabulous Ronettes."

The story of The Ronettes begins in New York City on the upper West Side of Manhattan, known as Washington Heights. Veronica (Ronnie) Bennett, her sister Estelle and their cousin, Nedra Talley, all started on the road to a singing career by entertaining their family members. Get-togethers were an exciting time for the young girls, because it meant that they got to perform for an audience.

The Ronettes, 1963, (L-R) Nedra Talley, Veronica (Ronnie) Bennett, Estelle Bennett.

There was a wealth of talent to draw on if one was growing up during the 1950s on W. 165th and Amsterdam Ave. This was the stomping ground of many a vocal group, such as The Valentines, Jimmy Castor and The Juniors, and The Teenagers, featuring Frankie Lymon, (one of young Ronnie Bennett's idols). When she sang, she prided herself on singing Frankie's tunes effectively. Her sister and cousin dutifully sang the background parts. Ronnie was the one who had the sound, desire and drive to be out front, and her distinctive voice allowed her to do just that.

As time progressed, and the girls grew up, developing into shapely young ladies, they dressed in atypical styles of the early 1960s, knee-length skirts and high, teased hair, with heavy makeup a part of that glamorous city image which set them apart from other girls. Of course, with young people, styles are often taken to extremes, and Ronnie, Estelle and Nedra were no exceptions, taking their cues from the older girls in their neighborhood. They wore heavy eyeliner and wore hair piled high on their heads. The girls were exotic looking because they came from a mixed racial heritage. This added to their overall image of three alluring Hollywood starlets.

As the three young ladies matured, so did their pursuance of being in the music business. No longer content with singing and entertaining at family functions, the girls began singing at dances and local teen spots. In 1960, all the girls were in high school and began calling themselves Ronnie and The Relatives. They signed to Colpix Records in 1961 and worked under the attention of producer Stu Phillips.

The group decided to change its name to a composite of each of the girls' names, The Ronettes, but their first single is billed as Ronnie & The Relatives. Colpix Records was part of Columbia Pictures. The record label was associated with Don Kirshner's and Al Nevins' Aldon publishing operations in New York. Although Phillips was from the West Coast, he was assigned to the young group. The Ronettes recorded lightweight group harmony records for the parent label and for the May subsidiary during 1961 and 1962, including a cover of The Rays hit, "Silhouettes." Some of the writers contributing songs for the group during this period were Jackie DeShannon, Sharon Sheeley, Carole King, Helen Miller and Willie Denson. There was enough material to release several singles, but many songs remained in the can.

Unfortunately, the label didn't know what to do with The Ronettes. None of the prolific writers came up with a hit for them. After a year of this, Stu Phillips stopped producing them. The Ronettes had more fun as backing vocalists on other artists' records, like Joey Dee's "Getting Nearer" and Del Shannon's "Wamboo."

The Ronettes' sense of style got them noticed at The Peppermint Lounge, where they would go to dance and have a good time. They often dressed alike, and were all good dancers. Murray The "K" spotted them at the Peppermint Lounge while vacationing in Miami. He told them he could use them in New York. The Ronettes became part of The Peppermint Lounge's official dancers, featured in many shows, including Murray The "K" packages. Through all this exposure, they were noticed and eventually introduced to producer Phil Spector, who was now hot, having had three hits by The Crystals on his own label, Philles Records.

After meeting and hearing the group, Phil convinced them to get out of their former contract. Since their records weren't going anywhere, Colpix Records obliged. Phil spent almost a year with them before announcing that The Ronettes were signed to Philles Records. Phil came up with a song co-written by him, Ellie Greenwich, and Jeff Barry entitled, "Be My Baby," a prophetic title, because Ronnie and Phil were beginning their now-famous love affair. Another song being considered for the debut release of The Ronettes was another Greenwich-Barry-Spector tune called "Why Don't They Let Us Fall In Love," which would be released in 1964 on the Phil Spector label as "Veronica." This action signaled the beginning of Phil's efforts to present Ronnie as a soloist.

"Be My Baby" was a smash hit for Philles, taking off and not stopping until it reached number one in America and was a hit all around the world. Artists like Brian Wilson and Marshall Crenshaw revere "Be My Baby" as one of their favorite records of all time. "Be My Baby" is a prime example of a "good record"; a distinctive lead vocal, a good song and an effective production. The song went to number one in the summer of 1963.

Spector then showered all his attention on The Ronettes, eclipsing The Crystals and Darlene Love in the process. None of The Crystals' or Darlene Love's tunes broke into the Top 40 after the release of "Be My Baby." Spector was no longer concerned. He even pulled a Darlene Love record in favor of a Ronettes single. "Be My Baby" is probably the best representation of a Phil Spector record if one needed to present evidence to anyone not familiar with the Spector sound. The sheer presence of this record is probably why their next single, issued in the fall, bore a close resemblance to its predecessor. "Baby I Love You" also scored high on the charts, although not as high as "Be My Baby."

There were plans to record Brian Wilson's "Don't Worry Baby" as the next single, but Phil could not get a co-writing credit. At this time, Spector had his eye on the British Invasion bands that were about to grace American shores. Through Phil's association with The Rolling Stones' producer Andrew Loog Oldham, The Ronettes were being prepped to be the American ambassadors of music in England.

By the time their third and fourth singles appeared on the American charts, The Ronettes were sent to win over audiences in England, and win them over they did. Personal and television appearances abounded. The Spector groups and The Motown groups were probably the most closely linked to the British Invasion groups because of the degree of instrumentation on their recordings. The Ronettes were clearly the representatives for Spector's camp. He had all but washed his hands of The Crystals and Darlene Love's departure was not far behind. Spector wanted to be a part of the next big thing, and The Ronettes were the connection, although he was very protective of them when they first visited England.

The Ronettes next two singles, "(The Best Part Of) Breakin' Up" and "Do I Love You," were equally as brilliant as their forerunners. These songs were delivered by the writing team of Vinnie Poncia and Pete Andreoli (Anders), former members of The Videls and relatively new to the songwriting world. Despite the vibrancy of the production, the two subsequent singles did not get as high as the first two singles, although both made the Top 40.

The group was touring like crazy, and the possibilities seemed endless. The more ensconced Phil and Ronnie became in their personal relationship, the less he was comfortable with her being a Ronette. Spector had begun his goal of separating Ronnie from the group by issuing two singles on the Phil Spector subsidiary label. The first single billed as Veronica, was a cover of The Students' opus, "I'm So Young," which would also appear on their LP. The second single, "Why Don't They Let Us Fall In Love," was a contender as the first Ronettes single for Philles, but lost to "Be My Baby." Neither charted. Phil had also inserted Ronnie's voice on two songs used as filler for a Crystals LP. In the fall of 1964, the group scored big again with "Walking In The Rain." Their LP, "Presenting The Fabulous Ronettes," was a compilation of their singles, a Veronica single, and some non-45s, including a live version of Ray Charles' "What'd I Say" and a version of "I Wonder," a song already released as a single in England by The Crystals. The album was released in late 1964. Screen Gems (formerly Aldon) tried to cash in on the success of The Ronettes by releasing an LP by the group containing all the previously recorded Colpix material. There also was a planned single, "He Did It/Recipe For Love," slated for release on the now floundering Dimension Records, but the single was never pressed.

The year of 1965 brought success to Spector with another Philles act, The Righteous Bros. They had a huge hit with "You've Lost That Lovin' Feeling." The Ronettes were gaining exposure in the Rock & Roll movie, The Big TNT Show, for which Spector was the musical director. However, The Ronettes needed another hit single to keep their momentum going.

The first of two singles in 1965 was "Born To Be Together," which enjoyed success in New York and other big cities, but only made the middle of the national charts. The second single, "Is This What I Get For Loving You," fared even worse on the national charts. Many on the scene thought Spector needed to break new ground, and that his singles were slipping. Many in the business also felt he was too arrogant.

Phil let The Crystals go in 1964, and by the end of 1965, he had lost The Righteous Bros. and Darlene Love. The product at Philles was not forthcoming because there were no new acts. Phil had wanted to record Tina Turner for a long time. He got his wish and released the critically acclaimed "River Deep, Mountain High." When it was not well received, Phil decided to let Philles Records languish. When The Ronettes were scheduled to appear as the opening act for a Beatles tour, Phil asked Ronnie not to join them. The last Ronettes single for Philles, "I Can Hear Music," was produced by Jeff Barry. It briefly appeared on the national charts at 100, then disappeared. This officially marked the end of The Ronettes.

Phil and Ronnie were married in 1968. Phil kept his hands in the business by producing for The Beatles, and a series of singles for A&M Records. He found success

recording Sonny Charles and The Checkmates, "Black Pearl." He did find time to record Ronnie on one song entitled, "You Came, You Saw, You Conquered," billing it as a Ronettes single. The tunes for both artists were co-written by Spector, Toni Wine and Irwin Levine. The B-side for The Ronettes single was "Oh I Love You," recycled from the flip side of "Is This What I Get For Loving You." Ronnie recorded "Try Some, Buy Some/Tandoori Chicken" in 1971 for Apple Records, with Phil and George Harrison as co-producers. Some tracks were recorded for a Ronnie Spector LP, but Phil's erratic behavior in the studio caused Harrison to abandon the project. In 1973, Ronnie ended her tumultuous five-year marriage to Phil Spector and hit the comeback trail.

Ronnie corralled two new Ronettes, Chip Fields and Denise Edwards, and recorded two singles for Buddah Records in 1973. The result was "Lover Lover/Go Out and Get It" and a reworking of a Greenwich/Barry/Spector song, initially recorded during the Philles days, called "I Wish I Never Saw The Sunshine," flipped with "I Wonder What He's Doing." All tracks were providential songs, featuring a mixture of Rock and Rhythm & Blues, well suited to Ronnie's voice. Ronnie began making appearances in person and on television, notably on the Midnight Special.

Ronnie continued with her career throughout the 1970s. Not wanting to be pigeonholed as an "oldies act," she dropped The Ronettes moniker. Ronnie recorded contemporary songs at various labels, garnering notice for her interpretation of Billy Joel's tribute to her, "Say Goodbye To Hollywood" with Bruce Springsteen's E Street Band and her duet with Southside Johnny on "You Mean So Much To Me." In 1978, Ronnie recorded an expressive version of "It's A Heartache," but the song got pushed aside by Bonnie Tyler's version, which climbed the charts to number one. Juice Newton also had a version released at that time. Bonnie had the publishing rights and her single came out a few weeks before.

Impelling her voice to sing songs with a harder edge, Ronnie worked with singer/producer Genya Ravan in 1980 and released "Siren," an album that netted her AOR airplay, particularly with the song "You've Got A Hell Of A Nerve." Unfortunately, this song was not chosen as the album's single. In 1983, Ronnie appeared in the video "Girl Groups, The Story of a Sound," based on Alan Betrock's book and in "Da Doo Ron Ron," a film about Phil Spector, recounting her days as a Ronette. In 1986, Ronnie was a guest vocalist on Eddie Money's nod to her, "Take Me Home Tonight," which introduced her voice to another generation. The association with Columbia Records led to an album entitled "Unfinished Business," released in 1987, reuniting Ronnie with her old label mate, Darlene Love, who also had an LP released on Columbia the same year. More recently, she recorded a version of Frankie Lymon's "Creation Of Love" for a Christmas CD and "Brace Yourself" for a tribute CD to songwriter Otis Blackwell.

Ronnie Spector has been a mainstay of the New York rock club circuit for over twenty-five years, appearing at The Left Bank and The Ritz, reprising mostly her Philles material. Ronnie has made guest appearances with Billy

Joel, Eddie Money and Joey Ramone. She was a frequent guest on Late Night With David Letterman and Conan O'Brien. Ronnie appears once a year for her "Christmas Spectacular" Show at The Bottom Line in Greenwich Village. She and her husband/manager Jonathan Greenfield live with their family in Connecticut.

Estelle Bennett recorded one single for Laurie Records in 1967, the morose, prophetic "The Year 2000," written by Teddy Vann. Today, she no longer performs. Nedra Talley recorded two Gospel LPs in the late 1970s. She and her husband, Scott Ross, record and produce albums and films for The Christian Network. In 1987, The Ronettes filed suit against Phil Spector over monies and rights due them for the work they did with him, winning the suit in June, 2000.

Although The Ronettes were at the forefront of American popular music for a relatively short time, their impression was well established. A blend of the right voices, the right look and the right sound made it all possible. The Ronettes were the epitome of sound and style. Their image in the world of popular music remains a beacon for all female groups to come.

The Ronettes Discography

45s

	Label	Number	Year
(as Ronnie & The Relatives)			
I Want A Boy/Sweet Sixteen	Colpix	601	1961
Ronettes			
I'm On The Wagon/I'm Gonna Quit While I'm Ahead	Colpix	646	1962
Silhouettes/You Bet I Would	May	114	
Good Girls/Memory		138	
Be My Baby/Tedesco and Pitman (Inst.)	Philles	116	1963
Baby I Love You/Miss Joan and Mister Sam (Inst.)		118	
(The Best Part Of) Breakin' Up/Big Red (Inst.)		120	1964
Do I Love You/Bebe and Susu (Inst.)		121	
Walking In The Rain/How Does It Feel		123	
Born To Be Together/Blues For Baby		126	1965
Is This What I Get For Loving You/Oh I Love You		128	
I Can Hear Music/When I Saw You		133	1966
You Came, You Saw, You Conquered/Oh I Love You	A&M	1040	1969
Be My Baby/So Young	Collectables	3205	1983
Baby I Love You/(Best Part Of Breakin' Up)		3206	
Do I Love You/Chapel Of Love		3207	
Walking In The Rain/Born To Be Together		3208	
(as Ronnie Spector & The Ronettes)			
Lover, Lover/Go Out and Get It	Buddah	384	1973
I Wish I Never Saw The Sunshine/I Wonder What He's Doing		408	
Ronnie Spector			
Try Some, Buy Some/Tandoori Chicken	Apple	1832	1971
You'd Be Good For Me/Something Tells Me	Tom Cat	10380	1975
Paradise/When I Saw You	Warner-Spector	0409	1976
Say Goodbye To Hollywood (w/The E Street Band)/Baby Please Don't Go	Epic	8-50374	1977
It's A Heartache/I Wanna Come Over	Alston	3738	1978
Darlin'/Tonight	Polish	202	1980
I Saw Mommy Kissing Santa Claus/Rudolph The Red-Nosed Reindeer (Crystals)	Pavillion	8-03333	1981
Take Me Home Tonight (w/Eddie Money)/Calm Before The Storm	Columbia	38-06231	1986
Who Can Sleep/When We Danced		38-07082	1987
Love On A Rooftop/Good Love Is Hard To Find		38-07300	
Estelle Bennett (as Estelle)			
The Year 2000/The Naked Boy	Laurie	3449	1967

LPs

	Label	Number	Year
Ronettes			
A Christmas Gift For You	Philles	4005	1963
Today's Hits By Today's Artists		4007	1964
Presenting The Fabulous Ronettes		4008	1965
The Ronettes	Colpix	486	1965
Phil Spector's Greatest Hits	Warner/Spector	9104	1977
Rare Masters	Phil Spector Int'l. (UK)	2335 233	1977
Nedra Talley (as Nedra Ross)			
The Court Of The Kings	New Song	004	1977
Full Circle		005	1978
Ronnie Spector			
Siren	Polish	808	1980
Unfinished Business	Columbia	40620	1987
She Talks To Rainbows (UK only)	Creation	305	1999
She Talks To Rainbows	Kill Rock Stars	348	

EPs

	Label	Number	Year
Christmas EP	Philles	X-EP	1963

The Rosebuds

Members:

(1957-58)	Dorothy Pasqualini, Lead	*(1959)*	Rosemarie De Santis
	Rosemarie De Santis		Mary Salta
	Mary Salta		Virginia Petasso
	Virginia Petasso		

Seldom is it possible to have a chance to be part of a winning team for one time only. The Rosebuds, four singers from Brooklyn got such a chance in 1957 when they were part of a winning roster of talent, scoring a run in the process.

The Rosebuds were from the Bay Ridge/Bensonhurst area of Brooklyn. The quartet enjoyed singing for fun, never thinking that they would actually record anything. Through a parent's contact, the girls landed a deal with Gee Records, known for its Rhythm & Blues and Rock & Roll acts. The girls recorded two sides for Gee. The A-side was "Dearest Darling," a warm ballad with Dorothy deftly handling the lead role. The song merited local airplay around New York City. Since most acts singing for the label in 1957 were black, this foursome of Italian-American girls stood out on the roster when they made a personal appearance with the rest of the Gee/Rama roster at the Brooklyn Paramount Theatre. It was truly an experience for the group, because they were singing with all

The Rosebuds on stage, 1957, (L-R) Mary Salta, Rosemarie DeSantis, Dorothy Pasqualini, Virginia Petasso. (Photo courtesy of Steve Blitenthal)

of their idols, Frankie Lymon and The Teenagers, The Valentines and The Cleftones. Their passing fancy for singing did not go unrewarded.

After the initial single, Dorothy left to pursue a solo career. The remaining trio recorded one more single for Lancer Records entitled, "Kiss Me Goodnight/Joey" in 1959, before the group broke up. Dorothy and Virginia spent the late 1950s and 1960s singing in separate bands managed by Virginia's husband, doing mostly pop and big band music. All of the members except Dorothy have left the New York area. Dorothy occasionally appeared on New York radio during the 1980s, talking about her experiences and reliving the evening that she and her friends got to sing on stage with the artists they admired so much, feeling that they didn't really belong "up there" with all their idols. Dorothy sang briefly with the Long Island a cappella group, Champagne in 1998.

The Rosebuds Discography

45s	Label	Number	Year
Dearest Darling/Unconditional Surrender	Gee	1033	1957
Kiss Me Goodnight/Joey	Lancer	102	1959

The Royalettes

Members:

(1962-67) Sheila Ross, Lead
               Anita Ross
               Veronica (Roni) Brown
               Terry Jones

Take four beautiful young girls with fabulous voices and winning harmonies. Place them in a setting full of horns and strings with lush arrangements. Then wrap them in an array of packages from hip pants suits to form-fitting gowns. The result is the sharp looking, trend setting Royalettes, a group whose graceful sound and style are considered top shelf.

Sheila and Anita Ross had music in their lives ever since they can remember. As a young man, their father, Mr. Ross, had put together a small combo, playing on a makeshift bass fiddle. His brother James and Charlie Pace played guitar. They called themselves Dot, Dash and Comma. Naturally, these talents were passed on to his children. Sheila recounts her days as a child when her entire family would entertain themselves at home: "We came from a musically inclined family. Dad played the piano, bass fiddle and guitar. Our mom tap-danced on the Royal Theater stage along with Roni's mom, my aunt

THE ROYALETTES   Personal Management   CAPITOL
                      Leonard Stogel & Assoc., Ltd.   BOOKING
                                            CORPORATION

The Royalettes, 1965, (L-R) Sheila Ross, Roni Brown, Anita Ross, Terry Jones. (Photo courtesy of Sam Carson)

Mary Ruth. My two brothers played the piano, drums and organ. My two younger sisters simply sang along and observed. Dad taught us all how to play the piano and organ. Anita later took lessons, and I took a couple of summer courses at Peabody Institute here in Maryland when I was about 10 or 11 years old."

The girls' uncle, James Ross, had gone on to be a professional musician and singer who traveled with Dinah Washington and Louis Armstrong's band. He would often critique Sheila's performances. With such a wealth of musical knowledge and exposure on the home front, it's a small wonder that the Ross sisters turned their attentions to singing and entertaining.

Sheila and Anita continued exercising their musical talents as they entered high school. While in high school, they got together to sing for fun with their cousin Veronica (Roni) Brown and good friend, Terry Jones. Sheila and Ronnie attended Edmonson High School, while Anita and Terry attended Douglas High School. Sheila, Anita, and Terry all lived in the same neighborhood, while Roni lived in another. As a result, she would often spend weekends at the Ross house. Again, this was the meeting place where the girls "jammed." They officially formed The Royalettes in 1962. The group's plan was to enter the myriad of talent shows held in the Baltimore area. Before embarking on their career as singers, they needed a name that suited their talents. Anita suggested the group's stately moniker, "We needed to be called something, so we named ourselves after the Royal Theatre, calling ourselves the Royalettes. Everyone thought it sounded nice."

Indeed, the name implies the regal tones that emanated from the group. The young ladies had quite a polished sound due to their frequent rehearsals. After competing in numerous talent contests, they often walked away with a first place trophy. Their signature song was a version of The Chantels' hit "He's Gone." This was the song that The Royalettes sang when they entered a statewide talent contest presented on "The Buddy Deane Show" in Baltimore. The Royalettes were among one thousand contestants to enter, were in for the picking of the thirty-one semi-finalists, and made the last round of six acts, finally winning the contest.

This time, instead of a trophy, the group won a recording contract with Bob Marcucci's Chancellor Records. One of the representatives for Chancellor on hand at the contest was Harold Berkman. Berkman was the record distributor for Chancellor Records, which was distributed nationally by ABC-Paramount Records. He also became the manager of The Royalettes.

The Royalettes recorded some sides for Chancellor during 1962-63, joining the roster with popular teen idols, Frankie Avalon and Fabian, as well as The Hearts (the male group) and Claudine Clark. Two singles were released while The Royalettes were signed to Chancellor. The first single was "No Big Thing," a catchy dance tune with a mashed-potato beat, made popular by Dee Dee Sharp's "Mashed Potato Time" and The Blue Belles' "I Sold My Heart To The Junkman." This single received local attention in the Philadelphia and Baltimore areas. It seemed to Anita that the song was almost inescapable, "We were very lucky to have won the contest and the opportunity to record a song. 'No Big Thing' was played a lot. Every time you turned on the radio in Baltimore, it was playing."

Their second single was a more sophisticated sounding, mid-tempo song called "Blue Summer," which showcases the softer side of Sheila's lead, much different from her delivery on the first single. The group's harmonies were also showcased with this soft, charming ballad. "Blue Summer" foreshadowed the willowy, elegant sounds that would emerge from The Royalettes as they became more adept at blending their voices, which would become well-suited to ballads.

Harold Berkman moved quickly when it came to getting the best deal for The Royalettes. Berkman worked distribution at ABC-Paramount where singer/songwriter Teddy Randazzo was signed as an artist. When The Royalettes' contract lapsed at Chancellor Records in 1963, he informed Teddy of their existence.

Randazzo, a performer in his own right, both with The Three Chuckles and as a soloist, recognized the group's talent. Teddy saw a chance to tailor this talent to his ideas for conducting and arranging. Teddy was a partner with writer and arranger Don Costa in a recording studio in New York City. Costa had started a new label, DCP, and Teddy stepped into the role of producer for the label, working with veteran group Little Anthony and The Imperials, with his songwriting partner, Bob Weinstein. Randazzo's efforts were the key in The Imperials' crossover from 1950s group harmony to 1960s satin soul. These same efforts would sustain the talents of his new proteges.

Shortly before their work with Teddy, The Royalettes released one single while they were placed with Warner Bros. Records in 1964. "Come To Me," the uptempo arrangement, was written by former Kodaks lead singer Pearl McKinnon. The flip side is a cover of The Velvelettes tune, "There He Goes," which has an adult contemporary sound, similar to the recordings of Dionne Warwick. Sheila exudes a supple and full-bodied lead on these recordings.

The Royalettes' stay at Warner Bros. was brief, however. Not only did Harold Berkman arrange a new deal with MGM Records, but also had MGM contract Teddy Randazzo to be the group's exclusive producer and arranger. In just two years, The Royalettes had gone from local talent shows to a favorable association with a major label. They also had Berkman, who was an assertive manager, premium booking agent Leonard Stogel, and creative input from Randazzo, one of the hottest producers in the business at the time. Now all they needed was a hit. The talents of all involved were that much closer to their principal achievement.

The Royalettes were brought to New York for the MGM recording sessions. In fact, most of the business of The Royalettes would now emanate out of New York. Roni tells of the transition both in location and in sound: "Our business was mostly conducted out of New York and we traveled back and forth quite a bit. Our arranger and producer, Teddy Randazzo, gave us the change in sound when we moved to New York to record. He was a great arranger of strings and it showed up a lot in his work. He picked out most of our songs ...."

Randazzo's dramatic use of strings and horns graced a version of The Chantels classic, "He's Gone," the song that The Royalettes sang to win trophies in the talent shows. This version of "He's Gone" begins with a deftly orchestrated build-up, introducing the vocalists. The song moves at a comfortable stride, showing an emphatic lead accompanied by confident group sounds. It goes out the way it came in, with a mammoth string finale. Sweet soul with a light, bounding beat was the flip, entitled "Don't You Cry." These two songs were paired for the first single placed with MGM Records in the fall of 1964. The second single was an Academy Award nominated, Michel LeGrand composition from the critically acclaimed French movie, "The Umbrellas of Cherbourg." "Watch What Happens" provides a relaxed setting for The Royalettes' vocals. Sheila receives a featured credit on the label, which would prevail on future singles. The first two singles did not chart, but their arrangements were the platform for a style that would help the group eventually achieve chart success.

"It's Gonna Take A Miracle" was released in the spring of 1965. Sheila's tender delivery, the group's perfectly honed "oohs" and the flowing musical arrangement with the punchy hook line, sent the single soaring both through the Pop and the R&B charts. "...Miracle" possesses all the qualities of an enduring love song: a memorable melody and lyric, strong, yet winsome voices and a stunning arrangement. The song was so beautiful, that in the years following its release, many artists like Laura Nyro, Honey and The Bees, The Shirelles, Bette Midler with The Manhattan Transfer and Deniece Williams have recorded their versions of the song, none getting too far away from the original. Besides The Imperials, Randazzo now had another successful act with a recognizable sound, a sound that was fast becoming his identifying hallmark. Roni remembers being struck by the song she and her group mates recorded: "When we first heard 'It's Gonna Take A Miracle' on the radio, we were very excited, especially with the new and fuller sound. It sounded so professional."

Sheila recounts the events that just landed in their laps in the weeks following the success of "It's Gonna Take A Miracle": "Immediately, our bookings increased. We had extensive TV work where we performed on such shows as 'American Bandstand,' 'Where The Action Is' and 'The Lloyd Thaxton Show,' just to name a few. We began to travel more often, covering most of the states in the union. We went on tours, performed in Greenwich Village and Central Park in New York, performed at county fairs, country clubs and did many interesting one-nighters. Many doors opened for us and we began to get offers in Canada and England."

Now that The Royalettes' recordings had an established style, other impressive singles were released. "I Want To Meet Him" heralded the same qualities as "It's Gonna Take A Miracle." This marked the second chart hit for The Royalettes. Next came "You Bring Me Down," a variation on the melody of the Little Anthony and The Imperials' hit, "Hurt So Bad." The flip was the quintessential "Only When You're Lonely," featuring engaging call and response vocals. The group's first LP, "It's Gonna Take A Miracle," released in 1965, consisted mostly of their singles. The chance to have an album, though, was a positive prospect for the girls. They were confident in Teddy Randazzo's ability to pick out songs, produce and arrange for them, giving them their polished sound. Sheila reflects with nothing but praise for the group's mentor, "Working with Teddy was one of the highlights of our career. We simply loved him. He brought out so much in us, musically. In addition, . . . he became our friend. I cannot say enough about him. I was very impressed with Teddy and trusted his judgment in selecting songs for The Royalettes to record."

The Royalettes worked hard in the studio, too, recording four to six songs in one session. In fact, everyone in The Royalettes camp worked so hard, promotions were in order. Harold Berkman became the International Promotional Manager for MGM, so he turned over his duties as manager of The Royalettes to a close associate, Zachary Glickman, who was the girls' road manager. The group felt just as close to him as they did to Teddy. There would be no break in the quality of care that The Royalettes received.

Glamorous and elegant, The Royalettes, 1966, (L-R) Sheila, Anita, Ronnie, Terry. (Photo courtesy of John Grecco)

Television appearances and touring dates were also a significant part of The Royalettes' existence. The group appeared on "American Bandstand," "Where The Action Is" and "The Lloyd Thaxton Show." They played to sold-out crowds in clubs and on college dates, sometimes with their British label mates, The Animals. Of course, The Royalettes sang for the tough crowds on the Chitlin Circuit. If you were well received by the discerning crowd, it meant that you were good, but if you weren't, they'd let you know it.

The Royalettes made appearances on the one-night tours with Gene Chandler, The Flamingos, The Marvelettes, and Otis Redding. The Apollo and other theatres on the circuit had a hierarchy. If the group was very popular, they closed the show. If they weren't so popular, they'd open the show. The dressing room assignments reflected the same stature. The Royalettes made it to the second floor at the Apollo, then moved around a few times, but it was always the chance to perform at the famed theatre that was the true allure.

The group hoped for that chance on a proposed tour with The Beatles in 1966, which Harold Berkman was trying to negotiate. Anita remembers being disappointed when the deal fell through: "Harold was trying to negotiate a tour with the Beatles. He told us we were up for this tour, but we lost the chance to The Ronettes."

The Royalettes sailed into 1966 with three more illustrious singles. Randazzo sought to capitalize on success with sounds similar to "...Miracle" like "It's Better Not To Know" and "I Don't Want To Be The One." The positive response from these singles yielded a second LP for the group, "The Elegant Sound of The Royalettes," featuring the group's next few singles, complete with Teddy's signature arrangements. The girls rehearsed at Teddy's house, where he had a piano in his living room. Then they moved on to the studio, recording fifteen tracks for this album, many of them standards, in three days. For each song, Teddy went over the melody with Sheila, she would listen to it, then record a reference vocal and listen to that in preparation for recording the actual take. After the lead was established, Roni, Terry and Anita's backing vocals were polished to perfection. The Royalettes recorded with the entire 20-piece orchestra present in the studio, playing right alongside them. On the cover of the LP, the group is depicted in an opulent mansion, decked out in mauve gowns, flaunting their image as glamorous starlets. This was indeed a very enticing package.

Despite valiant efforts to keep the luminous orchestrations alive, tastes in Pop and R&B were changing. When the singles from The Royalettes' second album did not chart nationally, MGM decided it was time to assign a new producer to The Royalettes. Righteous Brother Bill Medley was given the job to fill Teddy Randazzo's shoes. Medley was himself signed to MGM as a recording artist at this time. Sheila was flown out to Los Angeles to prepare for her session with Medley. One single, "My Man/Take My Love" was the result of his efforts.

Although closely aligning himself with Randazzo's productions, Medley favored a slightly more soulful sound. Still, Anita felt that MGM had made the wrong choice, "I just thought that they were going on a different avenue. I didn't know they had dropped Teddy and I was mad about that. Teddy had given us an identifiable sound. After he stopped producing us, we lost something."

The Bill Medley-produced single didn't return The Royalettes to the charts. After a two-year association with MGM, The Royalettes' management got them a new deal with Roulette Records. The group released a token single, "River Of Tears," in 1967. The single did nothing to keep the group at the forefront of the popular music world, so bookings began to fall off. Without the benefit of a hit record, an artist must work harder to earn a living based solely on live performances.

The Royalettes decided to cease performing in order to concentrate on other aspects of their lives. At the time, Roni experienced overwhelming disappointment, "When The Royalettes disbanded, it was an awful time for me. I was still very young and had no other experience in holding and obtaining a job. I was very grateful that my parents made me at least graduate from high school to prepare me for the future."

Although the group disbanded, the members of The Royalettes continued to sing on their own in some capacity. Roni sang locally with groups around the Baltimore and Washington DC area for more than twenty years. Since caring for her family became the primary concern, Roni limited her singing to special occasions. She is currently a legal secretary.

After her marriage, Terry Jones Flippen went into the medical field in Baltimore before moving to the West Coast, where she currently resides. Anita Ross Brooks' job took her south to Florida. She is currently a secretary with CSX Railroads.

Sheila Ross Burnett continued singing, often coming to New York to record backing vocals for other artists that Teddy Randazzo was recording, particularly Derek Martin. In 1973, Sheila recorded "Miracle Of Miracles" and "You Hold My Life In Your Hands" for Teddy and Zachary Glickman. When they decided the recording

needed backing vocals, Sheila suggested The Royalettes. The ladies rose to the occasion. After that, Sheila performed in clubs, at weddings and at other occasions.

Sheila became a Playboy Bunny during the 1970s and performed on the Playboy circuit as a singer in Playboy clubs across the country. Sheila was voted "Bunny of The Year" in the Baltimore club. She has also been the star of her own PBS special, "This Is Sheila Ross." Sheila is currently an administrative assistant in Baltimore. She gives public performances, as well as performances at private affairs. In her act, Sheila performs jazz and pop, as well as a segment showcasing her days as a Royalette. Sheila did this all while raising a family.

Teddy Randazzo retired to Florida and is still writing songs. Teddy made a special appearance in 1999 at The United In Group Harmony Association, reprising his days as a soloist and as one of The Three Chuckles.

The Royalettes look back on their career with fondness and very little regret. To be able to sing and perform gave them confidence and brought happiness and positive energy, tools that they used to succeed in other facets of their lives. They are all thankful to Teddy Randazzo for recognizing their talent and believing in them. Sheila says it all with her warmhearted reflection of her first days as an entertainer: "The Royalette era in my life brought me nothing but happiness . . . and so much more. We were very fortunate to have won that talent contest . . . This business is such a tough, competitive one and there's only room for a few. Thank God we were blessed to have had that opportunity and that there was room for us."

The Royalettes were able to work their musical magic on the listening audience with their unforgettable sound and style. "It's Gonna Take A Miracle" is one of the most enduring songs of its time. The provision for the song's long-lasting influence comes from the direction of producer Teddy Randazzo, channeled through the utmost vocal abilities of The Royalettes, striking exemplars of 1960s popular vocal group music.

The Royalettes Discography

45s

	Label	Number	Year
No Big Thing/Yesterday's Lovers	Chancellor	1133	1962
Blue Summer/Willie The Wolf		1140	1963
Come To Me/There He Goes	Warner Bros.	5439	1964
He's Gone/Don't You Cry	MGM	13283	
Watch What Happens/Poor Boy		13327	1965
It's Gonna Take A Miracle/Out of Sight, Out of Mind		13366	
I Want To Meet Him/Never Again		13405	
Only When You're Lonely/You Bring Me Down		13451	
It's Better Not To Know/It's A Big Mistake		13507	1966
I Don't Want To Be The One/An Affair To Remember		13544	
When Summer's Gone/Love Without An End		13598	
(He Is) My Man/Take My Love		13627	
River Of Tears/Something Wonderful	Roulette	4768	1967

Sheila Ross

	Label	Number	Year
Miracle Of Miracles/You Hold My Life In Your Hands	Kwanza	7685	1973

LPs

	Label	Number	Year
It's Gonna Take A Miracle	MGM	4332	1965
The Elegant Sound of The Royalettes		4366	1966

The Shangri-Las

Members:

(1964-67) Marguerite (Marge) Ganser
Mary Ann Ganser
Elizabeth (Betty) Weiss
Mary Weiss, Lead

In the realm of the entertainment business, artists are usually given material to record that suits their voices and styles. In 1964, one such group recorded material that not only suited their voices, but their attitudes as well. Four insurgent girls of the 1960s proved themselves the anomalous characters in "Remember (Walkin' In The Sand)" and "Leader of the Pack," sob stories on vinyl, written for them by the writers at their record label.

The Shangri-Las grew up in Cambria Heights, one of the many neighborhoods that comprised the southeastern portion of Queens, New York. To say that the four-some were typical teenagers of the day is an

understatement. The two sets of sisters were the epitome of teenage girls who hung out in the park. They were schooled in urban slang and faddish dress. Their demeanors reflected such societal no-nos like chewing gum, as a cow would chew grass, and using language unbecoming to young ladies. The girls put these same raw emotions into street corner singing, as so many teens did on the streets of New York in the early 60s. These were the qualities that would allow them to stand out as singers and performers. Their chance would come soon.

In 1963, The Shangri-Las were high school students. Betty Weiss (a senior), twins Marge and Mary Ann Gan-

The Shangri-Las as a quartet, 1964, (L-R) Betty Weiss, Mary Ann Ganser, Marge Ganser, Mary Weiss.

ser (juniors), and Mary Weiss (a sophomore), all attended Andrew Jackson High School. They sang at dances and record hops, and acquired quite a bit of local notoriety. In early 1964, they recorded a single with Artie Ripp for his new Kama Sutra Productions. The single was released on Spokane Records, then being distributed by Florence Greenberg's Scepter complex.

"Wishing Well" was a formulaic single, complete with chimes and an upbeat tempo. The single didn't fare well, so the girls went back to their well-appreciated live performances. One such live performance was captured on tape. Joe Monaco, the co-writer of "Wishing Well," thought favorably of the group's performance and would keep them in his thoughts. His suggestion to a friend would set the girls on their path to stardom.

George Morton was an acquaintance of songwriter Ellie Greenwich. George knew Ellie from their neighborhood on Long Island. Hearing about Ellie's success, he visited Ellie in New York, with the yearning to write songs of his own and get into the music business. George boasted to Ellie and her husband, Jeff Barry that he could write a hit song and would come back to them with such a product. Morton began gathering his forces. He booked time in a studio on Long Island, hired musicians, and went searching for a group to record a song he had written called "Remember (Walkin' In The Sand)." Joe Monaco told George about The Shangri-Las. Monaco had remembered their performance on the isolated single for Kama Sutra Productions. He suggested that George record them.

The original version of "Remember" was quite long and served as a demo for the song. Ellie and Jeff were sold on the idea and especially, on the group, whose lead singer had a mysterious, almost spooky delivery in her voice, well suited to the melancholy lyrics of the song.

The Shangri-Las, 1965. (L-R) Mary Ann, Mary, Marge.

The Shangri-Las were now recording artists for the fledgling Red Bird Records, who had scored big in the spring with "Chapel of Love" by The Dixie Cups. Right before the release of the single, Artie Ripp stepped in to remind Red Bird that the group was technically signed to Kama Sutra. The two companies worked out a deal and the single was released in the summertime of 1964. It was an instant hit. No other song on the radio sounded like it. The Shangri-Las went from local celebrity to national prominence in a few short weeks. In order to capitalize on the newfound success, their single on Spokane was re-released on Scepter Records and a live performance of "Simon Says" was released on Smash Records, with the group billed as The Shangra-Las. The Smash single was given an open release number, therefore dating it in 1963, but it was actually released in 1964. The group was now soaring, but unbeknownst to them, they had yet to reach the apex of their success.

During the mid-1960s, motorcycles were becoming quite popular. The album cover of "He's A Rebel" by The Crystals depicted a biker to represent the rebel set. Ellie, Jeff and "Shadow," as George was nicknamed, started tossing around ideas about bikes and, of course, a tie-in to a romantic relationship. They came up with the premise for a song called "Leader of The Pack." The record features Mary's sullen approach to what was fast becoming her signature sound. The production was replete with "good girl loves the bad boy" imagery, complemented by attention-grabbing back beats, sound effects and ominous sounding responses from the background vocals.

The writers/producers topped themselves, once again. "Leader of The Pack" had no competitors on the charts. People who thought Rock & Roll listeners were the devil's disciples immediately put down the song as a bad influence on the youth culture. Popularity won out and the song became a huge hit, spawning a few carbon copies, plus a parody called "Leader of The Laundromat," by Ron Dante under the name The Detergents.

The Shangri-Las were now part of the endless stream of artists who made the rounds on the television dance shows and Rock & Roll tours. The group was featured on "Clay Cole," "Hullabaloo," "Lloyd Thaxton" and "American Bandstand," where they would act out their stories with precise dance steps and serious looks on their faces. Sometimes they'd sing live and sometimes they'd lip-sync. They did Dick Clark's Caravan of Stars Tours and Murray the "K" shows.

Touring seemed almost endless, except to come in off the road to do some recording. The Shangri-Las maintained a grueling touring pace, both in The United States and in England, where they were equally popular. They appeared on "Ready, Steady, Go" and hit every major city in the UK for a live performance. Some of their touring mates included The Drifters, Jive Five, Vibrations, Marvelettes and Zombies. The Shangri-Las became the most successful group at Red Bird, with two hit singles under their belts in three months. In order to capitalize on the demand for their sound, Red Bird issued two more singles for 1964, the bold "Give Him A Great Big Kiss" and "Maybe," the latter record almost an afterthought, but it did chart high in New York, where the group's following was strong. An LP entitled "Leader of The Pack" was released in early 1965.

The theme of the good girl loving the tough guy continued with the poignant "Out In The Streets," the story of how an outcast found it hard to live in his girlfriend's straight and narrow world. Although it charted in the top 60 nationally, it was all over East Coast radio. As a testament to the song's influence, it gave way to another song with a variant theme. "Out In The Streets Again" was written by Nik Ashford, Valerie Simpson, and Jo Armstead, and was recorded by Candy and The Kisses.

The rock band, Blondie, covered "Out In The Streets" twice, once at the start of their career in 1975 and again on their 1999 CD, "No Exit." "Out In The Streets" was followed by "Give Us Your Blessing" a song previously recorded by Ray Peterson. This song was in keeping with the adolescent vs. parents theme. A creative trend began with this record. The spoken word was now Mary's lead. The formula worked, so once again the group was on the charts with another death disc. This one displayed much more directness, making use of the word "dead" in the recitation. The couple in the story dies on a rainy highway.

B-sides like "Heaven Only Knows" and "The Boy" were where the group showed they could handle serene harmonies as well as their ascending choruses of despair. The group's sustained popularity prompted their second LP, "Shangri-Las 65!" released in the spring.

"THE SHANGRI-LAS"

Red Bird
RECORDS
1619 B'WAY., N. Y. C.   LT 1-3420

A rare, formal shot of The Shangri-Las, 1965, (L-R) Mary Ann, Mary, Marge. (Photo courtesy of John Grecco)

Since image as well as sound was becoming more evident in the selling of an artist, The Shangri-Las' ensemble consisted of spiked-heeled boots, tight pants and leather jackets. Their publicity pictures sometimes showed three members and sometimes four. Betty did not like to tour, so she was often left out of photographs—but they were always a quartet on vinyl. Later on in their career, they rotated members in trios, Marge, Betty and Mary or Mary Ann, Betty and Mary.

Their appearance as delinquent girls went hand in hand with their records and the images those songs projected. Ironically, this was when Red Bird released "Right Now and Not Later," a complete departure from the group's previous A-side theme. The song charted on the strength of the group's urban following. The B-side was a previously recorded track written by Ellie and Jeff called "The Train From Kansas City." This song was in a style closer to what Ellie would fashion for herself in the late 1960s.

It seemed like a recovery for Red Bird when "I Can Never Go Home Anymore" was released, placing The Shangri-Las back in funeral mode. This time, Mother was interred. The single charted high. Their second LP was repackaged with the new hit, and received a completely new cover, dubbed, "I Can Never Go Home Anymore." Another parody by The Detergents, "I Can Never Eat Home Anymore," also appeared. Incidentally, "The Train From Kansas City" was the last appearance of a Barry/Greenwich production for The Shangri-Las. The hit-making duo moved to Bang Records in 1965 to pursue other creative endeavors, most notably, to produce Neil Diamond.

During 1966, Shangri-Las records continued to sell, but it became a much harder climb to the top. Fortunately, they maintained their following in New York and other major cities. Spoken word singles like "Dressed In Black" and "Past, Present and Future" were emotional eulogies on vinyl. A cover of Jay and The Americans' "He Cried" and the very beautiful "Paradise," penned by Harry Nilsson, certainly was in keeping with the dramatic, melancholy mood of previous Shangri-Las singles, but the company didn't move fast enough to change what was becoming an old formula for the A-sides.

It seemed that the group was singing its own epitaph. The girls were still touring, but getting restless, as the demands of the road became too much. When the hits slowed, so did the choice spots on the circuit. Still very young, the quartet needed to get on with their lives outside the music world. Back at Red Bird, Leiber and Stoller felt the same way, exiting the company soon after Barry and Greenwich. Red Bird was the speeding train full of hits and this was the end of the line. When Shadow Morton took The Shangri-Las to Mercury in the fall, there were no more premier groups left at Red Bird. By early 1967, the company folded.

The Shangri-Las recorded two singles for Mercury Records. The upbeat and contemporary "Sweet Sounds of Summer" charted in New York in the fall of 1966. The single highlights Mary's vital singing voice amidst pleasant group harmony and features a transcendent guitar and organ bridge. The second single, released in 1967 was "Take The Time" depicting the duties of American young men during the Vietnam War. The song urges reflection for our boys fighting overseas, especially those that didn't make it home. The group that exhorted impulsive behavior was now singing about a thought-provoking topic. The maturity was refreshing and the production commendable. Mercury had also purchased The Shangri-Las' Red Bird releases. Instead of developing the group for a potentially new phase in their career, the label elected to push "The Golden Hits of The Shangri-Las," a greatest hits LP covering the group's past efforts. The Shangri-Las' time in the limelight was over.

After the breakup of The Shangri-Las, Mary moved west for awhile, settling in California. Later on in the early 1970s, she returned to the East Coast, married, and went into private business with her husband. Betty also settled down to raise her family. Sadly, Mary Ann Ganser died from encephalitis in 1971. During the late 1970s, the underground rock music scene sported The Shangri-Las' sound as one of its influences.

In 1979, Mary Weiss guest starred on Aerosmith's "Night In The Ruts" LP, singing backup on their version of "Remember (Walking In The Sand)." Mary, Betty and Marge made a brief comeback at CBGB's in New York City in 1980. An album was planned for Sire Records, but unfortunately, nothing ever came of it. In the 1980s, the name of the group lay dormant. Promoter Dick Fox registered the trademark and sent out a group working as The Shangri-Las.

The original Shangri-Las planned to appear at a Palisades Park reunion show in 1989, but were stopped by an injunction by Fox and Mars Talent Agency, claiming the original group was in violation of trademark law. The original group disputed the idea of sending out a group who had not recorded the hits, resulting in the original group suing over The Shangri-Las' name. Fox and Mars

lost, partly because in performance, their Shangri-Las inferred recording the original hits. The original Shangri-Las performed at Richard Nader's Palisades Park Reunion Show as planned. The reunion, however, was ephemeral. In the summer of 1996, Marge Ganser died after a battle with breast cancer. Two original members are now gone, and the remaining two original members no longer have the desire to perform. Fans can no longer contemplate another reunion.

Since the early 90s, a Shangri-Las act tours the country, possibly through a mutual settlement between the remaining original members and Mars Talent Agency. They bear no association with the original recording group, except for the use of the name. As a result of court proceedings involving group trademarks like The Shangri-Las, many venues that book veteran vocal groups now stipulate that at least one original member needs to be a part of the act. Other promoters issue disclaimers at the end of radio spots saying that groups on a given show may or may not contain original members. Some groups containing non-original members now choose their words carefully on stage.

The practice of having multiple groups under the same name, bearing no affiliation to the individuals that recorded the hits and made the group popular, is a major point of contention among original members of 1950s and 60s vocal groups. Artists have lobbied in Washington, trying to have the trademark laws amended, so original members may benefit from reputations they helped build during the group's initial existence. Controversy aside, the original Shangri-Las, their sound and the impression they created in the public consciousness during the mid-60s are indelible marks in the history of American music culture. Mary, Betty, Marge and Mary Ann will always be remembered as the renegade girls of Rock & Roll.

The Shangri-Las Discography

45s

	Label	Number	Year
Wishing Well/Hate To Say I Told You So	Spokane	4006	1964
Wishing Well/Hate To Say I Told You So	Scepter	1291	
Simon Says/Simon Speaks	Smash	1866	
Remember (Walkin' In The Sand)/It's Easier To Cry	Red Bird	10-008	
Leader of The Pack/What Is Love		10-014	
Give Him A Great Big Kiss/Twist and Shout		10-018	
Maybe/Shout		10-019	
Out In The Streets/The Boy		10-025	1965
Give Us Your Blessing/Heaven Only Knows		10-030	
Right Now and Not Later/The Train From Kansas City		10-036	
I Can Never Go Home Anymore/Sophisticated Boom Boom		10-043	
I Can Never Go Home Anymore/Bull Dog		10-043	
Long Live Our Love/Sophisticated Boom Boom		10-048	1966
He Cried/Dressed In Black		10-053	
Past, Present and Future/Paradise		10-068	
Past, Present and Future/Love You More Than Yesterday		10-068	
The Sweet Sounds of Summer/I'll Never Learn	Mercury	72645	
Take The Time/Footsteps on the Roof		72670	1967

LPs

	Label	Number	Year
Leader of The Pack	Red Bird	20-101	1965
Shangri-Las 65!		20-104	
I Can Never Go Home Anymore		20-104	
The Golden Hits of The Shangri-Las	Mercury	61099	1967
The Golden Hits of The Shangri-Las		824 807-1	1985

The Sharmeers

Members:

(1958-59) Gloria Huntley
Costella Riley
Mitzi Ross
Majidah (Mattie) Williams

The Sharmeers were a quartet of girls from Philadelphia who recorded one marvelous single for Red Top Records. In 1958, "A School Girl In Love" struck the right chord with all the local teenagers and became a favorite among the Philadelphia record collectors.

Gloria Huntley and Majidah (Mattie) Williams grew up together in Northern Philadelphia. They were typical teenage girls who enjoyed listening to music and hanging out with friends in their neighborhood. In fact, the girls were so close that their mothers insisted that they attend different high schools so they could concentrate on their studies. Gloria went to Bok Vocational and Mattie went to Kensington. This ploy did little good, for Mattie would take the bus down to Gloria's school and spend time there. Gloria jokingly says that everyone thought Mattie attended Bok, she was there so much.

Two other local spots were Barber's Hall, where shows were performed and The Northern Liberties Recreation Center, an after-school center for young people. Many activities took place here, like basketball, knock hockey, dances and, for those so inclined, singing.

Impromptu groups sprang up at every teenage meeting place, imitating those from the neighborhood who were fortunate enough to have recorded a few sides for the myriad of labels operating in Philadelphia. All the teens admired those who had "made it," like Al Banks and The Turbans, Ronnie Jones and The Classmates, Little Joe Cook and a favored female group from New York, The Clickettes. It was during these sessions that Gloria and Mattie got together with Mitzi Ross and Costella Riley. Theirs was the sound that blended just right. Gloria and Mitzi even meshed in the ability to write songs for the group to sing. Since the girls' singing enchanted so many at the center and around the neighborhood, the group christened themselves The Charmers. The Charmers, all high school freshmen, performed at dances and parties, singing the ditties made up by Gloria and Mitzi. Mattie and Costella threw in some accents for good measure.

One evening, The Charmers decided to put their vocal prowess to the test at a local nightspot. Gloria remembers the chain of events. "We did a show at the Northwest Club. The Quintones were performing that night. The prize for winning the contest was a contract with Red Top and that's how we got our recording contract."

It certainly would have been an envious position for the group to wind up at Red Top Records. Red Top was the home of the already established Ivy Tones, who had a big hit with "Oo Wee Baby" and The Quintones, a quintet from York, Pa. who mesmerized everyone with the sultry "Down the Aisle of Love." The Charmers' parents wouldn't let them go to clubs, so the girls told their mothers they were singing at the church. When they got to the club, the quartet decided it would be best to look older. They immediately went into the bathroom and stuffed their bras. Mattie recalls the humorous turn of events. "Before the performance, we all went into the bathroom and stuffed our bras with toilet tissue. During the performance we looked over at Mitzi and discovered she had three breasts."

The group had decided to sing "Down the Aisle of Love," despite their discovering that the group scheduled to perform that night was The Quintones. Besides breaking up on stage over Mitzi's predicament, the group sang their version of "Down the Aisle of Love," winning the contest. They were soon approached by one of their singing idols, Donnie Elbert. Donnie was the one who had told them about the contest when he listened to the group one night while they were singing in line, waiting to get into a show. Elbert gave them the information about the session for Red Top. When the girls arrived at Red Top, owners Red Schwartz and Irving Nathan asked if they had any songs they'd like to sing. They went back to Barber's Hall and wrote "A School Girl In Love." The owners also informed them that the name "Charmers" was taken and suggested they change the C to an S, thus renaming them The Sharmeers.

The girls were quite excited about their first recording session. The group had written three of the four songs to be recorded. They had rehearsed "A School Girl In Love," "You're My Lover" and "The Night Was All Around Us," as well as a version of The Crickets' 1954 tune, "The Man From The Moon." Red Top decided to release "School Girl" and "You're My Lover" as the first single. Mitzi is featured as the lead on "School Girl." Doc Bagby's band backed the group on the session. The release of this single netted the group a niche in their neighborhood as a premier group, now held in the esteem of those groups they emulated.

The Sharmeers were now one of the featured local acts on a bill when Rock & Roll shows came to town. They had a brother group called The Cardells, featuring Earl Young, which first transformed into The Volcanos during the 1960s, and eventually into the disco 1970s icons, The Trammps. Fighter Bob Montgomery was also a promoter in Philadelphia, and would feature The Sharmeers at his shows. Bob's young niece, Tammy, took notice of The Sharmeers and other performers, and would eventually perform herself, first as Tammy Montgomery, then as the more famous Tammi Terrell.

Despite all this local publicity, there was one faction in Philadelphia that had no idea that The Sharmeers were local celebrities, the group's parents. It wasn't until plans were being made for the group to sign with Red Top that anyone's mother or father got wind of the fact that none of the "shows" were at the church, but in venues where the girls were not allowed. Mattie had taken to sneaking in and out of the house via the window. The girls felt that the notion of catching grief from their parents was worth the opportunity to jam at Barber's Hall and to walk from one end of their neighborhood to the other, meeting all the other groups and singing all night. Once back inside her house, Mattie would hear Bunny Sigler on his way home, playing guitar and singing up a storm. She would stop to listen to his sweet voice.

The Sharmeers were not exempt to the pitfalls of being young female singers, eager for a chance to perform and to even get paid for it. A few times their services were rendered for a show and the promoters refused to come up with some money. The ladies recalled one time in particular. "We sang at a show with Bobby (Charles) Peterson, a blind performer. We did the show, then got locked out of the theater and they didn't pay us a dime. We had no way to get home and it was late at night."

The group enjoyed local status, appearing on "The Mitch Thomas Show," a local Delaware dance show. The group covered popular songs of the day like The Chantels', "He's Gone," The Cookies', "In Paradise" and Ronnie Jones and The Classmates', "Lonely Boy" changing the lyrics to "Lonely Girl." They wondered when their next single was forthcoming. Although "School Girl" hadn't yet charted, radio listeners knew of its existence. Unfortunately, before the single really had a chance to break out, Red Top was being investigated in the payola scandal. As a result, singles on the label garnered little airplay. The Sharmeers hoped for the release of their next single, but they never got a second chance.

After the time for The Sharmeers had passed, Gloria sang with various local bands during the 1960s and 1970s. She appeared with The Orkettes, Andy Aaron and The Soul Machine, Snookie Jones and The Five Sharps and Tommy Keiths & The Marlboro Men, to name a few. Mattie had married and lived in Chicago for many years before returning to Philadelphia. Mattie recently received her degree at Temple University. She is currently working on a book about the origin of The Nation of Islam in Philadelphia. Mitzi Ross had a career singing cabaret and jazz for a time in Philadelphia. Gloria and Mattie have appeared informally at shows sponsored by The United In Group Harmony Association, chatting with fans about their single. They have even been known to sing a few songs. They are considering regrouping if conditions permit. That schoolgirl charm still has much appeal.

The Sharmeers Discography

45s	Label	Number	Year
The Sharmeers A School Girl In Love/You're My Love	Red Top	109	1958
Mitzi Ross Guarantee Me The Weekend/Man Hunt	CRS	007	1974

The Shirelles

Members:

(1958-66) Shirley Owens (Alston), Lead
Adeline (Micki) Harris
Doris Coley (Kenner), Lead
Beverly Lee

(1967-73) Shirley Alston
Adeline (Micki) Harris
Beverly Lee

When four girlfriends got together in school one day to sing a street rhyme they had written, they never dreamed it would take them places beyond the stoops of their modest homes in New Jersey or that their recordings would become Rock & Roll classics. These teenagers started by singing heartfelt choruses in a school hallway and became one of the most successful and significant female groups in popular music, enjoying a career that would span over forty years. They are the incomparable Shirelles.

The Shirelles formed at Passaic High School in Passaic, New Jersey in 1957. The four girls, Shirley, Micki, Doris and Beverly, were friends from childhood. Doris developed her voice singing in her minister father's church. All the girls liked listening to popular music. The group got together to sing at home and in school, making up little ditties of their own.

Singing was never more than a lark for the young group, all in their junior year at school. Sometimes they'd

THE SHIRELLES

Direction
SHAW ARTISTS CORPORATION
565 Fifth Avenue
New York 17, New York

The Shirelles first photo session, 1958, (clockwise from top) Doris Coley, Micki Harris, Shirley Owens, Beverly Lee.

sing and not keep their minds on what they were doing. One time, they were singing in the gym and not paying attention to their instructor. As a consequence, they had to enter the school talent show. To their surprise, they were well received. New attentions came their way, especially from one classmate, Mary Jane Greenberg, whose mother, Florence, was in the music business, running a small label named Tiara Records.

The group was not interested in recording and told Mary Jane just that, but she was persistent. The girls even resorted to dodging her, but she kept on. The group finally relented, auditioning for Florence right in her living room. They sang a song they had written themselves, which they sung in a round-robin fashion. The song was called "I Met Him On A Sunday."

Florence Greenberg recorded The Shirelles and released "I Met Him On A Sunday" in early 1958. The song started to make noise locally. The Shirelles started making personal appearances in and around the northern New Jersey area. Greenberg received an offer from Decca Records to distribute the single and re-release it on Decca. This meant national exposure for the single and for the group, something the tiny Tiara label could not provide.

The deal was made and the single climbed the charts to #50 nationally, its strongest appeal in and around the New York area. Decca picked up an option to release two more singles by The Shirelles. Florence's son Stan produced the first single, but as part of the deal with Decca, the production and arranging fell to famed orchestra leader Buddy Johnson.

The Shirelles' second single was "My Love Is A Charm," an emphatic, lamenting ballad with Shirley taking the lead vocals and Doris providing a recitation for the bridge. The interesting novelty tune on the B-side called all dancers to the floor for "Slop Time," a breezy rocker. Apparently the company liked the feel of "Slop Time," so the A-side for the last single for Decca was the similar "I Got The Message" written by Shirley and Stan. Its flip, "Stop Me" featured Doris on lead.

Varying the sound of the group was easy, with Doris' potent, passionate delivery and Shirley's coy, girlish eloquence. The producers could experiment until they hit upon the right mixture of voice, arrangement, and song. Having a hit with that formula was not far away. However, The Shirelles were not to be consistent hit makers at Decca. The follow-up singles to "I Met Him On A Sunday" produced no chart action. When the initial agreement with Decca ended, the label did not pick up another option. The Shirelles returned to work with the Greenbergs.

Florence Greenberg had released a series of singles on Tiara that were not as successful as "I Met Him On A Sunday." She decided to rename her company Scepter Records, after her music publishing company. The Shirelles were now Scepter recording artists along with Eddie & The Starlites and a fellow resident of Passaic, Joey Dee.

The first effort by the group on Scepter was a version of The Five Royales tune, "Dedicated To The One I Love." The teenaged females gave the song a completely different treatment than the original, with Doris' fervent voice out front. "Look A Here Baby," written by the group, graced the B-side. The song was a strong attempt to update the story in "I Met Him On A Sunday." The single had an auspicious beginning and entered the national charts on the strength of East Coast airplay, but Scepter didn't have the resources to push the song nationally, so it floundered at the bottom rungs of the pop charts.

The second Scepter single, "A Teardrop and A Lollipop," did not chart. "Doin' The Ronde" was again another play on the riff sung by the group in "I Met Him On A Sunday." The vocal arrangement was sung in a round robin style. The group pressed on with a tender ballad for the third Scepter single in 1960, "I Saw A Tear," flipped with "Please Be My Boyfriend," a distaff version of The Cadillacs tune. Doris provided her wonderful vocals for both. Again, no interest was generated for the single. With musical tastes changing in 1959, these singles seemed dated and too simplistic. It was time for a different approach.

In 1959 and 1960, the payola scandals were raging. Disc jockeys were admitting to taking money for playing records on the air. This was not a crime, but it fueled the extremist view that this was the only way Rock & Roll could get on the radio. Many Rock & Roll producers were sweetening the recordings by adding strings and other embellishments to broaden their appeal.

Florence Greenberg felt that the talents of The Shirelles should be matched with songs written by composers with proven track records. She made arrangements for songwriter Luther Dixon to supply her stars with premium material. Dixon was a singer as well as a songwriter, having been a member of The Four Buddies. Now he was writing and publishing his own songs. His first efforts with The Shirelles brought forth "The Dance Is Over" and another song co-written with Shirley entitled, "Tonight's The Night."

According to the single's label information, "The Dance Is Over," a sorrowful ballad, led by Doris, was the intended A-side. "Tonight's The Night" was lead by Shirley, with the rest of the group chanting the title line in the background, while the drums beat out a Latin flavored rhythm. The lyrics told the tale of uncertain love. This side took off in New York, making the top forty. The Shirelles' version had met early competition from a version by The Chiffons (no relation to the group that recorded "He's So Fine") on Big Deal Records. Even the same backing tracks were used. The Shirelles' version was clearly superior, with much stronger voices and tighter harmonies. This was the second glimmer of hope that The Shirelles would become consistent hit makers. Dixon's next production would open the floodgates, not only for The Shirelles, but also for many female groups to follow.

Many young people were coming to New York to try their hands at songwriting. The Brill Building at 1619 Broadway was the Mecca for song spinners eager to have their compositions placed with established artists. One such young girl had started in the music business in 1957, while still in high school. Carole King and her new husband, Gerry Goffin, began collaborating under the supervision of Al Nevins and Don Kirshner, who were publishing songs sung by Bobby Darin and Connie Francis through their Aldon publishing company. Luther Dixon brought one of Goffin/King's demos for The Shirelles to hear. The Shirelles initially rejected it, but after Luther convinced them he could tailor the song to their sound, they agreed to try it.

Since Shirley had success with "Tonight's The Night," she was selected to sing lead. "Will You Still Love Me Tomorrow" starts with a band of violins to introduce the song. From the moment Shirley sings her first line the listener is captured. The melodious backing vocals, swirling violin break and poetic lyrics keeps the production in stride. This production is a perfect example of the marriage of song-voice-production to produce a bona fide hit. The song took off and did not stop until it reached the top spot on the charts. In response to The Shirelles success, "Dedicated To The One I Love" joined the new single in the top ten. The Shirelles were now national singing sensations.

Starting with "Will You Still Love Me Tomorrow," The Shirelles embarked on a career that would make them the sweethearts of the airwaves. They provided fellow Scepter artist Lenny Miles with admonishing responses on his weepy "Don't Believe Him, Donna." Luther Dixon produced hit single after hit single for the group, featuring Latin tempos and sweet violins, under the auspices of his Ludix Productions. "Tomorrow" was followed by the mindful "Mama Said," flipped with the belated Christmas tearjerker, "Blue Holiday." Again, Shirley led the A-side and Doris the B-side. Then came the double-sided hit, Carole King and Jerry Goffin's "What A Sweet Thing That Was" backed by "A Thing of The Past."

Next was "Big John." All were chart toppers that put The Shirelles at the forefront of radio station polls for favorite artist among teens. Of course, countless Rock & Roll tours and television appearances followed. The Shirelles seemed to mesh well with the songs coming from the established publishing houses. Burt Bacharach, Mack David and Barney Williams provided the next rocket with "Baby It's You," a haunting single with a cool delivery by Shirley featuring some great vocal dynamics. The song was matched on the flip with the touching "Things I Want To Hear (Pretty Words)," led by Doris. Shirelles singles were now the models that other aspiring producers were imitating in 1961.

As 1962 began, Shirelles singles were now leaning towards a more pop sound than an R&B sound. Doris' vocals proved too strong for this direction, so most leads now went to Shirley, whose sound fit well with the avenues on which Florence Greenberg wanted her charges to travel.

The Shirelles, 1962, (clockwise from top) Micki, Shirley, Beverly, Doris.

The Shirelles had three LPs to their credit as well as numerous singles. The albums featured marvelous productions of potential singles like "Make The Night A Little Longer" and their version of Chuck Jackson's "I Don't Want To Cry." However, the choice for the next single was almost an afterthought. "Soldier Boy," recorded at the end of a session, was simplistic enough to have mass appeal. It became the biggest hit The Shirelles would have. Two mild singles, "Welcome Home Baby" and "Stop The Music" followed.

Luther Dixon's involvement was absent on the latter of the two. Van McCoy produced "Stop The Music," while Leiber and Stoller took credit for "It's Love That Really Counts." Unbeknownst to The Shirelles, Luther Dixon's involvement with Scepter was about to end. The last single for 1962 was a reworking of the standard "Everybody Loves A Lover," with a back beat and instrumentation borrowed from Barbara George's "I Know." The onset of The Shirelles' struggle to stay on top was about to begin.

Luther Dixon's contract with Scepter Records had come to an end. Dixon was starting his own label, Ludix Records and his association with Capitol Records. Creatively, Dixon felt he wanted to move on. The job of producing The Shirelles fell back to Stan Greenberg, or Stan Green, as it appeared on the record labels. Green scored with the group's first single for 1963, "Foolish Little Girl," the story of a young lover's bid for too little, too late. This single features a rare secondary lead by Beverly as the lamenting former paramour.

The Shirelles were again in the top ten. The backside, "Not For All The Money In The World," also charted. This was a favorable continuation for the group. However, new sounds were appearing on the charts, so Shirelles records had to stay current. Leiber and Stoller, Stan Green and, singer/songwriter Ed Townsend, now Scepter's A&R man, would all take turns producing for The Shirelles. Townsend won for the most creative success with the thought provoking "What Does A Girl Do" and the theme song from the hilarious movie, "It's A Mad, Mad, Mad, Mad World."

Although many singles were chart items, only two made the upper echelons of the pop charts, not like the half dozen of just two years before. One more single was released for 1963, seemingly a leftover Ludix Production. "Tonight You're Gonna Fall In Love With Me" heralded the group foray into 1964, with its Spector-like production. Newer, more contemporary musical influences continued to compete with sounds produced for The Shirelles, a fate that needn't have happened to a group that was still winning radio station polls and wowing everyone at concerts.

During 1963 and 1964, another, more hurtful revelation came to light for the group revered as the top female group in the country. When The Shirelles signed contracts, it was stipulated that a certain amount of money would be put aside for them when they turned twenty-one. When the group became of age, no such endowment was available. These circumstances led to a mounting legal battle between the group and the record company. The two principal sides would not enter court until the end of 1964, but the results of the obviously strained relationship between them was reflected in the product released.

In 1964, so many new companies were joining the ranks of successful hit makers. Motown was in full swing and the British Invasion had taken hold of American radio. The Beatles owed part of their popularity to The Shirelles when the band covered "Boys" and "Baby It's You." Also, pioneer producers George Goldner, Jerry Leiber, and Mike Stoller started a new company.

Red Bird Records featured its own warm twist on the female group sound, brought to everyone by Ellie Greenwich and Jeff Barry. Many R&B vocal groups were leaning toward a more soulful sound, with different arrangements and patterns for the backing vocals, almost always eliminating the need for a bass singer. Scepter Records was moving into the adult contemporary sounds with a former session singer, fresh from her family singing group, emerging to become the inimitable

Dionne Warwick. By 1964, she was Scepter's bright star, a solo act with the potential for broader appeal.

The Shirelles had four singles released during 1964. The first, "Sha La La," was a mock-live rocking hand clapper, complete with horns. "His Lips Get In The Way" graced the flip. Unfortunately, all it did was to serve as a demo for Manfred Mann's version, which became a bigger hit a few months later. The gentle "Thank You Baby" written by Beverly Lee, came next. Two more singles followed, each doing worse on the charts than the one before. Speculation has it that since The Shirelles and Scepter were in dispute over monies owed the artist, there was no reason to feed the pot. Whoever won or lost in the end didn't matter, for Scepter's former gold mine was now a dim prospect.

From 1965 to early 1967, it seemed as if Scepter was trying to avoid having a hit with The Shirelles. Admirable efforts by The Tokens, Nik Ashford, Valerie Simpson, Jo Armstead, and Tommy Kaye went unnoticed by radio stations. The productions seemed adrift, much too mild in execution compared to other sounds on the radio during the mid-60s. A promising LP, released on Scepter's Pricewise series, "The Shirelles Swing The Most," featured more interesting cuts than Scepter was releasing as singles, such as the Toni Wine/Steve Venet composition, "A Girl Is Not A Girl," and an old Motown cut called "Lonesome Native Girl."

One notable exception in the singles department was a cool discotheque-sounding version of The Shirelles' first hit, aptly entitled "I Met Him On A Sunday '66." Wildly uptempo, this rousing version could keep a dance floor going with snapping drums and frantic guitars. The vocals seemed almost secondary. Unfortunately, few would even know of its existence. It wasn't until 1967 that the in-house producers at Scepter would find the happy medium between what had become The Shirelles jazzy style and popular late 1960s arrangements,

The Shirelles in "Let The Good Times Roll", 1973, (L-R) Shirley, Micki, Beverly.

like those chosen by Chris Montez and Bobby Hebb. The Shirelles' new producer, Paul Vance, scored with "Don't Go Home (My Little Darling)." This remake of the old Playmates tune made it to the New York charts in January. Although its appearance was brief, it was a signal that The Shirelles were still a viable commodity.

The group was now a trio, Doris having left at the end of 1966. They were still touring and making personal appearances on the college circuit. Scepter was still releasing LPs including the live "Spontaneous Combustion," documentation of a particular college date at NYU. The same snazzy production by Vance continued with "Too Much Of A Good Thing," arranged by veteran Hutch Davie. The last in the trio of singles catering to this style put The Shirelles back on the national charts for the first time in three years. "Last Minute Miracle" slid The Shirelles right back where they should have been two years before, with a driving beat and familiar Shirelles harmonies showing up once again.

For their last Scepter single, The Shirelles' vocals were treated to a full dose of Chicago soul with Bill "Bunky" Sheppard as producer. "Wait 'Til I Give The Signal" was the first flat-out soul record by the group, released in early 1968. Sheppard had been working with his group, The Esquires, on Wand Records and he worked his magic with The Shirelles' single. Another single, "Hippie Walk," was planned but never released. After almost ten years with Scepter, hanging in there through the ups and downs, The Shirelles decided it was time to move on.

In 1968, The Shirelles hooked up with producer Randy Irwin and arranger George Andrews. The duo continued the trend started with the Bill Sheppard single on Scepter, releasing two uptown soul records for Mercury's revived subsidiary, Blue Rock Records, including the dynamic "There's A Storm Goin' On In My Heart," a favorite on the UK northern soul charts.

Three singles for Bell Records came next in 1969. The Shirelles benefited from the talents of Kenny Gamble, Leon Huff, and Jerry Butler; recording songs flavored with the Philly sound, like "Playthings" and "Never Give You Up." For the Bell singles, the group was billed as Shirley and The Shirelles. Since Doris' departure, Shirley was the sole lead singer. Although Doris' absence left the backing vocals a bit milder, Micki and Beverly rose to the occasion to blend for effective unison and smooth harmonies. Randy Irwin's production company again switched labels in 1970 to United Artists.

The Shirelles enjoyed a comfortable home at the label where other veteran vocal groups like Jay & The Americans and Little Anthony and The Imperials were enjoying chart success. These groups were having luck with updated arrangements of early 1960s hits. The Shirelles got on the bandwagon with their versions of "It's Gonna Take A Miracle," a "There Goes My Baby/Be My Baby" medley and a modernized take of "Dedicated To The One I Love." Still, another chart hit was elusive.

In 1971, The Shirelles switched labels again, this time to RCA Records, another company friendly to proven R&B vocal groups. The Shirelles joined the roster that included The Moonglows, Tymes, The Jimmy Castor Bunch and The Main Ingredient. Two albums and four

singles, including the marvelous "Brother, Brother" and "Let's Give Each Other Love," yielded no hits for the group. Also, another force was gaining momentum in the music industry by the early 1970s, the nostalgia craze. People who were approaching thirty longed for the music of their adolescence.

There was a new market forming, ironically for what groups like The Shirelles had been working to overcome, an association with an older sound. In 1973, The Shirelles appeared with The Five Satins, Coasters, Chuck Berry, and other stars of the 1950s and early 1960s in "Let The Good Times Roll," a documentary about the 1950s, combined with a live concert. The Shirelles became anchors at Richard Nader's Madison Square Garden reviews and other shows popping up in The New York area in the early 1970s. Easily able to capitalize on the laurels of their early hits, The Shirelles ceased recording new material to concentrate on their allure as an "Oldies But Goodies" attraction.

The Shirelles joined the party of yesteryear and never looked back. Shirley tried a contemporary solo career, recording an album in 1976 entitled "Lady Rose," but could never shake her identity as the girl who sang "Will You Still Love Me Tomorrow." Even though she returned to The Shirelles for a time, Shirley eventually went on her own, preferring to stick to her Shirelles material. Doris returned to the group, just in time for The Shirelles to celebrate twenty-five years in the business. A lavish party took place at the Ritz in New York. Many illustrious artists came out for the event, including The Crystals, Chuck Jackson and Florence Greenberg.

Tragically, not long after this celebration in 1982, Micki Harris McFadden died from a heart attack, backstage after a performance. The group carried on with Micki's cousin in her place. During the 1980s, Doris and Beverly had to fight off other groups claiming to be The Shirelles, but eventually won out.

Shirley, Beverly and Doris were honored with their induction into The Rhythm & Blues Hall of Fame in New York in 1994, and The Rock & Roll Hall of Fame in 1997. Although time and space have kept them apart, it was easy to see the old magic in their faces when they performed their hits at the ceremonies.

Doris Jackson lived on the West Coast, where she had her own group of Shirelles, the cream of the California singers, Blossoms Fanita James, Gloria Jones and, on occasion, Honey Cone member Carolyn Willis. Sadly, Doris passed away on February 4, 2000, from breast cancer. Only a few months before, she had given a powerful performance at Madison Square Garden, in New York. Beverly continues to this day with her group of Shirelles and Shirley Alston-Reeves appears on her own. Their one time mentor, Florence Greenberg, passed away in 1997.

The stellar efforts of The Shirelles have taken them around the world. They are an identifiable, pivotal and influential force in Rock & Roll. The Shirelles were the leaders to the next phase for female singing groups, achieving consistent mass acceptance in popular music. They were the trailblazers for all female groups of the 1960s and beyond.

The Shirelles Discography

45s

	Label	Number	Year
I Met Him On A Sunday/I Want You To Be My Boyfriend	Tiara	6112	1958
I Met Him On A Sunday/I Want You To Be My Boyfriend	Decca	30588	
My Love Is A Charm/Slop Time		30669	
Stop Me/I Got The Message		30761	
Dedicated To The One I Love/Look A Here Baby	Scepter	1203	1959
A Teardrop and A Lollipop/Doin' The Ronde		1205	
I Saw A Tear/Please Be My Boyfriend		1207	1960
Tonight's The Night/The Dance Is Over		1208	
Tomorrow/Boys		1211	
Will You Love Me Tomorrow/Boys		1211	
Don't Believe Him Donna (w/Lenny Miles)/Invisible (No Group)		1212	
Mama Said/Blue Holiday		1217	1961
I Met Him On A Sunday/My Love Is A Charm	Decca	25506	
What A Sweet Thing That Was/A Thing Of The Past	Scepter	1220	
Big John/Twenty One		1223	
Baby It's You/The Things I Want To Hear		1227	
Soldier Boy/Love Is A Swingin' Thing		1228	1962
Welcome Home Baby/Mama, Here Comes The Bride		1234	
Stop The Music/It's Love That Really Counts		1237	
Everybody Loves A Lover/I Don't Think So		1243	
Foolish Little Girl/Not For All The Money In The World		1248	1963
Don't Say Goodnight and Mean Goodbye/I Didn't Mean To Hurt You		1255	
What Does A Girl Do/Don't Let It Happen To Us		1259	
It's A Mad, Mad, Mad, Mad World/31 Flavors		1260	
Tonight You're Gonna Fall In Love With Me/20th Century Rock & Roll		1264	
Sha La La/His Lips Get In The Way		1267	1964
Thank You Baby/Doomsday		1278	
Maybe Tonight/Lost Love		1284	
Are You Still My Baby/I Saw A Tear		1292	
March (You'll Be Sorry)/Everybody's Going Mad		12101	1965
My Heart Belongs To You/Love That Man		12114	
Soldier Boy/My Soldier Boy Is Coming Home		12123	
I Met Him On A Sunday '66/Love That Man		12132	1966
Que Sera Sera/Till My Baby Comes Home		12150	
Look Away/Shades Of Blue		12162	
After Midnight/Shades Of Blue		12162	
When The Boys Talk About The Girls/Shades Of Blue		12162	
Teasin' Me/Look Away		12178	
Don't Go Home (My Little Darling)/Nobody Baby After You		12185	1967
Too Much Of A Good Thing/Bright Shiny Colors		12192	
Last Minute Miracle/No Doubt About It		12198	
Wait 'Til I Give The Signal/Wild and Sweet		12209	1968
Sweet, Sweet Lovin'/Don't Mess With Cupid	Blue Rock	4051	
There's A Storm Goin' On In My Heart/Call Me		4066	
A Most Unusual Boy/Look What You've Done To My Heart	Bell	760	1969
Playthings/Looking Glass		787	
Never Give Up/Go Away and Find Yourself		815	
There Goes My Baby/Be My Baby/Strange, I Still Love You	United Artists	5064	1970
It's Gonna Take A Miracle/Lost		50693	
Dedicated To The One I Love/Take Me For A Little While		50740	
Strange, I Still Love You/No Sugar Tonight	RCA	48-1019	1971
Brother, Brother/Sunday Dreaming		48-1032	1972
Let's Give Each Other Love/Deep In The Night		74-0902	1973
Touch The Wind/Do What You've A Mind To		APBO0192	

Shirley Alston as Lady Rose

	Label	Number	Year
If You Want Me/Dream Express	Strawberry	105	1976

LPs

	Label	Number	Year
Tonight's The Night	Scepter	501	1960
The Shirelles Sing To Trumpets and Strings		502	1961
Baby It's You		504	1962
The Shirelles and King Curtis Give A Twist Party		505	
The Shirelles' Greatest Hits		507	1963
Foolish Little Girl		511	
The Shirelles Sing Their Songs In The Great Movie "It's A Mad, Mad, Mad, Mad World"		514	
Shirelles Sing The Golden Oldies		516	
The Shirelles' Greatest Hits Volume II		60	1964
The Shirelles Swing The Most	Pricewise	4001	1965
Hear And Now	Pricewise	4002	
Spontaneous Combustion	Scepter	562	1967
Eternally, Soul (w/King Curtis)		569	
Happy and In Love	RCA	--	1971
Shirelles		--	1972

Shirley Alston as Lady Rose

	Label	Number	Year
Lady Rose	Strawberry	6004	1976
Lady Rose Sings The Shirelles Greatest Hits		6006	1977

The Socialites

Members:

(1962-63) Lorraine Anthanio, Lead
Eloise Covington
Gloria Meggett
Delores Rainey
Mildred (Kym) Trant

(1963-64) Lorraine Anthanio
Eloise Covington
Gloria Meggett
Delores Rainey

(1964-65) Lorraine Anthanio
Eloise Covington
Gloria Meggett
Sandra Durant (?)

During the early 1960s, the music business was set up so that anyone with talent and ambition could have their chance to be heard. Groups were forming in junior high schools and high schools in every major city in America. At one high school in the North Bronx, a quintet of girls were winning accolades for their talents and becoming singing sensations.

The Socialites were formed at Grace Dodge High School, on E. 189th St. and Crotona Ave., in The Bronx around 1960. Before that, Lorraine Anthanio, Mildred "Kym" Trant and Eloise Covington attended Junior High School 40 in their Morrisania neighborhood. They developed their love of singing by listening to the radio and joining the school glee club, becoming friends in the process. Lorraine was content with singing in the background, but her instructor had other plans; "I was very shy. I was singing in the back of the group. She heard my voice and said to come down front. I represented The Bronx in a talent show as a soloist in 1958. I sang 'Chances Are'."

When the girls entered high school, they again joined the school glee club. At Dodge, the trio joined Gloria Meggett and Delores Rainey to form the group. They rehearsed the popular songs heard on the radio. A day of reckoning came when The Socialites were asked to perform at one of the weekly assemblies held in the school auditorium. The girls were all sophomores and juniors, but they were asked to sing for the senior assembly. This warranted a show of strength, because they knew none of the seniors wanted to hear a group of underclassmen. Kym recalls the group's apprehension, "We were very afraid to perform for the seniors, but we went over very well. For the senior assembly, we performed 'Down The Aisle of Love'."

After this auspicious onset, the group performed more and more, not only in their school, but also as part of a youth organization tour. The Socialites appeared at record hops and summer concerts in the park, mainly on Long Island. Sometimes they did three or four events in one night, loving every minute of it. Gloria became confident in the group's ability to command an audience: "What I remember most about singing with The Socialites is the applause we always received when we did appearances. I also enjoyed how the kids were so eager to receive our autographs."

The Socialites w/Sunny & Horizons at an Alan Fredericks show, 1962, (L-R) Lorraine Anthanio, Eloise Covington, Gloria Meggett, Delores Rainey, Kym Trant. (Photo courtesy of Lorraine Anthanio Lofaso)

These events would have been the extent of their career, but now, Lorraine was making plans for the group. A fellow classmate, who occasionally played piano for the group, had suggested they go and see Joe Simmons, a songwriter and producer who was associated with a local Bronx label called Arrawak Records, which had some local success with a single entitled, "No Money" by The DeVilles. Simmons was already working with The Laddins and The Janettes. The normally shy Lorraine was now orchestrating an audition for the group. This took the rest of the members by surprise. Kym was startled by the thought, "It (singing) was something recreational for me, something I enjoyed. Every song I heard, I learned. I never thought of music as a career. We sang in the hallways a cappella, but the thought of going to an audition was kind of scary. I was wondering if people would like us."

The Socialites went into Manhattan for the audition. In addition to Simmons, singer/songwriter Carl Spencer was also in attendance. Kymberly remembers that they had originally been slated to work with Spencer, but ended up working with Simmons. Not only was Simmons taken with the group, he also liked the songs that Lorraine had written, two tunes called "Jimmy" and "The Click." An ethereal ballad, "Jimmy" was an ode to an old boyfriend, written by Lorraine at the age of 15. The group had been performing it. These two songs were released as the first Socialites single in 1962.

Another figure who factored into the success of The Socialites was Joe De Angelis, a songwriter from Brooklyn who met the group when they were at 1650 Broadway. De Angelis expressed an interest in managing the group. He soon proved himself to be a fair and earnest businessman. Lorraine marvels at how he took care of his charges: "We met Joe De Angelis downtown and he was interested in us. He spoke with our parents and then we signed contracts. Not only did he make sure we got paid, but also that people didn't bother us. When we performed, some neighborhoods were all right, but in other neighborhoods, people would scream and yell at us to sign autographs. On Sundays, we would go to his house in Brooklyn, on Kingsland Ave. His mother would say we were too skinny and feed us."

Through the astute management of Joe De Angelis, the group performed in many local hot spots. The Socialites performed at Freedomland Amusement Park in The Bronx. Freedomland proved to be an awakening experience one afternoon, as Lorraine recalls: "Once, when were singing at Freedomland, the exhibit next to us was a man being blown out of a cannon. Just as we're getting to our climax in the song, the cannon explodes and the audience runs off. We were like 'what did we do?'"

Meanwhile, "Jimmy" was enjoying local airplay on WWRL and Jocko was spinning the disc on WADO. Arrawak's owner had a local radio show broadcasting out of his home on Elton Ave. The Socialites were busy with engagements and radio interviews at Arrawak's home-made station and on Alan Frederick's "Night Train Show."

In 1963, Joe Simmons negotiated a deal to have the second Socialites single placed with Mercury Records. "The Conqueror" made it onto the Chicago label, with the artists billed as Lorraine and The Socialites and enjoyed local popularity in New York. The group continued to appear around New York. The Socialites appeared with other stars like The Four Seasons. Before his hit single "But, It's Alright," fellow Bronxite J.J. Jackson was their accompanist on piano, but

sometimes they held the marquee by themselves. After a continual chain of appearances in New York, New Jersey, Pennsylvania and Connecticut, Kym decided to leave the group. She was married and in nursing school, so the time demands of personal appearances were too much. The group continued as a quartet.

The last Socialites single was made under the supervision of Artie Ripp's Kama Sutra Productions. "You're Losing Your Touch" was co-written by Joe De Angelis. Motown rhythms were in full force in 1964 and New York was not going to be left behind. The song possesses a driving beat with each word of the lyrics accenting each thump of the drum. Independent producer and songwriter Van McCoy wrote the enchanting flip, "Jive Jimmy."

Once again, a teenage interlude is effectively delivered in just two and a half minutes. The Socialites continued to make live appearances during 1964 and 1965. By this time, Delores had departed and was replaced by Sandra Durant (?). This quartet made a personal appearance at the New York World's Fair, where they received a letter of thanks from Gov. Rockefeller for their part in the festivities.

As time went on, all the young ladies got married and their focuses changed. Kym Trant Smith went into nursing, and Lorraine Anthanio Lofaso became a liaison within the oil industry. Gloria Meggett Dorsey stayed in the business of entertainment for a time, as a professional dancer. Gloria has also managed and owned two nightclubs. She is now a social worker for New York City. Eloise and Delores have moved out of state.

In February of 1998, Kym, Lorraine and Gloria were interviewed on The R&B Serenade on WRHU at Hofstra University, where they spoke with hosts Gordon Skadberg and Frank Gengaro about their time as Socialites. During the last few years, Lorraine attended Juilliard School of Music. She has studied voice, opera and musical theatre. She has also studied with Jimmy Willis and the famous jazz pianist Barry Harris. Lorraine often performs at Iridium, one of New York City's premier jazz clubs, where she also serves as producer and as executive producer for shows exposing new musical talent. Lorraine and Kym were part of The Great Day In Harlem photo shoot, which took place on June 6, 1999, and were also part of the festivities for its dedication at The Smithsonian Institution in February, 2000. Along with The Socialites, members of countless vocal groups gathered to preserve their slice of musical history. These appearances have sparked renewed interest in The Socialites' music. By their recent efforts, The Socialites have demonstrated consideration for their craft and have participated in its preservation. That's no "jive."

The Socialites Discography

45s	Label	Number	Year
The Socialites			
Jimmy/The Click	Arrawak	1004	1962
You're Losing Your Touch/Jive Jimmy	Warner Bros.	5476	1964
(as Lorraine & The Socialites)			
The Conqueror/Any Old Way	Mercury	72163	1963

The Starlets

Members:

(1961-64) Maxine Edwards
Jane Hall
Mickie McKinney
Jeanette Miles
Liz Walker (Danetta Boone)

One measure of a group's success is to have a hit record and make personal appearances. It's quite another measure of success when the group's endeavors launch the career of another group. Such was the case with The Starlets, a quintet from Chicago whose early soul sound and stark harmonies paved the way for other female groups in the Chicago area. Unfortunately, their most popular record did not give them the kind of recognition they originally sought.

The Starlets began their career in 1960, when group founder, Jane Hall, met Mickie McKinney, Liz Walker and Jeanette Miles while working for the same employer. The quartet came to the attention of Bernice Williams who ran a small record label in Chicago with veteran Chicago producers Bill Sheppard and Carl Davis. The label was called Pam Records. With its companion label, Nat Records, both labels carried acts that did very well locally.

This yet unnamed female group got together at Bernice's house to sit in on the rehearsals of another group, The Dukays. One evening, Earl Edwards, a member of The Dukays, brought his sister, Maxine, to a rehearsal. Earl informed Bernice that Maxine also sang, so Bernice suggested putting Maxine with the other girls. Maxine joined and the group became a quintet. Bernice christened them The Starlets.

They were signed to Pam Records and Bernice began managing the group. It wasn't long before the group had their first single, released in 1961, called "Better Tell Him No." The song's catchy "Mama, should I . . ." lyrics, with Maxine trading lead lines with guest star Bernice, garnered airplay in Chicago, New York, and other cities. By the springtime of 1961, "Better Tell Him No" had jumped onto the national charts. The dreamy flip, "You Are The One," also received attention. The producers were now enjoying success with two singles, The Starlets single and "Duke Of

Earl," by The Dukays, featuring the inspiring voice of their lead singer, Gene Chandler. Another Starlets single, "My Last Cry," was rushed out, this time with Mickie singing lead. Bernice did another guest vocal on the novelty flip, "Money Hungry."

Based on the success of "Better Tell Him No," The Starlets embarked on an endless stream of tours. Excitement fueled their spirits, as they were now appearing with artists they admired, like Gladys Knight & The Pips, The Spinners, Van McCoy and a young singer from Philly named Tammy Montgomery, who later became Tammi Terrell. They also appeared on television on "The Jim Laudsberry Show." The Starlets' stage shows proved to be energetic and invigorating. At their first performance in Gary, Indiana, Maxine literally danced right out of her costume. The group was dressed in flair dresses with full slips, doing their version of "The Twist." Maxine laughingly recalls their maiden performance. "We were twisting and my heel got stuck in my petticoat. I did the twist all the way down to the floor and kicked that petticoat right into the audience."

The group was enjoying the best of everything, but not always without a catch. One night after a show in Philadelphia, the girls had to sneak out of The Benjamin Franklin Hotel, leaving all their belongings behind because the bill wasn't paid. Two men that the girls didn't know drove them back to Chicago. When the bill was finally paid, their costumes were returned. Philadelphia would soon prove to be an interesting town for The Starlets.

On one of the group's excursions to Philly, they were approached by Harold B. Robinson, a car salesman and record producer, who admired their sound and thought he could help them. Maxine remembers how their wariness gave way to the desire to move upward: "Harold Robinson saw us at this revue and came back to our dressing room. He wanted us to meet with him. He sent us a limousine. We thought he had all this pull, and that Carl and Bill were going to work with him. We saw all these riches and thought that this was a way to better ourselves."

The girls listened to his pitch, and told him that they were contracted to Pam Records and could not record for him. Robinson assured them that recording a few sides would be no problem. He said he would take care of everything with Bill and Carl. The group was staying in Philadelphia, so in no time at all, Robinson informed them that he had cleared the path for them to do a session for him. The song that he had in mind was a version of "I Sold My Heart To The Junkman."

The Starlets, 1961, (L-R) Mickie McKinney, Maxine Edwards, Jane Hall, Jeanette Miles. (Photo courtesy of Maxine Edwards Smith/Earl Edwards)

The arrangement was much different from the mellow version recorded by The Silhouettes. This version was wildly uptempo with rolling drums and screeching violins. Liz Walker had not made the trip with the group this time, so the recordings were made by the quartet. Maxine sang the lead. Jane hastily wrote a flip entitled "Itty Bitty Twist," a derivative of their show-stopping live version of "The Twist."

Three other songs were recorded at the session, but left in the can. Bobby Martin and Phil Terry arranged the session. Everyone was satisfied with the results. The group thought that this time they would go over the top. After the session, The Starlets went back to Chicago; it was business as usual. The group felt secure that their Philadelphia recordings would bring them more good fortune. It never dawned on the young group, all still in their teens, to ask Carl Davis or Bill Sheppard about the "arrangements" that were made for them to record for Harold B. Robinson. They were soon to discover that Davis and Sheppard knew of no such plans.

One evening in 1962, Maxine received a call from her mother in Memphis. ". . .Junkman" was playing on the radio down in Tennessee. Maxine immediately telephoned Jane. This would have been a happy occasion, except for one thing. The deejays introduced the group that recorded this hot new single as The Blue Belles. A short time later, the single was on the charts. Then came a personal appearance on "American Bandstand" by a quartet from the Philadelphia-Trenton area, appearing as The Blue Belles and lip-syncing this song.

Knowing that he couldn't use the group that had recorded the single, Robinson put a call out to audition a new singing group. Patricia Holt, Nona Hendryx, Sarah Dash and Cindy Birdsong got the job. The powerful, commanding voice of young Patsy Holt would front this group. Eventually, the group name was changed to Patti La Belle and The Blue Belles. Robinson had the new group record a version of ". . . Junkman," but The Starlets' version was the single version. The Starlets were embarrassed and furious. The matter would have died there had it not been for a phone call placed by Phil Terry to Davis and Sheppard.

Terry, feeling that Robinson had not given him his due, encouraged the group to institute a lawsuit against Robinson. According to Maxine, Robinson tried to deny that the group ever recorded for him, but he relented and the suit was settled in favor of The Starlets. The group members were paid a portion of the profits from the hit single, a restitution that Maxine feels fell far short of what the entitlement was.

The group may have settled with Robinson over their role in the launching of a top-twenty single, but the matter wasn't over where Carl Davis and Bill Sheppard were concerned. The Starlets were lambasted for attempting to go into a situation like that on the blind side, breaching their contract in the process. Even worse than that, Davis and Sheppard washed their hands of the group. Davis and Sheppard had already parted ways with Bernice Williams. Maxine recounts how the events cost The Starlets their career; "Bill and Carl wanted to know how we could do something like that. We had settled out of court, but after that, nobody wanted to touch us."

A single had already been released on Okeh Records with Liz singing lead, billed as Danetta and The Starlets, a stage name that Liz sometimes used. "You Belong To Me" was a swirling ballad with Liz's lead effortlessly carrying the record. It was simply allowed to wither on the vine as Carl Davis exercised his apathy toward the group. Davis would go on to have a fruitful career at Okeh, producing The Artistics, Vibrations, Major Lance and Billy Butler, among others. Sheppard found success with The Esquires. The fate of The Starlets was not so positive. The group stayed together for a short while, then Jane got married and left. Maxine departed soon afterward.

During 1964 and 1965, the songs that had remained in the can from the session that produced "... Junkman" surfaced on budget singles. The members of the group weren't even aware of their existence. Two of the songs, "I've Got To Let Him Know" and "You Better Move On" cast the group in a reworking of the "Junkman" groove. Of the three songs, "You're Just Fooling Yourself" showed the promise of thrusting the group through the changing sounds of R&B, with its horn accents and Chicago soul oriented groove. Unfortunately, the belated singles were also billed as Blue Belles singles, no one suspecting the charade.

After the demise of The Starlets, Jane Hall Stovall moved to California, where she formed another group and continued to write songs. Maxine Edwards Smith began singing as a soloist in nightclubs in Detroit. In 1965, she joined a touring group comprised of female impersonators called "The Adam & Eve Revue." Maxine was their opening act. The work was both interesting and rewarding. Maxine remained with the revue until 1980, when she decided to devote her life to church work. Today, Maxine works with the physically challenged, preparing them for day to day living situations. The other members of The Starlets scattered and disappeared. Maxine regrets not having the business savvy to have clearly understood the business end of the music industry when she was younger, but is very proud of the role that The Starlets played in shaping Rock & Roll history, even if it was an inadvertent self-sacrifice. One listen to "...Junkman" will prove that the high note had definitely been hit.

The Starlets Discography

45s

	Label	Number	Year
Better Tell Him No/You Are The One	Pam	1003	1961
My Last Cry/Money Hungry	Pam	1004	
(as Danetta and The Starlets)			
You Belong To Me/Impression	Okeh	7155	1962
(as The Blue Belles)			
I Sold My Heart To The Junkman/Itty Bitty Twist	Newtown	5000	1962
You Better Move On/You're Just Fooling Yourself	Rainbow	1900	1964
(some pressings say Original Blue Belles)			
I've Got To Let Him Know/I Sold My Heart To The Junkman	Peak	7042	1964
(issued with a picture sleeve of The Starlets)			

LPs

	Label	Number	Year
The Girl Groups Are The Best (Peak cuts)	Pricewise	4004	1965

The Supremes

Members:

(1960-61) Florence Ballard Barbara Martin Diana Ross Mary Wilson	*(1967-70)* Cindy Birdsong Diana Ross Mary Wilson	*(1975-76)* Cindy Birdsong Scherrie Payne Mary Wilson
(1962-67) Florence Ballard Diana Ross Mary Wilson	*(1970-71)* Cindy Birdsong Jean Terrell Mary Wilson	*(1976-77)* Susaye Green Scherrie Payne Mary Wilson
	(1972-73) Lynda Laurence Jean Terrell Mary Wilson	

The success of many talented artists seems to happen almost overnight. What the public never sees is the hard work, preparation and sacrifice that go into readying an act for public view and acceptance. The year 1964 may have been a turning point for their fame, but The Supremes had been climbing the stairway of achievement for five years before that. For any performer, a combination of talent, perseverance and endurance, combined with the proper direction can mean the difference between lasting success and a fleeting career. The Supremes rocketed to stardom in 1964 with these qualities and the help of the tightly controlled, efficient, and sensible Motown Records.

The Supremes got their start at the various talent shows open to young people in Detroit during the 1950s. Mary Wilson entered a talent show at the local high school in 1958, where she met Florence Ballard, who was also performing that night. They thought much of each other's talent, and promised that if any opportunity came up for them to sing together, one would let the other know. One day in school, Florence came up

The Supremes' first photo session as a trio, 1963, (from top) Diana Ross, Florence Ballard, Mary Wilson.

to Mary to tell her about a local group called The Primes, who were looking for a sister group to complement their talents. This certainly was a perfect opportunity for the girls to sing together. When Florence and Mary showed up at the rehearsal, two other girls were waiting there, too. Betty McGlown and Diana Ross also hoped to become part of the group that the locally popular Primes wanted to annex to their entourage. The girls found that they had a nice blend. The quartet fittingly became The Primettes.

It wasn't long before the young group of girls was as popular as their male counterparts, appearing at local dances and state fairs. All this time was spent enjoying themselves and polishing their act, always looking their best as well as sounding vibrant and exciting. Justifiably, they developed a fair amount of bravado. As time went by, they were seasoned performers. The group thought it was time that The Primettes record. Mary recounts their decision: "We had been singing from 1959 through 1960, doing local record hops and state fairs. We had gotten a following. It finally dawned on us to do some recording. Motown was the only company that was going strong."

Motown Records was the Detroit label already famous for hit records by The Miracles, Marv Johnson and Mary Wells. When the girls went to Motown, however, they were declined. Berry Gordy, the founder and president of the label, thought the group was talented, but too young.

He told them to wait until they finished high school. This did not prevent the group from making plans for themselves. Just as The Primettes hit a steady stride, however, Betty McGlown announced that she was leaving the group to get married. Betty was not as serious about making singing a long time career.

The remaining trio still wanted a record of their own. They recorded a single in 1960, "Tears Of Sorrow/Pretty Baby," for Richard Morrison on another, less successful Detroit label, Lupine Records. This single remained unreleased until their fame in 1964. After trying to recruit girls in Betty's place, Flo, Mary, and Diana selected the enthusiastic Barbara Martin. The girls also decided to associate themselves with Motown Records. The quartet would show up at the Motown studios daily, just to be seen. They were often asked to provide handclaps on records, or just bang tambourines.

Finally, in 1961, they were given the chance to record something of their own. Gordy thought highly of the talents of The Primettes because he had often seen them in action around Detroit. They had good singing voices, beauty, poise and, most of all, determination. Their chance to prove what they could accomplish had finally come. Mary knew what everyone else saw in them, "We knew we were good. We were not mediocre. Being able to sing was not the only criteria. We knew we had a spirit amongst us. We knew we were great."

Berry produced the first efforts by the quartet. Before the release, Gordy decided the name "Primettes" wouldn't do, so

Florence picked The Supremes from a list of names. With the group now billed as The Supremes, "I Want A Guy," flipped with "Never Again" appeared on Tamla Records in 1961. The strange arrangement kept the single out of the charts. Another female group at the label had better luck with their first single; the Marvelettes' recording of "Please Mister Postman" reached the top spot in 1961.

The Supremes had more luck with the second single that received much airplay in Detroit and other nearby cities. "Buttered Popcorn," a novelty dance tune, was led by Florence. During the group's early days, all the members had a chance to sing lead. Each member's voice had an identifiable approach. There was no decision to settle on a specific style or configuration for the group. Soulful ballads like "The Tears," led by Mary and an imposing lead by Florence on "Save Me A Star" remained unreleased. The group's releases were switched to the parent Motown label in 1962. Since Gordy had no luck getting them a hit, Smokey Robinson was assigned to work with the young group. It was at this time Barbara Martin announced she was leaving the group. Tired of replacing the fourth member, the young ladies decided to remain a trio.

During 1962 and 1963, Smokey managed to come up with the dreamy, soldier boy anthem, "Your Heart Belongs To Me" and the wistful "Breath Taking Guy." These songs charted in the top 60. "Let Me Go The Right Way" had barely clung to the bottom of the charts. The Supremes were now part of The Motown Revue packages sent out by the company, where they sang their minor hits. By this time, the decision had been made to feature Diana's untrained lead on singles, the sentiment being that her voice had the most commercial potential.

There was also another force at work already. Berry Gordy saw special qualities in Diana, qualities that showed she would work hard to reach the top of her game and then some. Berry Gordy's plans for the group, and especially for Diana, would open many doors for Motown. However, this would not be apparent for a few years. The main priority in 1963 was to get a hit for The Supremes.

After six singles showed no lasting success, Gordy handed the job of transforming the lustrous Supremes into a hit-making act to songwriters Lamont Dozier, Brian Holland and Eddie Holland. All singers in their own right, the trio found more success and satisfaction writing and producing for other artists. They proved themselves with hit records by Mary Wells, Martha and The Vandellas, and The Marvelettes. Now it was The Supremes' turn.

In a complete change of style, the team came up with a gospel-tinged stomper called "When The Lovelight Starts Shining Through His Eyes." Full of grinding saxes and clanging tambourines, the song fared well for The Supremes, putting them in the top 30 for the first time. The next record would tell whether the mating would prove fruitful. "Run Run Run" was bland in comparison to "Lovelight," and by the time 1964 came, so many new sounds were crowding the charts, Holland-Dozier-Holland couldn't repeat the formula of "Lovelight." It was already a tried and true format for Martha and The Vandellas. They had to create a new one for The Supremes. The result was "Where Did Our Love Go."

Even though they didn't think it would be a hit, The Supremes recorded it. They sang the song on a summer tour they were doing for Dick Clark called "Dick Clark's Caravan of Stars." It seemed that every city they went to, the applause was getting louder and louder each time they appeared on stage. By the time the tour wound down, The Supremes had the number one record in the country.

Although The Supremes had already considered themselves professionals, a hit single of the magnitude of "Where Did Our Love Go" began the process of making them household names, at least to the teenage public. This was the nucleus of a larger plan for Motown to endear The Supremes to adult audiences as well as the teen market. The primary interest at this time was to keep the group's records in the upper echelons of the pop charts.

The Holland-Dozier-Holland sounds for The Supremes can be broken down into three phases, the hand clapping phase, including "Where Did Our Love Go," "Baby Love" and "Come See About Me." The release of "Come See About Me" was an afterthought, released only because Wand Records had released a version by singer Nella Dodds and it was climbing the charts. The original quickly surpassed it. The second phase for 1965 was a sound like a steady heartbeat, including "Stop In The Name of Love" and "Back In My Arms Again." This was proceeded by "Nothing But Heartaches," which culminated that sound.

A change in the back beat occurred on "I Hear A Symphony," and continued to pick up speed on "My World Is Empty Without You" and "Love Is Like An Itchin' In My Heart." "You Can't Hurry Love" and "You Keep Me Hanging On" shook like no other Supremes records before them. By the third phase, with "Love Is Here and Now You're Gone" and "Reflections," the Motown groove had taken on a slow, marching beat. Soul sounds in general were becoming more sophisticated. The Supremes records were no exception, with a more acceptable place for the organ sounds and strings placed further back in the mix.

From 1964-1966, public appearances at some of the best venues in the country and television appearances on "American Bandstand," "The Ed Sullivan Show," and movies like "Beach Ball," were coming at The Supremes at warp speed. As far as the group was concerned, they were unstoppable.

Mary said, "We had all that time that we were laying the groundwork. We were well prepared. During 1963-65, we had done the Motown tours, Dick Clark tours and the Murray The

THE SUPREMES

The first tide of change for The Supremes, 1967, (L-R) Cindy Birdsong, Diana, Mary. (Photo courtesy of Yellowlinda, Inc.)

"K" shows. The world was our oyster. As a whole, we knew there was more. I was having a ball, going to Europe and getting the same type of hype that The Beatles were getting. Then America embraced us. We were international stars."

The seemingly endless one-nighters had paid off. Now The Supremes were strutting their stuff at such top notch places here and abroad, like Talk Of The Town in London, Burns Café in Sweden and The Olympia in France.

In 1966, rumors started circulating about the possibility of Diana having a solo career. Florence and Mary would not begrudge Diana a career of her own, if that's what she wanted, but they would not allow their own ambitions to fall by the wayside. All three women had already invested years in their careers. It was hurtful and embarrassing to hear whispers about a situation that the group had not discussed amongst themselves or with the company. The first concrete evidence came in the change on the record labels, from simply "The Supremes" to "Diana Ross and The Supremes." This distinguished moniker was also given to Smokey Robinson and Martha Reeves, but it had a special meaning for The Supremes. It implied that they were no longer a unit. Evidence of this began under the guise of publicity photos and interviews, where Diana got most of the attention, as per Motown's directive.

There was also another unforeseen crack in the substructure that held The Supremes together. It had become apparent that Florence had started to drink, and her already candid personality had become somewhat overblown and brutal. Mary felt the same degree of anger toward what was becoming increasingly obvious. Unfortunately, Florence's unhappiness within the group came in the form of misguided rage left over from a brutal rape that she suffered at the hands of an acquaintance when she was sixteen. She never received counseling and buried her fury for years.

When the opportunity came for this emotional baggage to surface, the eruption was uncontrollable. Florence gained weight, missed interviews, performances, and on one occasion, went onstage with alcohol in her system. After one chance to straighten herself out, her fate in the music world was sealed. In an attempt to manipulate the situation on her own terms, Florence forfeited her coveted position in the most successful female group in the world.

In order to protect business, a replacement had to be found. Cindy Birdsong of The Blue Belles was selected to become the new member of The Supremes in 1967. Mary felt that the bond between the trio had been severed, "We were so close, then we started disintegrating. It was over when Florence left."

Despite the turmoil involved with their most successful group, Motown Records was going stronger than ever. Hits by The Supremes, as well as other artists on the roster, continued to appear. "Reflections" heralded a new sound for Supremes records. They were moving in what some collectors term their "psychedelic" period. As the sounds of pop music changed in the late 1960s, so did the sounds of Motown. Keeping The Supremes on top as a recording unit became a harder job, as different sounds contributed to change people's musical tastes. Motown became less concerned with individual efforts, and more concerned with keeping the pace of the company moving, a company that was making plans to branch out into other venues besides producing Rock & Roll artists. This was also true of Motown's hit making songwriting team of Holland-Dozier-Holland, who left Motown in 1968 amidst heated controversy over their role in the company.

Although Supremes singles were still successful, the climb to the upper reaches of the pop charts became labored. Several singles did not reach the top 20. Also, these singles, including the two most successful singles, "Love Child" and "Someday We'll Be Together" were recorded without Mary and Cindy. The Andantes, Ashford & Simpson or any available personnel not on the road at the time were recruited for recordings. It was only on the series of singles and LPs that The Supremes

recorded with The Temptations during 1968-69, that Mary and Cindy were included in the recordings. One single, a version of Jerry Ross and Kenny Gamble's "I'm Gonna Make You Love Me," was a huge hit for the two superstar groups. The Supremes continued as a viable force, but it was now common knowledge within the company that the decision-making body of Motown thought that Diana Ross' voice was the voice of importance. After a perfunctory farewell performance in January of 1970, Diana Ross officially left The Supremes. She was replaced by Jean Terrell. Jean had originally come to Motown to be a solo artist. As far as Mary was concerned, this was a chance for The Supremes to be a unit once again. It's a shame she was the only one who held that sentiment to heart.

For The Supremes, 1970 was another banner year on the charts. Glorious singles like "Up The Ladder To The Roof" and "Stoned Love" soared to the top spots. This was an especially uplifting experience for the group, because, once again, the voices in the group were being heard without the augmentation of studio singers. This was the chance for The Supremes to renew their stature as a bona fide group. For almost two years, singles appeared at the peak of the charts, including a duet with The Four Tops on "River Deep, Mountain High." Cindy left in 1971 to have a baby, so Mary hired Lynda Laurence. Lynda came from a singing family. Her father is Ira Tucker, leader of The Dixie Hummingbirds and her sister Sandra sang with Patti La Belle as a part of The Ordettes and performed for a short while with The Three Degrees. The Supremes kept up their live appearances in clubs both in America and overseas. Their performances continued to be showstoppers, featuring all types of American music, as well as their hits.

The momentum gained by the reconfigured group would eventually slow in 1972 and 1973 when the group realized that Motown Records was not putting its all into keeping The Supremes at the pinnacle of success. The company had moved to Los Angeles in 1972. Berry Gordy set his sights on conquering Hollywood with the making of a movie based on the life of singer Billie Holiday, entitled "Lady Sings The Blues," starring his protégé, Diana Ross.

Supremes' singles were no longer on the priority list. "Automatically Sunshine," "Your Wonderful Sweet Sweet Love" and "I Guess I'll Miss The Man," a song from the musical, "Pippin," didn't particularly burn up the charts. The only single for 1973, "Bad Weather," a fabulous record written and produced by Stevie Wonder, made an auspicious start, but floundered and died. Motown just didn't seem interested anymore. Numerous LPs were also ignored. Promotion of the records was not being handled astutely.

Jean and Lynda wanted to leave Motown and start over at a new label, but this would have meant leaving The Supremes' name behind, something Mary did not want to do. She had spent her adult life building the reputation of the group, and was not about to abandon it. Jean and Lynda held no such allegiance to either the company or the name, and left the group at the same time in 1973.

Mary strove to hold the group together, despite the downward spiral of attentions from Motown. Mary asked Scherrie Payne to join as the lead singer and Cindy Birdsong returned. Scherrie is the sister of singer Freda Payne and had been a member of the group Glass House. Again, The Supremes had another exquisite lineup. However, without a string of hit records to give the group a break from incessant touring, the members would be worn out. Also, they needed time to refurbish the act. The group noticed that their bookings were slipping, too. Once booked into the best houses in the country, The Supremes were relegated to smaller venues, not always conducive to their stage act.

One saving grace is that the reception for the group was still warm in Europe. Problems also began to arise when Mary's husband, Pedro Ferrer, began managing the group. The group continued with a few more singles, including the steaming disco hits, "He's My Man," "Where Do I Go From Here" and "I'm Gonna Let My Heart Do The Walking." Three LPs were released during 1975 and 1976. Disagreements over policies within the group caused Cindy Birdsong to leave a second time.

Susaye Green replaced Cindy in 1976. She recorded the last LP with the group. Growing unrest within the group led Mary to the realization that she couldn't put off the inevitable. In 1977, The Supremes held their farewell performance in England.

Through miscommunication and legal entanglements, Mary Wilson had to keep The Supremes going beyond their farewell performance, billed as "Mary Wilson and The Supremes." After a solo single and album with Motown in 1979, Mary left Motown and continued with her career. She divorced her husband, Pedro in 1981, and continued to build her talents as an actress as well as a singer, all while raising her children. She appeared in the play "Beehive" all across America and in Canada and made a guest appearance in "Grandma Sylvia's Funeral" in New York.

Mary, Cindy and Diana participated in the Motown reunion television show in 1983, amidst controversy that Diana had acted improperly during the taping by pushing Mary's microphone away from her mouth. Mary has written two books, "Dreamgirl" and "Supreme Faith," documenting her life and the career of The Supremes. Mary recorded some songs for Ian Levine's Nightmare Records in 1989. She is currently working on a plan to turn the story of The Supremes into a film. Mary is also attending New York University for her degree.

Diana Ross left The Supremes and moved on to a fruitful and lucrative career as a soloist and actress. Numerous, successful singles for Motown were released, including "Love Hangover" in 1976 and "Upside Down" in 1980. Diana departed Motown in 1981 for a profitable contract with RCA. Her huge hit for the label was with Frankie Lymon and The Teenagers', "Why Do Fools Fall In Love." Diana returned to Motown in the early 1990s, but to a Motown far different than the one The Supremes joined. Berry Gordy had sold Motown to MCA in 1988, which in turn sold the label to Polygram, which is now owned by Seagrams, Inc.

Florence Ballard was never able to overcome her fall from grace. After a brief, unsuccessful attempt at a solo career, she died in 1976 in Detroit. Cindy Birdsong stepped back into the limelight in 1988 to record one single, "Dancing Room," released in the UK. Jean Terrell recorded an album for A&M Records in 1977 entitled "I Had To Fall In Love," before retiring as a full time singer. Scherrie Payne and Susaye Green recorded one LP for Motown as Scherrie and Susaye in 1979, entitled "Partners." Jean, Lynda and Scherrie have toured as The Flos, (Former Ladies of The Supremes) since 1990. Jean left in 1992 and was replaced by Freddi Poole.

The Supremes were the depiction of both struggle and triumph in the music industry. They worked well within the machine that was Motown, but the same machine eventually rolled right over them. Their recordings are timeless. The Supremes were given their due once again when they were inducted into the Rock & Roll Hall of Fame in 1988. Mary and Florence's daughters cordially accepted their honors. Artists like Phil Collins, Soft Cell, Elvis Costello, Bonnie Pointer and others too innumerable to mention have paid tribute to the efforts of The Supremes. Their work in the field of popular music shows that nothing worthwhile comes easy. The Supremes' success will always be the example of what anyone can achieve if they want it badly enough.

The Supremes Discography

45s	Label	Number	Year
The Supremes			
I Want A Guy/Never Again	Tamla	54038	1961
Buttered Popcorn/Who's Loving You		54045	
Your Heart Belongs To Me/He's Seventeen	Motown	1027	1962
Let Me Go The Right Way/Time Changes Things		1034	
My Heart Can't Take It No More/You Bring Back Memories		1040	1963
A Breath Taking Guy/Rock & Roll Banjo Band		1044	
When The Lovelight Starts Shining Through His Eyes/Standing At The Crossroads of Love		1051	
Run Run Run/I'm Giving You Your Freedom		1054	1964
Where Did Our Love Go/He Means The World To Me		1060	
Baby Love/Ask Any Girl		1066	
Come See About Me/Always In My Heart		1068	
Stop! In The Name Of Love/I'm In Love Again		1074	1965
Back In My Arms Again/Whisper You Love Me Boy		1075	
Supremes Interview/The Only Time I'm Happy	(George Alexander)	1079	
Nothing But Heartaches/He Holds His Own		1080	
I Hear A Symphony/Who Could Ever Doubt My Love		1083	
Twinkle, Twinkle Little Me/Children's Christmas Song		1085	
My World Is Empty Without You/Everything Is Good About You		1089	
Things Are Changing/same	EEOC	--	
Love Is Like An Itching In My Heart/He's All I Got	Motown	1094	1966
You Can't Hurry Love/Put Yourself In My Place		1097	
You Keep Me Hanging On/Remove This Doubt		1101	
Love Is Here And Now You're Gone/There's No Stopping Us Now		1103	
The Happening/All I Know About You		1107	1967
Diana Ross and The Supremes			
Reflections/Going Down For The Third Time		1111	
In And Out Of Love/I Guess I'll Always Love You		1116	
Forever Came Today/Time Changes Things		1122	1968
Some Things You Never Get Used To/You've Been So Wonderful To Me		1126	
Love Child/Will This Be The Day		1135	
I'm Living In Shame/I'm So Glad I Got Somebody		1139	
The Composer/The Beginning Of The End		1146	1969
No Matter What Sign You Are/The Young Folks		1148	
Someday We'll Be Together/He's My Sunny Boy		1156	

45s	Label	Number	Year
The Supremes			
Up The Ladder To The Roof/Bill, When Are You Coming Back	Motown	1162	1970
Everybody's Got The Right To Love/But I Love You More		1167	
Stoned Love/Shine On Me		1172	
Nathan Jones/Happy		1182	1971
Touch/It's So Hard For Me To Say Goodbye		1190	
Floy Joy/This Is The Story		1195	
Automatically Sunshine/Precious Little Things		1200	1972
You're Wonderful, Sweet, Sweet Love/Wisdom Of Time		1206	
I Guess I'll Miss The Man/Over and Over		1213	
Bad Weather/Oh Be My Love		1225	1973
He's My Man/Give Out, But Don't Give Up		1358	1975
Where Do I Go From Here/Give Out, But Don't Give Up		1374	
I'm Gonna Let My Heart Do The Walking/Early Morning Love		1391	1976
You're My Driving Wheel/You're What's Missing In My Life		1407	
Let Yourself Go/You Are The Heart Of Me		1415	1977
(with The Temptations)			
I'm Gonna Make You Love Me/A Place In The Sun	Motown	1137	1968
I'll Try Something New/The Way You Do The Things You Do		1142	1969
The Weight/For Better Or Worse		1153	
(with The Four Tops)			
River Deep, Mountain High/Together We Can Make Such Sweet Music		1173	1970
I'm Glad About It/You Gotta Have Love In Your Heart		1181	1971
(as The Primettes)			
Tears Of Sorrow/Pretty Baby (rec. 1960)	Lupine	120	1964
Florence Ballard			
It Doesn't Matter How I Say It/Goin' Out Of My Head	ABC	11074	1968
Love Ain't Love/Forever Faithful		11144	
Scherrie Payne (w/Glass House)			
Crumbs Off The Table/Bad Bill Of Goods	Invictus	9071	1969
I Can't Be You, You Can't Be Me/He's In My Life		9076	1970
Stealing Moments From Another Woman's Life/If It Ain't Love, It Doesn't Matter		9082	1971
Touch Me Jesus/If It Ain't Love, It Doesn't Matter		9090	
I Don't See Me In Your Eyes Anymore/Thanks		9129	1972
Let It Flow/--		--	
Diana Ross*			
Reach Out And Touch/Dark Side Of The World	Motown	1165	1970
Ain't No Mountain High Enough/Can't It Wait Until Tomorrow		1169	
Remember Me/How About You		1176	
Reach Out I'll Be There/Close To You		1184	1971
Surrender/I'm A Winner		1188	
I'm Still Waiting/A Simple Thing Like Cry		1192	
Good Morning Heartache/God Bless The Child		1211	1972
Touch Me In The Morning/I Won't Last A Day Without You		1239	1973
Last Time I Saw Him/Save The Children		1278	
Sleeping/You		1295	1974
Sorry Doesn't Always Make It Right/Together		1377	1975
Theme From Mahogany/No One's Going To Be A Fool Forever		1377	
I Thought It Took A Little Time/After You		1387	1976
Love Hangover/Kiss Me Now		1392	
Smile/One Love In My Lifetime		1398	
Getting Ready For Love/Confide In Me		1427	1977
Baby It's Me/Your Love Is Good For Me		1436	
You Got It/Too Shy To Say		1442	
Pops, We Love You/Inst.		1455	1978
What You Gave Me/Together		1456	
The Boss/I'm In The World		1462	1979
It's My House/Sparkle		1471	
I'm Coming Out/Give Up		1491	1980
Upside Down/Friend To Friend		1494	
It's My Turn/Together		1496	
One More Chance/After You		1508	
To Love Again/Crying My Eyes Out For You		1513	1981
My Old Piano/Now That You're Gone		1531	
Old Funky Rolls/We Can Never Light That Old Flame Again		1626	1982
Diana Ross w/Marvin Gaye			
You're A Special Part Of Me/I'm Falling In Love With You	Motown	1280	1973
My Mistake (Was To Love You)/Include Me In Your Life		1269	1974
Don't Knock My Love/Just Say, Just Say		1296	
Diana Ross w/Michael Jackson			
Ease On Down The Road/Poppy Girls	MCA	40947	1978
If We Hold On Together/Inst.		53448	
Diana Ross w/Lionel Richie			
Endless Love/Inst.	Motown	1519	1981
Jean Terrell			
I Had To Fall In Love/--	A&M	--	1977

45s	**Label**	**Number**	**Year**
Mary Wilson			
Red Hot/Midnight Dancer (45 and 12")	Motown	1467	1979
Don't Get Mad, Get Even/--(UK only)	Nightmare	39	1987
Ooh, Child/--		C7	1989
LPs			
Meet The Supremes	Motown	606	1963
Where Did Our Love Go		621	1964
A Bit Of Liverpool		623	
Country, Western and Pop		625	1965
More Hits By The Supremes		627	
We Remember Sam Cooke		629	
Meet The Supremes (repackaged)		606	
At The Copa		636	
Merry Christmas		638	
I Hear A Symphony		643	1966
Supremes A Go Go		649	
Sing Holland-Dozier-Holland		650	1967
Sing Rodgers & Hart		659	
Greatest Hits Vol. 1&2		663	
Reflections		665	1968
Love Child		668	
Sing And Perform Funny Girl		670	
Live At London's Talk Of The Town		676	
Let The Sunshine In		689	1969
Cream Of The Crop		694	
Greatest Hits Vol. 3		702	
Right On		705	1970
Farewell/Captured Live The Final Performance		708	
New Ways But Love Stays		720	
Touch		737	1971
Floy Joy		751	1972
The Supremes Prod. & Arr. By Jimmy Webb		756	
The Supremes		828	1975
High Energy		863	
Mary, Scherrie & Susaye		873	1976
At Their Best		904	1978
From The Vaults	Natural Resources	4014	1979
Supremes 25th Anniversary		5381ML3	1986
Motown's Brightest Stars	Motown	5380ML	
(with The Temptations)			
Supremes Join The Temptations	Motown	679	1968
TCB		682	
Together		692	1969
On Broadway		699	
(with The Four Tops)			
The Magnificent Seven	Motown	717	1970
The Return of The Magnificent Seven		736	1971
Dynamite		745	
Scherrie Payne (w/Glass House)			
Inside The Glass House	Invictus	7305	1971
Glass House		9805	
Thanks, I Needed That		9810	1972
*Diana Ross**			
Reach Out	Motown	711	1970
Diana (TV Special)		719	1971
Surrender		723	
Everything Is Everything		724	
Lady Sings The Blues		758	1972
Touch Me In The Morning		772	1973
Live At Caesar's Palace		801	1974
Diana & Marvin		803	1973
Last Time I Saw Him		812	
Mahogany		858	1975
Diana Ross		861	1976
Greatest Hits		869	
An Evening With Diana Ross		877	1977
Baby It's Me		890	
Ross		907	1978
The Boss		923	1979
Diana		936	1980
To Love Again		951	1981
All The Greatest Hits		960	
Anthology		60449	1983*
Jean Terrell			
I Had To Fall In Love	A&M	--	1977
Mary Wilson			
Mary Wilson	Motown	927	1979

*Since ample documentation exists on Diana Ross' discography, this listing ends with her departure from Motown Records in 1981.

The Sweet Inspirations

Members:

(1967-70) Emily (Cissy) Houston
             Estelle Brown
             Sylvia Shemwell
             Myrna Smith

(1970-79) Estelle Brown
             Sylvia Shemwell
             Myrna Smith

Deep-rooted, heartfelt emotion, resplendent harmonies and intense vocal styling define many great Gospel singers, both past and present. Many of these singers who learned how to reach for the sky also reached for a profession in the field of popular music, many shirking the elders' forewarning of eternal damnation for singing "the devil's music." Fortunately, for the world of popular music, no one was struck by lightning. Starting in the early 1960s, soul styling acquired an earthier feeling, with vocal runs and choruses closer to the roots of spirituals and Blues. Singers like Aretha Franklin, Freddie Scott, and Percy Sledge personified the formula for the 1960s pop roots music, all with their musical experience in Gospel music.

THE SWEET INSPIRATIONS

The Sweet Inspirations after Cissy's departure, 1973, (L-R) Estelle Brown, Sylvia Shemwell, Myrna Smith. (Photo courtesy of Yellow-linda, Inc.)

Producers like Jerry Wexler, Jerry Ragovoy, Bert Berns, Isaac Hayes and David Porter knew exactly how to handle the musical aspects of the idiom. Muscle Shoals Studios in Memphis became the hub for artists eager to acquire this ambience. Not only did this entail the direction of a capable artist and adept producer, but also required the expertise of proficient musicians and, last but not least, backing vocalists. There existed one such family of backing vocalists whose abilities on vinyl are so far-reaching that their influence is present even in today's music.

The Sweet Inspirations were indeed an inspiration, put together during the 1960s, through the visualization of one Emily (Cissy) Houston. As a young girl living in Newark, New Jersey, Cissy began singing with her brothers and sisters in a Gospel ensemble known as The Drinkard Singers, their family name. The troupe was featured in the choir of The New Hope Baptist Church, where their father was pastor. The elder Drinkard had given the group the direction they needed, and with God as the enlightenment to bring His message to the world, the singers gladly obliged. After her father's death in 1952, Cissy took over the job of directing the choir at the church. The Drinkard Singers, consisting of Cissy, her sister, Lee, her brother Larry on piano, Judy Guions, Marie Epps and Ann Moss, continued their quest for jubilant singing, recording two LPs. They appeared at the 1957 Newport Jazz Festival, winning accolades and a chance to record their third LP for RCA in 1958, judiciously entitled, "A Joyful Noise."

The Drinkard Singers' career as background singers for other artists during the 1960s didn't begin until the family began branching out into secular music. By 1961, The Drinkard Singers consisted of Cissy, Judy, Marie, Ann, and Sylvia (Guions) Shemwell, with Cissy's brother, Nick on piano. This configuration recorded two more Gospel LPs for Choice Records. In addition, Lee had two daughters, Dionne and Dee Dee, who were rotating in and out of The Drinkard Singers, as well as getting work as background singers for Drifters' sessions in New York.

Arrangers were using female choruses to sweeten the sound of many recordings, including those by vocal groups. Also, the popular female group, The Shirelles, was using Dionne as an occasional sub for live appearances. It was during this period that she was spotted by songwriter/arranger/producer Burt Bacharach, who heard the possibilities in Dionne's distinctive voice. In 1962, she was given the chance to have a singing career of her own, under Bacharach's direction. Dee Dee's turn came a year later, with producer/songwriter Van McCoy. In 1963, Judy also left the fold to have a successful solo career as Judy Clay. This was when Myrna Smith and Estelle Brown came to the group that would transform into The Sweet Inspirations.

By 1963, the sound of The Drinkard Singers was in demand and they worked nonstop as backing vocalists for many up and coming artists. Naturally, they were the voices behind the many recordings of Dionne Warwick. Producer Jerry Ragovoy decided to use them as The Enchanters behind Garnet Mimms on "Cry Baby." The Drinkard Singers were the vocal padding added to many group sounds on recordings between 1961 and 1967. Finally, the chance came for the quartet to become recording artists in their own right, after years of painting aural canvases for others. The ladies configured a name from the spiritual inducement they felt when they sang. A sweet inspiration hearkened back to their religious roots, the reason why they sang in the first place. The perfect name for them was The Sweet Inspirations. The soulful foursome netted a contract with Atlantic Records in 1967.

Despite their immense talent and versatility, the group's accomplishments at Atlantic were surprisingly spotty, considering the resources available to them. The first two singles, an intense version of The Drifters' "I Don't Want To Go On Without You" and "Let It Be Me," made both the R&B and the pop charts, but failed to really break out. The group's solid renditions of other

Cissy Houston at the Rhythm & Blues Awards, 1998.

proven hit songs like Otis Redding's "I've Been Loving You Too Long" and Aretha Franklin's "Do Right Woman, Do Right Man" did not affect the public in the same way.

Their 1968 single, "Sweet Inspiration" was recorded down at Muscle Shoals on a break, but did the best for them to date and was nominated for a Grammy Award. The group continued, however, putting their stamp on covers of classic Rock and Soul, turning in spirited versions of The Bee Gees' "To Love Somebody" and The Everly Brothers' "Crying In The Rain." Although The Sweet Inspirations were not making consistent inroads into the top 40, they had long since acquired the renown as the singers' singers.

The foursome continued with their session work, helping out singer/songwriter Ellie Greenwich on her classy solo LP, "Ellie Greenwich Composes, Produces, and Sings," and also joined Ellie on Aretha Franklin's testament, "Chain of Fools." The group often accompanied Aretha on her numerous tours. A handful of R&B chart singles followed in 1969 and 1970, such as the haughty "A Brand New Lover" and the enlightening "This World." When the group's contract with Atlantic Records ended in 1970, Cissy went on her own.

The remaining members of The Sweet Inspirations continued without Houston and forged an ephemeral recording assignment with Stax Records during 1973 and 1974, releasing two singles and one LP entitled, "Estelle, Myrna and Sylvia," co-produced by David Porter. At the time, Stax Records was in turmoil and on the verge of shutting down, so suffice it to say that the handling of the group was less than prudent. A much more illustrious and profitable position for The Sweet Inspirations was the job of being the featured singing group behind Elvis Presley.

From 1970 until his death in 1977, the group toured with Presley on countless tours in The United States and Europe. The vocal trio was part of the ensemble at Elvis' celebrated concerts, along with J.D. Sumner and The Stamps Quartet, and vocalist, Kathy Westmoreland. As the 1970s drew to a close, The Sweet Inspirations found themselves in the studio for RSO Records, recording "Hot Butterfly" in 1979, a tune previously recorded by Luther Vandross, with Bionic Boogie, in 1978. With no success for the single and same titled LP, Estelle, Myrna, and Sylvia refrained from further recording. Recently, they were part of the Elvis screen tribute, "This Is Elvis–The Concert" where they appeared live in front of screens of Presley's image, with other musicians who toured with him back when.

After leaving The Sweet Inspirations, Cissy Houston recorded a solo LP in 1971, "Presenting Cissy Houston." She enjoyed brief status as a disco diva with the 1978 disco hit, "Think It Over," for Private Stock Records. Apart from occasional recording, Houston lends her voice to jingles and background singing, as well as honing her skills as a vocal coach, songwriter and an actress on Broadway.

Houston co-wrote "Out of My Hands" for Dionne Warwick's critically acclaimed comeback LP with Barry Manilow as producer in 1979. She was standing by when her now famous daughter, Whitney Houston, started her singing career. Mother Cissy is featured on Whitney's "How Will I Know" and "I Wanna Dance With Somebody." Cissy recorded a CD of Gospel material for House of Blues Records called "Face To Face" in 1997. Cissy Houston has accepted many awards for her work, including a special Grammy and a Touchstone Award celebrating women in music.

Cissy is still the director of the choir at The New Hope Baptist Church. In 1995, The Rhythm & Blues Foundation honored all of The Sweet Inspirations at their annual award ceremonies. No other group can boast such an illustrious and inspired career, started by the yearning use their voices to spread the good news of God, indeed their first inspiration.

The Sweet Inspirations Discography

78s	Label	Number	Year
The Drinkard Jubilairs			
When I Rise/A Sinner Like Me	Savoy	4053	1954
Walk Together Children/I'm Troubled		4074	1958

45s	Label	Number	Year
The Drinkard Singers			
Rise, Shine/My Rock	RCA	47-287	1958
Out Of The Depths/You Can't Make Me Doubt Him	Choice	24	1962
Do You Love Him/Holding The Saviour's Hand		30	
Joy Unspeakable/--		36	
The Sweet Inspirations			
Why/I Don't Want To Go On Without You	Atlantic	2410	1967
Let It Be Me/When Something Is Wrong With My Baby		2418	
I've Been Loving You Too Long/That's How Strong My Love Is		2436	
Don't Fight It/Oh What A Fool I've Been		2449	
Do Right Woman, Do Right Man/Reach Out For Me		2465	
Sweet Inspiration/I'm Blue		2476	1968
To Love Somebody/Where Did It Go		2529	
Unchained Melody/Am I Ever Gonna See My Baby Again		2551	
What The World Needs Now Is Love/You Really Didn't Mean It		2571	

45s

Crying In The Rain/Every Day Will Be Like A Holiday		2620	1969
Sweets For My Sweet/Get A Little Older		2638	
Don't Go/Chained		2653	
A Brand New Lover/Part 2		2686	
At Last I Found A Love/That's The Way My Baby Is		2720	1970
Them Boys/Flash In The Pan		2732	
Glory Glory/You Don't Know (w/The Young Rascals)		2743	
This World/Light Sings		2750	
Evidence/Change Me Not		2779	
Emergency/Slipped and Tripped	Stax	0178	1973
Try A Little Tenderness/Dirty Tricks		0203	1974
Black Sunday/Inst. Caribou90221977			
Love Is On The Way/Inst.	RSO	932	1979
Hot Fun/Love Is On The Way		1013	

Cissy Houston (as Susie Houston)
Bring Him Back/World Of Broken Hearts	Congress	268	1966

Cissy Houston (as Sissie Houston)
Don't Come Running To Me/One Broken Heart For Sale	Kapp	814	1967

Cissy Houston
I'll Be There/So I Believe	Commonwealth Unltd.	3010	1970
I Just Don't Know What To Do With Myself/Empty Place	Janus	131	
Be My Baby/I'll Be There		145	1971
Hanging On To A Dream/Darling Take Me Back		159	
I Love You/Making Love		177	
Didn't We/It's Not Easy		190	1972
Will You Still Love Me Tomorrow/Midnight Train To Georgia		206	
I'm So Glad I Can Love Again/One Time You Say You Love Me		230	1973
I Believe/Nothing Can Stop Me		255	1975
Love Is Something That Leads You/It Never Really Ended	Private Stock	137	1977
Love Is Something That Leads You/If I Ever Lose This Heaven		137	
Tomorrow/Love Is Holding On		153	
Things To Do/It Never Really Ended		171	
Think It Over/An Umbrella Song		204	1978
Warning, Danger/An Umbrella Song	Columbia	11058	1979
Break It To Me Gently/The Easy Way Out		11208	

Sylvia Shemwell
He'll Come Back/Funny What Time Can Do	Philips	40149	1962

LPs

The Drinkard Singers
This Man Jesus	Regent	6080	1954
Walk All Over God's Heaven	Verve	8245	
A Joyful Noise	RCA	1856	1958
--	Choice	508	1961
--		513	1962

The Sweet Inspirations
Songs of Faith and Inspiration	Atlantic	8182	1968
What The World Needs Now Is Love		8201	1969
Sweets For My Sweet		8225	
Sweet, Sweet Soul		8253	1970
Estelle, Myrna & Sylvia	Stax	8155	1973
Hot Butterfly	RSO	3058	1979

Cissy Houston
Presenting Cissy Houston	Janus	--	1971
I'll Take Care Of You (w/Chuck Jackson)(CD only)	Shanachie	9002	1992
Face To Face (CD only)	House of Blues	--	1997

The Teardrops

Members:

(1964-65) Linda (Lin) Schroeder, 2nd Soprano/Lead
Pat (Punkin) Strunk, 1st Soprano
Dorothy (Sunni) Dyer, 2nd Soprano/Lead
Wanda (Wendy) Sheriff, Alto

(1965-66) Linda Schroeder
Hazel (Tinker) Smiddy
Pat Strunk
Wanda Sheriff

The port city of Cincinnati, located on the Ohio River, is residence to many engaging points of interest, such as The Cincinnati Zoo, Union Terminal and The Krohn Conservatory, as well as being the abode of The Bengals and The Reds. This great city is also the home of one of the best examples of the genre of female singing groups, keeping them almost exclusively as the city's own for many years.

The Teardrops are a quartet of females who were one of Cincinnati's premier talents throughout the 1960s and whose benefaction to the world of Rock and Roll consists of an eclectic body of recordings. The Teardrops had four releases for the fledgling Saxony Records, owned by writer Paul Trefzger and arranger George (Bud) Reneau. Their best known recording is "Tears Come Tumbling/You Won't Be There," originally released in 1965. The song made enough noise to be picked up by Musicor Records for national distribution. The Teardrops are far from one-hit-wonders, however. Their story is one of tremendous local success and acclaim.

The Teardrops began as a trio, 1962, (L-R) Pat Strunk, Linda Schroeder, Dorothy Dyer. (Photo courtesy of Linda Schroeder Milazzo/Dorothy Dyer Wethington)

The story of The Teardrops starts in 1961. Linda Schroeder, Dorothy Dyer and Pat Strunk all attended Hughes High School in the Clifton area of Cincinnati. Linda and Dorothy sang in the school choir and, through other mutual interests, had become friends. Together, they began hanging out in Inwood Park where many street singers would gather to pass the time singing the popular Rock and Roll group harmony songs of the day. Even though Linda and Dorothy were younger than the crowd of teen guys, they had an "in" because they sang. Linda remembers: "Even though we were younger than most, we were pretty much accepted because we could sing and even protected like little sisters would be."

Not only did the girls hone their talents in the park, but they were students of the varied singing styles of their racially mixed high school. There, Linda and Dorothy emulated the Rhythm and Blues style of the black students who sang along with them in the bathrooms, while taking advantage of the proper acoustics for singing a cappella. In fact, when deejays heard The Teardrops on tape, then met the group in person, it was a surprise to the local deejays to see that the girls were white. Outside of the singing experiences the girls had in school, none of them had any formal musical training. Linda's father played guitar and she dabbled on the ukulele, guitar, and accordion. When Wendy joined later on, her influences came from a mixture of bluegrass and southern gospel. This combination definitely accounts for the use of unusual tones and harmonies in their recordings.

One evening, Linda and Dorothy went to The Tulu Club, a non-alcohol teen club that was sponsored by local radio station WSAI, run by deejay Ron Britton. While sitting in the audience, listening to the band on stage, Linda and Dorothy started singing background. The bandleader heard them and asked them to come up on stage to sing behind the lead singer. This is how they caught the "bug" to sing. Afterwards, someone approached them and told them how much he enjoyed their performance. It was suggested that they start a singing group of their own and if they did, he would like to manage them. Linda remembers, "A band was playing on stage and Dorothy and I were singing in the audience. The bandleader asked us to get on stage and sing. We did, and a man named Mike Mesley approached, stating that we were good and he'd like to manage us. He suggested that we add another girl . . . Voila! The Teardrops were born."

Linda and Dorothy decided they would do it. The girls had formed a trio with another girl, Diane Barstow, but Diane's interest quickly waned, so Pat was asked to replace her. It was Dorothy who had come up with the name "Teardrops" while she and Linda were walking home after a rehearsal. Since they were all going through "boy" problems, tears symbolized the full range of their emotions, thus, the name fit.

Not only did the group acquire a name, so did everyone in the group, thanks to Linda. Linda liked to pin nicknames on people. She christened herself "Lin" and "Lacey." Dorothy was named "Sunni" because of her outgoing personality. When Wanda joined, she became "Wendy" because it seemed less formal, but the best moniker of all was Pat's name change to "Punkin"

because she sported a big, red bouffant hairdo, just like a pumpkin. Dorothy recalls everyone being given the new labels, "The nickname thing is definitely Linda's doing. She loved to stick nicknames on everyone. And nearly everyone seemed to accept whatever handle she gave them! I guess no one really likes their name. Twenty years later someone was telling me that they met a woman named Lacey, who said she'd sung with The Teardrops back in the sixties. I explained that no one by that name was ever in our group, but when they described Linda I realized that she had taken a new identity!"

Rehearsals took a long time to get up to speed. It involved great difficulty gaining the self-control to rehearse on a regular basis, what with homework, family matters and, since they were only fourteen years old, occasionally being grounded. Once the group was disciplined, it became easier to establish both a repertoire and dance routines. Dorothy believes that coming up with the routines was a more arduous task than learning the songs.

Since the group had a premium vocal sound, they wanted the dance steps to be just as sensational. Mike Mesley had made good on his promise to get the trio some work. The Teardrops worked the teen circuit, singing at non-drinking teen socials and special events. On one occasion, the group was booked to sing on a show with a band called The Matadors, the house band at a local club. Bud Reneau was the lead guitarist and arranger for The Matadors. Bud heard potential in the girls' performance that night, so he arranged for his partner, songwriter Paul Trefzger, to hear them sing and to pitch some of Paul's songs to the group.

Paul Trefzger started his musical career in the late 1950s, singing in a trio called The Profiles. The Profiles sang the popular songs of the day as well as favorite standards, but the group did not record. One member, Kay Willis, was the wife of Rollie Willis, a member of Otis Williams and The Charms, who had a huge hit with "Hearts Of Stone" in 1954. Rollie was also Otis' cousin. Kay was the female voice on "The Secret" by Otis Williams and The Charms and The Checkers' "Nine More Miles."

Paul was also doing some songwriting. He had placed one song, "Where Is The Boy Tonight," with The Charmaines, who recorded it for Dot Records in 1962. Paul and Bud met in 1962 after Paul worked with Bud's piano player, Tom Dooley, and his drummer, Dave Listerman, on some demos they were making with Rollie Willis and his group, The Contenders. Paul needed a band for a party so he hired The Matadors. Paul and Bud immediately struck up a friendship and started Saxony Records soon after that.

When Rollie decided to record, Paul was asked to lend a hand. The first release on Saxony, in July of 1962, was Rollie Willis and The Contenders' single, "Whenever I Get Lonely/That's The Way." "Times Is Tough" by The Matadors soon followed as the second Saxony release, with a few more Matadors' singles to follow. Paul and Bud's greatest triumph, however, was yet to come.

Before asking The Teardrops to hear material, Paul heard the group sing at The Olympian Club one afternoon during an alcohol-free teen party. Paul didn't hesitate at the time, "To me, they sounded adult enough and I guess we introduced ourselves and I never had any problem with their ages unless there was some kind of inconvenience associated with working with them and their still being in high school and having parents to please."

The Teardrops, at this point, were already seasoned performers, entertaining at socials and teen clubs for almost two years prior to meeting Bud and Paul, so there was very little polishing to do. The group agreed to meet at Paul's house. He played them some songs, which they sang back to him per his arrangements. Paul was elated to find that the girls learned quickly. His collaboration with The Teardrops was now in motion. Paul remembers that it was not long after meeting the group that they went into the studio to record. The trio signed contracts with Paul, Bud and investor, Joe Sheets. Of course, with the girls' being underage, their parents also had to sign.

It was not long after this signing that Wendy joined the group. Linda had met Wendy at Colerain High School. Linda had moved and switched schools. Wendy's voice rounded out the harmonies for a fuller sound. Dorothy recalls that when Wendy joined the group, she had to wear a dress of the same style, but in a different color because they could not find a fourth dress to match, thus, breaking the tradition of groups who dressed alike. Wendy also lent her coifing expertise to come up with some seriously outlandish hairstyles for the girls to wear on stage.

The first session was recorded at King Records Studios on September 2, 1964. Dorothy recalls being very excited and honored to stand where so many prominent recording artists stood to lay down tracks for their songs. This was The Teardrops' first effort in the studio and the experience was exhilarating. They listened to different instruments being utilized, all at the same time. The result of their efforts was "Tonight, I'm Gonna Fall In Love Again/That's Why I'll Get By." "Tonight . . ." opens with the baion beat drum that Phil Spector made so popular, then the unique blend of vocals. Linda's sweet, cultured voice carries the message of how this girl has just lost her love, but she's not going to sit around brooding. She's going right back into the field.

The flip side utilizes a group vocal for the chorus and Linda's lead for the bridge, an effective counterpoint all under the guise of clever lyrics by Paul with a potent use of the acoustic guitar and the flute. Motown had tried

The Teardrops (L-R) Wanda "Wendy" Sheriff, Pat, Dorothy, Linda. (Photo courtesy of Linda Schroeder Milazzo/Dorothy Dyer Wethington)

using flutes during its early days, but never quite achieved what Bud achieved. Bud and Paul effectively used influences from other musical trends at that time, like country music. Using their expertise at writing and arranging and top-notch local musicians for the sessions, they metamorphosed these concepts into The Teardrops' particular body of tunes. Paul reflects on their compositions, "I think I tried not to have songs sound like each other and when Bud would pick out songs I'd written that he liked, I think he intentionally (or unconsciously) tried to not duplicate a sound."

The Teardrops' first single for Saxony netted the group much local airplay. "Tonight…" was in the top 20 Hit List on WCPO and on Bobby Wayne's show on WSAI in late 1964 and early 1965. It even became number one in Okinawa. The group certainly did their part, playing clubs throughout Ohio and Kentucky, such as Ben Kraft's Guys 'N Dolls in Cold Spring, and Arcaro's in Erlanger. Arcaro's was owned by Eddy Arcaro, the noted horse jockey.

Other acts appearing in these clubs at the time were Billy Joe Royal and Jerry Lee Lewis. The group also made many personal appearances on Cincinnati's local teen dance shows like Tony Reisig's "Between Time" and "Upbeat." The girls were frequently mobbed and asked to sign autographs when they shopped for new dresses in the heart of the city. So venerable was the group's reputation that they were often asked to appear as the opening act for such national notables as The Beach Boys and Sonny and Cher when these acts came to town.

In addition to the recognition via their first single, The Teardrops continually concentrated their efforts on their live act, not only performing their own recordings, but the popular songs of the day. Everyone in the group sang lead at their live shows. Even Paul was corralled to sing a version of The Diablos' "The Wind" with the girls singing background. The Teardrops live shows contained plenty of R&B-flavored tunes to showcase their versatility. Paul and Bud showed evidence of this on the group's next single. Dorothy lead the frenetic dance track, "I'm Gonna Steal Your Boyfriend," delivering the lead with as much attitude as the title implies. The fast pace of the tune gives Dorothy a chance to breathlessly render her message to an unsuspecting competitor that she has given up the rights to a guy she treated like dirt, and Dorothy will haughtily pick up her slack.

"Call Me And I'll Be Happy" gives Linda a chance to float freely throughout the song, with the backing vocals rising and falling along with her. It is Linda's peerless inflections and her use of R&B runs that give this side a sophisticated appeal. The picture she paints of selfless love is completed with the soft-spoken vocal break. Paul remembers the studio take, "Linda was so taken with the result of "Call Me . . ." in the studio that she cried upon hearing its playback."

The first two Teardrops singles were indeed outstanding not only for their clever executions, but also for their purposeful disunity in style. Paul pointed out that he and Bud weren't fishing for a style which would net the group and themselves some commercial recognition. They didn't think of the singles in terms of items to be marketed. They wanted songs that showed off the group, which they achieved; though Paul freely admits he could have been more formulaic: "Had 'Tonight…' sold nationally in the top Ten, I'd have tried to write a song along the 'same sound' lines, but as it was, we just kept trying to put out songs that fit and sounded good by the girls. I think we felt that they had a sound that was a signature."

Paul and Bud's ventures into the recording and music industry were endeavors they undertook in addition to their regular jobs. Paul once had to leave his job to take records to a distributor and to cart the records around to radio stations, a job he didn't quite care for. The Matadors' reputation for their work at local deejays' record hops helped in some ways, but these producers definitely cast their fates to the wind. It seemed a strong wind was on the horizon.

The next single sealed Paul and Bud's fate as premium producers and arrangers. "Tears Come Tumbling" begins with a jazz-inspired guitar and Linda's soft-spoken voice. The bass drum enters, with an updated, marching band beat, while the lead voice peaks, reciting her tag line, with an echo from the backdrop. Then, bursting forth into glorious harmonies, the group delivers all the ingredients of an emotional rainstorm.

The treatment of "Tears Come Tumbling" enhanced the inherent style of the group. This song and its flip, the drum-driven dance tune, "You Won't Be There," were recorded in the new RCA studios in Nashville. During recording, the group was excited to meet Roy Orbison, who was recording in the studio nextdoor. After the tune began climbing local charts in Boston, Cleveland, and Philadelphia, Paul sent copies of these local charts along with the records to various labels. Musicor Records in New York, the label which famed crooner Gene Pitney called home, decided to pick up "Tears Come Tumbling" for national distribution. Although the single did well in many local markets during late 1965 and early '66, it failed to break into the national charts. The people at Musicor could have done more in promoting the record, but they didn't, and the distributors for Saxony, which took care of part of the market, didn't have the scope needed to properly promote the disc.

The Teardrops themselves continued their relentless efforts on the live entertainment circuit. The girls were still doing teen dances for free to enhance their exposure, as well as their regular nightclub work. Their repertoire consisted of a variety of pop songs of the day from Frankie Valli, The Shirelles, and The Supremes to The Beach Boys, Brenda Holloway, The Dave Clark Five, and The Dells. Many bands they worked with could not transpose the keys needed for female voices, so the girls could aptly accommodate the band by singing songs usually sung by males.

Because of their ages, they still needed a chaperone whose services were provided by Dorothy's brother Bob, who also managed them for a while. Bob obtained all the bookings and only took a pittance for his efforts. His enthusiasm and faith played a significant part in pushing the group to the forefront. He made sure that these four pretty girls were a safe distance from admiring male fans. Bob also made sure the group got to their gigs safely, got paid, and he even showed his devotion by tutored Linda in chemistry.

Before recording "Tears Come Tumbling," there was a change in the lineup. Dorothy had graduated high school early and married, so she decided to assign herself full time to her marriage. Hazel Smiddy, christened "Tinker" by Linda, took Dorothy's place. She also recorded on the next and final Teardrops single released in 1966 on Musicor, the patriotic "I Will Love You Dear Forever." In keeping with the war-conscious times, the song tells the tale of a soldier going to war, his girl saying good-bye, describing in detail her unwavering devotion to him. Linda sang the lead and Tinker did the spoken verses. Despite the premium productions, Musicor just did not put all their efforts into the record, probably considering that none of the previous Teardrops singles had made it onto the national charts. Plus, stations were increasingly encouraged to tighten their playlists to include what were perceived as sure-fire tunes. By 1966, only Motown was managing to continually put any vocal groups, let alone female groups, in coveted positions on the national charts. Paul recalls that the group's final single did not even receive adequate airplay in their native Cincinnati. Paul continued to write songs for The Teardrops to record. They have one unreleased song that was recorded for Musicor, called "Here Comes Loneliness." A rough demo of the song exists on tape, but to this day, Sony, who acquired the Musicor catalogue, cannot locate the finished master. Another project was taking Paul and Bud's time; a group called The Ditalians. Not long after that project was finished, Bud decided to continue his career in Nashville.

The Teardrops continued to get steady club work in the Cincinnati area. After the last recording, Wendy left the group and got married. Then, Punkin got married and moved to Virginia. Two girls who auditioned for the spots replaced them. Barbara "Bobbie" Frost was a University Of Cincinnati student who filled the top soprano spot. Susann "Susie" Leicht was a fourteen year-old powerhouse who could really belt out a song. She was very mature for her age and had to have a watchful eye kept on her. Her fun-loving personality gave the group an added edge on stage. This configuration had even signed contracts with Paul and Bud, but never recorded anything. Also, eighteen months after her exit, Dorothy returned to take Tinker's place. Tinker had decided to go on her own and Dorothy was asked to come back to the group. Dorothy felt she could now fit the group's solid weekend work schedule into married life.

The Teardrops were still making personal appearances at concerts and on teen dance shows. Linda recounts the continued excitement of performing, "We had a terrific time playing for larger concerts and opening for bigger acts. I also recorded on a few tunes for James Brown, Lonnie Mack, a few locals, etc. We played at Music Hall with Sonny and Cher, opened at Cincinnati Gardens for

The Teardrops, 1965, (L-R) Wendy, Pat, Linda, Hazel "Tinker" Smiddy. (Photo courtesy of Linda Schroeder Milazzo/Dorothy Dyer Wethington)

The Beach Boys, worked steadily at a club called The Olympian, working with Ruby & The Romantics, The Matadors, many, many bands. We performed on quite a few television shows, such as "Five A Go Go" in Cleveland and "The Bob Braun Show Teen Dance Party" here in Cincy. We didn't get to go on tour because of school being so important to each of us."

The group's pace didn't slow with the personnel changes. Dorothy remembers having to lip-sync Tinker's part on "I Will Love You Dear Forever" after frantically rehearsing the words on the way to the station. As time went on, public tastes were changing and the group was not excepted from the wake of these forages into other genres of music. By 1969, The Teardrops' career was winding down. Linda and Dorothy had kept The Teardrops going as a successful live act through the acquisition of numerous, albeit temporary replacements. Much to Bob Dyer's disappointment, it was time to move on.

After The Teardrops dissolved, Linda and her fiancé moved to Santa Monica, where Linda was part of an act, working in Dean Martin's Lounge. Her accompanist was Billy Marx, son of Chico Marx of the famous Marx Bros. Linda had a very tempting offer from Dean Martin to become one of his Golddiggers, but turned him down, a decision Linda says she regrets.

Eventually returning to Cincinnati, she and Susie sang in a band called The Happy People for a few months, singing exclusively for Arcaro's nightclub. Linda formed and managed a Christian band, Reaching Out, singing with her sister Phyllis Ann and Dorothy. She has also recorded radio jingles for local companies in Cincinnati, such as Cobbie Cuddler Shoes. In 1990, Linda helped form a band called The Avenues, with guitarist Paul Milazzo, whom she eventually married. Linda has one son, Adam Bruce, who is also a musician, as well as an accomplished painter. Adam is part of The Aronoff Center in Cincinnati, which showcases new commercial artists.

In 1996, Linda recorded a demo about AIDS, which was shopped around to prospective labels. Linda coaches voice, both privately and for Jewel Recording in Cincinnati, where she is also a sales representative. Its owner, Rusty York, was inducted into The Rock & Roll Hall Of Fame.

Dorothy did backup work over the years and she, Linda, and Wendy sang backup on a Lee Greenwood session. Dorothy is now a nurse and Clinical Coordinator at The University Of Cincinnati. She and her husband, Harold Wethington, have been happily married for over

thirty years. Dorothy has kept her voice in shape doing choral singing. As of 1992, Dorothy and Wendy were still hooking up for studio work. Dorothy is quite fond of what can be accomplished in a studio, so she tries to get in there whenever she can. Wendy is now a mother of four and works as a legal secretary, a far cry from her days as a free spirit throughout the late 1960s and 1970s: "After my hippie days of travelling the states and commune hopping, I actually settled down to raise a family and picked up the guitar and stayed busy in gospel music locally for several years. I've also done a lot of studio back-up work and sang with Dorothy in a country/southern rock band called 'Country Flair.' We had so much fun together on stage during that time. People told our guitarist they had come just to watch the two of us have such a great time together!"

Pat Strunk lives in Florida, although no one hears from her. Tinker continued to perform for many years in a local band in Cincinnati. She is now a special education teacher with two children. Susie Leicht now sings contemporary Christian music. Bud Reneau is a successful songwriter in Nashville. Paul Trefzger lives in San Francisco, making his living as a probation officer, and still running Saxony Records. All the releases are still available as reissues.

In 1989, The Teardrops reunited to perform at a benefit to raise money for homeless Vietnam veterans. The Clarion Hotel in Cincinnati donated their Grand Ballroom and the place was packed with hundreds of well wishers. Linda, Dorothy, Wendy and Tinker were met with enthusiasm. This was the first time Dorothy and Tinker sang in The Teardrops simultaneously. Many old friends and fans turned out to hear The Teardrops, as well as a host of other local groups.

As a result of this benefit and other reunion shows, a local music renaissance in Cincinnati was born. The Teardrops were called upon to appear once again. The group also had the chance to record again, but the project never materialized. For a time, Dorothy, her daughter Jessica, Wendy, and a friend, Karen, put a group together to perform at some of these reunion shows. The act was aptly called Teardrops Too.

Neither The Teardrops, nor their producers have any regrets about their years performing and recording. Even though they never achieved a high level of national fame, the love of performing, recording and standing before thousands of people who validated their talents is enough reward for the group who reigns as Cincinnati's champion female vocal quartet. No "tears" here.

The Teardrops Discography

45s	Label	Number	Year
Tonight I'm Gonna Fall In Love Again/That's Why I'll Get By	Saxony	1007	1964
I'm Gonna Steal Your Boyfriend/Call Me And I'll Be Happy		1008	1965
Tears Come Tumbling/You Won't Be There		1009	
Tears Come Tumbling/You Won't Be There	Musicor	1139	
I Will Love You Dear Forever/Bubblegummer		1218	1966
I Will Love You Dear Forever/Bubblegummer	Saxony	2002	1993

The Teen Queens

Members:

(1956-62)   Rosie Collins
Betty Collins

Every part of America can revel about a special style of R&B vocal music unique to that particular region. Philadelphia boasts the floating high tenor leads amidst relaxing, relenting harmonies. New York had its suave sounding groups trading off street tunes, many making it to the vinyl shrine. Los Angeles had its tightly knit stable of singers who thrived on interesting arrangements for the backing vocals, bringing them to the forefront of the song alongside the lead. LA also wins hands down for the sheer number of popular vocal duos in Rhythm & Blues, like Marvin & Johnny, Jessie & Marvin, Bob & Earl and Gene & Eunice. Another entry on the roster of distinctive West Coast duets sang of true love, the likes of which has departed, leaving them as withering posies.

Forget about Bobby or Jimmy, Johnny or Tommy; no one broke a heart like Eddie, the lost love of The Teen Queens.

Rosie and Betty Collins liked to practice their singing in front of a mirror, never dreaming that it would be preparation for the one day they would be trying out their act in front of an audience. The duo came to the attention of RPM/Modern Records in 1955 through their brother, singer/songwriter Aaron Collins, a member of the Cadets/Jacks.

By January of 1956, the girls had their first single released. "Eddie My Love," co-written by Aaron, tells of an angst ridden lover, begging her boyfriend to come home because she is just wilting away from being without him. The song's arrangement contains low blowing saxophones and slow, countering piano chords to introduce the song and ends just the same way. The pace of the tune is meant to evoke the sentiment of a funeral dirge. This arrangement would become a trademark in Teen Queens recordings.

"Eddie My Love" climbed the charts, becoming a huge hit in the winter of 1956. The flip side of this gem was the jumping blues tune, "Just Goofed." The harmonies contain a third, male voice, a voice that would make intermittent guest appearances on future Teen Queens singles.

Since the formula for "Eddie My Love" worked so well, RPM followed with the similar, "So All Alone," utilizing the same instrumentation. The third single, "Until

The TEEN QUEENS

Direction
SHAW ARTISTS CORPORATION
565 Fifth Avenue
New York 17, New York

The singing sisters, The Teen Queens, Rosie and Betty Collins, 1956.

The Day I Die" seeks to speed up the formula, while still holding on to the mid-50s, California sound of a horn-dominated arrangement. This single features a male responding during the bridge. The use of slow, horn-laden orchestration reflected a specific style, but was no longer working as a hit formula for the duo, so the company decided to concentrate on the uptempo numbers that the sisters sang with clarity and gusto. The band was able to really jam on these cuts, showcasing instrumental Rock & Roll at its best.

A fine example of this is The Teen Queens' fifth single, "Rock Everybody," which can work dancers into a jitter-bugging frenzy. One more single, "Two Loves and Two Lives" was released at the beginning of 1957. The Teen Queens received an offer to record for RCA Records. This, of course, meant a more elaborate recording studio, sophisticated arrangements, wider distribution and the potential for greater success. Or, so they thought. RCA was certainly considered one of the major forces in the music industry in the mid-1950s. In addition to having Elvis Presley and an artist roster of pop performers like Perry Como and Eddie Fisher, the label looked to broaden its appeal among the younger crowd of record buyers by featuring vocal groups like The Four Lovers. RCA mined the vein Rhythm & Blues acts in the late 1950s. In 1958, RCA signed The Teen Queens. Unfortunately, RCA placed the duo in a purely pop setting, giving them songs like "You Good Boy, You Get Cookie" and "Movie Star" singing in a style so straight, the records reverberate like cuts from a Broadway soundtrack. The label was obviously trying to change the image of The Teen Queens, but at the same time stripped them of their Rhythm & Blues style, the factor that made The Teen Queens so popular in the first place. Major labels often did this with dismal results.

The allure of a major record label was enticing, but it was often a dead end, as arrangers and producers used to dealing with pop orchestral acts often didn't know what to do with Rock & Roll artists. The Teen Queens were gone from RCA within a year. It wouldn't be until the 1960s that major record labels would show consistently good taste and effort in producing Rock & Roll acts.

After almost two years of not recording, the sisters made four sides for Antler Records, alongside a roster of other legendary, veteran California artists like The Colts, The Flairs, and Linda Hayes. The Teen Queens' first single was an answer record to Big Jay McNeely's "There Is Something On Your Mind," entitled, "There's Nothing On My Mind." Each of the sisters takes her turn singing a line, interspersed with a stern spoken lecture. Other novelty tunes like "Politician" and "Magoo Can See" were also issued.

Kent Records was issuing new product by other West Coast artists like The Senders, Etta James and Tony Allen, but The Teen Queens were conspicuously absent from the roster. A token nod to the popularity of "Eddie My Love" was its official re-release on Kent in 1961. After one more single on Press Records in 1962, as Rosie & Betty, The Teen Queens ended their recording careers. The two sisters, tragically, met untimely deaths; a fate more realistically unfortunate than the melodramatic end they predicted in their renowned hit single.

The Teen Queens Discography

45s

	Label	Number	Year
Eddie My Love/Just Goofed	RPM	453	1956
So All Alone/Baby Mine		460	
Until The Day I Die/Billy Boy		464	
Red Top/Love Sweet Love		470	
Rock Everybody/My Heart's Desire		484	
Two Loves & Two Lives/I Miss You		500	1957
You Good Boy, You Get Cookie/Dear Tommy	RCA	47-7206	1958
Movie Star/First Crush		47-7396	
There's Nothing On My Mind/Part 2	Antler	4014	1960
Politician/I'm A Fool		4015	
Donny/Instrumental		4016	1961
McGoo Can See/I Heard Violins		4017	
Eddie My Love/Just Goofed	Kent	359	
(as Betty & Rose)			
That Twistin' Feeling/Doodle Doo Doo	Press	2805	1962

LPs

	Label	Number	Year
Eddie My Love	Crown	5022	--

Jean Thomas

The scene is summertime in New York City, 1964. Music listeners are enjoying a new single by The Four Seasons called "Rag Doll." This hit was another notch in the belt of producer Bob Crewe, who had been consis- tently scoring with the New Jersey quartet since 1962. Female artists were happening on the charts in the early 1960s, too, so why not have the same hit sounds grafted onto productions featuring a female? The auspicious

One of Jean's groups, The Rag Dolls, 1965, (L-R) Mickie Harris, Jean Thomas, Susie Lewis.

result was a sweet sounding response to "Rag Doll" appropriately called, "Society Girl," sung by a group fittingly called The Rag Dolls. The Rag Dolls, however, were a conglomeration of studio singers, fronted by a young lady who was getting a lot of attention from producers as the featured voice on numerous demos, as well as having releases under her own name. Jean Thomas found herself at the threshold of a scene that was moving forward so quickly, she could barely catch her breath.

During The Brill Building Era, pop hits were churned out faster than an automated assembly line at a canned goods factory. Business during this time was so fast-paced, a song was recorded on Monday, mastered on Tuesday, pressed on Wednesday, released on Thursday, and landed on the charts by Friday. The profession was also about having that new gimmick, something just ahead of everything else to catch the ear of the teenage record-buying public. Since new ideas bounced around so quickly, demos often became the actual releases. The idea of working with a smaller group of musicians and singers seemed more efficient in order to keep up with the competitive pace. A particular idea or trend could be worked out with a succinct team of session people. A desired sound could be achieved and gotten to market in a shorter amount of time. The actual group was secondary, and this sometimes led to fictitious groups. A producer wouldn't have to worry about artists because there were only session fees to pay. Then, if a group were needed, singers would be hired to go out on the road.

Jean Thomas was born in Weymouth, Massachusetts and grew up in the coastal town of Hull. Jean's parents ran a business in Sarasota, Florida, so Jean's family would go back and forth, eventually settling in Sarasota when school started. Jean started singing while in high school. Through a gentleman named Bill Blackburn, who had been given a half hour of time for a radio show at station WKXY each week, Jean gained exposure as his featured soloist. As a result of working with Blackburn, Jean became part of a larger ensemble. This entailed much preparation, "I would go down to the community center and rehearse before the show, then we would go on the air. I was the solo vocalist. Also, I sang duets, leads and was part of a group. We started a rock group called Preacher John (Feight) and The Five Saints. We became popular because of the radio show."

Jean's younger brother Don had picked up the guitar when Jean was a senior in high school. After Jean left for Florida State University, Don's interest in music had grown. So had his guitar-playing ability. Don became quite popular at school and eventually helped start a folk group, The Merry Men. After gaining popularity on the local level, The Merry Men were asked to participate in the Coca-Cola sponsored Talentsville, a showcase for local talent. After winning for Sarasota, the band won in the state and regional competitions. When the group came to New York for the finals, Archie Bleyer, owner of Cadence Records, spotted them and signed them to his label, after they won the national competition. The Merry Men had a handful of releases for the pop-oriented label and were included on a tour in 1960, with Chubby Checker, Fabian and Brenda Lee.

After the tour was over, two members of The Merry Men quit to concentrate on their studies. Jean saw her chance and encouraged her brother to return to New York with her to make their marks in the business of music using the contacts Don had acquired from his first encounters in New York. Soon after their arrival, Don and Jean began writing songs for Paul Anka's publishing company, Spanka Music. Anka had offered Jean a contract, but before she accepted, Jean and Don had run into Archie Bleyer.

Bleyer offered Jean an audition. Jean opted for Bleyer's offer, signing on as a singer with Cadence Records. Her first recording was a stark version of "Moon River." Exercising perfect diction, Jean's alto stands alone, save for the guitar and harmonica, appropriating a fanciful mood for this splendid version of the theme from the movie "Breakfast At Tiffany's." Kudos also went to the similarly styled flip, "My Ideal." "Moon River" went to number one in Syracuse in the spring of 1962 and also went to the top five in New England. Jean began making personal appearances to promote the record, going on tour with Jay and The Americans, Brian Hyland, and Del Shannon. She was also busy collaborating on songs with her brother Don, as well as with Barry Richards, and Peggy Santiglia of The Angels. Jean was featured on other pop standard productions for Cadence during 1962-63. Teen idol sounding songs like "He's So Near" and "The Boy I Want Doesn't Want Me" were the given venues for Jean's voice, a little more musically daring for a label like Cadence, known for mellow songs with more of an adult appeal. Jean was usually backed by a chorus. For Jean, productions with more of a Rock & Roll edge were soon to come.

As time went by, Jean began cutting demo records to help make her way in New York. Many demos were cut at Associated, Dick Charles, or Bell Sound. Everyone on the circuit used these studios for demo work and constantly crossed paths. Once in this network, Jean met other songwriters and producers and began collaborating on more and more compositions. Jean worked with many producers who wanted to use her voice to achieve a certain sound on their recordings. This demand for the Jean Thomas sound kept her in the studio. Jean worked with Robert Feldman, Gerald Goldstein, and Richard Gottehrer on particularly anonymous projects like "Treat Him Tender, Maureen," a nod to Ringo Starr's wife, and another local hit in New York City. Members of The Angels helped with that single, and it was released as Angie and The Chicklettes.

Jean and The Angels also worked with FGG on projects under the name The Beach Nuts, recording "Out In The Sun," which fared favorably in many markets both in America and in Europe. While associated with Bob Crewe, Jean recorded "Midnight Mary" with Joey Powers, which she also arranged. The song was a top ten hit. It was through this alliance with Crewe that Jean would record her most notable work in female group music. Jean eventually worked with Bob Crewe and Charlie Calello, first recording for MGM in 1964.

Answer records were nothing new. The Harptones had responded to Maxine Brown's "All In My Mind" with "All In Your Mind" and Motown's Satintones replied to The Shirelles' "Will You Still Love Me Tomorrow" with "Tomorrow and Always." Even Bob Crewe had cut an answer record to "Sherry" with Tracey Dey called "Jerry, I'm Your Sherry." Crewe had the idea to answer his own Four Seasons hit, "Rag Doll," with a continuation from the girl's point of view entitled, "Society Girl." This production blended just the right amount of similarities in melody and harmony without copying the exact composition.

Originally, there was no group. Session singers Carol Fran, Marilyn Jackson and Ann Phillips provided the backing vocals to Jean's lead voice, laid over the classic Bob Crewe instrumentation, complemented by Charlie Calello's arrangement. Suddenly, the style formerly reserved for Tracey Dey and Diane Renay had taken on a new dimension. At the opposite end of the spectrum from R&B vocalists, Jean's sweet voice exudes the onset of pubescence, the antithesis of the tough-sounding female voice prevalent in many recordings during this period. Her innocent plea won the listeners' hearts and sympathies. "Society Girl" became a hit in New York and many other regions, jumping on to the outer rungs of the pop charts.

Now, with a hit to The Rag Dolls' credit, a group is needed to promote the single. Jean was surprised at the fact that Crewe wanted to run with the idea of a real Rag Dolls group. She wondered what was to happen with her solo projects. Crewe assured Jean that they would run concurrently, so Jean agreed to go out on the road. As Ellie Greenwich was appearing with her sister Laura and Beverly Warren as a live Raindrops group, Jean had to be prepared. She originally corralled her friend, Lesley Hamlett, to help her out for the ad hoc group. Eventually, Jean brought in Mickie (pronounced Mikey) Harris, her singing buddy from Sarasota, for session work and for work as a Rag Doll. Mickie, Jean, and Jean's other roommate, Susie Lewis, posed for the publicity photos as The Rag Dolls.

Jean agreed to continue on the road provided that Bob Crewe eventually find replacement Rag Dolls, because she had no intention of doing extensive touring. Steadier and more lucrative work could be found in demo and session singing. Jean crossed paths with Ellie Greenwich many times at these sessions. They enjoyed each other and the sound they created together. When Mickie Harris came from Florida, she completed an incredible trio in the studio, "I brought Mickie up from Florida to sing with me. Ellie and I would be hired separately to sing backgrounds and we said 'wouldn't it be nice to have a third person'. Usually, we bounced back and forth on two tracks. Four tracks were still a luxury. On those recordings, Ellie was responsible for vocal arrangements."

Jean, Ellie and Mickie were the schoolgirl-sounding backgrounds on Lesley Gore's "Look Of Love," as well as other recordings. However, Jean's association with The Rag Dolls would continue. Bob Crewe was so satisfied with "Society Girl" that he decided to go ahead with more Rag Dolls singles.

During late 1964 and early 1965, Crewe produced more singles with Jean singing the lead. One was a chart item, this time on the Bell-related Mala label. "Dusty" rang out as another distaff version of The Four Season's style. This netted The Rag Dolls their second winning single. The pleasant B-side, "Hey Hoagy," also received significant attention. These productions were now being done under Crewe's newly christened Genius, Inc. production company that he shared with his brother, Dan. Denny Randell and Sandy Linzer provided their writing skills for these productions, along with the tried and true Charlie Calello. Linzer and Randell were just months away from success with their own female proteges, The Toys.

Even though success for the Rag Dolls was forthcoming, only one more production was created before the concept was abandoned. "Baby's Gone" was another successful release on Mala in 1965. The Toys would later cut an emotional version for their Dyno Voice LP. Session musicians and singers are generally where they are because they prefer the behind the scenes activity to performing. Jean was no exception.

Crewe was busy with The Four Seasons, Diane Renay, and Tracey Dey. Yet he never missed a beat, ultimately finding a replacement for Jean, so she didn't have to continue touring as part of The Rag Dolls. Jean remembers how cavalier she was about the end of her days as a Rag Doll, "I told Bob I would go out on the road until he had another group. 'Dusty' was a big record. When I would go to a performance everyone would crowd us. I remember one time I had to do a record hop as myself. The crowd had no idea who I was. I went offstage to polite applause. The headliners turned out to be The Rag Dolls. I watched from backstage and it was interesting to see other people lip-sync to my voice, but I was surprised to find out that it didn't bother me, which proved to me I didn't really want to be a Rag Doll anymore."

Jean Thomas continued with her career as a singer/songwriter throughout the 1960s and 1970s, appearing with Kenny Karen and Lesley Miller on hundreds of songs by artists like Ella Fitzgerald, Sarah Vaughn and Barbra Streisand. There were also notable appearances on Neil Diamond's "Sweet Caroline" and Jeff Barry's neo-Spector version of "Baby I Love You" by Andy Kim. Jean provides the soaring soprano backing that helps sell the song.

Another lucrative venue for singers was the world of jingle singing. To Jean's surprise, when she first auditioned for a commercial, she beat out seasoned jingle singers for the role. Jean's voice appeared on commercials for Noxema Skin Crème and Newport Cigarettes, among others. Through her extensive work in commercials, she became associated with jingle producer Joe Brooks, making a notable appearance as a guest vocalist on his movie soundtrack for the cult hit, "The Lords of Flatbush" in 1974.

She continued to write with Jeffrey Richards and her brother Don, inadvertently placing a song with John (Johnny Rotten) Lydon's Sex Pistols. "Don't Give Me No Lip, Child" struck the punk band's fancy, so they recorded it for their controversial long player, "The Great Rock and Roll Swindle," in 1979. "We were all afraid that we were going to be fired as songwriters if we didn't come up with some songs. We got together one morning and we wrote 'Don't Give Me No Lip, Child' and we laughed at how silly we thought it was."

Jean has been married to author, screenwriter, and songwriter, Ray Fox since 1966. Ray's documentary, "Preserving The Past" was nominated for an Academy Award. They have two daughters. Lauren is an actress, singer and the writer of an upcoming movie, "Bar Hop." Haley is a writer and will direct "Bar Hop." Jean is the head of her own talent management company, Fox-Albert. Talented actors and actresses like Mira Sorvino, Noah Fleiss and Rebecca Pidgeon are some of the company's illustrious clients. Jean Thomas made many pivotal songs of the early 1960s genre of teen pop. With the help of her producers, she established a pleasant, distinct sound and created an identity for herself, ironically, while remaining somewhat shrouded in mystery.

Jean Thomas Discography

45s

	Label	Number	Year
Jean Thomas			
Moon River/My Ideal	Cadence	1419	1962
He's So Near/Seven Roses		1435	1963
The Boy I Want Doesn't Want Me/He's So Near		1438	
Don't Make Me Fall In Love With You/I Don't Miss You At All	MGM	13263	1964
(as The Beach Girls)			
Skiing In The Snow/Goin' Places	Dyno Voice	202	1965
(as The Beach Nuts w/The Angels & FGG)			
Out In The Sun (Hey-O)/Someday Soon	Bang	504	1965
(as The Calendar Girls)			
People Will Talk/Sha-Rel-A-Nova	4 Corners	118	1965
(as Angie & The Chicklettes w/The Angels)			
Treat Him Tender, Maureen/Tommy	Apt	25080	1964
(as The Powder Puffs)			
My Boyfriend's Woody/Woody Wagon	Imperial	66014	1964
(as The Rag Dolls)			
Society Girl/Ragen (Inst.)	Parkway	921	1964
Dusty/Hey, Hoagy	Mala	493	1965
Baby's Gone/We Almost Made It		499	

LPs

	Label	Number	Year
(as Jeanne Thomas Fox)			
The Lords Of Flatbush – "Oh What A Night For Love"	ABC	828	1974

The Three Degrees

Style and grace, perfection in performance, and high quality entertainment. This is an all-too-short roster of chartered qualities belonging to The Three Degrees, the best all around female group in the business, whose illustrious endeavors have proven that these capabilities are the building blocks of a fruitful career in music.

The Three Degrees were formed at Overbrook High School in 1964. Fayette Pinkney, Linda Turner, and Shirley Porter started singing at dances and other functions on the weekends. It was through this exposure that the trio of high school girls came to the attention of Richard Barrett.

Richard had just parted ways with The Chantels, and he was looking for a group that he could mold as premium entertainers as well as singers. The group had another name, which nobody seems to remember, when Richard heard them, liked them and christened them The Three Degrees.

The Three Degrees in a group hug, 1973, (L-R) Valerie Holiday, Fayette Pinkney, Sheila Ferguson. (Photo courtesy of Weldon A. McDougal III)

After managing The Chantels and his own vocal group, The Valentines, Richard was a professional, having been in the business for almost ten years. His visions were more far-reaching for his next project. Not only should the group look and sound good, they had to be adept dancers and charismatic performers as well. After much rehearsal for a debut release, the solid "Gee Baby, I'm Sorry" scored on the charts in the fall of 1964. One surprise on this fluid single is that the high, floating tenor was provided by Richard himself.

Helen Scott and Sheila Ferguson lived in Germantown, Pa., where they attended Germantown High School. Helen and Sheila knew each other since they were toddlers, had grown up together, and sang in the school chorus. When a teacher at the school heard them, he knew they had the right voices to succeed in music. He told them about this group that he heard of through a friend that was in need of two vocalists. The group had one single to their credit that had done fairly well in local markets, and their manager didn't want to break up the act. They were losing two singers at once. Helen recalls her beginnings as a member of the group: "Sheila and I used to sing at talent shows. A teacher named Gene Harris said he knew of a group that needed singers. He asked Sheila and me if we would audition. I got into the group and Sheila received an offer to record as a soloist. Another girl who was hired was Janet Jones."

A few months after the initial release of "Gee Baby I'm Sorry," the group was back in business. Sheila began her solo career first, even making a few appearances with the initial trio of girls. When Helen and Janet became permanent members, they fully immersed themselves in rehearsals, in order for the group to succeed. The eager trio worked on dance routines and made their own costumes. Since Helen and Fayette were still in high school, their public appearances were limited to local venues and weekend engagements. The group appeared at record hops and colleges, as well as venues like The Apollo and The Uptown Theatres.

This trio of Helen, Janet and Fayette, with its perfected harmonies, recorded the balance of the recordings for Swan, except for the last single. Sheila had a single placed with Landa Records before recording three releases for Swan. The trio backed Sheila on her singles and in turn Sheila completed the triad in the background while Helen sang the lead parts.

Their string of singles and Sheila's solo efforts certainly were not telling of their teenage years as the songs tailored for both acts were demure and alluring. One of the strongest aspects of their prowess as artists was their ability to deliver not only strong, impermeable harmonies, but seamless unison as well. On songs like "I'm Gonna Need You" and "Just Right For Love," the group floats effortlessly between lush harmonies and tight unison. The latter skill would forever set The Three Degrees apart from other female vocal groups, using it to effectively deliver either arousing musical messages or soft, sensual lullabies.

The group's tenure at Swan included versions of two Chantels standards, "Look In My Eyes" and a Latin-tinged version of "Maybe." They also backed "American Bandstand" producer and Swan Records partner Tony Mammarella on his novelty answer record to "Eve Of Destruction," called "Eve Of Tomorrow." Another novelty tune, "Let's Shindig," recorded with The Showmen, was released as The In Crowd. A couple of smooth ballads, "Close Your Eyes" and "I Wanna Be Your Baby" rounded out the Swan years. All the singles did well in local markets although "Look In My Eyes" was the only single to chart nationally. Richard Barrett, Leon Huff, Norman "General" Johnson and Ugene Dozier, some of Philadelphia's best songwriters, provided the tunes.

Sheila's singles were also inviting, with beguiling dance tunes like "How Did That Happen" and "Signs of Love" and also, "Little Red Riding Hood," an adult contemporary-sounding ballad. The two acts officially came together for the last Swan single, as Helen left to marry and have a family. Sheila stepped into the vacated spot. The last Swan single was "Love Of My Life." Not long after the release of this single, Swan Records closed its doors.

The year of 1966 saw many changes for the group. Helen left the group to tend to family business. Swan Records closed, leaving the group temporarily without a label, and now Janet, who had come to the group married, decided to leave the group. At this point, the group was out of school and touring. Many dates still had to be honored. Richard asked Sonia Goring of The Chantels to step in for one show in Las Vegas.

Sandra Tucker, daughter of Ira Tucker, founder of The Dixie Hummingbirds, then filled the spot for about a year. Sandra had experience with groups, starting out with Patti La Belle in The Ordettes. Unfortunately, disagreements with Richard Barrett during her stay with The Three Degrees prevented Sandra from becoming a permanent member. She would go on to fill in for Cindy Birdsong as a live replacement in The Blue Belles in the late 1960s. Of course, this meant that the group was still looking for a permanent third member. They found a suitable partner, not in or around Philadelphia, but in Boston.

While on a trip to Boston, Richard and a friend spotted young Valerie Holiday singing in a club. He thought she would be perfect for the Three Degrees. Valerie had the right amount of spunk in her voice that would complement the developing sounds of the group by adding a dimension of soulfulness. Valerie recalls when she decided to join the fold, "A friend of Richard's, Frank Hatchett, told me about the group and invited me to come and check out the act. I went to see them and liked what I heard. I was impressed with the group's appearance and sound, so I decided to join the act."

Since Valerie had experience entertaining an audience, it was not long before the group was running at full stride. Live appearances were becoming their bread and butter. Recordings were now sporadic as the ladies concentrated on constantly improving and refining their live act. A single was released on ABC and one on Warner Bros., the gentle ballad "No Not Again," followed by two single on Metromedia and one on Gamble and Huff's Neptune Records. The fortuitous nature of these releases, songs that did not capture the full potential of the group, is proof that recordings took a back seat to sustaining the act in live performance. Barrett would just keep striking recording deals until the right one came along. This situation was not far off.

In 1970, Barrett signed the group to Roulette Records. Richard was no stranger to the company that bought out the efforts of his old friend George Goldner. The Three Degrees stayed for two years, recording numerous singles and an LP. Their first hit single for Roulette was another version of the Chantels hit, "Maybe." Sounding nothing like their version on Swan, this interpretation starts with an emphatic recitation, followed by an unsurpassed lead vocal by Valerie, which absolutely tears your heart out. No female group had ever recorded a pop song like this before, with both style and soul.

"Maybe" was the beginning of a string of creative, heartfelt singles that the group recorded from 1970-72. Other singles like "I Do Take You" and "Trade Winds" also made the charts. By this time, the group was performing at every major venue in the country. This kind of exposure afforded the group a unique opportunity to appear in a major motion picture. Valerie recounts the group's fling with filmdom, "We just happened to be booked at The Copacabana when the movie "The French Connection" was being filmed there, so we received our union cards and we were in. The song we sang was a version of "Everybody's Gone To The Moon."

By 1973, the group left Roulette and returned to Philadelphia to do some recording. Gamble and Huff's hometown operation, now named Philadelphia International Records, was turning into what was to become the major force in the music industry during the 1970s. Gathering the cream of Philly session musicians and veteran artists together on one record label proved a powerful formula when mixed with Gamble and Huff's writing and producing abilities.

The Three Degrees were to be a part of this bandwagon. The trio's first release for the label in the fall of 1973 was the tough standing "Dirty Old Man," featuring those soaring, close harmonies with full orchestrations behind them. This single and its follow-up, the socially conscious "Year of Decision," made a significant impact on the R&B charts. The next single would reintroduce the ladies to the pop world. As the theme song for the hit television dance show, "Soul Train," "TSOP" or The Sound Of Philadelphia featured them singing the invaluable hook during the mostly instrumental song.

This was followed by their biggest selling single to date, "When Will I See You Again," from the LP, "The Three Degrees," featuring Sheila's silky lead vocal. A string of singles and LPs flaunting the group's versatility followed in 1974-75, including the critically acclaimed "International"

LP, where the group sings in different languages to accommodate their overseas fans that were quickly overtaking those who noticed them in America. More and more work in Europe and Japan had acquainted vast, new audiences with The Three Degrees. Eventually, the group would find their niche with audiences abroad, playing to sold out houses all across Europe and Japan.

As The Three Degrees' chart impact in The United States waned, it boomed in places like France and Belgium. This was now the place for them to be. Fayette had left the group on maternity leave, scheduled to return, but the reluctant new mother had a change of heart and decided to leave the group for good. After a ten-year absence, Helen Scott returned to take her place. Also at this time, the group left Philadelphia International in 1976 to record a token LP and single for the parent Epic Records. There were many dates to fill with Fayette gone. Helen was the logical choice, says Valerie, "We needed a replacement for Fayette, because there were still many dates to fill. It had to be someone who could hit the ground running."

Since most of The Three Degrees' sustained popularity was concentrated in Europe, it was a good idea for the group to be placed with a label that concentrated on acts with a following abroad. The group was still touring Europe and Japan, playing to sellout crowds, week after week. It had been almost four years since the group's biggest chart topper in the States and the forgetful American audiences had forsaken them. This was not so with audiences across the Atlantic. Richard had gotten them a deal with Ariola Records, joining other successful American R&B artists such as Eruption, Amii Stewart, Chanson and Deborah Washington, all having success in Europe. The label then placed the trio into the hands of one of the hottest producers of the day, Giorgio Moroder.

Giorgio Moroder had started as a singer/songwriter in Germany, having his LP, "Son of My Father," released on Atco Records in 1974. By 1975, he and his partner, Pete Bellotte, were having success with a rising disco diva, Donna Summer. As 1978 drew to a close, Summer was extremely successful, thanks in part to the Moroder/Bellotte production team. They were now assigned to merge their talents with The Three Degrees, and a talented production they assembled.

The result was the driving "Giving Up, Giving In." With The Three Degrees vocals soaring high above the scorching, synthesizer-laden Eurodisco, the song catapulted to the top of the charts in Europe, and made a significant inroad on the American pop charts. The single's greatest American success was on the Hot Disco Singles chart. It spun on every deejay's turntable, keeping dance floors crowded in every city in The United States. Favorable sequels, such as "Woman In Love," "The Runner," penned by Sheila, and "My Simple Heart" followed in 1979 and 1980. "My Simple Heart" allowed the group to get back to a softer, more demure sound, while maintaining that European flavor.

By now, the group was revered by fans in Japan and in every country in Europe. They were guests at the wedding of Prince Charles and Princess Diana. They were also the only group to ever sing in Buckingham Palace for Prince Charles' 30th birthday. It seemed the road of success was paved as smooth as satin.

In 1981, The Three Degrees made a major decision. They decided to part ways with Richard Barrett. This resulted in a continued dispute over the use of the group's name. Barrett felt it belonged to him because he created the group, put them together and guided them through their career. The ladies felt the use of the name belonged to them because they worked hard to maintain a premium image, and, in the end, it was they who got out onto the stage every night to entertain the fans. The existent battle over the trademark of The Three Degrees wouldn't actually happen until 1989. Meanwhile, accolades were continually bestowed upon the group. Their hand imprints are encased in cement in Rotterdam and they are in the Guinness Book of World Records as the longest existing female group in the world. Multitudes of fans continue to greet them in Belgium, The Netherlands, France and Germany, and they have appeared on numerous television shows in Japan.

During the 1980s, the group released several LPs on their own, most notably, 1983's "Album of Love," produced by Irwin Kaelis, which includes an outstanding cover of The Police song, "Every Breath You Take," and "Live In The UK," which features their exciting showstoppers. In 1986, Sheila Ferguson retired from the group to raise her children, although she has made occasional appearances as a soloist, performing Three Degrees material. Helen and Valerie tried several ladies in the third spot, including Victoria Wallace, who stayed long enough to have her image grace the cover of a CD. In 1989, they signed with John Abbey's Ichiban Records (which means Number One in Japanese) recording the CD "And Holding."

The woman chosen to permanently fill the spot vacated by Sheila was Cynthia Garrison, a seasoned session singer whose vocals appeared on the popular Change LPs, behind Luther Vandross. She also had worked extensively with Millie Jackson and Kathy Sledge. Cynthia's presence has solidified the group for the last eleven years.

In 1989, The Three Degrees were part of a reunion package of a Philadelphia International tour that reunited them with old Philadelphia International label mates Billy Paul and Harold Melvin & The Blue Notes. This concert resulted in a live album recording. As fate would have it, in 1989, Richard Barrett petitioned the court over the use of the name Three Degrees in America. After lingering in the courts for three years, Richard won the rights to the group name in The United States. The ladies were exhausted by the court battle and learned quite a bit about the laws governing the entertainment industry. Helen puts it succinctly when she talks of the acquired knowledge, "At the end of the proceedings, I was ready to study law."

Despite this setback for the group, Cynthia, Helen and Valerie continue to captivate audiences around the world. Another first for the group is the recording of a Christmas LP. They have recorded many acclaimed CDs, available at their performances. Their older material is constantly being repackaged for consumption by new fans hungry for the sound of The Three Degrees. All the Three Degrees' recordings are ample, creative evidence of their longevity, proving that The Three Degrees will maintain their status as the longest running female group of all time, continuing to perform as long as fate will allow, a class act that can stand the test of time.

The Three Degrees Discography

45s	Label	Number	Year
Gee Baby I'm Sorry/Do What You're Supposed To Do	Swan	4197	1964
I'm Gonna Need You/Just Right For Love		4214	1965
Close Your Eyes/Gotta Draw The Line		4224	
Eve Of Tomorrow/Love Letter (w/Tony Mammarella)		4226	
Look In My Eyes/Drivin' Me Mad		4235	1966
Maybe/Yours		4245	
I Wanna Be Your Baby/Tales Are True		4253	
Love Of My Life/Are You Satisfied		4267	
Tear It Up/Part 2	ABC	10991	1967
Contact/No No Not Again	Warner Bros.	7198	1968
Down In The Boondocks/Warm Weather Music	Metromedia	109	1969
Feeling Of Love/Warm Weather Music		128	
What I See/Reflections Of Yesterday (Inst.)	Neptune	23	1970
Melting Pot/The Grass Will Sing For You	Roulette	7072	
Maybe/Collage		7079	
Maybe/Sugar On Sunday		7079	
I Do Take You/You're The Fool		7088	
You're The One/Stardust		7097	
Yours/There's So Much Love All Around Me		7102	1971
Lowdown/Ebbtide		7105	
Trade Winds/I Turn To You		7117	1972
I Wanna Be Your Baby/Find My Way		7125	
I Won't Let You Go/Through Misty Eyes		7137	
Dirty Ol' Man/Can't You See What You're Doing To Me	Phil. Int'l.	3534	1973
Year Of Decision/A Woman Needs A Good Man		3539	1974
When Will I See You Again/Year Of Decision		3550	
I Didn't Know/Dirty Ol' Man		3561	1975
Take Good Care Of Yourself/Here I Am		3568	
Free Ride/Loving Cup		3585	1976
What I Did For Love/Macaroni Man	Epic	50283	
Standing Up For Love/In Love We Grow		50330	1977
Giving Up, Giving In/Woman In Love	Ariola	7721	1978
Out Of Love Again/Woman In Love		7742	1979
The Runner/Out Of Love Again		7746	
Jump The Gun/Falling In Love		7776	
My Simple Heart/Hot Summer Night		7801	1980

UK Singles			
Dirty Ol' Man/Can't You See What You're Doing To Me	Phil. Int'l.	1860	
Year Of Decision/A Woman Needs A Good Man		2073	
Get Your Love Back/I Like Being A Woman		2737	
When Will I See You Again/I Didn't Know		2753	
Toast Of Love/Do It (Use Your Mind)		4215	
Jump The Gun/Looking For Love	Ariola	--	

(as The In Crowd)			
Let's Shindig/You're Gonna Miss Me	Swan	4204	1965

(w/MFSB)			
TSOP/Something For Nothing	Phil. Int'l.	3540	1974
Love Is The Message/My One And Only Love		3547	

Sheila Ferguson			
Little Red Riding Hood/How Did That Happen	Landa	706	1965
I'll Weep For You/Don't (Leave Me Lover)	Swan	4217	
And In Return/Are You Satisfied		4225	
Heartbroken Memories/Signs Of Love		4234	1966

LPs and CDs			
Maybe	Roulette	42050	1970
The Three Degrees	Phil Int'l.	32406	1973
International		33162	1975
Three Degrees Live		33840	
Standing Up For Love	Epic	34385	1976
A Toast Of Love	--	--	--
Live In Japan	--	--	1982
Album of Love		--	1985
Live In The UK		--	--
And Holding	Ichiban	--	1989
Best and New Hits		--	1990
Out Of The Past, Into The Future		--	1992
Christmas With The Three Degrees		--	1998

The Toys

Members:

(1963-68)   Barbara Harris, 1st Soprano/Lead
June Monteiro, 2nd Soprano
Barbara Parritt, Alto

By the time the mid 1960s arrived, Rock & Roll had already borrowed from many a musical genre, blending and synthesizing to further change and broaden what had become an already homogenized musical mix. It only seemed natural to reach back further than the influences of American sounds, to the sounds of old Europe, the classical sounds, the music that was written by the great masters of the 16th century. These melodies weren't to be simply set to teenage lyrics. Just an appropriation of the sweetness of the pieces to accompany the sweet sound of female voices was used to create a new approach.

Bob Crewe was working with Jean Thomas, Tracey Dey and, most notably, Diane Renay in productions which featured more elaborate musical arrangements. Sandy Linzer and Denny Randell were two students of the Bob Crewe sound. They had the idea for turning sweet female voices into well-crafted pop operas with this newly found classical angle. The duo needed singers who would be suited to create and enhance this sound. Linzer and Randell found the qualities they were looking for in three young girls from Queens.

The Toys were from St. Albans, Queens in New York City, the town that the famed Count Basie called home. Barbara Harris and Barbara Parritt knew each other from Woodrow Wilson High School and started singing together as teens. June, attending Van Buren High School, met the other girls while visiting her sister. Barbara Parritt and June initially formed the group with Dottie Berry and Betty Stokes. Stokes missed one too many rehearsals, so Barbara Harris quickly replaced her. Their favorite songs to sing were the songs of Motown by Mary Wells and The Miracles.

The girls had some friends who were dancers and drummers, so they enjoyed African rhythms as well. Eddie Chase, a local agent, heard the girls sing and heard potential. He christened them The Charlettes and introduced them to producer Bob Yorey. They recorded one single entitled, "The Fight's Not Over/Whatever Happened To Our Love," on the Angie record label in 1963. The girls began singing at high school dances and talent shows. Their manager decided to shop the group to producers in the city. The Charlettes got work singing backgrounds.

The Toys, 1965, (L-R) June Monteiro, Barbara Harris, Barbara Parritt.

THE TOYS

Their first assignment was to sing background for Barbara Chandler on Kapp records. The Charlettes can be heard painting the aural picture on Chandler's version of The Tokens-penned tune, "It Hurts To Be Sixteen." Their work on Chandler's singles was so impressive that Chandler's husband, Vince Marc, became their new manager. Dottie dropped out in 1964, so the group continued as a trio. Marc worked to get the girls jobs singing backup on other recording sessions.

Marc eventually shopped the group to producer Bob Crewe and arranger Charlie Calello, who were trying to create another hit for their long-time protégé, Diane Renay. Normally, Crewe used a pop-chorale type of sound on Renay's records, in keeping with her undiluted, clean-cut sound. Crewe had placed Renay with MGM in 1965 and decided to use vocals with more tone and distinction. "I Had A Dream" features The Charlettes prominently in the mix. Taking note of the group's ability to weave almost operatic harmonies in and out of leads, Crewe decided that he wanted to showcase the group on their own. He turned the project for this latest venture over to his associates, the capable producing and songwriting team of Denny Randell and Sandy Linzer.

The group was taken into the studio in 1965 and recorded two songs, "Deserted" and "On Backstreet." Vince Marc also thought the group needed more of a catchy name than The Charlettes. Marc is the one responsible for naming the group The Toys, a name the girls abhorred. All the members of The Toys sang lead, but it was Barbara Harris who led the group on their hits with her steady, piercing voice. Even though the group had a few tunes already in the can, Linzer and Randell wanted to try out a theme with which they were experimenting. The duo had a song based on a classical piece of music written by Bach. The song was aptly entitled "A Lover's Concerto." Although the melody borrowed cues from classical music, the bass line bore much of a resemblance to accents featured in the Motown sound. The meshing of the ideas of pop and classical was the key to opening the door of fame for The Toys' debut single on the Dyno Voice label. The airiness of the song allows Barbara's lead to ride comfortably over its hills and valleys, leaving room for effective unison in the background. The mellifluous carol steadily climbed the charts in October of 1965 and landed squarely at number one, staying there for six weeks. This well-crafted tune was also a hit around the

THE original TOYS
"A LOVER'S CONCERTO"

Trumbull Productions
60 SEAMAN AVE
NEW YORK, NEW YORK 10034
(212)-304-1598

The Toys, reunited in 1986, (L-R) Barbara Harris, Barbara Parritt, June.

world. The flip was an epilogue to the A-side, the laconic "This Night."

The group's sudden popularity in America and abroad prompted Vince Marc to immediately book The Toys on a European tour. This did not sit well with Linzer and Randell, who wanted the group to do more promotion in the states to capitalize on the success of their single. The business-minded team was also looking to the future and wanted to start on the follow-up single. This caused an almost contiguous rift between Marc and the production team, with The Toys caught smack-dab in the middle. The group did not wish to pay this adversity any mind. They wanted to concentrate on what they loved to do, which was singing. Barbara often wished she could avoid the pitfalls of the business and concentrate on the frills of being a global celebrity, "Going to England and Germany, all these countries I used to dream about—it was wonderful. People ask me about where I've been, and I start telling and I can't stop. I enjoy telling about our experiences."

The group did not realize what the impact of the tumultuous relationship between their manager and their producers would have on their career. After returning from a successful tour of England and Europe, The Toys were now ready to record the follow-up to their huge hit. Again, Linzer and Randell applied the usual rule so apparent in pop music at this time. Follow a huge hit with a sound-alike formula.

Once again they employed a classical piece for the introduction, this time using a melodic variant of "The Nutcracker." "Attack" was lyrically tougher than "Lover's Concerto," with a more aggressive story line. The arrangement stayed basically the same, engaging a gamboling lead amid reliable unison backups, but featured more emphatic horns. "Attack" modulates to a climax, sending the group's seamless harmonies soaring, casting the voices into roles reserved for strings.

The group rose to the occasion, reverberating as violins magically granted the gift of speech. In addition to her lead, Barbara Harris was also in the background, enrapturing the listener with a commanding resonance. She is complemented by June's supple soprano and by Barbara Parritt's proportionate alto. The group's secondary effort reached number 18 on the pop charts and was again a hit worldwide. The Toys had a chance to go to Hollywood with their second single, singing "Attack" in the beach party comedy movie, "It's A Bikini World," starring Tommy Kirk and Deborah Walley.

The Toys now had two top twenty tunes to their credit. The company wanted to capitalize on this by releasing an album. It certainly was the way to go as far as The Toys and the Linzer-Randell machine were concerned. The success of "Attack" should have at once precipitated the release of The Toys' long player, but bickering between the interests were delaying its release. Vince Marc wanted the girls out on the road so he could reap the benefits of his efforts. Linzer and Randell wanted the group in the studio at once to capture the momentum created by two hits in a row. True, there were some songs in the can, but this project was not to be a rush job. By the time the two sides reached an agreement,

the excitement generated by "A Lovers' Concerto" and "Attack" was waning.

Although it was too late for true success on the heels of two monster singles, the quality of production and arrangement for the group's debut LP was certainly apparent. This effort turned out to be a superlative album entitled, "The Toys Sing." In addition to the group's two hits and their accompanying B-sides, the package includes cuts containing more of the same qualities appreciated in the group's previous endeavors. Almost every cut could have made its mark as a single release. The songs included were the shaking "Deserted" and the party-time tune, "On Backstreet." The album also contained "Can't Get Enough Of You Baby" which was eventually a single. All cuts are fine efforts, especially "What's Wrong With Me, Baby," the driving, foot-stomping dance tune, complete with a blaring sax break. Utilizing more of her range for effect, Barbara Harris' voice reaches for the sky in parts of this gutsy tune.

Originally slated as a single, The Toys' version was passed over by Linzer and Randell. Instead, they released a cover of the tune by a male group, The Invitations. Maybe the production team thought the song too bold for young girls. The song did not receive a single release until the 1980s on Virgo Records, a reissue label. June exercised her willowy soprano on a cover of Paul McCartney's "Yesterday." Barbara Parritt used her far-reaching range on the sassy "Hallelujah" (also released as a single by The Invitations). Barbara refers to these works as a superb selection of songs from the group's only LP for Dyno Voice Records, "I enjoyed all the cuts on our LP. I loved the way Sandy and Denny used to write, and Charlie Calello's arranging. It was refreshing, their sound. To me it was different than what was being played at the time—it was unique. Bernard Purdy was one of the musicians on the recordings. He was funky, and Chuck Rainey. They chose the best musicians for our recordings."

While the girls were enjoying creative and commercial success in America, Europe, and Japan, their producers were at war with their manager. Vince Marc did not see eye to eye with Linzer and Randell on touring arrangements. Marc was determined to make his part in the career of The Toys pay off for him, and he was tired of what he saw as an infringement on his abilities as a manager. Meanwhile, Toys singles continued to be released. Dyno Voice issued "May My Heart Be Cast Into Stone" and "Can't Get Enough Of You Baby" as singles in 1966. "Silver Spoon" followed the classical theme motif and made an appearance as a B-side. Both A-sides were pleasant mid-tempo stompers, but did nothing on the charts.

Linzer and Randell fought back with one of the most intricate productions, with an arrangement by Jimmy Wisner. "Baby Toys" starts out with a tooting toy trumpet, then transcends into the bass-laden shuffling beat found on their other singles, but with more determination. A few seconds into the song, soaring violins take over with breaking drum licks every few seconds. The vocal pattern then enraptures with chords seemingly coming from every direction, while similes and metaphors abound. It was almost too sophisticated for pop radio, although it did chart.

The flip side was the dramatic, dirge-like "Happy Birthday Broken Heart." A marvelous single, it would be their last production with Linzer and Randell. Plans for a second album, which were to include already recorded versions of The Four Seasons' classics "Let's Hang On" and "Opus 17," did not materialize. Vince Marc got the group a production deal with Alan Lorber, who placed the group's productions with Philips Records in 1967.

Under Lorber's direction, the group waxed four sides. One was "Ciao Baby/I Got Carried Away," a pop sounding single similar to light Euroballads which were becoming so popular among vocalists during the late 60s. The next single, "Love Sonata," was more reminiscent of their Dyno Voice singles. The flip "I Close My Eyes," delivers the story of a wartime romance. The Toys' association with Alan Lorber lasted only a year. In 1968, they signed with Art Talmadge's Musicor Records. The group worked under the supervision of veteran songwriter and producer Helen Miller, and sang arrangements by Gene Redd and Charlie Calello. This relationship yielded two more singles, including a version of Brian Hyland's "Sealed With A Kiss." Although the group continued to work, growing disagreements concerning the group's direction caused The Toys to disband in 1969.

During the 1970s and 1980s, all the members of the group worked on various musical projects. Barbara Parritt and June worked as The Marvelettes for awhile, and Barbara Harris kept her voice in tune singing studio jingles. Through the efforts of Dennis Garvey and Ed Hawkins, The Toys briefly reunited in 1986, appearing at Danceteria in New York, and at the United In Group Harmony Association's monthly meeting in North Bergen, NJ. June remains in the old Queens neighborhood where she produces music videos.

Barbara Harris currently sings with her husband, Ken Wiltshire, in a blues band called Rhythm & Babs. In addition, Barbara occasionally appears with Joe Rivers as Johnnie and Joe, who brought us "Over The Mountain." Barbara also appears as a soloist, entertaining enthusiastic crowds in New York City in trendy rooms like Le Bar Bat. In 1998, Barbara released a CD entitled, "Barbara Now." Although she loves her work with The Toys, she has a special place in her heart for her current efforts, "I feel that at this age, being able to produce, arrange and write the songs on this CD, I feel blessed. Any obstacles that came along were quickly overcome and put down. This project just fell into place. This is a culmination of all my influences, Gospel, R&B and especially Blues, because we have an old blues tune on the CD, Robert Johnson's "I Need Your Love So Bad."

Barbara has no regrets about her career and the choices that she's made that have given her a beloved family and an extended career in the music business: "I'm thankful for my family. I'm glad I stopped to have children. In fact, my two sons sponsored this CD project. They started their own computer business and they backed us on this project. I'm especially thankful for my husband, Ken. He is the greatest inspiration in my life. He is constantly pushing me to do better. He is always there to lift my spirits. I can't see myself without him. He is always positive and has a lot of faith in me."

Barbara recalls the days of The Toys with fondness, a chance to work with talented songwriters, creative producers, great singers and good friends. The Toys are as their recordings were; true classics.

The Toys Discography

45s

	Label	Number	Year
(As The Charlettes)			
The Fight's Not Over/Whatever Happened To Our Love	Angie	1002	1963
The Toys			
A Lover's Concerto/This Night	Dyno Voice	209	1965
Attack/See How They Run		214	
May My Heart Be Cast Into Stone/On Backstreet		218	1966
Can't Get Enough Of You Baby/Silver Spoon		219	
Baby Toys/Happy Birthday Broken Heart		222	
Ciao Baby/I Got Carried Away	Philips	40432	1967
My Love Sonata/I Close My Eyes		40456	
You Got It Baby/You've Got To Give Her Love	Musicor	1300	1968
Sealed With A Kiss/I Got My Heart Set On You		1319	

LPs

	Label	Number	Year
The Toys Sing	Dyno Voice	9002	1966
Girls About Town -- "Let Me Down Easy"	Impact	006	1985
(Previously unreleased Musicor session, UK Import)			

CDs

	Label	Number	Year
Barbara Harris			
Barbara Now	Baheeja	--	1998

Martha & The Vandellas

Members:

(as The Del-Phis/Vells)

(1960-62) Rosalind Ashford, Soprano
Annette Beard, Alto
Martha Reeves, 2nd Soprano
Gloria Williamson, Lead

Martha & The Vandellas

(1962-64) Rosalind Ashford
Annette Beard
Martha Reeves, Lead

(1964-68) Rosalind Ashford
Betty Kelley, Alto
Martha Reeves

(1968-69) Rosalind Ashford
Lois Reeves, Alto
Martha Reeves

(1970-72) Lois Reeves
Martha Reeves
Sandra Tilley, Soprano

They possess voices that have the fiery delivery of a Baptist sermon, rising higher than the stratosphere, more emphatic with each passing word. Almost every single recording that this group released hit the charts with an incendiary blast, knocking every listener out of his/her socks and into a pair of dancing shoes. Of the four main female vocal groups at Motown Records, Martha and The Vandellas reigned memorably as the vocal powerhouses that Motown had in their stable of hit makers.

The splendor that is The Vandellas was formed out of another group in 1960, The Del-Phis (or Del-Fis, as some recordings spell the name). The Del-Phis had quickly metamorphosed from a trio to a quintet. Rosalind Ashford remembers that her singing sister managed to get things off

THE VANDELLAS
GORDY RECORDING ARTISTS

Personal Management
Berry Gordy, Jr. Enterprises, Inc.
Detroit 8, Michigan

The Vandellas first photo session, 1962, (L-R) Martha Reeves, Rosalind Ashford, Annette Beard. (Photo courtesy of Rosalind Ashford Holmes)

the ground for the eager soprano, "My sister, Geraldine Ashford, sang with two guys. A gentleman named Edward Larkin, whom we called "Pops" started managing them. Since he had a group with guys, he wanted a girl group, so Geraldine suggested me. Gloria Williamson had worked with him a lot, so she got in. There was also a girl named Trudy and a girl named Beatrice. They needed an alto, so Annette got in."

Gloria Williamson joined as a lead and Annette Beard lent her alto to the group of young singers. Actually, Annette's inclusion in the group was a surprise to her, because she had only gone to the audition to keep company with her friend. By the time the audition was over, Annette was a member of the group, "The Del-Phi's just sort of came about. The group was originally five girls, then four girls and a guy. I went with Beatrice for the ride. I didn't go to audition."

The girls didn't consider this group a serious venture; they joined because of their love for singing, and to pass the time after school. After a time, Trudy and Beatrice became tired of the ritual and dropped out. Since the remaining and increasingly earnest members weren't doing anything noteworthy yet, they took care in finding a replacement for the two departed vocalists. Gloria knew of a young lady who was performing around Detroit both as a soloist and as part of another vocal group, The Fascinations, but was not a permanent member. Gloria asked Martha Reeves to come to an audition for the group. All it took was one tryout and Martha was in as a tenor and second lead. As Martha puts it, there was instant magic, "The minute we heard our voices, we knew we had a blend."

The cogent and solidified group now wanted to show off their talents and make personal appearances. Pops did not seem capable of getting the group any bookings, so The Del-Phis switched management and went with Fred Brown, a postman who dabbled in the music business. Through Fred, the group began performing at local venues. Annette saw the experience in Fred Brown that she did not see in Pops, "We left Pops and went with Fred Brown. He had a little bit more of a connection than Pops did. With Fred, we did sock hops, lawn parties and afternoon teas. Fred also managed J.J. Barnes."

Through an arrangement with Fred Brown, The Del-Phis backed J.J. Barnes on his local hit "Won't You Let Me Know." Soon the capable quartet was getting work recording vocal backgrounds for other artists as well. The Del-Phis appeared as guests on recordings with Leon Peterson and with Mike Hanks on a bizarre record called "The Hawk." The capabilities of the group allowed Fred Brown to arrange a session for The Del-Phis to record an answer record to J.J. Barnes' hit on the Chess subsidiary, Check-Mate records. "I'll Let You Know" met with mild success in the Detroit area. Concurrently, Martha made appearances as a soloist at The Twenty Grand Lounge, a popular night-spot in Detroit.

At a show at The Twenty Grand, Martha met songwriter William "Mickey" Stevenson, who was associated with the budding Motown Records. After hearing the singer's performance, he gave Martha a card and told her to drop by the studio. Thinking this was an invitation for a position as a vocalist, Martha quit her day job and showed up at Hitsville the next morning. To Martha's surprise, Stevenson guessed that she had misunderstood him. There was no place for another singer under his wing at this time. Before the disappointed Martha could say anything, Stevenson asked her to stay for a few minutes to answer the telephone, then disappeared for three hours.

Martha & The Vandellas, sizzling hot after the success of "Heat Wave", 1963, (L-R) Annette, Martha, Rosalind. (Photo courtesy of Rosalind Ashford Holmes)

While Martha stood there, the phone started ringing off the hook, "Mickey told me to stay and answer the phone. About fourteen different writers came in, waiting to use the piano. Then, Benny Benjamin and James Jamerson came in. They said they wanted their money. So I called accounting and said I was the A&R secretary. A lady named Louise Williams said there was no A&R secretary. I told her 'these gentleman want to speak to you'. I spent the whole eight hours there, organizing. From then on, session notes were made."

Martha did such a good job straightening out the office that Clarence Paul came to her house to ask her father if she could continue at the Motown offices. Martha's father would allow her to return only if they agreed to pay her. Motown certainly agreed and Martha knew she had her right foot in the door.

Martha's chance to get the rest of The Vandellas to Motown came in the form of utilizing the group for backing vocals and hand clapping. In 1962, the quartet backed Lamont Dozier on a minor effort entitled "Dearest One," released on Mel-O-Dy Records, a small label Motown had acquired. This led to The Del-Phis having a chance to record a single of their own. Fearing that someone associated with the group's past accomplishments would complain, Motown did not want to take any chances using the name Del-Phis, so they called the group The Vells.

The maiden single was "You'll Never Cherish A Love So True/There He Is (At My Door)." Unlike the other girls, Gloria was married and had two small children. When the single didn't make any noise, Gloria left the group. Since Martha had originally joined The Del-Phis as the second lead, she took over Gloria's spot as lead singer. By the fall of 1962, the group recorded behind singer LaBrenda Ben as The Beljeans and had a few tunes in the can that were not released. They had also been prominently featured on some recordings by an up and coming singer named Marvin Gaye.

The Del-Phis were happy to be a part of the company doing whatever they could to make music. Annette remembers the trio's enthusiasm: "We used to do a lot of filling in of whatever they wanted, hand clapping, foot stomping. It was like, once we went down there, they became familiar with us and we became family to them. We would just go down and hang out. They always needed voices to fill in here or handclaps there. They would pay us five or six dollars per session. At the end of the week, we'd go down and pick up our checks. In the studios, we went where we wanted. We weren't forbidden to go anywhere. Singing became the thing to do after school."

The Del-Phis next shot at recording their own single would come when Mary Wells failed to show up for a recording session. Since the union had a rule that no tracks were to be recorded without a vocalist present, Martha was called out of the office to be in the studio when representatives made a surprise inspection. When Martha saw a spot open up, she called the rest of the group to the studio to record a song called "I'll Have To Let Him Go." Motown realized the potential of this powerful trio who utilized Gospel shouts and responses sung in scorching soprano harmony. The sound of The Del-Phis was much different from the other two female groups at Motown at the time, the hit-making Marvelettes, and another group that was trying to get a hit, but having no luck, The Supremes. One last detail was that the group needed a permanent name and The Del-Phis was no longer an option. Rosalind recounts how the name Del-Phis was permanently dropped, "Somebody came up with this song and we recorded it. Motown didn't want to go through the hassle of finding out if Fred Brown owned the name The Del-Phis. Berry said we couldn't use the name. He gave us half an hour to come up with a new name."

Annette concurs that the decision was ultimately up to Berry Gordy, "He put us in a room and we tossed around lots of names. He poked his head in and said, 'You're going to be called The Vandellas.' We didn't say we didn't like the name. We just went along with it."

At the close of 1962, "Stubborn Kind of Fellow," was released by Marvin Gaye, with the name The Vandellas underneath. Another Marvin Gaye single, "Pride and Joy," also featured The Vandellas, but did not give the group credit on the label. "I'll Have To Let Him Go" was officially released as the first Gordy single of 1963, billed as Martha and The Vandellas, as a nod to Martha's capable lead voice. Martha co-wrote the flip, "My Baby Won't Come Back." Unfortunately, the single did not receive any attention. From here, though, the only place for this group to go was up.

At The Vandellas next recording session, the group worked their magic on some tunes that were tailor made for them. "Jealous Lover" was a wistful ballad and "Come and Get These Memories" showcased the group's spectacular blend. "Come and Get These Memories" climbed into the Top 30, giving the group their first hit. With more pushing, perhaps the single would have gone higher.

Motown thought enough of the single to subsequently release an album of the same title, featuring the hit as well as other popular songs of the day, like "Can't Get Used To Losing You" and "Moments To Remember." Other songs were recorded during the winter months of 1963, a rocking recording called "Spellbound" and another, especially fiery production called "Heat Wave," featuring instrumen-

tation appropriate for a Pentecostal testament. The best was yet to come.

While "Come and Get These Memories" had established The Vandellas as credible artists, the Rock & Roll world was definitely not prepared for the third single released by this cogent trio. The group was busy singing behind other artists, backing Marvin Gaye at live venues and promoting themselves, enjoying the favorable response to "Memories." "Heat Wave" had been held back until the summertime of 1963, when, in the middle of a particularly scorching month of August, this brash single hit the airwaves with the almighty strength and intensity of a meteor shower.

The single was everything its title implied. As the drum breaks into a stride at the beginning of the recording, one is grabbed by the guitar, passed on to the horns and ravaged by the honking, grinding saxophone and shimmering tambourines. The playful drum and guitar break teases the listener before the vocals enter, assailing the mind with a message of burning passion. Martha puts her all into the lead vocal, her voice abounding with incautious impetuosity, revealing all her desires, while the harmonies in the background echo her sentiment. Rosalind's soaring soprano and Annette's equally elevated alto ride high above the melody line, gaining altitude and momentum with every note, like two jet planes breaking the sound barrier.

This was a hot record, and no other record in 1963 sounded like it. Since then, few artists have attempted to capture its intrinsic fervor. Linda Ronstadt successfully paid homage to the song in 1975, but did not venture to recreate the intensity of the original. No artist can aspire to a better delivery of "Heat Wave" than Martha and The Vandellas can.

"Heat Wave" was an unprecedented recording, brought about by the group's association with the talents of Holland-Dozier-Holland. Eddie Holland, Brian Holland, and Lamont Dozier had written songs and produced hits for other artists, but the blending of their talents with the talents of The Vandellas was like a potent mixture of nitroglycerin. Considering the conflagration created by the pairing, saying that it was a match made in heaven would be paradoxical.

Martha & The Vandellas on "Ready, Steady, Go" in England, 1966, (L-R) Rosalind, Betty, Martha. (Photo courtesy of Betty Kelley)

Martha and The Vandellas were now at the forefront of the mounting Motown empire. Their second chart topper was followed by their second LP, "Heat Wave" featuring the hit and premium covers of several popular songs of the day by female artists, like "Just One Look" and "Then He Kissed Me." The Vandellas also showed their softer side on songs like "More" and "Danke Schoen." They appeared on the all-star Motown Revues that traveled on The Chitlin Circuit, wowing audiences in cities all over the map.

Motown wanted to maintain this momentum, so the producers copied the approach used on "Heat Wave." The next single released was the similar and almost as gutsy "Quicksand," followed by "Live Wire," the latter beginning to sound a bit contrived. By early 1964, that particular sound had run its course with "In My Lonely Room," having just enough punch left for Kenny Gamble, Jerry Ross, and Jimmy Wisner to borrow some for their production of "The 81" by Candy and The Kisses. With the advent of The British Invasion, American sounds had to be kept constantly fresh and on the cutting edge. Vandellas records wouldn't disappoint.

By 1964, Martha and The Vandellas were constantly in demand and, therefore, on the road. Annette Beard had married and was now Annette Sterling. The demands of domestic life were upon her. When she became pregnant, Annette had to make a decision. Although Motown encouraged her to stay, Annette opted to leave for obvious reasons, "It was my choice. Actually, I would have stayed in the group longer, but I had gotten pregnant. They said they could make maternity uniforms, but I could not see myself on stage in a maternity outfit. I remember once, a dress that I had on, a zipper unzipped. When I got out of the group, I was four months pregnant with my son."

The group was ready to tour England in the fall, so a replacement for Annette was needed. Berry Gordy looked no further than to his newly acquired female group, The Velvelettes. Since some of the members were still in school and not able to tour, Gordy simply pulled member Betty Kelley out and inserted her into The Vandellas. He thought that she and Annette had a similar stature and complexion. He wanted the change to be subtle. The Velvelettes weren't running at full stride, so this was a favorable opportunity for Betty. After a few months of a trial run, Betty signed a contract to be a Vandella, "I joined The Vandellas in the summer. They had to go to Washington D.C. for a show at The Howard. At first, when I went into The Vandellas, Berry wanted to see whether or not it was going to work, so I was on salary. Then, later on, we signed contracts."

The group certainly didn't miss a beat with Annette's exit and Betty's entry. The hits kept coming. Mickey Stevenson had a song he had written with Marvin Gaye called "Dancing In The Street." Martha had sung the demo and Mickey felt it was a most favorable effort. He had originally intended to give it to his wife, Kim Weston, but Kim didn't care for it, so he took advantage of his initial instinct.

"Dancing In The Street" is said to have been a message to quell the string of riots breaking out in big cities all over America during the turbulent 1960s. It turned out to be the biggest chart hit Martha and The Vandellas had, reaching the top spot. "Dancing In The Street" is a good song and has been honored with many cover versions from all types of genres in rock music, by artists like Van Halen, The Mamas and The Papas, The Grateful Dead, and Mick Jagger with David Bowie. As an example of how quickly things happened in the music world in 1964, Betty's first recording with The Vandellas was "Dancing In The Street," but a picture sleeve released with the single features Annette in the photo. Of course, there was the obligatory sound-alike follow-up, "Wild One." Another LP was in the works. Originally entitled, "Wild One," the third long player by the group was called "Dance Party."

As the popularity for Motown artists grew, the acts eventually outgrew The Motown Revue and were ready to head venues on their own. Martha saw how the packaging had to change, "Thomas "Beans" Bowles had created The Motown Revue. They were three months of endless touring. I was on all three of the tours. Then Motown became too big."

Indeed, it had. With an A-list of 1960s Rock & Roll, Motown needed to create an independent vein for all of its big acts. In addition to Murray the "K" shows and visits to The Apollo and The Uptown Theatres, Martha and The Vandellas also did college dates and shows at The Blue Note and The Twenty Grand in their home base of Detroit. The group was allowed more creative freedom, singing songs like "Canadian Sunset." The trio also sang more ballads, allowing them to demonstrate other facets of their vocal abilities. Betty saw this as a nice change of pace, "College dates were really big back then. We were doing a lot of them. And fraternity dances. It was another side of the coin. We sang supper club songs and sang our slow songs. We did a medley of our dance tunes."

As the 1960s progressed, Martha and The Vandellas scored again and again, continuing in 1965 with the dynamite hit, "Nowhere To Run," which was accompanied by a video of the girls at the Ford factory in Detroit. The tender "Love Makes Me Do Foolish Things" and "My Baby Loves Me" shows Martha's affinity for straightforward ballads as well as flaming dance hits. After a string of milder songs like "What Am I Going To Do Without Your Love" and "Go Ahead and Laugh," The Vandellas were cast right back into their primary mold as the heralds of the hottest vocal dance records. "I'm Ready For Love" can stand alone as a prime example of Martha's ability to handle rock arrangements with a seriously harder edge. Had she so desired, she could have fronted a band like Led Zeppelin. Different facets of augmentation on both instrumental and vocal productions were emerging at Motown, in order to keep up with changing trends.

The way the records sounded was an aspect of mighty importance to Motown. Many groups at the company had the sound of their recordings enhanced by either extra or different backing vocals by The Four Tops or The Andantes. One such recording for The Vandellas was the audience favorite, "Jimmy Mack." Originally recorded by Martha, Rosalind, and Annette back in 1964, a new version was released in late 1966, featuring vocal abilities of The Andantes as well as Martha, Rosalind, and Betty. Martha's normally potent approach is tempered by the treatment of this production. The Andantes are prominent only at the refrain, and one can't miss Rosalind and Betty's high hoots at the end of this buoyant hand clapper. It was well worth the effort to bring the three year-old song out of the vault.

As the dawn of the 1960s had brought changes to the sounds of popular music, so had the late 1960s. Motown Records, in its infancy in 1960, had succeeded and became a rapidly growing commodity. Motown artists in particular had come into their own, burgeoning with the image of the organization. Evidence of this growth came in the form of separating lead singers from their respective groups. The most celebrated was Diana Ross, depicted in the change of the group name from The Supremes to Diana Ross and The Supremes, a foretelling of her imminent departure from the group. Motown also bestowed this honor on Smokey Robinson and Martha Reeves. Having conquered the world of popular music, Motown was now ready for other ventures. Much attention was paid to Diana Ross, readying her for solo stardom, not only in music, but also in film. In 1967, as the names changed, so did the balance of power. No situation stays the same forever. Some artists and producers like Mary Wells, Kim Weston, Mickey Stevenson, and Clarence Paul had left the company and Holland-Dozier-Holland was getting ready to walk due to a personal dispute with

Motown over money and position. Artists like Marvin Gaye and Gladys Knight & The Pips, however, were enjoying much more success during the late 1960s than at the beginning of their careers with Motown. All these factors played a part in the shift in fortunes.

During 1967, The Vandellas had three chart singles. "Jimmy Mack" was very successful, but "Love Bug Leave My Heart Alone" met with mild acclaim. "Honey Child," a bluesy number featuring Martha's emphatic delivery climbed into the Top Twenty in late 1967. Unfortunately, it would be the group's last major hit. Other singles followed in 1968, placing midway on the charts, including a recording that Martha had refused to complete. Martha asked writer/producer Deke Richards to change some lines in the song she felt did not belong. When he refused, she would not go on with the production. To her surprise, she found that Syreeta Wright was brought in to sing the lines Martha had left out, and "I Can't Dance To That Music You're Playing" was released, "I had never before had trouble with a writer changing some lines in a song when I had requested it. But when that single came out, that was a low blow."

Other troubles were mounting in the ranks of The Vandellas. In 1968, Betty Kelley left the group amidst internal conflict and failing health. Martha brought in her sister, Lois, as a replacement. The group carried on with pleasant singles and LPs, but the hits were no longer forthcoming, despite marvelous efforts from producers Richard Morris and Henry Cosby on singles like "Honey Love" and "Sweet Darlin'."

Controversy again hit The Vandellas, this time with Rosalind Ashford's ousting from the group. The Motown office told Rosalind that she was no longer wanted in the group. Martha then recruited Sandra Tilley from The Velvelettes. Since The Velvelettes were virtually not doing much, Sandra had worked briefly as a member of The Orlons, then came to join The Vandellas. A handful of singles followed, including the anti-war anthem, "I Should Be Proud." An early version of "I Want You Back," recorded in late 1968, was held in the can too long. When The Jackson Five scored with the tune, any hope for The Vandellas version was dimmed.

Finally released in early 1972, Martha and The Vandellas version of "I Want You Back" would be their last single, never even reaching the charts. The trio of Martha, Sandra and Lois worked until Motown moved west. By this time, Martha was in dispute with Motown over earnings. She effectively ended her association with Motown, paying back all studio costs. It seemed this was a bitter end to a partnership that had flourished out of enthusiasm, talent and love.

Martha continued recording after leaving Motown, finishing a critically acclaimed LP for MCA Records, with producer Richard Perry, which, unfortunately, never got off the ground. She continued recording during the 1970s for Arista and for Fantasy Records, which released the disco hit "Love Don't Come No Stronger." In 1983, Martha briefly appeared on Motown's Twenty-Fifth Anniversary celebration. In 1995, Martha toured in a production of Fats Waller's "Ain't Misbehavin'" with Janice Singleton and Joan Crawford, two of her backing vocalists. Martha had performed sporadically as a soloist and with her sisters, but is now more visible with the reformed Vandellas. Martha is currently working on a CD of her own compositions and has high hopes for the project, "Some of the subjects I've chosen are from my own creation. It will be an expression of my ideas and descriptions of my feelings."

Betty Kelley moved west after leaving The Vandellas and paid more attention to herself, "When I left The Vandellas, I concentrated on pulling my health together. Then I said I'd try something different. I went to dental hygienists school and worked as a hygienist in California. I worked for Home Savings Bank."

Now retired from the bank and living in California, Betty revels in her role as a Vandella. She appears at autograph parties and gives radio interviews. Betty was the mistress of ceremonies at Sunset Junction; a non-profit organization aimed at youth and designed to keep them off the streets. She works closely with the director, Michael McKinley. The organization hosted The Velvelettes at a street festival in August of 1999. After leaving Motown, Annette Sterling concentrated on raising her family. Today, she is Annette Helton, a medical technician at St. John's Hospital in Detroit. After two years of being a "lady of leisure," as she puts it, Rosalind Ashford Holmes landed a job at Ameritech, where she has been employed for almost thirty years. Sadly, Gloria Williamson passed away in 1999.

In 1988, Rosalind and Annette received a call from Martha, asking if they would accompany her on a tour. There was renewed demand for the original Vandellas. With their families now grown, Annette and Rosalind accepted the offer, to the delight of Vandellas fans everywhere. During the last ten years, Rosalind, Annette, and Martha have appeared at events both in America and abroad.

On a rotating basis, Martha also appears with her sisters Lois and Delphine. All of The Vandellas received their accolades by rightfully being inducted into The Vocal Group Hall of Fame, The Rhythm and Blues Hall of Fame and The Rock & Roll Hall of Fame. All of the ladies view the Motown experience as a wonderful trip, affording them the opportunity to do what they enjoyed, which was singing. Making outstanding recordings and burning up the charts was the calling for Martha and The Vandellas. Their fans are thankful that they answered the call.

Martha And The Vandellas Discography

45s	Label	Number	Year
(as The Del-Phis)			
I'll Let You Know/It Takes Two	Check-mate	1005	1961
Worthless Love/--	Mahs	1001	
No More/The Magic Of Your Love	Cadette	8010	
(as The Vells)			
You'll Never Cherish A Love So True/There He Is	Mel-O-Dy	108	1962
Martha & The Vandellas			
I'll Have To Let Him Go/My Baby Won't Come Back	Gordy	7011	1963

45s

	Label	Number	Year
Come and Get These Memories/Jealous Lover		7014	
Heat Wave/A Love Like Yours		7022	
Quicksand/Darling, I Hum Our Song		7025	
Live Wire/Old Love		7027	
In My Lonely Room/A Tear For The Girl		7031	1964
Dancing In The Street/There He Is		7033	
Wild One/Dancing Slow		7036	
Nowhere To Run/Motoring		7039	1965
Love (Makes Me Do Foolish Things)/You've Been In Love Too Long		7045	
My Baby Loves Me/Never Leave Your Baby's Side		7048	
What Am I Going To Do Without Your Love/Go Ahead and Laugh		7053	1966
I'm Ready For Love/He Doesn't Love Her Anymore		7056	
Jimmy Mack/Third Finger, Left Hand		7058	
Love Bug Leave My Heart Alone/One Way Out		7062	1967

Martha Reeves & The Vandellas

	Label	Number	Year
Honey Chile/Show Me The Way		7067	
Forget Me Not/I Promise To Wait My Love		7070	1968
I Can't Dance To That Music You're Playin'/I Tried		7075	
Sweet Darlin'/Without You		7080	
Honey Love/I'm In Love		7085	1969
Taking My Love/Heartless		7094	
I Should Be Proud/Love, Guess Who		7098	1970
I Gotta Let You Go/You're The Loser Now		7103	
Bless You/Hope I Don't Get My Heart Broke		7110	1971
Your Love Makes It All Worthwhile/In and Out of My Life		7113	
I Want You Back/Tear It Down		7118	1972

(as The Beljeans w/LaBrenda Ben)

	Label	Number	Year
The Chaperone/Camel Walk	Gordy	7009	1962

(as The Del-Phis w/J.J. Barnes)

	Label	Number	Year
Won't You Let Me Know/My Love Came Tumbling Down	Kable	437	1960
Won't You Let Me Know/My Love Came Tumbling Down	Kable	913	
Won't You Let Me Know/My Love Came Tumbling Down	Rich	1005	1961

(as The Del-Phis w/Mike Hanks)

	Label	Number	Year
The Hawk/When True Love Comes To Be	Spartan	401	1961
The Hawk/When True Love Comes To Be	Mahs	0003	
I Think About You/Part 2		0004	

(as The Del-Phis w/Leon Peterson)

	Label	Number	Year
Together Just We Two/Silver and Gold	Kable	438	1960

The Vandellas w/Lee Alan*

	Label	Number	Year
Set Me Free/--	(no label)	94422	1962

The Vandellas w/Marvin Gaye

	Label	Number	Year
Stubborn Kind of Fellow/It Hurt Me Too	Tamla	54068	1962
The Vandellas w/Saundra Mallett			
The Camel Walk/It's Gonna Be Hard Times	Tamla	54067	1962

Martha Reeves

	Label	Number	Year
Power Of Love/Stand By Me	MCA	40194	1974
Wild Night/Stand By Me		40274	
My Man/Facsimile		40329	
This Time I'll Be Sweeter/Love Blind	Arista	0124	1975
Now That We Found Love/Higher And Higher		0160	
The Rest Of My Life/Thank You		0211	1976
You Lost That Lovin' Feeling/Now That We Found Love		0228	1977
Love Don't Come No Stronger/Special To Me	Fantasy	825	1978
Dancing (Skating) In The Streets/When You Came		868	1979
Really Like Your Rap/That's What I Want		887	

LPs

	Label	Number	Year
Come and Get These Memories	Gordy	902	1963
Heat Wave		907	
Dance Party		915	1965
Greatest Hits		917	
Watchout!		920	1966
Martha and The Vandellas Live		925	1967
Ridin' High		926	1968
Sugar 'N Spice		944	1969
Natural Resources		952	1970
Martha & The Vandellas Greatest Hits		--	1975

Martha Reeves

	Label	Number	Year
Martha Reeves	MCA	414	1974

*The Vandellas provided unaccredited backing for Marvin Gaye, Lamont Dozier and Mary Wells.

The Velvelettes

Members:

(1962-64)	(1964-66)	(1984-Pres.)
Caldin (Carolyn/Cal) Gill, Lead	Carolyn Gill	Carolyn Gill (Street)
Mildred (Millie) Gill	Millie Gill	Millie Gill (Arbor)
Norma Barbee	Norma Barbee	Norma Barbee (Fairhurst)
Bertha Barbee	Bertha Barbee	Bertha Barbee (McNeal)
Betty Kelley		
	(1966-69)	
	Carolyn Gill	
	Sandra Tilley	
	Annette Rogers (MacMillan)	

Who says you can't have it all? This female group had the looks, brains, talent, and timing, converging on the most prolific recording company of its time. The Velvelettes were quintessential schoolgirls whose talent paved the way to the most innovative recording company in America. They formed at Western Michigan University in Kalamazoo, Michigan in 1962. After some prompting from the son of a Motown executive, this group signed to the now infamous record label and turned out a most compelling body of singles ever to come out of the Motor City.

Unlike other Motown acts, the young ladies did this while keeping careers outside of the music business, a juggling act that was worthwhile. It also depicts the notion that success is best measured in the self-fulfillment brought about by personal achievement. Bertha and Norma Barbee are two cousins who grew up in Flint, Michigan. Superior vocal ability was a common strand in the Barbee family. Bertha and Norma's uncle, Simon Barbee, was an accomplished singer and songwriter.

Simon needed a group to sing his songs, so he corralled Bertha, Norma and Joyce, a cousin by marriage, to be his backing group, while he sang the lead. The girls were twelve, thirteen and fourteen at the time. The chance to sing with their favorite uncle on his songs was very exciting. After some rehearsing, the group began getting some local gigs both in Flint and the surrounding towns. The group was very well received. Encouraged by the positive response, Simon announced that they were going to record two of his songs, "The Wind" and "Que Pasa." Bertha tells of the events surrounding their first recording: "I

remember my uncle saying that we were going to make a record. He said, 'I want you to meet a producer from Detroit'. He mentioned Berry Gordy, who was only a songwriter at that time. The producer came from Detroit and it was Mickey Stevenson. He was talented, but struggling at that time."

The resulting recording of "The Wind/Que Pasa" was released on the small Stepp Records in 1957. Although the record didn't take off, its presence on local radio netted the group some work. Norma remembers the enjoyment of being a part of The Barbees, but she didn't view singing as a career possibility, just as a chance to exercise the family talent.

"I heard the record played in Flint. It was just something that our uncle led us into, but it was something that we didn't intend to do for the rest of our lives. Our uncle was very, very talented. I was taking voice lessons and piano lessons. We performed at prisons, nursing homes. Not only did we have the ability, but we also made people happy. We did pop tunes and Christmas carols." The isolated recording by The Barbees created a connection that would have far reaching effects, but it would take five years to realize the significance of that connection.

Mildred and Caldin Gill grew up in a large family in Kalamazoo, Michigan, the daughters of a Baptist minister and a nurse. "Millie" and "Cal" got their singing experience from singing in church. When they were not worshiping, the youngsters listened to popular music. Although Rock & Roll and Rhythm & Blues were frowned upon in the Gill household, Cal often stayed up late listening to the radio. Her dad knew, but didn't scold her about it. Cal absorbed every tune she heard, learning the parts to the songs, especially the leads. This talent would later come in handy. Millie had gone off to college, but she would soon call upon Cal's flair for memorizing lyrics.

Bertha was a student at Western Michigan in Kalamazoo in 1961. One evening, Bertha went with her roommates to the Student Union freshman social. Upon her arrival, Bertha noticed a beautiful piano sitting in the corner. Bertha was trained on the piano and her background was in classical music. She sat down to play. Instead of turning out a classical piece, Bertha tried out some rock chords that Joyce had taught her. Rock & Roll was still relatively new, so when people heard the sounds emanating from the piano, they gathered around. One audience member was fellow student, Millie Gill, who hadn't planned on a night of performing; she was just hungry, "I went up to the Student Union to get something to eat. I heard this girl playing the piano. There were other girls listening to Bertha playing piano. Twenty of us started singing. A month later, we sang at an affair. We sang "Ya Ya" by Lee Dorsey."

This informal get-together eventually turned into a regulated ritual, when someone suggested that the chorus become a reality. As the rehearsals increased

The Velvelettes after a performance, 1963, (L-R) Millie, Norma, Cal, Betty, Bertha. (Photo Courtesy of Bertha Barbee McNeal)

and the group became more polished, the group was asked to sing at campus affairs, performing popular songs of the day like, "Twist and Shout." After a time, though, fifteen to twenty voices became too much to handle, so Millie suggested to Bertha that they trim down the group to a more manageable size.

Instead of utilizing the girls singing in this choir, Bertha suggested her cousin, Norma and Millie suggested her sister Cal and Cal's close friend, Betty Kelley. Millie remembers that some of the girls they sang with were not happy about the group's reformation. Cal, Betty, and Norma made the trip to the university by bus on the weekends to rehearse. Norma was in junior college, but Cal and Betty were in their last year in junior high, so they needed their parents' permission. Since big sister would be looking after them, this was no problem.

The newly formed quintet had just weeks to rehearse for a very important appearance. A talent show was coming up at the Alpha Phi Alpha Fraternity. When the group spent the weekend on campus, they stayed with Bertha in the dormitory, then made their way over to the music rooms, where a piano was available for rehearsals. Bertha remembers the theatrics involved in setting the group apart from the rest of the show's acts, "Alpha Phi Alpha was having a talent show, offering twenty-five dollars to the first prize winners. For the show, we wore long, black gloves that went over our elbows. I went over to the piano and took off my gloves one finger at a time, to be sexy. It must have worked, because we won first prize."

After their memorable performance, the yet unnamed group began getting offers to sing at fraternity parties and other socials around the campus. At their first performance as an official group, Robert Bullock, a nephew of Motown chief Berry Gordy, approached the young ladies. Bullock was impressed with their satin sound. He said that his uncle owned a record company that was having success with acts like The Miracles, The Marvelettes and Mary Wells. Cal remembers his enthusiasm when he told them of the company's potential, "Robert Bullock was a student at Western. He approached us about going to Motown. He pointed to records that were lying on the table that the deejay was playing, Tamla and Gordy. He said he would clear a path for us."

Of course the girls had heard of, and were fans of all the popular artists at Motown. They set out to convince their parents to drive them down to Detroit for an audition with the up-and-coming company. It took quite a bit of convincing for Millie and Cal because their parents had to take time off from work to accompany them to Detroit. The girls had said that they had an audition, but in actuality, they were only hoping for an audition, they had no appointment. They had picked out a name for themselves, derived from the positive comments received from various admirers. Cal recollects how the group decided on The Velvelettes, "We already had our name when we came to the audition. We had to get a name before we came to Detroit. It was suggested that we pick a name that sounded like smoothness."

Unfortunately, the trip to Detroit was not so smooth. It was quite a journey, driving in a snowstorm to get to Detroit, because in 1962, the interstate roadway system in the United States was not yet complete. After a long excursion on the highway, sometimes losing their way, The Velvelettes finally arrived at Motown. Upon their arrival, the girls were in awe once they were inside the studio on West Grand Boulevard. They saw Smokey Robinson and Marvin Gaye walking through the lobby. Much to their dismay, they were turned away by a tall, skinny girl named Wanda, who was the receptionist. Even the Rev. Gill was pleading for a chance, considering the risk they took, driving in such foul weather. Bertha recalls the nerve-racking event, "We drove for four hours in a snowstorm and we couldn't find it. When we finally found it, we went in to audition. There was this girl at the desk, chewing gum. We told her we were here to audition. She said, 'I'm sorry, we don't have auditions on Saturday.' We had tears in our eyes

and we were all choked up. We were all set to go out the door, when who comes into the lobby, but Mickey Stevenson, dressed in a sharp suit. He said, 'What are you girls doing here?' We ran over and hugged him. Mickey is responsible for us getting our foot in the door."

Thank goodness that the forces of fate all came together in the lobby that day. Stevenson had recognized Bertha and Norma from his session with them years before. As the group walked past the contrary receptionist, they all gave her little side-glances. Once inside the studios, the girls heard other groups in rooms, rehearsing, preparing to record. Cal recalls the event as a magical experience, "As we walked down the hall, we heard different girls singing. We auditioned with "There He Goes" and "Should I Tell Them."

The Velvelettes planned to audition using their two original songs. Norma had written "There He Goes" and the group collaborated on the endearing ballad, "Should I Tell Them." Bertha played piano and the group sang. Immediately following the audition, Stevenson told them that they were in.

Toward the end of 1962, The Velvelettes began travelling to Detroit to lay down tracks for possible releases. Meanwhile, papers were being drawn up for the girls to sign. Their parents also went into action, concerning the legal aspects of joining Motown. Millie and Cal had an aunt and uncle who lived in Detroit, who provided the attorney who would look over the girls' contracts. Motown was not pleased with this, but the formalities were eventually worked out and The Velvelettes became Motown recording artists in 1963.

The first single scheduled for release was a version of "There He Goes." Not only did Mickey Stevenson produce "There He Goes," he credited himself as the writer. Another Velvelettes composition, "That's The Reason Why," graced the B-side of the single. "There He Goes" features a tender lead vocal by Cal, backed by the group's silky harmony, angelically rising and falling throughout the song, carrying the somber message.

A complementary accent to the song, augmenting its mellow mood, was the use of a harmonica. This accompaniment was provided by a blind, twelve year-old musical prodigy that Motown had under contract. Young Stevie Wonder was anxious to play on The Velvelettes session. In fact, Little Stevie would run rampant through the studios at Motown, insisting that he sit in on recording sessions by all the artists at Motown. The Velvelettes returned the favor by providing vocals for his big hit, "Fingertips." Stevie was a fan of Norma's five-octave range, "I remember sitting at a piano stool with Stevie. He would ask me to hit this note and I would sing it. He used to call me the 'songbird'."

Oddly, when "There He Goes" was released, it was issued on the Detroit based IPG record label, which stood for Independent Producers Group. It is speculated that Motown did not want to take a chance on the group until all legalities were taken care of. In case there was a problem, Motown would not be directly connected to The Velvelettes. Fortunately, their stay at Motown would not only be ongoing, but prolific as well.

Besides being from out of town, The Velvelettes were different from other groups at Motown Records in other ways. Unlike many other acts signed to Motown, the girls all played piano and were able to sight-read music. Another characteristic was that they all were in school when they signed to Motown in 1962.

By 1963, Millie was married, then Norma got married. Bertha, Millie and Norma also had regular jobs. Cal and Betty were still in high school. Their parents stressed that education and self-sufficiency must come first, and the girls were not about to stray from that advice. This "9 to 5" schedule prevented The Velvelettes from touring on a full time basis. They recorded material, but Motown knew that the group could not effectively promote any singles until their schedule permitted. Personal appearances were usually confined to weekends and summers.

In 1964, Motown Records was moving full speed ahead. In addition to the Motortown Review Tours, Motown was sending out the acts separately, because their acclaim was now more widely renowned. Mary Wells had a big hit with "My Guy" in the spring of 1964, and by the end of the summer, The Supremes would take the pop music world by storm with "Where Did Our Love Go," the first of their string of big hits.

Following their first single in1964, Martha and The Vandellas had to find a replacement for Annette Sterling, who had married and was planning to leave the group. Berry Gordy was a stickler for image. He wanted to make sure that few people would notice a change in the group lineup. He thought that substituting girls who had similar features would ensure public integrity. He called Betty to his office to ask her if she was interested in become part of The Vandellas. Betty went to Cal to ask her what she thought. Since The Velvelettes weren't touring because of their schedules, Cal told Betty to grab the opportunity to perform. After rehearsals for a show at The Howard Theater and a summer tour to England, Betty was officially a Vandella. Betty had recorded some sides as a Velvelette, but Motown was not releasing anything by the group. When "Needle In A Haystack" was released in September of 1964, it was from a session recorded by the remaining quartet.

The Velvelettes did finally tour during the summer of 1964, joining Bobby Freeman, The Crystals, The Drifters, The Supremes and Dee Dee Sharp, but it was a prelude of greater things to come. Their first chart single would not be released until the end of this tour. Unlike The Velvelettes first recording, "Needle In A Haystack" came from the songwriting efforts of one of Motown's in-house writing and production teams. Mickey Stevenson and Norman Whitfield, years away from his success with The Temptations, collaborated for this Velvelettes session, which yielded "Needle In A Haystack," a fresh, effervescent dance tune with killer backing vocals from the group, singing the wild and unexpected three part "wah dahs," after the unison. They borrowed the background pattern from a recent Chiffons' hit. Cal's persuasive lead delivers the learned message. The song did well, reaching #45 on the pop charts. Bertha tells how the group had free reign on the vocals, "We were recording with Norman Whitfield, who let us make up our own background. We thought of 'doo doo lang, doo doo lang, like 'He's So Fine'."

Released on Motown's VIP subsidiary, the energetic single was a hit both in America and abroad, prompting producer Tony Hatch to record a version of the song with British Invasion songstress Tawny Reed, released on Leiber and Stoller's Red Bird Records in 1965.

Now with a major hit to their credit, The Velvelettes were on their way. But, if The Velvelettes were going to promote this single, it would have to be as schedules permitted. Millie had to take a leave of absence from her job as a medical technician to be able to participate in the tour, "I took a leave of absence from my job to do the Washington, DC tour. That's when we met Flip Wilson before he was famous. He was also the MC at The Apollo."

Millie was also a mother by this time and often took her daughter to Motown rehearsals. Marvin Gaye did duty as a diaper changer. The lines were clearly drawn between the domestic lives that The Velvelettes were living, certainly not in keeping with the fast-paced lives of many other Motown artists. Sometimes, after witnessing events on the road, The Velvelettes would swear each other to secrecy, fearing what their parents would say or do. Millie remembers one startling incident that unfolded right in the middle of a performance, "We had red roses on our dresses. We were on stage performing, when this man jumped up on the stage and ripped those red roses off our dresses. We didn't miss a beat and kept right on singing."

The next Velvelettes release was "He Was Really Sayin' Something," a confident song with a rocking piano intro and just about the best background hooks Motown ever set to vinyl (bop bop sookie do wah dah). As usual, the superb vocals sell the song, with Cal's courteous, yet sassy vocals. The girls also proved that they could handle ballads with "Should I Tell Them." They further exhibiting this versatility with the heart wrenching "Throw A Farewell Kiss." No one at Motown doubted the vocal prowess of The Velvelettes. When Berry Gordy held his "Battle of the Stars" exhibitions, The Velvelettes often won out over The Supremes. The Velvelettes had the right stuff, but singing would still be secondary to their education. Everyone at Motown had already dubbed them "the college girls." They did get a chance to be in on several tours when the time was right.

The Velvelettes made television appearances on "Shindig" and "Hullabaloo," two popular teen dance shows. They sometimes joined The Dick Clark Caravan of Stars show for appearances on weekends and did full tours in the summer. They also appeared at The Twenty Grand and The Graystone Ballroom in Detroit and at Leo's Casino in Cleveland, a popular venue famous for featuring Motown artists. Once, in Los Angeles, after an engagement at The Roxy, The Velvelettes were invited to the home of Ike and Tina Turner, which Cal remembers as being very lavish. The Velvelettes were hobnobbing with Rock & Roll stars, while still maintaining their weekly schedule of work and school.

In 1965, The Velvelettes released two more moving singles, "Lonely, Lonely Girl Am I," flipped with the light ballad, "I'm The Exception To The Rule" and "A Bird In The Hand," paired with "Since You Been Loving Me," featuring Cal's quivering, emotional lead. During this time period, The Velvelettes often went on tour as a trio. The demands of motherhood kept Millie off the road, and Norma also had a family, so they rotated appearances. Motown was planning to release an album of Velvelettes' material, when Bertha, also married, became pregnant. The responsibilities of family life were now weighing more heavily on the group. Shortly before the release of "A Bird In The Hand," Millie, Norma and Bertha left the group permanently. Cal wanted to continue, so two recruits were needed to fill the spots. Four Tops' member Duke Fakir brought Sandra Tilley to the group. Sandra, a Cleveland native, used to follow the groups, so when the chance to be a part of Motown came, she auditioned. Annette Rogers was from Detroit.

The new Velvelettes recorded versions of "A Bird In The Hand" and another song, "These Things Will Keep Me Loving You." Although they were given release numbers, these versions remained in the can. Despite having two new group mates in The Velvelettes, Motown released the vibrant "These Things Will Keep Me Loving You" by the original lineup in 1966. The company switched both the label (to the Soul subsidiary) and the writing and production team to Harvey Fuqua, Johnny Bristol and Sylvia Moy for what would be the last Velvelettes single. It didn't disappoint, charting high on the R&B charts and capturing everyone's attention in England. Cal, Annette, and Sandra continued recording and making personal appearances into 1967 and 1968.

An interesting fact at this time was, although the original group was out of the picture and adjusting to family life, Norma auditioned for Florence Ballard's spot in The Supremes in 1967, but did not get the job. Cal was dating Richard Street, a former member of The Distants and member of the fellow VIP group, The Monitors. Richard was also in the quality control department of Motown and is credited with the push for Velvelettes singles. As their relationship grew into courtship, the two planned to wed. Even though Cal and her new partners were recording, Motown wasn't following up, "Even though Motown was recording us, they weren't releasing anything on us. I had to go back to business college. Ford Motor Company was recruiting, so I took a job."

Also, Annette Rogers was now Annette MacMillan, and her husband was giving her a hard time about being in show business. Sandra Tilley was subbing as a member of The Orlons. Since work for The Velvelettes was almost at a standstill, Sandra accepted a position as a member of Martha and The Vandellas, replacing Rosalind Ashford. When Cal and Richard tied the knot in 1969, Richard was subbing in The Temptations for the ailing Paul Williams and would eventually become a permanent member. It was agreed that one entertainer in the family was enough. This sequence of events prompted Cal's decision to disband The Velvelettes.

By the 1980s, Motown Records had changed quite a bit, expanding throughout the two previous decades. The material of the groups that pioneered the Motown sound was constantly referenced and repackaged. Many of the Motown stars of the 1960s found lasting fame, but some faltered. The Four Tops, Gladys Knight and The Pips, The Isley Bros. and The Temptations continued to record into the 1990s. With the exception of The Supremes, who recorded for Motown until 1977, none of the female groups found success as entertainers beyond the confines of Motown. Only Martha Reeves had continued to record. This notion rang true for Bertha Barbee McNeal, now a junior high school music teacher in Kalamazoo, until a fateful committee meeting, "I thought we weren't ever going to sing again. I was on the music committee for Concerned Black Women of Kalamazoo. We were putting together a show, documenting women in music through the ages. Someone turned to me and said 'weren't you in a group?' They suggested putting The Velvelettes on the show."

Millie, Norma, Bertha and Cal agreed to do the show, just as a token gesture. What they did not expect was the overwhelming response of their presence on stage. All the members figured that if ever there was a time that fate stepped in to deliver a message, this was it. In 1984, The Velvelettes were officially reformed.

After a series of engagements, including a Motown reunion at The Fox Theater in Detroit, The Velvelettes traveled to England to join other former Motown artists like The Andantes, Brenda Holloway, Carolyn Crawford, and Mary Wilson, to record for Ian Levine's Nightmare Records. The group rerecorded some of their hits, including "Needle In A Haystack," featuring some percussive updates, plus a version of "Come See About Me" and Van McCoy's "That's When The Tears Start." They were released as dance singles and as an LP in Europe from 1988 to 1990. Even though the releases did not make an impact on American shores, the reputation of The Velvelettes was reestablished both as a significant part of the Motown culture and as American recording artists.

The group's resurgence even scared off a bogus group of Velvelettes, performing in Europe under the guise of a misspelled name and singing all the authentic group's hits. The Velvelettes themselves didn't realize their impact until the British group, Bananarama, had a hit with their version of "He Was Really Sayin' Something" in 1982 and acknowledged that The Velvelettes had a direct influence on their career. In 1999, as a further testament to the impact that the group has as a resurgent attraction, Motown Records released a CD compilation of Velvelettes material, including all their hits, plus a few unreleased gems. Motown boasts more unreleased Velvelettes material in the vaults, awaiting future release.

After their stay at Motown, all the members of The Velvelettes chose other career paths, in addition to raising families. Millie Gill Arbor became a registered nurse, Norma Barbee Fairhurst is a director of sales for Radisson Hotels, Carolyn Gill Street is a coordinator at Upjohn Laboratories and Bertha Barbee McNeal is a music teacher and choir director at a junior high school in Kalamazoo, Michigan. Betty Kelley moved west, worked in the medical field for awhile, then became a bank executive until her retirement.

Sadly, Sandra Tilley died of complications resulting from a brain tumor in 1985. Millie, Norma, Bertha and Cal are now traveling around, performing and revisiting places where they performed in the 1960s. Shortly after their reunion, they performed at a show with other Motown artists at Leo's Casino, honoring the owner for his years of supporting the acts that kept his business on top.

In August of 1999, The Velvelettes participated in a festival hosted by Sunset Junction in Los Angeles, a non-profit organization that provides guidance counseling for young people. The Velvelettes are considering holding workshops for young people who aspire to careers in entertainment. Norma puts it succinctly when she tells how her experiences have enabled her to put many things into perspective and how the group would like to pass on that experience to others, "The Velvelettes are very important to me, they are a part of my life. It certainly made a big difference in my character and made me a better person. It was a part of my learning process. I want to spend my life sharing what I learned."

Perhaps The Velvelettes were not as celebrated as a group like The Supremes, but they certainly embodied what Motown Records was all about a sincere, unique sound, a sound that no one was able to copy, a sound that brought people together and made them feel good. The recording stars that built the Motown empire created the pulsating sounds of a generation. The Velvelettes are "no exception to the rule."

The Velvelettes Discography

45s

	Label	Number	Year
The Barbees			
Que Pasa/The Wind	Stepp	236	1957
The Velvelettes			
There He Goes/That's The Reason Why	IPG	1002	1963
Needle In A Haystack/Should I Tell Them	VIP	25007	1964
He Was Really Saying Something/Throw A Farewell Kiss		25013	
Lonely, Lonely Girl Am I/I'm The Exception To The Rule		25017	1965
A Bird In The Hand/Since You've Been Loving Me		25030	
These Things Will Keep Me Loving You/Since You've Been Loving Me	Soul	35025	1966
Needle In A Haystack/remix	Nightmare	28	1988
Running Out Of Luck/Dub Mix		60	
Pull My Heartstrings/remix		116	1989

LPs

	Label	Number	Year
One Door Closes	Motorcity	43	1990

CDs

	Label	Number	Year
The Very Best of The Velvelettes	Motown	31454 95072	1999

The Veneers

Members:

(1959-63) Barbara Joyner
Lorraine Joyner
Annette Swinson (Smith)
Valerie Swinson

(1964) Lorraine Joyner
Barbara Joyner
Valerie Swinson

The Veneers made only a handful of recordings together, but, as the old saying goes, quality is better than quantity. These four relatives knew how to record melodious sounds together. The Veneers came from Manhattan and from Brooklyn, in New York City. Sisters, Lorraine and Barbara Joyner, joined their cousins Valerie and Annette Swinson, to sing in the park for fun and at family functions. Lorraine explains that she and Barbara looked forward to spending time with their cousins, because they got to sing, "My sister and I lived on the Lower East Side of Manhattan and Annette and Valerie were from Brooklyn. They would come and spend holidays with us. We were very close; we grew up together. Our mothers, Annabelle Swinson, and Millie Joyner, were sisters."

In the late 1950s, Manhattan teenagers were imitating sounds they heard on the radio. Running into the subway to get a perfect echo for a cappella singing was common among young men who liked harmonizing voices. Since the advent of female groups like The Queens, Cookies, Chantels, Bobbettes and Shirelles, it was now both acceptable and fashionable for their counterparts to do the same.

The cousins' ability and desire to sing was inherent. Annabelle Swinson had been part of a singing group called The Ginger Snaps. Annabelle and Millie also sang together with their other sisters at holiday time, singing spirituals like "The Lord's Prayer." Annabelle encouraged her girls to sing and even coached them for awhile. As a young girl, Annette was fortunate enough to gain exposure on television. Lorraine relates how her mother was instrumental in gaining Annette's appearance on a renowned show, "My mother wrote such a sensitive letter to the 'Paul Whiteman Show' and got an answer. Then, the whole family was screaming and yelling. They called Annette for an audition. It was the week before Christmas."

In addition to a few featured spots on local shows, Annette was featured in a show staged in celebration of the retirement of world middleweight boxing champ, Sugar Ray Robinson. At a 1951 Christmas show at The Apollo, Annette performed in a skit where she sat on Santa Claus' lap, telling him what a good girl she was and what she deserved for Christmas. Santa told her that he would grant her wish if she sang a song for him. On cue, Annette sang a version of "Pretend You're Happy When You're Blue." The audience was impressed. After the show, Sugar Ray exclaimed that he wouldn't touch that song after hearing Annette sing it.

As a young adult, Annette's vocal capabilities became quite diverse. Her singing talents came directly from Annabelle. Her deliberate phrasing, supple movement and reserved power, enabled her to sing all types of styles. This endowment would net her a chance to step into various roles with almost no effort.

As for singing in the family quartet, Annette's lead, combined with the versatile harmonies of Valerie, Barbara, and Lorraine, the yet unnamed group was quickly becoming a local attraction, "We would get free canoe rides in camp because the counselors would grab us and make us sing. Everyone would discover our music. Community centers would gather us up. They would pass money and say 'we'll give you a dollar if you sing'. We used to sing modern jazz like The Hi-Los. 'Summertime', that Annette recorded with The Chantels, was our arrangement."

The young teens' singing began getting the attention of local songwriters looking for recording artists. As The Swensons (sic), Annette and her mother recorded one single for X-Tra Records in 1957, entitled, "Remember Me To My Darling." The single did not gain much radio attention, but furthered the talk of the talented young ladies. A short time later, a young man came to call on the group. Lorraine remembers his first visit, "Eddie Jones came to our house. He introduced himself, saying 'I am in show business'. He's the one who took us to Richard Barrett."

Eddie was a songwriter and the former lead singer of The Demens who wrote and recorded "Take Me As I Am". He also sang with The Emersons, who recorded "Joanie, Joanie." Eddie was now playing piano, arranging, and co-writing songs with his friend, Richard Barrett. Barrett is the man responsible for the rise of vocal groups like Frankie Lymon and The Teenagers, The Chantels and his own Valentines. He was also George Goldner's right hand man in the End-Gone-Gee complex of labels before they were bought out by Roulette. Richard and Eddie were now producing records independently and striking deals with interested labels. In 1959, the quartet, now known as The Cashmeres, recorded a novelty tune with Eddie called, "Daddy Can I Go To The Hop?" Herb Abramson, founder of Jubilee and Atlantic Records, produced the single. Abramson had left Atlantic about a year prior and was now freelancing. Unfortunately, the single was not released.

In 1960, The Cashmeres were being produced and managed by Richard Barrett. He had written two songs for the group, "Believe Me (My Angel)" and "I." At this time, the young ladies decided to change their name because too many groups had already recorded under the name "Cashmeres." They wanted a name that showed off their polish, they chose the name "Veneers."

Two songs were recorded and released on Barrett's short-lived Princeton Records. The double-sided ballad showcases Annette's full, stalwart lead. She had earned the nickname "Pepper" because her voice was thought of as "hot, like pepper." The record achieved a level of success in New York, but failed to chart nationally. The single secured The Veneers a successful run of live per-

The Veneers, backstage at The Celebrity Club in Freeport, LI, 1960, (clockwise from top) Annette Swinson Smith, Valerie Swinson, Barbara Joyner, Lorraine Joyner. (Photo courtesy of Lorraine Joyner/Jerry Zwecher)

formances in and around the New York area. Lorraine's mother worked diligently on the group's costumes for these appearances. Since saving money was a consideration, Millie Joyner put her talents as a seamstress to good use, "My mother would cash her bill money orders just to get us shoes. We would get satin shoes, glue glitter onto them and you couldn't tell the difference. My mother would make all of our clothes. She would copy the pattern of expensive dresses and make our clothes."

Even though "Believe Me" gained attention, Annette was disappointed, thinking that she could have improved on her performance. She had high hopes for the record. Her chance to achieve another level of success would soon be upon her.

The Chantels had stopped recording in 1959. They had been released from their contracts when End Records was sold to Roulette. The group finished their education and some members went into private business. During 1960, no Chantels group existed, although End Records released a single. In 1961, Richard Barrett wrote a song for The Chantels, and he gathered three of the original young ladies together to hear it. Jackie Landry, Sonia Goring, and Renee Minus agreed that this song would make its mark.

They wanted Arlene Smith, the original lead on their previous records, to join them, but she was contractually bound to another project. Richard thought it viable to take Annette from The Veneers and place her as the lead singer of the regrouped Chantels. Annette rehearsed with The Chantels until they achieved the required sound. Richard's arrangement worked beyond everyone's expectations. "Look In My Eyes" was a phenomenal success that put The Chantels back on the top of the charts for the first time in three years.

Although The Veneers were not entirely happy about this change of plans, they knew that they could not stop Annette, who needed to be out on the stage. In 1961, she officially joined The Chantels. With Annette as the new lead for the renowned Chantels, the group recorded three singles for Carlton Records, topping it off with an LP entitled, "The Chantels On Tour," featuring the group and other artists like Little Anthony and The Imperials and former Del Viking, Gus Backus. The group's second single, "Well I Told You," was an answer record to Ray Charles' "Hit The Road Jack" and featured Richard Barrett as the ousted male. This single also climbed high on the pop charts. The Chantels' renewed success prompted Roulette Records to lease and release The Veneers' Princeton single as a Chantels single.

"Believe Me/I" also appeared on a Chantels LP, entitled "There's Our Song Again," along with other, previously released Chantels recordings. The group toured incessantly, amazingly amidst marriages and pregnancies. One tour in particular featured one of Annette's idols, Duke Ellington. On this tour, the group performed a version of "Autumn Leaves." This did not make Ellington happy, as he had an interpretation of the song in his act. Though, after hearing The Chantels' on stage, he had to impart his approval of their rendition.

Annette Smith recorded one more single with The Chantels in 1962, the expressive, "Here It Comes Again," flipped with a pensive rendition of Gershwin's "Summertime," an arrangement originally sung by The Veneers. This tune revealed Annette's potential as a jazz singer. After a year of recording and touring, Annette departed The Chantels to start a family and was replaced by the rotating roster of subbing Chantels, Yvonne Fair, and Helen Powell, although by 1963, Sandra Dawn was featured on the two recordings produced for Luther Dixon's Ludix label. In 1963, Annette rejoined her Veneers for one more ingratiating single, "With All My Love." Annette also worked with producers Burt Bacharach and Teddy Randazzo before leaving the business.

In 1964, The Veneers, without Annette, recorded as The Relatives for the Canadian-American related Almont Records, with Lorraine taking the lead for "Never Will I Love You Again." The trio worked for a time in the entertainment field, appearing as Jackie Wilson's Wilsonettes, on some of his live shows. They also worked with artists like Gloria Lynne and recorded with Titus Turner on "The Return of Staggerlee." Lorraine also did studio work on her own, "I did some demo work with a girl named Denise Gorme, who needed some direction. I sang some parts, showing her how to sing, so the producers said, 'Lorraine, why don't you sing it yourself?' The tune was 'Johnny Casanova'." Lorraine recorded the tune, leaving the artist's name on the production. For a time, Lorraine continued in the music business before turning her priorities elsewhere.

Today, Valerie Swinson lives in the New York area, working for Harlem Hospital. Barbara Joyner was married to Eddie Jones until her death in 1972. Her torch in the entertainment field is carried by her daughter, Milira, who in 1990, recorded a version of Marvin Gaye's "Mercy Mercy Me" for the Apollo/Motown label. She is now recording and producing a CD of spirituals on her own Arilim Records.

In 1995, Annette Smith was given an award with the rest of The Chantels at Ronnie I's United In Group Harmony Hall of Fame Ceremonies, held at Symphony Space in New York. It was there that Annette met producer Jerry Zwecher, who encouraged Annette to record again. Zwecher produced a compilation CD featuring Annette with a new group called Rendezvous. Her recording of "Moonlight" captures the feel of earlier R&B recordings. In August of 1999, Annette recounted her days as a Veneer and a Chantel on Don K. Reed's Doo Wopp Shop on WCBS-FM, in New York.

Lorraine Joyner is now employed as a social worker in New York City. Lorraine is also the newest member of The Clickettes, joining original members Barbara Jean English, Trudy McCartney-Cunningham, and Sylvia Hammond Akridge. The longing to sing has returned, but in reality, never really went away. Lorraine gives credit to her mother and aunt, and especially to Eddie Jones for guiding The Veneers and looking out for them during their glory days. For The Veneers, singing together was one of the strongest family ties, and everyone knows that family ties are the ties that bind.

The Veneers Discography

45s	Label	Number	Year
The Veneers			
Believe Me (My Angel)/I	Princeton	102	1960
With All My Love/Recipe Of Love	Treyco	402	1963
(as The Chantels)			
Believe Me (My Angel)/I	End	1104	1961
(The Chantels w/Annette Smith)			
Look In My Eyes/Glad To Be Back	Carlton	555	1961
Well I Told You/Still		564	
Summertime/Here It Comes Again		569	1962
(as The Relatives)			
Never Will I Love You Again/I'm Just Looking For Love	Almont	306	1964
My Heart Goes Zigga Zigga Zoom/I'm Just Asking For Love	Almont	303	1964
The Swensons			
Remember Me To My Darling/Golly Boo	X-Tra	100	1957
Annette Smith (as Annabelle Fox & Doris)			
Lonely Girl/Little Boy Go Away	Spin	--	1964
Getting Through To Me	Satin	400	1965

LPs	Label	Number	Year
The Cashmeres w/Eddie Jones			
R&B Laff Blasts From The Past			
Daddy, Can I Go To The Hop (rec. 1959)	Red Lightnin'	0059	1959
(as The Chantels)			
There's Our Song Again (2 cuts)	End	312	1961
(The Chantels w/Annette Smith)			
The Chantels On Tour	Carlton	144	1962
Arlene Smith And The Chantels	Murray Hill	000385	1987

CDs	Label	Number	Year
Moonlight – Annette Smith & Rendezvous	Chicago	CD200	1997

Beverly Warren

The early 1960s New York music scene is known as the Brill Building era, where many songwriters were crammed together inside cubicles in several offices, trying to come up with the next big hit. Many were successful. Several recording artists would forever be associated with these hitmakers. One formidable artist who made her mark while working with the best, and releasing consistently premium product.

Beverly Warren was born in Gary, Indiana and moved to New York City when she was a year and a half. Beverly knew she had a talent for singing, because every time she sang, people paid attention, "I never knew I could sing because I always sang. Singing was just like breathing in and out. It was always there."

While in school, Beverly pursued her innate sense of musicianship by auditioning for the school band. Everyone else she knew was taking up an instrument, namely the clarinet. Since there were no more clarinets when it was Beverly's turn to audition, she accepted the flute. This outlet enabled Beverly to shine at something she liked, in spite of her shyness.

For enjoyment, Beverly listened to her favorite artists on the radio like Frankie Lymon, The Marvelettes, and The Blue Belles. She also favored Latin tunes. As Beverly's ability to sing emerged, her talent landed her in a series of groups around her Queens neighborhood. The other girls in the crowd resented Beverly because she was attractive and she was in the thick of where they wanted to be…right along side their boyfriends.

Beverly sang with many ad hoc groups consisting of varying personnel. Sometimes one configuration had the sound that would take them to the next level. One group from Astoria

BEVERLY WARREN   Professional Management
                     Seymour Barash
                     1 Hanson Place, Brooklyn, N.Y. 11217
                     NE 8-9777

Beverly Warren, 1965. (Photo courtesy of Beverly Warren)

that had made it past the casual stage was The Devotions, who recorded "Rip Van Winkle" in 1961. So many of the other groups longed to follow on their heels. Beverly sang with various makeshift groups in Long Island City, at Pops Candy Store by Long Island City High School. Beverly often traveled to other neighborhoods to sing with other groups. One of these impromptu groups meshed enough to prompt the quintet to go into Manhattan, looking for a recording deal. Ricky and The Hallmarks were from Sunnyside, Queens.

The group, consisting of Beverly and four guys, were singing under the elevated train, when they were heard by a gentleman who admired their sound. That gentleman was songwriter and producer Bert Berns, who had written "A Little Bit of Soap" for The Jarmels and "Twist and Shout" for The Isley Bros. He asked that the group meet him to audition for songwriters Ellie Greenwich and Jeff Barry. Beverly remembers that Ellie had the group stand in a room while she tested their abilities to sing. There were other artists in the studio working on other projects at the same time, "In the room was a snare drum. Somebody told me that the Coasters were rehearsing nextdoor. The bass singer's voice was so powerful, that from the next room, he made the snare drum vibrate."

In turn, the group was introduced to Jerry Leiber and Mike Stoller. The songwriters who brought The Coasters to the music world were producing acts with Jerry Ragovoy. After working with Greenwich on possible songs, the group proceeded to the recording studio. There were two songs selected, "Like A Million Years," with Ricky leading and another, "It Was Me Yesterday," with Beverly on lead. When the group reached the studio, to everyone's surprise, Beverly was asked to sing lead on Ricky's tune. Beverly nervously sang, not quite knowing how to handle this turn of events. She sang the song like a country tune. The producers said they liked the songs and wanted Beverly, but not the group. The other members left the studio, leaving teenage Beverly on her own. Beverly was then assigned to Leiber and Stoller as her producers and Ellie Greenwich and Jeff Barry as her managers. Ricky and The Hallmarks eventually recorded "Joanie Don't You Cry" for Amy Records in 1963.

Beverly's first assignment was to record "It Was Me Yesterday" and "Like A Million Years." Greenwich had originally auditioned "It Was Me Yesterday" for Phil Spector. Having just met Ellie, he paid no attention to the tune, so Ellie had this song for use by Beverly. The single was released on United Artists Records in the spring of 1963. Beverly recalls King Curtis playing on the session. She also remembers standing in the cavernous vocal booth to sing her lead. This exciting experience was still just fun to her.

The groups that usually backed Beverly at this time on record were The Cookies and The Bobbettes. Beverly remembers how encouraging The Cookies were at one of the shows where they were both appearing. Despite positive attitudes all around, Beverly's first single did not take off. She continued to be the typical teenager, going to school during the week, but rehearsing and planning for more recordings on the weekends.

Beverly was now busy cutting demos with Ellie and her new husband, Jeff Barry. Beverly's clear, enticing voice was soon to be used for a vehicle that Ellie and Jeff had kind of fallen into while writing a possible follow-up for a Philadelphia group, The Sensations. Ellie and Jeff had produced a demo of a song called "What A Guy" with Ellie singing all the vocals except bass, which Jeff sang. When Leiber and Stoller heard it, they insisted on releasing it, issuing the single on Jubilee Records. "What A Guy" made the Top 40, climbing even higher in New York. The Raindrops are now in demand, but there is no group. Ellie quickly commissioned her sister, Laura, and shy Beverly to be the road Raindrops. Beverly remembers Ellie calling her and asking if she was interested, "I remember Ellie phoning me and saying 'Beverly, do you want to be a Raindrop?' And I answered 'sure, what's a raindrop?' Ellie had to be my guardian on the road."

Now, as well as her solo career, Beverly was the road crew for a "group" which would have six successful singles between the fall of 1963 and early 1965. Bob Bosco was recruited to sing bass, as Jeff was not interested in performing. Since The Raindrops were successful, there was no big push to be Beverly Warren. Despite "It Was Me Yesterday" being a wonderful record, it garnered no airplay. Beverly's main job now was to be a Raindrop, and that was only on the weekends.

Even though Ellie and Jeff tried to write a song that would put Beverly on top of the charts, it seemed elusive. Beverly remembers that Ellie would rehearse her, having her sing Mary Wells' "You Beat Me To The Punch." Try as they might, the duo never came up with material for Beverly that they felt was ready for release. Beverly was interested in a tune that Ellie had sitting on the piano, "Ellie had this old piece of paper with coffee stains and cigarette burns on it. I would sing the tune and ask Ellie if I could record it. She said no, that wasn't for me."

The song that seemed to be languishing on the piano turned out to be "Look Of Love"; a big hit for Lesley Gore, one of two songs written for her by Greenwich and Barry. Beverly dutifully made her appearances as a Raindrop, performing in Philadelphia and Chicago with other notables as The Rocky Fellers, The Volumes, Johnny Thunder and Linda Scott. Of course, being on the road was grueling, but not as nerve-racking as a memorable performance at New Jersey's Palisades Amusement Park, "I remember Cousin Bruce Morrow coming over to ask me my name. He was famous and I was so nervous. We had to do a dance step, crossing one leg over from side to side, wearing stiletto heels. I got my heel caught in a wooden slat and I couldn't move. I kept pulling my foot, but it wouldn't come out. I kept swaying back and forth, but I was stuck. I was so embarrassed. I felt like a big deal signing autographs, but Monday I was back at school."

Beverly's excursion as a Raindrop ended when the singles stopped coming. Jeff and Ellie's attention focused more on their work at Red Bird Records. Beverly then began her association with The Tokens' Bright Tunes Productions and a management association with Seymour Barash. The Tokens made several recordings with Beverly between 1965 and 1967. Beverly recorded the marvelous "Let Me Get Close To You," a tune written by Carole King and Gerry Goffin. The Tokens released this single on the Laurie Records subsidiary, Rust Records. Beverly's subsequent releases were issued on The Tokens' own B.T. Puppy Records. One novelty single, "Would You Believe," modeled on a saying by Don Adams' character in the television series, "Get Smart," did make some noise in the New York area, landing Beverly a spot on "The Clay Cole Show."

Beverly was put through the star-making process. Beverly remembers the grooming tips she was given. No heavy makeup or teased hair was to be worn. She was even sent to a cosmetologist, but didn't like the way her hair was done or her makeup was applied, so she did it herself, much to the dismay of Seymour Barash, who wanted her to go for the natural look. Beverly also had the chance to be a part of Italy's San Remo Festival, but somehow the arrangement fell through. Beverly followed "Would You Believe" with a marvelous version of The Chiffons' hit, "He's So Fine," but with no lasting success, Beverly and The Tokens ended their collaboration in 1967.

Beverly continued her career in music, making personal appearances in clubs and committing to session work. She recorded radio jingles, including the memorable Dodge Rebellion commercials for Chrysler Corporation. During the late 1960s and 1970s, Beverly did much travelling. She lived in various parts of the country, including Miami, Buffalo, New Orleans, and parts of Canada. Beverly hooked up with a New Orleans act called Vince Vance and The Valiants.

She is part of the ensemble of Valianettes, Valerie, Veronica, and Vicki (Beverly is Valerie). This band did well touring the country, playing to appreciative crowds familiar with the band's prowess. To this day, Beverly has standing club dates with The Valiants. As an artist and entertainer, Beverly continued to absorb all different styles evolving within popular music. Beverly became especially influenced by the compositions of singer/songwriter Laura Nyro, taking to heart Nyro's introspective lyrical approach.

In the late 1970s, Beverly returned to the New York area, and sang with various local bands like The Jerry Lawrence Band and Peggy Senders and The Stepsisters. Beverly eventually joined a group of singers that she knew from the old days at Pops Candy Store in Queens, called The Blendaires.

She and fellow members Larry Galvin, Sam Wood, Al Vieco and singer/arranger Jack Scandura had graduated from the simplistic harmonies of their youth to a more sophisticated, close harmony. They worked very hard, recording songs for Roy Adams' Story Untold Records and appearing with Don K. Reed on WCBS-FM. Once that group had disbanded, Beverly continued with her session work, expanding her range with Gospel, Country and dance-oriented music. Beverly also returned to singing in clubs, performing her jazz favorites as well as popular tunes.

Today, Beverly is Vice President of Sales at Jerry Kravat Entertainment in New York City. She provides guidance for other artists as she was guided. Beverly has sung with many local New York groups including the notable a cappella group, Brooklyn Queens Expressway (BQE). Beverly is currently a vocalist with The Tercels. Beverly has become an accomplished blues and jazz vocalist as well as having an excellent track record as a pop vocalist. A love of singing and a desire to entertain keeps Beverly Warren ensconced in the fabric of popular music.

Beverly Warren Discography

45s	Label	Number	Year
It Was Me Yesterday/Like A Million Years	United Artists	543	1963
Let Me Get Close To You/Baby, Baby Hullabaloo	Rust	5098	1965
Would You Believe/So Glad You're My Baby	B.T. Puppy	521	1966
He's So Fine/March		526	
(with The Blendairs)			
Shouldn't I/Gee Whiz	Story Untold	501	1978
I Beg For Your Love/Don't Leave Me		503	1982
LPs			
Side By Side – Andrea Carroll and Beverly Warren	B.T. Puppy	1017	1970

Appendix: Female Groups From A-Z

*(A comprehensive listing of female rock & roll groups
(1950s–1990s) and their respective record labels.)*

Name	Label
1. Accents	Karate
2. Accents, Sandi & the	Charter/Challenge/Commerce/ CRC
3. Adorables	Golden World
4. Adorables	Peacock
5. Affections, Judy & the	Dode/Top Ten
6. Afternoon Delights	MCA
7. Alexys	Dot
8. Allisons	Smash
9. Allison Sisters	Vellez
10. All Saints	London
11. Allure	Crave
12. Allures	Melron
13. Ambers	Todd
14. American Spring	Columbia {Ginger & The Snaps/ Honeys/Spring}
15. Andantes	Motown/VIP {Darnells}
16. Angelettes	Josie
17. Angelettes	London
18. Angelos	Tollie/Vee Jay
19. Angels	Ascot/Caprice/Smash/ Polydor/RCA {Delicates/Dusk/Halos/ Starlets}
20. Angel Sisters	Cue
21. Angorians	Donna/Tishman
22. Antoinetts	Karen
23. Antwinetts	RCA
24. Apollas	Loma/Warner Bros.
25. Apollonia 6	Motown/Warner Bros.
26. April, May & June	RCA
27. Aprils	Ran Dee
28. Arketts, Argie & the	Ronnie
29. Arnells	Roulette
30. Arvettes	Ideal
31. Atlantics	Marquee
32. Attractions	B&B
33. Attractions	June Bug
34. Attractions	Main Attraction
35. Aubry Twins	ABC
36. Austin Sisters	Edison International
37. Avalons	Dice {Clickettes/Loreleis}
38. Avons	Abet/Groove/Ref-O-Ree/ Sound Stage 7
39. Azaleas	Romulus
40. Babes In Toyland	Reprise/Sub Pop
41. Babies	Dunhill
42. Baby Dolls	Boom
43. Baby Dolls	Gamble/Maske/Elgin/RCA/ Warner Bros.
44. Baby Dolls	Hollywood
45. Back Beats, Terri Cirell & the	Veko
46. Baker Sisters	Mercury/RKO Unique
47. Bananarama	London
48. Band Aids, Suzanne & the	Liberty/Trump
49. Band Of Angels	Mums
50. Bangles	Columbia/Down Kitty {Bangs}
51. Bangs	Down Kitty {Bangles}
52. Barbara & Brenda	Avanti/Heidi
53. Bardeau	Enigma
54. Barry Sisters	Cadence/Colpix/Roulette
55. Basic Black Pearls	Polydor
56. Beach Girls	Dynovox/Vault
57. Beas	Chattahoochee/Dee Gee
58. Beatle-ettes	Assault/Jamie/Jubilee
59. Beau Belles	Arrow/Planet
60. Bedwells	Del-Fi
61. Beechwoods	Smash
62. Bees, Honey & the	Pentagon

Name	Label
63. Bees, Honey & the	Acadamy/Arctic/Bell/Chess/ Josie/North Bay
64. Belgianetts	Ember/Okeh/USA
65. Belginetts	Cheer
66. Believers, Barbara & the	Capitol
67. Bel Jeans, LaBrenda Ben & the	Gordy
68. Belle Aires	RCA
69. Belle Stars	Stiff
70. Belles, Glorious Wilson & the	Choice/Fairbanks
71. Belles	Mirwood
72. Belles, Terry & the	Ducky/Hanover/Vernon
73. Bell Sisters	Bermuda
74. Bennetts	Amcan
75. Bermudas	Era
76. Betty & Karen	MGM
77. Beverly Sisters	Mercury
78. Bey Sisters	Decca/Jaguar/King
79. Big Town Girls, Shirley Matthews & the	Atlantic
80. Big Trouble	Epic
81. Bikini Kill	Kill Rock Stars
82. Birdies	CRC
83. Birds	Sue
84. Birds Of A Feather	DJM/Page One
85. Bits O' Honey, Sharon &	Penthouse
86. Bits Of Honey	Shout
87. Bittersweets	Cameo/Tema
88. B-Girls	Bomp
89. Blackgirl	RCA
90. Black Magic	Avco
91. Black Pearls	Tupelo Sound
92. Black Velvet	Black Top
93. Blaque	Columbia
94. Blended Spice	Queen Bee
95. Blenders	Witch {Blenders, Goldie Coates & the}
96. Blenders, Goldie Coates & the	Cortland {Blenders}
97. Blends	Talent
98. Blondettes	MGM
99. Blossoms	Bell/Capitol/Challenge/Classic Artists/EEOC/Epic/Lion/ MGM/Ode/Okeh/Reprise {Bob B. Soxx & The Blue Jeans/Coeds/Crystals/ Dreamers/Girlfriends/ Hushabyes, Hale & the/ Playgirls/Rollettes/Wildcats}
100. Blue Angels	Crazy
101. Blue Angels	SSS International {Butterflys/ Buttons}
102. Blue Orchids	London
103. Blue Belles	20th Century Fox
104. BlueBelles (Early)	Atlantic
105. BlueBelles, Patti LaBelle & the	Atlantic/Newtown/Nicetown/ King/Parkway {Labelle}
106. Bluebelles	Newtown/Peak/Rainbow {Original Bluebelles/Starlets}
107. BlueJeans, Bob B. Soxx & the	Philles {Coeds/Crystals/ Dreamers/Girlfriends/ Hushabyes, Hale & the/ Playgirls/Rollettes/Wildcats}
108. Bo-Bells, Jackie Burns & the	MGM {Raindrops, Jackie & the}
109. Bobbettes	Atlantic/Diamond/End/ Galliant/Gone/Jubilee/ King/Mayhew/RCA/Triple X {Sophisticated Ladies/Soul Angels}
110. Bobbi-Pins	Mercury
111. Bobby Pins	Okeh
112. Body	MCA

Name	Label
113. Bohemians	Chex
114. Bon Bons	Apollo
115. Bon Bons	Columbia/Coral/London
116. Bon Bons	Samson
117. Bon Bons, Bee Gee Kay & the	Dore
118. Bones	Jet
119. Boney M	Atco/Sire
120. Bongi & Judy	Buddah/Epic
121. Bonnets	Unical
122. Bonnie Sisters	Rainbow
123. Bookends	Capitol
124. Boomerang	Atlantic
125. Boone Girls	MGM
126. {Boones}	
127. Boones	Warner Bros. {Boone Girls}
128. Bootiques	Date
129. Boquets	Vest
130. Bouquets	Blue Cat/Mala {Bouquets, Tootie &}
131. Bouquets, Tootie & the	Parkway {Bouquets}
132. Boyd Sisters	Roulette
133. Boys	Kama Sutra
134. Boystown Gang	Moby Dick
135. BPS Revolution	Jewel
136. Bracelets	Congress
137. Bracelets	20th Century Fox
138. Brand New Faces	Lujuna
139. Brandye	Kayvette
140. Breakaways	Cameo
141. Breeders	4 AD/Elektra
142. Breeze	Fantasy
143. Brentwoods	Talent
144. Brides of Funkenstein	Casablanca {Par-Let}
145. Brigidi Sisters	Chancellor
146. Bronzettes	DoubleSoul/Parkway
147. Brood	Dionysus/Estrus/Get Hip/ Skyclad
148. Brooktones	Coed
149. Brother Sisters	Mercury
150. Brownettes	King
151. Browns, Barbara & the	Cadet/Stax/Wilmo/XL
152. Brown Sisters	Golden Crest
153. Brownstone	Epic/MJJ
154. Brown Sugar	Bullet/Capitol/Chelsea {Raeletts}
155. Brown Sugar, Co Co &	Vestpocket
156. Bunnies	Roomate
157. Burners, Allison Gary & the	Royo
158. Burns Sisters Band	Columbia
159. Burton Sisters	RCA
160. Buttercups	Silver Star
161. Butterflies, Bonnie & the	Smash
162. Butterflys	Red Bird {Blue Angels/Buttons}
163. Buttons	Columbia/Ember {Blue Angels/ Butterflys}
164. Buttons & Beaus	Zen
165. B*Witched	Epic
166. Cake	Decca
167. Calamities	Posh Boy
168. Calendar Girls	Four Corners/Kapp
169. California Girls	Doorway
170. Campus Queens	Gone
171. Canaries	Dimension
172. Candies	Ember
173. Candies	Fleetwood
174. Candletts	Ronda/Vita
175. Candy Girls	Rotate
176. Candy Stripers	Vim
177. Cannon Sisters	Real Fine/Valiant
178. Capitols	Omen
179. Capri Sisters	ABC-Paramount/Cadence/ Dot/Hanover/Jubilee/ Newtown/Warwick
180. Caravans	Vee Jay
181. Caravelles	Columbia/Smash
182. Cardigans	Mercury
183. Carletts	Capitol

Name	Label
184. Carmelettes	Alpine
185. Carmel Sisters	Jubilee
186. Carolines	Roulette
187. Carol & Cheryl	Colpix
188. Carol & Connie	Imperial
189. Carol & Joan	Pioneer
190. Carole & Sherry	MGM/Popside
191. Carolinas, Tammy & the	Larson
192. Carols	Lamp
193. Carols	TCP
194. Carol Sisters	RCA
195. Carousels	Guyden
196. Carrie Nations	20th Century
197. Carvels	Twirl
198. Cashelles	Decca
199. Castles, Barbara & the	Ruby-Doo
200. Castle Sisters	Roulette/Terrace
201. Castanets	TCF
202. Castanets, Yolanda & the	Tandem {Charmanes, Yolanda & the/Naturals, Yolanda & the }
203. Castells	United Artists
204. Catholic Girls	MCA {Double Cross Schoogirls}
205. Celestrals	Alpha/Don-El/RCA
206. Chadons	Chattahoochee
207. Chains	HBR
208. Chalfontes	Mercury
209. Chances	Airway/Bea & Baby
210. Chanels	Deb {Five Chanels/ Four Chanels, Virgil & the}
211. Chansonettes, Les	Shrine/Mon'ca
212. Chantelles	GNP Crescendo
213. Chantells	Aqua/Soul Kitchen
214. Chantels	Carlton/Crackerjack/End/ Ludix/Mem-O-Ree/RCA/ TCF-Arrawak/Verve
215. Chantels	End {Relatives/Swensons/ Veneers}
216. Chante's	Prism
217. Chantique	AIP International
218. Chants	Capitol
219. Chapter Four	PIP
220. Chapter Three	Dial/Grand Grove/New Moon
221. Charades	Warner Bros.
222. Charlettes	Angie {Toys}
223. Charlotte & Emily	
224. Charmaines	Dot/Saxony {Charmaines, Gigi & the}
225. Charmaines,	Gigi & the Columbia/Date/ Fraternity/Minit/Red Leaf {Charmaines}
226. Charmanes, Yolanda & the	Smash {Castanets, Yolanda & the/Naturals, Yolanda & the}
227. Charmells	Volt {Charmels/Tonettes}
228. Charmels	Volt {Charmells/Tonettes}
229. Charmers	Aladdin
230. Charmers	JAF/Pip
231. Charmettes	Federal
232. Charmettes	Mala
233. Charmettes	Marlin/Mona/Tri-Disc
234. Charmettes	Kapp/World Artists
235. Charmettes, Bonnie & the	Markay
236. Charmetts	Philomega
237. Charmonaires	Knick
238. Chatters	Viking
239. Cheerettes	Vita
240. Cheese Cakes	Laurie
241. Cheetah	Atlantic
242. Chelette Sisters	NRC
243. Chell-Mars	Hi Mar/Jamie
244. Chelmars	Select
245. Cherries	Big Beat
246. Cherries	Della
247. Cherry Blend	King
248. Cherubs	Blend
249. Chevelles	Butane
250. Chevelles, Betty Turner & the	Crescent
251. Chicklets	Lescay

Name	Label
252. Chicklettes, Angie & the	Apt {Powder Puffs/Rag Dolls}
253. Chic-Lets, Josie & the	{Darlettes/Darlettes, Diane & the/Liberty Belles/ Patti Lace & The Petticoats/ Rosettes}
254. Chiffons	Big Deal/Reprise/Wildcat
255. Chiffons	B.T.Puppy/Buddah/Laurie {Four Pennies}
256. Chiffons, Ginger & the	Groove
257. Chips	ABC/Mercury/Philips
258. Chirades	Colt-Virt/Virtue
259. Chix, Heidi Hall & the	Superior
260. Chora Leeters	Duke
261. Choralettes	Fargo
262. Chordettes	Cadence/Columbia
263. Chums, Mary Eustice & the	Apt
264. Chymes	Okeh
265. Cinderellas	Dimension {Cookies/Honey Bees/Palisades/Raeletts/ Stepping Stones}
266. Cindarellas	Escapade
267. Cinderellas	Columbia
268. Cinderellas	Decca/Mercury
269. Cinderellas	Tamara
270. Cinders	Original Sound
271. Cindy & Sue	Era
272. Cineemas	Dave
273. Cinnamons	B.T. Puppy
274. Claremonts	Apollo {Tonettes}
275. Clark Sisters	A&M/Dot/Elektra
276. Classinettes	Markay
277. Clementines	Round-Up
278. Clickettes	Checker {Hearts/Hearts, Ena Louise & the/Jaynetts/Patty Cakes/Poppies/Z-Debs}
279. Clickettes	Dice/Guyden {Avalons/ Fashions}
280. Clingers	Columbia/MGM {Clinger Sisters}
281. Clinger Sisters	Tollie {Clingers}
282. Coasterettes	Coast To Coast
283. Cochrane Twins	Garpax
284. Coconuts	Sire
285. Cocquettes	RCA
286. Cody Sisters	Arch
287. Co-eds	Cha Cha
288. Coeds	Challenge {Blossoms/ Bob B. Soxx & The Blue Jeans/ Crystals/Dreamers/ Girlfriends/Hushabyes, Hale & the/Playgirls/ Rollettes/Wildcats}
289. Coffee	De-Lite/Love Life/MIR
290. Coffee, Cream & Sugar	Both Sides
291. Colpixies	Colpix
292. Combonettes	Combo
293. Commotions	Blue Rock/Capitol
294. Company B	Atlantic
295. Confessions	Epic
296. Confidentials	Masterpiece
297. Contessas	WGW/Witch
298. Contessas	GeorgeClements/E
299. Continettes	Richie
300. Cook County	Motown
301. Cookies	Atlantic/Dimension/Josie/ Lamp/Warner Bros. {Cinderellas/Honey Bees/ Palisades/Raeletts/Stepping Stones}
302. Cooperettes	Brunswick/IDB
303. Cooperetts	ABC
304. Copesetics	Premium
305. Copycats, Susie & the	Brent {Fidels, Holidays}
306. Coquettes	Epic/Mercury
307. Coquettes, Joann Bon & the	MTA
308. Coralites	Carib
309. Coralettes	Brunswick

CoName	Label
310. rals	Cheer/Kram/Rayna
311. Corlettes	Kansoma/Nita
312. Cornell Sisters	Label
313. Coronadas	Bright Star
314. Coronados	Parliament
315. Corvells	Lupine
316. Corvettes, Nikki & the	Bomp
317. Cosmopolitans	Shake
318. Cotillions	ABC/CB/Ascot
319. Cottonblossoms	Gramophone
320. Cover Girls	Conte
321. Cover Girls	Epic/Fever
322. Coyote Sisters	Morocco
323. Cozy	Fortune
324. Crampton Sisters	ABC/DCP
325. Crayons	Counsel
326. Crayons, Ronnie & the	Domain
327. Creations	Radiant
328. Creslyns	Beltone
329. Crystalettes	Crystalette
330. Crystal, Ronette, & Chiffon	Geffen
331. Crystals	Aladdin
332. Crystals	EEOC/Philles/Michelle/UA {Blossoms/Nelson, Group, Teri}
333. Crystals, Claudia & the	Dore
334. Cupcakes	Diamond
335. Cupcakes	Time
336. Cupids, Sandy & the	Charter
337. Cupids, Paulette & the	Prism
338. Cupons, Materlyn & the	Impact
339. Curls	Everest
340. Cute-Teens	Aladdin
341. Dabettes	Advance
342. Dacrons	Hit
343. Dahlias	Big H
344. Daisies	Capitol
345. Daisies	Roulette
346. Danielle	Casablanca
347. Darby Sisters	Cub/Metro
348. Darlene & Darla	IPG/Neptune
349. Darlenes	Stacy
350. Darlettes	Dunes {Chiclets/Darlettes, Diane & the/Liberty Belles/ Rosettes}
351. Darlettes, Diane & the	Dunes {Chiclets/Darlettes/ Liberty Belles /Rosettes}
352. Dar-Letts	Shell
353. Darletts	Mira/Taffi {Sweet Things}
354. Darling DearsFlower	
355. Darlings	Penguin
356. Darlings	Dore
357. Darlings	Kay-Ko/Mercury
358. Darling Sisters	
359. Darlings, Jeanne & the	Volt
360. Darnells	Gordy {Andantes/Del Rhythmetts/Marvelettes}
361. Dash & Dot	Skyla
362. Date With Soul	York
363. Daughters Of Eve	Cadet/Spectra Sound/USA
364. Davenport Sisters	Tri Phi
365. Dawn	Apt/ABC/UA
366. Dawn	Laurie
367. Dawn Sisters	Southtown
368. Daydreams	Dial
369. Daylights	Propulsion
370. DC Blossoms	Shrine
371. Deadly Nightshade	Phantom
372. DeAngelis Sisters	ABC
373. Debanairs	W-BS
374. Debanettes, Marlene & the	--
375. Debelaires	Lectra
376. Deberons	Bond
377. Debonaires	Maske
378. Debonaires	Golden World/Solid Hit
379. Debonaires	Soul Click
380. Debonairs	Harmon

Name	Label
381. Debonairs	Warner Bros.
382. Debonettes	Merry
383. Debrells	Ace
384. Debs	A&M
385. Debs	Bruce {Leslie Sisters}
386. Debs	Crown/Keen {Three Debs}
387. Debs	Double L/Mercury
388. Debs	Infinity
389. Debs	Squalor
390. Debteens	Boss
391. Deb-Tones	RCA
392. Debutantes	Kayo
393. Debutantes	Savoy
394. Debutantes	Standout
395. DeCastro Sisters	ABC-Paramount/Abbott/RCA
	Marie & the Cub
396. Deccors,	Ramarca
397. Dedications	Acclaim/Keen
398. Dee & Di	Britton
399. Dee Lites	Epic/Sunbeam
400. DeJohn Sisters	Arrawak
401. Del-Airs	Shikari
402. Delanettes	World Pacific
403. Delegates	Blue Rock
404. Deletts	Challenge/Celeste/Dee Dee/
405. Delicates	Pulsar/Soul Town
	{Wild Honey}
406. Delicates	Roulette/Tender/UA/Unart
	{Angels/Dusk}
407. Delights	A&M
408. Delights	Arlen
409. Delights, Barbara & the	UA
410. Delights,	Lorraine & the Barry
411. Del Phis	Checkmate {Martha & The
	Vandellas/Vells}
412. Del Rays	Stax
413. Del-Rhythmetts	JVB
{Darnells/Marvelettes}	
414. Del Rios	Neptune
415. Delrons, Reparata & the	Kapp/Laurie/Mala/RCA/
	World Artists
416. Deltairs	Felsted/Ivy {Tranquils}
417. Deltairs	Vintage {Del-Tears}
418. Deltanettes, Lena & the	Uptown
419. Deltas	EMP
420. Del-Tears	Rayborn {Deltairs}
421. Delteens	Federal
422. Delltones	Baton/Brunswick/Rainbow
	{Enchanters}
423. Delvets	End
424. Del-Vetts, Bettye Scott & the	Teako/One-Way
425. Dematrons	Southern Sound
426. Demures	Brunswick
427. Denims, Bonnie & the	LLP
428. DePippo Sisters	Magnifico
429. Desirables, Mary & the	Checker
430. Desires	Herald {Passionetts}
431. Destiny, Alton McClain &	Polydor
432. Destiny's Child	Columbia
433. Devastating Affair,	
Suzee Ikeda &	Mowest
434. DeVaurs	D-Tone/Moon/Red Fox
435. De Velles	Emanuel
436. DeVille Sisters	Imperial/Spry
437. Devines, Angel & the	Siana
438. Devonairs	Devon
439. Devonnes	Colossus
440. DeVonns	Parkway/Redd {DeVons}
441. DeVons	Decca/King/Mr. G {DeVonns}
442. Devotion	Colossus {Devotions/Superbs}
443. Devotions	J-City/Silver Dollar {Devotion/
	Superbs}
444. Devotions	Tri-Sound
445. Dew Drops	Jeff
446. Dew-Drops, Honey & the	MMC
447. Dial Tones	Best/Lawn
448. Diamonettes	Alston/Dig {Friday, Saturday
	& Sunday}

Name	Label
449. Dielles	D.C. & B.
450. DiMara Sisters	Pip/Roulette/Slicko
451. Dimensions	D-Town
452. Dimples	Cameo
453. Dimples	Dore/Era/JK
454. Dinning Sisters	Capitol/Essex
455. Diplomettes	Diplomacy
456. Direct Current	Tec
457. Dispoto Sisters	Verve
458. Divine	Pendelum
459. Dixiebelles	Sound Stage 7
460. Dixie Chicks	Monument/Sony
461. Dixie Cups	ABC-Paramount/Red Bird
462. Docketts	Botanical
463. Do Drops, Misty & the	Imperial
464. Dolby's Cube	MCA
465. Dolletts	ABC-Paramount
466. Dolls	Okeh/Teenage
467. Dolls	Kangaroo
468. Dolls	Loma/Maltese/Toy
469. Dolls	NCG
470. Dolls, Spongy & the	Bridgeview
471. Dolly Dots	Atlantic
472. Dolphin Dolls	Scarpa
473. Domineers	Roulette
474. Donays	Brent
475. Donnels	Alpha
476. Donettes	Rona
477. Dooley Sisters	R-Dell/Tampa
478. Dorelles	Atlantic/GEI {Dorells}
479. Dorells	RSVP {Dorelles}
480. Dorells	Bronze
481. Dorell Sisters	RCA
482. DoRey Sisters	Poplar
483. Dorothy, Oma & Zelpha	Chisa
484. Dotty & Kathy	Charter
485. Double Cross Schoolgirls	Cinema {Catholic Girls}
486. Doves	Big Top
487. Drake Sisters	Chattahoochee
488. Dramatics, DeNielle & the	Margate
489. Dream Girls	Cameo/Big Top/Twirl {Dream
	Girls, Bobbie Smith & the}
490. Dream Girls, Bobbi Smith & the	Big Top/Metro {Dream Girls}
491. Dreamers	Apt/UA
492. Dreamers	Aladdin/Flair/Flip {Blue Jeans,
	Bob B. Soxx & The/Blossoms/
	Coeds/Crystals/Girlfriends/
	Hushabyes, Hale & the/
	Playgirls/Rollettes/Wildcats}
493. Dreamers	Fairmount
494. Dreamers	Manhattan
495. Dreamettes	Dream Makers
496. Dreamettes	UA
497. Dreamliners	Cobra/Jox
498. Dreams	Kellmac
499. Dreams	Smash
500. Dreams, Joann Jackson &	Harthon
501. Dream Team	Epic
502. Dream Timers	Flippin'/London
503. Dreamtones	Mercury
504. Drew-Vels	Capitol/Quill
505. Drummonetts	Bradley
506. Duchesses	Chief {Four Duchesses}
507. Duets, Judy & the	Ware
508. Du-ettes	Mar-V-lus/M-Pac/One-derful
	{Uniques, Barbara & the}
509. Duncans	Malaco
510. Duncan Sisters	Earmarc
511. DungareeDarlings	Karen {Dungaree Dolls}
512. Dungaree Dolls	Rego {Dungaree Darlings}
513. Durettes	SVR
514. Dushons	Golden Gate/Down To Earth
515. Dusk	Bell {Angels/Halos/Starlets}
516. Dynels	Atco/Blueberry/Dot
517. Dynettes	Constellation
518. Dynette Set	Rhino
519. Earthquake	Motown

Name	Label
520. Easy Credit	Mopres
521. Ebonettes	Ebb
522. Echolettes	Imperial
523. Edward Sisters	Junior/Kaiser
524. Edward Twins	Twistime
525. Eight Feet	Columbia
526. Electric Banana	Flip-O
527. Electrodes	Fran
528. Electras	CVS/De-Lite
529. Eligibles, Gaye Merritt & the	Pillar
530. Elites	Hi-Lite
531. Ellingtons	RCA
532. Embraceables	Sidra
533. Embraceables	Sound
534. Emeralds	Jubilee
535. Emotions	ARC/Brainstorm/Columbia/ Motown/Red Label/Stax/ Twin Stacks/Volt {Sunbeams}
536. Empress	Prelude
537. Enchanters	Jubilee {Delltones}
538. Endeavors	J & S {Clickettes/Hearts/Hearts, Ena Louise & the/Patty Cakes/Poppies/Z-Debs}
539. Enlightenment	NRR
540. English Muffins	B.T. Puppy {Three Pennies}
541. En Vogue	Atlantic/East-West
542. Ervin Sisters	Tri-Phi
543. Essence	Interstate
544. Etiquettes	Clock
545. Evaros	Al Globe
546. Evaros	Roulette
547. Evels	Tra-X
548. Exciters	Bang/Fargo/Roulette/RCA/ Shout/Today/UA {Masterettes}
549. Expose	Arista
550. Extensions	Success
551. Eye Shadows, Merle Lee & the	Debbie
552. F. J. Babies	Apt
553. Fabians	Blue Rocket
554. Fabulettes	Kangi/Monument/Phil L.A. of Soul/Sound Stage 7
555. Fabulous Chimes	Invincible Recording Artists
556. Fabulous Jades	Rika {Jades}
557. Fair Play	Silver Blue
558. Fallen Angel Choir	Angelic
559. Family Cookin', Limmie &	Bareback
560. Fantaisions	Satellite/Thomas
561. Fantastic Vontastics	Tuff
562. Fanny	Reprise
563. Farleys	Jody
564. Fascinations	Mayfield {Fasinations}
565. Fashionettes	GNP-Crescendo
566. Fashions	20th Century Fox
567. Fashions	Cameo
568. Fashions	Elmor/RouletteWarwick {Avalons/Clickettes/ Fashions, Barbara English & the}
569. Fashions	Amy/Ember/Felsted
570. Fashions, Dolly & the	Ivanhoe/Tri Disc
571. Fashions, Barbara English & the	Roulette {Avalons/Clickettes/ Fashions}
572. Fasinations	ABC-Paramount {Fascinations}
573. Fawns	Apt
574. Fawns	CapCity/New Frontiers/ RCA/Tec
575. Fayettes, Hattie Littles & the	Gordy
576. Femm-Eles	Do-Kay-Lo
577. Femmes, Les	Power Pack
578. Femme, Les Tre	Uptite/20th Century/Phil LA of Soul
579. Feminetts	Gramo
580. Feminine Society	Sure Hits
581. Fem 2 Fem	Critique
582. Ferris Wheels	Philips
583. Fidels	Warner, {Holidays, Susie & the Holidays}

Name	Label
584. Five Chanels	Deb {Chanels/Four Chanels, Virgil & the}
585. Fire	Sunshine Sound
586. First Choice	Gold Mind/Philly/Groove/ Scepter/Warner Bros.
587. First Love	CIM/Dakar/HCRC
588. Five Cookies	Everest
589. Five Rocquettes	Decca
590. Five Sable Sisters	Dixie
591. Flair	Flash
592. Flamettes	Laurie
593. Flirtations	D&D/Deram/Festival/ Josie/Passion/Parrot {Gypsies}
594. Flirts	By-Lew
595. Flirts	CBS/O {Heartbreak U.S.A}
596. Flowers	Chant
597. Forbidden Circle	Down Home
598. Forevers	Weis
599. For Real	Rowdy
600. Fortune Cookies	Smash
601. Four Calquettes	Capitol/Liberty {Four Coquettes}
602. Four Chanels, Virgil & the	Deb {Chanels/Five Chanels}
603. Four Chicadees	Checker
604. Four Coquettes	Capitol {Four Calquettes}
605. Four Darlings	Forte
606. Four Dolls	Capitol
607. Four Duchesses	Chief {Duchesses}
608. Four Havens	Veep
609. Four Jewels	Checker/Start {Jewels/Impalas}
610. Four J's	Four J
611. Four Making Do	WDR
612. Four Pennies	Rust {Chiffons}
613. Four Queens	ABC-Paramount/Teron
614. Four Teens	Three H's
615. Foxes	ABC
616. Foxes	Titanic
617. Foxes	Pickwick
618. Foxettes, Lady Fox &	Don-El
619. Foxy Ladies	Tapestry
620. Fragile Rock Valley	Earth
621. Francettes	Besche/Challenge/Kentone/ Sleeper/MM/Valiant/Wolfie
622. Fran & Flo	Jupiter
623. Freckles	Madison
624. Freeze	Streetwise
625. French Coffee	Pick-A-Hit
626. Friday, Saturday & Sunday	Dig {Diamonettes}
627. Friends	Gold Future
628. Front Runners	Tom Cat
629. Funky Sisters	Aurora
630. Fuzzbox	Geffen
631. Fuzzy Bunnies	Decca/Philips {Meantime/ Raindrops}
632. Fuzz	Calla {Passionettes}
633. G-Notes	Jackpot
634. Gail & Sandra	Radio
635. Gailtones	Decca
636. Gales	Debra
637. Gambrells	Carla/Cub/Pioneer
638. Gay Charmers	Grand
639. Gayles	King/Media
640. Gayletts	Black Jack
641. Gayletts	Hour Glass/Steady
642. Gaynels	Okeh
643. Gaynotes	Aladdin
644. Gay Notes	Post {Honey Bees}
645. Gee Sisters	Palette
646. Geminis	RCA
647. Gems	Chess {Lovettes/Pets/Starlets}
648. Gems	Riverside
649. Gems, Pearl Woods & the	Wall
650. Genies	Lenox
651. Genies	Ronn
652. Gentle	Leo Mini
653. Gentle Persuasion	Capitol
654. Gentle Rain	Fee Bee
655. Georgettes	Challenge/Ebb/Hit/Jackpot/ Trey {Georgettes, Geri & the}

Name	Label
656. Georgettes	Goldisc/Sabre
657. Georgettes	Yodi
658. Georgettes, Geri & the	Hit {Georgettes}
659. Gibralters	A&W
660. Gigi On The Beach	Scotti Bros.
661. Gingerbreads, Goldie & the	Atco/Spokane
662. Gingers	Radiant
663. Ginger Snaps	RCA/University/V-Tone
664. Ginger Snaps	Dunhill
665. Gingersnaps	Kapp
666. Girlfriends	Colpix {Blossoms/Blue Jeans, Bob B. Soxx & The/Coeds/ Crystals/Dreamers/ Hushabyes, Hale & the/ Playgirls/Rolletes/Wildcats}
667. Girlfriends	Melic/Pioneer
668. Girlfriends, Erlene & the	Old Town
669. Girls	Atco
670. Girls	Capitol/Scepter
671. Girls	Columbia
672. Girls	Memphis
673. Girls, Les	Laurie
674. Girls At Our Best	Records
675. Girls Can't Help It	Sire
676. Girls From Petticoat Junction	Decca/Imperial
677. Girls From Syracuse	Palmer
678. Girls Next Door	Atlantic/MTM
679. Girls Three	Chess
680. Girls Together Outrageously	Straight
681. Givens Four	Venture
682. Glitters	Big
683. Global Gonks	Heartstrings
684. Gloo Girls	Bible Belt
685. Glories	Date {Quiet Elegance}
686. G-Notes	Remember
687. Go-Go's	IRS/Stiff
688. Golden Girls	Tommy Boy
689. Goodees	Hip
690. Goodies	Blue Cat
691. Good Girls	Counsel
692. Good Girls	Motown
693. Goodnight Kisses	Atco
694. Gorman Sisters	Arrow
695. Green's III	HCRC
696. Groovettes	Reness
697. Gross Sisters	Checker
698. Guinn	Motown
699. Gum Drops	Coral
700. Gypsies	Caprice/Old Town {Flirtations}
701. Hairdooz, Henrietta & the	Liberty
702. Half-Sisters	Chattahoochee
703. Halos	Congress {Angels/Dusk/ Starlets}
704. Hamilton Sisters	Columbia/King
705. Happy Teens	Paradise
706. Harvey Sisters	Newtime
707. Harts, Toni & the	Path
708. Hayden Sisters	Royce/Tilt
709. Haywoods, Kitty & the	Capitol
710. Heartbreakers	Atco/MGM/P&M
711. Heartbreak U.S.A.	Preppy {Flirts}
712. Hearts	Baton/J & S/Tuff/Zell's {Clickettes/Endeavors/ Hearts, Ena Louise & the/ Jaynetts/Patty Cakes/ Poppies/Z-Debs}
713. Hearts, Ena Louise & the	Argyle {Clickettes/Endeavors/ Hearts/Jaynetts/Patty Cakes/Poppies/Z-Debs}
714. Hearts, Joan & the Hunter	
715. Hearts, Sherry Gibbs & the	TNT
716. Hearts, Toni & the	Path
717. Heartstoppers	London House
718. Heatwaves	Enjoy
719. Hellcats	New Rose
720. Hesitations, Dorothy &	theJamie
721. Heyettes	London

Name	Label
722. Hi-Fashions	Paris
723. Hi-Fashions	Dyno Voice
724. Hi-Fi's	AVR
725. Hi-Lights	JR
726. Hi-Lites	Reno {Joytones}
727. High Inergy	Gordy/Motown
728. Hill Sisters	Anna/Choice/Space
729. Hodges, James	& SmithLondon/People/ 20th Century {Hodges, James, Smith & Crawford}
730. Hodges, James, Smith & Crawford	Mpingo
731. Holiday	Brent {Fidels, Susie & the Holidays}
732. Holly Twins	Rendezvous
733. Hollywood Chicks	Class
734. Hollywood Jills	Capitol/Tune-Kel
735. Holy Sisters Of The Gada Dada	Bomp
736. Honey Bees	Fontana {Cinderellas/Cookies/ Palisades/Raeletts/Stepping Stones}
737. Honey Bees	Imperial/Pentagon {Gay Notes}
738. Honey Bees	Garrison/ Vee Jay/Wand
739. Honey Bees	Roxbury
740. Honeybirds	Coral
741. Honeycombs	Pro
742. Honey Cone	Hot Wax
743. Honey Duo Twins	Yam Bo
744. Honey Ltd.	LHI
745. Honeys	Capitol/WarnerBros. {American Spring/Spring/Ginger & The Snaps}
746. Honeytones	Mercury/2-Mikes/Wing
747. Hot	Big Tree/Boardwalk {Hot Chocolate}
748. Hot Chocolate	Bell/Big Tree {Hot}
749. Hot Sauce	Stax
750. Houstons	Hit
751. Hush-a-byes	Signature
752. Hushabyes, Hale & the	Reprise {Blossoms/Blue Jeans, Bob B. Soxx & The/Coeds/ Crystals/Dreamers/ Playgirls/Rolletes/Wildcats}
753. Hutch Stereos	Local
754. Idolls	Atlantic
755. Ikettes	Atco/Modern/Phi- Dan/ Pompeii/Teena/UA {Mirettes}
756. Ila	Star Record Co.
757. Illicit	Pink Street
758. Illusions	Sheraton
759. Impalas	Checker {Four Jewels/Jewels}
760. Imported Moods	Hi
761. Inception	RCA
762. In Crowd	Swan
763. Indeep	Sound Of New York
764. Indigo Girls	Epic
765. Indigos	Verve-Folkways
766. Inspirations	Black Pearl
767. Instants	Rendezvous
768. Inticers	HLS
769. Intros	Jamie
770. Invictas	Mavis
771. Irresistables	Imperial
772. Ivorys	Despenza/Wand
773. Ivys	Coed
774. Jackie & Gayle	Capitol/Mainstream/UA
775. Jackson Jills	Dot
776. Jackson Sisters	Mums/Polydor/Prophecy
777. Jade	Giant
778. Jade & Sarsaparilla	Submaureen
779. Jades	Imperial/Liberty {Fabulous Jades}
780. Jades	MGM/Verve
781. Jades	Port
782. Jamells	Crosley
783. Jan & Jill	20th Century
784. Janettes	Goldie

Girl Groups

Name	Label
785. Jaye Sisters	Atlantic/UA
786. Jaynetts	J & S/Tuff {Clickettes/ Endeavors/Hearts/ Hearts, Ena Louise & the/Patty Cakes/Poppies/Z-Debs}
787. Jays, Janit & the	Hermitage/Hi
788. Jeans	Laurie
789. Jelly Beans	Eskee/Red Bird
790. Jenny's Daughters	Buluu/Dunhill
791. Jets, Ellie Gee & the	Madison {Meantime/Raindrops}
792. Jet Set, Liza & the	Capitol
793. Jewels	Dimension/Dynamite/King/ Federal/Tec {Four Jewels/ Impalas}
794. Jewels	MGM
795. Jewels	Olimpic
796. Jewels, Jenny & the	Hit
797. JGs, Beverlie & the	Pre-Teen
798. Jillettes	Amazon/Carbs/Philips
799. Jills, Jacqueline & the	Goldisc
800. Joan & Joy	Hull
801. Jobettes	Kevin
802. Jodarettes	Jocida
803. Jogettes	Mar
804. Johnson Sisters	Broadway/Josie/Swan
805. Jomanda	Big Beat
806. Jones Girls	Curtom/GM/Music Merchant/ Paramount/Phil. Int'l./RCA
807. Jonesettes	Cougar
808. Jovialetts	Josie
809. Joyettes	Onyx
810. Joylets	ABC-Paramount
811. Joy Of Cooking	Capitol
812. Joy Sisters	Whirl
813. Joys	Master
814. Joys	Valiant
815. Joytones	Coed/Rama {Hi-Lites/Love Potion}
816. Joy Unlimited	Mercury
817. Judy & Joyce	Dot
818. Juliettes	Catamount
819. Juliettes	Chattahoochee
820. Junior Misses	Rendezvous
821. Just Us Girls	Cleveland Int'l./Epic
822. Kane Triplets	Kapp
823. Karrians	Pelpal
824. Kavettes	Okeh
825. Kaye Sisters	Philips
826. Keefer Sisters	Swan
827. Kendall Sisters	Argo
828. Keynoters	Pepper
829. Kimberlys, Verna & the	Happy Tiger
830. Kim Sisters	Epic/Monument
831. Kisses, Candy & the	R&L
832. Kisses, Candy & the	Cameo/Decca/Scepter {Love Notes, Harriet Laverne & the/ Love Notes, Honey Love & the/Sweet Soul}
833. Kittens	ABC/Chess/Vick
834. Kittens	Alpine/Unart
835. Kittens	Chestnut/Don-El
836. Kittens	Herald
837. Kittens	Murbo
838. Kittens, Kelli & the	Sound Stage 7
839. Kittens, Terri &	theImperial
840. Kittens Three	Newark
841. Klymaxx	Constellation/MCA/Solar
842. Knickers	Rhino
843. Knick Knacks	Columbia
844. Knight Sisters	Tempwood
845. Knott Sisters	Big Top
846. Known Facts	Pawn
847. Kolettes	Barbara/Checker
848. Krystal Generation	Buddah
849. Krystol	Epic
850. Ladelles	Debonaire
851. La Dell Sisters	Mercury

Name	Label
852. Ladybirds	Atco/Lawn/Wickwire
853. Lady Bugs	Chattahoochee/Del-Fi
854. Lady Bugs	Legrand
855. Lady Flash	RSO
856. Lady Luck	First American
857. La Fons	Invinsible
858. Lalarettes, Lala & the	Elpeco
859. Lambs, Mary	Hurt & the Zebra
860. Lamp Sisters	Duke
861. Lane Sisters	Landa
862. Lanas	Laurie
863. Lang Sisters	Dore
864. LaNiers	River City
865. Larkettes	Hey-Day
866. Laurie Sisters	Mercury
867. Laurie Sisters	MGM/Port/Vik
868. Lavells	CTB
869. Lavells	Mercury
870. Lavenders	Dot
871. Lavenders	Mercury
872. LaVerne & Shirley	Atlantic
873. La Salles	VIP
874. La Vettes	Philips
875. Lazy Susans	Kapp
876. Leamon Sisters	Monument
877. Lenettes	Zepp
878. Leroys	Cabot
879. Leslie SistersMarble	{Debs}
880. Leverett Sisters	Kayden
881. Levettes	Unity
882. LeVons	Columbia
883. Lewis Explosion	Pleasure
884. Lewis Sisters	VIP
885. Libby & Sue	Era
886. Liberty Belles	Shout {Chiclets/Darlettes/ Darlettes, Diane & the/Rosettes}
887. Lilith	Galaxia
888. Lindettes, Linda & the	Laurie
889. Lindreals	Kim
890. Linettes	Palette
891. Linneas	Diamond
892. Little Bits	Dyno Voice
893. Little Coquettes	Colpix
894. Little Dippers	University
895. Little Foxes	Okeh {Trinkets/Versalettes}
896. Little Girl Blue	Universal
897. Little People, Janice & the	Mercury
898. Little Sister	Stone Flower
899. Little Sisters	MGM
900. Live Experience	E&B
901. Liverbirds	Philips
902. Living Dolls, Bee Jee & the	Vita
903. Lockets	Argo
904. Lockettes	ABC-Paramount
905. Lockettes	Flip
906. Lollipops	Atco/RCA/Smash
907. Lollipops	Impact/VIP
908. Lollipops, Becky & the	Epic/Troy
909. Lolly Pops	Jamie/Kandee
910. Loose Change	Casablanca
911. Lonesome Rhodes	RCA
912. Lonnie's Legends	Playboy
913. Lorelei	Columbia
914. Loreleis	Bally
915. Loreleis	Brunswick {Avalons/Clickettes}
916. Lori & Lee	Columbia
917. Lornettes	Galleo
918. Lovables	Toot
919. Lovations	Cap City/Part III/Segue
920. Love Chain	Minit/UA
921. Love Children	GreGar
922. Love, Devotion & Happiness	Black Magic/PEO Jaden
923. Loved Ones	Roulette
924. Lovejoys	Red Bird/Tiger
925. Love Kittens	Mos-ley
926. Lovelets	CapCity/Doin' Our Thing/ Laurie

L*Name*	*Label*	*Name*	*Label*
927. Lovelights	Phi-Dan	988. Mello Moods	Gamble/North Bay {Mellow Moods}
928. Lovelites	Bandera/Cotillion/Lock/ Lovelite/Uni/20th Century {Lovelites, Patti & the}	989. Mellowettes, Judy McDonald & the	VRC
929. Lovelites, Patti & the	Cotillion/Lovelite {Lovelites}	990. Mellow Moods	We Make Rock n Roll {Mello Moods}
930. Lovelles	Atco	991. Melodears	Gone
931. Lovells	Brent	992. Michele	West End
932. Lovells, Laurie & the	Canadian American	993. Milky Way	4 Radio
933. Love Notes	Cameo {Kisses, Candy & the/ Love Notes, Harriet Laverne & the/Love Notes, Honey Love & the/Sweet Soul}	994. Milky Ways	Liberty
		995. Miller Sisters	Acme/Glodis/GMC/Herald/ Hull/Onyx/Rayna/ Riverside/Roulette/ Stardust/Sun
934. Love Notes, Harriet Laverne & the	Brenne {Kisses, Candy & the/ Love Notes/Love Notes, Honey Love & the/Sweet Soul}	996. Millington	UA
		997. Minits	Sounds of Memphis
935. Love Notes, Honey Love & the	Cameo {Kisses, Candy & the/ Love Notes/Love Notes, Harriet Laverne & the/ Sweet Soul}	998. Minks	Ermine
		999. Minx	Mercury
		1000. Mirettes	Minit/Mirwood/Revue/Uni/ Zea {Ikettes}
936. Love Notes, Sybil Love & the	Valex	1001. Misfits, Melinda & the	U-Nek
937. Love Potion	Kapp/TCB {Hi Lites/Joytones}	1002. Mitlo Sisters	Klik
938. Love Salvation	Bell	1003. Mizz	Casablanca
939. Love Squad, Linda Carr & the	Roxbury	1004. Models	MGM
940. Love Unlimited	20th Century Fox/Unlimited Gold/Uni	1005. Mod Singers	Savern/USA
		1006. Mohawks	Cotillion
941. Lovettes	Knight	1007. Moments	Deep
942. Lovettes	Carnival/Checker{Gems/Pets/ Starlets}	1008. Monique's	Darrel'Rie
		1009. Monster Girls	Tone-Science
943. Lullabies, Lady Luck & the	Philips	1010. Montclairs	ABC-Paramount
944. Lullabyes	Dimension	1011. Montells	Golden Crest
945. Luscious Three	T'Suga Rays	1012. Moppets	Spirit
946. Lusters	Curio	1013. Morrison Sisters	Decca/Deed
947. Luv Bugs	Stone Rock/Wand	1014. Mother's Finest	Epic
948. Luvs	Stallion	1015. Motor Scooters, Beverly & the	Epic
949. Lyrics	Bell	1016. MSDs	O'Retta
950. Lyrics, Musique & the	Valiant	1017. Mulberry Lane	MCA
951. M'Lady	20th Century Fox	1018. Murmaids	Chattahoochee
952. Madame X	Atlantic	1019. Musique	Prelude
953. Mademoiselles, Michelle & the	Admiral	1020. Mystic Five	Leo/Unity
954. Mai Tai	Critique	1021. Natura'Elles	Venture
955. Magic Lady	Motown	1022. Naturals, Yolanda & the	Kimley {Castanets, Yolanda & the/Charmanes, Yolanda & the}
956. Magic Touch	Black Falcon/Falcon's Roost/ Sirco		
957. Magnificent Montagues	Ro Yo	1023. Nature's Gift	ABC
958. Magnolias	Mastercraft	1024. Neevets	Reon
959. Maidens	Lenox	1025. Nelson, Group, Teri	Kama Sutra {Crystals}
960. Main Attraction	Black Hawk	1026. Neptunas	SFTRI
961. Mamselles	Diamond	1027. New World & Mary Lou	Vault
962. Majestics	MGM	1028. Nightingales	Ray-Star
963. Majorettes	Regency Int'l./Troy	1029. 9.9	RCA
964. Majorlettes	Mercury	1030. Noreen & Donna	Carlton
965. Margaret & Carol	Checker	1031. Nornetts	Wand
966. Marie Sisters	Brunswick/Capitol	1032. Norwood Singers	Savoy
967. Marionettes	London	1033. Novelairs	Shar
968. Marlettes	Howfum	1034. Nuance, Vikki Love with	4th & Broadway
969. Markettes	Big 20	1035. Nu Girls	Atlantic
970. Markeys	RCA	1036. Nu Shooz	Atlantic
971. Marriots	ABC	1037. Nu-Luvs	Clock
972. Marshans	Etiquette/Johnson	1038. Nu-Luvs	Mercury
973. Marshmellows	Veep	1039. Null Set	Date
974. Martin Sisters	Barry	1040. Obsession	Happy Tiger
975. Marvelettes	Tamla {Darnells/Del Rhythmettes}	1041. Odds & Ends	Today
		1042. Omens, Carol & the	Cody
976. Mar-Vells	Angie/Butane/Yorey	1043. Oncoming Times	Duo/Turbo
977. Marvells	Watch	1044. On The Air	Pulse/Rhino
978. Marvettes, Margo & the	American Arts	1045. Opals	Beltone
979. Mary Jane Girls	Gordy/Motown	1046. Opals	Laurie
980. Masterettes	Le Sage {Exciters}	1047. Opals	Okeh
981. Maura & Maria	Cameo	1048. Optimists	Crystalette
982. McKetney Sisters	Lota	1049. Orchids	Columbia/Roulette
983. McKinleys	Swan	1050. Original Bluebelles	Rainbow {Bluebelles/Starlets}
984. MDLT Willis	Ivory Tower Int'l.	1051. Orlons	ABC/Calla/Cameo {Zip & The Zippers}
985. Meantime	Atco {Fuzzy Bunnies/Jets, Ellie G & the/Raindrops}		
		1052. Other Kind	Afro-K
986. Medallions	Lenox	1053. Otisettes	Epic/Jonco
987. Mello Maids	Baton	1054. Our Ladies of Soul	Kelton

Name	Label
1055. Overtones	Rim
1056. Overtures, Ovella & the	Columbia
1057. Ozells	Cub
1058. Pace Setters	Correc-Tone
1059. Pacettes	Regina
1060. Pages	Sunstruck
1061. Page Sisters	Zephyr
1062. Palisades	Chairman {Cookies/ Cinderellas/Honey Bees/ Stepping Stones}
1063. Pams	Catamount
1064. Pams	MG
1065. Pandoras	Imperial/Liberty/Oliver
1066. Pandoras	Moxie
1067. Pandoras	Voxx
1068. Paper Dolls	Uni/MGM/Warner Bros.
1069. Paper Dolls	Sky
1070. Para-monts	Ole
1071. Paretti Sisters	Al-Brite
1072. Par-Fays	Fontana
1073. Paris Sisters	Capitol/Cavalier/Crescendo/ Decca/Gregmark/Imperial/ Mercury/MGM/Reprise
1074. Par-Let	Casablanca {Brides of Funkenstein}
1075. Parlettes	Jubilee
1076. Parleys, Ronnie & the	Kerwood
1077. Parliaments	Jubilee/Symbol
1078. Party Favors	RSVP
1079. Party Lights, Shona & the	Chicory
1080. Passionettes	Klik
1081. Passionettes	Path/Uni {Fuzz}
1082. Passionetts	Mother Earth/SoulBurst {Guinn}
1083. Passions	Cylyn
1084. Passions	El Virtue/Electrified Satellite
1085. Passion, Betty Fikes & the	Southbound
1086. Pastels	Pastel
1087. Pastels, Dawn & the	Steady
1088. Patettes, Patti & the	UA
1089. Pat & Pam	Our Town
1090. Patience & Prudence	Liberty
1091. Patterns	ABC-Paramount
1092. Patty & Margie	Roulette
1093. Patty Cakes	Tuff {Clickettes/Hearts/Hearts, Ena Louise & the/ Jaynetts/Poppies/Z-Debs}
1094. Paulette Sisters	Capitol
1095. Peaches	Bumps/Constellation
1096. Peaches	Modern
1097. Peachettes, Lynn Taylor & the	Black Hawk/Clock
1098. Pearlettes	Craig/Go/Segway/Vault/ Vee Jay
1099. Pearl	London
1100. Pearls	Bell
1101. Pearls	Warner Bros.
1102. Pebbles	Sussex
1103. Pebbles	Planet Pimp/Repent
1104. Pelicans, Moose & the	Vanguard
1105. Penetts	Becco
1106. Penny Candy Machine	Strobe
1107. Peppermints	Ruby Doo
1108. Percells	ABC
1109. Perfections	Pam-O
1110. Perigents	Maltese
1111. Permanents	Chairman
1112. Perris	Madison
1113. Perry Sisters	Decca
1114. Persianettes	Olympia
1115. Persianettes	Open/OR/Strata/Swan
1116. Persians	Pageant
1117. Personal Touch	PAP
1118. Petals	Mercury
1119. Petites	Ascot/Columbia/Spinning/ Troy
1120. Petites	Cub
1121. Petites	Teek
1122. Petite Teens	Brunswick
1123. Pets	Carnival
1124. Pets	MGM {Gems/Lovettes/Starlets}
1125. Petticoats	Challenge/Prep/RKO Unique
1126. Petticoats, Patti Lace & the	Kapp {Chiclets/Darlettes/ Liberty Belles/Rosettes}
1127. Phenominals	AVI
1128. Philettes	Fleetwood/Hudson
1129. Pinafores	Capitol
1130. Pink Lady	Elektra
1131. Pinups	Columbia
1132. Pin-Ups	Stork
1133. Pinz, Karen Lawrence & the	RCA
1134. Pirouettes	Diamond
1135. Pixies	AMC/Don-Dee
1136. Pixies	Beau Monde
1137. Pixies Three	Mercury
1138. P.J.s	Audio Fidelity/Roulette
1139. Playgirls	RCA {Blossoms/Blue Jeans, Bob,B. Soxx & The/Coeds/ Crystals/Dreamers/ Girlfriends/Hushabyes, Hale & the/Rollettes/Wildcats}
1140. Playgirls	Galaxy
1141. Playgirls	Toga
1142. Playmates, Cindy & the	Kemp {Playmates, Sandy & the}
1143. Playmates, Sandy & the	Jay Pee {Playmates, Cindy & the}
1144. Playthings	Liberty
1145. Pleasures	RSVP
1146. Pleasure Seekers	Capitol/Mercury
1147. Plus 4	Warner Bros.
1148. Pointer Sisters	Atlantic/Blue Thumb/ Columbia/ERG/MCA/ Motown/Planet/RCA
1149. Poison Dollys	Invasion
1150. Poni Tails	ABC-Paramount/Point
1151. Poppies	Epic
1152. Poppies	Tuff {Clickettes/Hearts/Hearts, Ena Louise & the/Jaynetts/ Patty Cakes/Z-Debs}
1153. Popsicles	GNP Crescendo
1154. Portraits	RCA/Tribune/Tri-Disc
1155. Postalettes	Dore
1156. Poussez	Vanguard
1157. Powder Puffs	Imperial {Chicklettes, Angie & the /Rag Dolls}
1158. Powell Sisters	Kaydee
1159. Preachers	Challenge
1160. Precious Three	Ref-O-Ree
1161. Precious Metal	Mercury
1162. Prelude	Pye
1163. Pree Sisters	Capitol
1164. Pre-Teens	J&S
1165. Primettes	Lupine {Supremes}
1166. Pristines	Date
1167. Pristines, Gari & the	Cameo
1168. Profiles, Reval Jordan & the	Keetch
1169. Promise	Great Potential/New Directions
1170. Promises	Ascot
1171. Promises	BRC
1172. Promises	Columbia
1173. Prophets	Advance
1174. Puffs	Dore
1175. Pussycats	Columbia/Keetch
1176. Pussycats	Dynamic
1177. Pussycats, Josie & the	Capitol
1178. Pussywillows	Telstar
1179. Queens	Flair
1180. Quiet Elegance	Hi {Glories}
1181. Quiet Fire, Destiny Sills &	Philly Town
1182. Quintones	Chess/Hunt/Red Top
1183. Quinto Sisters	Columbia
1184. Raeletts	Tangerine {Cookies/Sisters Love}
1185. Rag Dolls	Mala/Parkway {Chicklettes, Angie & the/Powder Puffs}
1186. Rainbows	Capitol
1187. Rainbows	Dot

Name	Label
1188. Raindolls	AVI
1189. Raindrops	Jubilee {Fuzzy Bunnies/Jets, Ellie Gee & the/Meantime}
1190. Raindrops, Jackie &	Colpix/Jaylee {Bo-Bells, Jackie Burns & the}
1191. Raindrops, Nita Neely & the	Preview
1192. Ramblettes	Four Corners/Decca
1193. Ramsey Sisters	Smash
1194. Rare Pleasure	Cheri
1195. Raunchettes	Bomp
1196. Ravenettes	Josie/Moon/Shurfine/Vertigo {Ravenettes, Diane & the}
1197. Ravenettes, Diane & the	Rack {Ravenettes}
1198. Rayons	Decca/Forte
1199. Reasons	UA
1200. Reasons, Ria & the	Amy
1201. Rebel Pebbles	IRS
1202. Redd, Hedwig, & Crossley	Columbia
1203. Reginas	Raio & Raio
1204. Relatives	Almont {Chantels/Swensons/ Veneers}
1205. Relatives	Musicor
1206. Relatives, Ronnie & the	Colpix {Ronettes}
1207. Renegaids, Bonnie Wagner &	Impact
1208. Renes	Riba
1209. Results	Apt/Philips
1210. Revelaires	Crystalette
1211. Revellons, Ria & the	RSVP
1212. Revlons	VRC
1213. Rev-lons	Garpax/Reprise/Starburst/Toy
1214. Rhodes, Chalmers, Rhodes	Warner Bros.
1215. Rhythmettes	Brunswick/Coral/RCA
1216. Rhythmettes	Manhattan
1217. Ribbons	Marsh/Parkway
1218. Richettes	Apt
1219. Ricochettes	Destinations
1220. Ridley Sisters	Del-Pat
1221. Riels	Laurie
1222. Ripples	Apache
1223. Rita & Robin	Unical
1224. Ritchie Family	Marlin {Honey & The Bees}
1225. Ritchie Family	Casablanca/Marlin
1226. Robin Sisters	Polaris
1227. Robins	New Hit/Sweet Taffy
1228. Robyns, Tiny Dahl & the	UA
1229. Rochelles	Spacey
1230. Rockabyes, Baby Jane & the	Port/Spokane/UA
1231. Rockets	Cool
1232. Rock Flowers	Wheel
1233. Rock Goddess	A&M
1234. Rockin' Kids	Dot
1235. Roleaks	Hope
1236. Rollettes	Class {Blossoms/Blue Jeans, Bob B. Soxx & The/Coeds/ Crystals/Dreamers/ Girlfriends/Hushabyes, Hale & the/Playgirls/Wildcats}
1237. Rollettes	Melker
1238. Ronettes	A&M/Buddah/Colpix/ May/Philles {Ronnie & The Relatives)
1239. Rosebuds	Bobwin
1240. Rosebuds	Gee/Lancer
1241. Rosebuds	Tower
1242. Roses	Dot
1243. Roses, Sally & the	Columbia
1244. Rosettes	Atlantic
1245. Rosettes	Decca
1246. Rosettes	Herald {Chiclets/Darlettes/ Darlettes, Diane & the/ Liberty Belles}
1247. Rosie & Betty	Press {Teen Queens}
1248. Rosie's Baby Dolls	Fargo
1249. Rouge	Capitol
1250. Roulettes, Yvonne Caroll & the	Domain
1251. Rouzan Sisters	Frisco
1252. Royal Debs	Tifco

Name	Label
1253. Royalettes	Chancellor/MGM/Roulette/ Warner Bros.
1254. Royalettes, Bunny & the	Cavalcade
1255. Royalites, Jo Paris & the	Countess
1256. Royalty	Sire
1257. Ru-Be-Els	Flip
1258. Rubies	District
1259. Rubies	TNT
1260. Rubies	Vee Jay
1261. Rubys, Janice & the	Swan
1262. Rude Girls	Flying Fish
1263. Rums & Coke	Bram
1264. Russells	ABC-Paramount
1265. Sables	RCA
1266. Salem 66	Homestead
1267. Salisbury Twins	ABC
1268. Sallycats, Sally & the	Rendezvous
1269. Salt Water Taffy	Metromedia
1270. Salvadors	Nike
1271. Same	Barrington
1272. Sandelles	Alto
1273. Sandetts	Smokey
1274. Sandi & Salli	{Sandy & Sally}
1275. Sandpapers	Charger
1276. Sandpipers	Tru-Glo-Town
1277. Sandy & Sally	Capitol {Sandi & Sally}
1278. Santells	Courier
1279. Sassafras	H&L
1280. Sa-Shays	Alfi/Zen
1281. Satin Bells	Shamley
1282. Satin Dolls	Gold Soul/Shamley
1283. Satinettes, Laura Otis & the	Caljo/Mexie
1284. Satisfactions	Imperial
1285. Satori	ABC
1286. Savettes	Choice
1287. Savoys, Marva & the	Coed
1288. Scharmers	Vintage
1289. School Belles	Crest/Dot
1290. School Girls	Express
1291. Schoolgirls, Wendy & the	Golden Crest
1292. Schoolmates, Colleen & the	Coral
1293. Scotts, Irene & the	Smash
1294. Screaming Sirens	Enigma
1295. Scuzzies	CRS
1296. Sea Larks	Dot
1297. Seashells	Columbia
1298. Second (2nd) Verse	IX Chains
1299. Secrets	Columbia
1300. Secrets	DCP/Red Bird
1301. Secrets	Omen
1302. Secrets	Philips
1303. Secrets	Wand
1304. Secrets, Colleen Kaye & the	Big Top
1305. Seduction	A&M
1306. Seekers	Cougar
1307. Sensationals	Candix
1308. Sensations, Sonya & the	Gend
1309. Sentimentals	Knap Town
1310. September	Brunswick
1311. Sequal	Capitol
1312. Sequence	Sugar Hill
1313. Sequins	Ascot
1314. Sequins	BAB
1315. Sequins	Cameo
1316. Sequins	A&M/Crajon/Fantasy/ GoldStar
1317. Sequins	Detroit Sound/Renfro
1318. Sequins	Terrace
1319. Sequins, Janice Rado & the	Edsel
1320. Serenadetts	Enrica
1321. Sessions	Guyden
1322. 702	Motown
1323. 7669	Motown
1324. Seven Teens	Golden Crest
1325. Shaddows	United Audio
1326. Shade of Soul	Sunburst/Unity
1327. Shades	Fujimo

Name	Label
1328. Shades of Love	Delon/Venture
1329. Shakers, Shelly Shoop & the	Groove
1330. Sha Says	London
1331. Shalimars	Brunswick/Mr. Maestro/Verve {Shalimars,Sari &}
1332. Shalimars, Sari & the	Veep {Shalimars}
1333. Sham-Ettes	Gold Dust/MGM
1334. Shane Sisters	Ford
1335. Shangri-Las	Mercury/Red Bird/ Scepter/Smash/Spokane
1336. Sharlets	Explosive
1337. Sharmeers	Red Top
1338. Shar-mels	Palm
1339. Sharmettes	King
1340. Sharpets	Sound City
1341. Sharp-etts	Perma Hit
1342. Shellets, La'Shell & the	Eagle
1343. Shepherd Sisters	Atlantic/Benida/Capitol/ Lance/Melba/Mercury/ 20thCent. Fox/UA/Warwick
1344. Sherrons	DCP
1345. Sherry Sisters	Cindy
1346. Sherry Sisters	Epic/Okeh {Sherrys}
1347. Sherrys	Guyden/Jamie/J.J./Mercury/ Roberts {Sherry Sisters}
1348. Sherwoods	V-Tone
1349. Shirelles	Bell/Blue Rock/Decca/RCA/ Scepter/Tiara/UA
1350. Shockettes	Symbol
1351. Shondelles	King
1352. Short Cuts	Carlton
1353. Signals	Rhino
1354. Significant Other	Critique
1355. Silk	Decca/Nation
1356. Silk 'n Soul	Pacemaker
1357. Silk Satin & Lace	Sunrise
1358. Silver Convention	Midland Int'l./Midsong Int'l.
1359. Silver Sisters	Candee/Shell
1360. Silver Slippers, Barbara J. & the	Lescay
1361. Simon Said	Roulette
1362. Simon Sisters	Columbia/Kapp
1363. Simplicities	Hull
1364. Simpson Sisters	DCP
1365. Sinceres	Epic
1366. Singing Belles	Madison
1367. Sisters	Del-Fi/September
1368. Sister Sledge	Atco/Atlantic/Cotillion
1369. Sisters of Righteous	King
1370. Sisters Love	A & M/ManChild/Motown/ Mowest {Raeletts}
1371. Slick	Fantasy
1372. Slits	Island
1373. Smith Sisters	Dot
1374. Snakes, Leila & the	Asp
1375. Snaps, Ginger & the	MGM/Tore {American Spring/ Honeys/Spring}
1376. So & Sos, Anita & the	RCA
1377. Socialites	Arrawak/Warner Bros. {Lorraine & the Socialites}
1378. Socialites, Lorraine, & the	Mercury {Socialites}
1379. Society Girls	Vee Jay
1380. Softouch	Prodigal
1381. Songettes, Katie & the	Decca
1382. Song Spinners	Leila
1383. Sonnets	Guyden
1384. Sonnettes	K.O.
1385. Sonoma	MCA
1386. Sophisticates	Janus/Mutt/Sonny
1387. Sophisticated	LadiesBareback/Mayhew {Bobbettes/ Soul Angels}
1388. Sophomores, Sandy & the	Columbia
1389. Sorrows, Joy & the	MGM
1390. Soul Aggregation	Capitol
1391. Soul Angels	Josie {Bobbettes/Sophisticated Ladies}
1392. Soul Club	MCA
1393. Soulettes	Dud Sound/Scope

Name	Label
1394. Soul Generation	Tru-Ba-Dor
1395. Soul Impacts	S.I.M.
1396. Soul Sisters	Guyden/Kayo/Sue/Veep
1397. Soul Teasers	Joker
1398. Sound of Experience	Bicentennial/Community
1399. Sound of Soul	Josie
1400. Sounds of Love	RCA
1401. Sparkels	Old Town
1402. Sparkletones	Pageant/Verve
1403. Sparks	Della/Path
1404. Specialties Ultd.	Sack
1405. Spice	Cle An Thar/Sound Gems
1406. Spice Girls	Virgin
1407. Spice Of Life	Poppy
1408. Spices, Sugar & the	Stacy/Swan/Tollie/Vee Jay
1409. Spyce	Moby Dick
1410. Spring	UA {American Spring/Ginger & The Snaps/Honeys}
1411. Squires, Shirley & the	Constellation
1412. Starbells, Terry Star &	New Art
1413. Starettes	Jewel
1414. Stargard	MCA/Warner Bros.
1415. Starlets	Astro {Angels/Dusk/Halos}
1416. Starlets	Chess {Gems/Lovettes/Pets}
1417. Starlets, Ella Thomas & the	Gedisons/Kelley/Middle C
1418. Starlets	Pam {Bluebelles/Original Bluebelles/Danetta & the Starlets}
1419. Starlets, Danetta & the	Okehm {Starlets}
1420. Starlets	Lute/Tower
1421. Starlets, Jenny Lee & the	Congress
1422. Starlettes	Checker
1423. Starlettes	Siana
1424. Starletts	Scarlett
1425. Starlites	Queen
1426. Starr Sisters	Lute
1427. Stepping Stones	Philips {Cinderallas, Cookies, HoneyBees, Palisades}
1428. Stepsisters, Cindy Rella & her	Carlton
1429. Stewardesses	Capitol
1430. Stewart Sisters	Specialty
1431. Storey Sisters	Baton/Cameo/Mercury {Twinkles}
1432. Stormy & Sunny	Inarts
1433. Stratavarious	Roulette
1434. Strollers	Jubilee
1435. Student Nurses	RCA
1436. Stylettes	Cameo/San-Dee
1437. Sty-Letts	Pillar {Sty-Letts, Sandy & the}
1438. Sty-Letts, Sandy & the	Rem
1439. Sugar & Spice	Groove/Kapp
1440. Sugar 'N Spice	Loma/White Whale
1441. Sugar Babes	MCA
1442. Sugar Beat	Peak
1443. Sugar Buns	Warner Bros.
1444. Sugar Cakes	Warner Bros.
1445. Sugar Lumps	Uptown
1446. Sugar Lumps	Virgil
1447. Sugarnettes	Conclave
1448. Sugar Plums	Phi-Dan
1449. Sugar Tones, Candy & the	Jackpot
1450. Summer's Children	Apt
1451. Summits	Harmon/Rust
1452. Sunbeams	Tollie {Emotions}
1453. Sunbeams, Donna Rae & the	Sattelite
1454. Superbs	Catamount/Sue/Symbol {Devotion/Devotions}
1455. Superbs, V.V. & the	Blue Rock
1456. Super Chicks	Roulette
1457. Supremes	Mark
1458. Supremes	Motown/Tamla {Primettes}
1459. Supreme Teens	Lowery
1460. Surf Bunnies	Dot/Goliath
1461. Surfer Girls	Columbia
1462. Surfs, Les	RCA
1463. Suzettes	Atomic
1464. Suzettes	Moonglow

Name	Label
1465. Swanettes	Beltone
1466. Swans	Cameo/Kapp/Parkway/ Roulette/Swan
1467. Swans	Dot/Reveille
1468. Sweet and Innocent	Act IV
1469. Sweet and Sassy	Del Pat
1470. Sweet Cherries	T-Neck
1471. Sweet Cream	Shady Brook
1472. Sweethearts	Brunswick/Como/D & H/ Harris/Kent/Ray-Star
1473. Sweet Inspirations	Atlantic/Caribou/RSO/Stax
1474. Sweet Delights	Atco
1475. Sweethearts	Discotek/Seeburg
1476. Sweethearts, Shirley & the	Twirl
1477. Sweethearts, Valentine & the	Big Top
1478. Sweet Honey In The Rock	Earthbeat
1479. Sweet Obsession	Epic
1480. Sweet Tarts	Whiplash
1481. Sweeties	End
1482. Sweet Marquees	Apache
1483. Sweet Music	Wand
1484. Sweet Nothings	Destination
1485. Sweet Nuthins	Swan
1486. Sweet Rain	Polydor/RCA
1487. Sweets	Soultown
1488. Sweets	Valiant
1489. Sweet Sensation	Atco/Next Plateau
1490. Sweet Sensation	Pye
1491. Sweet Soul	Mercury {Love Notes, Harriet Laverne & the/Love Notes, Honey Love & the/Love Notes/Kisses, Candy & the}
1492. Sweet Teens	Gee
1493. Sweet Teens	Bea & Baby/Federal/Flip
1494. Sweet Things	Capitol
1495. Sweet Things	Date {Darletts}
1496. Sweet Three	Cameo/Decca
1497. Swensons	X-Tra {Chantels/Relatives/ Veneers}
1498. Swinging Bridgettes	Bronze/Owl Sound
1499. Swinging Rocks, Ruby Yates & the	Hit
1500. SWV	Arista/RCA
1501. Sydells	Beltone/Lang
1502. Sylte Sisters	Coliseum
1503. Symbols	Stanson
1504. Symphonics	ABC/Brunswick/Wilson
1505. Symphonies	Carnival
1506. Syncapates	Times Square
1507. Tabulations, Brenda & the	Chocolate City/Epic/Top & Bottom
1508. Taffys	Amy/Fairmount/Pageant
1509. Tailor Maids	Capitol
1510. T'Aira's, Gloria & the	Betty
1511. Tammys	UA/Veep
1512. Tandells	Jam-Cha
1513. Tangenettes	Ran
1514. Tangerines	Wildcat
1515. Tantrum	Ovation
1516. Taste of Honey	Capitol
1517. Tattletales	Warner Bros.
1518. Tax Free	Foxcar
1519. Taylor Tones	Alton/C&T/Starmaker
1520. Teardrops	Musicor/Saxony
1521. Teardrops, Honey & the	Val
1522. Teardrops, Patti Jo & the	Crazytown
1523. Tears	Dig
1524. Tears	Smash
1525. Teddy Bear Co., Rena Faye & the	Melron
1526. Teenagers	Tahoe
1527. Teen-Aires, Carol Kay & the	Crest
1528. Teen-Clefs	Dice
1529. Teen Dreams	Vernon
1530. Teenettes	Brunswick/Josie
1531. Teenettes	Carellen/Sandy
1532. Teenettes	Crest
1533. Teenettes, Betty J. & the	Mona Lee

Name	Label
1534. Teen Queens	Antler/Kent/RCA/RPM {Rosie & Betty}
1535. Teens, Barbara Jean & the	Allison
1536. Teen Turbans	Loma
1537. Telltales	Decca
1538. Tempettes	Impresario
1539. Tender Loving Care	Renfro
1540. Tenderonies	Hip Spin
1541. Teques	Gary/Star-Vue
1542. Ter-Rells	ABC
1543. Terrifics	Diamond Jim
1544. Terry Girls	Mala
1545. Terrytones	Wye {Terrytones, Gayle Fortune & the}
1546. Terrytones, Gayle Fortune & the	{Terrytones}
1547. Tetes Noires	Rapunzel/Rounder
1548. Third Creation	Motown
1549. Third Degree	Music Factory
1550. Third Party	DV8
1551. Third Point	Tide
1552. 13th Amendments	News Maker
1553. Thomas Sisters	Chief
1554. Thorntonettes	Bobsan {Thornton Sisters}
1555. Thornton Sisters	Bobsan/Cuppy {Thorntonettes}
1556. Three Barry Sisters	London
1557. Three Belles	Jubilee
1558. Three Bells	Lawn
1559. Three Coquettes	Hope
1560. Three Debs	Crown {Debs}
1561. Three Degrees	ABC/Ariola/Epic/Ichiban/ Metromedia/Neptune/Phil Int'l./Roulette/Swan/ Warner Bros.
1562. Three Dolls	MGM
1563. Three Dolls, La Ronda Succeed & the	Magnificent
1564. Three Dots	Buzz
1565. Three Graces	Golden Crest
1566. Three Ks	Carousel
1567. Three Karats	Delray/D.W.
1568. Three Kittens	Brunswick
1569. Three Ounces Of Love	Motown
1570. Three Pennies	B.T. Puppy/Golden Crest {English Muffins}
1571. Three Playmates	Savoy
1572. Three Queens	J.O.B.
1573. Three Tons Of Joy	RCA
1574. Threeteens	Rev
1575. Thrillettes	Lawn
1576. Thrills	Capitol
1577. Tiaras	3D/Valiant
1578. Tiaras, Rita & the	Dore
1579. Tiffanies	KR
1580. Tiffanys	Arctic/Atlantic/Josie/MRS {Tiffanys, Cindy Gibson &}
1581. Tiffanys, Cindy Gibson & the	General {Tiffanys}
1582. Tiger Lily	Rhino
1583. Tikies	Wright Sound
1584. Tilton Sisters	Dot
1585. Tip Tops	Parkway
1586. TLC	La Face
1587. Tomboys	Swan
1588. Tom Tom Club	Sire
1589. Tonettes	ABC-Paramount/Doe/Modern {Claremonts}
1590. Tonettes	Dynamic
1591. Tonettes	Volt {Charmells}
1592. Tonettes, Gloria Scott & the	Warner Bros.
1593. Tonetts, Jackie & the	D-Town
1594. Total	Bad Boy
1595. Total Coelo	Chrysalis
1596. Toy Dolls	Era
1597. Toys	Dyno Voice/Musicor/ Philips/Virgo {Charlettes}
1598. Tracey Twins	East West/Reserve
1599. Tracynettes	Pearlsfar
1600. Tranquils	Hamilton {Deltairs}

Girl Groups

Name	Label
1601. Tran-Sisters	Imperial
1602. Traps, Mousie & the	Toddlin' Town
1603. Treasures, Bonnie & the	Phi Dan
1604. Treat	First Prize
1605. Trebelaires	Nestor
1606. Trells	Port City/Roal
1607. Triangles, Joanne & the	VIP
1608. Trilettes	Master
1609. Tri-Dells	Eldo
1610. Tri-Lites	Enith
1611. Trilons	Tag
1612. Trinikas	Pearce
1613. Trinkets	Cortland/Imperial {Little Foxes/ Versalettes}
1614. Triplets	Mercury
1615. Triplettes	Molly-Jo
1616. Tru-leers	Checker
1617. Tuesday's	Arista
1618. Tuesday's Children	Columbia
1619. Tulips	MGM
1620. Tuxedo Junction	Butterfly
1621. Twans	Dade
1622. Twilettes	Darcy
1623. Twilights	Capitol
1624. Twinkles	Peak {Storey Sisters}
1625. Twinkles	Musicor
1626. Twinettes	Vee Jay
1627. Twin Tones	Monte Carlo
1628. Twintonettes	Titan
1629. Two Notes	Coral
1630. Two Of A Kind	Planet
1631. Two Of Clubs	Fraternity
1632. Two Sisters	Sugarscope
1633. Two Tons Of Fun	Fantasy-Honey {Weather Girls}
1634. Ultimates	Capitol
1635. Ultimates	Valentine
1636. Unforgettables	Colpix/Titanic
1637. Uniques, Barbara & the	Abbott/Arden/New Chicago Sound {Du-ettes}
1638. Unit One	Jamie
1639. Unluv'd	MGM
1640. Upnilons	Lummtone
1641. Uptights	Columbia/Mala
1642. Uptights	Skye
1643. Utmosts	Pan-Or
1644. Utopias	Fortune/Hi-Q
1645. Valerons, Vala Reegan & the	Atco
1646. Valentines	Ludix/UA
1647. Valons	Mark III
1648. Vandellas, Martha & the	Gordy/Tamla {Del Phi's/Vells}
1649. Vandelettes	Mellow Town
1650. Van Dorn Sisters	Phil Tone
1651. Vanity 6	Motown/Warner Bros.
1652. Vareeations	Dionn
1653. Vashonettes	Checker
1654. Vashons	Delle
1655. Vells	Mel-o-dy {Del Phi's/Martha & The Vandellas}
1656. Velvelettes	IPG/Soul/VIP
1657. Velveletts, Dot & the	Teek
1658. Velveteens	Laurie/Stark
1659. Velveteens, Terri & the	Arc/Kerwood
1660. Velvetones	Ascot/Verve
1661. Velvets	Number One
1662. Vel Vettes	Round
1663. Velvetts	Dore/20thCent. Fox
1664. Veneers	Princeton/Treyco {Chantels, End 1104 /Relatives/Swensons}

Name	Label
1665. Vernons Girls	Challenge/Mala
1666. Versalettes	Witch {Little Foxes/Trinkets}
1667. Versatiles, Tootsie & the	Elmor
1668. Ve-Shellles	Boola Boola
1669. Vestelles	Decca
1670. Viadettes, Irma & the	Upset
1671. Viceroys	Imperial
1672. Victorians	Liberty
1673. Vignettes	Empala
1674. Violetts	Diamond/Herald
1675. Virgos	Pioneer
1676. Voices	Marlu/Victoria
1677. Voices	Zoo
1678. Voices of Joy	Paramount
1679. Vonettes	Cobblestone
1680. Vonns	King
1681. Vonnair Sisters	Buena Vista
1682. Vont Clairs	Double R
1683. Vontones	Al King
1684. Vydells	Happy Fox
1685. Wagnon Sisters	RCA
1686. Watesians	Donna
1687. Waitresses	Clone/Polydor/ZE
1688. Watts Line	Bullet/Capitol
1689. Wednesday Week	Enigma/Warf Rat/Rhino
1690. West Winds	Kapp
1691. Weather Girls	Columbia {Two Tons Of Fun}
1692. Wendy & Bonnie	Skye
1693. Wendy & Lisa	Columbia
1694. What Four	Capitol/Columbia
1695. Whippets	Josie
1696. Whispering Winds	MGM
1697. Whyte Boots	Philips
1698. Wildcats	Reprise {Blossoms/Blue Jeans, Bob B. Soxx & The/ Coeds/Crystals/Dreamers/ Girlfriends/Hushabyes, Hale & the/Playgirls/Rollettes}
1699. Wild Flower	Dash
1700. Wild Honey	Dash/Drive/Georgia Peach/ Houston Int'l./P&P {Delicates}
1701. Wil-ettes	Jamie
1702. Willis Sisters	ABC-Paramount/Cameo/ Columbia/RCA
1703. Willows	MGM
1704. Wilson-Phillips	SBK
1705. Wilson Sisters	Bethlehem/Freedom
1706. Wish, Fonda Rae &	Personel
1707. Witches & A Warlock	Calla/Sew City
1708. Woman	Shock
1709. Womanfolk	RCA
1710. Wonderettes	Enterprise/Ruby/UA/Veep
1711. Wonderlettes	Baja
1712. Wonders, Ruby & the	Normar
1713. Wooden Nickels	Omen/Philips/Vault
1714. Wright Sisters	Cadence
1715. Xscape	Columbia
1716. Young Generation	Red Bird
1717. Young Generators	Mary/Star Ship
1718. Young Ladies	Stang
1719. Young Sisters	Mala/Twirl
1720. Youngsters	Apt
1721. Young World Singers	Decca
1722. Y-Pants	99
1723. Yum Yums	ABC
1724. Z-Debs	Roulette {Clickettes/Hearts/ Endeavors/Jaynetts/Poppies}
1725. Zippers, Zip & the	Pageant {Orlons}

Hottest 500 Collectible
Girl Group Records Value Guide

The pricing for the following selection of records has been
compiled by the staff of *Goldmine* magazine. These suggested values are for
Near Mint condition items only. Values will very with condition, region,
and demand so check out the trends in your locale.

Group	Record	Label/Number	Year/Value
1. Adorables	Be/School's All Over	Golden World 10	1964 ($25)
2. Andantes	Like A Nightmare/If You Were Mine	VIP 25004	1964 ($2,500)
3. Angels	Boy From Cross-town/World Without Love	Smash 1931	1964 ($15)
4. Angels	Cotton Fields/A Moment Ago	Caprice 121	1963 ($15)
5. Angels	Cotton Fields/Irresistible	Ascot 2139	1963 ($12)
6. Angels	You Should Have Told Me/I'd Be Good For You	Caprice118	1962 ($15)
7. Attractions	You Don't Know, Boy/Think Back	June Bug 697/698	1966 ($25)
8. Avalons	Louella/You Broke Our Hearts	Dice 90/91	1958 ($150)
9. Baby Dolls	Go Away Baby/I'm Lonely	Maske 103	1960 ($50)
10. Baby Dolls	Thanks Mr. DJ/What A Wonderful Love	Maske 701	1961 ($120)
11. Barbees	Que Pasa/The Wind	Stepp 236	1957 ($200)
12. Beach Nuts	Out In The Sun (Hey-O)/Someday Soon	Bang 504	1965 ($50)
13. Bees, Honey & The	Inside O' Me/Two Can Play The Same Game	Academy 114	1965 ($12)
14. Beljeans, LaBrenda Ben & The	Camel Walk/The Chaperone	Gordy 7009	1962 ($50)
15. Berry, Richard	Wait For Me/Good Love	RPM 477	1956 ($30)
16. Big Town Girls, Shirley Matthews & The	Big Town Boy/Count On That	Atlantic 2210	1963 ($12)
17. Big Town Girls, Shirley Matthews & The	Private Property/Wise Guys	Atlantic 2224	1964 ($12)
18. Blossoms	Deep Into My Heart/Let Your Love Shine On Me	Reprise 0522	1966 ($15)
19. Blossoms	Good, Good Lovin'/Deep Into My Heart	Reprise 0639	1967 ($15)
20. Blossoms	Have Faith In Me/Little Louie	Capitol 3878	1958 ($25)
21. Blossoms	I'm In Love/What Makes Love	Okeh 7162	1962 ($20)
22. Blossoms	Move On/He Promised Me	Capitol 3822	1957 ($30)
23. Blossoms	My Love Come Home/Lover Boy	Reprise 0475	1966 ($15)
24. Blossoms	No Other Love/Baby Daddy-O	Capitol 4072	1958 ($25)
25. Blossoms	That's When The Tears Start/Good, Good Lovin'	Reprise 0436	1966 ($15)
26. Blossoms	Things Are Changing/same	EEOC T4LM 8172	1965 ($150)
27. Blossoms	Write Me A Letter/Hard To Get	Challenge 9122	1962 ($20)
28. Blu, Nikki	(Whoa, Whoa) I Love Him So/Inst.	Parkway 931	1964 ($10)
29. Blue Belles	Cool Water/When Johnny Comes Marching Home	Newtown 5009	1963 ($20)
30. Blue Belles	I've Got To Let Him Know/I Sold My Heart To The Junkman	Peak 7042	1964 ($25)
31. Blue Belles	Story Of A Fool/Cancel The Call	Atlantic 987	1953 ($150)
32. Blue Belles, Patti LaBelle & The	Academy Award/Decatur Street	Newtown 5019	1963 ($20)
33. Blue Belles, Patti LaBelle & The	Down The Aisle/C'est La Vie	King 5777	1963 ($15)
34. Blue Belles, Patti LaBelle & The	Love Me Just A Little/Pitter Patter	Newtime 510	1963 ($20)
35. Blue Belles, Patti LaBelle & The	Oh My Love/I Need Your Love	Atlantic 2446	1967 ($10)
36. Bobbettes	I Shot Mr. Lee/Billy	Triple-X 104	1960 ($20)
37. Bobbettes	I Shot Mr. Lee/Untrue Love	Atlantic 2069	1960 ($30)
38. Bobbettes	Looking For A Lover/Are You Satisfied	King 5551	1961 ($15)
39. Bobbettes	Oh My Papa/Dance With Me Georgie	King 5490	1961 ($15)
40. Bobbettes	Oh My Papa/I Cried	Gallant 1006	1960 ($20)
41. Bobbettes	Over There/Loneliness	Jubilee 5427	1962 ($12)
42. Bobbettes	The Dream/Um Bow Bow	Atlantic 1194	1958 ($20)
43. Bobbettes	Don't Say Goodnight/You Are My Sweetheart	Atlantic 2027 (stock)	1959 ($20)
44. Bobbettes	Have Mercy Baby/Dance With Me Georgie	Triple-X 106	1960 ($20)
45. Bobbettes	Mr. Lee/Look At The Stars	Atlantic 1144	1957 ($25)
46. Bobbettes	My Dearest/I'm Stepping Out Tonight	King 5623	1962 ($15)
47. Bouquets	Girls, Girls/Yeah, Babe	Vest 8000	1963 ($15)
48. Bouquets	Welcome To My Heart/Ain't That Love	Blue Cat 115	1965 ($30)
49. Bouquets, Tootie & The	The Conqueror/You Done Me Wrong	Parkway 887	1963 ($25)
50. Bronzettes	Run, Run, You Little Fool/Hot Spot	Parkway 929	1964 ($12)
51. Butterflys	Goodnight Baby/The Swim	Red Bird 10-009	1964 ($25)
52. Butterflys	I Wonder/Gee Baby Gee	Red Bird 10-016	1964 ($25)
53. Cake	Baby That's Me/Mocking Bird	Decca 32179	1967 ($10)
54. Carols	My Search Is Over/Keko	Lamp 2001	1956 ($50)
55. Carroll, Bernadette	All The Way Home I Cried/Nicky	Laurie 3217	1963 ($15)
56. Carroll, Bernadette	Happy Birthday/Homecoming Party	Laurie 3268	1964 ($15)
57. Carroll, Bernadette	Party Girl/I Don't Wanna Know	Laurie 3238	1964 ($15)
58. Castanets	I Love Him/Funky Wunky Piano	TCF 1	1963 ($10)
59. Chantels	Eternally/Swamp Water	Ludix 101	1963 ($20)
60. Chantels	Goodbye To Love/I'm Confessing	End 1048	1959 ($25)
61. Chantels	I Can't Take It/Never Let Go	End 1037	1958 ($25)

Group	Record	Label/Number	Year/Value
62. Chantels	I Love You So/How Could You Call It Off	End 1020	1958 ($40)
63. Chantels	It's Just Me/Indian Giver	Verve 10435	1966 ($15)
64. Chantels	Look In My Eyes/Glad To Be Back	Carlton 555	1961 ($20)
65. Chantels	Love Makes All The Difference In The World/I'm Gonna Win Him Back	RCA 74-0347	1970 ($10)
66. Chantels	Maybe/Come My Little Baby	End 1005 (Black)	1957 ($80)
67. Chantels	Summertime/Here It Comes Again	Carlton 569	1962 ($20)
68. Chantels	Sure Of Love/Prayer	End 1026	1958 ($25)
69. Chantels	Take Me As I Am/There's No Forgetting You	TCF/Arawak 123	1965 ($15)
70. Chantels	There's Our Song Again/I'm The Girl	End 1105	1961 ($25)
71. Chantels	Whoever You Are/How Could You Call It Off	End 1069	1960 ($25)
72. Chantels	Believe Me/I (Veneers)	End 1103	1961 ($60)
73. Chantels	Congratulations/If You Try	End 1030	1958 ($25)
74. Chantels	Every Night/Whoever You Are	End 1015	1958 ($30)
75. Chantels	He's Gone/The Plea	End 1001 (Black)	1957 ($80)
76. Charlettes	The Fight's Not Over/Whatever Happened To Our Love	Angie 1002	1963 ($25)
77. Charmaines	Where Is The Boy Tonight/On The Wagon	Dot 16351	1962 ($20)
78. Charmers	He's Gone/Oh, Yes	Aladdin 3341	1956 ($60)
79. Charmers	Johnny, My Dear/All Alone	Aladdin 3337	1956 ($60)
80. Charmettes	Johnny Johnny/School Letter	Federal 12345	1959 ($40)
81. Charmettes	Ouzi Ouzi Ooh/He's A Wise Guy	Kapp 570	1964 ($25)
82. Charmettes	Stop The Wedding/Sugar Boy	World Artists 1053	1965 ($25)
83. Chicklettes, Angie & The	Treat Him Tender, Maureen/Tommy	Apt 25080	1965 ($30)
84. Chic-lets	I Want You To Be My Boyfriend/Don't Goof On Me	Josie 919	1964 ($15)
85. Chiffons	Just For Tonight/Teach Me How	Laurie 3423	1967 ($10)
86. Chiffons	Love Me Like You're Gonna Lose Me/Three Dips of Ice Cream	Laurie 3497	1969 ($10)
87. Chiffons	Lucky Me/Why Am I So Shy	Laurie 3166	1963 ($15)
88. Chiffons	My Boyfriend's Back/I Got Plenty O' Nuttin'	Laurie 3364	1966 ($10)
89. Chiffons	Sailor Boy/When Summer's Through	Laurie 3262	1964 ($12)
90. Chiffons	Secret Love/Strange, Strange Feeling	B.T. Puppy 558	1969 ($10)
91. Chiffons	So Much In Love/Strange, Strange Feeling	Buddah 171	1970 ($10)
92. Chiffons	What Am I Gonna Do With You/Strange Strange Feeling	Laurie 3275	1964 ($12)
93. Chiffons (w/Hoagy Lands)	The Next In Line/Please Don't Talk About Me	Laurie 3381	1966 ($25)
94. Chiffons	Dream, Dream, Dream/Oh My Lover	Laurie 3648	1976 ($10)
95. Chiffons	My Sweet Lord/Main Nerve	Laurie 3630	1975 ($10)
96. Chiffons, Ginger & The	She/Where Were You Last Night	Groove 58-0003	1962 ($30)
97. Christian, Diane	Has Anybody Seen My Boyfriend/There's So Much About My Baby That I Love	Smash 1862	1963 ($10)
98. Christian, Diane	Little Boy/Why Don't The Boy Leave Me Alone	Bell 617	1965 ($10)
99. Christian, Diane	Wonderful Guy/It Happened One Night	Bell 610	1964 ($10)
100. Cinderellas	Baby, Baby I Still Love You/Please Don't Wake Me	Dimension 1026	1964 ($40)
101. Cinnamons	I'm Not Gonna Worry/Strange, Strange Feeling	B.T. Puppy 503	1964 ($8)
102. Claremonts	Angel Of Romance/Why Keep Me Dreaming	Apollo 517	1957 ($60)
103. Clickettes	Jive Time Turkey/A Teenager's First Love	Dice 83/84	1959 ($150)
104. Clickettes	Lover's Prayer/Grateful	Dice 96/97	1959 ($150)
105. Clickettes	To Be A Part Of You/Because Of My Best Friend	Dice 92/93	1959 ($120)
106. Clickettes	Warm, Soft And Lovely/Why Oh Why	Dice 94/95	1959 ($120)
107. Clickettes	Where Is He/The Lone Lover	Guyden 2043	1960 ($30)
108. Clickettes	But Not For Me/I Love You I Swear	Dice 100	1958 ($120)
109. Clickettes	I Just Can't Help It/Inst.	Checker 1060	1963 ($20)
110. Cookies	Down By The River/My Lover	Atlantic 1110	1956 ($25)
111. Cookies	I Never Dreamed/The Old Crowd	Dimension 1032	1964 ($15)
112. Cookies	In Paradise/Passing Time	Atlantic 1084	1956 ($30)
113. Cookies	Later, Later/Precious Love	Atlantic 1061	1955 ($30)
114. Cookies	Mr. Cupid/Hang My Head And Cry (Big Guys)	Warner Bros. 7047	1967 ($10)
115. Cookies	Wounded/All My Trials	Warner Bros. 7025	1967 ($10)
116. Cookies	Don't Let Go/All Night Mambo	Lamp 8008	1954 ($40)
117. Cookies	King Of Hearts/Hippy Dippy Daddy	Josie 822	1957 ($30)
118. Cookies, Varetta Dillard & The	Star Of Fortune/Rules Of Love	RCA 47-7144	1958 ($20)
119. Copesetics	Bohemian/Believe In Me	Premium 409	1956 ($200)
120. Crayons	Love At First Sight/I Saw You	Counsel 122	1963 ($30)
121. Crystals	He Hit Me/No One Ever Tells You	Philles 105 (Blue/Black)	1962 ($80)
122. Crystals	He Hit Me/No One Ever Tells You	Philles 105 (Orange)	1962 ($100)
123. Crystals	He's A Rebel/I Love You Eddie	Philles 106 (Orange/Black)	1962 ($60)
124. Crystals	I Do Believe/I Love My Baby	Aladdin 3355	1956 ($60)
125. Crystals	I Got A Man/Are You Trying To Get Rid Of Me Baby	United Artists 994	1966 ($15)
126. Crystals	I Wonder/Little Boy (UK only)	London 9852	1964 ($25)
127. Crystals	My Place/You Can't Tie A Good Girl Down	United Artists 927	1965 ($15)
128. Crystals	Please Be My Boyfriend/Things Are Changing (Blossoms)	EEOC T4LM 8172-1	1965 ($150)
129. Crystals	The Screw Pt. 1/The Screw Pt. 2 (DJ Only)	Philles 111	1963 ($4,000+)
130. Cute-Teens	From This Day Forward/When My Teenage Days Are Over	Aladdin 3458	1959 ($250)
131. Darlettes	Here She Comes/Just You	Dunes 2026	1963 ($15)
132. Darlettes, Diane & The	Just You/Wobble	Dunes 2016	1962 ($25)
133. Darnells	Too Hurt To Cry, Too Much In Love To Say Goodbye/Come On Home	Gordy 7024	1963 ($80)
134. Debs	Johnnie Darling/Doom-A-Roca	Keen 34003	1957 ($25)
135. Debs	Just Another Fool/Danger Ahead	Double L 727	1964 ($12)

Group	_Record_	_Label/Number_	_Year/Value_
136. Debutantes	Going Steady/Memories	Kayo 928	1958 ($250)
137. Deccors, Marie & The	I'm The One/Queen Of Fools	Cub 9115	1962 ($25)
138. Del-Phis	I 'll Let You Know/It Takes Two	Check-mate 1005	1961 ($200)
139. Del Rios	Wait Wait Wait/I'm Crying	Neptune 108	1959 ($60)
140. Delicates	Comin' Down With Love/Stop Shoving My Heart Around	Challenge 59304	1965 ($15)
141. Delicates	The Johnny Bunny/My First Date	Tender 818	1959 ($20)
142. Delltones	Baby Say You Love Me/Don't Be Too Long	Baton 212	1955 ($30)
143. Delltones	I'm Not In Love With You/Little Short Daddy	Rainbow 244	1954 ($100)
144. Delltones	My Heart's On Fire/Yours Alone	Brunswick 85015	1953 ($200)
145. Delltones	My Special Love/Believe It	Baton 223	1956 ($30)
146. Del-Rhythmetts	Chic-A-Boomer/I Need Your Love	JVB 5000	1959 ($60)
147. Delrons	Your Big Mistake/Leave Us Alone	Laurie 3252	1964 ($30)
148. Delrons, Reparata & The	Captain Of Your Ship/Toom Toom	Mala 589	1968 ($12)
149. Delrons, Reparata & The	I'm Nobody's Baby Now/Loneliest Girl In Town	RCA 47-8820	1966 ($15)
150. Delrons, Reparata & The	The Boy I Love/I Found My Place	World Artists 1062	1965 ($12)
151. Delrons, Reparata & The	A Summer Thought/He's The Greatest	World Artists 1057	1965 ($12)
152. Deltairs	Lullaby of The Bells/It's Only You Dear	Ivy 101 (yellow)	1957 ($150)
153. Deltairs	Standing At The Altar/I Might Like It	Ivy 105	1958 ($30)
154. Deltairs	Who Would Have Thought It/You Wont Be Satisfied	Felsted 8525	1958 ($30)
155. Del-vets	Repeat After Me/Will You Love Me In Heaven	End 1107	1961 ($20)
156. Del-vetts	Repeat After Me/I Want A Boy For Christmas	End 1106	1961 ($30)
157. Demures	He's Got Your Number/Raining Teardrops	Brunswick 55284	1964 ($100)
158. DeVaurs	Baby Doll/Teenager	D-Tone 3	1958 ($250)
159. DeVaurs	Where Are You/Boy In Mexico	Moon 105	1959 ($200)
160. DeVaurs	Where Are You/Boy In Mexico	Red Fox 104	1965 ($40)
161. DeVons	Groovin' With My Thing/Wise Up And Be Smart	Mr. G 825	1968 ($12)
162. Dixie Cups	Gee The Moon Is Shining Bright/I'm Gonna Get You Yet	Red Bird 10-032	1965 ($20)
163. Dixie Cups	Two Way Poc-A-Way/That's Where It's At	ABC-Paramount 10692	1965 ($12)
164. Dodds, Nella	Come Back Baby/Dream Boy	Wand 187	1965 ($12)
165. Dodds, Nella	Gee Whiz/Maybe Baby	Wand 1111	1966 ($15)
166. Dodds, Nella	Honey Boy/I Just Gotta Have You	Wand 1136	1967 ($80)
167. Dodds, Nella	Ps and Qs/Your Love's Back	Wand 178	1965 ($12)
168. Dodds, Nella	Come See About Me/You Don't Love Me Anymore	Wand 167	1964 ($12)
169. Dolls	And That Reminds Me/The Reason Why	Loma 2036	1966 ($15)
170. Dolls	In Love/Please Come Home	Okeh 7122	1959 ($12)
171. Dolls	Just Before You Leave/I Love	Teenage 1010	1958 ($1,000)
172. Dorells	Maybe Baby/The Beating Of My Heart	Atlantic 2244	1964 ($15)
173. Dorells	Maybe Baby/The Beating Of My Heart	GEI 4401	1963 ($30)
174. Dorrelles	You Are/Good Luck To The Lucky Girl	RSVP 1108	1965 ($12)
175. Douglas, Kellie	My Mama Don't Like Him/Big Honky Baby	RCA 47-8005	1962 ($12)
176. Dream Girls	Oh This Is Why/Don't Break My Heart	Cameo 165	1959 ($25)
177. Dream Girls	Oh This Is Why/Don't Break My Heart	Twirl 1002	1959 ($50)
178. Dream Girls, Bobbie Smith & The	Mine All Mine/The Duchess Of Earl	Big Top 3100	1962 ($20)
179. Dream Team	I'm Not Afraid/Inka Dinka Doo	Epic 9701	1964 ($12)
180. Dreamers	Do Not Forget/Since You've Been Gone	Flip 319	1956 ($40)
181. Dreamers	Do Not Forget/Since You've Been Gone	Flip 354	1961 ($20)
182. Dreamers	No Obligation/Lips Were Meant For Kissing	Manhattan 503	1956 ($100)
183. Dreamers, Eloise Brooks & The	Charles My Darling/My Plea	Aladdin 3303	1955 ($200)
184. Dreamers, Richard Berry & The	At Last/Bye Bye	Flair 1052	1955 ($60)
185. Dreamers, Richard Berry & The	Daddy Daddy/Baby Darling	Flair 1058	1955 ($60)
186. Dreamers, Richard Berry & The	Do I Do/Besame Mucho	Flip 339	1958 ($30)
187. Dreamers, Richard Berry & The	Together/Jelly Roll (no group)	Flair 1075	1955 ($50)
188. Drew-vels	It's My Time/Everybody Knows	Capitol 5145	1964 ($10)
189. Dungaree Darlings	Boy Of My Dreams/Little Wallflower	Karen 1005	1959 ($100)
190. Dungaree Dolls	Boy Of My Dreams/Little Wallflower	Rego 1003	1958 ($250)
191. Eady, Ernestine (w/Candy & The Kisses)	The Change/That's The Way It Goes	Junior 1007	1963 ($30)
192. Eady, Ernestine (w/Candy & The Kisses)	The Change/That's The Way It Goes	Scepter 12102	1965 ($12)
193. Earl-Jean	Randy/They're Jealous Of Me	Colpix 748	1964 ($10)
194. Elena	Evening Time/Road Of Love	Roulette 4605	1965 ($15)
195. Emotions	Brushfire/I Love You But I'll Leave You	Twin Stacks 130	1968 ($10)
196. Emotions	Brushfire/Somebody New	Twin Stacks 126	1968 ($10)
197. Emotions	I Can't Stand No More Heartaches/You Better Get Used To It	Brainstorm 125	1967 ($8)
198. Emotions	Never Let Me Go/I Can't Control These Emotions	Brainstorm 129	1968 ($8)
199. Enchanters	I've Lost/Housewife Blues	Jubilee 5080	1952 ($200)
200. Enchanters	Today Is Your Birthday/How Could You	Jubilee 5072	1952 ($250)
201. Endeavors	Suffering With My Heart/I Got The Feeling	J&S 254	1960 ($1,200)
202. English, Barbara	Small Town Girl/Tell Me Like It Is	Reprise 0349	1965 ($25)
203. English, Barbara Jean	(You Got Me) Sittin' In The Corner/Standing On Tip Toe	Aurora 55	1966 ($80)
204. English, Barbara	Because I Love Somebody/Good Times Gone	Warner Bros. 5685	1966 ($20)
205. English, Barbara	I've Got A Date/Shoo Fly	Reprise 0290	1964 ($25)
206. Estelle	The Year 2000/The Naked Boy	Laurie 3449	1968 ($100)
207. Evels	The Magic Of Love/Wonderful Guy	Tra-X 14	1960 ($60)
208. Exciters	Blowing Up My Mind/Don't Know What You're Missing	RCA 47-9723	1969 ($30)

Group	Record	Label/Number	Year/Value
209. Exciters	Soul Motion/You Know It Ain't Right	Shout 214	1967 ($10)
210. Exciters	You Better Come Home/Weddings Make Me Cry	Bang 518	1966 ($30)
211. Exciters	You Got Love/Number One	Shout 205	1966 ($10)
212. Exciters	Alone Again, Naturally/--	Fargo 1400	1972 ($8)
213. Exciters	If You Want My Love/Take One Step (I'll Take Two)	RCA 47-9633	1968 ($30)
214. Fashions	Fairy Tales/Please Let It Be Me	Elmor 301	1961 ($25)
215. Fashions	Baby That's Me/Nick and Joe Callin'	Cameo 331	1964 ($10)
216. Fashions	Dearest One/All I Want	Warwick 646	1961 ($20)
217. Fashions	When Love Slips Away/I.O.U.	Twentieth Cen. Fox 6703	1968 ($8)
218. Fashions, Barbara English & The	We Need Them/Ta Ta Tee Ta Ta	Roulette 4428	1962 ($30)
219. Fashions, Barbara English & The	Bad News/Fever	Roulette 4450	1962 ($30)
220. Fascinations	Mama Didn't Lie/Someone Like You	ABC-Paramount 10387	1963 ($20)
221. Fascinations	Tears In My Eyes/You Gonna Be Sorry	ABC-Paramount 10443	1963 ($25)
222. Fawns	Until I Die/Come On	Apt 25015	1958 ($30)
223. Ferguson, Sheila	And In Return/Are You Satisfied	Swan 4225	1965 ($30)
224. Ferguson, Sheila	Heartbroken Memories/Signs Of Love	Swan 4234	1966 ($40)
225. Ferguson, Sheila	I'll Weep For You/Don't (Leave Me Lover)	Swan 4217	1965 ($40)
226. Ferguson, Sheila	Little Red Riding Hood/How Did That Happen	Landa 706	1965 ($30)
227. First Choice	This Is The House/One Step Away	Scepter 12347	1972 ($6)
228. Flirtations	Stronger Than Her Love/Settle Down	Festival 705	1967 ($60)
229. Flirtations	Change My Darkness Into Light/Natural Born Lover	Josie 956	1966 ($15)
230. Flirtations	How Can You Tell Me?/Someone Out There	Parrot 40028	1968 ($12)
231. Four Chicadees	Ding Dong/Teenage Blues	Checker 849	1956 ($60)
232. Four Jewels	All That's Good/I Love Me Some You	Start 641	1963 ($30)
233. Four Jewels	Johnny Jealousy/Someone Special	Start 638	1963 ($30)
234. Four Jewels	Loaded With Goodies/Dapper Dan	Checker 1039	1963 ($20)
235. Four Jewels	Time For Love/That's What They Put Erasers On Pencils For	Checker 1069	1964 ($20)
236. Four Jewels	Loaded With Goodies/Fire	Start 638	1962 ($40)
237. Four Pennies	When The Boy's Happy/Hockaday Part 1	Rust 5070	1963 ($25)
238. Gay Notes	Hear My Plea/Crossroads	Post 2006	1955 ($60)
239. Gaye, Ellie	Cha-Cha Charming/Silly Isn't It	RCA 47-7231	1958 ($40)
240. Ginger Snaps	The Sh Down Down Song/I've Got Faith In Him	Dunhill 4003	1964 ($20)
241. Girlfriends	My One and Only Jimmy Boy/For My Sake	Colpix 712	1963 ($20)
242. Girlfriends, Erlene & Her	Because Of You/Casanova	Old Town 1152	1963 ($20)
243. Gray, Maureen	I'm So Young/There Is A Boy	Chancellor 1100	1962 ($25)
244. Gray, Maureen	The Story Of My Love/Summertime Is Near	Mercury 72131	1963 ($12)
245. Gray, Maureen	Crazy Over You/Today's The Day	Chancellor 1082	1961 ($25)
246. Greenwich, Ellie	You Don't Know/Baby	Red Bird 10-034	1965 ($40)
247. Gunter, Shirley	Believe Me/Crazy Little Baby	Tender 511	1958 ($30)
248. Gypsies	Hey There, Hey There/Blue Bird	Old Town 1168	1964 ($20)
249. Gypsies	Jerk It/Diamonds, Rubies, Gold and Fame	Old Town 1180	1965 ($20)
250. Gypsies	Look For The One Who Loves You/Oh Girl	Caprice 8442	1966
251. Gypsies	Oh I Wonder Why/Diamonds, Rubies, Gold and Fame	OldTown 1193	1966 ($25)
252. Gypsies	They're Having A Party/It's A Woman's World	Old Town 1184	1965 ($80)
253. Halos	Since I Fell For You/You're Never Gonna Find	Congress 249	1965 ($12)
254. Hearts	Going Home To Stay/Disappointed Bride	Baton 222	1956 ($30)
255. Hearts	Gone, Gone, Gone/Until The Real Thing Comes Along	Baton 215	1955 ($50)
256. Hearts	I Couldn't Let Him See Me Crying/You Weren't Home	J&S 1181	1961 ($50)
257. Hearts	I Had A Guy/He Drives Me Crazy	Baton 228	1956 ($25)
258. Hearts	I Want Your Love Tonight/Like Later Baby	J&S 1626/1627	1958 ($50)
259. Hearts	If I Had Known/There Are So Many Ways	J&S 10002/10003	1958 ($50)
260. Hearts	My Love Has Gone/You Or Me Has Got To Go	J&S 425/426	1959 ($50)
261. Hearts	There's No Love At All/Goodbye Baby	J&S 4571	1959 ($40)
262. Hearts	A Thousand Years From Today/I Feel So Good	J&S 995	1960 ($40)
263. Hearts	All My Love Belongs To You/Talk About Him Girlie	Baton 211	1955 ($50)
264. Hearts	Dancing In A Dream World/You Needn't Tell Me, I Know	J&S 1657	1957 ($60)
265. Hearts	Lonely Nights/Oo-Wee	Baton 208	1955 ($50)
266. Hearts	So Long Baby/You Say You Love Me	J&S 1660	1957 ($60)
267. Hearts, Ena Louise & The	From A Cap And A Gown/A Prisoner To You	Argyle 1635	1959 ($50)
268. Hi Lites	Please Believe Me I Love You/Sweet And Lovely	Reno 1030	1958 ($250)
269. Hill, Vernell	Long Haired Daddy/Sometimes Love	Tuff 381	1964 ($8)
270. Honey Bees	Endless/Let's See What's Happening	Imperial 5400	1956 ($40)
271. Honey Bees	One Wonderful Night/She Don't Deserve You	Fontana 1939	1964 ($20)
272. Honey Bees	Some Of Your Lovin'/You Turn Me On Boy	Fontana 1505	1965 ($20)
273. Honeys	He's A Doll/Love Of A Boy and Girl	Warner Bros. 5430	1964 ($600)
274. Honeys	Pray For Surf/Hide Go Seek	Capitol 5034	1963 ($200)
275. Honeys	Shoot The Curl/Surfin' Down The Swanee River	Capitol 4952	1963 ($150)
276. Honeys	The One You Can't Have/Jimmy With Tears	Capitol 5093	1963 ($200)
277. Honeytones	False Alarm/Honeybun Cha Cha	Wing 90013	1955 ($30)
278. Honeytones	Too Bad/Somewhere, Sometime, Someday	Mercury 70557	1955 ($25)
279. Hughes, Carol	Let's Get Together Again/Don't Turn Your Back	Corby 212	1966 ($10)
280. Humes, Anita	Just For The Boy/I'm Making It Over	Roulette 4575	1964 ($15)
281. Hushabyes, Hale & The	Yes Sir, That's My Baby/Bee Side Soul (Inst.)	York 408	1967 ($50)
282. Hushabyes, Hale & The	Yes Sir, That's My Baby/Jack's Theme (Inst.)	Reprise 0299	1964 ($200)
283. Hushabyes, Hale & The	Yes Sir, That's My Baby/Quetzals (Inst.)	Apogee 104	1964 ($300)

Group	Record	Label/Number	Year/Value
284. Ikettes	Down Down/What'cha Gonna Do	Phi-Dan 5009	1966 ($10)
285. Ikettes	Help Wanted/John's Big Chance	Minit 32045	1968 ($10)
286. Impalas	For The Love Of Mike/I Need You So Much	Checker 999	1961 ($12)
287. In Crowd	Let's Shindig/You're Gonna Miss Me	Swan 4204	1965 ($15)
288. Jackson, Shirley (The Dream Girls)	Wait For Me/The Wedding	Metro 20031	1959 ($12)
289. Jaynetts	Chicken, Chicken, Cranny Crow/Winky Dinky	J&S 1468/69	1964 ($8)
290. Jaynetts	Cry Behind The Daisies/Is It My Imagination	J&S 1177	1964 ($8)
291. Jaynetts	Looking For Wonderland, My Lover/Make It An Extra	J&S 1686	1965 ($8)
292. Jaynetts	There's No Love At All/Tonight You Belong To Me	Tuff 377	1964 ($12)
293. Jaynetts	Vangie Don't You Cry/My Guy Is As Sweet As Can Be	J&S 4418/4419	1965 ($8)
294. Jaynetts	Who Stole The Cookie/That's My Baby	J&S 1477	1965 ($10)
295. Jaynetts	I Wanted To Be Free/Where Are You Tonight	J&S 1765/66	1958 ($10)
296. Jelly Beans	You Don't Mean Me No Good/I'm Hip To You	Eskee 10001	1965 ($15)
297. Jets, Ellie Gee & The	Red Corvette/I Go You Go	Madison 160	1961 ($30)
298. Jewels	Baby It's You/She's Wrong For You Baby	Tec 3007	1964 ($25)
299. Jewels	Papa Left Mama Holdin' The Bag/This Is My Story	Dynamite 2000	1966 ($15)
300. Jewels	This Is My Story/My Song	Federal 12541	1964 ($20)
301. Jones, Dorothy	It's Unbearable/Taking That Long Walk Home	Columbia 42062	1961 ($10)
302. Jones, Toni	Dear (Here Comes My Baby)/Love Is Strange	Smash 1814	1963 ($10)
303. Joyettes	Story Of Love/Boy Next Door	Onyx 502	1956 ($100)
304. Joytones	Gee What A Boy/Is This Really The End	Rama 202	1956 ($300)
305. Joytones	My Foolish Heart/Jimbo Jango	Rama 215	1956 ($500)
306. Joytones	This Love/I Wanna Party Some More	Coed 600	1965 ($12)
307. Joytones	You Just Won't Treat Me Right/All My Love Belongs To You	Rama 191	1956 ($150)
308. King, Carole (w/The Cookies)	It Might As Well Rain Until 308. September/Nobody's Perfect	Companion 2000	1962 ($300)
309. King, Carole (w/The Cookies)	School Bells Are Ringing/I Didn't Have Any Summer Romance	Dimension 1004	1963 ($20)
310. Kisses, Candy & The	Sweet and Lovely/Out In The Streets Again	Scepter 12125	1966 ($15)
311. Kisses, Candy & The	Tonight's The Night/The Last Time	Scepter 12136	1966 ($12)
312. Kisses, Candy & The	Soldier Baby (Of Mine)/Shakin' Time	Cameo 355	1965 ($20)
313. Lalarettes, La La & The	This Day Of Ours/Getting Ready For Freddy	Elpco 2922	1963 ($60)
314. Linneas	My Baby Comes Home Today/Born To Be Your Baby	Diamond 248	1968 ($12)
315. Little Eva	Makin' With The Magilla/Run To Him	Dimension 1035	1964 ($10)
316. Little Eva	Takin' Back What I Said/Wake Up John	Dimension 1042	1965 ($10)
317. Loreleis	Why Do I Put Up With You/Strange Way	Brunswick 55271	1964 ($8)
318. Love Notes	Baby Baby You/Beg Me	Cameo 409	1966 ($12)
319. Love Notes, Honey Love & The	We Belong Together/Mary Ann	Cameo 380	1965 ($12)
320. Love Potion	This Love/Moby Binks	Kapp 979	1969 ($8)
321. Love Potion	This Love/Mr. Farouk (inst.)	TCB 1601	1968 ($15)
322. Love, Darlene	Christmas (Baby Please Come Home)/Winter Blues	Philles 125	1964 ($400)
323. Love, Darlene	Christmas (Baby Please Come Home)/Harry and Milt Meet Hal B.	Philles 119	1963 ($40)
324. Love, Darlene	Christmas (Baby Please Come Home)/Winter Wonderland	Philles 125x	1964($25)
325. Love, Darlene	Stumble And Fall/(He's A) Quiet Guy	Philles 123	1964 ($800)
326. Lovelites	I Found A Lover/Stop It	Bandera 2515	1967 ($15)
327. Magic Touch	Step Into My World/Part 2	Black Falcon 19102	1971 ($8)
328. Mar-vells	Go On And Have Yourself A Ball/How Do I Keep The Girls Away	Angie 100	1963 ($20)
329. Mar-vells	Go On And Have Yourself A Ball/How Do I Keep The Girls Away	Butane 778	1963 ($15)
330. Masterettes	Never Ever/Follow The Leader	Le Sage 716	1961 ($150)
331. Maye, Hartsy	As The Years Go By/Heigh Ho The Merry O	Zell 4397	1962 ($75)
332. McCrea, Darlene	I Feel A Little Bit Better/Soulful Feeling	Jubilee 5524	1965 ($10)
333. McCrea, Darlene	My Heart's Not In It/Don't You Worry Baby	Tower 104	1964 ($10)
334. McCrea, Darlene	You Made A Fool Of Me/You	Roulette 4173	1959 ($12)
335. Medallions	You Are Irresistible/Why Do You Look At Me	Lenox 5556	1962 ($20)
336. Miller Sisters	Let's Start A New/The Flip Skip	Acme 721	1957 ($40)
337. Miller Sisters	My Own/Sugar Daddy	Onyx 507	1957 ($50)
338. Miller Sisters	You Made A Promise/Crazy Billboard Song	Acme 717	1957 ($40)
339. Nelson Group, Teri	Sweet Talkin' Willie/The Backside	Kama Sutra 245	1968 ($10)
340. Opals	Love/Hop Skip & Jump	Beltone 2025	1962 ($25)
341. Orchids	That Boy Is Messing Up My Mind/The Harlem Tango	Columbia 42913	1963 ($20)
342. Original Blue Belles	You Better Move On/You're Just Fooling Yourself	Rainbow 1900	1964 ($25)
343. Orlons	Come On Down, Baby Baby/I Ain't Comin' Back	Cameo 352	1965 ($12)
344. Orlons	Don't You Want My Lovin'/I Can't Take It	Cameo 372	1965 ($12)
345. Orlons	Happy Birthday, Mr. 21/Please Let It Be Me (w/organ) Cameo 211 (B2 in deadwax, possibly dj only)		1962 ($50)
346. Orlons	Happy Birthday, Mr. 21/Please Let It Be Me (w/strings)	Cameo 211	1962 ($50)
347. Orlons	I Ain't Comin' Back/Envy	Cameo 346	1964 ($12)
348. Orlons	I'll Be True/Heart, Darling Angel	Cameo 198	1961 ($50)
349. Orlons	Keep Your Hands Off My Baby/Everything	ABC 10894	1967 ($10)
350. Orlons	No Love But Your Love/Envy	Cameo 384	($40)
351. Orlons	Once Upon A Time/Kissin' Time	ABC 10948	1967 ($10)
352. Overtones, Penny & The	What Made You Forget/--	Rim 2021	1958 ($100)
353. Palisades	Make The Night A Little Longer/Heaven Is Being With You	Chairman 4401	1963 ($25)
354. Pearls	If I Had A Choice/Happy Over You	Warner Bros. 5300	1962 ($20)
355. Peppermints	My First Love/--	Ruby Doo 3	1966 ($20)
356. Pixies Three	Love Me, Love Me/Your Way	Mercury 72357	1964 ($15)
357. Pixies Three	Love Walked In/Orphan Boy	Mercury 72331	1964 ($15)

Group	Record	Label/Number	Year/Value
358. Pointer Sisters	Destination, No More Heartaches/Send Him Back	Atlantic 2893	1972 ($20)
359. Pointer Sisters	Don't Try To Take The Fifth On Me/Tulsa County	Atlantic 2845	1972 ($20)
360. Poppies	There's No Love At All/Johnny Don't Cry (promo only)	Tuff 377	1964 ($15)
361. Poppies	Johnny Don't Cry/Inst.	Tuff 372	1963 ($15)
362. Powder Puffs	My Boyfriend's Woody/Woody Wagon	Imperial 66014	1964 ($25)
363. Primettes	Tears Of Sorrow/Pretty Baby	Lupine 120	1964 ($300)
364. Queens, Shirley Gunter & The	That's The Way I Like It/Gimme, Gimme, Gimme	Flair 1070	1955 ($30)
365. Queens, Shirley Gunter & The	You're Mine/Why	Flair 1060	1955 ($30)
366. Queens, Shirley Gunter & The	Baby, I Love You So/What Difference Does It Make	Flair 106	1955 ($30)
367. Queens, Shirley Gunter & The	Oop Shoop/It's You	Flair 1050	1954($30)
368. Quinn, Carole	What's So Sweet About Sweet Sixteen/Good Boy Gone Bad	MGM 13265	1964 ($10)
369. Quin-Tones	Down The Aisle of Love/Please Dear	Red Top 108	1958 ($120)
370. Quin-Tones	Heavenly Father/I Watch The Stars	Red Top 116	1959 ($100)
371. Quin-Tones	What Am I To Do/There'll Be No Sorrow	Hunt 322	1958 ($60)
372. Quintones	Ding Dong/I Try So Hard	Chess 1685	1957 ($40)
373. Ray, Alder	Cause I Love Him/A Little Love	Liberty 55715	1964 ($15)
374. Relatives	Never Will I Love You Again/I'm Just Looking For Love	Almont 306	1964 ($40)
375. Relatives, Ronnie & The	I Want A Boy/Sweet Sixteen	Colpix 601	1961 ($100)
376. Rockabyes, Baby Jane & The	Heartbreak Shop/Dance 'Til My Feet Get Tired	Port 3013	1964 ($30)
377. Rollettes	More Than You Realize/Kiss Me Benny	Class 203	1956 ($40)
378. Rollettes	Sad Fool/Wham Bam (Googie Rene Orch.)	Class 201	1956 ($40)
379. Ronettes	Good Girls/Memory	May 138	1962 ($50)
380. Ronettes	I Can Hear Music/When I Saw You	Philles 133	1966 ($30)
381. Ronettes	Silhouettes/You Bet I Would	May 114	1962 ($50)
382. Ronettes	You Came, You Saw, You Conquered/Oh I Love You	A&M 1040	1969 ($16)
383. Ronettes	I'm On The Wagon/I'm Gonna Quit While I'm Ahead	Colpix 646	1962 ($60)
384. Ronettes, Ronnie Spector & The	I Wish I Never Saw The Sunshine/I Wonder What He's Doing	Buddah 408	1973 ($20)
385. Ronettes, Ronnie Spector & The	Lover, Lover/Go Out and Get It	Buddah 384	1973 ($20)
386. Rosebuds	Dearest Darling/Unconditional Surrender	Gee 1033	1957 ($50)
387. Rouzan Sisters	Men Of War/Dance Every Dance	Frisco 113	1965 ($10)
388. Royal Debs	Jerry/I Do	Tifco 826	1961 ($25)
389. Royalettes	Blue Summer/Willie The Wolf	Chancellor 1140	1963 ($15)
390. Royalettes	He's Gone/Don't You Cry	MGM 13283	1964 ($12)
391. Royalettes	River Of Tears/Something Wonderful	Roulette 4768	1967 ($10)
392. Saint, Cathy	Big Bad World/Mr. Heartbreak	Daisy 501	1963 ($50)
393. Sans, Peggy	Snow Man/Give Your Love	Tollie 9018	1964 ($10)
394. Sa-Shays	Boo Hoo Hoo/You Got Love	Alfi 1	1962 ($25)
395. Satisfactions	Daddy, You Just Gotta Let Him In/Bring It All Down	Imperial 66170	1966 ($20)
396. Serenadetts	Boyfriend/The Big Night	Enrica 1008	1961 ($12)
397. Shangri-Las	Simon Says/Simon Speaks	Smash 1866	1964 ($40)
398. Shangri-Las	Take The Time/Footsteps on the Roof	Mercury 72670	1967 ($20)
399. Shangri-Las	The Sweet Sounds of Summer/I'll Never Learn	Mercury 72645	1966 ($20)
400. Shangri-Las	Wishing Well/Hate To Say I Told You So	Scepter 1291	1964 ($20)
401. Shangri-Las	Wishing Well/Hate To Say I Told You So	Spokane 4006	1964 ($30)
402. Sharmeers	A School Girl In Love/You're My Love	Red Top 109	1958 ($150)
403. Sharmettes	My Dream/Answer Me	King 5648	1962 ($15)
404. Sharmettes	Tell Me/I Want To Be Loved	King 5686	1962 ($15)
405. Sherry Sisters	The Prize/--	Cindy--	1957 ($100)
406. Sherrys	Slow Jerk/Confusion	Roberts 701	1965 ($12)
407. Shirelles	A Teardrop and A Lollipop/Doin' The Ronde	Scepter 1205 (white)	1959 ($30)
408. Shirelles	Dedicated To The One I Love/Look A Here Baby	Scepter 1203 (white)	1959 ($40)
409. Shirelles	Don't Believe Him Donna (w/Lenny Miles)/Invisible (No Group)	Scepter 1212	1960 ($12)
410. Shirelles	I Saw A Tear/Please Be My Boyfriend	Scepter 1207 (pink)	1960 ($30)
411. Shirelles	My Love Is A Charm/Slop Time	Decca 30669	1958 ($40)
412. Shirelles	Stop Me/I Got The Message	Decca 30761	1958 ($40)
413. Shirelles	There's A Storm Goin' On In My Heart/Call Me	Blue Rock 4066	1968 ($10)
414. Shirelles	Wait 'Til I Give The Signal/Wild and Sweet	Scepter 12209	1968 ($10)
415. Shirelles	I Met Him On A Sunday/I Want You To Be My Boyfriend	Tiara 6112	1958 ($800)
416. Shirelles	Tomorrow/Boys	Scepter 1211	1960 ($40)
417. Shirelles	Tonight's The Night/The Dance Is Over (pink)	Scepter 1208	1960 ($30)
418. Shondelles	Special Delivery/Muscle Bound	King 5706	1962 ($20)
419. Silver Slippers, Barbara Jay & The	Laughing At Me/Love Is The Thing	Lescay 3001	1961 ($30)
420. Socialites	You're Losing Your Touch/Jive Jimmy	Warner Bros. 5476	1964 ($12)
421. Socialites	Jimmy/The Click	Arrawak 1004	1962 ($20)
422. Socialites, Lorraine & The	The Conqueror/Any Old Way	Mercury 72163	1963 ($12)
423. Sonnets	Forever For You/I Can't Get Sentimental	Guyden 2112	1964 ($15)
424. Spotswood, Kendra	Jive Guy/Stickin' With My Baby	Tuff 407	1965 ($10)
425. Starlets	Better Tell Him No/You Are The One	Pam 1003	1961 ($20)
426. Starlets	My Last Cry/Money Hungry	Pam 1004	1961 ($20)
427. Starlets, Danetta & The	You Belong To Me/Impression	Okeh 7155	1962 ($100)
428. Starlettes	Please Ring My Phone/Jungle Love	Checker 895	1958 ($150)
429. Sunbeams	Good Old Days/Sing A Song	Tollie 9022	1965 ($12)
430. Supremes	Buttered Popcorn/Who's Loving You	Tamla 54045 (lines)	1961 ($125)
431. Supremes	I Want A Guy/Never Again	Tamla 54038	1961 ($125)
432. Supremes	My Heart Can't Take It No More/You Bring Back Memories	Motown 1040	1963 ($40)

Group	_Record_	_Label/Number_	_Year/Value_
433. Supremes	Run Run Run/I'm Giving You Your Freedom	Motown 1054	1964 ($25)
434. Supremes	Supremes Interview/The Only Time I'm Happy	George Alexander/ Motown 1079	1965 ($60)
435. Supremes	Your Heart Belongs To Me/He's Seventeen	Motown 1027	1962 ($25)
436. Swans	Please Hurry Home/The Boy With The Beatle Hair	Cameo 302	1964 ($40)
437. Sweet Marquees	I Love My Baby/You Lied	Apache 1516	1961 ($300)
438. Sweet Teens, Faith Taylor & The	I Need Him To Love Me/I Love You Darling	Bea & Baby 104	1959 ($50)
439. Sweet Teens, Faith Taylor & The	Your Candy Kisses/Won't Someone Tell Me Why	Federal 12334	1958 ($50)
440. Sweeties	After You/Paul's Love	End 1110	1961 ($20)
441. Sweet-Teens	With This Ring/My Valentine	Gee 1030	1957 ($60)
442. Swensons	Remember Me To My Darling/Golly Boo	X-Tra 100	1957 ($200)
443. Swisher, Debra	You're So Good To Me/Thank You and Goodnight	Boom 60001	1965 ($12)
444. Sydells	In The Night/The Hokey Pokey	Beltone 2032	1963 ($15)
445. Taffys	Can't We Just Be Friends/Peter Cottontail	Pageant 608	1963 ($10)
446. Tammys	Egyptian Shumba/What's So Sweet About Sweet Sixteen	United Artists 678	1964 ($12)
447. Teardrops	I Will Love You Dear Forever/Bubblegummer	Musicor 1218	1966 ($15)
448. Teardrops	I'm Gonna Steal Your Boyfriend/Call Me And I'll Be Happy	Saxony 1008	1965($25)
449. Teardrops	Tears Come Tumbling/You Won't Be There	Musicor 1139	1965 ($15)
450. Teardrops	Tears Come Tumbling/You Won't Be There	Saxony 1009	1965 ($20)
451. Teardrops	Tonight I'm Gonna Fall In Love Again/That's Why I'll Get By	Saxony 1007	1964 ($80)
452. Teen Clefs	Sputnik/Hiding My Tears With A Smile	Dice 98/99	1959 ($150)
453. Teen Queens	Red Top/Love Sweet Love	RPM 470	1956 ($25)
454. Teen Queens	Rock Everybody/My Heart's Desire	RPM 484	1956 ($20)
455. Teenettes	My Lucky Star/Too Young To Fall In Love	Josie 830	1957 ($60)
456. Thomas, Jean	Don't Make Me Fall In Love With You/I Don't Miss You At All	MGM 13263	1964 ($10)
457. Thomas, Jean	The Boy I Want Doesn't Want Me/He's So Near	Cadence 1438	1963 ($10)
458. Three Degrees	Close Your Eyes/Gotta Draw The Line	Swan 4224	1965 ($12)
459. Three Degrees	Contact/No No Not Again	Warner Bros. 7198	1968 ($10)
460. Three Degrees	Eve Of Tomorrow/Love Letter (w/Tony Mammarella)	Swan 4226	1965 ($12)
461. Three Degrees	I Wanna Be Your Baby/Tales Are True	Swan 4253	1966 ($12)
462. Three Degrees	I'm Gonna Need You/Just Right For Love	Swan 4214	1965 ($12)
463. Three Degrees	Look In My Eyes/Drivin' Me Mad	Swan 4235	1966 ($12)
464. Three Degrees	Love Of My Life/Are You Satisfied	Swan 4267	1966 ($12)
465. Three Degrees	Maybe/Yours	Swan 4245	1966 ($12)
466. Three Degrees	Tear It Up/Part 2	ABC 10991	1967 ($10)
467. Tiffanys	Please Tell Me/Gossip	MRS 777	1964 ($80)
468. Tonettes	He Loves Me, He Loves Me/Uh-Oh	Doe 103	1958 ($60)
469. Tonettes	Oh, What A Baby/Howie (long version)	Doe 101	1958 ($80)
470. Toys	Ciao Baby/I Got Carried Away	Philips 40432	1967 ($10)
471. Toys	My Love Sonata/I Close My Eyes	Philips 40456	1967 ($10)
472. Tranquils	You're Such A Much/One Billion, Seven Million And Thirty Three	Hamilton 50005	1958 ($30)
473. Trebelaires	There Goes That Train/I Gotta	Nestor 16	1954 ($100)
474. Trueleers	Waiting For You/Forget About Him	Checker 1026	1962 ($12)
475. Unforgettables	It Hurts/Was It Alright?	Colpix 192	1961 ($30)
476. Vandellas, Saundra Mallet & The	The Camel Walk/It's Gonna Be Hard Times	Tamla 54067	1962 ($1,000)
477. Vareeations	The Time/Ssab Berom	Dionn 506	1968 ($15)
478. Vells	You'll Never Cherish A Love So True/There He Is	Mel-O-Dy 108	1962 ($100)
479. Velvelettes	A Bird In The Hand/Since You've Been Loving Me	V.I.P. 25030	1965 ($20)
480. Velvelettes	Lonely, Lonely Girl Am I/I'm The Exception To The Rule	V.I.P. 25017	1965 ($20)
481. Velvelettes	These Things Will Keep Me Loving You/Since You've Been Loving Me	Soul 35025	1966 ($30)
482. Velvelettes	There He Goes/That's The Reason Why	IPG 1002	1963 ($100)
483. Veneers	Believe Me (My Angel)/I	Princeton 102	1960 ($40)
484. Veneers	With All My Love/Recipe Of Love	Treyco 402	1963 ($15)
485. Veronica	So Young/Larry L.	Phil Spector 1	1964 ($200)
486. Veronica	Why Don't They Let Us Fall In Love/Chubby Danny D.	Phil Spector 2	1964 ($200)
487. Vestelles	Come Home/Ditta Wah Doo	Decca 30733	1958 ($30)
488. Victorians	Happy Birthday Blue/Oh What A Night For Love	Liberty 55693	1964 ($15)
489. Victorians	Monkey Stroll/If I Loved You	Liberty 55728	1964 ($15)
490. Victorians	What Makes Little Girls Cry/Climb Every Mountain	Liberty 55574	1963 ($20)
491. Victorians	You're Invited To A Party/Monkey Stroll	Liberty 55656	1964 ($15)
492. Warren, Beverly	He's So Fine/March	B.T. Puppy 526	1966 ($10)
493. Warren, Beverly	Let Me Get Close To You/Baby, Baby Hullaballoo	Rust 5098	1965 ($12)
494. Warren, Beverly	Would You Believe/So Glad You're My Baby	B.T. Puppy 521	1966 ($10)
495. Warren, Beverly	It Was Me Yesterday/Like A Million Years	United Artists 543	1963 ($15)
496. Wellington, Mary Sue	Spoiled/Save A Little Monkey	Tuff 400	1964 ($8)
497. Wonderettes	I Feel Strange/Wait Until Tonight	Ruby 5065	1965 ($40)
498. Woods, Kenni	Do You Really Love Me/Back With My Baby	Philips 40156	1963 ($10)
499. Woods, Kenni	That Guy Is Mine/Can't He Take A Hint	Philips 40112	1963 ($10)
500. Zippers, Zip & The	Where You Goin', Little Boy/Gig	Pageant 607	1963 ($25)

Bibliography

Beckman, Jeff, Jim Hunt, Tom Kline, *Soul Harmony Singles 1960-90*, Three On Three Publishing Elizabeth, New Jersey, 1998.

Betrock, Alan, *Girl Groups The Story Of A Sound*, Delilah Communications Ltd., New York, NY, 1982.

Crenshaw, Marshall, *Hollywood Rock*, Harper Collins Publishers Inc., New York, N.Y., 1994.

Gonzalez, Fernando L., *Disco-File-The Discographical Catalog Of American Rock & Roll and Rhythm & Blues Vocal Harmony Groups-Second Edition*, Fernando L. Gonzalez, Flushing, New York, 1977.

Greig, Charlotte, *Will You Still Love Me Tomorrow,* Virago Press Limited, London, UK, 1989.

Groia, Philip, *They All Sang On The Corner*, Phillie Dee Enterprises, Inc., Port Jefferson, NY, 1983.

Kreiter, Jeff A., *Group Collectors Record Price Guide 6th Ed*, Jeff Kreiter, Bridgeport, Ohio, 1996.

LaBelle, Patti w/Laura B. Randolph, *Don't Block The Blessing–Revelation of a Lifetime*, Riverhead Books New York, NY., 1996.

Redmond, Mike & Steve West. *Arlene Smith & The Chantels, A Recording History.* New York: Outlet Book Co., Inc., 1987.

Ribowsky, Mark, *He's A Rebel*, E.P. Dutton Books, New York, New York, 1989.

Schwartz, Phil. "The Quintones", Keystone Record Collectors Recorder Fall, 1986: 1-3.

Wilson, Mary w/Patricia Romanowski, *Dreamgirl, My Life As A Supreme*, St. Martin's Press, New York, NY, 1986.

Interview List

The following artists have contributed information
and/or quotes to articles in this book:

The Andantes: Louvain Demps, Jackie Hicks, Judith (Marlene) Barrow Tate

The Angels: Peggy Santiglia Davison, Tom DeCillis, Phyllis (Jiggs) Allbut Sirico

Honey & The Bees: Phil Hurtt

The Blossoms: Fanita Barrett James, Gloria Jones, Darlene Love

The Bobbettes: Laura Webb Childress, Emma Pought Patron, Reather Dixon Turner

The Chantels: Jackie Landry Jackson, Lois Harris Powell, Arlene Smith, Renee Minus White, Sonia Goring Wilson

The Charmettes: Kenny Young

The Clickettes: Sylvia Hammond Akridge, Trudy McCartney Cunningham, Barbara Jean English, Charlotte McCartney Ford

The Cookies: Darlene McCrea Jackson, Dorothy Jones Johnson, Earljean McCrea Reavis, Margaret Ross Williams

The Crystals: Barbara Alston, Delores "LaLa" Brooks, Fatima (Frances)Collins Gueye, Dee Dee Kenniebrew

The Darlettes: Shirley Crier Fields, Gale J. Noble, Dianne Christian Toppin

The Delltones: Della Simpson Griffin

Reparata & The Delrons: Nanette Licari, Mary "Reparata" Aiese O'Leary

The Deltairs: Carol Stansbury Johnson

The Dixie Cups: Barbara Ann Hawkins

Nella Dodds: Sam Carson

The Exciters: Carolyn Johnson, Lillian Walker Moss, Brenda Reid

The Flirtations: Dr. Wayne Bickerton

Maureen Gray: Maureen Gray

The Hearts: Rex Garvin, Lezli Valentine Johnson, Louise Harris Murray, Justine "Baby" Washington

The Honey Cone: Shelly Clark White, Carolyn Willis

The Ikettes: Shelly Clark White

The Jaynetts: Lezli Valentine Johnson, Louise Harris Murray

The Jewels: Sandra Peoples Bears, Margie Clarke, Grace Ruffin

The Joytones: Vikki Burgess, Margaret Moore

Candy & The Kisses: Jerry Ross

Little Eva: Little Eva

The Marvelettes: Gladys Horton, Juanita Cowart Motley, Katherine Anderson Schaffner

The Orlons: Audrey Brickley, Stephen Caldwell

Teri Nelson Group: Steve Camhi, Elliot Chiprut

The Pixies Three: Debra Swisher Horn, Kaye McCool Krebs, Bonnie Long Walker

Shirley Gunter Queens: Piper Alvez (Lula B. Kenney)

The Quintones: Phil Schwartz

The Raindrops: Ellie Greenwich

The Ronettes: Jonathan Greenfield, Ronnie Spector

The Royalettes: Anita Ross Brooks, Veronica (Roni) Brown, Sheila Ross Burnett, Teddy Randazzo

The Sharmeers: Gloria Huntley, Majidah Williams

The Socialites: Gloria Meggett Dorsey, Lorraine Anthanio Lofaso, Kym (Mildred) Trant Smith

The Starlets: Maxine Edwards Smith

The Supremes: Mary Wilson

The Teardrops: Wanda (Wendy) Sheriff Engelhardt, Linda Schroeder Milazzo, Paul Trefzger, Dorothy Dyer Wethington

Jean Thomas Fox

The Three Degrees: Richard Barrett, Valerie Holiday, Helen Scott

The Toys: Barbara Harris Wiltshire

Martha & The Vandellas: Rosalind Ashford Holmes, Annette Beard Helton, Betty Kelley, Martha Reeves

The Velvelettes: Mildred (Millie) Gill Arbor, Norma Barbee Fairhurst, Betty Kelley, Bertha Barbee McNeal, Caldin (Carolyn) Gill Street

The Veneers: Lorraine Joyner

Beverly Warren: Beverly Warren